The Guide to Norfolk Churches

D.P. Mortlock: Born in Suffolk in 1927. Spent most of his childhood at Mildenhall where he was a choirboy at St Mary's – one of the finest churches in East Anglia. Grammar school was followed by war service in the Indian Grenadiers. His library career begain in 1947 with the old West Suffolk County. By this time 'church crawling' was a compulsive habit and continued in the West Riding and in Derbyshire before he came back to East Anglia in 1960 as Deputy and then County Librarian of Norfolk, retiring in 1985. He went on to complete his coverage of all the churches in East Anglia by publishing the *Popular Guide to Suffolk Churches* , which will be published as a companion revised edition to this book shortly. His other published works include *Holkham Notes & Annals*, 2002; *Holkham Library: A History and Description*, Roxburghe Club, 2006; *Aristocratic Splendour: Money and the World of Thomas Coke, Earl of Leicester*, Sutton, 2007. The last mentioned has been nominated for the Duff Cooper Prize. He has been Librarian to the Earl of Leicester at Holkham since 1990.

C.V. Roberts: Former literary editor and drama critic of the *Eastern Daily Press*. He came to Norfolk, he recalls, on a six month stop gap: 'But the place quickly put its spell on me,' he says, 'and I'm now very firmly adopted.' As a schoolboy in his native North Staffordshire one of his absorbing pastimes – in company with a friend who was subsequently ordained – was to cycle around the villages in the area, exploring their churches and writing accounts of them. His later newspaper and magazine work, first at various points in this country and then abroad, enabled that old interest to broaden – with a change to mosques and temples when he lived and worked in the Middle East for 2½ years. Having retired, he now lives in France.

Little Snoring, St Andrew by Gwyneth Cook

D.P. Mortlock and C.V. Roberts

The Guide to
Norfolk Churches

With an encyclopaedic glossary

2nd revised and enlarged edition

Foreword by the Countess of Leicester

The Lutterworth Press

The Lutterworth Press
P.O. Box 60
Cambridge
CB1 2NT

www.lutterworth.com
publishing@lutterworth.com

First published in three volumes, 1981 and 1985
Second revised edition in one volume, 2007

ISBN: 978 0 7188 3064 9

British Library Cataloguing in Publication Data
A catalogue record is available from the British Library

Printed in the United Kingdom by

Contents

'Walk about Sion, and go round about her:
　　and tell the towers thereof,
Mark well her bulwarks, set up her houses,
that ye may tell them that come after.'

Psalm XLVIII

'O go your way into his gates with thanksgiving,
and into his courts with praise.'

Psalm C

Foreword

As a child I used to be taken, unwillingly, around Norfolk churches by my Father. I am fairly certain I didn't much enjoy the experience at the time, but those visits must have instilled a residual interest in, and affection for our churches, as I have now been a committee member of the Norfolk Churches Trust for several years, and indeed, I now very much enjoy visiting them myself.

The parish church is perhaps the definitive icon of rural England, and it, together with the village green, the pub and the cricket field, is the picture that so many, especially English expatriates abroad, carry with them, and remember with nostalgia as quintessential England.

Some years ago, in high summer, I was driving from Holkham to mid Norfolk, when I saw a tiny village dominated by its church tower; on impulse I turned off the main road to the village. It was a hot afternoon, no one was about and the only sound the calling of jackdaws. Inside, the well-kept church was an oasis of calm and restfulness. As I read the names of all the incumbents over the centuries, it struck me as to how very important it was to ensure that our churches continue to be well cared for, so that one's successors are able to read a similar list with all its associations of continuity, stability and peace.

In Norfolk and Suffolk, we have the highest concentration of Mediaeval churches in Europe; 659 altogether, in a relatively small area. I urge you to spare a few minutes out of your busy lives and explore some of these beautiful buildings. I am certain you will find it as rewarding as I do.

In this, his revised guide to Norfolk churches, Mr Mortlock has provided us with a fascinating and illuminating description of each and every one he has visited. Armed with this guide the visitor cannot fail to enjoy exploring our lovely churches and having done so, it is my earnest hope that he or she will be inspired to lend their support to these marvellous symbols of our heritage.

The Countess of Leicester

Introduction

Another book on Norfolk churches? Yes. But this is a revised edition of the first one which, we believe, combined a straightforward guide to every 'living' medieval church in the county, with a substantial reference back-up in encyclopaedic form to a host of questions and queries which may tease the church visitor. All technical terms are pinpointed in the main body of the text by being printed *in italics*, indicating that they will be found in the Glossary and Appendices.

This book, moreover, is not written by specialists, but by enthusiasts, whose declared object is to share, as widely as possible, their own lively pleasure and fascination with the subject in hand. To us the real appeal is that once you have broken the code and learned the language, then every church is different; every single one, be it ever so humble, has something of its own to offer.

The essentials of a good building, wrote Sir Henry Wotton, early in the seventeenth century, are 'commoditie, firmness, and delight'. Lovely! But what he did not mention were the delights to be found inside these commodious buildings – spelled out, in our churches, in centuries of additions and oddities, glories and disasters, eccentricities and ornamentations, which can turn a simple visit into a voyage of discovery.

At random: Why does that painted saint hold a *scallop shell?* – or that one have a couple of deer skipping round her feet? (See *St James the Great* and *St Withburga*, one of Norfolk's own saints.) South Walsham's medieval *screen* reminds us that there was serfdom and slavery hereabouts. At Great Snoring, a 1710 memorial records the death of three brothers who all 'fell to the same shaft from the quiver, namely smallpox', bringing home the epidemic horrors of that time. And who occupied the three seats in the the *three-decker pulpit* at Warham St Mary, or the *sedilia* beside inumerable Norfolk altars? On a grand tomb effigy at Ashwellthorpe, a nobleman has a *Collar of S's* around the neck – an introduction to an ancient world of rank and favour. In Norwich, the church of St Giles has a curious iron basket in the s. aisle – so what was that for? And so the questions go on – and we have tried to answer as many of them as we can.

But a church is not just a building, constructed to specific architectual patterns, interesting though they often are. It is, much more importantly, an enduring witness to faith, a mirror of the community it has served for centuries, and a microcosm of the history of England itself. In a moving, indefinable way, it is a living thing, an ageless symbol of continuity, the links of its chain formed through the years by the countless good souls who have worshipped there, loved the place and have, at last, been buried in and around it. Sister Hilary Markey once said of a country church: 'The very stones can speak, causing hearts to open in this holy place, where prayer and worship ceaselessly offered for centuries are part of the fabric'.

If, by chance you walk into a church that is neglected, damp, dismal, unloved, the sadness you feel is much more than regret at seeing the beautiful work of men's hands being neglected. Rather, the sadness is contained within the stones themselves, as though the very place mourns its desertion. In Norfolk there are a number like that. But there would be many more if it were not for the splendid work of the Norfolk Churches Trust who keep many churches open, for worship and for visitors, which would otherwise have closed their doors forever. Added to that, the tremendous work being doing by the *Churches Conservation Trust* across the country have saved over a score of Norfolk churches and guarantees their presence for future generations to use and enjoy.

Not that problems of upkeep are a modern phenomenon. In 1562 *The Second Book of Homilies* talks of '. . . sin and shame to see so many churches so ruinous and so foully decayed in almost every corner . . . suffer them not to be defiled with rain and weather, with dung of doves, owls, choughs . . . and other filthiness.'

It our good fortune that so many of our heritage still remains to us. Especially so in Norfolk, with its rich profusion of well over 600 medieval churches individually detailed in this book. Our policy has been to include only medieval churches (plus some later buildings of merit and interest, and the number of these has been significantly enlarged in this edition) which are 'in use', including buildings used only occasionally.

Almost all church towers contain bells, but unfortunately quite a number of them cannot be rung for a variety of reasons. For those that are in use, brief details are appended to the entries, giving the weight of the tenor and an indication of the quality of the best.

A final point. That so many churches are kept locked today is an unhappy reflection on our society and its rising numbers of thieves and vandals. We have visited every church listed and the matter of obtaining keys was sometimes a challenge. Leafing through an 1846 copy of *Sketches for an Ecclesiology of the Deaneries of Sparham, Taverham and Ingworth*, one realises that this is another age-old problem: 'It is very tiresome when one has travelled so far – in our case 12 miles – to see a church, to find that the *parish clerk* lives a mile off: and on reaching his cottage to hear that he has gone out, and has taken the key in his pocket . . .'

Could we make this appeal to todays clergy: That a clear notice should be sited where it is easily seen, saying not only who has the key, but where they live and giving a telephone number if at all possible.

To all those incumbents, church-wardens, key-holders and the countless people who have extended to us their help and kindness, we return our warmest thanks, and a special thank you to Michael Daley for all his assistance in the preparation of the illustrations for this edition.

D.P.M. & C.V.R.
Norwich, 2007

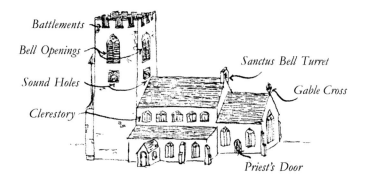

Battlements
Bell Openings
Sound Holes
Clerestory
Sanctus Bell Turret
Gable Cross
Priest's Door

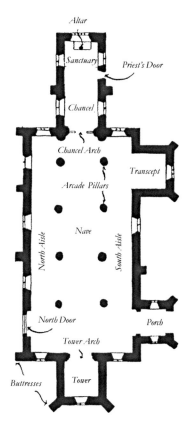

Altar
Sanctuary
Priest's Door
Chancel
Chancel Arch
Transcept
Arcade Pillars
North Aisle
Nave
South Aisle
North Door
Porch
Tower Arch
Buttresses
Tower

Elevation and Ground Plan of a Medieval Church

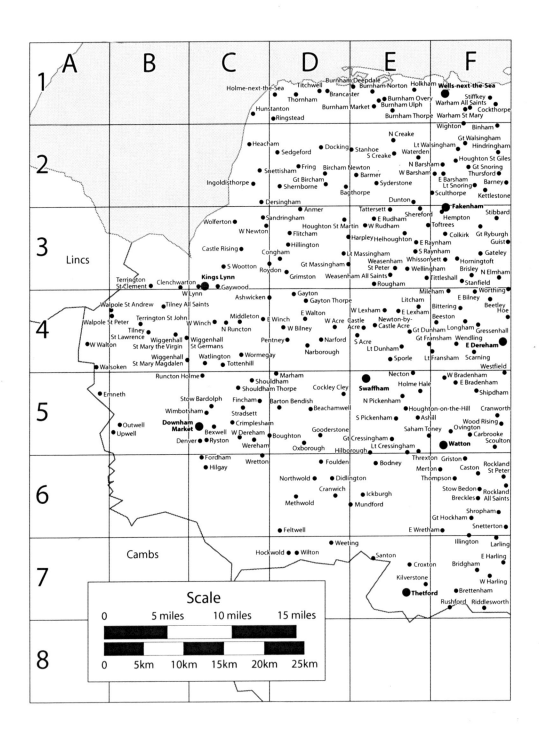

A   B   C   D   E   F

1
Holme-next-the-Sea
Titchwell Burnham Deepdale
Burnham Norton Holkham Wells-next-the-Sea
Brancaster
Thornham Burnham Overy Stiffkey
Hunstanton Burnham Market Burnham Ulph Warham All Saints Cockthorpe
Ringstead Burnham Thorpe Warham St Mary

Wighton Binham
N Creake
2
Heacham Docking Stanhoe Lt Walsingham Gt Walsingham Hindringham
Sedgeford S Creake Waterden Houghton St Giles
Fring Bircham Newton N Barsham Gt Snoring
Snettisham Barmer Thursford
Gt Bircham W Barsham E Barsham Barney
Ingoldisthorpe Shernborne Syderstone Lt Snoring Kettlestone
Bagthorpe Sculthorpe
Dersingham Dunton

Anmer Tattersett Fakenham Stibbard
3
Wolferton Sandringham Shereford Hempton
E Rudham Toftrees
W Newton Houghton St Martin W Rudham Colkirk Gt Ryburgh
Flitcham Harpley Helhoughton E Raynham Guist
Castle Rising Hillington S Raynham Gateley
Congham Lt Massingham Weasenham Whissonsett Horningtoft
Lincs S Wootton Gt Massingham St Peter Brisley N Elmham
Roydon Grimston Weasenham All Saints Wellingham Stanfield
Terrington Clenchwarton Kings Lynn Rougham Tittleshall
St Clement Gaywood Mileham Worthing
W Lynn Gayton Litcham E Bilney
4
Ashwicken Gayton Thorpe Bittering Beetley
Walpole St Andrew Tilney All Saints E Walton W Lexham Litcham Hoe
Terrington St John Middleton E Winch W Acre Castle Newton-by- Beeston
Walpole St Peter W Winch Acre Castle Acre Gt Dunham Longham Gressenhall
Tilney N Runcton W Bilney Gt Fransham Wendling
St Lawrence Wiggenhall Wiggenhall Pentney Narford S Acre E Dereham
W Walton St Mary the Virgin St Germans Lt Dunham
Wiggenhall Watlington Wormegay Narborough Sporle Lt Fransham Scarning
Walsoken St Mary Magdalen Tottenhill Westfield
Runcton Holme Marham Necton W Bradenham
5
Shouldham Cockley Cley Holme Hale E Bradenham
Emneth Shouldham Thorpe Swaffham Shipdham
Stow Bardolph Fincham Barton Bendish N Pickenham
Wimbotsham Stradsett Beachamwell Houghton-on-the-Hill Cranworth
Downham Crimplesham S Pickenham Ashill Wood Rising
Outwell Market Bexwell W Dereham Boughton Gooderstone Saham Toney Ovington Carbrooke
Upwell Denver Ryston Wereham Gt Cressingham Watton Scoulton
Oxborough Hilborough Lt Cressingham
Fordham Threxton Griston
6
Hilgay Wretton Foulden Bodney Merton Caston Rockland
Northwold Didlington Thompson St Peter
Cranwich Stow Bedon Rockland
Methwold Ickburgh Breckles All Saints
Mundford Shropham
Gt Hockham
Feltwell E Wretham Snetterton

Illington Larling
Weeting
7
Cambs Hockwold Wilton Santon E Harling
Croxton Bridgham
Kilverstone W Harling
Thetford Brettenham
Rushford Riddlesworth

8
Scale

0   5 miles   10 miles   15 miles

0   5km   10km   15km   20km   25km

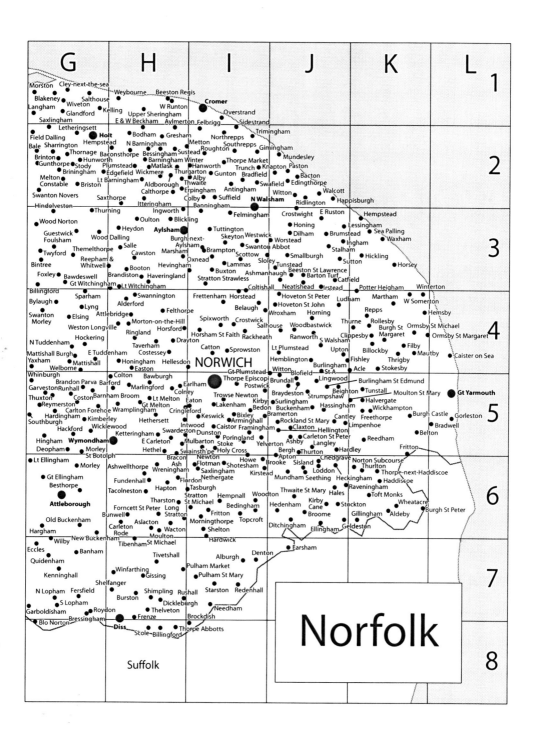

Styles of Architecture

Monarchs

An instant check-list – but see 'Appendix 2 – Styles of Architecture' for detailed background. All dates are approximate only.

Saxon – C7 to the Conquest (1066)

William I, 1066-87
William II, 1087-1100
Norman – 1066 to about 1200   Henry I, 1100-35
Stephen, 1135-54
Henry II, 1154-89
Richard I, 1189-99

John, 1199-1216
Transitional/Early English – 1200 to 1300   Henry III, 1216-72
Edward I, 1272-1307

Edward II, 1307-27
Decorated – 1300 to 1350   Edward III, 1327-77
Richard II, 1377-99

Henry IV, 1399-1413
Henry V, 1413-22
Perpendicular – 1350 to 1500   Henry VI, 1422-71
Edward IV, 1461-83
Richard III, 1483-85

Henry VII, 1485-1509
Henry VIII, 1509-47
Tudor – 1500 to 1600   Edward VI, 1547-53
Mary I, 1553-58
Elizabeth I, 1558-1603

Map references in brackets after the church names refer to the map on pp. 12-13. References to Glossary and Appendix entries in the text are printed in *italics*.

Alphabetical Guide to Churches

Acle, St Edmund (K4): Many Norfolk church towers have a mark showing where an earlier roof has been superceded by one of lower pitch, but here the thatched *nave* roof partially obscures the *lancet* bell opening in the e. face of the octagonal top and is obviously not original. The round lower stages of the tower probably date from before the Conquest. Entry is by way of the C15 n. *porch*, which has an interesting carving in the left-hand *spandrel*. A couple kneel with their rosaries and may well be the donors. Inside the porch, the e. window still has 'God Save the King 1616' roughly carved, and one wonders whether the King James' Bible of 1611 had just reached the village to prompt a loyal response. The font is a fine piece and is one of the few that can be dated accurately. On the top step is incised in Latin, 'Pray for the souls of those who gave this font to the glory of God A.D. 1410.' The bowl panels have: e., the *Trinity* – God the Father crowned and bearded, with a cross between his knees (from which the figure of Christ has been removed) and a (replacement) dove on his shoulder; s., an angel holding a *Trinity* shield; w., a *Pietà* with the head of the Virgin re-cut; n., an angel with a shield depicting the *Instruments of the Passion*; the four *Evangelistic Symbols* in the other four panels. The stem has alternating *woodwoses* and lions. A great deal of the original colour survives. The C15 *rood screen* is said to have come from elsewhere and it enhances the church wonderfully. It was well restored in the 1920s and has two lovely ranges of tracery, one above the other. The panels are dappled with *sacred monograms* and 'E's for St *Edmund* with crossed arrows as the sign of his

martyrdom. The *rood stairs* were in a C16 brick and flint exterior turret, and the base of this has been converted into a *sacristy* behind a grill. At a glance, this seems to have a fireplace but it is really a collection of fragments from a *Norman* doorway discovered in the nave wall in 1927. On the n. wall of the *chancel* a board labelled 'Do not remove' covers the fascinating remains of an inscription in Latin which translates:

O lamentable death – how many dost thou
　　cast into the pit.
Anon the infants fade away, and of the
　　aged, death makes an end;
Now these, now those, thou ravishest, O
　　death on every side.
These that wear horn (head-dresses) or
　　veils, fate spareth not.
Therefore while in the world the brute
　　beast plague rages hour by hour.
With prayer and with remembrance deplore
　　death's deadliness.

Although *Dr Pevsner* dates it as C15, Dr M.R. James, a leading antiquary of a previous generation, picks out the reference to 'ladies' horned hats' as a pointer to the period of the *Black Death* in 1349. Below it, a *brass* to Thomas Stones (d.1627). This is a very late date and is one of only six known from the reign of Charles I. In beautiful condition, it bears the lines:

The Lord has caused this painful [i.e.
　　diligent] shepherd die,
To live with Him in joy eternally.

The church has a ring of 6 bells, tenor 9-1-19 cwt.

Alburgh, All Saints (I7): Known locally as 'Arbrough'. For a relatively small church, the tower is tall but was probably not always so. The buttresses go only to the second stage and the belfry is a late *Perpendicular* addition. On top are elaborate stepped battlements and corner pinnacles which have most unusual little flying buttresses. One Sunday afternoon in 1895, during the service, two of the pinnacles came crashing down, leaving the rector preaching to an empty church after the entire congregation had fled! The niches by the w. window have lost their canopies but the door below has attractive *flushwork* panelling on either side. The big s. *porch* was built by the local family of Wright in 1463 and was subject, like the rest of the church, to full scale restoration by the rector in 1876. He raised the *chancel* walls by 6ft., installed a waggon roof there, built a new vestry, took down the old w. *gallery* and opened the tower arch. It was then that the *piscina* in the *nave* was uncovered, and in 1936 the base of the *rood screen* was restored and put back into its proper place. The work was well done, and the red and green stencilled panels have very fine tracery which is both intricate and crisp. There is a lot of the original *gesso* ornament on the leading edges, you can see that the main uprights had a continuous series of little saints in niches, of which four remain. Note that the *wall plate* of the *arch-braced* roof has a cresting that matches the one along the top of the screen. On the n. wall, matching tablets – one, to a 2nd lieutenant of the Warwickshire Regt., has a military shako hat in bas relief; the other, to a captain in the Queen's Bays, has a plumed helmet. The church has a good ring of 8 bells, tenor 9-3-13 cwt.

Alby, St Ethelbert (I2): C15 tower, but the *nave* is earlier and has *clerestory* windows although there is no trace of *aisles* having been built. There is a coarse unadorned *piscina* in the *chancel* with two *credence shelves* that might well be original. Another rudimentary piscina for the nave altar is cut in the step below the window on the s. side, and opposite there are stairs to the *rood loft*. One can still see the stub of the *rood beam* and loft floor high on the n. wall. There are four *consecration crosses* incised in the walls on either side of the chancel arch, and the heavily varnished bottom half of the *screen* remains.

Aldborough, St Mary the Virgin (H2): Well away to the s.w. of the village, on the Matlask road and, having lost its tower in the C18, easy to miss. The church was extensively restored in

1847, and the perky bell-turret of 1906 renovated in 1968. *Carstone quoins* at the w. end of the *nave* and halfway along the s. wall indicate *Norman* origins, but the windows and much of the present building are C14. The n. *aisle* was probably added in the C13 and the piercing of the nave wall was roughly done. The three good *brasses* in the nave were moved to their present position early in the 1900s. Close to the *chancel* step, the brass to Anne Herward (d.1485) shows the elegant *butterfly head-dress* of the period. West of this is a brass to a civilian c.1490, and further w. still is the brass to Robert Herward (d.1481), Anne's husband, shown in armour. There is an interesting series of small *corbels* in the *porch*, nave and aisle, and the exterior modern metal *gargoyles* are an unusual feature. The statues of the Virgin and Child in the sanctuary and in the niche over the s. door are by H. Rogers.

Aldeby, St Mary (K6): There was a Benedictine Priory here in the C12 and that explains why this small village church is quite elaborate, with a central *crossing tower*, a n. *transept*, evidence of a s. transept, and a s. *chancel aisle*. Although one enters now by a richly decorated C14 *porch*, the w. front has a lovely *Norman* doorway with three columns on each side topped by individually carved *capitals* supporting an arch full of zigzags and cones. Inside, the *nave* with its plain white plastered ceiling, the narrow arches of the central tower, and the darker chancel beyond with a glow of stained glass in the e. window, provide a vista hard to match in many a larger church. The C15 font has plenty of space round it at the w. end and the painted cover is very beguiling – *Jacobean* in spirit but probably late C17. Although the tower is Norman, there are none of the usual clues and it was partially rebuilt in 1833. The tablet on one of the n. *piers* compounds the confusion: 'This Stepll was belt 1633'! A modern partition has been inserted to make the n. transept into a self-contained (and no doubt warmer) chapel; the altar here is an unusually lightweight *Stuart* table. The chancel is largely C13 and the *piscina* with stepped two-seat *sedilia* are of that period, although sharply restored. Above them, a curiosity – the memorial to Henry Carpenter who died in 1888 aged 85 and Ellen Lucy his wife. She has doubtless gone to her rest, but the stone still waits for the blanks to be filled in. The 1888 glass in the e. window is anonymous but extremely pleasing. Rich foliage background to the figures, and strong crimson, blue, and apricot colours in the robes are effectively balanced with pale lilac and yellow.

Aldeby, St Mary: Norman w. doorway

For those with a taste for euphony, there is in the chancel the grave of Thomasine Trott who died in 1652. One of the happy accidents of matrimony. The church has a ring of 5 bells, tenor 9 cwt.

Alderford, St John the Baptist (H4): One of the thin C14 towers with added w. buttresses which are common in the county – made to look taller than it is by having small and narrow bell openings very close to the top. There was a C14 n. *aisle* but this has gone, leaving the *arcade* embedded in the *nave* wall. The s. side of the continuous nave/*chancel* has a nicely varied range of windows – two with flowing (slightly different) tracery, one with a four-centred *Perpendicular* arch, and eastern-most (blocked) with three *ogee*–headed lights under a square label. Over the *porch* door, a wooden sundial (C19?) with 'Redeem the time' in raised letters. The *seven sacrament font* is unusually placed just e. of the n. door and, being on two deep steps, it dominates the little nave. Some of the figures round the shaft are identifiable – St *James the Great* (pilgrim's purse), St *Andrew* (cross saltire), St *John the Evangelist* (chalice), St *Philip* (loaves). There are demi-figures of angels with scrolls in the corona, and the bowl panels are (clockwise from the e.): baptism, ordination, mass, penance (note how the angel all in feathers drives the

devil back), confirmation, marriage, extreme unction and the Crucifixion. Traces of colour remain. The altar *reredos* is made up of recoloured panels – probably from the former *rood screen*, and the stairs for the *rood loft* are set in the s. wall, marking the division between nave and *chancel*. As you leave, have a look at the old knocker in the centre of the door – it has been there at least 600 years.

Anmer, St Mary (D3): Reached by a winding drive, the church stands close by Anmer Hall in a very pretty setting. The early-C14 *nave* has its original n. doorway, and there are two varying *Perpendicular* windows on that side. Although the C13 *chancel* was over-restored in 1880, it still has wrap round buttresses typical of the period, and the e. window was faithfully reproduced; there are fascinating *grotesques* at the gable ends and as stops for the e. window – teeth bared and tongues out. The C15 tower has a little *flushwork* on the buttresses and large *gargoyles* below the battlements. The early-C14 s. *porch* is very robust, with an unusual stone *tunnel vault* on transverse *ribs*. Inside, there is a modern *screen* just e. of the door, leaving the w. end mainly clear around the simple C15 font. In the gloom, one can just about see six *hatchments* of the Coldham family and a big *Royal Arms* of George III on canvas; it is a complete achievement. Like the nave, the s. chapel is C14 and has very nice flowing tracery in the e. window. The *rood stairs* rise from here and must be contemporary with the chapel. The screen across the entrance is modern, there is an C18 *baluster* font, and the *reredos* is a memorial to Admiral Sir Henry Keppel. The two monuments on the s. wall are interesting because one was used as a pattern for the other; they are handsome *cartouches*, with a little drapery, and coloured crests on top – Rachel Coldham's inscription in Latin (1727), Thomas and Elizabeth Patrick's in English (1730). On the n. wall of the chancel, three pictures by Sir Noel Paton: 'The Man of Sorrows' and 'The Good Shepherd' flank a larger 'Watch and pray'; dated 1883 and typical of the period, they were given by Queen Mary, who took a personal interest in this church.

Antingham, St Mary (I2): Two churches in one churchyard and an old wives' tale that they were built by two sisters, virtuous Mary whose church remains intact and dissolute Margaret, whose church lies ruined and swathed in ivy. St Mary's is mainly mid-C14 with a later variation to the top of the tower, and the windows have a common theme of *reticulated* tracery. The wide and high *arch-braced roof* runs right through with no division between *nave* and *chancel*, but there are extra struts at the e. end so it may have had a ceiling at one time. The chancel *piscina* is matched by another just e. of the *rood loft* stairs so there was a nave altar nearby. The two head *corbels* set in the chancel walls are puzzling. *Munro Cautley* suggests that they were used for the *Lenten Veil*, but they are awkwardly sited and may have been moved. The s.e. window is good C19 glass by *Morris & Co.* – two sisters again, Martha and Mary on either side of the Virgin. Martha endearingly has a saucepan tucked under her arm as well as carrying a spoon and a leather bottle. At the e. end of the nave is a good *brass* to Richard Calthorp (1562), a 17in. bearded figure in full armour. His wife's brass is gone, but below a long inscription there is a separate plate with 19 of their progeny grouped in mourning.

Arminghall, St Mary (I5): The peculiarly bold flintwork of the outside of this church immediatly catches the attention, its strong colouration suggesting rather sea-shore shells than flint. Nonetheless the hand of restoration lies heavily on the exterior. The tower is in the *Decorated* style of the first half of the C14, though it was actually built in the second half of that century – a common example of time-lag in styles. It has battlements picked out in battle-grey flints, and pleasant geometrically-styled belfry openings, with *quatrefoils* in the tracery heads. The body of the church is earlier, of the C13, with an unusual profusion of simple *lancet* windows, and a neatly restrained *Perpendicular* e. window of the late C14/early C15. Inside, a simple 'single hall' with a modern barrelled roof; and a wooden *chancel* arch with open fretwork in the *spandrels* and a neat *king post* between its *tie-beam* and the roof (see Fig 3, *Roofs*). Beside the filled-in n. door is the niche of a *holy water stoup*. On the same side, against the chancel arch, is a large, pointed indentation in the wall whose purpose is puzzling. The charming little chancel has lancet windows on the n., deeply splayed; and on the s. a most attractive double lancet, with *dropped sill sedilia*, next to a large *piscina* niche with a restored plain arch. Nearby note the deep embrasure containing both a lancet and, below it, a *low side window*, its opening casement long since replaced. There are two fine late-C17 *ledger-stones* in the sanctuary, with splendid incised coats-of-arms of the Herne family, and of the Herne coat conjoined with that of the Cookes. Another Herne is

remembered only by a tiny, faded slab in the pavement in front of the sanctuary step – in contrast, on the wall above, with a large painted wall monument, of much pomp and circumstance, to John Herne, 1661, topped by a war helmet with its crest of a coroneted swan (?). The choir stalls, though largely modern, have built into them some attractive old *poppy-head* medieval remnants, gone silvery grey with age.

Ashby St Mary, St Mary (J5): The tower, with a lot of red brickwork in its construction (a common feature in this immediate locality) is C15 *Perpendicular*, but the body of the church is much older – though on first appearance this is not evident, as it has been so thoroughly restored and, during the C19, had its windows replaced. The antiquity is evident once you look inside the *porch* (with its charming *Tudor* red-brick outer arch) – for the s. doorway there is *Norman*, its splendid arch has seven different patterns of carved decorations and sits on an assemblage of little pillars. There is a tiny *mass dial* carved into the *capital* on the left and what looks like a crude 'graffiti' attempt at one (albeit scratched out long ago) to the right. On the n. side of the *nave* is a Norman slit window, and on the s. side of the basically C13 *Early English chancel*, a clean-lined little contemporary *priest's door*. A lovely, simple interior, a single 'hall' for nave and chancel, cosy and intimate under a plain plaster barrel ceiling for the nave and a modern panelled one, in similar shape, for the chancel. There is a plain but stylish font with an elegant, carved wooden cover – C17 or C19. By the s. door is a deep *holy water stoup* recess, next to a solid old chest and a poorman's box, like a stubby wooden pillar with three business-like locks, and possibly C17. The furnishings otherwise are modern, with the exception of the robust and enormously pleasing *communion rails*, which again are C17. As you go, notice the amusing conceit of a screen wall across the tower arch, complete with 'mediaeval' battlements. Outside, near the porch, don't miss the wonderfully evocative Victorian tombstones to George and Ann Basey, who in carved relief scenes are shown surrounded by their geese and turkeys – harking back to the days when the 'Norfolk turkey' tradition was at its height – and factory farming wasn't even a bad dream.

Ashill, St Nicholas (E5): A neat church, set snug within its village, and radiating strong character the moment you see it from the *lych-gate*. The tower and *chancel* are *Decorated*. The s. aisle is *Perpendicular*, the *clerestory* is either very late Decorated, or early Perpendicular – harking back to the earlier form but presenting together a most striking ensemble. Perpendicular too is the most attractive two-storey *porch*, with its miniscule figure niche over the outer arch. Among the big, powerful tower's special features are a splendidly traceried w. window, in exuberantly flowing lines, and a positively buoyant doorway below it, under a deeply recessed *ogee* arch, a composite picture not easily forgotten. Three very large Perpendicular windows almost fill the n. wall of the *nave*. The n. door however is patently *Early English* in character, pointing to the church's C12 heritage. At the e. end of the nave's n. wall, the faint oblong outline, almost obscured by lichens, was presumably associated with the *rood stairs*. Notice the *put-log* hole in the centre of the otherwise blank chancel n. wall. Back on the s. side, we return to this church's most eye-catching feature: late Perpendicular windows with flattened arches in both clerestory and *aisle*, those above with crisp and lively tracery, and set in a wall beautifully patterned in chequerworked flint, stone and red brick, and below, the bold windows having richly adorned *transoms*. After all this, the interior is plain, with a big, no-nonsense nave roof, supported by massive cross beams, dated 1618. The s. *arcade* of six bays is elegantly of the Decorated period, as is the curiously compressed chancel arch. There are some good fragments of C15 glass in the nave n. windows; and equally small traces of original work in the otherwise modern *screen*. Notice the slim shafts with ring *capitals* to either side of the e. window – another C13 survivor, as is the rather coarse *angle piscina*, with its little supporting pillar and rough capital carved askew. Of the modern *reredos* here, perhaps the less said the better. Before you leave, look at the handsome little carved set of *Royal Arms* (for George IV) on the nave n. wall. The church has an excellent ring of 8 bells, tenor 9-2-0 cwt.

Ashmanhaugh, St Swithin (J3): Nicely set at the end of a narrow lane in a neat churchyard. The round tower was rebuilt in 1849 and, with a diameter of only 10ft, it is the smallest in the county. Just inside the door, the back of the nearest bench has an interesting series of shields carved with the *Five Wounds of Christ*, and another range below carry initials and the date 1531. The *rood loft stairs* are in the n. wall and the sockets for the front floor beam of the loft itself still remain. The lower doorway has been fitted with neat oak half-doors to form a seemly

cupboard for the electrical mains panel. The sanctuary has a large *aumbry* in the n. wall, and in the s.e. corner is the tomb of Honor Bacon who, in 1591 died on the eve or the morning (tradition varies) of her wedding day. The epitaph is decayed and hard to decipher in full, but plainly begins, 'A better mayden lived not then / And now her lyke doth lacke'.

Ashwellthorpe, All Saints (H6): From the road, the *nave* seems very high for its length and this is accentuated by the range of tall C15 windows. The C13 tower has little *quatrefoil sound-holes*, heavy buttresses with *flush-work* and gables on the lower ones, and a later addition of chequer-work battlements. Like the nave, the *porch* is *Perpendicular* but is disguised by having a C18 Dutch gable on top. There are large shields low down on either side of the door, plus flanking niches that have lost their canopies; by the door, a *holy water stoup* under a battered but still pretty *ogee* canopy. Inside, two good things at the w. end; first, the font given by the Knyvett family in 1660 (unusually late) – it has coloured coats of arms around the bowl and stands on a tall shaft with attached columns. Just beyond it is a C17 Italian chest, brown as a conker, with the front all carved in low relief and decorated with poker-work. The scenes have soldiers and a tented camp, and the inside of the lid is covered with mildly bacchanalian scenes, again in poker-work. The gem in this church is the alabaster tomb of Sir Edmund de Thorp and his wife Joan. He died at the siege of Louviers Castle in Normandy in 1417 fighting under Henry V, and was brought home for burial. On each side of the tomb, four standing angels bear the family arms (beautifully re-coloured); on top, the figures of the knight and his lady are of very high quality. Her hair is caught up in wide jewelled snoods and two angels with outstretched arms bear her pillows; two lap-dogs play at her feet, one plucking at the hem of her gown. Sir Edmund's moustaches lap the edges of a helmet crowned with a chaplet wreath and his head rests on a mighty helm and plume. Most unusual to see that both of them wear the mark of privilege, a *collar of S's*. For three centuries, ignorant minds and idle fingers have devised banal mementos on this lovely alabaster but have not yet subdued its beauty. Don't miss the C13 priest's grave slab in the n. e. corner of the sactuary. The Knyvets followed the Thorps and were some-times equally martial. Round the corner in the n. chapel is an oval tablet recording that Major Knyvet Wilson of the Inniskillen Regt. fell on St Lucia in 1796, 'bravely leading on the Gallant Regiment to a Glorious Victory over the French Republicans'. Still the same old lot after nearly 400 years! As you go out, note the medieval closing ring on the door.

Ashwicken, All Saints (D4): A very neat churchyard at the end of an avenue of chestnuts. There is a band of *carstone* in the middle stage of the early-C14 tower, massive C16 brick buttresses, a two-light w. window with *cusped lancets*, and single lancets above. There were battlements at one time but the top is now capped with a little pyramid. The *nave* has brick buttresses too, and a new vestry has been built on the n. side of the *chancel*. Both nave and chancel are basically C15 but there was a big restoration in 1860 and this is very evident inside, where all the fittings are Victorian. The font, curiously, was carved in Benares in an overdone C14 style. The solid C19 benches have *poppy-heads* and for a change, the lectern is carved wood rather than brass. But why was the eagle on its ball made to revolve?

Aslacton, St Michael (H6): An extremely pretty, compact little church on its gentle hill. It has a round *Anglo-Saxon* tower which, typical of its period, has two-light, triangular-headed windows, the arches sitting on heavy slabs and sturdy central *mullions*. The battlements are a later, *Perpendicular*, addition. Perpendicular too is the charming s. *clerestory* over the *nave*, with little two-*light cusped* windows under bold square hoods. From the same period comes the s. *aisle*, though its geometrically styled s.windows are modern. Again Perpendicular is the s. *porch*, with its surprisingly ambitious gable end: This has traceried *flushwork*, and a good arch under a square *hood mould*, with tracery, *quatrefoils* and floral motifs in the *spandrels*, which sits on slim rounded pillars with battlemented *capitals*. Above is a beautifully canopied figure niche – in which stands a modern effigy of a martial St *Michael*, armoured, winged and standing on the dragon of evil. The *chancel's Early English/early Decorated* origins show in its n. wall (remodelled) *lancet* and its s. wall 'Y' traceried window. There is also here a *low side window* of two *lights*, cusped, and under a square hood. The interior of this church, so small and inviting, is most pleasing – an effect underlined, as you go in, by some very low bench pews with *poppy-head*-shaped cut-out benchends, rudely adzed from single hunks of wood. Roofs and furnishings are otherwise modern, including the clumsy little deal pulpit,

crammed into a corner against the chancel arch but relieved by a canopied wood carving, attached to its front. The carving shows David holding the severed head of Goliath, and on the plinth on which the hero stands, a scene in miniature of he and the giant about to join in battle – C16, and Flemish, says *Dr Pevsner*; C17, says *Munro Cautley*. The arch from the Saxon tower is not original – it has been given a point – but almost undoubtedly original Saxon are the *imposts* on which the arch sits. The s. *aisle*, the charming little three-bay *arcade* on its trim octagonal pillars, and the graceful chancel arch, are all C15; as is the plain octagonal font, with shields carved round its bowl and floral motifs alternating with funny little grotesque faces around the foot of the stem. By the s. door, a *holy water stoup*; in the s.e. corner of the aisle, the diminutive entrance to the *rood stair*, which emerges in the nave at *rood loft* level. In the heavily restored chancel, a *double piscina* (with ugly remodelled arch) and *dropped sill sedilia*; and in the n. wall, by the chancel arch, another recess (again remodelled), which may have been an *Easter Sepulchre*. The church has a ring of 5 bells, tenor 7 cwt.

Attleborough, The Assumption of the Blessed Virgin Mary (G6): The first impression of the visitor is that the tower of St Mary's is at the wrong end and, as far as the original builders' intention is concerned, it is. The *Norman* church which was raised here sometime between 1075 and 1135 had a *nave* and *chancel* e. of the tower, and of that building only the lower stage of the tower remains. In 1386 Sir Robert Mortimer founded and endowed the College of the Holy Cross – a community of five priests whose sole duty it was to say masses for his soul and for those of his ancestors. For this, Sir Robert took over the whole of the old church, and by way of reparation, he began to build the parishioners a new nave and *aisles* w. of the old tower. The new parish church was completed in its essentials in 1405 and coexisted happily with the secular college, housed in its predecessor, for over 100 years until the Dissolution in the 1540s. Then the college and its possessions were given to the Earl of Sussex who destroyed the choir of the old church and made off with much else; in 1602 it was reported 'there ys no chancell there, nor hath been most these threescore yeares'. The second stage of the tower dates from the C12, and the two-*light* bell opening to the n. has the distinctive *plate tracery* in its head. There was

Attleborough, The Assumption of the Blessed Virgin Mary: Rood screen and mural

once a tall spire which, had it survived, would have made a tremendous difference to the look of the church we see today – alas! it fell at the end of the C17. A stroll round the spacious churchyard confirms much of this chequered history, particularly at the e. end. The three *lancets* in the e. face of the tower are imitations, but below them one sees the Norman arch which led into the old nave, and on the e. wall of the s. transept there is the roof line to show where it joined a side *aisle* of the old college. The window in that wall was taken from the former buildings when they were demolished. On the s. wall above the new vestry, note the *flushwork* false window which matches the rest of the range – placed there presumably to give wall space inside for the big St *Christopher* that faced the n. door. All the windows except two at the w. end of the *aisles* of the 'new' church have attractive four-petalled flowers, characteristic of *Decorated* architecture but, as *Pevsner* points out, it is unusual to find a church finished in the early 1400s betraying nothing of the new style of *Perpendicular*. The C15 n. *porch* entrance is badly eroded, as is the flushwork above it. A big two-light window has half-angels as stops to the *hood mould*, and two of the three niches have little heads at the bottom of the shafts, with a half-angel between. The corner buttresses carry seated figures just below the parapet, and beasts serve as corner pinnacles with a seated figure at the top of the gable. The inside of the church is almost square at first glance, and the eye is taken up by the grace of the slender columns of the *arcades* – they are so tall that they seem to sway slightly outward at the top, under the gently cambered timbers of the roof. Turning to the e., the real treasure of the church awaits. From wall to wall stretches one of the most interesting and impressive *rood screens* in the country – and only by chance is it still here. It was covered in limewash, probably in the C17, and in 1842 the parish sold it to a Norwich antique dealer for £40. Luckily the diocesan authorities would not grant a faculty and the Bishop asked for an expert assessment. That described it in glowing terms and said, 'it ought on no account to be removed either from the church or from its present position'. Baulked at the sale, the parish was not to be beaten and moved the whole thing to the w. end in 1845, and even had another go at selling it in 1852. There matters rested until 1932, when it was repaired, restored and returned to its rightful place. There is not another church in East Anglia that can match this *screen* for size and completeness. Given by the Rattcliffe family in 1475, it stretches 52ft. from wall to wall and, with its *loft* intact, rises to nearly 20ft. The sections facing the aisles had lost their vaulting and this was replaced, as were some of the front panels, but the rest of the work is original. One of the most striking features is the array of heraldry in the panels of the loft. Painted in the early C17, the shields, with little arabesques above and below, carry the episcopal arms of all the Welsh and English dioceses, and a chart in the n. aisle will help you to identify them. Looking closely, you will see that the panels had been used previously for Elizabethan 'fruitful and profitable sentences', and along the top is an inscription of the same period recording profound advice from the Book of Proverbs. The remains in the arches serve to show how delicate the lacy *cusping* was, and the valance of the loft is still rich. The arches that led originally to the part of the building used by the college of canons could be blocked off, and you can still see the grooves in the uprights for boards to be slotted in. Because the e. end of the church was not for parochial use, two altars were set against the front of the screen, and the panels covering the pillars on either side of the entrance formed *reredoses*. To the n., the tall and stately figures of St *John the Baptist* and St *John the Evangelist* flank a queenly Madonna – richly robed against a red ground and holding a sceptre. To the s., St *Thomas of Canterbury*, a *Holy Trinity group* (Christ on the cross before the Father, with the Dove of the Spirit) and St *Bartholomew*. All of the figures represent unequivocal English work at its best. Above the screen is a great mural, painted about 1500, which is one of the most outstanding to have survived anywhere. It was discovered in 1844 but promptly limewashed again, and in opening up the two Norman windows of the tower, the upright of the great foliated cross was destroyed. Nearly 100 years later it was again uncovered, cleaned and treated. At the top, just below the roof is an *Annunciation* scene (quite unusual in this position), and the figures of God and the angel can be picked out clearly. Two rows of lifesize figures flank the huge centre cross – top left: David, with Jeremiah beyond; top right: Moses, and an unidentified figure; angels hold *Instruments of the Passion* at either side. Below, seraphim with calm, beautiful

faces *cense* the cross, and the figures of the Virgin in dark green cloak and red gown, and St *John* stand to left and right There were series of figures up each side too, but only traces of those on the left remain. It is worth taking a pair of binoculars to study the detail of this fine mural. Beyond the screen, it is two steps down into the space under the Norman tower – now a sanctuary. The arches have three sturdy attached shafts, and there are two more at the angles. The n. transept was built as a chapel by Thomas Chaunticlere who was buried there in 1378, but it is now chock full of the organ. The s. transept was built by another of the Mortimers – William, who was buried here in 1297. By one of those odd quirks of fate, the font that Whitwell Elwin threw out when he rebuilt Booton has found its way here, having spent the intervening 100 years or so in St *Mary Magdalen*, Norwich. Attleborough has a most unusual lectern – not the customary brass, but all in cast iron painted black and relieved with gold. The steps that go with it rest on sinuous snakes and the handrails are in the form of palm leaves. This quietly exotic tour de force was the gift of the churchwardens in 1816. Across the nave is an exceptionally fine early-C18 pulpit which came to the church in l845 after its previous home, Broadway Chapel, Westminster, had been demolished – all of it exudes an air of lavish quality. Note the *consecration crosses* in the s. aisle, the remains of a St *Christopher* above the s. door, and a curious alms box below it – a solid baulk of timber with three overlaying hasps and with pebbles driven into the wood at the bottom. The church has a good ring of 6 bells, tenor 12-2-18 cwt.

Attlebridge, St Andrew (H4): A thin un-buttressed tower with a niche below the *lancet* window on the ground floor. The triple lancets of the early-C14 e. window are contained within one arch, and it has particularly good *headstops* outside which turn toward each other. They look unrestored. The 1864 restoration was almost certainly responsible for the curious wooden *chancel* arch which rests on stone *corbels*. In the chancel s. wall, a *low side window* in the bottom third of a lancet, a blocked *priest's door*, and *dropped sill sedilia*. There is a *squint* in the n. wall of the chancel, cut through from the *aisle*, but the angle is not acute enough for it to align with the high altar and so its use is doubtful. The bulbous *baluster* lectern recorded by *Pevsner* has given way to a very plain reading desk-cum-pulpit in Columbian pine, but the priest's desk has ten C17 turned balusters with acanthus leaf carving which must have been taken from something else. There is a little *chalice brass* to George Conyngham (d.1525) by the sanctuary rail.

Aylmerton, St John the Baptist (H2): The upper stage of the *Norman* round tower was rebuilt to the old design in 1912, when a long-blocked doorway was discovered at its base. The two-storey s. *porch* is tall and shallow, and looks well as one comes up the steep approach path. Its staircase fits snugly in the angle with the *nave*, and the original entrance door inside is beautifully solid and iron banded. The *chancel* was rebuilt in the mid-C14 and has a pretty *piscina* and two-bay *sedilia*, with a *cusped* and *crocketted* canopy over it. The little round faces of the *headstops* crop up again at the w. end of the church by the *holy water stoup*, which was discovered behind plaster in 1840. Before you leave, note the most unusual *capitals* of the s. doorway. They are castellated with arrow slits, and are reminiscent of the arms of Castile, in Spain. John of Gaunt (a great landowner in this part of Norfolk in the C14) was the patron here, and through marriage he inherited the Crown of Castile in 1371 – which may account for this minor architectural puzzle.

Aylsham, St Michael (H3): At a distance, the C17 spike on the top gives the tower a distinctive silhouette, particularly from the n.e. and the whole exterior of the church is impressive in its size when approached from the nearby market-place. The s. *porch* was enlarged to two stories in the late C15, and has rich *flushwork* panelling, the arms of France and England, and a beautiful canopied niche flanked by windows above the arch. The alternating circular and octagonal pillars of the early-C14 *arcade* are very effective, and the later *transepts* and *chancel* chapels are on a generous scale. The font is early-C15, with *Symbols of the Evangelists*, *Instruments of the Passion*, and the Crucifixion around the bowl. The shaft carries four shields, one of which is John of Gaunt's, who is credited with the building of the church. The base of the *rood screen* has been beautifully restored by Miss Pauline Plummer. The sixteen painted figures in the panels include the donor Thomas Wymer, who died in 1507 and whose *brass* is on the n. side of the sanctuary. The little *gesso* figures on the screen buttresses are very similar to those at Cawston. Bishop Jegon, a chaplain to Queen Elizabeth and successively Dean and Bishop of Norwich died in Aylsham in 1617, and his monument is on the n. wall of the chancel. The eccentric *reredos* was put together by John Adey Repton in 1833; besides incorporating pieces of the top of the rood screen, it has some *misericords* built in. Humphrey Repton, the renowned landscape gardener, has his memorial outside the church against the s. wall of the chancel. Composed by himself, his epitaph reads:

Not like Egyptian tyrants consecrate,
Unmixed with others shall my dust remain;
But mold'ring, blending, melting into
    Earth,
Mine shall give form and colour to the
    Rose,
And while its vivid blossoms cheer Mankind,
Its perfumed odours shall ascend to
    Heaven.

The church has a good ring of 10 bells, tenor 17-1-6 cwt.

Baconsthorpe, St Mary (H2): A restrained, yet elegant little church. The tower was rebuilt in 1740, having fallen down the previous year – a neat reproduction, in the *Perpendicular* style. The body of the church is mainly of the *Decorated* period, except the Perpendicular windows. The *chancel* is older, pre-1300, but fairly heavily restored. There are some things inside: the little *screen* at the end of the n. *aisle* (it used to be in Bessingham Church, a few miles away) is beautifully simple, unaffected Perpendicular; another under the tower arch looks as if it was made up from old bench backs. The angled double *piscina* in the chancel is lovely, and like its adjoining *sedilia* is C13. Opposite, a C14 *Easter Sepulchre* – a bit of pomp in miniature, all *crockets* and arches. Crammed into the s. aisle is a huge monument to Sir William Heydon and his wife, 1592 (for about a century, the Heydons were great folk hereabouts). It is a typical example of a commission carried out in a London workshop and was just too big when it arrived. Note in the s. aisle window the remnants of heraldic stained glass – they are bits rescued after the rectory next door received a direct hit from a stray German bomb in 1941 which blew out the church windows. See also the charming little *brass* to Anne Heydon, 1561, set in the wall to the left of the big Heydon monument.

Bacton, St Andrew (J2): Approached from the s., an avenue of trees, grazing black sheep and a donkey provided a fitting foreground for this pretty church when visited, though beyond the scene changes drastically, to the hard-edged sprawl of the great gas terminal complex. The church tower is neat *Perpendicular*, with contrasting battlements, and *sound-holes* with shields set in tracery; and large carved figure niches set low down in the angle buttresses. *Nave* and *chancel* are a mix of *Decorated* and Perpendicular. Indeed, the early Perpen-dicular windows of the nave have more than a hint of Decorated nostalgia in their tracery. The e. window has been renewed in Decorated style. An agreeable, meticulously cared for interior, with the blue-roofed chancel, richly-coloured e. window glass and the particularly lovely *decalogues* painted on the e. wall like ancient illuminated manuscripts. A C19 *reredos* lurks behind curtains on the e. wall. There is a C15 *piscina* with handsome *cusped* arch, and shields in the *spandrels* with a lot of original colour remaining, adjoining very small triple *sedilia*, also C15, all plain, under flattened arches. Placed here is a dumpy stone angel with a scroll, said to have come from one of the tower buttress niches. In the nave, a few old *poppy-heads* remain at the w. end. Very good and unusual font, the finely carved rectangular bowl having angels with shields alternating with *Symbols of the Evangelists*; immediately under the bowl and flowing down to the base are more angels and garland-like canopies, whilst around the base are indeterminate animal heads – though the n.e. one surely suggests a calf.

Bagthorpe, St Mary (D2): This little redundant church retains its original *Norman* font – the rest is totally 1853 by W.J. Donthorne – you will see by the neat red notice board that the *Norfolk Churches Trust* have taken it under their wing and it is used for services. Inside, on the s. wall, framed copies of contemporary pen sketches show the old church before, and during demolition in June 1853. The font is a simple square, with columns at the angles and a pattern of interlaced cords on the n. side only. On the s. wall a large tablet to George William Chad (1849) takes some pains to chart his diplomatic odyssey as a minister plenipotentiary and an envoy extraordinary all over the place. It must have impressed the villagers no end. Good 1850s glass in the e. window and a curious cast iron hexagonal container in the vestry. It has been described as a chest, but there are lugs for a vertical partition inside and a section of the back is not solid. Some form of heating apparatus perhaps? The church has an excellent ring of 6 bells, tenor 7-0-3 cwt.

Bale, All Saints (G2): A magnificent group of 18 ilexes – evergreen small-leafed oaks – provide a noble entrance to this attractive church. The grove, which since 1919 has been in the care of the National Trust, replaces the huge and famous Bale Oak which, 36ft. in circumference, had to be removed in 1869 when it became unsafe. The C14, late *Decorated,* tower has below its west window, with its pretty Decorated tracery, a figure niche – a feature to be found in several towers hereabouts. The *nave* dates from the late C14, but the superb glass assembled in the s.e. window in 1938 is mostly C15 Norwich work. Gabriel, Mary, and a fine old bearded saint dominate a splended *Annunciation* scene. Above Mary, a delightful feathered Angel. Below her, two *apostles* against dark red backgrounds – high quality and possibly C14. Note the tiny black-and-white heraldic shields right at the bottom of the window – they bear the arms of Thomas Wilby, lord of the manor here in the reign of Henry IV (d.1413), who probably built the present church. A wonderful window, deserving of your time. Don't miss the candle beam pulley-block high up at the e. end of the nave roof – a very rare survival, it was used to raise and lower the candle beam which lit the *rood*. Handsome font, dated 1470, showing the *Instruments of the Passion* etc. The *Royal Arms* are a nice example of patch-and-make-do – they were originally *Stuart* arms but are dated 1698, which is *William & Mary,* and initialled for George I, who came still later. In the nave and in the pretty n. *transept* (with its well preserved *rood stair* entrance) are remnants of wall paintings, the *consecration crosses* on the e. walls of nave and transept being the best. Lovely *chancel* of about 1300, with possibly original rafter roof; splendid e. window with very distinctive, generous tracery; and simple side windows, deeply recessed and standing out beautifully against the white painted walls. Simple *angle piscina*. Deep, flat and oblong recess, low in wall to left of altar, is an enigma. The church has a good ring of 5 bells, tenor 9-2-0 cwt.

Banham, St Mary (G7): Long before you get there you can see the 125ft. high ribbed lead spire – and when you arrive, threading round the pleasant tree-lined village green with its coterie of medieval and later houses, you see at once that this is a sparkling building, predominantly of the *Decorated* period – all of the first two thirds of the C14. The spire sits on a fine C14 tower and has, jutting out on its e. side, a tiny *sanctus bell cote*, lead covered too. The

Banham St Mary: Elizabethan Royal Arms

tower has two-light belfry openings with 'Y' traceries, big *quatrefoil sound-holes* in round frames, and a tall and slender w. window, again with 'Y' tracery. The *chancel* e. window, facing you dramatically as you approach from the gate, is a Victorian replacement with tracery which, though somewhat excessive in its exuberant version of C14 Decorated, is nonetheless very striking and complements the wealth of flowing and geometrical patterns which characterise this church. Notice also the *low side window* in the usual place on the s. side of the chancel – a large *lancet* shape with a *trefoil* arch. Decorated too is the fine s. *porch*, with trefoil headed figure niches in both angle buttresses and over the outer arch, the arch itself having floral motifs carved around it. To each side of the porch, unusually, are two two-light windows, again beautifully traceried. Tremendously spacious and light inside, with *clerestory* windows shedding light onto the 'bleached look' timbers of the *nave* roof, with its massive *tie-beams* and *king posts* and dated, large and clear, 1622, with the initials of the churchwardens of the time. Not to be outdone, the restoring wardens of the n. and s. *aisle* roofs responded in due course – in 1845 and 1892 respectively – a nice continuity of tradition. High in the w. wall is a *sanctus bell opening* (immediately below that little lead cote on the spire) giving the ringer an uninterrupted view of the high altar; just below, the *Royal Arms*

of George III. Noble late Decorated *arcade* of five bays, on quatrefoil pillars. In the s. aisle, a good *piscina*, built into the base of a window, with *cusped* arch and, inside, a stone *credence shelf*; immediately to r. a painted *consecration cross*. In the n. aisle at the e. end, in a deep wall recess under a flowing *ogee* arch (complete with carved leaves and a flower in the head of the arch and a *crocket* on top), a rare wooden effigy, of early-C14 date, of a knight in armour, perfectly preserved – even to his aquiline nose. He is reputed to be Sir Hugh Bardolph, founder of this church, who died in 1203, but the armour of his effigy points to about a century later than that. In the angle of the small 'cut off' arch between n. aisle and chancel is a very large figure niche. Opposite, the low side window noted from outside. The rather bare chancel has a low tomb recess in the n. wall, a piscina and triple *sedilia* opposite, all wholly reconstructed. Two items of glass of interest. First, the Elizabethan Royal Arms in stained glass, in a small leaded panel on the s. of the chancel – a rare item (see also Thursford). Then, before you leave, spend a few minutes in front of the enchanting stained glass in the s.e. window of the s. aisle, a radiant Christ in what is patently an English landscape peopled with a profusion of flowers and fruit and ferns, trees and grasses and corn, birds and rabbits and lambs – all in beautifully blending colours by *Henry Holiday*. The church has a good ring of 6 bells, tenor 10-1-11 cwt.

Banningham, St Botolph (I3): The C15 tower is beautifully proportioned with more than the usual number of *drip courses*, and the detailing of the parapet and *sound-holes* is particularly good. The inside, with its C14 *arcades*, has a spacious feeling mainly because there are no choir stalls in the *chancel* which opens to the Lady chapel on the s. side. The *spandrels* of the *nave hammer-beam roof* have varied tracery and the two at the e. end have lovely carvings of angels swinging incense *censers*, one standing in a boat set in a choppy sea. The beam of the *rood* is still there above the chancel arch and is an unusual survival. There are two wall paintings above the nave n. arcade and one is a St *George* (minus his head) and the Dragon. The other was apparently a St *Christopher* but is now hard to make out. The font cover is rather good late-C17 in pine, with slim classical columns supporting an *ogee* shaped top. The medieval glass collected in one of the s. *aisle* windows is interesting. Top left is part of the *Nine Orders of Angels* – the Seraphim is labelled and has purple feathers, and next to him a Cherub whose feathers are covered with eyes (A reference to Ezekiel 10:12: 'Their entire bodies, including their backs, their hands and their wings, were completely full of eyes'). For its date, the monument on the n. chancel wall to Samuel Wanley (d.1723) is surprisingly naive. His coat of arms rests against stacked books and at the bottom a fearsome skull clutches a bone in its teeth. He was rector for 38 years and gave his 'commodious and pleasant dwelling with its appurtenances for the parsonage house'. Below in the centre lies his wife Mary (d.1709): 'none at ye door would She let craveing stay / Or ever goe without an almes away.'

Barford, St Botolph (H5): The C13 tower has a brick *lancet* at ground floor level, and another was blocked up when the *quatrefoil sound-holes* were added – probably at the rebuilding in 1397. The e. buttresses are flush with the face and make it look wider than it is when one approaches. Inside, the *nave* is bare and very wide, and the little *corbels* of the old roof look hardly sufficient for so wide a span. The C14 font has a deep and slightly sloping bowl, and instead of the more usual carved panels it has attractive tracery patterns. There are crude steps to the *rood loft* in a n. window recess and, at the top, the sawn-off timber that supported the loft can be seen in the wall. Interesting that this is lower than the tops of the plain niches either side of the *chancel* arch – they must have been partially obscured when it was installed. They were for the altars of St *Nicholas* and *Mary the Blessed Virgin*, and there is a *piscina* within a *trefoil* arch by the latter on the s. side. The base of the small C14 *screen* is made up of roughly finished boards, and they contrast oddly with the pretty and varied tracery above the *ogee arches* and turned shafts. All of it was painted and grained ages ago and would look infinitely better if it could be stripped. The *priest's door* in the C13 chancel is blocked now, and so too is the *low side window* – look below the tall lancet to the w. on that side and you will see the original sill. An early priest's tomb slab is set in the chancel floor on the n. side and there is a double *aumbry* in the e. wall – the niche to the right of the altar could have been a piscina. The *Royal Arms* on the left of the chancel arch are for George III – well painted on wood and rather good.

Barmer, All Saints (E2): 'Very ruinously decayed' in 1602, neglected in the C18, restored as a mausoleum for the Kerslake family in 1885

and declared redundant in the early 1970s. That might have been that but for the inspiration and energy of the *Norfolk Churches Trust* who leased and restored it and who ensure that occasional services are still held – the vital difference between a church and a museum piece. Although Barmer is scarcely even a hamlet now, there was a *Saxon* settlement around this tiny church, romantically isolated, with clouds of rooks in its grove of oaks, elms and sweet chestnuts. The round tower is *Norman*, but the flint *quoins* at the w. end of the *nave* suggest a Saxon beginning. The C12 doorway was fitted with a cast iron *tympanum* and lining to the door in 1885, and it was then that the C13 *chancel* was so thoroughly rebuilt that only the external shafts of the e. window are original. Inside, both the massive Norman chancel *arch*, with its simple stop chamfers and rudimentary *imposts*, and the tower arch were altered in the C13 to a pointed outline, and the nave *lancets* date from the same period. The *arcade* and the e. and w. *aisle* windows are C14. The wooden shelf on three medieval pillars in the s. e. corner of the nave defies explanation, and the recess in the s.w. corner is also puzzling. Large enough for a tower stair doorway but in the wrong place, it could have been a *banner-stave locker*; if so, it is much shorter than others in the county, and I think it may have been a large *aumbry*. Standing in the base of the tower you can see right to the top – the silence broken only by the soughing wind that sweeps across the open fields and through the trees.

Barney, St Mary (F2): A church full of interest, though much restored. A very simple, early-C16 *Perpendicular* tower. Beside the s. *porch*, note outline of a roundheaded doorway, probably *Saxon* and as early as C10, with typical tile *jambs*. In the angle of s. *transept* and *chancel* (behind large tomb slab) is more Saxon work – tiles and a hunk of dark brown stone – built into fabric. Note too the windows of the late-C13 chancel: contemporary *Early English* double *lancets*. The e. window is very pretty C15 *Decorated*. On n. side of church is another filled-in doorway, C13 *Early English* – and a diminutive 27in. wide. Back now to the s. porch, with its pleasingly rustic inner doorway, dated about 1200. Inside, a really charming little church. The age-mellowed roof of the *nave*, decorated with angels and *bosses* with *Tudor* roses, is simple *arch-braced* and mainly C15. Excellent C15 font, richly carved on its eight faces with sacred emblems: clockwise from the e. face – *Agnus Dei*; the *IHS*; *Mary the Blessed Virgin*; *Holy Trinity*; St *Peter*; pelican; St *Andrew*;

arms of Lords of the Manor. There is a *Jacobean* pulpit, delightfully carved. Fine *rood stairs* with immediately above and opposite, enchantingly carved roof *corbels*. All the nave corbels are worth a careful look – portraits, *Tudor roses* and a grotesque. In the chancel, an attractively solid angle *piscina*, with a tiny niche to left, all of a C13 piece with the *lancet* windows in their deep recesses, and the *dropped sill sedilia*. As you leave, notice the high, carved Jacobean bench-back by the door and, right, the homely hat pegs from the C18.

Barnham Broom, St Peter & St Paul (G5): In its rural retreat, this neat church is dominated by its big, handsome tower which, with the rest of the building, is *Perpendicular*. It has battlements with *flushwork* panelling, surmounted at the corners by three of the four *Evangelists* – the fourth, St *Matthew*, was knocked from his perch in a storm a few years ago. He lies in the *porch*, on a bench, on his back, a seraphic smile on his face, a figure of infinite unconcern. Through a massive ancient door into an interior of great charm, with simple *arch-braced roofs*, white painted between the timbers in the *nave* – and deep red in the *chancel*, which is not perhaps entirely successful. In the nave there are beautiful carved *wall plates*, and deep *wall posts* standing on stone *corbels* – mostly portrait heads, one unusually showing also hands in prayer, another an angel with a book. A little *gallery* houses a perky organ with a *crocketted* organ case. On the front of the gallery, a super little painted *Royal Arms* of George III, signed and dated by its painter in 1803. Below the gallery, an odd font with buttressed corners and battlemented frieze, which could be C19 or medieval. Nearby, a remnant of a *brass* figure and inscription to Edmund Brighteve, 1467, and in the *aisle* pavement, to John and Ellen Dorant, 1503. In the s.e. corner of the nave, a plain *piscina*, and an *aumbry* with a modern door, all indicating a side altar here prior to the *Reformation*. Opposite, the entrance to the old *rood stairs*. The well-carved pulpit is, like the pews, Victorian. Lovely C15 chancel *screen*, with crisp, confident carving in its tracery – and a fine selection of painted saints in its lower panels. N. side: a very faint figure wearing a papal tiara – St *Gregory* (?); *Clement*, with anchor; *Walston of Bawburgh*, the local saint, in a full green robe with a white collar, and his two oxen at his feet; and a bishop (?). S. side: *Edward the Confessor*, with staff and ermine collar and cuffs; *Etheldreda*; *Ursula* (a rarity), crowned, a sheaf of arrows in one hand, and young

women in some profusion at her feet; St *Withburga* of Dereham, with church in hand and doe at feet; *Dorothy*, with basket and flowers; and a problematical one, a lady with a vase and loaves on a tray – either *Elizabeth of Hungary* or *Joan of Valois*. A snug little chancel behind the screen, with a large *angle piscina*, unusual in having a motif of tiny shields carved around both its main arch and its small 'angled' arch, letting on to the adjoining *dropped sill sedilia*. On the n. wall, a monument evidently to a couple of book lovers, for to either side of the flowing Latin inscription to Nicholas Canning, rector here, died 1680, and his son Samuel, 1708, are neat piles of little sculpted books. Notice on leaving that one of the porch windows has been filled in with a remnant of an early medieval stone coffin lid.

Barningham Winter (or Town), St Mary the Virgin (H2): A little difficult to find, as the church is set in the centre of Barningham Park, next door to the fine hall which was built in 1612 for Sir Edward Paston. Once found, the effort is worth it for the pleasure of the setting and the generally picturesque impression of a curiously shaped building approached through ruins. You go in through the remains of the s. *porch*, *nave* and tower which have been ruinous since the early C17. The original C14 *Decorated chancel*, with its elegantly traceried windows, now serves as the church: onto it the Victorians built a small west-end addition, vestries below, a *gallery* above, with an outside entrance and stairway (for the servants and estate workers) and incorporating the original chancel arch. Most attractive inside, light, airy and meticulously looked after. A fine *Royal Arms* (with initials 'CR', for one of the Charleses) in mellow colours is the only stained glass in the e. window (save for some older fragments in the tracery above) and so presents a fine central feature. Two C18 *hatchments* dominate on the e. wall to left and right of the window: Paston impaling Barney, another old Norfolk family; right Mott impaling Partridge (The Motts bought Barningham from the *Pastons* in 1785). Attractive *piscina* and graduated *sedilia*, all under continuous arches; fine remounted and repaired *brass* to John Wynter, about 1410, in full armour. No font – a portable one is used these days. But there is an old one under the ruined tower, which was used a few years ago for the baptism of the Barningham gamekeeper's child – a nice continuance of tradition.

Barton Bendish, St Andrew (D5): The late-C14 tower has large *ogee*-headed niches in the two western angle buttresses at the second stage, *Decorated* bell openings, and a pyramid cap above a plain parapet. Stout stair turret in brick up to ringing chamber; base of tower repointed. There are *Norman lancets* on the n. side of the *nave* and on the s., a tall late-C13 window with 'Y' tracery and a low *transom*. The C14 *chancel* has windows with nice flowing tracery and one on the s. side was extended downwards to form a *low side window* which is now blocked. The C15 s. *porch* leaves no doubt about the church's dedication, for there are St *Andrew's* crosses in *flushwork* on the buttresses and either side of the entrance, one on the gable, and an original figure of the saint with his cross in a shallow niche just below it. The inner doorway of about 1200 shows how the Norman style merged into Gothic – the shafts and *capitals* are Norman but the arch is pointed, even though it still has *billet* decoration on its outer edge. To the right, a small *holy water stoup* and just inside, a small medieval poor box attached to the back pew. The n. side of the nave is filled with attractive oak *box pews* which are lower than usual and have turned *finials* at the corners, simple strapwork and gouge decoration in the top panels, and are dated 1623. Beyond them, a C15 pulpit disguised by C19 additions and heavy varnish stands in front of a tall C14 niche – very handsome with its *cusped* and *crocketted ogee arch* and floral motifs in the surrounding moulding. The stairs to the *rood* are in the wall nearby and note that the vanished loft was lit by a lancet behind the top doorway. The chancel sanctuary is particularly interesting because it still has its complete floor of 4in. square medieval tiles with varying patterns. Not only that, below the C14 *piscina* with its beautiful pierced tracery is a very rare floor piscina. It has a double drain (unlike the other Norfolk example at Wilton) and was probably in use in the late C13, when the ritual called for piscinae with two drains. There is no other known example of this combination of two drains in the floor and one in the wall.

Barton Bendish, St Mary (D5): A lovely little church of great simplicity which was vested in the *Churches Conservation Trust* in 1976. The tower collapsed in the early C18, destroying part of the *nave*, and as the village's third church of All Saints was ruinous (demolished 1787) its late *Norman* n. doorway was removed here to become the w. door of a shortened nave. It is quite elaborate, with *dog-tooth* and beakhead

motifs in the outer arch and the shafts are lapped by a large leaf design, with bobbins on the inner shafts and arch moulding. The whole church is thatched and the minute n. vestry has a blind window, cleverly painted on the outside to resemble *Decorated* tracery. The nave and *chancel* windows all have attractive C14 tracery – note that the one in the s. nave wall has most unusual asymmetrical *ogees* and that the *priest's door* boasts an extremely decorative *hood mould* outside. Within, there are rustic benches at the w. end dated 1637 and some plain deal *box pews*. On the nave s. wall is a large but very faint painting of St *Catherine* with a big wheel emblem and (possibly) a coffin lying on a *bier* underneath. Her face is just discernible and there are similarities with the more elaborate example at Sporle. In the chancel, a line of *quatrefoils* is carved under the *dropped sill sedilia*; no *piscina* survives but there is a small *aumbry* in the e. wall and a larger one in the n. wall which has been enhanced by a carved wooden frame and lining of high quality.

Barton Turf, St Michael & All Angels (J3): The C15 tower is handsomely proportioned, and entry to the church is through a two-storied n. *porch* which is quite elaborate. It has three niches above the arch, *flushwork* panelling, a *base course* of shields, and a vaulted ceiling. The church is renowned for its *screens*. The head of the *chancel* screen is coved with a graceful *crocketted* centre arch, and there are twelve painted panels of exceptional merit. From left to right they represent St *Apollonia*, St *Citha* (or *Zita*), Powers (Raphael fighting a devil), Virtues, Dominions, Seraphim, Cherubim, Principalities, Thrones, Archangels, Angels and St *Barbara*. Those of the Virgin Saints are lovely, with a naive and sweet demureness characteristic of English work of this period at its best. The Angel Hierarchy is a rare subject (*Nine Orders of Angels*), and there is no other screen example in Norfolk, although part of a series can be seen in the e. window at Salle. Here, details of the armour dates the work as mid-C15. The s. *aisle* screen has four kings: *Henry VI*, Edmund, *Edward the Confessor*, and St *Olaf* (or *Holofius*) King of Norway, He is distinguished by the punning emblem of a whole loaf of bread. There are two more panels of St *Edmund* and St *Stephen* above the n. aisle altar which came from Rackheath church. In the s. *aisle* chapel is a fine wall monument to Anthony Norris (d.1786), one of Norfolk's earliest antiquaries, and by some happy chance, the copy of Rubens'

Barton Turf, St Michael and All Angels:
Rood screen detail

'Descent from the Cross' in the chancel once belonged to Dawson Turner, the C19 Gt. Yarmouth historian. A walk round the outside will lead you to a monument on the e. wall of the s. porch to the four young sons of Mr and Mrs Doyley. They were all drowned in Barton Broad on Boxing Day 1781, and one reflects on 'the changes and chances of this fleeting world'. The church has an excellent ring of 6 bells, tenor 10-2-14 cwt.

Bawburgh, St Mary & St Walstan (H5): It takes imagination to people this quiet lane and little churchyard with the stream of pilgrims that once came to pray at St *Walstan's* shrine – one of Norfolk's own saints, but it must have been a rich and bustling spot in the Middle Ages. His well can be seen by asking at the nearby farm, and details of his legend are given in Appendix 1. The *chancel* was rebuilt in 1309, and a splendid shrine chapel added to the n. of the *nave*. For a time, this was a wealthy church, served by a vicar and six *chantry* priests, but at the *Reformation*, Walstan's bones were burned and scattered, the shrine demolished and the building left to decay. So much so that by the C17 the parishioners had to walk to Barnham Broom for services. In 1633, repairs were put in hand and the crow-stepped gables probably date from then. The oldest part of the building is the *Saxo-Norman* round tower, and its candle snuffer cap is now topped by a flame carved in wood as a *Pentecostal* symbol. Just inside the door on the w. wall is a fragment of wall painting, probably part of a much larger scheme; there are texts, and two figures at top and bottom can just be made out. The tub font may be Norman, but if so, it has been totally re-worked. The arch which led to the shrine is on the n. side, and there is a fine modern figure in wood of St Walstan with his scythe on the ledge. There are two C14 angels at the very top of the window overhead, and below them, a line of roundels with the text of the 'Nunc Dimittis' canticle. Further down, two heads (possibly from a Coronation of the Virgin) flank a small head of St *Gregory* wearing his cap as one of the *Four Latin Doctors* of the Church. The nicest piece of glass in the church is in the opposite window on the s. side – a lovely pale yellow C15 St *Barbara* with a palm in one hand and a tower in the other. Most of the *screen* is new work, but the heavy *rood beam* is original. The pulpit came from the cathedral nave in 1892, and it is strange that such a crisp copy of a good medieval design was carried out in pitch pine rather than oak. Opposite stands a dumpy medieval poor-box – a turned shaft with a domed top. Parish churches do have some strange benefactions and Bawburgh is no exception; the churchwardens' staves were once the Drum Major's staff and baton of the Queen's Royal Regiment and are very handsome, with Charles II's loyal Queen, Catherine of Braganza's *Agnus Dei* modelled on one and engraved on the other. Examine the C17 *communion rails*, with their pairs of simply turned *balusters*, and note that they have been joined in two places – a sure sign that they once stood on three sides of the altar and not straight across the chancel. In front of the *priest's door* is a *brass* for vicar William Richers (1531) that has the chalice held by hands, and in the centre of the chancel, a *shroud brass* for Philip Tenison (1660) – he was Archdeacon of Norfolk and kinsman of the Archbishop who crowned Queen Anne. On the same slab, another much larger *shroud brass* – this time to vicar Thomas Tyard (1505) with a big 'black letter' inscription. Lastly for brass lovers, halfway down the nave, the 10in. figure of Robert Grote (1500).

Bawdeswell, All Saints (G3): A delightful reversion to the C18. The little brick and flint Victorian church which replaced a 'pseudo classical building' was itself destroyed by an aircraft crash in 1944. In 1950, J. Fletcher Watson used local flint pebbles and brick as primary materials for the new church which, with its little shingled lantern topped by a weathercock, would not look out of place in colonial Virginia. The interior is charming. It has a w. *gallery* with balustrade and classical columns for the organ, matching columns flank the *apse*, and a suite of solid comfortable panelled pews is complemented by what is surely the only modern *three-decker pulpit* in the country. It needs only an *hour-glass* and wig stand to complete the illusion. Small roundels of Flemish glass have been inserted effectively in the *nave* windows, and a fine melon-legged table is in use as a side altar. It may be unfashionable to imitate but Bawdeswell needs no justification. Go and see.

Beachamwell, St Mary (D5): A weather and time-scarred, but appealing little place, with thatched *nave* and *chancel*, lead-roofed s. *aisle* and a pretty tower. The latter is two thirds round, and *Saxon*, with an octagonal *Perpendicular* top third. The Saxon part has coarse two-*light* triangular-headed bell openings to n. and w. and round-headed ones to the e. and s., with a variety of rough mullions between them. The octagonal top has two-light, *cusped* windows on four sides – alternating with *flushwork* 'mock' window outlines on the rest. The body of the church comes largely within the C14, *Decorated* and Perpendicular, fairly modest on the n. side, more ambitious in the later, s. aisle side, where the *Tudor* windows are *transomed* and generously cusped. Look at the n.w. corner of the nave – the *long and short work* there, retained from an earlier building, is Saxon, and of the same era as the tower. The nice little C15 n. *porch*, with its stepped gable, has its original moulded timber *wall plates* inside. Charming, uncluttered interior under a single plaster ceiling to nave and chancel, with no interruption between the two. Solid rounded tower arch, totally unadorned and

without *imposts*. Above it, high in the wall, is a distinctive door opening either for refuge or valuables belonging to the parish. Low *arcade* of four bays: the two at the w. end are early Perpendicular, the other two of C19 origin. Don't miss the scratched graffiti on the column at the w. end of the arcade, s. side. These are thought to date from the mid-C14 – one is a demon, of remarkable liveliness and quality of drawing, let alone of imagination; to his left you can just make out the outline of a lady wearing a *wimple* head-dress. Above her are details of what appear to be an inventory of materials delivered for the purposes of the rebuilding going on at the time – '600 quarters, 3 lbs', reads one line, 'Four hundred and thirty four lbs', another. Not for nothing have antiquarians described these 'scratchings' as being among the best preserved of their kind in the kingdom. In the s. aisle is a good multi-cusped *piscina* niche under a square hood, its central position in the aisle indicating that the aisle itself was formerly much shorter. In the chancel, behind the nice little *Jacobean* pulpit, is an opulent carved square hood, 'embattled' along the top and with big traceries in the *spandrels*, over the handsomely moulded arch of a filled-in doorway. Also Jacobean appears to be the reading lectern attached to one of the choir stalls nearby. In the chancel floor are two *brasses* to former rectors: one, late-C14, to a priest in his full vestments, but no inscription; the other, a half-figure remembering John Grymeston, and dated 1430. (See Litcham for another interesting example of medieval graffiti).

Bedingham, St Andrew (I6): In the C14, one of Bedingham's manors belonged to the rich and famous Priory of Walsingham and this perhaps explains why a small hamlet has such a spacious and handsome church – there were once two in the same churchyard but all trace of St *Mary's* has long gone. Originally *Norman* (see the round base of the tower and the buttresses on either side of the *chancel*), the present building is largely late-C13, with typical intersected and simple 'Y' tracery in the e. window and in the *aisles*. The *priest's door* in the s. chancel wall is a beauty – graceful triple *colonettes* with carved *capitals*, *dog-tooth* in the arch and rich moulding. Inside, simple braced roofs in unstained pine, fresh white walls and lots of windows combine to make it a delight of light and peace, and the undulating brick and *pamment* floors in *nave* and chancel are enchanting. The font stands high on two steps with *quatrefoil* tracery round the top one. There are battered lions round the stem, but unlike most of the others in the area, this one has big roses in the bowl panels with the *Symbols of the Evangelists*, and an angel playing a lute on the w. side. The pews were originally backless and the w. pair have a pair of heads, a woman in a *kennel head-dress* on the s. and a man in *Tudor* cap on the n. It could be that this marks the old custom of splitting up the sexes during service time, except that it was more usual to place the women on the n. side. Part of the back of the third bench from the back on the s. side must have come from a *screen*. There is an inscription asking one to pray for Simon Tillas and his wife, with a tiny pointing finger at the left hand end in case you miss it! The *aisles* have a range of stark *box pews*. One doesn't often see late-C17 pulpits in country churches, and this one says it was given by Thomas Finderne. Possibly a local product, it has stiff and rustic swags carved on the *pilasters*. Beyond that, a most beautiful C15 *rood screen*. Apart from the top of the screen, all the colouring is original; the *ogee arches* have luxuriant *crocketting* and *cusps*, with tiny heads carved above the entrance. The tracery between is like a series of *transomed* windows. The s. aisle chancel chapel was altered to make it into a *transept* with its own roof, and you will see how the *clerestory* range was blocked in so doing. It has *reticulated* tracery in the large s. window and a *trefoil piscina* below which has a stone *credence shelf* at the back. The angle piscina in the chancel is both attractive and unusual. It has a trefoil arch on a *Purbeck marble* shaft and is next to *dropped sill sedilia*. Then comes its twin on the w. side and the pair, with the tall window between, make a nicely balanced unit which must have been designed to please the eye. The late-C17 *communion rails* are very attractive. They have delicate *balusters* that combine barley sugar and dumb-bell sections very elegantly. The chancel also has some fine monuments to the Stone family – lords of the manor from the C16 to the C19. On the s. side, *Thomas Rawlins'* tablet to William Stone, 'whose blooming Virtues were faded by the nipping blast of a Consumption of which he died at Bristol hot-wells' in 1765 aged 18. This obelisk with urn and shell sconces either side in multi-coloured and white marble was copied accurately by R. De Carle & Son in 1808 for George Stone on the n. wall, its quality having been appreciated forty years on. In the *lancets* of the n. aisle e. window, there is a modern resetting of some interesting glass. The centre section has two early-C15 figures from an *Apostles* sequence, either St *James the Less* or St

Thomas on the left and St *Philip* with his basket of loaves on the right The two big roundels illustrate a different and much later technique with coloured enamels applied to the glass and fired. This provides the brilliant colour in the scenes of the stoning of St *Stephen*, and St *Paul* on the road to Damascus – both vivid and full of action. This church is so nice that one cannot but feel that the lease of it is in the hands of the special providence looking after the things that cannot look after themselves.

Beeston, St Lawrence (J3): There was still a small village here in the C18 but now there are only a few houses within sight of the church. The lower part of the tower and the n. wall have a lot of *carstone* work and probably pre-date the Conquest. The *nave*, with a *porch* added, was rebuilt in the early C14. The *chancel* followed a little later in rather more lavish style; the buttresses have decorative gables, the corners have battlements, and there is a wide band of *flushwork* under the e. window. The inside was transformed in 1803 when the church was 'new roof't and repair'd'. The ceiling is gently coved with widely spaced gothick ribs, and the alternating shields and ornament on the cornice have now been picked out in bright colours – with all the whiteness, this gives the effect of a birthday cake inside-out. The chancel has a fine collection of Preston family monuments, of which the earliest is the tomb chest of Jacob (d.1673). Coloured shields set in curly *cartouches* flank the inscription on the front. Sir Isaac Preston not only has a *ledger-stone* in the sanctuary with curly italic script, but also a big architectural tablet in white marble on the wall above. Opposite, the monument to Alicia Preston (d.1743) is quite grand – a sarcophagus topped by a small urn in an arched recess, with curtains drawn back to reappear again outside the frame and drop in folds. A long Latin inscription is cut on marble drapery below the plinth.

Beeston-next-Mileham, The Nativity of the Blessed Virgin (F4): One of a number of *isolated churches* in this area and by far the largest and most interesting. One can seldom particularize over dedications to St *Mary*, but in the Beeston registers a note of 1598 says that the church was dedicated to the Nativity of the Virgin, as a parish fair was always held on that festival day. The tower and spire were badly damaged by lightning in 1872, and the old spire-cum-cupola (photo inside the church) was replaced by a conventional spire with horizontal bands of lighter slates. The tower has *quatrefoil sound-holes* and 'Y' tracery bell openings, with new work in *Perpendicular* style above that. The main building is early-C14, with *reticulated* tracery in the big e. window and fine *aisle* windows of the same period. The *clerestory* had round windows (see the rims outside), but by 1410 an ambitious roof and range of Perpendicular windows had been completed. Once inside, look immediately overhead at the *boss* in the n. *aisle* roof; it is carved with a black ploughshare which was the fine that had to be paid in Beeston manor on the death of a copyholder. This is a lovely interior in many ways; the marvellous *hammer-beam roofs* of *nave* and aisles are all light untreated wood, and the nave *wall posts* have tall canopied figures, still impressive even though their faces have been chopped away, as have the smaller figures lying under the intermediate principals. Below, the nave pews, again in untreated oak, have pierced and traceried backs, *poppy-heads*, and pretty runs of carving along the top rails. The pews angle away at the w. end to leave a comfortable space around the plain font standing on its high plinth. The *arcades* match the *chancel* arch and are an interesting mixture of slender *Decorated piers* and Perpendicular *capitals* and bases. *Pevsner* believed that this is an overlapping of styles rather than, as *Cautley* would have it, evidence of rebuilding. The *rood screen* presents a very odd sight – the cornice has disappeared and the spikes of the *ogee arches* stick up into nothingness; the delicate carving has broken raggedly at the edges, but below, in the *spandrels* of the panels one can find a unicorn and a mutilated St *George* to the left of the centre arch. The painted figures are too badly defaced to be identified, except that the lamb in the third panel from the left might indicate St *Agnes*. As a consolation there are two *parclose* screens and the one in the n. aisle has exceptional tracery over the heavily *crocketted ogee arches*. The bottom panels are no longer painted on the face side, but the backs still bear a diaper pattern. The pulpit, with its tall panels, dates from 1592 and has been given a new base and top. You will see from the Latin inscription by the n. door that John Forbie gave a set of chancel stalls in 1598 but, unlike those at East Bilney, they have not survived. Going back down the path to the gate, lovers of the fancy should not miss the white cross to the left, proudly inscribed 'Jem Mace, Champion of the World'. The famous boxer was born at Beeston in 1831, lived many years in Norwich; he was one of the first Englishmen to fight abroad, and lies buried at

Liverpool. 'A few of his Old Friends' thought it right that he should be remembered here. There is a stone across the path for a Henry Cooper but then, life is like that!

Beeston Regis, All Saints (H1): Lovely position, alone on rising land above the sea (if one can ignore the unfeeling sprawl of caravans which disfigure the meadow to the n.w.). The tower, unlike most of its C11 and C12 Norfolk contemporaries, is square, and has *quoins* formed of large flints. The *nave arcades* are of the same date as the e. window, with its pretty *Decorated* tracery. But the *sedilia* are *Perpendicular*, and their awkward insertion into a window embrasure suggests that they originally belonged to nearby Beeston Priory. The C15 *rood screen* is beautiful, and alone makes the church well worth a visit. Carefully restored after many misfortunes, its twelve panels of Apostles still have their original colour, and not one has been defaced. The saints' names have been discreetly added recently above the middle rail to help the visitor. Nice plain set of *Laudian communion rails* and a super Elizabethan 'melon legged' communion table in the s. *aisle*. Thoughtful reminder inside s. door of the last of a dynasty of vergers who died in 1975.

Beetley, St Mary Magdalene (F4): Goats in safety grazed, and placidly too, in the big, well-grassed churchyard around Beetley Church when I visited. On a summer's day it all presents a most attractive picture – a largely *Decorated* church, with a solid tower (the battlements are modern) facing the roadway; its fine w. window displaying confidently flowing tracery above a deeply inset and heavily moulded (filled in) w. door. Save for the *nave* n. side (cheaply replaced wooden interlacing tracery) all the windows and doors in the body of the church show the same Decorated form and flow, those on the nave n. side having *butterfly tracery*, while to n. and s. of the *chancel* they are reaching, gingerly, towards *Perpendicular*. There was once a n. *aisle* – thus those unlovely window replacements. Inside, the old three-bay *arcade* is still there, outlined in the wall, and is delicate and attractive. Clean-lined modern *hammer-beam* and *arch-braced* roofs. An enormous C14 chancel arch is supported on rounded triple pillars, forming a frame for the splendidly light and spacious chancel. Chief feature here is a lushly carved *piscina* – five-leaf, *ogee arch*, richly moulded and carved with *crockets*, plus foliage and curious little fauna carvings in the *spandrels*. This pattern at one time evidently extended across the *sedilia* – now wholly disappeared except for the side shafts – and must have been a fine sight. *Rood stair* entrance in s.e. corner of nave. High up in the n. e. corner notice the large wall *corbel* – Was this to support the *rood beam*? Neatly and simply carved octagonal font. Under the tower is the original *Jacobean* altar table – adjacent to the most delightful little doorway, with an *ogee arch*, which leads to the tower stair. As you leave, look at the massive, cracked step inside the w. door: it is thought this might be the pre-*Reformation mensa*, deliberately put here so that everyone who stepped on this 'Popish' relic would thus 'defile' it. Pause again outside the *porch* and pick out the notably preserved *mass dials*, one on each side of the outer arch. The church has an excellent ring of 8 bells, tenor 4-0-7 cwt.

Beighton, All Saints (J5): The C14 tower has a renewed top stage and the battlements, with their prominent corner figures, are dated 1890. The thatched roof of the *nave* forms attractive hoods over the *clerestory* windows, and inside the reeds show through the pattern of *scissors-braced* beams. In the *chancel* the early-C14 stepped *sedilia* and *piscina* are grouped under a range of handsome *ogee arches*, but only one of the *headstops* survives. With the exception of the middle rail, the *screen* is mainly restored work and the modern *rood* has four attendant figures instead of the more usual two. There are two medieval stall ends in the chancel but the rest look like good C19 work and so does the excellent sow with suckling litter on a bench end at the w. end of the n. *aisle*.

Belaugh, St Peter (I4): The church stands on a rise, and the land falls steeply away w. of the tower down to the river, as it does at nearby Wroxham. There are signs of *Norman* work in *carstone* at the n.e. corner of the *chancel*, and there are blocked round-headed arches to be seen on the outside of the s. wall which may be earlier still. The font is a heavy Norman bowl, which has large shallow arches linking the four supporting columns. The tall *screen* has traces of gilding on the upper tracery, and the base panels have painted saints which are of good quality, although their faces have been obliterated. From left to right they are: SS. *James the Less, Philip, Thomas, Bartholomew, John Baptist, Peter, Paul, John the Evangelist, Andrew* (with a rustic cross), *James the Great, Simon, Jude*. The *rood*

stair remains in the angle of the chancel and the n. aisle.

Belton, All Saints (K5): By 1849 all that was left of the round tower was a heap of rubble, and what you see now is a total rebuilding. In 1880 the *nave* received its staring red tile roof and the *chancel* was totally reconstructed. Inside, much the same – *Three-Decker Pulpit* that used to stand on the s. wall surrounded by matching pews, a *barrel organ* with 60 tunes, a w. *gallery* – all made way for standard fittings of the period. There are still good things to see however. Both n. and s. doorways have big *headstops* (the n. still in unrestored condition) and *crocketted* arches with a hint of the *ogee* shape to come. The C13 *Purbeck* font with *blank arcading* on its sloping surfaces was given a high polish by the restorers, but an older *Norman* font which they found underneath has been pieced together and stands opposite the door. There are three windows in the nave that have a *Decorated* (*reticulated*) pattern in the head while the others have a *quatrefoil* design. The square headed *screen* is a better version of the one at Fritton St Catherine. The lower half is made up of oak wainscot boards, on which can be traced the original flower-trail patterns that must have been most attractive in their colour. It still has doors to the full height and, instead of mullions it has turned shafts, each with a host of rings at the top. Tracery wheels sprout in pairs from the columns, each wheel filled with a typical *mouchette* design – very pretty. The sanctuary has an *ogee arched* recess low in the wall on the n. side which was no doubt a tomb designed to do duty as an *Easter Sepulchre*, and the heads on either side are delicately carved inclining inwards, The 1896 *Kempe & Co.* glass in the e. window has typically cool colour: Christ the Vine, with his branches the Saints – a gallery of figures from the *Evangelists* to St *Augustine* of Canterbury and St *Etheldreda*. Below it, a *reredos* of 1887 by James Elwell of Beverley. Most of the figures are conventional but the Crucifixion anticipates the style of Eric Gill and his contemporaries. On the n. nave wall, a chaste tablet to John Ives – local historian and antiquary who died tragically young in 1776. The elegant Latin epitaph (Eheu! Abreptus – Alas! snatched away) has a fine medallion below of a riven oak. There were huge C15 wall paintings uncovered in 1848 of St *James the Great* and the legend of the *Three Living* *and the Three Dead* on the n. wall of the nave, but hardly anything recognisable remains. Strangely, more can be made out of the big C13 St *Christopher* that preceded them, and which now shows through.

Bergh Apton, St Peter & St Paul (J5): This much restored and remodelled church stands on a commanding hilltop site, in a well-timbered churchyard and in the midst of rich farming country. The tower, with its Victorian battlements, is *Decorated*, as is the *nave*, with its 'Y' traceried windows of C19 insertion, plain but pretty s. doorway, and endearingly amateurish *corbel* heads both at the ends of the *hood mould* and at the top of the arch. Nice *Perpendicular* square-headed window in w. face of tower, but the n. *transept* is Victorian, and the s. transept and *chancel* complete re-modellings of the same era of little charm. Spacious, but rather sparse inside, with an unexpectedly pleasing panelled roof in the nave which, at the *crossing* between the transepts, is shaped into pyramidal gables with a wooden hanging pendant in the centre. West *gallery*, cheerfully panelled in green, white and gilt; and a colourful roof to the Victorian chancel, from which hangs a gleaming brass six-branch candelabra. Good octagonal C14 font, with angels and the *Symbols of the Evangelists* around the bowl, and round the base, lions, two robed figures and what could be two very broken and battered *woodwoses*. The church has a good ring of 6 bells, tenor 8-3-15 cwt.

Bessingham, St Mary (H2): A delightful little church, perched up on its mound in a neat and well-kept churchyard. The venerable, time-grained round tower is one of the earliest in the county and certainly pre-Conquest. Built of *carstone* rather than flint it has splendid, rough-built bell openings with triangular heads, the classic *Saxon* outline; equally typical of that period is the interior tower opening high up and looking into the *nave*. Little of interest inside – largely *Perpendicular*, but heavily restored in the C19. Pulpit is about 1500.

Besthorpe, All Saints (G6): There is a handsome uniformity about this early-C14 church that is not disturbed by the C19 restorations – save a vestry leading from the old n. door, and a new e. window. The tower has some unusual features – there are blocked n. and s. windows in the ground floor, the

buttresses change from right-angle pairs to single diagonals at the first stage, and the *sound-holes* are *quatrefoils* set in circular frames. Within, the *transepts* are on a generous scale, and the arches to the *nave* have unusually good *headstops* – a king and a bishop on the n. and civilians on the s. The n. transept *piscina* has a *squint* by it, cutting through the *chancel* arch and giving a view of the high altar. The s. transept is altogether more elaborate; its s. window has attractive *butterfly* tracery, and on the e. wall there are two large niches – not a pair, but contemporary with the rest of the fabric. The r.h. niche matches a piscina nearby in the s. wall, and the same C14 style is to be found in the chancel. There, the piscina and *sedilia* are lovely; *crocketted* gables over *cusped, ogee arches*, with slim pillars which carry through to become pinnacles above. The *Stuart* holy table has been given extra length on new brackets and raised on block feet (when it would perhaps have been better left alone and placed on a low platform). As you can see from the inscription, it was the gift of George Copping in 1624; he was vicar here for 54 years, and in his time Sir William Drury was building the hall across the fields. Sir William's wife, Lady Mary, commissioned *Gerard Christmas* in 1639 to carve the splendid monument to his 'deer and lasting memory' that stands on the n. side of the chancel; Sir William in armour, propped on cushion and rolled mat, looks bland and enigmatic with his neat beard and moustaches, but his widow who kneels at his head and the group of children at his feet are expressively modelled, with more than a touch of family resemblance. The church has a ring of 5 bells, tenor 8 cwt.

Bexwell, St Mary (C5): A farm and a few houses cluster round the church which stands attractively on its small mound just off the main road. There is a range of small *Norman lancets* fairly high in the round *carstone* tower, but the doorway halfway up on the w. face suggests a *Saxon* origin and a place of refuge. The octagonal top is probably early-C16, when money was left for 'the building of the stepyl'. To the left of the n. door, a Norman lancet, with its twin blocked on the s. side of the *nave*, and there are tall renewed lancets in both walls that seem to be C13. The *chancel* was repaired in 1878 and a four-light window was exchanged for the present three lancet arrangement. Have a look at the e. buttress on the s. side – a block of stone at the bottom is hollowed out to form a bowl with a hole in the middle, which suggests that it was once a floor *piscina* that has been taken up and put to a new use (as possibly at South Lopham). The s. *porch* has a new outer arch but the plain C14 doorway has large *headstops*, and the large niche overhead with remnants of canopy and pinnacles contains a modern Virgin and Child. The hall interior of nave and chancel is very simple and the C19 open timber roof is stark with no concessions to beauty at all. At the w. end, a large parish chest with three hasps, a *Stuart* table with a new top, and a C13 grave slab. On it, a stone bowl almost big enough to be a font but shaped like a *holy water stoup*. Was it? On the s. wall of the nave is a small *touchstone* tablet to Henry Bexwell (1581) within an alabaster frame which has carved and painted emblems of mortality, the hour-glass and the scythe. Opposite and slightly larger, a memorial for Francis Bachcroft (1658) in white marble, with stiff little drapes, bows, and a cherub's head on the frame, with arms in a small *cartouche*. The upper door to the *rood loft* shows in the n. wall, and further e. a blocked doorway at an angle may have led to an outside stair. C14 piscina under a five-leafed arch, with stone *credence shelf* and, next to it, plain stepped *sedilia* in the lowered windowsill. There is a memorial here to men of the R.A.F. who flew from the wartime aerodrome across the road and who used this as their church. Extreme old age has a fascination of its own and s.w. of the tower outside you will find the small gravestone of Frances Smith, wife of the *parish clerk*; she died in 1858 aged 106.

Billingford, St Leonard (H8): Take the track up from the main road, and there is a beautiful view across the spread of the Waveney valley into Suffolk – with the brick tower and white cap and sails of Billingford mill as a centre-piece. Local tradition says that the top half of the church tower collapsed 'years ago', but a more considered view is that it was never completed. Anyway, the low pyramidal roof sits sweetly on it. At one time the tall porch had an upper room but the roof was restored with much else in 1881. The main fabric is a mixture of C14 and C15 – the windows in the *chancel* have *Decorated* tracery, those in the *nave Perpendicular* with embattled *transoms*. In the porch there are remains of a *holy water stoup* to the right of the door under a *trefoil* arch and the original door is decorated with floral motifs. Inside it, to the left, note the door to the porch room – a lucky survival with pretty tracery. The nave roof is fine – single framed with *wall posts* on stone *corbels*.

These have excellent heads and an angel bearing a monogrammed 'M'. The font has a tall bowl, the panels carry big *Evangelistic Symbols* and shields – St *George*, the donor's arms, the *Trinity*, and St *Edmund's* crown and arrows. Smiling lions guard the shaft and there is a modest C17 cover. The octagonal pulpit is the same period as the font cover and the two back panels are taken up to support a *tester* which has turned pendants – similar in style to the cover and possibly by the same craftsman. By it, fixed to the *screen* is the old *hour-glass stand*, and on the other side the *rood stairs* go neatly up from a window embrasure through a little arch in the wall and retain their wooden treads. The C15 screen is square headed with tracery around the *ogee arches* and has been successfully restored and partly re-coloured. There are ten old bench ends (to which pine pews have been added) which have floral motifs carved on the bevels, and two of the *poppy-heads* have masks carved in them – one with its tongue out! Chancel roof of 1881 and below it a C13 trefoil *piscina*, and instead of the common *dropped sill* next door to form *sedilia*, here it is only partly done and gives room for one person only. The homely *Stuart* table has been given a broader top and continues in use as the altar, and on the n. wall there is a monument to Christopher le Grys (1601) – badly cracked black marble tablet set in an alabaster frame with his coat of arms on top. There are fragments of C14 and C15 glass, including shields of the Hastings (n. chancel), the de la Poles (s. chancel – this powerful Suffolk family are much in evidence in the Waveney valley), and the Brewses (n. w. nave). From this tiny village came a V.C. of the first World War. Lieut. Gordon Flowerdew had emigrated to Canada, but came back with Lord Strathcona's Horse and led a charge on the Somme. It cost him his young life – and gained half a mile:

> Was it for this the clay grew tall?
> – O what made fatuous sunbeams toil
> To break earth's sleep at all?

Billingford, St Peter (G3): This is a big church for what is no more than a hamlet, but because the ground slopes quite steeply from e. to w. the tower, though more modest in size, holds its own against the rest of the building. Like the *nave* and *chancel*, it is C14, and, unusually, octagonal all the way, with buttresses to the w., with attractively panelled battlements. The chancel e. window was bricked up at some time and the smaller *Perpendicular* style replacement

Binham, St Mary

looks like Victorian work. Just round the corner on the n. side is the *priest's door*, and the *lancet* beyond has a blocked *low side window* below it. Entry is by way of a red brick *porch* and a C14 door, and the interior is very spacious and uncluttered – a broad nave with narrow *aisles* under steep roofs beyond C14 *arcades*; overhead, a range of *quatrefoil clerestory* windows. The font is not the usual Norfolk style, but late-C13, and the sloping sides of the bowl each have a double arcade – very like *sedilia* of the period and most attractive. The pitchpine pews and enormous stone pulpit are Victorian, but the C16 lectern with its mighty eagle is unusually interesting. It is cast in unpolished latten (the amalgam of metal used for memorial *brasses*), and it is strange to think that another like it from the same foundry can be seen in St Mark's, Venice, as well as the one in St Nicholas, King's Lynn, nearer home. The sanctuary *piscina* is one of those with a stone *credence shelf*, and as you come back to the nave, note that tracery from the old *rood screen* has been used again in the front row of pews. Thomas Leeds (1836) has a very wordy epitaph by the pulpit, but see the simple slab of Ruth

Green (1691) just to the e. – country mason's lettering and full of character.

Billockby, All Saints (K4): All alone in the fields shielded by tall trees, this late-C14 church must have been exceptionally fine. Already in decay, it was struck by lightning in a great gale of 1762, leaving the tower, *porch* and *nave* all in ruins. The *chancel* remained to serve as the present church and is 'clean and decent'. It is worth looking at the ruins to appreciate the obvious quality of the original work. There is a good n. doorway, the *rood loft* stairs are virtually complete, and on the s. side of the nave, note the curious 'ragged staff' set at an angle in the *flushwork* by the side of each window.

Binham, St Mary (F2): Approached across the rolling landscape from the direction of the great pilgrimage centre of Walsingham, this must in its prime have been a glorious and inspiring sight, when the church was the centrepiece of a vast Benedictine house. Even now, the great west front of what remains of the majestic priory church – the *nave* only – is a fine spectacle, despite its battered details and its huge west window bricked in. This magnificent example of *Early*

English work can be accurately dated, since it was built during the time of Prior Richard de Parco, 1226-44. This gives it an added interest and importance, for the west window has *bar tracery*, which indicates that this could be the very earliest tracery of its kind in England. Inside, the scene is superb: soaring *Norman* strength, massive yet not weighty – most of the great rounded arches are plain, but those either side of the altar have fine *billet* and zig-zag moulding. The arches were bricked in soon after Henry VIII's Dissolution of the Priory, leaving the *aisles* beyond, and the *transepts*, to decay – and *Tudor* windows, with their typical depressed arches, inserted into the new brickwork. Note that not all the interior is Norman – at the west end it is Early English work of the C13, like the west front, either an extension or a rebuilding. Very interesting in the sanctuary are a triple *sedilia* and blocked *priest's door*, under one continuous Early English moulding. The nail-studded frame set into the wall, above right of the altar, is a puzzle. The lovely early *Stuart* altar table is exposed to view; whilst now serving as sanctuary chairs are two exceedingly ill used *misericords*, rescued from the troublous past. There are some fine original benches and excellent *poppy-head* bench ends carved with figures; look for the little lion, the only individual here not to lose his head at the *Reformation* – perhaps his Royalty saved him. Which leads us on to the *Royal Arms* at the back of the church, originally set up in 1815, the year of Waterloo, painted by William Archer of Foulsham, whose name appears on the back (his tombstone is at Foulsham church). The Arms were for long left to decay in a dark corner, but in 1969 they were restored well and placed in a gothicky wooden frame. Just below the arms, a mutilated *holy water stoup*. The C15 *seven sacrament font* is fine, though much defaced. Remnants of an old *screen*, painted over with 'goodly texts', now serves as a bench back to the rear pew.

Bintree, St Swithin (G3): One of four churches in the county dedicated to the saint of Winchester. There is a modern statue of him in the niche over the s. *porch* entrance. The tower is early-C14 with simple Y-tracery in the w. window. The same style is found in the *transept* e. windows, but the s. window is much more ambitious with fine *reticulated* tracery enclosing smaller designs. The transept was restored in 1928 and now forms an attractive Lady chapel. The C14 font has unusually fine panels of shallow tracery in a variety of forms. The greater

part of the *chancel* collapsed in 1806 and was rebuilt to half its original length. There is a tablet outside over the e. window 'I.A. Rector 1761', but this must have been re-set. Rediscovered in 1903, the C12 pillar *piscina* has survived at least two rebuildings, and a short column of the same date or a little later has been let into the *jamb* of the chancel s. window. A bell was sold in 1864 to provide the present pulpit – a monstrous cube on four elephantine legs. Near the font there is a *chalice brass* to a C16 rector, Thomas Hoont, and an epitaph to another incumbent in the C17, Ralph Outlaw: 'Reader pray stay, death's trophies view and see...In them what thou thyself ere long must be.' The processional cross is a reminder of an almost forgotten facet of Anglican history. It belonged to Fr. William Enracht, rector 1895-1898, who was the last priest to be imprisoned for introducing Roman ritual into his services. The indictment was brought under the Public Worship Regulation Act, a piece of legislation that was soon withdrawn following a public outcry.

Bircham Newton, All Saints (D2): A neat, compact C13 church, with pairs of *lancets* in the s. wall of the *nave* and in the base of the unbuttressed tower, and 'Y' and intersected tracery in the *chancel* which dates from around 1300. Inside, the square *Norman* font tapers slightly and is devoid of ornament save for nooks at the head of the corner chamfers. There was wholesale restoration in 1858 and the oak *box pews* have that date and a church-warden's name cut carefully on an end panel. They have quaint Victorian versions of *poppy-heads* and are altogether a strange mixture (The same joiner was at work at Gt Bircham). The simple semi-circular chancel arch has the slightest of *imposts* and a crude recess on the s. side once led up to the *rood*. It now houses a two-decker pulpit in grained deal which is probably a century older than the pews. Over the chancel arch, a large *Royal Arms* of George III, painted on boards and framed. The chancel has a small early-C14 *piscina* with pierced *trefoil* tracery, and in the opposite corner, a fine recumbent figure of a C14 priest – worn but most impressive. He is fully vested, and above his head, a symbol of the sun on one side and a fascinating head of a child on the other. It might be taken for a soul symbol, except that in 1832 the tomb was opened, and the skeletons of a man and a child were found buried together. I do wish we knew why! On the chancel s. wall an oval tablet records the death in 1829 of John Stephens, two-year old son of the Rev

Philip Ward and Horatia Nelson. Thus in this quiet backwater we find a grandson of 'The Norfolk Hero', and an echo of his romantic liaison with Lady Hamilton.

Bittering, St Peter (F4): Down a narrow twisting lane then up a field track, and you'll find this church amid the fields, lonely but not forgotten, for it is still looked after with affection, and a service held here once a month. It is a 'single hall' building, about 50ft. long by 18ft. wide, with a C17 bell-cote on the w. gable. Mainly mid-C13 *Early English* work, the church has a simplicity which gives it great charm, its walls being picked out by *lancets* (the e. window is a pretty set of three) and some later, very plain, *Perpendicular* windows under square hoods. Inside it is as simple and homely as one could have hoped. White painted walls under the plainest of roofs – and white painted too is the late *Norman* font, with its severe round bowl standing on four unadorned shafts. There is a tiny pipe organ; a *Jacobean* pulpit, with several benches nearby of the same period, all distinctively carved; a solid, straight-forward C15 wooden *screen*; a charmingly rustic Early English *angle piscina* in the *chancel*, and *sedilia* nearby (What could that curious, now defaced carving have been at the top right hand side of the *sedilia*?) and a couple of ancient stone coffin lids with remarkably well preserved carvings. The *communion* rails are cast iron, and rather pretty. Notice as you leave the unusual feature at the w. end, where arches set into the wall are fitted with stone benches.

Blakeney, St Nicholas (G1): A large, powerful *Perpendicular* building of the first half of the C15, with a great lofty tower (104ft. high), and enormous four-light *aisle* windows and three-*light clerestory* windows, presenting an impressive pattern of mathematical order. The odd little tower at the n.e. angle of the *chancel* – again C15 Perpendicular – was probably a lighthouse of sorts, containing a beacon light to guide mariners in the days when Blakeney was a bustling port. A large-scale restoration of the church in the 1880s took place when the tower and complete outer walls of the church were given a new 'skin' – thus its well preserved appearance now. Base of the tower is richly panelled, and the buttresses are decorated with *flushwork* and, at the n. and s. corners, with shields representing the arms (inaccurately?) of the bishoprics of Thetford and Norwich. The n.w. buttress of the n. aisle has a shield bearing

Blakeney, St Nicholas

the *Instruments of the Passion*. At the e. end of the church, note the small window high over the *Early English* chancel window – this lights a vault above the *groined* chancel cieling. The church inside is impressive, albeit a trifle gloomy. A lofty *nave* of six great bays, its handsome *hammer-beam roof* carved with figures on the beam angles and with decorative fretted work in the *spandrels*. Up above the chancel arch is the original *rood beam*, carved with fleur-de-lys. Despite the mutilated faces of its carved figures – the four *Evangelists* with their symbols – the C15 font is fine. Other shields carry the *Instruments of the Passion* and the *Five Wounds of Christ*. Under the tower, note the little recess (n. side) with holes in its base – probably a rare *cresset stone*. Both *aisles* have some original C15 open-work benches and *poppy-heads* (The nave pews are Victorian.), and their window sills are let down to form seats as in some other churches locally. In n. *aisle*, some good C15 glass in window adjacent to pulpit; in s.e. corner, stairs to former *rood loft* (The present great *rood screen* and loft date from 1910, with the exception of two small original panels.); over entrance door, *Royal Arms* of George III, dated 1818 – though the Arms shown were not by then in use in that form. Immediately opposite, on wall of s. aisle, handsome painted *decalogue boards*, with Lord's Prayer and creed, with a framing of cherubs' heads. Set into the pavement in front of the screen is a tiny *brass* with shield to John Calthorp, 1508, one of the benefactors of the Carmelite Friary whose church this originally was. Calthorp was precise in his Will – his 'Synfull body' was to be buried 'in the myddys of the chancel'. And what a chancel this is – a feast of subdued C13, Early English beauty, with its groined and vaulted ceiling with boldly-leafed *bosses*, its fine e. window of seven *lancets*, an *Easter Sepulchre* (with a Victorian canopy), attractive triple *sedilia* on s. side; and a few original *misericords* among the otherwise modern reproductions. Both inside and outside this church, several memorials testify to Blakeney's sea-going past and the price so many paid for it. Like John Easter, whose stone is in the churchyard, dated 9th Feburary 1861:

I with seven others went
Our fellow men to save
A heavy wave upset our boat
We met a watery grave.

Blickling, St Andrew (H3): Conveniently placed, by the entrance to Blickling Hall. The tower, *porch*, and much of the exterior is Victorian, although the s. door is C13, and the *arcades* C15. A massive iron-banded chest with five locks stands just inside the door, and is inscribed, 'Mayster Adam Ilee mad ys chest and Robert Filipis payed yer for God have mercy on yar soules'. Beyond it is a font in the conventional E. Anglian style, but a profusion of remarkably smug lions, and traces of colour give it a highly satisfactory feeling. Still at the w. end, within the n. arcade, is the large monument to the eighth Marquis of Lothian by G.F. Watts (1878). Considering that he was buried elsewhere it is a somewhat overstated reminder. Two life-size angels strike attitudes of concern at head and foot of the recumbent figure which, swathed in a generous shroud, sports a beard of Old Testament proportions. His widow's memorial by the door, by A.G. Walker, is comparatively tame. There are many *brasses*, and a series of replicas grouped in the n. *aisle* for the convenience of rubbers is a very sensible idea. The original to Sir Nicholas Dagworth (d.1401) lies before the tomb-chest at the e. end of the s. aisle. He built the first Blickling Hall, and is shown in full armour, with a massive helm behind his head and with a lion at his feet. Nearby, the brass to Anne Astley (d.1512) shows her with two babes in arms, and the Latin inscription describes her death after the birth of twins. In

front of the pulpit, the brass to Roger and Cecily Felthorp (1454) portrays their sixteen children as well, and in the *chancel*, Isabelle Cheyne's effigy depicts the fleeting style of the *butterfly head-dress* of the 1480s. The chancel has a nice *angle piscina*, with a tiny eagle and young in a wicker nest serving as a stop to the arches. In the s. wall is the alcove monument to Elizabeth Gurdon, who died at seventeen on a visit to Blickling, just before the Armada. Rigid in cap and ruff, and with sadly mutilated stumps for hands, she half turns her head; a wide-eyed girl wearing a faint smile. Sir Edward Clere provided her memorial, and his own is the large alabaster tomb-chest at the e. end of the s. aisle. Now lacking its effigy, it carries an armorially illustrated pedigree around the sides which stretches fancifully back to the Conquest. Outside the church, on a stone n.w. of the tower, there is a salutory corrective to all the temporalities inside. It concerns James Howard, *parish clerk* for fifty years, who died aged 88 in 1829: 'Praises on tombs is oft times vainly spent / Mans good deeds is his best Monument.'

Blo Norton, St Andrew (G8): In deepest rural S. Norfolk, this church stands amid arable fields and twisting lanes, with a dark hallway of evergreens from gate to *porch*. Plain battlemented tower, with two-light belfry windows, solidly traceried and *Tudor* arched, though the tower is basically of the *Decorated* period (Notice the perfectly Decorated style outline of the partially filled-in w. doorway). 'Single hall' *nave* and *chancel*, with a pleasant variation of windows from single large *lancet* (one on each side, though their originality as we see them now is not wholly certain), 'Y' traceried examples and simple *Perpendicular* of both square-headed and pointed patterns. The triple-lancet e. window is a C19 replacement. We enter the church through a special little survivor – a C16 wood-framed porch, neatly carved in the *spandrels* over the outer arch. The low n. door, with its moulded hood and arch, is early-C14, with beside it a charming, tiny *holy water stoup*, under a *cusped* arch. An interior of country simplicity and instant appeal, with the plain-glassed low windows, in their deep, light-reflecting embrasures, looking out on quiet churchyard and serene fields. Simple C14 font, the eight panels of its bowl carved with various window designs, a *quatrefoil*, a six-pointed star, and the 'X' cross of this church's dedicatory saint. Well-preserved *rood stairs*; and in the embrasure of the sanctuary s. window, a three-stepped-levels arrangement of *piscina* drain on the highest 'step', and *sedilia* seats formed by the other two. Under the tower is a good set of *Royal Arms* for James I, dated 1610. Facing the main door in the nave will be seen a classically simple wall monument, with gilded crest and crown, 'To the memory of His Highness Prince Frederick Victor Duleep Singh M.V.O. 3rd son of Their Highnesses the Maharajah and Maharanee of Lahore. Born 23rd January 1862, died 15th August 1926.' The Royal Family of the Punjab were exiled from their state by the Imperial Government of India, and here in Blo Norton, at the hall, Prince Frederick made his home, and was a benefactor of this church. Later the family acquired the large Elveden Estate near Thetford, and it is there, in Elveden churchyard, that Duleep Singh lies buried – though in recent years attempts have been made by Sikh religious leaders to have his remains returned to his native Punjab. The church has an excellent ring of 6 bells, tenor 8 cwt.

Blofield, St Andrew (J5): An impressive church with a fine, soaring *Perpendicular* tower, beautifully panelled with *flushwork* around the base and on the faces of the buttresses; the modern shield carvings handsomely adorn the battlements; there are enormous three-*light* belfry windows; *sound-holes* with unusual, honey-comb tracery in the third stage; and a great west window with an imposing doorway below it (The cross of St *Andrew* and keys of St *Peter* are carved in the *spandrels*.) in stylish harmony. The n. *porch* used to have an upper room, now gone, which for many years housed the village school. We pass through it to a grand interior, with lofty arcades (with *quatrefoil* grouped pillars) of five bays, of the late-C14. Note that the easternmost bay on the s. side has 'slipped' badly – and a massive transverse arch in the *aisle* been put in to take the strain. The *clerestory* is Perpendicular, around 1400. The roof above, supported on deep *wallposts* and battlemented *corbels*, is modern. Raised up at the back of the nave are some old C18 *box pews*; a lot of old benches and *poppy-heads* here, some with carved figures, those on the arms of the front benches being particularly good. The *chancel* arch is enormous, yet has a look of lightness and fragility; and is complemented by an equally lofty tower arch, framing the w. window. The aisle windows are replacements, as is the e. window, but are Perpendicular in style and carefully in sympathy with all. At one time the chancel must have been a grand sight-but three of its great

side windows have been blocked in. The sill of one of these is dropped to form plain *sedilia*, adjoining a Perpendicular *angle piscina*, with good pierced tracery. The stone *reredos* is brisk C19 Gothic. On the n. wall is a formalised marble monument to Edward *Paston*, 1630, who was attached to the court of Henry VIII: it has mother and father, with children two deep, five sons and four daughters; a lugubrious skull tops all. Hanging above it, a helmet of about 1530. Nearby, up in the chancel n.w. corner, is the blocked-off entrance to the *rood loft*, its stair entrance being in the n. *aisle*. The remains of the *rood screen* has restored paintings of the apostles and, on top, modern carvings of St *Andrew* and St *Peter*. Note, under centre window in n. aisle, the faded remains of a painted *consecration cross*. The roof here, with its plain, solid beams, looks original. Finally – the medieval font: it is extremely interesting in that the carvings set into the eight panels round its bowl represent incidents in the life of Christ, from Nativity to Crucifixion, most unusual subjects for a font. The church has a good ring of 8 bells, tenor 15-2-0 cwt.

Bodham, All Saints (H2): Recently rescued from neglect, this plain but pleasant little church is now as neat and well-kept, inside and out, as loving care can make it. It is mostly simple *Perpendicular* in style, with a neat, earlier tower. The unfortunate red-brick buttresses on the n. side are Victorian. In the *porch*, with its attractive *Decorated* outer arch, is a *holy water stoup* interestingly lined with old, rough-glazed tiles, and from the Bacon Papers, vol. 2, p. 19, we know that they were made by a brick maker called Blogge who re-roofed the church with tiles in 1578. There is another stoup on the inside wall. A bright, light uncomplicated village church inside, whose timeless character is enhanced by highly ornamental, but also very practical, hanging oil lanterns – there being no electricity here. The furnishings, including the splendidly solid, 'Town Hall Victorian' pulpit, are said to have come from Beckham Workhouse chapel. A plain figure niche above, a nice *piscina* to the right of the *nave* altar, no doubt there was originally a *guild altar* belonging to one of the three guilds who, *Blomefield* says, had their 'lights' in this church in medieval times. Entrance to *rood stair* may be seen at left of the early-C14 *chancel* arch. Two of the square headed Perpendicular windows on the n. side of the nave have interesting wooden frames, carved and coloured to match the surrounding stonework. *Royal Arms* of Queen Anne above indentation of old n. doorway (which is clearly defined outside).

Bodney, St Mary (E6): A pretty little chapel-like building, perched on a knoll in lovely countryside – but with virtually no village now to call its own, and less than 20 parishioners. It is a single small 'hall' building of continuous *nave* and *chancel*, no tower, and a small *bell cote* on the w. gable. Heavily restored in the late C19 when all the windows were replaced, though in most cases faithful copies of the originals, in simple *Decorated* and *Perpendicular* forms, as is made clear by a pre-restoration drawing of the church, displayed inside. At this time the whole fabric was 'made new'. Nonetheless a very ancient foundation, dating from *Saxon* days – fragments of the original structure are built in, against the buttress in the n.e. corner, for example. Close observation of the outside of the n. wall of the nave will reveal the head, footstones and tiny rounded arch of a very narrow slit window, no more than five inches across, of early though unclear date. Interior of utter simplicity and great charm. Plain modern roofs; severe C14 octagonal font; surprisingly spacious chancel arch (note immediately above its *capitals* the indentations where the *rood beam* sat). To the right, set into the wall, is the well-preserved *rood stair*, complete with loft level exit. This, together with the unadorned *piscina* in the chancel and the remnants of a painted *consecration cross* were brought to light during the Victorian restoration. Homely old low rustic pews in the nave, with pierced backs to the benches and nice old *poppy-heads*. The pulpit is panelled, unsophisticated *Jacobean*.

Booton, St Michael & All Angels (H3): The Reverend Whitwell Elwin was not only Rector for fifty years (1850-1900), he was also editor of the prestigious 'Quarterly Review', and entirely dissatisfied with the parish church. It was unprepossessing, in poor state, and he began to improve it. In the end, he rebuilt the whole thing, keeping only the walls of *nave* and *chancel* encased in new work. Lack of training as architect or draughtsman was not an impediment, and he gaily filched designs from here, there, everywhere and nowhere – nave windows from Temple Balsall, w. window from St Stephen's chapel, Westminster, n. *porch* from Burgh, the diagonally placed twin towers from a fertile imagination. The outside is a riot – pinnacles

Booton, St Michael and All Angels: Detail of s. nave window

of all shapes and sizes, some with *crocketting* so lush it verges on the fungoid. The *priest's door* has a porch like part of Peterborough w. front seen through the wrong end of a telescope. From a distance the fairytale outline of the towers looks like an errant fragment of Milan Cathedral peeping over the trees. The interior keeps it up. Enormous angels with upswept wings jut from the *hammer-beams*, and there is an extraordinary rounded triangle of a window above the chancel arch lighting nothing and giving no light. The *chancel* side windows are deeply recessed (to mask the old walls), and the glass is a series of angel themes from the Old and New Testaments. The glass in the nave windows is really pleasing, full of muted greens and blues, here and there a flash of brighter colour. A procession of musicians on the s. side is matched on the n. by female saints and attendant angels, all wending their way dreamily eastward. Designed by Cox, Sons & Buckley in the 1890s, this is a complete glazing scheme for the whole church – something very rare in East Anglia. Elwin has a simple memorial in his far from simple chancel. Below, one of the few survivals from the old church – a small *brass* with lettering of real quality: 'Here Lyeth The Bodi of Master Edward Fentone preacher of ye worde in Boton 46 yeares buried in the yeare of our Lord 1610.' In the n. *porch* another remnant – what must have been a beautiful statue of the Virgin and Child, but when found in a blocked doorway during the rebuilding, the heads had already been hacked away. Sir Edwin Lutyens, architect of New Delhi and Liverpool's Catholic Cathedral, called Booton 'very naughty, but in the right spirit'. Who shall say he was wrong? The church is now in the care of the *Churches Conservation Trust.* The floors have been handsomely renewed, and plans are in hand to replace the lamps that were originally suspended from the hammer beams in the roof.

Boughton, All Saints (D5): If there were star ratings for village ponds, Boughton's cottage-ringed example would get five at least. Just up a lane is the unassuming little church. Only the attractive tower is old, the rest having been rebuilt in 1872. Late-C13/early-C14 by the look of its w. and belfry windows, the tower has modestly panelled battlements and *crocketted* corner pinnacles, a *base course,* and defined only by two very heavy *string courses.* An unusual element is the centrally placed stair turret on the s. side, which goes right up to the belfry level and culminates in a neat little pyramid cap. In the rebuilding of the church, the s. doorway, with a *mass dial* carved into one of its *jamb* stones, was re-used; it appears to be of about the same date as the tower. The rest, in a very basic interpretation of *Early English* and *Decorated* styles, is Victorian to the last brick, nothing of the old remaining. Lovingly looked after, this is a village church with a palpable atmosphere of welcoming warmth.

Bracon Ash, St Nicholas (H5): Lying in a quiet sequestered churchyard it is a plain little church with no tower. There used to be a bellcote until early C20 but it was taken down and the single bell now hangs from a frame by the s. door.

The C18 Berney mausoleum juts out to the n. of the *chancel* and looks too squat and heavy for the parent building. The late-C13 chancel is best appreciated inside where you can see the lovely range of grouped windows n. and s. – slim shafts and carved *bosses* on the *hood moulds.* The rhythm of the arches differs from side to side and what a pity that the symmetry of those on the n. was broken for the 1694 Bedingfeld monument and then for the Berney mausoleum. The entrance to this is framed by a *Renaissance* monument in terracotta very like the Bedingfeld tombs at Oxborough, and one wonders whether it was complete before the Berneys came along. That family have left a grand array of *hatchments* in the chancel – hung almost haphazardly as pictures might be in a crowded room, The *low side window* on the s. side is blocked, but note that it was part of the window (about 1300) above. Over the chancel arch is a nice big set of *Royal Arms* for George III set in an architectural frame, and the *rood stairs* can be seen in the n. wall. The large C14 font is an unadorned octagon on a heavy shaft. The pews here are modern and a very good set too – traditional style, well made and well finished. The pale brick floors are more handsome than any carpet.

Bradfield, St Giles (I2): All alone up a narrow lane, with its fine four-stage *Perpendicular* tower dominating its surroundings – even though it is rather blunt on top, as it was never finished. Most attractive are the buttresses at the e. end of the *chancel,* with their sprightly carved pinnacles. *Nave* and chancel are basically mid-C14, but the church was much knocked about in an early-C18 'rebuilding' – which meant demolishing the nave *aisle* and walling in the *arcades,* as can be clearly seen inside. As you go in, you seem to step back a century and more – a slightly mouldering air, old hanging oil lamps and a little pedal organ in a beautiful mellow walnut case; time here has stood still. There is a C14 font. *Brass* memorial inscriptions let into the nave pavement are, w. to e., John Tebald and his wife Agnes, 1490; Margaret, wife of Thomas Heins, 1534; and John Tebald, 1506. Over chancel arch remains of the medieval painting about which the experts disagree: like a crude *Trinity,* says one; Christ on a rainbow displaying his wounds, says a second. The second, we think, wins on points. Now the chancel: C14, very fine, with good five-light e. window. In s. wall, a nice *Decorated piscina* with *cinquefoil* head; opposite, a big recess where there was probably an *Easter Sepulchre.*

Bradwell, St Nicholas (L5): Urban tentacles have crept out and surrounded this church which, forty years ago, stood in quiet countryside, but the leafy graveyard remains a quiet and pleasant place. Another of Norfolk's round towers – *Norman* with bands of thin red brick especially noticeable at the top, and simple early brick bell openings. The body of the church is early-C14 and a number of the buttresses have been repaired in C18/C19 brick. The *nave* has a tall 3-bay C14 *arcade* on *quatrefoil* pillars, and above each arch is a tiny circular *clerestory* window. There are two more circular C14 windows of differing designs in the w. walls of the *aisles*. A big drop in the roof level from nave to *chancel*, plus a relatively small chancel arch sets the chancel apart, almost as a separate space. Like the side windows, the e. window has a *reticulated* motif set within another in the tracery, but it's difficult to say whether this is original or C19. The 1898 glass has lots of yellow and cream in the colour scheme and is not unpleasing on a sunny day. The *sedilia* and *piscina* in the sanctuary are grouped under a range of *cusped* arches and the *quatrefoil* columns between the seats are free-standing to form a miniature *arcade*. Opposite, William Vesey's monument has been restored in full colour so that it probably looks much as it did when he died in 1644. He kneels, with his two wives facing each other primly in front and there are two elder children behind. On the frieze underneath, four more little girls with a brother stiffly propped up on one elbow. The late-C17 *communion rails* are unlikely to have been designed for the church but are an asset nonetheless. The heavy 6in. deep top rail is carved on one face with a succession of boisterous sea monsters being ridden by *putti*, and it is supported by excellent heavy barley sugar *balusters*. Both *aisles* had e. chapels and you can see the simple *trefoil*-headed piscina – the one on the n. is in the end pillar of the arcade by the organ. Looking up by the chancel arch on that side you will see the epitaph of Thomas Salmon (d.1829) – average conventional expression of grief. But read on. When his wife Ann died, the poet did much better, and a thoughtful 'ivy and the oak tree' theme was the result – worth reading. On the s. side of the chancel arch, a substantial staircase to the old *rood loft* is set in the wall with its entrance around the corner in the s. aisle chapel. The font is *Perpendicular,* in a familiar local style. The angels are in deep bas-relief carrying shields (emblems of the *Trinity*, the Passion, the *chalice* and *host*) and the lions below have snootily uplifted muzzles with plenty of whisker dots.

Bramerton, St Peter (I5): Snug within its village, the church has a time-mellowed, venerable look about it. It's mainly in the *Decorated* style, including the handsome *reticulated* e. window – *Blomefield* in his History gives a definite rebuilding date of 1462: but unless the Decorated style lingered on here for a surprisingly long time, then the real date could be anything up to a century and more earlier. *Dr Pevsner* dates the tower as late C13 to early C14. The window traceries in the tower, as in the *nave* and *chancel*, are in most attractive Decorated designs; and on the chancel s. side, a curiously appealing feature is the mellow *Tudor* red-brick square hooded *priest's door*, inserted in the late C15 or early C16. All the buttresses are faced in flint and stone *flushwork*, with little shields set into the bases of those at the angles of the chancel. Notice that in the w. face of the tower, a large *lancet* has been given *cusps* – and above it, a tiny slit lancet filled in. The n. *transept* is Victorian, and built in sympathetic style with the whole. Inside the church, you find with a start of pleasure that time here seems to have stopped at about the time the Blake family built their transept in 1860 – a combination perhaps of pew ends adorned with candelabra, and supporting unusual little globe shaped electric lamps which look like gas lights; more candelabra, and much polished brass in the chancel; all set under simple *arch-braced roofs*, whose timbers contrast with pristine white plaster. Behind the pulpit is the deep indentation of the old *rood stair* – with a coarsely carved *corbel* head, worn but intact, which has the disconcerting qualities of a death-mask. There's a plain C14 octagonal font; and inside the tower, the *Royal Arms* of George III. Specially noteworthy here is the most intriguing feature of this church – how the base of the tower is extended into 'wings' behind the nave w. wall, with *squints* to each side of the arch (one now blocked in) to give a view of the high altar, and the 'wings' themselves being 'bridged' under the tower by massive 4ft. thick arches. Notice as you leave the fine old timbered s. door, with its ancient iron handle and plate.

Brampton, St Peter (I3): The round *Norman* tower has a C15 brick octagonal top, and a single roof now covers what was *nave* and s. *aisle*. The *arcade* has disappeared and also the chapel that opened from it into the *chancel*. The s. door looks to be C19 but has fine C15 tracery with *crocketed* arches applied to it. By the door on the s. wall a very big and very curly *cartouche* to

Margaret Beevor (1716) sprouts acanthus leaves with two cherub heads below. The chancel has a fine array of *brasses*. On the s. side of the sanctuary are the delicately engraved figures of Edward Brampton and his wife Joan (1622). They turn towards each other and have most expressive faces. East of them, two shrouded figures, Robert Brampton and his wife, with a little Virgin and child inset above them. On the n. wall are the figures of John Brampton (d.1535) in armour and chain-mail with his two wives Thomaseyne and Anne wearing *kennel head-dresses*. As a mild eccentricity, a Roman urn dug up in a nearby field has found a resting place on a bracket above the pulpit.

Brancaster, St Mary (H3): A lovely ensemble of many-shaded flints with stone and a little old red brick is this attractive church beside the coast road. Many changes over the years have made it something of an architectural muddle, but this only adds to its character. Its principal characteristics now are *Perpendicular*, but it is, in essence, much older than that. The s. *porch* belongs to the C14, as its outer arch indicates (notice the door-bar slots on each side); the inner, much coarser doorway looks early-C14. To its right are the signs of a *holy water stoup* having been hacked away. Spacious interior, under eminently forgettable C19 roofs; clean-lined C14 *arcade*, with beyond, in the s. *aisle*, two windows – large, fat, simple *lancet* shapes. By both n. and s. doors are ancient poor-men's boxes, each triple padlocked and rudely made from a single piece of timber. The plain C14 font has in contrast a magnificent piece of the woodcarver's art as its crowning cover – a beautiful, tall tabernacle type of the C15. The wooden figure on the w. wall nearby is said to have come from a *wall post* of the original roof. On the w. wall in the n. aisle is a faded *Royal Arms*, dated 1832, of William IV. At the opposite end of this aisle may be seen the entrance to the old *rood loft*, with its exit at loft level in the *nave*. Notice too the slots and indentations in the *chancel* arch showing where the rood loft was fixed. In the chancel floor a *heart brass* has, sadly, long ago been ripped away, but its outline is clearly to be seen – the inscription, to William Cotyng, rector here, who died in 1490, is still in place. Look closely, however, and you'll see that the date shown is 1480 – MCCCCLXXX – he clearly had it put down in his own lifetime and left room for another X! As you leave, take a look at the remnant of the *rood screen*, which formerly stood across the chancel arch, and which

now is placed below the tower arch. Also here, in the n. wall, is a fireplace and flue.

Brandiston, St Nicholas (H3): This church, now in the care of the *Churches Conservation Trust*, is cosily tucked away, sharing a driveway with Church Farm, and the best approach is from the Felthorpe direction. A circuit of the churchyard reveals that the building has an eccentric layout – the tower stands at the w. end of the n. *aisle* but that was originally the *nave*.The old *chancel* at the e. end had gone by the C18., although two *corbels* that supported its roof remain high on the outside n. wall of the present chancel.The round tower was originally *Norman* but was almost entirely rebuilt in 1890 having been badly damaged in a gale, and the top section became octagonal. The aisle e. window dating from the middle of the C14 has excellent *reticulated* tracery, and in the C18 the chancel was reduced and had its e. wall rebuilt mainly in brick with heavy buttresses. The new nave was built in the mid-late-C14, and its windows provide a good example of the way in which the *Decorated* and *Perpendicular* styles merged and sometimes overlapped. The three tall Perpendicular windows in the s. wall have identical mouldings, but whereas the outer ones have Perpendicular tracery, the one in the centre employs the same pretty four-petalled motif at the top that occurs in the Decorated w. window. The tall and compact *porch* probably formed part of the nave rebuilding and the niche above the outer arch displays a 1930s carving of the church's patron saint. The large rectangular slab in the floor of the porch is possibly the original *mensa* reversed and put to new use at the *Reformation*. Moving inside, the immediate impression is one of unusual spaciousness for a small church. The three-bay arcade has *quatrefoil piers* with rounded caps and bases and double-chamfered arches, and overhead the nave roof has been ceiled in halfway up the braces. There is a *holy water stoup* in the wall by the door and in the floor nearby one finds an interesting example of an early-Victorian sepulchral *brass* for Edward Athill, 'late officer in the Windsor East Indiaman'. The replacement font was given in memory of a late-C19 rector, and the church's only modern stained glass is in the 'Decorated' window in the n. aisle, featuring unmemorable 1920s figures of St John and St Nicholas by Percy Bacon. Of more interest are the fragments of late-C14 glass in the tracery of the nave windows. They are very dark but three of the multi-coloured lozenges in the one nearest the door contain tiny faces, while fragments of tabernacle work survive in the tops of the main *lights*. Across in the aisle stands a handsome little chamber organ which came from Haveringland Hall, and it is a pity that the pierced *screen* in front partially obscures an important grave slab. The name 'Thomas' is cut in *Lombardic capitals* across one end, and remembering that Thomas Andrew was rector here from 1338 to 1349, it probably records the burial of the priest who was here just before the great rebuilding. The tall niche set in the n.e. angle of the aisle may mark the limit of the original nave. Edward Blore carried out restorations here in 1844 and the pine pews with *poppy-heads* in the nave may have come in then. There is no *piscina* in the truncated chancel and the plain oak *reredos* which was a 1914-18 thank-offering, is given a little style by the band of carving above the altar.

Brandon Parva, All Saints (G5): A quiet rural setting, up a lane and through a farmyard. *Decorated* period tower, with *Perpendicular* top and *flushwork* panelled battlements; good belfry windows with bold *quatrefoil* tracery. The body of the church is all of a Perpendicular piece, albeit with a lot of restoration work thrown in and a quite disastrous e. window, presumably Victorian, where a semblance of intersecting tracery is cramped under a flattened arch. The *nave* windows on the s. side have as *corbels* strange heads of a type which crop up at odd points in the county – if they look like anything, it's seahorses! (See also Swafield). These are nicely picked up in the adjacent modern metal guttering downpipe, where a little effort and imagination have made a real feature out of a purely functional article. On the n. side, the nave window corbels have three weird demon grotesques – and a dyspeptic lion. Inside this church there is retained an antique charm, accentuated by oil and gas lamps and strategically placed candelabra and a jolly little organ. Very wide nave (27ft.) and *chancel*, the former under a rebuilt Victorian roof (1860), so well done it could pass for original, the latter a good, simple *arch-braced* example with flowered and heraldic *bosses*, and retaining below its substantial *wall plates* and trim little *wall posts* the original *corbels*, rather roughly carved but tremendously attractive. The tower arch is eye-catching, being prominently and boldly carved around its *hood mould* with a trailing vine decoration, and sitting on two large corbel heads of a king and a queen. Don't miss in the tower the splendid little medieval door into the belfry turret, with its

studded, rounded panels. Very plain, whitewashed, C14 font. In the nave s.e. corner, the memorial to John Warner, who died in 1702 aged 21, is not to be overlooked – a riot of very fat cherubs, peculiar faces, swags and scrollery and below, a sculptural fancy of a kind of hammock, holding a whole jumble of bones. Notice on the end of the prayer desk, facing the nave, an ancient carving of a bird in landing position 'undercarriage down'. This was one of the bosses of the original nave roof. Another one, even better is fixed to the side of the organ – a *pelican* feeding her young with her own blood, a lovely piece. In the chancel, a rather heavy restored *piscina* next to *dropped sill sedilia*. Numerous excellent *ledger-stones*, including one just below the sanctuary steps, s. side, with a lugubrious skull and 'Hodie mihi eras tibi' – 'Today it is for me, tomorrow for you'. This is to John Utting, died 1658 aged 76, when Cromwell (whose turn came within months of old John) still ruled. For John was evidently a good Royalist: 'No faithful soule did e'er take more delight, God and his King and countrye more to right'.

Braydeston, St Michael (J5): Only about a quarter mile as the crow flies, southward from Brundall's great church, but a trek through winding lanes actually to reach its remote site. A neat little place, as interesting as it looks. The tower – *Decorated* originally, and with a nice *Tudor* w. window – is so over-restored that it looks like a rebuild. The *nave* has large and rather fine *Perpendicular* windows, with elegant tracery. The *chancel* is originally C13 *Early English* – the *lancet* in the n. wall looks contemporary. Beautiful C14 Decorated e. window with *reticulated* tracery. In the *porch*, with its attractive hooded outer arch, note on the old wooden benches, among assorted graffiti, the *Nine Men's Morris* boards, one at the centre of each side. Interior is small – but full of interest: under the tower, a rare *wafer oven*. Old font with coarsely carved six-sided bowl (The w. panel may be a rough copy of the e. window tracery; the e. panel, possibly one of the 'wheels with eyes' of the *Nine Orders of Angels*). Behind the font, a tiny inscription *brass*, restored to the church in recent years after unknown wanderings, to Henry Love of Norwich, 1518. A remnant of a pillar in the nave s. wall indicates an earlier, C13 Early English *arcade*, as does the triple pillar of the arch framing the organ. Note vestiges of colour on a *jamb* of one of the fine n. windows of the nave. On both sides, indications of the *rood* and stairs, with the entrance behind the sturdy little pulpit – the latter, like the rest of the furnishings, is modern, but it has on top an older and curious *hour-glass stand*. The *screen* is modern too – though the silvery-aged tracery in five of the six lower panels is evidently ancient, C15 by the form of it, with its leaves, flowers and cusps, and very good. Note especially, s. side, the lovely *pelican* feeding its young with its own blood. In the chancel pretty Early English C13 *piscina* with beside it a great rarity, a little corner shelf supported on large, coarse mouldings. Below sanctuary steps, extreme right, a small inscription in Latin is all that remains of a *brass* to Osbert, son of John Barney of Reedham, killed in 1469 by an arrow during the siege of Caister Castle. Note the *ledger slab* poignantly reminding us of the rate of child mortality in the past:

> Here lyeth the body of Ann, daughter of
> John & Eliz. Cotton, who died Aug
> 13,1727, aged 2 years and 6 months,
> adjacent lie nine more of their children.

Nearby are the graves of yet two more sons, who both died before reaching the age of 20. In the w. window – striking modern stained glass, with bold Faith, Hope & Charity, in memory of First World War fallen.

Breckles, St Margaret (F6): A round tower that is *Saxon* rather than *Norman*, judging by the blocked circular *sound-holes* halfway up and the trail of mixed carving in the arch *imposts* within. There is a slim *Perpendicular* window to the w., the C15 octagonal top has bold chequerwork on four faces, and a good line in grotesque *gargoyles* below the parapet. The rest of the building is a mixture of C14 and C15 work, and in 1970 the decline into decay was arrested by a courageous restoration effort by this small village – all now looks well cared for. The font is a big, square, oatmeal-coloured Norman showpiece – an exercise in lively and barbaric design; two of the sides are covered in writhing strap-work, and on the e. face four figures stand – each under an arch (possibly the *Evangelists*). All the corners vary, and that to the s.w. has a half-figure holding another head. Even the corners of the top surface are carved. An elegant C18 or early-C19 set of the Lord's Prayer and creed are framed above the tower arch and matching *decalogue boards* will be found in the *chancel*. The C15 *screen* is interesting because much of the carving is in the solid – rather than applied. Flowers are carved in the simple mouldings of the uprights, one of which has warped, accentuating the solidity. A rich band of flowers is worked along the centre rail, and the doors are quite lavish – the concave outlines of their tops *crocketted*; some restoration work but skilfully done. A *rood stair* was solidly constructed in the n. wall and on the s. wall, an *hour-glass stand* which has the happy addition of a modern replica glass (the pulpit is no longer close enough to turn it over for 'the second hour' however!). In the chancel by the *priest's door* is something very strange. John Webb, the son-in-law of Sir Thomas Richardson, the Lord Chief Justice, was buried here in 1658, and linked to his slab by a carved strap and buckle is a smaller stone oval – the grave of his daughter Ursula Hewyt, who died in the same year. She asked to be buried in an upright position, like Ben Jonson in Westminster Abbey. The stone says 'Stat ut vixit erecta', and so she was.

Bressingham, St John the Baptist (G7): Viewed in the distance as you approach along the main road from, Thetford, Bressingham's tower is striking enough – tall, slim C15 *Perpendicular*, its clean-cut lines standing out elegantly from its landscape. But as you draw up outside, what fairly stops you in your tracks is the *clerestory* – a splendid piece of *Tudor* showmanship in which the use of very light-coloured stone with very dark flints creates a quite dramatic effect. There are eight two-light windows, with excellent tracery, topped by crisply alternating stone and flint 'fingers', plus superb *flushwork* panels between the windows; and the whole drawn into an entity by the linking of the *drip moulds* of all eight windows into a continuous frieze. On the n. clerestory, facing the road, are the date 1527 and the initials of Sir Roger Pilkington, who rebuilt this church (excepting the tower). On the e. gable of the *nave*, a *sanctus bell turret*, rather depleted and skeletal. The tower incorporated into Sir Roger's new church, though Perpendicular, has belfry windows, which despite their Tudor arches and very deep drip moulds, nevertheless have tracery that is strongly geometrical and *Decorated* in character. Battlemented, flushworked parapet, and flushwork too down the faces of the diagonal buttresses and round the *base course*. The w. face is very individual, in that it has *trefoil* arched and canopied figure niches to each side of its fine w. window with its battlemented *transoms*; flint and stone chequerwork immediately below the window; and below again, a finely proportioned w. door, richly carved with crowns and floral motifs in the mouldings of its arch; which in turn has a square hood and shields in the *spandrels*. The church's interior is lofty and light, and fulfils the promise of the outside of the building. The nave roof is a splendid *arch-braced* and *hammer-beamed* example, the hammers richly carved like miniature castles, and with open wheel carvings in the spandrels. The *wall plates* are carved with equal attention to detail, and the deeply thrusting, moulded *wall posts* sit on strongly carved wooden *corbels* in a pendant shape. Above the slim and soaring tower arch, a *sanctus bell opening* gives a clear view of the high altar; low in the pillars of the arch, note the slots in the stone where presumably a *screen* was once fixed. Four-bay *arcade* with wide, flat *capitals* sitting on octagonal pillars which are correspondingly so slim that they look almost fragile. Big C14 octagonal font, with shallow *arcading* and leaf motifs carved around the bowl, and delicate tracery patterns around the stem. Nearby will be found three delightful, small collecting shoes, like neat little dust pans, each dated 1631. Nave benches and bench ends here, contemporary with the church, are a remarkable example of lushness of carving and variety of design, a marvellous riot of form and shape and movement. The pulpit, complete with *tester*, is *Jacobean* and excellent. In both n. and s. aisles, plain old roofs; and a few beautifully panelled old *box pews*. In the s. aisle, a large, plain figure niche is set into the *jamb* of the s.e. window; what looks like a smaller edition of same in the left jamb of the window by the s. door. Notice in this corner the rather fine *bier*, which needs only a black-plumed horse to complete an image of Victorian funereal pomp. In the n. aisle are two considerably more simple biers, one of which, with its collapsible arms, looks very like the 1666 example at Old Buckenham. Beside them, the C14 ark-type chest, its massive lid wrought from a single tree trunk and the whole thing girt about with iron strappings. Beside the n. door, a *holy water stoup*; set into the angle of the easternmost pillar of the aisle, the remains of a *piscina*. In the *chancel* (which *weeps* to the s.) is a large piscina with a boldly simple, moulded trefoil arch, the stone ledge of its *credence shelf* intact and inside it, a curious square niche inset low in the corner in its left jamb. Adjoining are *dropped sill sedilia*; and below that, lovely early-C14 double sedilia, each seat under a separate, plain arch inset into the wall, with small round pillars and flat, ring *capitals* – all pointing to the early origin of this otherwise Perpendicular chancel. In the e. window are some remnants of ancient stained glass. Above, a curious roof of timbers which look like those

of a simple make-shift barn – an odd contrast with the splendours over the nave. The church has an excellent ring of 6 bells, tenor 8-2-20 cwt.

Brettenham, St Mary (F7): This cannot be called medieval, but enough old work remains to justify a visit. The old church of St *Andrew* was badly damaged by fire in 1693, and after twenty years the *nave* was rebuilt and used. In the 1850s, the architect *S.S. Teulon* was transforming nearby Shadwell Park into fantastical Gothick, and he was also commissioned to deal with the church. He left the unbuttressed C14 tower alone – except for the battlements and windows, and re-used the *Norman* s. doorway. This has single shafts (zigzag on one side and spiral on the other), spiralled *capitals*, and zigzag and rope mouldings in the arch. Everything else is of 1852, and considering Teulon's other work, a remarkably restrained exercise in the *Decorated* style. The *porch* is decidedly pretty – all in imaginative timber tracery, and inside, the wrought iron screens to tower and *transepts* are excellent. The *chancel screen* is heavily encrusted woodwork on a monolithic alabaster base, and the *reredos* blanks off a good two thirds of the e. window. These two in combination have a most unfortunate effect on what would otherwise be a pleasing interior. Good solid woodwork in the chancel, with a very rich stall set in the embrasure of the *priest's door*. Except for the tower window and one in the nave, all the stained glass is en suite and suits the church perfectly.

Bridgham, St Mary (F7): A church with rather an odd profile – the *chancel* roof rises above the *nave*, and a very plain *bellcote* is completely boarded up (the single bell now rests in the nave by the *rood stairs* – is there anything aloft?). That there was once a tower may be seen by the doorway outline in the w. wall. Continuing the walk round, note the 'Y' tracery windows of about 1300 in the nave and the pretty *Decorated* windows in the chancel. There is a blocked *low side window* on the s. side, with an attractive *trefoil* head, and the iron bars show through the plaster (inside you will see the old shutter hinges as well). Past the exterior rood stair turret with its tiny window, and we are back at the *porch*. This was all *flushwork* originally, but over the years there has been much patching up in red brick. The porch roof is most unusual – like Anmer it has a *tunnel vault*. The C13 doorway has worn *headstops* and the door itself sags gracefully to one side with age – and see how the step is quite hollow in just the one spot where everybody puts their feet (and ponder on the generations that have come through that door before you). Immediately ahead, a fine C15 font with *quatrefoils* on the second step, and more round the base of the shaft with its defaced lions. The carvings in the bowl panels are of more than passing interest; clockwise from the e.: the *Trinity* (God the Father with the crucified Christ before Him, but lacking the dove of the Holy Spirit), Angel with Trinity emblem (odd to find two variations of the same theme side by side), a seated bishop, angel with the arms of the See of Canterbury, the *Assumption* (a rare subject on fonts – the only other in Norfolk is at Great Witchingham), angel with the arms of Ely, a seated figure (possibly another bishop). The cover is *Jacobean.* There are rood stairs in the n. wall, and a tall plain niche nearby. The *screen* has been reduced to the base panels – alternating red and green stencil work, and the s. side was cut into to give access to a re-sited Jacobean oblong reading desk now used as a pulpit. C17 panelling on two stall fronts beyond, and the little bench end just behind the n. side of the screen has an inscription: 'John Watson and Alys hys wyf', who left money for the painting of the screen in 1475. By the pulpit, a trefoil niche, and on the floor, the bowl of a rugged *Norman* font that came from nearby Roudham church – burned out and ruined in 1735. The *piscina* in this corner is puzzling; it looks as though the *capital* of a pillar piscina has been set in the recess – did that too come from Roudham? The chancel has one of the most handsome piscina/*sedilia* sets in the area. Although they are of different styles and dates (the piscina is slightly earlier) the stone matches, and the two blend beautifully. The piscina has a quatrefoil over two trefoil *ogees*, and the stepped sedilia are under a square hood, with a slim turned column with ring capital in the centre, and a good pair of *headstops*. The altar is a *Stuart* table and there is an *aumbry* in the n. wall. The church has few monuments, but George Comyn (1816) who died, 'having served his time in the Navy with honour to himself and highest Approbation of his Commander fell a victim to the climate of the West Indies', is the subject of an affecting verse. Back to the w. end under the bare and ugly plaster ceiling to see the high *box pews,* and two painted C18 panels fixed in the old w. doorway. They are Moses and Aaron, and will have flanked the missing *decalogue boards.* On Sunday 24th June 2007, St Mary's Bridgham celebrated its thousandth anniversary, and

Norwich Cathedral Choir sang evensong there as part of the thanksgiving.

Briningham, St Maurice (G2): A remarkable mid-C14 four-*light* window in the s. side of the *nave*, with beautiful, intricate flowing tracery, is one of the features of this church – it is of C14 date, probably about 1360, which makes it an interesting survivor of the *Black Death.* Inside, the *jambs* of this window have most curious little C12 *Norman* columns attached, less than three feet high: what their purpose originally was, one can only guess at. The purple Victorian glass in this window alas does no credit to a magnificent piece of medieval craftsmanship. The base of the C14 tower serves as a *porch,* leading into the earlier nave. Note the pretty fluted columns of the chancel arch as you go into the Decorated chancel. Attractive *arch-braced* roof, and a fine communion rail, about 1700, with plump *pilasters* like those round a gentleman's formal garden of the period. Finely traceried and deeply recessed e. window, flanked by huge *ogee*-headed niches now containing forbidding large wooden figures of the Virgin on one side and the church's dedicatory soldier-saint, *Maurice,* on the other. Nice *piscina* and interesting remains of *sedilia.* Equally interesting, a blocked-up, square *low side window* in the traditional place near the chancel arch. Also blocked, a plain, lop-sided little *priest's door.* Note the 1930 Brereton memorial on the n. wall, recalling through its names, continued in the family through the years, their descent from *Sir Clowdisley Shovel.* Outside, at e. end, a massive pyramid obelisque to the Breretons, topped by a haltered bear, their family crest.

Brinton, St Andrew (G2): Lovely setting in a pretty village. Church has lost its *chancel,* but has a fine *arch-braced roof,* restored (with the n. *transept* roof) in 1964, when the angels were re-coloured. Contemporary with the roof are the solid benches, which have good figures. Two of these are in the form of a *rebus* on the village name – Brinton = BRYNING A TUN (barrel), and BRIN (burnt) TUN. See the date and initials, '1544 R.P.', on the western-most bench end. Fine example of Elizabethan 'fruitful and profitable sentences' on n. wall, restored in 1869 when the *gallery* was removed. Fireplace in base of tower was still in use in the 1890s. Excellent *Jacobean* chest.

Brisley, St Bartholomew (F3): Brisley's notable four stage tower is a soaring landmark from

Brisley, St Bartholomew

whichever direction you approach it. Close up the tower, and indeed the whole of this church, is yet more rewarding. The tower, with deeply carved battlements and diagonal *flushwork* panelled buttresses topped by richly carved and canopied figure niches, is powerfully *Perpendicular*. The great four-*light* w. window and complementing, moulded w. door are its special feature, the window having a *drip mould* which goes deeply down each side, and then strikes off to go round three sides of the tower – a fine effect of composition. Walking round the church one is struck by the window designs; the *nave aisles, Tudor* Perpendicular with drip moulds extending low down each side; the *clerestory,* two-light under square hoods, with charming little *quatrefoils* studding the *spandrels;* in the *chancel,* flowing *Decorated* on the n. side, simple Perpendicular on the s. – a perfect example of the leap from the one style to the other during the one building operation, spanning the horrors of the *Black Death.* The slit openings, almost at ground level around the e. end of the chancel, are explained by the presence of an under-crypt which was almost certainly a *charnel* house. Inside the church there is much of interest. Plain modern roofs to chancel and nave, though the latter has its original *bosses* and *wall plates;* simple, heavily timbered medieval roofs in the aisles. Soaring tower and chancel arches,

and above the latter there is a small, filled-in e. window. Clerestory and five-bay *arcades* are Perpendicular, the arcade pillars (as also the e. ends of the two aisles) having some original colour remaining. This dates from the mid-C14, as do the faded wall paintings to n. and s. On the s. wall is a St *Christopher*, between St *Bartholomew* and St *Andrew*. Nearby to the left are the remains of a *consecration cross.* Opposite, by the n. door, the merest remains of another St *Christopher* and the Christ Child's head, complete with gold halo. At w. end, good *Royal Arms* of George II, dated 1753, and a rather ugly little *gallery,* on cast metal pillars, dated 1848. Splendidly rustic, low old benches fill two thirds of the nave; at the front they are 'regular' size and most appealing in their variety of carving – *poppy-heads,* pierced carving, animals (a dog with a goose in its mouth) and even a fitted cupboard for books. Equally nice is a rough and ready *three-decker pulpit,* a corner bench dated 1590 in the s. aisle, and another, clearly *Jacobean,* in the n. aisle. Very tall C15 *screen* with excellent tracery and spandrel carving, but generally much altered and over-painted. In the chancel is an especially fine *piscina* and triple *sedilia,* each under richly carved *ogee arches.* The piscina is in a panel studded with floral motifs, the sedilia canopies are supported by delicate clustered columns, and the *capitals* carved with tiny *pelicans* and fighting

Brisley, St Bartholomew: Three-decker pulpit

lions. The hole in the wall opposite is presumably associated with the crypt below the sanctuary, entry to which is by the door on the chancel n. side which has well-preserved 'portrait' *headstops* to its *hood mould*. Although the undercroft's original use was probably as a charnel or perhaps a treasury, it has been suggested that it was used as a jail to house prisoners who were being taken from King's Lynn to Norwich and were held overnight at Brisley.

Briston, All Saints (G2): There was a round tower here but it was pronounced unsafe in 1785 and removed; a n. *aisle* has also disappeared, leaving the *arcade* set in the *nave* wall. There are marks too of a *porch* over the blocked s. door. The early-C14 *chancel* is handsome. The *priest's door* has deep mouldings with good *headstops*, and a well defined *dripstone* runs below the windows. The e. window has a tight design, *reticulated* in the head which is very effective outside. Less so inside, but there the slender columns in the *jambs* are enhanced by battlemented rings halfway up – unusual and attractive. The C14 *sedilia* have clustered columns with *cinquefoils* and *ogee arches*. The elaborate double *piscina* has a pierced *quatrefoil* in the head and a stone *credence shelf* crossing it halfway up like a window division. Holes in both jambs look like hinge placements, so perhaps it doubled as an *aumbry* at some stage. The early-C18 *communion rails* are very sturdy – plump turning and broad mouldings. The parish chest in the sanctuary is huge (5ft. 6in. x 2ft. 6in.) and completely swathed in iron. It has four locks, and lugs for a long bar to cover them all. Briston has its own unique curiosity – a metal cello made by Mr. Clithero the village blacksmith in 1700 and apparently played by him for many years. It has been played in recent years, and when one listener was asked what it sounded like, the response was 'tinny'. The church also has one of the ugliest bell-cotes in Christendom – two brick pillars, late-C20.

Brockdish, St Peter & St Paul (I8): The church lies to the w. of the main village and has a lovely setting next to the old rectory. Approach is by a narrow path that winds round the edge of a field from the rectory gate and leads to a gate in the far corner of a churchyard that is almost a park, with a whole variety of big trees. The old *Norman* tower was demolished in 1864, and although the new one is in flint and stone, it is more like Somerset in style than East Anglia.

The s. *porch* was aggressively remodelled but the original parapet frieze and side windows were apparently incorporated. Inside, the church is rather dark, although the s. *clerestory* windows have an extraordinary array of gaudy C19 heraldic glass. The tower was kitted out with a fireplace of baronial proportions as well as a new font, but have a look at the two angel *corbels* resting on the s. window ledge. The restoration did uncover some interesting evidence of earlier building – a small *Saxon* slit can be seen in the n. wall of the *nave*, and there are Norman windows in the n. side of the *chancel*. All the other windows are the work of a Mr Marrable (surely he must have escaped from Dickens?) in 1864. Considering its size, the main timbers of the C15 *arch-braced roof* are decidedly slim. The base of the *rood screen* was re-coloured at the restoration and it was given a new top; but the original gates were dispensed with in 1899 on the orders of the Misses Kay who also thought that a plain cross on top was more appropriate than the previous *rood*. The early-C14 s. *arcade* has *quatrefoil* pillars which are set diagonally instead of the more normal e.-w. alignment, and the easternmost pillar was later altered to form the canopy for an image. The C14 table tomb of Sir Ralph Tendring in *Purbeck marble* has been let into the wall beneath the s. *aisle* e. window, and it now serves as an altar. By it, a handsome *piscina* which has all the signs of removal from elsewhere; the *dog-tooth* moulding and little stiff-leaf *cusps* point to a date 1230-1250. George France was rector here for over 50 years in the C19 and responsible for much of the restoration. He put in the extraordinarily pretty *reredos* of Minton tiles – a wall to wall treatment in the chancel, with two big side panels in a moulded six-leafed pattern linked by recessed *trefoils* – all in cream, gold and blue. The effect of the whole is largely lost now that the altar has posts and curtains. On the chancel s. wall, an austere but graceful tablet to Thomas Cotton (1778): 'If the Virtues which ADORN Life could PRESERVE it' there would be no need, it says, to record the passing of 'the tenderest Father, the faithfullest Friend, the best Husband'. How true, how true. The church has a good ring of 6 bells, tenor 12 cwt.

Brooke, St Peter (I6): Round *Norman* tower of the C12, with possibly *Early English* windows of the C13 at the top, and with an octagonal, chequer-work parapet in brick and flint which is C15-C16 *Perpendicular*. The body of the church is much restored (red brick buttresses support it at every point) but its ancient origins are still there in evidence. The *nave* and n. *aisle* are Perpendicular in character, the *chancel Decorated*, but there have been so many replacements and remouldings that one tends to be cautious. The nave s. windows are interesting – late Perpendicular with flattened *Tudor* arches, and the outline clear above them of much larger, earlier Perpendicular windows. Fairly definite in character is the Decorated *priest's door* on this side of the chancel. The *porch's* outer arch looks Early English; certainly the inner, s. doorway is of about 1200 with typical graceful pointed arch, flat *abacus*, leaf-curved *capitals* and slim round pillars; the door itself is ancient, with good carved *arcading* and *crocketted* pinnacles. The interior is spacious, the gloominess of the dark nave roof (*arch-braced*, carved *bosses* at the intersections, and shield-carrying angels on the *wall posts*) being relieved by the range of eight sweet little single-*light, cusped clerestory* windows over the arcade into the n. aisle. The arcade itself is a most curious mixture of forms and styles and arch-shapes. The colourful organ stands on a w. *gallery* supported by iron posts and carrying on its front a set of *Royal Arms* carved in wood. Beneath this hangs a constabulary truncheon, also painted with the Royal Arms. Immediately below is the *seven sacrament font*, much defaced but still fine: the panels show, clockwise from the e. face: mass, confirmation, penance, extreme unction, the Crucifixion, baptism, ordination and matrimony. Under the bowl are carved angels with scroll or bible, one of them holding a curious wheel or platter (?); round the stem, under rich little crocketted canopies, are various figures – all beheaded, alas. Overall can be seen traces of the original colour. Beside the pulpit, a C17 iron *hour-glass stand* – complete with hour-glass. Opposite, in the s. wall, a *piscina* niche has been given a door. In the big, wide chancel, a large plain double piscina has an arch merely cut into the wall, and supported at centre by a coarse round pillar – date about 1300. As you go, notice the ancient poorman's box, in solid chunks of timber, secured to the back pew. The church has a ring of 6 bells, tenor 14 cwt.

Broome, St Michael (J6): One of the county's extreme examples of the *isolated church*, over a mile from the present village and a quarter of that a stony track off the road across the fields. Broome Hall stood just beyond the church until it was demolished in 1825 and the original village nucleus may have been there. The position poses

a problem for the parish but it does enhance the building wonderfully and makes a visit there an occasion. The C15 tower is elaborate for a small church. Both base *course* and stepped battlements have *flushwork* and the w. facade is very good; w. door with shields of the *Trinity* and *Instruments of the Passion* in the *spandrels*, and a band of roses and shields in *quatrefoils* over the top which links the design with the big window. Over this, a niche under a beautifully delicate canopy, and quatrefoil *sound-holes* with square hoods. Inside, the *nave* is wide, and in the big *Perpendicular* windows of the s. range there is an interesting tracery pattern – a pair of small *lights* set above the main centre light with *ogee* shapes on either side. The *chancel* has windows of the same period but there are outlines of C13 predecessors, and in the s.e. corner, two slim shafts with tiny foliage *capitals* flank the old stepped *sedilia*. Opposite the *priest's door* in the s. wall is another which must have led to a chapel or sacristy no longer there. From the outside you can see that a buttress was built over it later. The blocked doorway just e. of the chancel arch led to the rood *stair turret* – again the evidence is outside in the form of a bulge in the corner between nave and chancel. The church has a very elegant *Regency* chamber organ (hand pumped of necessity) in a good mahogany panelled case; there is brass inlay on the front stiles and the swooping rows of diminutive pipes are on view behind glass doors. The one *brass* remaining is oddly placed, still on its slab, in a window embrasure and looks as if it has been there a long time. There were two figures but now only one and a bit of the scrolls remain, with two shields (the de Brome family, and de Brome impaling Winter). The smallest and oldest of the *hatchments* is Sir William Cooke's who died in 1681, and there are six more to make a fine array on the walls. Five of them are of the Fowle family, and Sir John Fowle has a long Latin epitaph on his monument to the left of the chancel arch. This has crossed trumpets and a wreath below, and two sizeable *putti* lounging on the pediment overhead.

Brumstead, St Peter (J3): Surprisingly fine, lofty tower to an otherwise unpretentious church; it is of early *Perpendicular* character, as is the *porch* – that is, very soon after the *Black Death* of 1349-50'. The body of the church is early-C14 *Decorated*, with three-*light* windows of simple intersecting tracery on each side – the tracery of those on the s. side has *cusping*, but on the n. side is totally plain. The large e. window is a

Victorian replacement of 1875. The signs of neglect evident outside the church are accentuated in the bleak, bare interior – a barnlike 'hall' with no separate *chancel*, under a plain boarded roof of 1834. There is a pretty traceried *piscina*, next to the bricked-in doorway to the old *rood stair*. Did the stone *corbel* immediately above the doorway, and that on the opposite wall support a low *rood beam*? Perhaps the square headed small windows placed just above this point on each side were put there to light the rood. Simple C14 font carved with *quatrefoils*. A first world war memorial on the n. wall is carved like an open book – most effective and tasteful.

Brundall, St Lawrence (J5): Set in a most beautiful garden-like churchyard, this is a charming little church, even though it is heavily restored and modernised (a n. *aisle* and vestry were added in 1900). A particular feature is its pretty double bellcote, which just could be a happy survivor from the late C13 – the tiny entrance door arch (entered through a diminutive *porch*) suggests that period too. Inside, almost everything is modern but in apple-pie order, including a handsome *screen*. In the vestry, a bland window by Charles Eamer *Kempe*. In centre window of the n. aisle a small roundel – about 10in. across, delicately coloured, and thought to be C16 – showing the church's dedicatory saint, *Lawrence*, with his grill. Finally, the church's treasure – a round, C13 font, lead-covered (the only one in Norfolk) and bearing tiny crucifixes punctuated by ornamental strips plus a lot of scratched on graffiti from several centuries.

Buckenham, St Nicholas (J5): Out of use for some years and now in the care of the *Churches Conservation Trust*. The octagonal tower has an *Early English* belfry stage with tall *lancets* in each face, giving it a very distinctive look. Vandalism has been rampant here and, despite the considerable amount of money spent by the Fund on urgent repairs during the statutory 'waiting period', the scene inside was depressing at the time of our visit. Apart from the block of C19 pews, only the font remains. This is a fine piece and has very well preserved figures of saints and apostles under flattened *ogee arches* in the panels. There are four civilians at the angles of the stem. A gilt crucifix and an alabaster panel of the martyrdom of St Erasmus were found under the *chancel* floor in 1840, and *Cautley* regretted that they were presented to Norwich Museum, instead of being preserved as objects of interest here. It is just as well that they were not.

Bunwell, St Michael & All Angels (H6): This is a wholly C15 *Perpendicular* building which looks well, with its great windows and soaring upward lines, as you approach it from the main Norwich road. The tower is tall and slim, with a battlemented parapet in notably detailed *flushwork*, with traceries, *quatrefoils* and other decorative devices; big two-*light* belfry windows with strong *cusped* tracery; and charming *sound-holes* in the form of tiny two-light windows under square hoods, with tracery as intricate and delicate as fretwork. Good flushwork too over the entire surface of the *porch* exterior, including its *base course* (the tower's, paradoxically, is plain). The porch's outer arch has a square hood, and in the *spandrels* are deeply cut quatrefoils with flower motifs at the centres. In a church of great windows, especially notable is the *chancel*'s magnificent five-light example at the e. end – purest Perpendicular of about 1450. A great pity that the walls of *nave* and chancel, overall, have had to be cement rendered, which inevitably spoils the general visual effect. Inside it is the sheer size of the nave which strikes one – 32ft.wide, and lofty too, with a vast roof which is a mixture of *arch-braces*, *tie-beams* and *hammer-beams*, all supported by enormous *wall posts* which sit on great, ugly, cheerlessly practical chunks of stone in lieu of *corbels*. High up in the n. e. corner is the *rood stair* exit at loft level and at such a level that the original rood and *screen*, now completely disappeared, must have been tremendously tall and impressive. Through the soaring chancel arch, plain save for embattled *capitals*, into the chancel under its good *arch-braced roof*. Furnishings here, as in the rest of the church, are modern. *Piscina* niche and *dropped sill sedilia*, like those hefty corbels to the nave roof, look as if they were built by quarrymen rather than by masons. The stained glass of the great e. window, unveiled on Easter Day 1914, shows Christ in glory surrounded by angels and saints, and with a series of biblical scenes at the foot of each light – all in rich glowing colours and excellent detail by *Hardman*. As you leave, notice the crisply carved C14 octagonal font with shields in its panels, a collection of grotesque animal heads and floral motifs under the bowl, and traceried 'windows' round the stem; up on the n. wall, a big framed set, much faded, of *Royal Arms* of Queen Anne; and by the font, an old panelled chest which is *Jacobean* in character. The church has a good ring of 6 bells, tenor 9 cwt.

Burgh Castle, St Peter & St Paul (K5): A straggle of houses down the lane away from the village and then the church, backed by a thick grove of trees which press close to the tower, Church Farm, and the Roman fort of Gariannonum to the s.; beyond, Breydon Water, often desolate, always lovely. The little round tower is C11 – see the large unfaced flints used at the base. The upper brickwork is C17 and the angled faces of the stubby battlements cap it neatly. Look at the s. side of the building where a C13 *lancet* is flanked by two tall and thin *Perpendicular* windows, and the C15 *chancel* had square-headed *Tudor* windows inserted later. The whole of the n. *aisle* including its *arcade* is Victorian, and the pair of windows from the old n. wall were reused at either end of the new aisle. The old n. door was also retained and there are two shields carved as if they hung on pegs in the *spandrels* of its arch. One has the *Instruments of the Passion* and the other could be the cross of St *Andrew*. Both tower and nave walls are studded with fragments of Roman bricks and tiles filched from the C3 fort a short distance away. Like a number of churches hereabouts, the C19 roof is *scissors braced* and the longish chancel has a panelled barrel roof done at the same time. The angels on the bowl of the C14 font are very like those at neighbouring Bradwell (and, like them, hold shields of emblems – the *Trinity*, the Passion, *hosts* above *chalices*, and the three crowns of old East Anglia). Here, the lions at the foot have had most of their features smoothed away by time. Behind the organ (by craning the neck you can just see it!), a tall C13 grave slab has been fixed to the wall. It has a long floriated cross on the lid and must have been made for the tomb of a high Ecclesiastic, possibly a Prior of St Olave's not far away – patrons of the living from 1273 to the Dissolution of the monasteries in the 1530s. The s. wall lancet has a fresh bright portrait of St *Fursey* who has a real claim to local veneration. He is shown with a rough staff in his hand and an ox lying behind him. The window by the pulpit has a unique theme for Norfolk. It is in memory 'of two great Christian monarchs of lineal descent though 1000 years apart 901-1901'. To the right, a good portrait of Victoria as she was in her youth, crowned and richly robed, with Windsor in the background; on the left, King Alfred, full of artist's licence, seen in a study stocked with his translations of Bede, Boethius, Orosius and Augustine, his fleet at sea beyond. Old and interesting things that people don't know what to do with, often end up in church, and Burgh Castle has an enormous beam clamped to the wall of the n. aisle. Parson

Thorne rebuilt the parish Guildhouse in 1548 and recorded the fact on this beam. It migrated to the school in 1836 and has finished up here. Full details on a plaque below.

Burgh, St Margaret (K4): The whole church has been virtually rebuilt, but entry is by a *Norman* s. doorway, with zig-zag and *billet* decoration in the arch. Remains of a second Norman doorway are still visible outside on the north. The C19 *gallery* is lit by a cottage-like dormer window in the thatched roof. There is a little *brass* to John Burton (d.1608) on the wall of the *chancel*, and the e. window has modern glass by Paul Jefferies depicting St *Margaret of Antioch*, St *Luke* and the Virgin. The C19 creed and *decalogue boards* in the chancel rest on re-used *corbels*, carved with foliage and animals, which are *Early English* in date.

Burgh St Peter, St Mary (K6): Hard by the Waveney and a long way from the village, the church has perhaps the most extraordinary tower in the county if not the country. The base of patterned brick and flint is early-C16, but the four stages of diminishing brick boxes with churchwarden gothick windows were built by Samuel Boycott, the rector, in about 1793. It was apparently inspired by a church that his son had seen in Italy, but the strongest resemblance is to the Ziggurat temples of Mesopotamia. Where would we be without our eccentrics? The rest of the church lies beneath a lovely uninterrupted run of reed thatch more than 100 feet long, and the diminutive brick *porch* fits snugly on the side. The *nave* has an *arch-braced roof* and there is a C14 font with angel heads in the corona and alternating shields and flowers in the panels round the bowl. Hefty C19 restoration did not disturb the simple C13 door and this could be the date of most of the

Burgh St Peter, St Mary

Burgh-next-Aylsham, St Mary: C13 chancel arch

building. The *chancel screen* is modern but the stair to the old *rood loft* remains in the wall behind the pulpit. The latter is well nigh covered in brass memorial plates to members of the Boycott family which supplied rectors for 135 years non-stop. Samuel was inducted in 1764 and William died in 1899.

Burgh-next-Aylsham, St Mary the Virgin (I3): Prettily placed with a path through the churchyard to a footbridge over the river Bure. The C15 tower has attractive *sound-holes* and a decorative series of Maria Regina monograms in the *flushwork* of the battlements. Inside this small church there is a delightful surprise for the newcomer. The *chancel*, lower than the *nave*, provides a lovely little vista of tall *lancets* and matching *arcading* below. Original work of about 1220 was extended eastwards two bays by R.M. Phipson in 1876, and it was done well. The n. chapel is also Victorian, but the splendid arch is original; the three shafts on either side have stiff-leaf *capitals*, and birds peck at the foliage on the e. side. It is intriguing to find such strong echoes of the work at Lincoln in this small Norfolk parish. The *seven sacrament font* is not as perfect as that at Sloley, but has the same *Evangelistic Symbols* at its base. As at Salle, the sacramental emblems are held by angels. The bowl panels are (clockwise from the e.): mass, mass of St

Gregory, extreme unction, matrimony, penance, baptism, confirmation (at an early age as was usual) and ordination. This font has the distinction of being signed – the mason's mark can be seen incised below the Penance panel. Under the tower is a set of George I arms in stone inscribed 'Matt Burr Gent Churchwarden 1721'. They are very weathered and must have been outside originally. Above them, a monument to Lt. John Woolsey, who served under Maj. Gen. Wolfe in the victorious expedition against Quebec in 1759 – and returned to live to a ripe old age in the peace of Burgh.

Burlingham St Andrew, St Andrew (J4): Neatly compact in its *Perpendicular* lines, in a well-groomed churchyard, backed by lofty trees – an agreeable picture. Nice tower, built about 1466, well panelled base (*flushwork*) and battlements, the latter inset with lozenge-shapes bearing shields carved with the cross of St *Andrew*. The bell openings have attractive tracery which is Perpendicular – but seems in its flow to want to be *Decorated*. On each side of the tower is a small square *sound-hole*, each set with different and most individual tracery – charming. Nave, *chancel* and aisle windows (all neatly set off by slim pink bricks over the heads) are Perpendicular, though the fabric is earlier, as the lovely flowing Decorated tracery of the e. window, and the bricked-in n. doorway, indicate; moreover, on the s. side of the chancel is a *low side window* which appears to be *Early English*. The entrance *porch* is Perpendicular, but note, over outer arch, a *hood-mould* which is re-used *Norman* material, studded with star moulding – tiny petal-like stars set in circles. Inside the church are rewarding surprises. A striking nave roof (a bequest dates it at 1487) with *arch-braces* plus *hammer-beams*, the first with fine *bosses* at the intersections, the second with lovely winged angels at the angles and all in the faded beauty of their original colouring; then there are rich, generously carved *wall plates* and deep *wall posts* sitting on *corbels* carved with delightfully funny faces – save for a very disturbing hollow-eyed creature at left above the *rood screen*. The nave's Perpendicular five-bay n. *arcade* is comparatively coarse. The *screen* is very interesting, dated 1536, the last addition to the church before the *Reformation* – and thus possibly the latest dated screen in Norfolk. The saints, painted on *gesso* with gilt decoration, are badly mutilated but still discernible: left to right, Norfolk's own *Withburga*, with her does – and Dereham church in her hand, *Benedict, Edward* the Confessor, Thomas of Canterbury, John the Baptist, Cecilia, Walston of Bawburgh, Catherine, an unidentifiable figure, and *Etheldreda*. At the modern top of the screen a medieval angel – he fell from the roof some years ago. The chancel has a plain (probably C18) plaster ceiling, *dropped sill sedilia* and severely simple *piscina*. Opposite, a fine memorial tablet (which came from the now ruinous Burlingham St Peter's) to Gregory Mileham, 1615, flanked by two *putti* – unusual in that one carries a spade, the other an extinguished torch. Below, a tiny inscription to one William Gilman:

> Wil Gilman heere lies buried in dust
> Who thirty two yeares was a servant just
> To masters twoe, the second whereof came
> First in his armes to church to get a name
> And least his name should with his bodye
>   die
> His master heere hath placed his memorye.

On the nave wall by s. door, and in pavement of n. aisle, two *palimpsest brass* inscriptions, one to Elizabeth Framlingham (1559), on the underside, part of a lady (about 1375); the other to John Randes and his wife (1503), on the reverse an inscription to Nicholas Man, Clerk (1441). Across the tower arch, a beautiful medieval screen (again, salvaged from St *Peter's*): it has two athletically lean and handsomely featured angels holding shields carved with the keys of St *Peter*; while the *cusps* of the elegant arches are carved with tiny floral motifs – and with miniature grotesques and animals, and one powerful human face. In the tower, an octagonal Decorated font; and on the walls a fine collection of tablets and *cartouches* to the Burroughes family, notably one to a gentleman who was evidently a paragon of all the virtues.

Burlingham St Edmund, St Edmund (J5): A lovely church full of character, with only the farm opposite to keep it company in the open fields. *Nave* and *chancel* are all under one continuous thatched roof and the *porch* is thatched too. There is a blocked *Norman* n. doorway which was evidently intended to have beakhead ornament in the arch, but the carving was never completed. The s. doorway is also Norman with a head above the arch. Both nave and chancel have Y-traceried windows of about 1300 – one in the s. nave wall has a *dropped sill* to form a seat, and on that side the outline of the *rood stairs* can be seen cut into the wall. The church's treasure catches the eye immediately – a pulpit which is the finest C15 example in Norfolk, beautifully restored

Burlingham St Edmund, St Edmund: C15 pulpit

with the help of the Pilgrim Trust in 1964. It has eight narrow panels, with a tall *crocketted* arch and canopy set in each; painted panels run below, and in the bottom third there is more rich tracery. An inscription is set midway like a band, 'Inter Natos Mulierum Non Surrexit Major Johanne Baptista.' (Among them that are born of women there hath not arisen a greater than John the Baptist. Matt. XI, 11). The upper stage of each buttress is ornamented with *gesso* and the whole piece glows with colour. Both the castellated rim and the base are carved from a single piece of timber – an eccentricity even for the period. Later additions are the *Jacobean* backboard and *tester*, and the *hour-glass stand*. The *screen* is a fitting companion to the pulpit, with fine open tracery, *ogee arches* and good cresting. Below the rail there are remains of a gilt diaper (surface decoration) pattern, but most of it was lost when the *box pews* (since removed) were built on to the screen. The nave benches have lovely solid ends with charming figures on the arms. An unlikely looking elephant has more of a proboscis than a trunk and a miniature castle on his back; there is a fox with a goose over its shoulder, and three figures seated in chairs. Some of the *poppy-heads* in the chancel incorporate faces – a bishop and a king. The *communion rails* are sturdy and unpretentious C17. The really interesting thing in the chancel is the big painting on the s. wall. Although virtually all the colouring

Burnham Deepdale, St Mary: Normal 'Seasonal' font

has gone, it is instantly recognisable as the martyrdom of St *Thomas Becket*, and is the only one on this scale to survive in Norfolk. Discovered in 1856, it shows St Thomas kneeling and being attacked by the four knights – one can be identified as Reginald Fitze Urse by the bear on his shield. The other painting in the church is a faint St *Christopher* on the n. wall of the nave. This delightful and most interesting church still relies on oil lamps and faces the problems of isolation and a tiny congregation – long may it survive.

Burnham Deepdale, St Mary (E1): This attractive little church beside the busy coast road has a neat, round *Anglo-Saxon* tower, studded with round-headed slit windows, and covered by a pert lead cap. On first sight the body of the church suggests a Victorian rebuild, since every single window is evidently a C19 replacement. But in fact, both *nave* and *chancel* are of late *Early English* origin. Pretty interior, colourful with modern rood, votive statuettes and hangings, contrasting with neat white walls. The round tower arch on simple 'lips' and the triangular-headed opening above it are typical of pre-Conquest architecture. The n. door is late-C12; the pretty three-bay *arcade*, on octagonal pillars, C14. Behind the pulpit in the s. e. corner of the nave is a small, oblong window, now attractively glazed with fragments of old glass – Could this have been a *low side window*, despite its unusual nave position? In the chancel – on a very much higher level than the nave – are simple *dropped sill sedilia* with the remnants of an eight-leaf *piscina* drain set into the sill. Lastly, to the great treasure of this church, a rare and remarkable example of a 'Seasonal Font'. The big, square *Norman* bowl, is carved on three sides with figures representing the months of the year, with 'activities' to match,

a frieze all round of foliage and splendidly feline lions, with linked tails. Starting on the n. side, and working right to left, we see: January, a seated man drinks from a horn; February, a seated figure warms himself at a fire; March, a labourer digs with a spade; April, tree pruning in progress. On the e. side: May, a man with a banner, in a *Rogation* procession of 'beating the bounds' and blessing the crops; June, weeding; July, reaping; August, binding a sheaf of corn. On the s. side; September, hand threshing with a flail; October, grinding corn with quern stones (a hand mill); November, killing a (surprisingly co-operative) pig; December, a jolly group celebrating Christmas at table. It is worth noting that this wonderful survivor almost didn't survive: in 1797, when an attempt was made to move it from the n. *aisle*, the font shattered into three pieces – and was then removed to the garden of the rectory at Fincham, way over in the w. of the county, where it remained for nearly half a century. It was then 'returned home' and partially repaired; another 50 years went by before the job was done properly, including the re-cutting, very ably, of the lower part of the October corn-grinding scene.

Burnham Market (Burnham West-gate), St Mary (E1): The really notable feature of this church is outside, and you need a pair of binoculars to appreciate it. It is the rather remarkable parapet to the tower; a *Perpendicular* addition to an otherwise early *Decorated* construction of about 1300-1310, with typical 'Y' traceries to the belfry windows. The parapet is carved with a richness of detail which is possibly unique, a whole series of panels carved with biblical figures and scenes under little *ogee*-headed canopies with *finials* and *cusping* above. In the centre of each side is the 'M' for Mary; and dating the work accurately are the Arms of William Lexham, Lord of the Manor, who died in 1500. The body of the church has been heavily restored, and all the window traceries are replacements, with the exception of the simple two-*light* Perpendicular examples in the s. *clerestory*, and possibly the *trefoil* and *quatrefoil* mouldings in their round frames in the C14 n. clerestory. At the w. end of the *chancel* s. wall is the filled-in square frame of a *low side window*. Entering through the C15 and formerly two-storey s. *porch* and the C14 Decorated s. doorway, one finds a simple interior on which the Victorian restoring hand shows heavily. C14 *arcades* on octagonal pillars, and a rather lovely and delicate tower arch, contemporary with the tower. Under the tower is a roughly carved stone effigy of a robed figure with his feet upon a dog, possibly dating from about 1300. In the sanctuary, plain *dropped sill sedilia* on three levels. On the opposite wall is displayed an attractive *brass* showing a woman and three children, a boy, and two girls with long hair. It is inscribed to John Huntely, 1523, and his two wives. But the figure depicting him has long since gone, leaving only one wife and his three offspring.

Burnham Norton, St Margaret (E1): This handsome, well proportioned church stands on a hilltop, well removed from its village. Its fine round *Norman* tower with later parapet has the virtue of having all its round-headed windows intact, with no subsequent additions. *Nave* and *aisles* are largely of *Perpendicular* character, with big, stately windows in the *aisles*. But note the 'Y' traceries, of about 1300, at the w. end of each aisle, and the C13 n. door, pointing to the earlier date of the fabric. The *chancel* is C14 *Decorated*, with good traceried windows on the n. side. The square headed e. window is modern, small and out of proportion to the whole. The interior of the church is a wonderful surprise, rich in character, detail and interest. A severely simple nave roof, of *arch-braced*, barnlike lines, steeply pitched, tops a tall narrow nave and range of small, two-light clerestory windows; below, a five-bay *arcade* which is C13 on the n. side (round pillars) and C14 on the s. (octagonal pillars). Over the chancel arch can be seen the outline of an earlier, lower ridge, marked with fragments of medieval colouring. Still remaining are the stone *corbels* which supported the *rood beam*; slots in the upper arch where a *tympanum* was fixed; and to each side, the gouged out indentations where the *rood loft* was positioned. In the corner of the n. aisle is the entrance to the *rood stairs*, with the painted head of a saint faintly discernible, under his halo, to the right of the doorway. There are two other stone brackets, lower down on each side of the chancel arch – what were they for? The *rood screen*, with its elegant carving and minimal remains of painted figures, is dated 1458. There are two pulpits: a richly painted six-sided one, dated 1450, portraying the *Four Latin Doctors* and donors John & Katherine Goldale, and standing on a wine-glass stem; the other is *Jacobean*, very simply carved and complete with backboard and *tester*. Spare a moment to take in the uncluttered beauty of the chancel. Notice as you leave the big, square Norman font on its five stumpy legs; the two *Royal Arms*, one initialled for William and dated 1697, the other

for George IV; the *decalogue boards*, painted on vellum (said to be early-C19); the *wafer oven* unusually sited to left of the n. door, with its flue within the wall; and a niche to right of the door which is all that remains of a *holy water stoup*.

Burnham Overy, St Clement (E1): This is a church whose history and fabric raise enough questions and intriguing puzzlements to make one dizzy. It stands prominent on a knoll within its village, and is made more distinctive by its squat central tower topped by a sturdy wood and lead C17 bell-cupola. It was a much grander, bigger church in times past, with its tower one stage higher and with *aisles* and *transepts*. The reasons for its reduction are open to conjecture. Observe the outline of an enormous *chancel* arch on the w. face of the tower, above the present roof. The tower is basically *Norman*, though the window insets are *Early English* and the top is C14. The body of the church much restored, with some curiously domestic windows on the n. side. The s. side, however, is very much Early English in character – a *lancet*, 'Y' and intersecting traceries with a nice suggestion of simple *ogee* heads. Over these windows and the blocked C14 *priest's door* are the outlines of arches indicating an *arcade* to a former aisle or chapel. Notice also the blocked oblong window, high at the e. end of the *nave* s. wall, which perhaps served to light a *rood* within the nave on the central tower's w. face. The chancel is altogether C13 Early English, with three delicate separate lancets forming the e. window, and double lancets to the s. The interior has an appealing air of rusticity about it. Severely simple *arch-braced roofs* to nave and s. aisle. Three bay arcade of the C13 with surprisingly wide arches and standing on round and *quatrefoil* pillars. One of the round pillars has stiff-leaf moulding round the *capital*; the quatrefoil ones have ring capitals, plain except for the addition of odd, fist-sized carved heads with vacant faces. The arches of the disappeared n. chapel/aisle are outlined in the wall; under the westernmost one are the faint remains of a very small St *Christopher* painting. On this wall also is a rather roughly carved and yet dynamic monument to Robert Blyford, 1704, and his wife, 1672 (She was but 35, he lived to 70). It has a big broken *pediment* inset with helmed and crested coat-of-arms; scrollery and cherubs down the sides; and below, a kind of hammock, with knotted ends, containing a grim jumble of skulls and bones (see also Brandon Parva). Over the cramped, round-headed arch into the tower are the old *decalogue boards*. High up on the right, notice the deep niche of a small round-headed window which, again, may have lit the *rood*. Take particular note of the filled-in arch at the e. end of the s. aisle – the only indication that there was formerly a *transept* on the s. side of the tower. Under the tower now, and under another simple arch, into the chancel – and a surprise. On the s. side is a three-bay, Early English arcade on round pillars, all leaning rather alarmingly outwards, and contained within the Early English wall seen from outside, barely a foot separating the two. Question: Was there an aisle or chapel, removed in a very short space of time? Notice at the base of one of the pillars a crude contemporary drain. Here in the chancel, the full beauty of the set of lancets in the e. wall can be appreciated, each deeply splayed and bounded by pencil slim shafts with ring capitals. As you leave, take in the lively and colourful *Royal Arms* of George III over the s. door.

Burnham Thorpe, All Saints (E1): This serene spot is deep rural England, undisturbed – and here *Nelson* was born. His father was rector of this handsome church, which stands now amid beautiful lawns and a surround of trees. The e. end, which fronts the lane, is impressive – the whole gable end, around a big (replacement?) *Perpendicular* window, is decorated in flint and stone chequerwork in two distinct colour schemes and *flushwork*. Above and to each side of the window are canopied and traceried figure niches. The *chancel* is *Decorated* but with Perpendicular window insertion (Notice the *Tudor* roses over the *priest's door* on the s. side). Early-C15 tower with a fine parapet, pinnacled and flushworked. A neat Perpendicular *clerestory* of four small, square-labelled windows each side. The s. *aisle* is a Victorian replacement, the original one having collapsed in the previous century. Surprisingly spacious interior, with a very fine early-C13 four-bay *arcade*, on slim round pillars. Modern roofs to *nave* and chancel, and modern furnishings throughout – though of special interest is the lectern, made of timbers from H.M.S. Victory, and given to All Saints by the Board of Admiralty. Large, fine and almost complete *brass* in floor of chancel to Sir William Calthorpe, 1420, lord of the manor and patron of the church, who is seen in full armour beneath a canopy set with shields, and birds holding scrolls. Notice particularly that Sir William is wearing the rarely seen mark of privilege, the *Collar of S's* (see also Ashwellthorpe). Beside the brass lies Nelson's

father under a plain slab simply inscribed: 'The grave of the Reverend Edmund Nelson, Rector of this Parish'. Impressive early-C15 *piscina* and triple *sedilia* with massive canopies and angel-headed *corbels*, and huge floral carvings in the *spandrels*. In the s.e. corner of the s. *aisle* is an arched recess containing an ancient tomb slab. See how the end arcade pillar has been cut away in this corner, presumably to fit a *parclose screen* when there was a side-chapel here before the *Reformation*. On the opposite side of the pillar, a *squint* gives a view of the high altar. Simple octagonal font bowl on a modern stem. Two points of interest outside the church before you leave: On the lower section of the s.e. buttress of the chancel are two *mass dials*; and on the n. side of the church will be found the graves of Nelson's much-loved sister Susannah and her husband, and of the Admiral's brother, Maurice.

Burnham Ulph, All Saints (E1): More properly, Burnham Sutton-cum-Ulph; to avoid possible map-reading puzzlement, this church is right in the centre of Burnham Market, a few minutes walk away from Westgate Church at the other end of the Green. It is a small building, *nave* and *chancel* only, with an C18 bellcote. First impression, on approaching from the s. side, is of a virtually Victorian rebuild. But though it was heavily restored in the latter years of the C19, it is a very ancient foundation, as we shall see. That slim little window in the centre of the nave s. wall, despite its replaced headstone, is in fact *Norman*, as is the very low, filled in arch on this side of the chancel. Nice C15 *Perpendicular porch*, with interesting multi-*cusped* openings to each side, set in square frames. The simple 'Y' traceried window in the w. end dates from about 1300. There is another round-headed window in the n. wall of the nave, with *dog-tooth* mouldings as a drip mould. It is credited with being original, but may be a re-use of original mouldings. In the chancel n. wall is a *lancet* with an inserted *cusped* head, with 'M' for Mary carved above it, somewhat crudely; and below it, the filled-in square of a small *low side window*. The e. window is C15 Perpendicular. The surprise comes inside the church, for though this is largely a very simple and pleasant Victorian interior, the chancel arch is a lovely example of the *Transitional* phase of about 1190. So we have slim rounded pillars, *capitals* with typical stiff-leaf carvings, and an elegant pointed arch. Notice the slots in the capitals and marks down the pillars where the *rood screen* was fitted; the *corbels* above the arch which supported the *rood*; and to left, the *loft* exit from the *rood stair,* whose floor-level entrance has been artfully incorporated into a window *jamb* (keeping two of its lovely little carved floral motifs) to form a figure niche. Don't miss either the splendidly grotesque carvings of the roof corbels to each side of the chancel arch. The *piscina* in the chancel once evidently had a fine *cusped* arch with *ogee* head and *finial,* but these have been hacked away, flush with the wall.

Burston, St Mary the Virgin (H7): The tower fell in 1753 and the *chancel* would seem to be a complete C19 reconstruction. The interior is rather barn-like under open pitchpine roofs, with a great blank wall at the w. end, redeemed by a fine and large set of James I *Royal Arms* (on boards) which has been well restored. Below, a plain octagonal C14 font with eight figures round the shaft. They have all lost their heads but one is St *Andrew* (n. side identified by his 'X' cross) and one on the s. side might be the Blessed Virgin with the Child. The blocked n. door has a *holy water stoup* by it and there is a simple medieval chest with chip decoration at the corners and on the ends of the top. Burston was famous for a while when, in 1914, the local school teachers, Mr and Mrs Higdon, clashed with the parson and the county education committee and were evicted from the school house. With local support and national trades union backing, they opened a rival establishment in 1917 – The Burston Strike School. Still to be seen on the village green, it finally closed in 1939. This is no place for its history, but you may feel moved to visit Ann and Tom Higdon's graves. They lie by the roadside hedge in the s. w. corner of the churchyard, in company no doubt with many that were for them and some that were against them.

Buxton, St Andrew (I3): The tower and some of the rest of the church was entirely rebuilt in1881, and the s. *porch* of similar date was set rather oddly at an angle to the *nave.* There are *quatrefoil clerestory* windows above the tall and graceful C14 *arcades.* The base of the C16 *screen* now stands between the *chancel* and the s. *aisle* chapel, and has been built up to full height with new work. There is a C13 *piscina* and *sedilia,* with plain arches and a single *headstop* at one end. On the chancel n. wall an alabaster monument to Margaret Robinson (d.1638) has black marble *Corinthian* columns, with a broken *pediment* above; cherubs peep out above the tablet, opposite is a tablet to Mary Ann Kent (d.1773 aged 4) who:

died under Inoculation... her fond parents deluded by prevalent Custom suffered the rough officious hand of Art to wound the flourishing root of Nature & rob the little Innocent of the gracious gift of life.

The church has a good ring of 6 bells, tenor 12-1-0 cwt.

Bylaugh, St Mary (G4): Ignore the necessary but unlovely sewage farm next door, and concentrate on St Mary's otherwise beguiling situation close to a curve in the infant Wensum. The round tower has a C14 octagonal top, but most of the rest was rebuilt in 1809 – the e. end completely, with short *transepts* and tall turrets at all corners. The interior has not in essence been disturbed from that day to this and therein lies its charm. It has, it is true, a small medieval font, and there is a fragment of C13 coffin lid by the s. door, but for the rest this is a church that the Victorians were not disposed to meddle with. There are pale cream walls and white plastered ceilings that meet in a smooth *Norman*-style four-sectioned vault at the *crossing.* Nave, transepts and *chancel* have a superb suite of *box pews* in oak the colour of a hazel nut, and the *three-decker pulpit* is undoubtedly the best in the county. It occupies the n.e. quadrant of the crossing and is a combination of quality joinery and astute design that would be hard to beat. The pulpit, under its *tester* is a 'walk through' – ascend by stairs on one side and descend by others on the far side to a mini-vestry, to be shielded from the public gaze by a curtain above the line of the wainscot. There is a semi-circular seat which the preacher may use while the service is read, and in the spacious reading desk below, an ingenious sliding block whereby the seat may be used at two levels for clerics short or tall. The *parish clerk's* pew is to the left and faces down the nave – snug but strategic. It would be an education to study the drawings for this piece, but no doubt the foreman joiner had, in the end, to be content with the age-old instruction 'fit on site'. Delicate candle sconces sprout from the tops of the pews, and the steep line of the tower arch is reflected in the curve of the half doors below- imaginative Georgian good taste. The *reredos* is black picked out in gold, with texts of the commandments, Lord's Prayer and creed, and again, a sweet curve downwards in the centre over the altar; *communion rails* of cast iron and of the period. It is worth the effort to draw back the matting (and to replace it) so that one may see the *brass* which lies in front of the pulpit.

The 3ft. 6in. figures of Sir John Cursun (1471) and his wife are excellent; he has a short rolled hairstyle, full armour, sword and dagger, and a smiling lion at his feet. She wears a *butterfly head-dress* with a high-waisted gown, and two little dogs snarl at each other round her skirts. On the e. wall of the sanctuary is the memorial to John Bendish (1707) – a very lively *cartouche* with three cherub heads at the top and another half hidden below. The Rev. Mr Norgate was vicar here from his ordination in 1836 until he died in 1908 aged 96. That means he lived out the whole of Victoria's reign here, and sitting in the blissfully civilised peace of his church it seems no more than reasonable.

Caister on Sea, Holy Trinity (L4): A church that is splendidly cared for. Slim C14 tower with buttresses to the w. only, and mid-C15 bell openings with *transoms*. The steep line of an old thatched roof shows clearly on the e. face, but since then the covering has been lead, then slate and now good looking pantiles. The *nave* still has a C13 *lancet* in the n. wall and in the C14 s. *aisle* the Lady chapel retains the original lower floor level. The *sedilia* and *piscina* in the *chancel* are nicely grouped under a range of *cinquefoil, ogee arches* with detached shafts. The church has what may be the biggest font in the county, and by chance rather than by design. There was originally a C13 *Purbeck* font but this was swapped in 1830 for a modern one, and then in 1902 the present C14 monster was discovered in a cottage garden at Eye, Suffolk and bought for £5. Even without steps it is 5ft. high and measures 3ft. 4in. across the bowl. The stem has shafts at the angles, highly individual tracery in four of the bowl panels and a castellated rim. It could look even better if the surface were relieved of its thick coating of staring whitewash. The *Royal Arms* hanging on the *arcade* pillar are dated 1786 for George III, but look at the initials and you will see that they have been altered; the shield is correctly painted for its date, 1786, but the motto – Exurgat Deus Dissipentur Inimic – strongly suggests that it was originally painted for James I. The arms are set in a square frame, but diamond-wise so that they look just like a *hatchment* from a distance. Also at the w. end, *decalogue boards* of well above average quality; on two panels 8ft. x 6ft. (Caister goes in for the ecclesiastical 'outsize'!) the figures of Moses and Aaron stand, each with their half of the decalogue. The paintings are well restored and good, and date from the late C17. The view into the chancel is narrowed by the twin organ cases

on the walls, but their curves effectively frame the e. window which is filled with a study of Christ and his fishermen disciples by Paul Woodroffe. It is a memorial to the nine Caister men who died when the lifeboat 'Beauchamp' was lost in 1901 trying to reach a stricken vessel. To the question 'Why?', came the reply 'Caister men never turn back' – simple statement of a great tradition. Also in the chancel, a memorial to Sir William Crowe (d.1668); a fine bust with shoulder-length hair and head half turned. In the churchyard w. of the tower you will find the grave of Sarah Martin (d.1843) She worked as a dressmaker, but found time to visit Yarmouth Jail each week to teach, hold services, and help the prisoners. Though not as well known as Elizabeth Fry, hers was and is a potent example.

Caistor St Edmund, St Edmund (15): In a lovely park-like, rural setting, a church of great antiquity, varied styles and much interest, with links to still greater antiquity. For here was the Roman town of Venta Iconorum, across whose moat and earthworks the long path to the church leads; and in the fabric of the church itself is much reused brickwork from the Roman fort. The C14 tower strikes interestingly at once, with its well-formed battlements in brick and flint; brick again, including the *mullions* and tracery outline (a curious effect) for the belfry openings; as also for the tiny *sound-hole* slits on each side. The w. window is a fine contemporary *Decorated* example. The rustic old *porch* looks most attractive with its preponderance of ancient red brick: note on its outer w. wall the extraordinary mixture of materials, including the thin, tile-like dark bricks of unmistakeable early origin. Inside the porch there is the coarse outline of a *holy water stoup*, and a severely simple but beautifully shaped n. doorway which is C13, with a heavy *hood mould* and large *corbel* heads – much ravaged by time and circumstance – of a bishop and a king. The *nave* is *Perpendicular*, with handsome, clean-lined windows to either side; the *chancel* is older, of C13 date, with large *lancets* to n. and s., and a striking little *priest's door* on the n. side, again in ancient red brick. The e. window is Perpendicular, but possibly a little earlier than those in the nave. A s. door, now partially filled in, is topped by a quite dramatic arch, badly time-worn, and built in this church's ubiquitous red brick: its opulence points to a Decorated period origin. A serenely plain interior, all being plastered and painted, including the roofs between beams of unsophisticated rusticity – these having been raised about 1800 using many of the old timbers from the original roof. Furnishings without exception are modern, including a charming little pulpit, dated 1937 and appropriately having an inscription plaque made out of Roman lead. A very faint, and very large St *Christopher* painting dominates the nave s. wall (note how this ancient wall leans heavily outwards); a smaller painting over the pulpit shows St *John the Evangelist* holding a chalice with a dragon emerging from it (*Appendix 1 – Saints*). The chancel arch has tall, slim and elegant C14 work, with carved 'battlemented' *capitals*. *Royal Arms* of Queen Anne, 1714, at w. end; and a fine C15 font in lovely mellow stone, whose eight panels are carved with four *Evangelistic Symbols*, alternating with angels holding shields which show the Arms of St *Edward the Confessor* (Three Crowns) and, clockwise, one of the usual *Emblems of the Trinity*, the Arms of the Diocese of Norwich, and the *Instruments of the Passion*; well behaved little lions support the base. In his 'History of Norfolk', *Blomefield* says that this font was made by Richard de Castre, a native of Caister and Vicar of St Stephen's in Norwich from 1402 to 1419. In the chancel is the over-restored outline of a *piscina* recess and to its left a much larger, lower arched recess, purpose unclear. The window behind the tiny organ (built locally at Norwich in the 1880s by Mark Noble Snr) has been lowered to form *sedilia*. There was a *low side window* on the s. side of the chancel which has been filled in.

Calthorpe, Our Lady & St Margaret (H2): Apart from the e. window of 1822, the *chancel* is C13 and in all probability so is the tower, although it looks as though it was updated when the *nave* was rebuilt in the C15. Inside, the tower arch is low and deeply moulded brick with no *capitals*. There was a s. *porch* originally and the recess above the n. door inside may have contained a St *Christopher* in the usual position opposite the main entrance. The C15 font is very robust and has four amiable and well fed lions at the angles of the stem, with varied tracery between them and in the panels of the bowl. It has a bright new cover in the style of the period. The *Laudian communion rails* have been carefully restored and the *balusters* are set diagonally – a thoughtful variation. The *consecration crosses* have been repainted and a fine new *rood* with its attendant figures has been placed on the original stone *corbels* above the chancel arch. This church is cherished and it shows.

Cantley, St Margaret (J5): There is a remnant of a *Norman* arch over the *priest's door* which gives a clue to an earlier building, but the bell openings in the tower and most of the *chancel* windows point to the early C14. The s. door is C14 too, and has good clusters of oak leaves with acorns as *stops* to the arch, and the finely traceried *spandrels* contain arms of the Philips and Bardolph families. There is a short s. *transept* chapel which is now stuffed with pews, with a flat panelled ceiling and a *piscina*. Some good memorials: that to the brothers Jonathan and Charles Layton of Reedham and Clippesby Halls (d.1801 & 1791) is striking – a gilded sheaf of wheat tied with a band stands against the obelisk, and there is a bull in bas relief on a roundel below. In the chancel, Simon Kidball (d.1735) – florid lettering with the names in Gothic, and a monogram in the *cartouche* above. On the chancel floor opposite, a lively epitaph to a local Jorrocks, Robert Gilbert (d.1714):

> ...That subtile FOX DEATH,
> Earth'd him here at last,
> And left a Fragrant Scent, so sweet behind,
> That ought to be persu'd by all Mankind.

Is he, I wonder, pursued across Eternity by the shades of all those foxes?

Carbrooke, St Peter & St Paul (F5): A church of impressive size and interesting history. Maud, Countess of Clare, founded a house for the *Knights Templar* here in the mid-C12; it stood in the field s. of the church and was the only one of its kind in the county. Under Edward II, the Templars' order was suppressed and their lands given to the Knights of St *John of Jerusalem*, and thus it stayed until the Dissolution of the Monasteries in the 1530s. The C15 tower is tall and stately and the *flushwork base course* continues all the way round to the *chancel*. The *sound-holes* have shields set in a circlet of small *quatrefoils*, and there are large three-*light* bell openings. The *nave* and chancel windows are C15 and generous in scale, but the e. window shows that the chancel dates from the late C13, and its tracery is highly original. There is a large n. *porch* with an upper room, but the doors are bricked up from the outside and locked from the inside. The s. doorway has an early-C14 *ogee* arch, and the s. *aisle piscina* matches it. This is a large and airy interior with graceful C15 *arcades* and a *clerestory* that is completed by a matching window over the chancel arch. The roof should be studied because it is a false *hammer-beam* (unusual for Norfolk); see how the big angels jut out from the arch-braces but do not support any of the weight. A further range of stiff little figures project from the bottom of the *wall posts*. The tall chancel arch has an attractive band of stone panelling on either side, and there are traces of a painting on the remains of the *tympanum* in the apex of the arch. At the e. end of the n. aisle, the bottom door of the *rood stair*, with its closing ring, is original and the nearby altar has a medieval stone *mensa* (look for the five *consecration crosses*). Within the tower arch there is a ringers' *gallery*, and a lively three-dimensional set of Hanoverian *Royal Arms* is fixed to the front. The painting just below, of David playing his harp, is dated 1747, and artistic licence has not only provided sheet music with modern notation, but the words are in Hebrew – just to give it a happy touch of verisimilitude! Some of the bench ends are original, but some are copies and you are free to exercise your talent for discrimination; on the arms, the *Evangelistic Symbols*, the *Agnus Dei*, and the *pelican* in her piety. On the e. wall of the s. aisle, an interesting coloured memorial in Franciscan mode to Elizabeth Chambers (1932) with cat, dog and birds. Moving past the big restored C15 *screen*, the chancel is spacious, and there are two grave slabs in the centre that carry the unmistakeable *cross patée* of the Knights Templar. The inscriptions are worn, but the Latin translates thus, 'A mother of the family of Clare, by a soldier of which family, England boasts herself renowned lies here' and 'A son rests at the right hand of his mother, returning to his own birth, he has sought his harbour'. One cannot be certain, but these are likely to be the graves of the foundress and one of her younger sons; they could well be the earliest burial slabs in Norfolk, dating from the early C13. The C13 *sedilia* have deeply moulded arches and there is a window sill *piscina* – one of the simplest forms used. The church has a ring of 6 bells, tenor 10-2-0 cwt.

Carleton Rode, All Saints (H6): A surprisingly large and impressive church in this small, secluded village, the initial impression – notably high pitched *nave* and *clerestory* and noble *Tudor* windows to the *aisles* – being of a generally *Perpendicular* building. But the tower is *Decorated*, as its w. window proclaims with its rather good tracery, and below it, a deep *cusped* figure niche. The tower is so squat that it doesn't look right at all – until you learn that by the opening years of the C18 it was 'in a state of grievous ruin'. Rescue work was put in hand. Then in 1755 the s.e. buttress collapsed, and fell onto the church.

Look at the e. face of the tower, the w. end of the clerestory on the s. side, and the e. end of the *aisle* immediately below, and you'll see where all the restoration, patching and panelling (some workmanlike *flushwork*) took place. The n. and s. aisles have fine big *Tudor* windows – including a particularly enormous one, easternmost in the n. aisle, which comes down to only three to four feet from the ground. The e. end aisle window at this point is different again – early Perpendicular with tracery of an easy flow. At the opposite end of the aisle, 'Y' tracery, of about 1300. All leading to the *chancel* – an especially fine construction of the C13. And although the exterior walls are unfortunately cement-rendered the splendid windows – 'Y' pattern, geometrical and, in the e. end, a superb four-light example of intersecting tracery, together with the outstanding *priest's door* – have a beauty which can not be dimmed. The e. window is further enhanced by pencil-slim shafts on the *mullions*, double ones on the *jambs*, and all dressed with delicate little shaft rings at the point where the tracery 'springs'. All have deeply carved foliage *corbels* to their *drip moulds* – as does the priest's door, elegant with its moulded arch, flat-ringed *capitals* and slimly rounded pillars. To the left of the door, a small *trefoil*-headed *low side window*. From this point, notice the most unusual window high in the e. gable of the nave – within a round frame, it is decorated with a profusion of *cusps*. Perpendicular clerestory. The porch looks earlier and is much restored, but retains a nice cusped figure niche over the outer arch. In 1875, *Thomas Jekyll*, that interesting and eccentric architect carried out his last restoration here, renewing the roofs and installing some of his most elaborate furniture. The nave pews have rich blind tracery and fine *poppy-heads* (all of which are different), a pulpit, and a rector's stall densely carved with flowers, angels and dragons. In the n. aisle chapel there is a substantial Elizabethan altar table and a fine C14 *piscina* with its original *credence shelf*. At the opposite end of the aisle, a niche for a *holy water stoup* by the n. door. In the s. aisle (crossing under the four-bay nave *arcades* of the C14) another C13 piscina, with a heavily moulded arched head, flat-ringed capitals and rounded pillars. Below the C14 chancel arch, the base of the old *rood screen*, with an excellent set of 12 painted panels showing the 12 apostles, all with their respective symbols. The figures, incidentally, are identical with those at Ranworth. Having walked under the chancel arch, turn back and look at the rim on its e. side and at the seven deep notches in the stonework.

This is where the *tympanum* would have been fixed. To your left, the low side window from which a *sanctus bell* would have been rung – though now, on the arch in that corner, a small modern sanctus bell has been fitted to continue ancient custom. Note that all the windows in this beautiful, light chancel, have lovely fluted shafts down their jambs, all with flat-ringed capitals; the e. window mirrors its own exterior by having shafts down the mullions too. In the sanctuary is a dramatic *double* piscina of the late C13, with an intricate abundance of open carving in the head of its stately arch. The *sedilia* that once adjoined it are filled in, leaving only a hint, in the jambs of the window above it. Of special interest here in the chancel are six painted *consecration crosses* in four distinct patterns – a direct link with the day on which this church, 600 years ago, was consecrated with due ceremony by the bishop. The church has an excellent ring of 6 bells, tenor 7-1-3 cwt.

Carleton St Peter, St Peter (J5): Marooned in fields in the deep countryside – but happily, still a well-used and cared-for little church. There were extensive C19 restorations but it maintains its own character very well. The C16 tower, with its jutting belfry stair, has a great deal of brick in it, including the belfry and w. window *traceries*. Nearly all the windows of the main body of the church have been replaced, but near the s. *porch* there is the outline of a C12 *Norman lancet*, and on the n. side, a C13 *Early English* lancet remains in use. Within, the *nave* and *chancel* are continuous, and the impression of length and narrowness is accentuated by the ceiled-in roof. Plain pews, choir stalls lit by candelabra, and the charming little organ under the tower with painted angels on its panels all combine to please the eye. The *rood screen* in largely C19 but some of the original C15 work has been incorporated. In the *chancel* the lovely late-C13/early-C14 *piscina* has fluted columns under a *trefoil* arch, and across in the n. wall an *Easter Sepulchre* was uncovered in 1897, revealing painted post-*Reformation* texts at the back, taken from St John's Gospel ch.14. The church has an excellent ring of 6 bells, tenor 12-1-26 cwt.

Carlton Forehoe, St Mary (G5): One of the pleasures of a visit here is the walk across the wide and open meadow to the church, and another is to collect the 2lb key that must surely be the biggest still in use in the county. The tower was completely rebuilt in 1713 – flint and red brick with a stone on the w. face that patriotically proclaims 'Vivat A (nne) Regina'. The rest of the building is *Perpendicular*, and the gable has a very decorative floriated cross. The tall white and bright interior has no masterpiece to offer but is lovely in itself. A simple w. *gallery* was installed in 1839 and there is a set of George III *Royal Arms* overhead. Traces of a *rood stair* in a n. window embrasure, and notice the drilled brackets high on the wall that once supported the *rood beam*. There were once two *nave* altars and the niches for images remain on either side of the arch. In the *chancel*, the *piscina* has a decorative leaf design around the drain, and the altar is a fine melon-legged late Elizabethan table. Thankfully, it has neither been lengthened nor set on blocks, and the replacement top rails are good work. The *communion rails* have the look of the 1830s – quality Gothick before the rot set in. This is a sympathetic place one feels – a notice says: 'Please leave organ open as mice get in and can't get out.'

Castle Acre, St James (E4): Placed in a strategic location on its hilltop, the only intact survivor of medieval glories of priory and castle, this fine church and its great tower present an imposing picture. The tower has battlements, *arcaded* and filled with *flushworked* flint; crisp *Tudor*-arched belfry windows and, on each side, two *sound-holes* side by side composed of multi-cusped *quatrefoils* in circular frames; also a huge four-light w. window magnificently proclaiming 'high *Perpendicular*'. Approached from the village street on the n. side, *aisles* and *clerestory* offer a brave display of windows in the church's predominant Perpendicular style, and three in vigorously flowing *Decorated* mode. The s. side is equally eye catching. The two-storey vestry, n. e. corner, is topped by three heraldic *talbots*. The circular tracery of the e. window is Victorian; but the *mullions*, with their slim shafts and ring *capitals*, look original late-C13 work. Of similar date, around 1300, is the *priest's door* on the *chancel* s. side. Notice above this door a filled-in outline culminating in a rounded arch (possibly *Norman*) showing that, originally, the doorway was quite amazingly high, 14ft. or more. The explanation is romantic but just could be true: that it was designed to allow a knight in full armour to ride in on his horse, so that he, his steed and his endeavours could be blessed. Back to the n. *porch* (with a big *holy water stoup* set deep in the gable end wall) and the imposing n. door, tall and deeply moulded. It is set off by an 'embattled' square hood with shields, bearing the carved

Castle Acre, St James: pulpit

arms of the Earls of Surrey (left) and Arundel set on backgrounds of floral motifs. Grandly spacious interior: but first to take the eye is the beautiful tabernacled C15 font cover, soaring to a height of 26ft. where a golden dove is in full flight. Coloured and gilded in russet, green and gold and intricately carved, it stands on a contrastingly severe C15 font. Nearby, the old *decalogue boards* have been tastefully re-used to form a *screen* below the new ringing chamber under the tower. The modern *nave* roof sits on older, central *arch-braces* which in turn are footed on massive, roughly-adzed cross beams. Below are five big bays, the arches Perpendicular but at least some of the pillars being apparently re-used C13 work. Above the tower arch is a big

Royal Arms for George II, dated 1748. Set within the s. *pier* of the chancel arch is the complete *rood stair*. Beside its entrance, a splendid pulpit of about 1400, six-sided, on wine-glass stem, is carved with tiny angels and richly painted overall, including representations on its panels of the *Four Latin Doctors* of the Church. The base of the screen, again of about 1400, remains, its 12 panels painted with figures of saints identifiable by their various symbols; left to right, *Philip, James the Less, Matthias, Jude, John, James, Peter, Andrew, Bartholomew, Thomas, Simon* and *Matthew*. Look closely at St Andrew – he's peppered with lead shot. A Civil War legacy? Marking the limits westward of the *aisle* chapels are rather lovely wooden arches, with remnants of original colour (Note on the s. side, the tiny dragon carvings in the *spandrels*). These are all that remain of the pre-*Reformation parclose screens*, though some of their panels, imprinted with Ns and mitres for St *Nicholas*, are in the s. chapel and built into choir stalls in the chancel. Also in the s. chapel, the remains have been exposed of a delicate painted *consecration cross*. In the window above, some remnants of medieval glass, including a much-restored St *George*. In both n. and s. aisles are some nice old low benches with poppy-head ends and animals carved on the elbows, and a big wooden chest dated 1636. There are two more old benches in the chancel, and three carved *misericords*. On the s. side of the sanctuary is a curious construction which may have been *sedilia*. It has a coarse arch, with a pillar down the middle; and above, within a huge triangle of stone set flush into the wall, a good deal of badly mutilated carving. Opposite there is a *squint* at eye-level from the *sacristy* – and a tiny window at first floor level, in the upper room where the priest would have slept. But keeping vigil now at the window, which is barred, is a human skull and a long bone. The church has an excellent ring of 6 bells, tenor 10-3-16 cwt.

Castle Rising, St Lawrence (C3): When the Norman, William de Albini built the castle in the mid-C12, he also built this church, and it is one of the finest of its period in the county. The *chancel* and s. *transept* were altered in the C13 and in the C19; *Anthony Salvin* in the 1840s followed by *George E. Street* in the 1850s supplied their versions of *Norman* – the top half of the tower, the s. transept and chapel, and the *porch*. The w. front is a piece of real Norman bravura – a doorway with two sets of shafts and multi zigzags in the arch, the window above has spiral columns with crouching figures on the *capitals* and, again, a pattern of overlaid zigzags in the arch; either side, *arcades* of very narrow arches, within larger ones that interlace. With massive walls and deep set Norman windows on the s. side only, the wide *nave* is always cool, with an exciting vista eastwards; the bowed C12 w. arch of the *crossing tower* frames the *Transitional* arch beyond and the three fine *lancets* of the e. window. The Norman font stands centrally and has three animal masks on the w. face amid the interlacing patterns of the bowl, with a tip-tilted head at each corner. Above the tower arch, a triple arcade with densely compacted arches stands on sturdy columns, and the tower itself has a vault with ribs that are deeply and unusually carved with the zigzag pattern. The altar niche on the n. side of the w. arch is also Norman and shows that this arrangement preceded aisle altars. The twin on the s. side is a little later and has a neat *angle piscina* combined with a *squint*. Within the altar recess, a wooden C15/C16 panel with angels holding a monogrammed shield. Notice how the C13 s. transept arch cuts into earlier Norman windows above, its deep mouldings carried on five shafts each side. Plain glass, with subtle striations and varying tones has replaced the Victorian medallions in the e. window, and it is now as John Sell Cotman sketched it in 1817. The slim shafts and leafy capitals support deeply

Castle Rising, St Lawrence: Norman w. front

moulded arches decorated with the *dog-tooth* motif. The very tall *ogee*-headed niche to the n. has been called a *banner-stave locker*, but the rich mouldings and shelving bottom make this very unlikely – an image on a pedestal would furnish a more reasonable explanation. If you have had a surfeit of black marble headstones, 'Peace perfect Peace', and oblongs of granite chippings sparkling like bath salts, then rejoice to see a modern table tomb n.w. of the w. door in the churchyard. Mary Rose Howard died at 23 in 1980, and her epitaph, cut in fine Roman capitals runs: 'You were as a noontide in our twilight and your youth gave us dreams to dream'.

Caston, The Holy Cross (F6): This is a dedication which is not very common (only five in Norfolk), although there were often altars of the Holy Cross in parish churches. The church looks well from the village green and the C14 tower has a fine w. front. The *ogee* arch of the door is deeply moulded and the window above it has that pretty conceit of the *Decorated* style – one *reticulation* set within another in each of the *lights*. There are tall, slim bell openings of the same period below a plain parapet. The *chancel* is of about 1300, and at one time there was a *porch* on the s. side as well as the n. – now the doorway there has a window set in it. The original thatched roofs were replaced by slate in 1853, and close by the fence on the s. side of the churchyard parallel to the e. end of the chancel is a poignant memorial; at 24, John Anderson fell from the shaft of a slate waggon and was crushed to death. His epitaph is from the Book of Samuel: 'There is but a step between me and death'. Unusually, slate gave way to thatch again in 1973 when a local craftsman re-roofed both *nave* and chancel handsomely in Norfolk reed. The nave windows are *Perpendicular*, but on the n. side there is the outline of a predecessor, and the remains of a shallow *rood stair* turret can be seen further along. The porch has an upper room which must be decidedly murky, judging by the size of the window over the arch. Entry is from the w. and there are three big steps down into the nave. A rather bare interior, with a wide expanse of waggon roof, panelled overall in chestnut boards. The ribs are picked out barber's pole fashion in the original green and white, and there are large lacy flower *bosses*. At the w. end, a fine range of large bench ends with endearing figures of animals and birds on the arms, and nicely varied tracery carved in the solid. Fragments of cresting from the head of a medieval *screen* stand in a n. wall recess. Much of the glass on the s. side of the church was blown out during the war, but one window has been re-glazed very successfully to display fragments of English and foreign glass of the C14 to C16. The *Stuart* pulpit, with simple panelling, has a new base and rim, and across the nave is a chest of very individual shape – 7ft. long and only 18in. wide, with the lid cut into two sections. Behind it, a simple sill *piscina*. On the right, just beyond the chancel screen, there are two stalls with *misericords* – just lift the seats to see the carved heads with the attendant leaf shapes. The nicest thing here is a big 18-branch candelabra which was given to the church in 1871. It was presented to Cheshunt church in Hertfordshire by Charles I and probably came from Hampton Court originally. A simple trefoil piscina in the sanctuary and opposite, an *Easter Sepulchre* (see how the arch was cut away when the Perpendicular window was inserted later). The *communion rails* are a very restrained Gothick set of 1852, and the altar itself is a Stuart table. This is well worth a closer look – if you turn back the cloth you will see where the bread used to be cut for the Communion or for 'the Holy Loaf' after the celebration at the n. end, leaving deep score marks in the wood.The church has a good ring of 6 bells, tenor 8-3-21 cwt.

Catfield, All Saints (J3): Most of the building is C14 and the *aisle* windows have a pleasing alternation of tracery patterns. There is no *clerestory*, but at one time the walls above the *arcades* and elsewhere were covered with paintings. Now, about all that can be discerned is the Stoning of *Stephen*, above the second pillar of the s. arcade. The *rood screen* has sixteen paintings of kings, somewhat mutilated. St *Edmund* can be seen with his arrow emblem to the right of the opening. In the embrasures of both easternmost *aisle* windows there are steps which evidently led up to the *rood loft*. It would appear that this originally stretched right across the church, some 10ft. w. of where the screen is now. Behind the ponderous pitchpine pulpit is an C18 echo – an *hour-glass* stand high on the wall. On the n. wall of the sanctuary is a tablet by the sculptor *William Groves*, with a peepul tree at the top, and a sheathed sword below, to Lt. Thomas Cubitt (d.1848) who 'met a soldier's death in his country's cause before Moultan' (Multan in the Punjab). The church has a good ring of 6 bells, tenor 10-0-23 cwt.

Catton, St Margaret (I4): Circular *Norman* tower with handsome later octagonal belfry. Rest of church, early-C14 *Decorated* and C15 *Perpendicular*. Very nice C15 *porch* with priest's chamber above, crow-stepped gables, niche containing figure of *Saint Margaret* (probably of Antioch); above her, an C18 sundial. The *chancel* – which is pebble dashed and, surprisingly, looks very acceptable – has a *priest's door* with Norman hood and *headstops* above it, a *consecration cross*. Inside, there's an C18 gothicky w. *gallery*; an interesting *Tudor* pulpit, dated 1537, bearing Arms of the *Guilds* of Norwich came from St George Colegate, Norwich in mid-C19. In n. *transept* (originally in chancel, from where it was moved by *Thomas Jekyll* in 1852 when the church was enlarged and restored) is a good monument, with two sad *putti* wringing their hands, to Bussy Green and family, 1745, by *Robert Page* of Norwich. Also a delicate and chaste memorial to Jeremiah Ives, Mayor of Norwich in 1820.

Cawston, St Agnes (H3): A big and impressive church which has, like many in Norfolk, a small village clustered round it. Apart from the *chancel* and s. *transept* which are earlier, the building dates from the early C15. The tower is tall and gaunt with a decidedly unfinished look at the top, but the rich combination of great w. window and deeply moulded doorway, with attendant wild man and dragon, more than compensates for this. The fine *base course* can be seen inside the church as well, and suggests that the tower was completed ahead of the rest of the work. The interior tower arch is very tall and is spanned by a C15 ringers' *gallery* resting on massive corner posts. Across its front runs an inscription which can be read more easily from the replica in the n. aisle:

> God spede the plow and send us ale corn
> enow our purpose for to make at crow of
> cok of ye plowlete of Sygate, be mery and
> glade wat good ale yis work mad.

Whether or no the last line is a reference to the profit from church ales or a pun on Walter Goodale's name, the connection of the plough *guild* with the church is maintained by the sign of the Plough Inn. It was hung above the n. door when the inn (formerly the guildhall) was closed in 1950. The *hammer-beam* roof of the nave is superb with each post backed by tracery, and supporting a standing angel with outspread wings. More angels line the cornice and the apex. Binoculars are a help here in appreciating the detail. At the e. end, the outline of the *rood*

Cawston, St Agnes: hammerbeam roof

(uncovered in 1911) can be seen above the chancel arch. Below is an unusually tall early-C16 *screen*, complete with doors to their full height. It was well restored in 1952, and the finely painted figures, some with most expressive faces, are ascribed to Flemish artists. From n. to s. the saints are: St *Agnes*, St *Helena*, St *Thomas*, St *John the Evangelist*, St *James the Great*, St *Andrew*, St *Paul*, St *Peter*, the *Four Latin Doctors*, St *James the less*, St *Bartholomew*, St *Philip*, St *Simon*, St *Jude*, St *Matthew*, St *Matthias*, and *Sir John Schorne*. The buttresses still carry traces of the tiny figures within canopies worked in *gesso*, a rich embellishment that can also be seen on the screens at nearby Aylsham and Marsham. The C15 pulpit is very well preserved and the treatment of the panels is reminiscent of the canopies seen on *brasses* of the period. The s. transept has a good roof with *bosses*, and traces of a painting on the e. wall, possibly of the Virgin. The *piscina* is extraordinary, and has a wild man and dragon with huge heads in the *spandrels*.

Chedgrave, All Saints (J6): A lovely situation, where the big high churchyard is bordered with Scots pine and looks out over heathy countryside. From the w. the building looks odd – the gable of the *Norman* nave side by side with that of the

brick n. *aisle*, and beyond, at the n.e. corner, a square Norman tower with original windows e. and w. and capped with thatch. Inside the 1880s *porch* we have the building's showpiece – one of those magnificent Norman doorways that are a feature of this part of the county. The shafts and *capitals* are richly carved, the arch has a heavy twisted rope moulding and a double zig zag that forms a lozenge pattern. Before you go in, note the *mass dials* by the entrance. The C15 octagonal font stands on a modern base and has angels holding shields on the bowl panels, with shallow five-leafed niches round the shaft. The glass in the e. window catches the eye straightaway. Restored in 1976, it was brought from Rouen Cathedral in the French Revolution by Lady Beauchamp Proctor, and there is more like it at nearby Langley, her family home.

Claxton, St Andrew (J5): Perched on a hilltop above its village, St Andrew's has the weathered look of centuries of buffeting by wind and rain. It is also one of those architectural bits-and-pieces buildings which give zest to the whole business of looking at old churches. The tower has been given red-brick corners and windows, which could be misleading in dating it – but the chances are that it was originally C14 *Decorated*, and the red-brick details of *Tudor* date. From the Tudor period too comes the attractive red-brick *porch*. There was a n. *aisle* to the *nave*, but that has long gone, and all that shows, inside and out, is the outline of the arches. The pillars so outlined inside, and the arch between tower and nave, point clearly to the early Decorated period – though the n. and s. doorways are equally clearly *Early English* – with the nave fabric being earlier still, C12 *Norman*. The *chancel* is a complete Victorian rebuild. The interior of this church is straight out of a Victorian print – plain varnished pews, with several *box pews* remaining from the C18; colour-washed walls and rush matting on the floors. The rebuilt chancel, with its lively *arch-braced roof*, retains a double *piscina*, which the Victorians meticulously restored with beautiful and authentic detail. Also given a new home was the monument – sanctuary, n. side – to Sir Henry Gawdy, who died in 1620; though this country-gentlemanly memorial, with decorous floral carvings and a dignified coat-of-arms, was not erected until 17 years later by his son. Very faded *Royal Arms*, quartered for Anne, and relettered for George I and a good C15 octagonal font, generously carved with two *Evangelistic* lions, two *Tudor roses*, St *Andrew's* cross, the shield-design *emblem of the Trinity*, a crowned lion rampant on a shield; and also on a shield, the *Instruments of the Passion*. adorable puppyish lions support the font's base. Notice as you leave, beside the s. door, a large and mildly adventurous *holy water stoup*, with a *cinquefoil* head topped by a square *hood mould*.

Clenchwarton, St Margaret (B3): The walls of this small church have a very pleasing mixture of brick, stone and flint and there is the fragment of a *holy water stoup* outside by one of the *Perpendicular* windows on the n. side. A great deal of thin red brick was used in the late-C14 tower and the bell opening to the e. has *plate tracery* although the divisions in the others have broken away. Above the plain *nave* parapets the line of a steeper and higher roof shows on the wall. The s. *porch*, restored in 1861, is largely brick with a sundial over the arch and pretty canopied niches at the angles. It has a vaulted roof with transverse ribs like the one at Runcton Holme and there is a *trefoil* niche over the *Early English* inner doorway. The octagonal font has roses within the *quatrefoils* of the bowl panels and could be mistaken for regular C15 work were it not known that it was made and installed in 1853. The tower arch beyond is low, with the mouldings fading into the *imposts* and the nave is plain and uncluttered. Standing on a new base, the late-C16 or early-C17 pulpit is intricately if somewhat coarsely carved – familiar blind arches and deeply cut panels above them. There is no *screen*, but a small *piscina* on the s. side shows that an altar once stood nearby. The whole of the e. end was rebuilt in the 1860s and there is

little to say of it, but do look at the tablet on the s. wall. Of Francis Forster (1741) it says:

> When the terrible inundation Feb 16 1735, Threatening the destruction of this whole Level, He with unshaken resolution when all around him droop'd under their Misery, Opposed the Flood, repaired the broken Ramparts, and sav'd the Land from that fatal ruin with which the next assault must have overwhelm'd it.

And so a local hero is remembered and it is interesting that the monument is signed by John Fellows of Kings Lynn, the 'free stone-mason' who, with John Parsons of Wells, built the new nave of St Margaret's Kings Lynn to the designs of Matthew Brettingham in 1742. On leaving, note the board of 1742 hung at the w. end of the nave roof bearing the churchwarden's name, and in the porch, a portion of lead roofing dated 1840 which has the plumber's name as well.

Cley-next-the-sea, St Margaret (G1): A marvellous, vital building, resplendent with carving and *crocketting*, niches and pinnacles – and a ruined s. *transept* adding to its visual impact; crowning all, a thoroughly individual *clerestory*. This is all from the s., from the delightful green which fronts the churchyard. The n. side is sober but nonetheless rewarding with, above the clerestory, a magnificent range of battlements in richly fretted stonework, beautifully inlaid with *flushwork*. The n. *porch* is a poor thing contrasted with its opposite

Cley-next-the-sea, St Margaret

number, but just around the corner is the splendid w. front with its huge dominant window. But then, the s.w. angle was intended to impress. Look across the serene meadows to Wiveton church on its own hill – 500 years ago that expanse between was a harbour, alive with the shipping and commerce of a prosperous port. Towards the mid-C14 the church took its present shape, on the back of a flourishing trade, virtually replacing its predecessor apart from the tall, slightly severe mid-C13 tower. This was the age of *Decorated* architecture, reaching in the ruined s. transept's beautiful window tracery, a peak of artistic opulence. Then came the *Black Death* in 1349 – and work stopped. When it resumed some years later, the consummate craftsmen were no longer available, and the *Perpendicular* style began to emerge. We have it grandly here in the *aisle* windows and the great w. window. Slowly from this time the sea withdrew, the river shrank – and with it went Cley's fat years, leaving a small coastal community with a huge church on its hands. Unable to maintain it all, they bricked off the transepts – already ruinous by the end of the C16. The s. porch is C15, of remarkably rich design, its upper chamber with handsome little windows, and a sundial between them. Above, battlements of beautiful filigree work, flanking buttresses highly ornamented with canopied niches; the outer arch and *jambs* carved with heraldic emblems, and inside, a *groined* roof with badly eroded *bosses* – though one has great vitality, with a fox making off with a chicken, pursued by a furious old woman. Inside, the church is a blaze of light, pouring in from the clerestory with its great *cinquefoil* windows alternating with a two-light design, from the soaring w. window, and from the aisles – where the dropped window sills all form seats. The C15 *arch-braced* aisle roofs have flower and foliage bosses and delicate tracery in the *spandrels*. In the *nave* and s. aisle are echoes of the exuberance outside – for between the arches of the elegant C14 *arcade* are some highly individual ornaments richly canopied. From e. to w. they represent an imp with a glass eye, a distinctly apprehensive St *George* wrestling with a very angry dragon, an enchantingly happy lion gnawing a bone, an angel with cymbals, a contortionist musician with pipe and tabor, and tucked away in the s.w. corner, a very sulky little man. On the other side of the arcade, acting as *hood mould* stops in the s. aisle, are more figures cavorting joyously, with one very naughty fellow mooning. Below is a fine *brass* for John Symondes (d.1511) and his wife Agnes (d.1508),

shown in their shrouds, with their eight children lined up below them, each with a 'name plate'. Other interesting brass remnants will be found westward in this aisle near the door, and in the n. aisle a splendid priest brass. Note in the n.w. corner of the nave the battered *Royal Arms*, crudely altered for Anne, from Charles II. The *seven sacrament font* is much defaced but still very fine, and there are some good bench ends – touched with the same buoyant humour which infects the arcade carvings. In the *chancel*, the *piscina, dropped sill sedilia* and the window above it are simple C14 Decorated, marrying happily with the earlier Y-traceried windows in the n. and s. walls. The large, five-light e. window is Perpendicular, but this too, with its uncluttered lines, remains in cool harmony with the rest. The altar stands on the medieval *mensa*, and there are six *misericords* carved with shields. The *rood stairs* are unusual – two entrances, one in the chancel, the other in the n. aisle. Outside, under the s. transept window seek out the tomb slab with interesting inscription to a loyal officer of *Sir Clowdisley Shovel*. The whole churchyard is worth exploring for the magnificent range of C18 headstones.

Clippesby, St Peter (K4): Buried in trees away from the road and easily missed. A typical round tower, this time with a C19 octagonal top. There is a *Norman* n. doorway, with remains of another in what is now the main s. entrance *porch*. There is a little *mass dial* here on the outer *jamb*. Early-C13 *lancets* in the *nave* are about the same date as the *piscina*, which has supporting shafts and simple spiralled *capitals*. In the same s.e. corner of the sanctuary is a good *brass* to the family of John Clippesby (1594) – two adults and three little maids with a *chrysom child*. Another brass in the nave also has two good figures, one with a man in a fur-lined gown with a purse at his belt. The inscription for this is probably the one fixed to the n. door (Thomas Pallyng, 1503). The excellent window of c.1919 with Christ and a group of children is by Margaret Rope, a fine Arts and Crafts artist whose work is found mainly in Suffolk churches such as Leiston and Little Glemham

Cockley Cley, All Saints (D5): A neat, pretty little church with the village pub (the splendidly named '20 Church-wardens') on one side, and a green river valley stretching away on the other. In 1866 the building underwent a restoration so drastic that now it gives the impression of a Victorian Gothic construction. Alas, the slim round tower (*Norman* in origin but rebuilt c.1300) collapsed in August 1991. The styles followed in the body of the church are *Early English* and *Decorated*, and there is good reason to believe that, in reconstructing the *chancel*, the Victorians followed the original plan of five bold *lancets* spaced out on each side. Certainly the interior detail, as we shall see, certifies the accuracy of the e. window's three grouped lancets with a continuous *drip mould* overall. In any event, the chancel as a whole is a most pleasing and successful composition. Nice s. doorway, early-C14, with devilish, pixie-eared *headstops*. An attractive interior, made spacious by the broad, light aisles to n. and s., and lofty and uncluttered *nave* and chancel under neat modern roofs. Pretty, original Early English *arcade* of three bays to the s., on *quatrefoil* pillars with ring *capitals*, all faithfully reproduced in the C19 n. arcade. The interior view of the e. window is a lovely Early English ensemble of 'pencil' – shafts (with tiny ring capitals) down the *jambs* of the three deeply-splayed lancets and, as outside, a continuous *hood mould* over the grouping. In the n. wall is a double *aumbry*, very businesslike and severe. In the s. aisle, a simple *piscina*, and a *holy water stoup* by the s. door on a pillar, both reconstructed. By this time no visitor can have failed to note that this is a church cared for with much love and even more elbow grease – the old quarry stones gleam as much as the woodwork, and you can literally see your face in the *ledger-stones* in front of the *communion rail*.

Cockthorpe, All Saints (F1): A most pleasing and welcoming little place. The tower, enhanced by a fine bit of restoration repointing work, is older than it looks on first glance: about 1300 in fact, as indicated by those Y-traceried (albeit bricked up) windows high up. Inside the church, the condition may be far from ideal – yet it was rescued from far worse decay and neglect through the excellent and invaluable work of the *Norfolk Churches Trust*, in whose care All Saints is now placed. The *nave* has a rather rustic *arch-braced* C15 roof, with surprisingly opulent carved *wall plates* on the n. side, and very long and carved wooden *wall posts*. The *clerestory* of the same C15 date, on the s. side only, was altered to fit the pitch of the roof. Below, an unsophisticated *arcade* of about 1300, very much at one with the sedate tower arch and the neat *chancel* arch. There is a lovely old knobbly bench end dated 1647, and a couple of earlier *poppy-heads*. Overhead, adding to the character and the lovely atmosphere of this little place, are

candelabra – there being no electricity here. The poor chancel has had a bad time of it – a lot of alterations, door and window now blocked and the upper tracery gone from the e. window. The s. *aisle* has a larger window partly filled in and replaced by a charming smaller one of two *lights*, seemingly to make way for the large *Jacobean* tomb chest below it to Sir James Calthorpe, 1615, which also shoves rudely into the simple little *angle piscina* (contemporary around 1300 with the *aisle*, the entrance door and the arcade) in the s.e. corner. Cockthorpe's other and famous Calthorpe monument is at the e. end of the aisle; the fascinating content of this alabaster and marble remembrance of Sir James and his dame reads:

> In assured hope resteth here the bodies of Sir James Calthorpe, Knight and Dame Barbara his wife, daughter of John Bacon Esq. of Hesset. By her he had 8 sons and 6 daughters, in whose severel marriages and issues the ancient glory of the name of the family (resting then chiefly and almost solely in himself), did reflourish and is dilated into many of the best houses in the country. He was buried the 16th day of June A.D. 1615 and of his age 57. The said Barbara, surviving him, and much comforted with the sight of 193 of their children and their offspring, at the age of 86 years exchanged this life for a better, upon the 3rd of November A.D. 1639.

Note that two of Norfolk's famous admirals were born in Cockthorpe and baptised here, *Sir John Narbrough* and *Sir Clowdisley Shovel*.

Colby, St Giles (I1): Apart from the old rectory, quite alone in the fields. A thin mainly C14 tower and a lovely C15 *porch*. Surrounded by *flushwork*, the doorway has St *George* and the Angel Gabriel in the *spandrels* and a niche between two windows above. The upper room has an open arch to the *nave* and was used as a Sunday school in the C19. There was a n. *aisle* but this was demolished in 1749 and a new wall of brick with arched windows replaced the *arcade*; the *chancel* arch was remodelled to match. The C15 font is interesting – the bowl panels have the *Evangelistic Symbols* interspersed with St *Giles* and his attendant hind, the Virgin on a settle with the Child standing on her knee, and the donors kneeling. The restrained architectural cover of 1848 is good – classical columns carrying a moulded flat canopy. Also at the w. end on the

n. wall in a glass frame hangs a beautiful C19 velvet altar frontal, richly embroidered and incorporating an earlier border. The chancel C14 *sedilia* and *piscina* are very shapely, with slender shafts carrying *ogee* arches, and the C17 *reredos* has painted panels of Moses and Aaron. The C15 glass in the e. window was arranged there by a C19 rector. The figures in the tracery are some of the Apostles, and in the main panels one sees in the centre St *Peter*, left and right at the bottom St *James the Great* and St *John*. The two angels standing on wheels refer to Ezekiel 10: 'Go in among the wheels beneath the cherubim'.

Colkirk, St Mary (F3): A small church, well proportioned, given individualism by the offset position to the s. of its tower, a strong, battlemented construction of the early C14 with sturdy belfry windows of contemporary style. Its base serves as a *porch*, with a big, handsome outer arch with noble-faced *headstops* to the *drip mould* and triple pillars supporting the arch – all very much in period. Both *nave* and *aisle* are late *Perpendicular*, all the windows having that special touch of elegance given by the steeply pitched 'basket' hood moulds extending well down below the curve of the arch, and by the impression of height afforded by the slimness of the windows. A *low side window*, heavily restored and filled in, is in the usual position at the w. end of the s. *chancel* wall. The n. aisle is a Victorian addition of 1872, which faithfully and most effectively echoes the Perpendicular character of the rest. Note that its n. door is re-used, C14 work. The interior is plain and unassuming, with modern furnishings throughout. Of strong interest is the big *angle piscina* in the chancel, with heavy *trefoil*-headed arches cut directly through the stone. Adjoining are simple, unadorned *dropped sill sedilia*; and to the left – not a usual position – an a *aumbry* under a big, plain pointed arch. On the opposite side of the sanctuary, placed against the wall, is the inscribed grave slab of 'Mistris Anne Jessop' who died in February 1639. It is a rather apprentice looking piece, with a grinning, gap-toothed skull at the top attended by that familiar warning, 'Hodie mihi cras tibi' – ('Me today, You tomorrow.'). Nonetheless 'Mistris Anne' was evidently concerned about the right connections in this world, for we are firmly told that she was 'daughter to John Hills Gentleman & grandchild to Sir John Potts Baronett'. At the w. end of the church, the chunky round font is *Norman* and rather unusual – four little moulded double *colonettes* on its otherwise plain sides extend down to stumpy supporting legs. The base is modern.

Colney, St Andrew (H5): Now that the main road has bypassed the village street, travellers cannot so easily read the homely admonition over the *porch* door, but perhaps they should! 'READER If thou drivest a team be careful & endanger not the Life of another or thine own'. John Fox's epitaph has recently been cleaned and re-cut, and you will want to read it before you go further. Half-way up the round tower there are blocked double-splayed windows, so this is probably *Saxon* rather than *Norman* work, and the w. end of the *nave* has *carstone quoins* – another clue to an early foundation. The rest of the building is basically early-C14 and there is pretty, small scale *Decorated* tracery in most of the windows. The C15 font is rather special; the design is imaginative – see how its vine trail decoration drops naturally down into the heads of the shaft panels, and the bowl panels have some unusual themes. Apart from the *Evangelistic Symbols*, there is a Crucifxion on the e. face, and on the w., a cowled figure prays to St *Sebastian* – bound and pierced by arrows. A nave n. window has some most peculiar glass of the 1870s by *Harry Wooldridge* – two patriarchs draped in a variety of dress fabrics have faces like weathered daguerrotypes. Behind the pulpit there is a small but heavy monument to Richard Browne (1674) – a black marble slab between reeded columns, with a coat of arms above. Just beyond the 1930s *screen* of plain oak, almost unadorned, is a little *chalice brass* to rector Henry Alikok (1502), and in the sanctuary, John Tomson's C16 tomb chest is let into the n. wall – fluted *pilasters* and a band of simple decoration along the top.

Coltishall, St John the Evangelist (I4): The C15 tower has a very nice w. front, with a small but tall w. window flanked by niches, and a frieze of alternating shields and *chalices* below. The chalice emblem of the Evangelist also figures in the *base course*. Two small round *Saxon* windows have survived, high under the eaves of the thatched roof on the n. side, but it is a pity that somebody in 1865 set a large and inappropriate circular window below them. The C13 square font of *Purbeck marble* stands on a central drum, with four supporting shafts, a type found in many churches in the county. On the n. wall of the *nave* is a monument to Sophia St John (d.1827); a female leans pensively against a tomb, posy basket in hand. On the s. *aisle* wall, James Perkins (d.1711/12) has a *cartouche* around which fat pink and gilt cherub heads are nicely arranged. The monument to John Hapman (d.1719) in the *chancel* has seated *putti*, one wiping his eye, and the candlesticks above, complete with candles, are rather an odd embellishment. A very fine tablet to Henry Smith (d.1743) and his wife states endearingly: 'they were happy in each other and their children in them'. The church has a good ring of 6 bells, tenor 10-0-25 cwt.

Colton, St Andrew (H5): A quite striking little church, with a late-C13 tower (complete with its original 'Y' tracery belfry windows), and the rest of the church reflecting the *Decorated* style of the first half of the C14. *Thomas Jekyll* carried out his first Norfolk restoration here in 1847, mainly in *Decorated* style. He removed all the external plaster and added buttresses to the *chancel*, restored the *porch* and re-roofed the church throughout. Within, George III *Royal Arms* loom darkly behind the C19 *gallery* and on the w. wall there is a faint remnant of C14 wall painting on the theme of gossiping – two women being encouraged by two devils, while a third dances above them. The panels of the octagonal C15 font are carved with quatrefoils, and there is a carved *consecration cross* on the *nave* n. wall. In the n.e. corner the 1715 monument for Philip Pooley has a portrait bust on top, with his armorials below, and to the l. a much simpler monument of 1741 for his wife Elizabeth. Jekyll replaced most of the C15 benches with pews and restored the *Perpendicular rood screen*, incorporating parts of the original. In the chancel, he provided a *communion rail*, a new altar, and the *reredos*. All the glass in the nave is by *Lavers & Westlake* and the s. chancel window of 1912 is signed by them. The rest of the patterned glass came from *Powell & Sons*, probably as part of the Jekyll restoration in 1847.

Congham, St Andrew (D3): A long narrow path between closely set trees makes a pleasant approach from the s. Slim early-C14 tower with small *trefoil sound holes* and 'Y' *tracery* bell openings, with a C19 w. door and window. The n. and s. *nave* doorways are C14, but heavy C19 restoration work obliterated most of what had gone before. Within, nave and *chancel* lie under one panelled roof. The octagonal font is a typical C13 pattern in *Purbeck Marble*, with pairs of blank arches in the bowl panels. The doors of the tower *screen* are made up from *Jacobean* panels

beneath a band of C15 carving, and the pulpit is a very pleasing piece. It was made by a Mrs Hilliam in the Sandringham wood-carving school around 1900, and with its walnut panels and graceful stair, it forms an excellent example of the work that came from that short-lived experiment on the royal estate. Behind it, and partially obscured, is a large slab with an inscription in fine italic which marks the entry to a vanished chapel built by Charles Spelman in 1684. More concerning the family can be found ay Narborough, but here their arms are engraved on a *ledger stone* in front of the altar. A C14 piscina sits in the e. wall and nearby there is a memorial for an early victim of the railway age. A 20 year old Ensign, Elsdon Edwards died 'by being knocked down by a locomotive, whilst crossing the Seaham and Sunderland railway… the high wind having prevented his hearing the signal whistle.'

Costessey, St Edmund (H4): A spacious, well-kept church in a well-groomed churchyard, and although much restored, still with a great deal of interest. The base of the tower is C14 *Decorated*, with a sturdy conical-capped bell-turret with more than a touch of the castle about it – which could be what prompted the style of the surprisingly successful brick belfry (topped by a lead spire) added in 1930 – battlemented, and with a raised frieze of small arches, mildly medieval Teutonic. A very good C15 *porch*, with stone/flint *flushwork* of notable extent and quality. The whole of the body of the church is C14 Decorated. But the big *nave* windows with their intersecting tracery are Victorian replacements, as is the effective Decorated window, with bold and handsome *quatrefoils* in its tracery. The other three *chancel* windows are most intriguing, with little *transoms* intersecting the tracery heads, that at the n.e. being a little riot of horizontals under a very tall, narrowed arch. The porch retains an attractive carved figure niche over the coarse Decorated entrance arch, which in turn sits on *jambs* of an earlier style which, if not original *Early English*, are certainly neat reproductions. To right, a *holy water stoup*, plainly restored, serves duty as a flower stand. Inside a solid modern *screen* partitions off the w. end to form a 'lobby' and vestry. Here stands the C14 font, carved with blank shields round the bowl and below them, curiously carved miniature human heads, half way between portrait and grotesque. Spacious nave and chancel, high, wide and light. Modern roofs and largely modern furnishings, the pews having come from Booton when that church was eccentrically rebuilt and refurnished; from the same source came the fine *Jacobean* pulpit, tastefully carved and distinctive of its period. Across the plain chancel arch is a special survivor – the old *rood beam*, set high up, which supported the *rood*. Below, a good C15 screen which retains short 'wings' to either side – were these, as *Dr Pevsner* suggests, to separate it from side altars, or did they complement 'the curve and projection of the *rood loft*', as *Munro Cautley* believed? In the chancel is a touching memorial in black and white marble by *Thomas Rawlins* to Mary Jerningham, who died, aged 4, in January 1733 – a child of '...affection that Endears, / And wit beyond an Infant's years'. Other Jerningham family memorials will be found here – Queen Mary I, who reigned 1553-58, gave them Costessey Park. Before you leave the churchyard, see if you can spot the *mass-dial* on the buttress immediately to the right of the porch – it's about 4ft. from the ground, very faint and cunningly disguised by lichens. The church has a ring of 5 bells, tenor 11-2-0 cwt.

Coston, St Michael (G5): This little church is set in quiet, deep countryside, serving one of the smallest of Norfolk's parishes, and by the 1970s it was in a sad condition, with holes in the roof and the tower unsafe. Thankfully, it has been taken under the wing of the *Churches Conservation Trust* and is now in beautiful order. Subject to small variations, all the indications are that it was built in one piece in mid-C13, and it is worth circling the building to see how a *string-course* below the *lancet* windows draws the composition together, rising up on the tower to bisect the w. window. The bell openings with their 'Y' tracery date from about 1300, and the battlemented parapet will have been added a little later. The lancet windows in the *nave* have *headstops*, and a *low side window* has been blocked in the s. wall of the *chancel*. A line on the e. wall of the tower shows that the original roof was much steeper and was probably thatched, but by 1763 it had become 'ruinous and decayed' and was replaced with tiles. In 1809 the chancel was shortened by one bay, given a new roof, the e. wall rebuilt in brick and the *Perpendicular* window re-inserted. The C16 brick *porch* is charming and in its old age the outer arch has gently splayed. Through the inner doorway with its canted headstops one enters a quiet, undemonstrative interior with faded, mottled walls and brick floor, lying under the starkly massive beams of the C15 roof. Beyond the plain octagonal font, the n. door that once led

to the parsonage house has been blocked but a plain *holy water stoup* survives alongside. The chancel arch is low and narrow and the *corbels* terminate in curious curlicues – no doubt a conceit by the same mason who added little leaves at the base of the window mouldings. The stair to the vanished *rood loft* was cleverly contrived within the thickness of the wall that separates nave from chancel on the n. side, and emerges just below the line that marks where the *rood beam* crossed the arch. An austere but handsome *Jacobean* pulpit with a canted book ledge stands on the s. side – the site of a nave altar whose *piscina* with its *trefoil* arch remains in the wall nearby. There are slim C18 gothick rails across the chancel step, and beyond, the *box pews* of the same vintage were formed into a priest's desk and choir stalls in 1850. In the shortening of the chancel the piscina was lost and, rather oddly, three corbels from the vanished bay were re-set low down in the e. wall. During the recent restoration the small *Jacobean* altar was rescued from the base of the tower, repaired, and placed once again at the e. end.

Cranwich, St Mary (D6): Tucked away behind the patrician hall, down a grassy field track, is this charming little church straight off a Victorian romantic print. Very slim, round *Saxon* tower; very small *nave* and *chancel* and neat little s. *porch*, all thatched; and everything with that weathered, lichen and ivy look which makes the building look as if it grew here, like its surrounding trees. The tower has excellent round *sound-holes* with tracery intertwined like a cub-scout's knot, each one, it seems, cut from a solid chunk of stone. The battlemented top of the tower is a C13 addition. Though the fabric of the nave is *Norman*, the rebuilders of the *Perpendicular* period left their mark on it with pretty little square headed windows. The chancel is of about 1300, with simple 'Y' traceries to each side, and a pleasant e. window of interlacing forms. All have tiny crude *corbels* to their *drip moulds*. Though the *porch* is Perpendicular, it's been given a round outer arch – in sympathy, no doubt, with the s. doorway, which is very elementary Norman work of about 1200, unadorned except for a *hood mould* carved with a single line of *dog-tooth* motifs. The interior perfectly complements the image presented by the outside of the building – complete simplicity, a calm which even the main road noises wafting across the fields cannot spoil; plain plastered ceilings and whitewashed walls throughout. Just a deal-panelled gable in lieu of a chancel arch; homely Victorian furnishings and well-worn brick floors. There's a very attractive C13 *piscina* in the sanctuary – a strongly moulded arch sits on stumpy little round pillars with ring *capitals*. Over the tower door at the w. end is a very small Hanoverian *Royal Arms*, undated, pale as a silvery water colour and very much at one with its surroundings.

Cranworth, St Mary (F5): There cannot be many villages in Norfolk that still boast a set of stocks; Cranworth's stand by the churchyard gate and have been well restored. There were C19 restorations at the church and the n. *porch* was rebuilt, but the building is virtually all of one period – early C14. Apart from the 'Y' tracery in the w. window of the tower all the windows have attractive *Decorated* tracery, and the outside drip moulds have *headstops* that turn inwards towards each other. You may find as you walk round that a great flock of pigeons rises from around the little spire to fill the air with the slap of their wings. Large heads of a king and queen flank the n. door – he with curly hair and beard. Inside, the *arcades* rest on *quatrefoil piers* and the whole of the s. range was renewed in the C19. Both the tower and *chancel* arches have head *corbels*, and though the former are difficult to see behind the organ, they have the look of Victorian work. With the *sedilia* in the chancel, it is plain that the square top is a C19 replacement, though the *double piscina* under its five-leafed arches was left alone. There is a blocked *low side window* on the s. side. In the n. *aisle* wall at the e. end is a tomb recess under a *cusped ogee* arch that might be the resting place of the founder, and nearby, a blocked arch once led to the *rood stair.* Cranworth has some excellent memorials – have a look first at the flamboyant *cartouche* over this doorway. It is to Sir William Cooke (1698); there is a host of little coats of arms, two cherub heads among the folds, and a sharply cut skull at the bottom. To the left, on the n. wall, a black tablet with flat alabaster drapes hung with bright shields; it records the annals of the Gurdons – rather confusing because most of them chose Brampton as a Christian name. However, this particular Brampton died in 1669 and, in his prime led the Suffolk Horse at Naseby (although in Good King Charles's Golden Days this is tactfully not mentioned). To the w. on the same wall, Thornagh Gurdon (1774); he wrote an early history of Norwich castle, and the monument by *Francis Stafford* is very elegant – a draped pyramid with his epitaph above inscriptions for his wife and family. Another good tablet in the s. aisle to (another) Brampton Gurdon (1691); this one has fine lettering on a marble drape,

and two *putti* recline nonchalantly, supporting shields on the broken *pediment*.

Crimplesham, St Mary (C5): Once on the main road but now insulated a little and approached via a cul-de-sac. The *Perpendicular* tower has a heavy stair-way bulking out its s. face, and there is a *Tudor* w. window. Walking round, note the *carstone* peeping through the plaster rendering of the *nave* walls, and the small *Norman lancet* on the n. side – first indications of the building's real age. The *chancel* was completely rebuilt in 1877 and there were new roofs twenty years later. The C17 *porch* of rich red brick, with very large side windows (now blocked) leads to a sizeable Norman doorway with two bands of decoration in the arch and single flanking columns. (Another Norman arch on the n. side now leads to a vestry). The tower *screen* incorporates parts of a late-C15 *rood* screen which came from North Weald Bassett in 1969; *linen-fold* panels, centre doors to full height with a band of foliage on the centre rail, part of a donor's inscription either side, and a section of loft coving at the top. The font is a very plain C14 octagon, and in the Victorian chancel, the late-C13 *double piscina* under twin *trefoil* arches, with deep *quatrefoil* drains, has been sensibly re-used. For those that like to seek them out, there are two *mass dials* on the right hand *capital* of the s. doorway.

Cringleford, St Peter (H5): The bypass has been merciful to St Peter's and one no longer risks instant translation to reach it. A chequered history here – n. and s. *aisles* demolished in the C15 and a new s. aisle with *arcade* added in 1898 when the church was thoroughly restored. For all that, there are windows in *nave* and *chancel* which have the splay both inside and out which is a sure sign of *Saxon* origin. The *lancet* embrasure in the chancel n. wall retains traces of *Norman* decoration – now faded to a dull red. The *low side window* on the same side just e. of the chancel arch is later, and its interesting feature is the *squint* cut through the w. *jamb* which originally enabled the celebrant at the altar in the now vanished n. aisle to see the high altar in the chancel. Incidentally, one of the old n. aisle *arcades* can be seen from the outside, by the side of a blocked Saxon lancet. In the chancel, the shallow and simple *piscina* no longer has a drain, but the original wooden *credence shelf* survives, albeit cracked and wormed. When the *rood stairs* were demolished in 1898 some Saxon stonework was found doing duty as steps, and it was re-assembled on the wall at the w. end to show its probable origin – part of a coffin lid. Also set in the w. wall is a fragment of a small Norman shaft. The early *Perpendicular* font is a fine example, standing on a Maltese cross base. The bowl panels have deep relief carvings of flowers and fruit and the shaft is deeply concaved to house strings of stubby flower motifs. In the s. aisle, a big oil of 'The marriage feast at Cana' by Bassano or his school, with all the figures in curiously frozen attitudes. Opposite, a much more sympathetic Virgin cradling the Babe's head in her hand while St *Francis* (?) leans over intently – cherub heads are dotted about and the painting is described as C17 Florentine. Under the organ, a framed tour de force in fretwork. A young apprentice cut the Lord's Prayer for his first test piece in 1906 and, after a long life as a local craftsman, he bequeathed it to the church. Touching.

Cromer, St Peter and St Paul (I1): The 160ft. tower is by far the highest in Norfolk and dominates the town, both from land and sea. Its impressive combination of strength and elegance is enhanced by the fine detail of *sound-holes*, double-opening belfry windows, and intricate parapet. The rest of the building is of the same C15 date, except the 1880s *chancel*. The church has three large *porches*, and the western one is lavish. It has a *groined* roof over a fine inner doorway enriched with a large moulding in which shields and angels alternate. The porch abounds with canopied niches, and is topped by traceried battlements and pinnacles. The interior of the church is outstandingly spacious, with very tall *arcades* and arches. Light floods through the great *transomed* windows. There is a good deal of C19 and C20 glass, and the *Pre-Raphaelite* figures by *Burne-Jones* in the e. window of the s. *aisle* are excellent. A variant provenance by Birkin Haward assigns the design to King of Norwich. The modern Rudland and Clark memorial windows in the s. aisle pick up a number of points of local interest, particularly those connected with the sea. The memorial to one of Cromer's most famous sons, Coxwain Henry Blogg, can be found beneath the tower where there is also a replica of the C15 font at Yaxham, near East Dereham. During the C18 and C19, Cromer church went through some bad times of neglect – it is recorded, in early Victorian times, that the churchwardens had to buy hedgehogs, at 4d each, to keep down vermin in the churchyard. It had some characterful vicars, however. There was Archdeacon George Glover, appointed about 1800, known as the 'Cardinal of Cromer', friend

of Coke of Norfolk and holing strong whig, controversialist views. His successor, William Sharp, was a very small man who required a hassock placed in the pulpit to give him a little more height. The story has it that one Sunday morning he was preaching on the text 'A little while and ye shall see me no more'. Alas, he slipped on his hassock, and to the dismay (or possibly delight) of his congregation, promptly disappeared from view. The church has a good ring of 6 bells, tenor 12-1-7 cwt.

Crostwick, St Peter (I4): Approached across the common from the road, and then up a short avenue of tall limes to the n. *porch*. The C15 tower is handsome, particularly the parapet, which has pierced tracery alternating with *quatrefoils* below the battlements. This, and the corner pinnacles are now very worn. The C16 porch is of brick, and so are the remains of the *rood loft stair* outside on the s. wall. Inside, there is a beautiful C15 font which has standing figures in niches round the shaft, and seated figures set in recesses round the bowl. On the s. wall opposite the door is the remains of a large St *Christopher* painting.

Crostwight, All Saints (J3): Set deep in fields, a church which has evidently gone through hard times – but its future is now assured, as is evident at once in its general condition and the neat order of its churchyard. The squat tower was once lofty, but its top had become so dangerous by 1910 that it was removed and capped in red tile. All the window tracery here seems to have been renewed, though the e. window has been done in an attractive *Decorated* style. The *porch* is very appealing, with its rough rural outer arch and 'battlemented' *capitals*, tiny figure niches above and a heavy, square *pediment* roofing it over. A *holy water stoup* has had a *piscina* drain put into it. Inside, the church is most attractive, with cream-washed walls and sympathetic modern furnishings. The much-restored C13 font is of the common design of double-arcading carved on its eight panels. Then there is a fine and important range of wall paintings on the n. side – and a really lovely C15 *screen* with carving which is intricate yet restrained: all its colour has gone, though traces of colour remain on the sturdy, Decorated *chancel* arch. In the chancel, there are heavy C13 coffin slabs either side of the altar; an unadorned piscina; and near the screen, two *brass* inscriptions, one dated 1447. To return to the C14 wall paintings, which were discovered originally in 1846: at the w. end is represented the *Seven Deadly Sins* in the form of a tree; a morality play sequence?; and a huge St *Christopher*. Between the two windows are numerous small scenes, among them, at top left, Christ with bound hands before Pilate; in the centre, very faintly, the Last Supper; below centre, what looks like a *consecration cross*; top right, Crucifixion; immediately below, the Crown of Thorns being placed on Christ's head; very good in the window splay is Christ's agony in the Garden of Gethsemene. Set into the opposite splay of the window is the old *rood stair* entrance, now filled in.

Croxton, All Saints (E7): The village street swoops up from a dip and the church perches close to it on the crest. The round tower has a C14 octagonal belfry stage which is topped by a small Victorian spire. The *chancel* is early-C13 judging by the *priest's door,* with its *hood mould* decorated with *dog-tooth,* although the side windows date from about 1300 – like two others on the n. side of the *nave;* a three-*light* e. window with *Decorated* tracery. There was a C14 s. *aisle* but by the early C19 this had gone, leaving the *arcade* embedded in the wall, and the present s. aisle and *porch* are Victorian work. The s. side of the nave has a pretty range of six *Tudor clerestory* windows in red brick, and inside they give light to a beautifully compact *hammer-beam* roof in pale oak. It is small in scale but quite elaborate, with braces between the *wall posts,* castellated corners to the hammer-beams and pendants at the apex. Rather odd to see the blank spaces on the n. side, but there is no sign that there was ever a second range of windows. The church is well blessed with fonts – an ancient one outside by the porch, and two inside. The first of these is a large C15 octagon with well defined but perfectly plain panels. *Cautley* thought that it must once have had carvings of the *Seven Sacraments* but, if so, there is absolutely no sign of them. The most that can be said is that the proportions would allow for it. Nearby is a simple C18 wooden *baluster* font painted grey; under the domed cover, the bowl has split and the lead lining has disappeared but it could be restored. The e. window has glass of the early 1900s reminiscent of Charles *Kempe* but not, I think, by him. The central figure of Christ is flanked by St *Edmund* and St *Felix,* the latter holding a model of Norwich Cathedral – a rather eccentric conjunction, since he died 500 years before it was built. While in the sanctuary, have a look at the *ledger-stone* of William Smith

(1682). It is a very good example of idiosyncratic lettering which has an innate sense of style.

Denton, St Mary (I7): A good view of the tower from down the hill to the w., an enticing approach over a sunken stream via an iron bridge, up the drive of the big house, and finally, two flights of steps into the churchyard. The tower is really quite odd – a *Saxo-Norman* round tower collapsed in the C18 and had a red brick back stitched on, and then in 1843 a new square top was added in flint. There were two more restorations in the C19 when all the windows and roofs of the church were re-done, the whole thing floored in Minton tiles and new seating throughout. The big, early-C15 n. *porch* has an outstanding set of roof *bosses*: e. the *Annunciation*; s. the Nativity, with the Holy Family on one side and the ox and ass on the other; w. the Resurrection, Christ rising from the tomb on one side and the sleeping soldiers on the reverse; n. the Ascension, Christ's feet have been chipped where they disappear into the cloud but there is a lovely group of the Apostles and the Virgin Mary looking up from below; centre, the *Coronation of the Blessed Virgin* – hardly damaged at all. Inside, there is an early-C14 *arcade* and over it, two pairs of large and handsome square *quatrefoil clerestory* windows. Look above the tower arch for another eccentricity – two big tie-beams protrude through the wall and are held there by great pegs at least 5ft. long. This is just how the rails of a medieval stool were secured through the solid ends, a simple and self-tightening brace. The big late-C13 *chancel* has a fine e. window with intersected 'Y' tracery filled with a brilliant gallimaufry of early glass – coats of arms, roundels and canopies. Not only is it one of the most pleasing arrangements of fragments that we have, but also the earliest in the county; collected by the rector John Postlethwaite who left £200 in his will for it to be installed. This was done in 1716 by a well known glass painter, Joshuah Price. There are lots of heraldic shields and the *Stuart Royal Arms* in a big oval are easy to pick out, but if you want to check them all there is a list handily framed on the *chancel* s. wall. Especially delightful are the tiny C15 roundels. Look for two birds playing trumpet and harp in the 2nd light from the left, just below and to the left of the Norwich arms, and the twin portraits of St *Christopher* and St *John* in the centre light just above the inscription about John Postlethwaite. At the top of the centre s. chancel window is a roundel of a man killing an ox from a 'Labours of the Months' series (binoculars are helpful to appreciate these). There is a C19 chest nearby which was made to display a range of medieval panels painted with saints. They have been grossly mutilated but a lot of the gilt *gesso* patterned background still adheres; left to right from the e. end they are: St *Agnes*, St *Dorothy*, St *Jude*, St *Peter*, a bishop, possibly St *Ambrose*, St *Zita*, St *Barbara*, St *Edmund*, *Edward the Confessor*, St *Walstan* and St *Paul*. They are only 12ins x 4ins, and if they came from a *screen* they must have been on the front of the *rood loft*. There is a small but good set of George III Royal Arms over the s. door, and Victoria's over the n. door in plain plaster; so with the *Tudor* and Stuart arms in the e. window, the church possesses four sets in all – more, I think, than any other in Norfolk.

Denver, St Mary (C5): Built of *carstone*, and that gives it the rich, dark colour of good plum cake. The C13 tower, with its small 'Y' tracery bell openings, had a leaded spire but it was blown down in a gale of 1895 (Norfolk has lost not a few this way). There had been wholesale restoration some 20 years earlier when the n. *aisle* was added but carstone blends and weathers very well. Although most of the detail has been renewed, note the *trefoil*-headed niches flanking the e. window. Inside, the *nave* has a panelled roof (also renewed) bearing original flower *bosses* and the series of small shields that adorns the cornice is quite unusual. In the *chancel*, an *angle piscina* with a simple trefoil arch and stepped *sedilia* in the window embrasure. The altar now hides half of Dr Robert Brady's *ledger slab* with its elaborate heraldry and Latin inscription. He was court physician to Charles II and Master of Gonville and Caius College, Cambridge for 40 years from the *Restoration* until 1700. Above, on the s. wall, a tablet by that rather uninspired partnership of *John Bacon* and Samuel Manning – for Lucy Smith (1843), but on the n. wall, a neatly turned epitaph for Thurlow Stafford (1760) carried out in stylish lettering on a cream marble tablet set between black classical columns under a plain *pediment*. Thomas Gaffin was another C19 sculptor who, with his father, turned out scores of memorials. Here, on the s. wall of the nave is one of his better efforts – a bas relief of a woman kneeling before a tomb, for John Dering (1836). There is a photograph of the church when it still had its spire on the n. aisle wall and with it, a variegated gallery of rectors spanning the best part of a century.

Deopham, St Andrew (G5): This must be one of the most distinctive towers in Norfolk, not only because it is so rich and splendid, but because it does not really seem to belong to the eastern counties, but rather to the West Country. It is pure *Perpendicular* of about 1450, at its most confident, in four thrusting stages divided by *string courses*. It has enormous right-angled buttresses, chequerworked down the faces and reaching right up to the opulent parapet with its octagonal, embattled corner turrets, and battlements intersected by triangular 'gables' crowned by luxuriantly carved crosses. Nobly traceried and *transomed* windows at three levels complete this sparkling piece of architecture. The body of the church is generally earlier, of the *Decorated* period, as indicated by the *aisle* windows – two-*light*, with big *quatrefoils* in the heads of the *ogee arches* and by the n. door. The rest of the windows, including the fine e. window, are all Perpendicular, that in the s.e. corner of the *chancel* being the latest of the group. The Perpendicular *porch*, which inside has shallow *arcades* recessed into the wall on each side, shelters a splendid s. doorway of similar vintage, with a square, embattled *hood mould* over its arch, and *cusped arcading* in the *spandrels*. The doors themselves should be noticed – they are C15, with excellent carved traceries. The interior of the church is spacious and lofty, albeit rather bare, with a plain *tie-beamed* roof which has moulded *wall plates* and deep *wall posts* with wooden angel *corbels*, immediately below which on the s. side are six large stone corbels, individually carved with human and animal heads – were these for the earlier, lower roof before the Perpendicular *clerestory* was added? Notice high above the soaring Perpendicular tower arch the *sanctus bell window*, giving a clear view of the high altar, The tall five-bay arcades are possibly separated in date by about a century: the s. pillars are octagonal and early-C14, those on the n. side square, with chamfered corners at the angles, are C15. On one of the n. arcade pillars is a small stone footing – possibly an effigy pedestal. Set into the e. end pillar is a very beautiful *piscina*, with a *trefoil* arch and protruding base; beside it, as also in the pillar immediately to the w., can be seen slots in the stonework where the *parclose screen* was fitted, when there was a chapel in this corner. Opposite, in the s. aisle, where there was another chapel (It is recorded that there were chapels here to the *Assumption of the Blessed Virgin* and to St *John the Baptist*.) a remnant of the old screen remains, with more pieces leaning against the wall. The steps to the old *rood loft* are here also, set into the base of a window; and a large traceried piscina under a square hood, with leaf shapes in the *spandrels*. Even grander is the piscina in the chancel, with a richly cusped, *ogee arch* and with shields in the spandrels. Adjoining are plain *dropped sill sedilia* on two levels. Notice again the grand five-light e. window; and above, the *hammer-beamed* and *arch-braced roof*, with its open-carved and battlemented *wall plates*. The font is plain, octagonal C16 work, with little *quatrefoil* motifs around the bowl.

Dersingham, St Nicholas (C2): An impressive early-C14 *carstone* church. The great five-light e. window of the *chancel*, restored in 1981, has a lovely web of *reticulated* tracery. *Aisle* windows, *clerestory,* and the top half of the tower are all C15 *Perpendicular,* although the angels at the top corners are modern. Entry by way of the C15 s. *porch* to a clean and bright interior – the ample width of both *nave* and chancel creates a great sense of space. The octagonal pillars of the C14 *arcades* have concave faces with little *trefoil* arches at the head of each – very effective, and the *headstops* are excellent (as they are everywhere in the church, both inside and out); spot the dragon opposite the s. door and the seal on the n.e. arcade column. The nave roof is a very good C19 *hammer-beam* replica, but see how the chancel *tiebeams* cut through the view of the e. window tracery. A very tall early-C14 tower arch, and above it, a large opening into the belfry that was probably a *sanctus bell window* rather than a door. The great chest by the font is one of the most interesting to be found anywhere. *Pevsner* calls it early-C16 but most authorities date it much earlier and it may be the one listed in the church's inventory of 1360 – certainly the panels of tracery at either end support this view; within a framework of rosettes and birds, the front has big relief carvings of the four *Evangelistic Symbols,* each bearing a scroll, and when it was complete the lid bore the inscription 'Jesus Nazarenus crucifixus Judeorum'. The C14 font is panelled with pairs of blank *ogee arches*, and this shape is seen again in the little s. aisle *piscina* of the same period. The C15 *rood screen* has a C19 top and the sensitive *rood group* was carved by a craftsman of the Queen's woodcarving school at Sandringham in 1917. When the screen was restored in 1877, the delicate *cusping* was renewed and six painted figures were found under the

paint; faded and mutilated, they are: St *Agatha*, St *Denys*, St *Agnes*, St *Hubert*, St *Martin* and St *Thomas of Canterbury*. The windows on the s. side of the chancel have *Decorated* tracery and one extends down to form a lovely *low side window,* four quatrefoils within a square. To the right is an exceptionally long *squint* into the s. aisle chapel. The window at the e. end of this wall was designed to sit centrally over the piscina and *sedilia*, and the latter have detached shafts with foliage decoration at the capitals. Across the chancel, a table tomb for John and Joanna Pell (1607); the black marble top is incised with their figures just as they would have been on a contemporary *brass*; his six sons kneel in the panels on one side, three daughters on the other. On the s. wall of the chancel, two good C18 monuments: Mrs Elizabeth Pell's by *Robert Page* – tablet with curtains drawn back to reveal the text, *putti* on the *pediment* and a pair of rather wooden cherub heads below; the other is for Mrs Hodgson by *Francis Stafford,* a free-standing marble column before an obelisk, with sensitive detailing in the surround. The *Royal Arms* over the n. door are unusual – the achievement is split into three and the robust, brightly painted wooden carvings came from the front of a local grocer's shop which had held the Royal Patent. The church has a good ring of 6 bells, tenor 9-0-8 cwt.

Dickleburgh, All Saints (H7): Now that the village is bypassed, the churchyard with its chestnuts, wellingtonia and mature holly trees is a place of calm and, incidentally, gives access to the neatly painted school of 1822. The plain unbuttressed tower of about 1300 has a 'Y' tracery bell opening to the w., but two are *Perpendicular* and a C19 stone clock face is set where the fourth was, with a *quatrefoil sound-hole* below it. The renewed *chancel* e. window is flanked by stately niches under *ogee arches* which have little king and queen *headstops* (only one is renewed). The ogee arch of the *priest's door* looks all C19 work except for the top, which has a head peaking out. *Porches* were often singled out for special treatment (marriage services began there and they were important in many other ways for both church and parish) and here again we see the evidence. There is elaborate *flushwork*, the outer arch has floral motifs in the moulding and fine headstops; ogee niches each side and a tall canopied niche above; in the *spandrels*, shields of the *Trinity* and the diocese of Ely, plus a shallow carved grotesque head to the right; on the buttresses crowned 'M's and 'RC's. The interior is well lit by the Perpendicular *clerestory* and the tall *transomed aisle* windows of the same period. The early-C14 quatrefoil pillars of the *arcades* are graceful, and see how a simple incision in the middle of each chamfer of the arch mouldings gives them much more character. The pale brown C14 font is so well preserved that one wonders whether it was plastered over in troublous times. Thin *woodwoses* with their clubs stand guard round the stem between fat lions (one licks his chops!); in the bowl panels are *Evangelistic Symbols*, together with angels both feathered and robed holding shields: emblems of the Passion, three *chalices*, the *Trinity emblem*, and the crowns of Ely. On the early-C19 *gallery*, an excellent set of *Royal Arms* on canvas, renovated by Professor Tristram. Dated 1662, it is just possible that it was originally made earlier for Charles I, judging by the style of the mantling. There are *decalogue boards* over the s. door and a single *hatchment* in each aisle. Although the roofs have been renewed, you will see the remains of a panelled *'canopy-of-honour'* at the end of the s. aisle – this was for the altar of the *guild* of St Peter and St Paul; the *piscina*, under a pretty *crocketted* ogee arch is in the s. wall, and the *aumbry* opposite has been given a convincing modern door carved in *linen-fold*. The *Stuart* pulpit is most attractive – the blank arches are carved with shallow arabesques and fitted with curly *capitals*, and each panel has a split egg-shape in the centre; oblong panels with deep leaf mouldings are ranged under the rim. The C19 added a plain but well designed stair, and beyond it stands the archway to the old *rood stair*. The *rood screen* has lost its top but the base is distinctly out of the ordinary. Apart from a narrow bottom course, the four panels are taken up with a large quatrefoil with square leaf terminations on all the *cusps*, and a positive riot of minor carving tucked into the various angles; a monk plays pipes with his habit blown back in the effort, there are dragons, a man catches two rabbits by the back legs, a goose drips blood in the fox's jaws, the devil is there looking pretty devilish – all very lively! The chancel has been heavily renewed, but in the sanctuary, a first class monument by Edward Marshall to Dame Frances Playters (1659); a tall composition with grey *Corinthian* columns under a scrolly open *pediment*. The alabaster demi-figure of Dame Frances stands in a deep niche, one delicate hand to her breast, the other holding a book, and a hood thrown loosely over her hair. The long inscription says of her husband Sir William:

Sometime one of ye Deputie Lieutenants & Vice Admiral of ye sd County (Suffolk) Justice of the Peace and Collonell of a Regiment of Foot till turned out of all by the then rebellious Parliam't & in fine out of the Hous of Parliam't whereof he had ye misfortune to be a member.

Read on to hear of the adventures of her equally Royalist son. By the organ is the grave of Christopher Barnard (1682). Like many Royalist clergy, he suffered cruel persecution and eviction by the parliamentarians, and he was:

well beloved by his parishioners who thought it a Judgement upon them when ye souldyers drag'd him away to carry him to Norwich Castle; but his beloved flock follow'd him and resqued him and hid him a long time after.

On his refusing the *Solemn League and Covenant*, his goods were plundered, but stout-hearted Dickleburgh people hid some of his corn and threshed it secretly – 'men, women and children assisting'. He lived to see King Charles II come in and was one of the first to be restored to his parish. He died 'much lamented in a good old age being 84, was translated to a better living to receive ye fruits of all his love and labours'. As did, I am sure, the good folk of Dickleburgh. The church has an excellent ring of 6 bells, tenor 11-1-7 cwt.

Didlington, St Michael (D6):

Didlington, St Michael (D6): Buried deep in wood and farmland, in a vast park which once centred on disappeared Didlington Hall, is this pretty and unassuming church. It is a development of three phases of medieval architecture and of heavy Victorian restoration thereafter. Fairly plain *Decorated* tower with battlements, belfry windows with boldly *cusped* contemporary tracery. *Aisles* and *clerestory* are strongly *Perpendicular* in character: the aisles have sturdy square-headed windows, but those in the clerestory are still echoing the Decorated tracery in the tower. The *chancel* is late-C13, with restored large *lancets* to each side and an unsuitable C19 e. window. On the e. end wall is a most beautiful figure niche with cusped head under an *ogee arch*, topped by a *finial*. In the chancel s. wall, w. end, is a *low side window* neatly leaded. The interior is extremely stark, *nave* and aisles having been cleared of virtually all furniture – an unusual opportunity to see a medieval church as it would have been originally. The chancel, however, behind a heavy curtain and glass panelling is neatly furnished. The big plain C16 nave roof, *tie beamed* and braced, has *wall posts* sitting on a mildly eccentric variety of carved *corbel* heads. Notice the subtle differences in the *arcades* and their pillars – early-C14 on the n. side with earlier *trefoil* pillars at each end, and trimmer C15 work on the s. side. Large stone-carved Victorian *Royal Arms* on the nave w. wall. Big octagonal C13 font of *Purbeck marble*, with typical *blank arcading*, on a C15 stem. A few good old benches placed around the walls – *poppy-heads* and carved arm rests, one displaying a most amiable shaggy dog which must surely be a portrait. *Hatchment* on the n. wall above a n. door which is set centrally in the aisle – did it perhaps give access to a *guild* chapel? Slots in the adjacent pillars where *parclose screens* may have been fitted certainly suggest this. At the e. end of the s. aisle a very attractive *piscina* is set into the sill of a window. The chancel has several notable C18 and C19 wall monuments, and the *decalogue* lettered on marble. Opulent C13 piscina with cusped head in pierced carving, and trim round pillars with ring *capitals*. The white marble *communion rails* on plump *balusters* topped with over-stuffed velvet runners are C18 – probably an Italian 'Grand Tour' acquisition. On the chancel n. side is a low blocked doorway with the outline of an arch over the adjoining window – evidence that there was a chapel or sacristry on that side.

Dilham, St Nicholas (J3): As long ago as 1700 the churchwardens reported that the church was 'much dilapidated, its buttresses much decayed, and the *porch* fallen down.' In 1775 it was meanly rebuilt in red brick with wooden windows, but in 1931 all this was pulled down and a new start made. The result is a simple, well finished, but unexciting building. The only things of interest are the base of the original round tower, the C15 font, and the arms of George III.

Diss, St Mary (H7): Cramped closely about by the attractive little market town it serves, this is a grand church, distinguished by a fine late-C13/ early-C14 tower which has a processional way underneath it. This has big, plain arches to n. and s., elegantly distinctive of its period, and a large w. door into the church. The tower has simple *flushworked* battlements, 'Y' traceried belfry windows and simple *lancets* at the second stage; and on two of the w. face buttresses, the remains of canopied figure niches. The metal framework on top of the tower, in a cupola shape, and holding a

weathercock, dates from 1906. Otherwise, this is in character a *Perpendicular* church, though basically of C13 fabric. Much Victorian restoration, and an extension to the *chancel*, have merged smoothly with the rest. The *clerestory*, of ten three-*light* windows under flattened arches and with embattled *transoms*, is very grand, with a parapet of battlements completing the effect. Below, the *aisles* with their enormous windows have a continuous frieze which is extended also round the chancel. There is an ancient *sanctus bell turret* on the e. gable of the *nave*. The splendid Perpendicular windows of the n. aisle are original; on the s. side, they are successful Victorian replacements. The Victorian e. window, however, despite following all the Perpendicular rules, signally fails to catch the spirit of the style. Both n. and s. *porches* are known to have been built about 1430-1440. That on the n. is very plain; but on the s., in common with that whole aspect of the church, the picture is striking. Notice the remnants of figure niches in the aisle buttresses – the beautiful canopy of one remains. All evidently had large carved animals, the full width of the buttress, lying at the feet of each saintly effigy. Running right round the aisle is a lovely frieze of floral motifs, occasionally punctuated by fierce little animal heads, and in turn by enormous grotesque *gargoyles*. The frieze is continued round the splendid two-storey n. porch, with its flushwork gable end and two orders of carving over its outer arch. The first of these is of large floral motifs (repeated in miniature around the *capitals*), the second of strange grotesque faces, of which only three discernibly remain. Even into the C19, it is said, the upper room of this porch was used as a hostel for visiting and itinerant priests. Inside, this large church is suddenly and surprisingly plain after the beauties of the exterior. A big, bland C16 roof, simply *arch-braced*, sits over the nave on contemporary, embattled *corbels* intricately carved with angelic figures. Five-bay *arcade* between nave and aisles, contemporary with the chancel arch of about 1300; modern *screen* and *rood* (1909) and furnishings. Extremely fine C15 w. doors, beautifully traceried, with tiny figures standing on wineglass-like pedestals between the mullions; and below, canopies and more pedestals. There is an arched niche in the n. aisle wall whose purpose is unclear. Hidden away in the n. side of the pillar against which the pulpit now stands, is the old *rood stair* entrance. Opposite, in the s. aisle, a quite enormous *piscina*, with a starkly dramatic single-leaf arch:

this marks the end of the aisle at an early point in the church's history, and before both n. and s. aisles were extended at the same time that the two porches were being built. The s. chapel, with its modern *parclose screen* and highly ornate stone *reredos* and window arch and *jambs* above it (a mass of flowers and vines, tracery and *crockets*) retains its beautiful, *trefoil*-arched piscina of about 1430-1440; with above it, the remains of a painted *consecration cross*. The chancel appears to be wholly Victorian, having been extended and remodelled in 1857, but re-using as far as the *communion rails* the original walls of about 1300. Retained too are its C18 *ledger-stones;* and just behind the screen, the imprint of a long-gone *chalice brass.* In the corner of the n. aisle, behind the pulpit, be sure to read the extremely lengthy inscription occupying the whole of the front of the table tomb of 'Mr. William Burton late of Cock Street, within this Parish'. Before his death in 1705, as is here set down in fullest detail, he left £100 vested in land so that 'this tombstone and the vault shall by the Churchwardens of Diss be constantly kept cleane and in good repair.' Any money over would go to the poor. But if the tomb should not be properly looked after, then the money would all go, forthwith, to Roydon instead for their poor, 'and if Roydon make default, then in like manner to Bressingham.' This pernickety gentleman need not have worried – his tomb is in splendid nick, its marble top polished to a turn. And, when visited, it was crowned withall by a magnificent display of 'everlasting' flowers, which may or may not mean something. The church has an excellent ring of 8 bells, tenor 22-2-17 cwt.

Ditchingham, St Mary (J6): A fine position above the junction of narrow lanes, well away from the village proper, and the 100ft. tower does justice to it. It has fine proportions, with the four stages defined by strong *drip courses* and angled buttresses that reach to the battlements. The *base course* is very rich and every other panel has a carved Sacred Heart encircled by thorns. The w. doorway has tracery and shields in the *spandrels* and the canopied niches each side have that rarity – original figures (albeit extensively repaired) that somehow escaped the iconoclasts, despite their size. The *sound-holes* are an intricate pattern of *quatrefoil* circles round a centre shield, and the tall three-*light* bell openings are in perfect proportion with the rest of the top stage. It is very satisfying to know who the begetters were of such a fine piece – James Woderofe was the master mason and Bishop Goldwell (who built

Ditchingham, St Mary: medieval statue

the presbytery vault at Norwich Cathedral) laid the foundation stone here in 1479. The only pity is that, as you circle the church to admire it, a quite nasty C19 brick chimney at the w. end of the C19 n. *aisle* keeps getting in the way. The tower building was part of a general reconstruction in the last half of the C15 and its base course theme is taken round the s. *porch.* The entrance *hood mould* has a little floral decoration which is also used round the niche above – once again containing a statue of the Virgin. Entry is by way of the original C15 doors and the first view is dominated by the massive black marble memorial to the dead of 1914/18. Along its base lies a life size bronze of a soldier by Derwent Wood, steel helmet laid above the calm young head, gaiters rucked about his boots. The C15 font stands on a quatrefoiled step with eight columns round the stem and alternating shields and roses in the panels of the bowl. The general feeling of the interior is dark, brought on, perhaps, mainly by the rebuilding and restoration which included a new n. aisle, *arcade* and *chancel* arch in the 1870s. The e. window is frankly garish but the gaily painted chancel roof (by the rector's wife) is much better, and the 'rector's' window in the s. e. corner is unique. In each laurel wreathed roundel is the name of a rector from 1609 to 1802, each set in a border of bronze coloured oak leaves. There is a good *brass* in the centre of the chancel to Philip and Margery Bozard (1490); 15in. figures, she with *butterfly head-dress*, he with heavily tasselled pouch and fur trimmed robe; five daughters at her feet, four sons at his. In the nave by the pulpit is another Bozard brass. It is only fifteen years later, but Roger and his son Philip have shoulder length hair instead of the short cut of their predecessor, and although the father's effigy is the larger, their dress is identical. There are many memories of Sir Henry Rider Haggard here. Famous author of 'King Solomon's Mines' and many other tales of adventure, a special window in the n.e. corner of the aisle is dedicated to him by *Powell & Sons*. Vignettes of his African farm, the Pyramids, and a view of Bungay from the Vineyard Hills close to his home draw together the strands of his varied life. The chancel *screen* was restored by his widow but little except the rails and frame look to be original C16. Murder always leaves a scar on a village community, although not often does one find tangible evidence of it – but a Ditchingham legend of a wife drowned by her husband is confirmed by a stone in the churchyard; s. w. of the tower, look for the grave of Mary Randalsome (1840) and read the sad story. The church has a good ring of 6 bells, tenor 12-3-12 cwt.

Docking, St Mary (D2): An elegant, crisply defined 'town' church, with a soaringly tall tower and extremely lofty *nave* of the 'high' *Perpendicular* period, about 1450, and a contrastingly small C13 *chancel*; neat Perpendicular *porch*; and n. *aisle* and associated organ chamber which are Victorian additions. The chancel e. window is a particular feature, of five *lights* with flowing *reticulated* tracery. In the s. chancel wall, low at the w. end, there appears to have been a *low side window*, the top and one side of its stone frame being visible. The interior of the church is impressive in its vast spaciousness, but has been restored with such single-minded thoroughness by the Victorians that one might, indeed, be inside a wholly C19 construction. However the C14 font is still there, and still beautiful in spite of its savage defacements. The big, octagonal bowl has figures of apostles in each panel, each under richly *cusped* and *crocketted* canopies; crocketted pinnacles

at the angles; winged angels, half-figures and flowers under the bowl; and around the stem, eight female statuettes, including St *Catherine* with her wheel and at least three figures carrying babies.

Downham Market, St Edmund (C5): A *carstone* church that stands on quite a little hill overlooking the town, and there are views w. across the level fens dotted with trees and punctuated by pylons. The *Early English* tower has two ranges of small *lancets* and the two-*light* bell openings have round centre shafts with a *quatrefoil* in the head of the arch. On the n. side, a later heavy turret reaches to the top, cutting through one of the windows on the way. Above the battlements, a short ribbed lead spire. There was a good deal of C19 restoration; the vestry was added in 1873 and you will see a vestige of the original *Norman* church embedded in its n. wall – a tiny section of spiral shaft. Most of the windows are *Perpendicular* but there are two lancets in the n. *aisle* wall which may have been re-set. Above the Victorian *priest's door* on the s. side of the *chancel* is a small relief of the Crucifixion which is a remnant of a medieval *churchyard cross*, and there is a curious little door tucked into the corner between s. chapel and chancel. The small figure of St *Edmund* over the *porch* entrance has an inscription dated 1886 but it looks convincingly older than that. A spacious church inside, with a deep w. *gallery* of the C18 which has a front of handsome marquetry panels. On the w. wall beyond and above it are the *Royal Arms* of Anne. A very murky inscription on top commemorates the union with Scotland: 'Henricus rosas, Anna Britannos' (Henry united the Roses, Anne the people of Britain). Below the gallery, the C15 font stands on a new shaft and base and its bowl panels are carved with angels bearing shields; clockwise from the e.: St *Paul*, St *George*, St *James the Great*, St *Edmund*, the *Instruments of the Passion* (2), St *Peter*, and St *Andrew*. A *clerestory* of small square-headed windows plus a three-light window over the chancel arch lights the *arch-braced, tie-beam nave* roof. It was repaired and stained in 1865 and restored again in 1899. There are coloured half-figures holding shields at the bottom of the *wall posts* and small angels on the intermediate timbers. The s. *arcade* is a very strange mixture of different sized arches and *Pevsner's* explanation seems reasonable – that there was originally a s. *transept* with a tall arch and, w. of it, a nave arcade of three lower, narrower arches. When the tower was built it was linked to the nave by the other two large arches. In contrast, the n. arcade is quite regular. There is a small *piscina* with a jumbled arch in the s. aisle and, beyond it, the lady chapel dating from about 1500. There you will find a heavily banded C14 chest with a waggon lid, and a modern uncoloured wooden sculpture of the Virgin in the corner niche. Nearby on the s. wall is a very elaborate *consecration cross* in red and green – the cross itself is floriated and set in a foiled circle, with a surrounding band of decoration. The Perpendicular chancel arch is filled with a *screen* and *rood* which is quality modern work in traditional style, and there is a matching pulpit on the n. side. Just in front hangs an eight-branch glass chandelier of about 1730. It was restored and rehung in 1967 and is the only one of its type known to hang in a parish church. There are a number of tablets on the walls but the best is high above the s. arcade: Edward Warmoll Apothecary and his wife Elizabeth (1761); fine lettering, a picture frame in coloured marbles with swags, coat of arms at the top, and all set off against a pale grey surround.

Drayton, St Margaret (H4): Architecturally over-restored, much interior 'beautifications' (also exterior 'homes & gardens' *lych-gate*) – and evidently all looked after with loving care. The old tower fell in December 1850, rebuilt the following year using the old materials. *Chancel* and *porch* rebuilt, *nave* restored 1866, n. *aisle* added 1908. Old portions of church, C13 and C14. Good C12 font and attractive C13 *piscina* in chancel. Good *Norwich glass* of about 1450 in a n. window, probably originally placed in e. window of s. aisle. Don't miss the poignant headstone to John Eke, 1856, on the church path. The church has an excellent ring of 6 bells, tenor 7-3-27 cwt.

Dunston, St Remigius (I5): This is a 'surprise' church – hidden down an unmarked grass track, but a step away from the vast Victorian pile of Dunston Hall (now an hotel). C19 restoration of the exterior was severe and although the trim, slim tower dates from the C14, from its perky pinnacles downwards, it has been thoroughly done-up. The body of the church has been refaced/rebuilt, including all the tracery of the *nave's* Perpendicular-style windows, which look renewed, as the e. window certainly is, in a slightly fanciful style whose exaggerated tracery shapes look more Eastern than Gothic. Only the plain *Early English lancets*, n. and s. in the *chancel* have an authentic look about them. Enter by the little

n. door and you are at once rewarded by an interior of great charm, beautifully maintained, with lovely wrought-iron hanging lamp pendants, fresh, white-painted walls contrasting with the timbers of a neatly simple *arch-braced roof* in the nave, and the similar modern replacement in the chancel. One of the church's most attractive features is the delicate and beautifully sculpted alabaster inner e. window behind the altar; unmatched anywhere in East Anglia, it is in elegant Perpendicular spirit and was installed as a memorial in 1907. The lancet windows of the tiny chancel are deeply splayed, with those on the s. containing some good C14 glass – the church's patron, Lady Margaret de Creke kneeling before the church's dedicatory saint *Remigius*, with 'R's all round the frieze. Alongside is a later and amiable St *Christopher* with the Christ child on his shoulder. The solid old choir stalls have medieval bench-ends topped with *poppy-heads*. A nearby *ledger-stone* 'to the memory of Susan, Relict of Matthew Long Esq. of this Parish who died 5th January 1734, aged 66', bears an inscription worth recording: 'Her bounty like a hidden spring was only visible in its Effects / And the glad hearts of those who were refreshed by its streams'. Numerous Long family memorials will be found in the church, all alike in having orotund epitaphs. Before leaving the chancel, have a look at an intriguing three-figure *brass* to 'Clere Talbot, Doctor of Lawe' and his two wives, they naively represented in shrouds – but with only one of them memorialised – 'Ann ye late Vertuous and Pious Wife' died in December 1649, making this a very late example of a sepulchral brass. There is a neat C15 *screen* with simple restrained carving and much original colour. In the upper *spandrels* of the centre section there is a *woodwose* on the left and a dragon on the right; within the carving of the centre arch find what looks like a wolf with its kill on the left and a lion and dragon sinking their fangs into each other on the right; below, in the arch's lowest splay, a bird. Note that the inner e. window tracery design echoes that of the screen. A very good font, in excellent preservation, has boldly carved lions, flowers and angels alternating in the panels of the octagonal bowl, while four lions sit on guard around the shaft. The decorative grills in the tower walls were once vents for a C19 heating system.

Dunton, St Peter (E2): A redundant church that has been rescued from the brink by the *Norfolk Churches Trust*. Probably *Norman* originally – see the remains of a thick *nave* wall on the s. side which is now capped with slates. The *chancel* and one of the nave windows are early-C14 and the rest of the building is C15 apart from the C19 rebuilt *porch*. Inside there are some interesting oddments. A small altar fronts the *piscina* on the s. side and beyond the modern *rood screen* the old lectern on its strange oblong base continues in use. Nearby is a pillar piscina, and in the floor a *ledger-stone* to Matthew Lancaster (d.1658) who claimed descent from 'John Lancaster ye first of Yt race in England & first founder of Lancaster castle from whom issued 50 or more knights Esquires & Gentlemen of qualitye'. On the n. wall, a marble tablet by Patteson of Manchester (odd, that) to Major William Case who fell at the defence of Lucknow in 1857. The e. window stained glass of 1863 by *Heaton, Butler & Bayne* commemorates one Clement Felton, whom the Guardians of the Poor of Walsingham Union evidently revered as their Chairman. In the nave s. window are gorgeous peacocks and on the other side, Gabriel greets the Virgin and Elizabeth in stained glass of 1882, also by Heaton, Butler & Bayne.

Earlham, St Mary (H5): The tower is a pleasing mixture of old irregular red bricks and flint; the top has been reconstructed, but at ground floor level there are two small *lancets* (one blocked) that suggest a *Norman* beginning. The gable and outer arch of the *porch* have been renewed, and the height of it shows that there was once an upper room which is no longer there. Inside, a small C19 w. *gallery* and a C14 traceried font with a shaft almost as wide as the bowl. Stone *corbels* that supported the old roofs of *nave* and *chancel* are still in position, and rough steps that led to the old *rood loft* rise from a s. window sill. Under them, a very elementary *piscina*. The dark stained C15 *screen* is complete to the cresting, and above the *crocketted* and *cusped ogee arches* the tracery is like a series of *Perpendicular* windows – very handsome. Someone acquired an angel from a roof *hammer-beam* and up-ended it to make a unique lectern. Polished to a nut-brown finish, it gives an opportunity to see the typically bold carving at close quarters. A Gurney *hatchment* hangs in the n. *transept*, and a *squint* through the chancel arch shows that there was once a *guild* or *chantry* altar here. There are big C14 blank arches in the chancel walls and a blocked C16 *priest's door* on the n. side. Near to it, an attractive monument with alabaster garlands, lettering on a black marble drape, and two weeping *putti*

on the *pediment*; for six Bacon children, it was moved by their surviving brother from the demolished London church of St Giles in the Fields to be near their parents' grave. On the s. wall, a large circular bas relief of the *Annunciation* carved in wood – probably C18 continental work, and given to the church in 1936.

Earsham, All Saints (J7): Not far from the river in the meadows of the Waveney valley, a church whose C14 tower is crowned by one of Norfolk's few spires. There is a line of dark red *carstone* high in both of the *nave* walls and so the church probably dates from the *Norman* period, but all the windows are *Perpendicular*. The n. *porch* has a *Tudor* outer arch with a *holy water stoup* beside it, and the inner C14 arch frames a lovely pair of medieval doors. They have simple wave mouldings (like those of Redenhall w. doors) between closely spaced uprights, and a band of *cusped* panels round the edge – all well restored and cared for. Inside, a wide vista through a laid back and reconstituted *chancel* arch to the e. end. The chancel itself, under a plain *hammer-beam roof*, is early-C14 (see the shafts of the windows), and the nave was heightened, probably in the following century. One of East Anglia's *seven sacrament fonts* is here, resting on a plain shaft. The figures have been completely chopped off the buttresses and the scenes in the panels very defaced, but they are still recognisable; clockwise from the e.: mass (note the *sacring bell* rope), penance, matrimony, extreme unction, the Crucifixion, confirmation, baptism and ordination. The nave has a C19 w. *gallery*, three *hatchments*, and a suite of *box pews* on the n. side. One is lined with red baize and has dinky brass curtain rails at the front, to impart that little extra exclusiveness with which one portion of society impressed its quality on the multitude. In a window opposite, there is a large C16 panel of the corn being shown to Joseph, and there are roundels of Flemish glass around it. The window next to it has a panel showing the Virgin and Child with St *Elizabeth* and St *John the Baptist*, and further along, a lurid window of the 1860s. The glass in the e. window was inserted in 1863 and is a mixture of foreign C16-C18 panels and roundels, including the head of a young girl in sepia which looks entirely secular. The late-C19 *reredos* is rather a stiff and flat design, but looks well from the body of the church and seems to anticipate the work of *Sir Ninian Comper*. On the sanctuary n. wall, a memorial to the Hon. Col. William Windham (1730): 'He distinguished himself in many Great Actions in the late wars, and Lost a Limb in the Defence of his Country at the Memorable Battle Of Blenheim.' Under the tower there is a 5ft. square set of Hanoverian *Royal Arms*.

East Barsham, All Saints (F2): A church of ancient foundation, much buffeted over the years, but having a great charm of its own. The *porch* is the first stage of what is left of the C13 tower, with its C17 top, and leads into the *nave*. *Chancel* and s. *transept* (more probably, a *chantry chapel*) long since gone, but foundations are still visible, with brick *groining* below ground level. The nave is a charming hotchpotch – bits of *Norman* (a blocked-up s. doorway), C14 and C15; most windows *Perpendicular*. Among lovely fragments of C15 *Norwich glass*, two delicious feathered angels, playing pipe and harp, in head of n. window. Of interest, an alabaster sculpture, probably from an altar, of St *Anne* teaching the Virgin to read – there were three pieces of it recovered from a C15 barn nearby when it was demolished but two have since been stolen. A very impressive wall monument to Mrs. Mary Calthorpe, 1640, full of detail and activity, and with a splendidly lofty inscription.

East Barsham, All Saints: Calthorpe monument

Harrod & Linnell's comment in their 'Shell Guide to Norfolk' (Faber, 1957) deserves repetition:

> Lady Calthorpe's shrouded figure rises from the grave with such vigour and movement that one feels impelled to rush to the roof of the church to applaud her arrival.

This delightful church, and the breathtaking *Tudor* manor house nearby, make a trip to East Barsham a 'must' for tourers in Norfolk.

East Bilney, St Mary (F4): Isolated above the village and main road, the building has seen many changes. The top of the unbuttressed w. tower was destroyed during Kett's 1549 rebellion and was not rebuilt until 1900, the double *lancet sound-holes* marking the division between old and new. The *chancel* fell into ruins in the C19 and was wholly rebuilt in 1883. At one time the *nave* had a *clerestory* but new large windows were put in, and the s. chapel was built on the site of a predecessor in 1886. What you see, therefore, is mainly Victorian replacement, but note that the *Early English* doorways are still there and there are male and female *headstops* at the entrance. Obscured glass makes for rather a dim interior, but in the chancel there is a handsome range of early-C17 stalls, a period noted more for pulpits and chests; they are in two tiers, tall, panelled fronts with shallow carving, and have turned knobs on the ends. Apart from the mosaic *reredos*, the e. wall is faced with attractive and unusual tiles in a matt, dusky pink, on which the *IHS* sacred monogram and a vine leaf design alternate. An 1885 window on the s. side in rich dark colours commemorates Thomas Bilney 'born in this parish 1495, suffered for conscience sake at Norwich 1531'; Latimer's 'Bilney, little Bilney, that blessed martyr of God', imprisoned by Wolsey and finally condemned to burn in the Lollards' Pit by Bishop Nykke. His ashes were brought home, but precisely where they lie no one but God now knows.

East Bradenham, St Mary (F5): Now vested in the *Churches Conservation Trust*. The *Perpendicular* tower has heavy buttresses that reach to the belfry stage, and the *aisles* lap each side so that the appearance is rather heavy from the w.. On three faces of the tower, in the second stage, there is the outline of a broad arch in brick stretching right across which is very puzzling. On the e. side, note the line of an earlier roof which was much steeper, and the *sanctus bell window* which became redundant when the roof changed. The early-C14 circular *clerestory* windows are *quatrefoils* and two larger Perpendicular windows were added at the e. end to give more light to the *rood*. There was a window over the *chancel* arch too, but it was cut into by the lower roof and blocked up. There are traces of a chapel on the s. side of the chancel and the *priest's door* is opposite. The e. window is *Decorated,* with all the rest in both chancel and aisles later Perpendicular. The n. *porch* is tall and solid, but although the stair turret still nestles in the angle of the wall outside, the floor to the upper room has been taken out and the window blocked. Just inside the church is a big and very plain C14 font, and its *Jacobean* cover has a centre spike supported by eight radiating brackets. The early-C14 *arcades* have octagonal *piers* and there are subtle variations in the mouldings of the *capitals*. The altar in the s. aisle chapel carries a fine medieval stone *mensa,* five inches thick, bevelled on the underside, with the five *consecration crosses* cut in the top. Nearby, a typically good tablet by *Thomas Rawlins* of Norwich for Gibson Lucas (1758); in white and multi-coloured marble, it has a *cartouche* set on the obelisk above a finely lettered tablet, with a pair of cherubs' heads below. On the chancel s. wall, a much larger monument for John Greene (1684); busts of man and wife – oddly stiff with heads inclined, he in full-bottomed wig. Skulls and bones lodge in the palm fronds at the bottom, while weeping *putti* hold a drape overhead. On the floor below, a *ledger-stone* epitaph with a distinctive turn of phrase: 'Here vertuous, Pious, Sarah Townsend lyes / Whose Soule Enamel'd thus to heaven fflyes.' (1667).

East Carleton, St Mary (H5): Back from the village street, and approached by a shady avenue; if you look to the right before turning into the churchyard there is the vestige of a second church, St *Peter's*. There are all the evidences here of a complete restoration – cum – re-building. The tower was dismantled, rebuilt and then heightened in 1895, and at that time had a spire which has since gone. The C13 doorway has a deep moulding and worn *headstops* and there is a *holy water stoup* just inside. The tall tower arch is in brick with a wide moulded *Tudor* arch and appears to have been undisturbed by the C19 work, but the n. *aisle arcade* was treated to new smooth round pillars. On the sanctuary n. wall, a tablet to Peter Coppinam who was rector here for 48 years and died in 1728. It still has the feel

of the C17, with its plain black tablet and simple sprays of foliage on the side *pilasters* – perhaps he wanted it that way. Acourt Dod (1783) has a grey obelisk on the s. wall with his arms in colour against it, a plain tablet and winged cherub's head below. Further e., a distinguished modern memorial to Nathaniel Baron Lindley (1921), the last created and last surviving Serjeant at Law. In the *nave* aisle we come again upon that favourite C17 admonition 'Hodie mihi, cras tibi' ('Today it is my turn, tomorrow it will be yours') – here for Anne Snell who died in 1676.

East Dereham, St Nicholas (F4): This is the church that George Borrow remembers nostalgically in 'Lavengro': 'Pretty, quiet Dereham, with thy venerable church, in which moulder the mortal remains of England's sweetest and most pious bard.' (William Cowper, author of hymns like 'Hark, my soul! it is the Lord', as well as the rollicking 'John Gilpin'). A building impressive in its solidity and variety and the sheer size of it, with the massive C16 bell tower standing by. This tower was built specifically to house the clock and bells, and is plain to the point of starkness – the only vestiges of decoration are small *flushwork* panels on the second stage of the buttresses and some tracery in the w. door *spandrels*. There was a church here long before the present building, and first have a look at St *Withburga's* well, just beyond the w. end. She was a daughter of Anna, King of East Anglia, and she founded a nunnery here in 654. It became a place of pilgrimage, but as you will see from the C18 tablet, the Abbot of Ely and his monks stole her body away to lay it with her saintly sisters at Ely. From her first grave 'issued forth a spring of purest water gifted with many healing virtues', and under the vaulted arch shaded by dog roses, ferns and honey-suckle, it still tinkles over the stones. After the Danes had burned the first church and the nuns had fled, the Normans built another, and two traces of it survive – firstly, the s. door (which has almost certainly been moved w.) which has two blunt heads at the spring of the arch, and secondly, sections of spiral moulding in the *chancel* arch. Although there is quite some scope for argument, it is probable that the *Norman* central tower was e. of the present one, and that the remnants in the chancel arch were part of its pillars. The massive *piers* of the *crossing tower* are C13 and the original tower may have collapsed westward, forcing a change of plan. Entry is by way of a large and elaborate s. *porch* which was built about 1500 at the behest of Roger and

Margaret Boton. Their names can be seen (his on the left, hers on the right) above the lushly canopied niches which may once have contained their statues. The flushwork buttresses stop short half way up, and have a variety of grotesques on top which formed the base for something else – either pinnacles or statues. In the arch spandrels, the *Annunciation* – a favourite theme in that position. Inside, the *nave* has sparkling white walls and a new waggon roof. The *arcades* are C13, except the w. bay with its octagonal pillars. That shows that there was a C14 extension, and the w. front with its great window (*cusped* and intersected tracery) was rebuilt. The n. *aisle* of the same period has an *arch-braced roof* with varied tracery in the *spandrels*. Before moving into the body of the church, study the font. At 6ft. 9in. this is certainly the tallest of the East Anglian *seven sacrament fonts*, and can be precisely dated 1468. It cost £12.13.9, of which the mason carver received £10. A very rich piece, but every figure is mutilated and not one has its face intact. The tall niches round the shaft have vaulted canopies and under the bowl there are carved angels, each under a curved *hood mould*. All the bowl buttresses had yet more figures under canopies, and each of the scenes in the panels lies under a vaulted ceiling. Clockwise from the e., mass (note the whole scene is viewed from the e. facing the priest – an unusual variation), ordination, matrimony, extreme unction (see how the bed clothes are turned back to expose the wasted body for anointing), the Crucifixion, baptism, confirmation, penance. By the nave altar stands a fine late-C15 brass lectern – three lions at the foot standing well out, and an alert looking eagle poised on the ball, with a deep curve to the underside of its wings. At your feet (under a carpet square) is a *brass* to Etheldreda Castell (1486); a 17in. figure in *butterfly head-dress* and plain gown – the inscription is readable but her shield of arms has gone. Looking up from the crossing, a lovely *gallery* range of arches on *quatrefoil* piers comes into view, with large double windows above. This C14 lantern had yet another stage but was reduced to its present height in 1501. The little *sacring bell*, under the weather vane with its hart emblem, is still put to its proper use. The s. *transept* is more or less filled with the organ, but the n. transept has a tall *screen* to the w. This belonged to Oxborough but was brought here when the tower of that church collapsed into the nave in 1948. Dated about 1480, its well restored panels have paintings of (from left to right) St *Thomas of*

Canterbury, St *John*, St *John the Baptist*, St *Withburga*, St *Mary Magdalen* and St *Etheldreda*. How appropriate that St *Withburga* and one of her sisters should come back to Dereham! This transept has a particularly fine modern roof, panelled and *arch-braced*, with angels below each main timber. Both transepts have C15 e. chapels (there are in effect two crossings one after the other), and both have very good roofs. The ceiling on the s. side has panels with *cusped* intersections, and in each, the *Agnus Dei* stands on a book surrounded by a garland of flowers that sprouts tendrils – all in red, green and gold. The n. chapel roof is *arch-braced* and panelled, the timbers enlivened with a carved frieze, panels painted with double headed eagles and crowned roses; in all, a very rich effect. In this chapel stands a splendid Flemish early-C16 chest. An elegant oval of C18 brass on the lid will tell you all about its origin and donation. The twelve tall figures in their swirling robes are those mysterious beings, the Sibyls, representing the ancient prophecies that foretold the coming of the Messiah. Below the figure of the bound Christ on the lock plate, a lovely Nativity vignette. At the n. end of the chapel is the William Cowper memorial by *Flaxman* at his least inspiring. Thank goodness that the window, by *Heaton, Butler & Bayne*, marking the centenary of his death in 1800, does justice to that gentle spirit whose final years were spent in Dereham. The colour is warm and rich, and the scene in the two centre *lights* combines around the poet's figure the things he loved – a portrait of his mother, his three pet hares and his dog in the foreground, flowers from the garden beyond pushing in at the window, and his books; four flanking scenes illustrate themes from the poems. To the right of this, a 1975 St *Withburga* window by Stammers of York (whose work can also be seen at Ormsby St Margaret and elsewhere in the county). A bright and somewhat bizarre composition in which the legendary does are puce coloured and one of the nuns sports speckled orange. The chancel *screen* and *rood* form a First World War memorial, and to the e. of it is a very elegant open tread spiral staircase with turned *balusters*, which now gives access to the old muniment room over the s. transept chapel. The chancel is late-C13 and was thoroughly restored and given its *reredos* in the mid-C19 (the paintings came later in 1929). The old *priest's door* – now blocked, was supplemented by another further e., and it is interesting to know that most of the congregation came in via the chancel then because it was nearer the town. There is, by the way, a small brass in the back pews on that side – a demi-figure with inscription for Edmund Kelyng (1479). The C13 *double piscina* has *dogtooth moulding* in its *trefoil* arches and down the sides, and like the stepped *sedilia*, it was heavily re-cut in the restoration. Only two of the *headstops* were left alone – the others are pure Victoriana. Across in the n. wall is a fine *aumbry* under a trefoil arch, with a head at the apex. It is presumed that this was originally an *Easter Sepulchre*, and this is more than likely in view of its elaborate form. Dereham has no ancient glass, but standing under the crossing, the great w. and e. windows by Heaton, Butler & Bayne complement each other very well at either end of the long vista, with a preponderence of pale yellow in the colours. For a quick contrast, look behind the organ for an 1862 window full of bright clean colours, and see if you make the total of figures come to 56! The church has an excellent ring of 8 bells, tenor 22-3-1 cwt.

East Harling, St Peter & St Paul (F7): A most impressive church inside and out, with lots of interest. There are tall niches under *crocketted* gables in the bottom stage of the tower buttresses, and all is early-C14 up to the belfry; then pretty C15 battlements – stepped, pierced, and decorated with emblems of the Harling family, with pinnacles and figures on the parapet. The lovely slim spirelet, rising from a close circle of wooden shafts and flying buttresses is exactly the right weight and height to complement the tower. Apart from a small niche, *flushwork* is the only decoration on the s. *porch*, but it was higher originally and, having become dilapidated, was rebuilt in 1840. The s. doorway is early-C14 and inside, above it, part of a window of the same date (later builders re-used the same wall). By and large, you stand in a church that was rebuilt in the first half of the C15 – *arcades* with graceful *quatrefoil* pillars, and a great range of 18 *clerestory* windows over them. The *hammer-beam roof* is splendid – long *wall posts*, traceried *spandrels*, and a *tie-beam* at the e. end that still has the pulley from which hung the rowell to light the *rood*. The s. aisle roof is wide and almost flat, and in every other spandrel look for the bull and unicorn badges of the Harlings. Another family emblem is used there too, the homely 'frail' – a soft rush holdall that workmen used well into the C20 to carry both their tools and their dinner. The late-C14 font is very solid on a tall step – simple tracery panels to shaft and bowl, and a *Jacobean* cover with brackets rising to a turned

E. Harling, St Peter & St Paul: E. Window detail

centrepiece. East Harling is well blessed with screens and the base of the main *rood screen* has now been moved to stand at the w. end. *Decorated* in the favourite red, green and gold, the top panels have intricately carved quatrefoils that sprout foliage from the *cusps*, and contain a helm, a garter, shields, and (2nd from left) most interesting of all, a Christ crucified on the stem of a *Jesse Tree*. The s. aisle chapel is approached through a beautiful C15 screen that rises to its full height and has a lovely wide canopy, and even part of the original top cresting. The *ogee arches* of the bottom panels have close *reticulated* tracery in the spandrels, and see how the doors are carved to match the main uprights when they close (splendidly careful work!). To the n. of the chapel, a *parclose screen*, earlier in date, with turned uprights and traces of colour. And the front of the pews in the chapel is made from the top of yet another screen – heavy ogee cusped arches of high quality. While in this chapel, there are two big tombs to study. In the corner, Sir Robert Harling – the brass inscription translates:

> Within this polished marble is entombed Robert Harlyng knight – a man noble in feats of arms. His fame flourished well known amongst many of its natives of France – at length mangled by force of arms he died at Paris in 1435.

The cusps of the ogee arch terminate in roundels of angels, an eagle, and a *pelican* in her piety. There is some doubt as to whether both effigies on top really belong here; you have to peer over the top of Sir Robert to see the lady in a crinkly lace hood, and his wife was actually buried at Rushford – perhaps the figure came from there when the College of Canons was dispersed and the buildings ruinated. Next door lies Sir Thomas Lovell (1604) and his wife – a heavily resplendent alabaster tomb restored in 1958; large canopy on three *Corinthian* columns, five coats of arms on the chest, plus the original railing. The two rigid figures are all in black, relieved by touches of gold; his head rests on a plain helm, hers on a rich tasselled cushion, and there are big painted crests at their feet – peacock's feathers and a Saracen's head held aloft. The C15 rebuilding was the work of two of rich Anne Harling's three husbands. She lies with the first, Sir William Chamberlain (1462) under the lavish tomb between *chancel* and n. chapel. The brass effigies have been ripped from the top, but the elaborate stonework is well preserved – large coat of arms with supporters and helm, canopied niches under the main arch, and more of the family emblems we saw in the s. aisle roof. There is a *piscina* with *credence shelf* on the chapel side and, unusually, two *squints* through the buttresses – one to the high altar and one to the nave. In the corners of the sanctuary, two surprisingly plain monuments to Sir Francis and Sir Thomas Lovell (1551 and 1567), in complete contrast to the showy magnificence of the later Sir Thomas in the s. aisle chapel. There are *misericords* to see here, with some interesting figures on the arms of the stalls: s. side, a bearded and turbanned Turk with raised scimitar, dragon, leopard, eagle; n. side, a *pelican* in her piety, *griffin* (the unicorn and lion are new work). The four misericords themselves are all heraldic. The e. window is full of the pale and unmistakeable loveliness of C15 glass, enlivened by sudden splashes of bright colour. Hidden in the Manor House attics during the Civil War, it

East Lexham, St Andrew

was brought home in 1736, taken out for safety in 1939, and finally restored in 1947. Lady Anne's second husband Sir Robert Wingfield gave it in 1480 and his portrait is in the bottom left hand corner, while his predecessor Sir William Chamberlain kneels in the right hand panel – both wearing rich tabards. Pick out the main sequence (using binoculars if you have them): scenes from the life of the Blessed Virgin; *Annunciation, Visitation,* Nativity (the pale red ox and ass are joined, unusually, by two midwives), Adoration of the shepherds (one plays a pipe, the others hold crook and lamb), Adoration of the Magi, Presentation in the Temple (2nd from left 2nd row), Christ among the Doctors (the Virgin is there), first miracle at Cana, Betrayal (2nd from left 3rd row), Crucifixion, *Pietà* (the tears spring from the Virgin's eyes), Resurrection (2nd left, bottom row – note the soldiers are awake), Ascension (see the feet of Our Lord with the mark of the nails, and the prints He has left on the ground below), *Pentecost,* and the *Assumption* (far right 3rd row). Scenes from this window figured on a Christmas Air Letter form some years ago and are justly famous. Many other things tempt one to linger here, *hatchments* and a *Royal Arms* for heraldry enthusiasts, and at least one oddity – a pillar piscina that was re-used as a *holy water stoup* by the n. door. The church has an excellent ring of 8 bells tenor 8-3-22 cwt.

East Lexham, St Andrew (E4): It presents an odd face to the visitor, this little church marooned in the middle of an enormous farmyard. The tower is round, narrowing towards the top, and tough and coarse as an ancient military fortification. Ancient it is, being pre-Conquest in date. Local belief is that it was built about 900 A.D., which would make it the oldest round tower in the kingdom. Its only contemporary relief is provided by three small openings at belfry level, one massively supported by a crude round pillar; the other by a typical *Saxon* balluster; and the third – looking down on the *nave* roof – having as tracery a roughly carved Maltese cross, of unknown date. The *lancet* in the lower, w. aspect of the tower is clearly C13. The body of the church – a 'single hall' construction – has been heavily restored, and on the n. side is completely rendered over. Save for the e. window, a handsome *Perpendicular* example, all the windows are replacements, without style in every sense. The extreme n. w. corner of the nave has fortunately not been rendered; because its Saxon *long and short work* in the *quoins* is very evident; also in the corresponding s.w. quoins. Both the n. and s. doors (the latter filled in) are *Early English*, wholly simple and unadorned, of about 1200. The beautifully cared for interior is an oasis of calm with a wonderful atmosphere. Particular points of interest are the beautiful Perpendicular *angle piscina* in the sanctuary, delicately *cusped* and leaf-carved; the adjoining cusped figure niche in the e. wall; the old *misericorde* seat (said to have come from Castle Acre priory); the *rood stair* entrance in the nave n. wall, covered by a modern door; and on the w. wall, a Hanoverian *Royal Arms* for George IV.

East Raynham, St Mary (E3): This church was designed in 1868 by Clark & Holland, somewhat obscure architects from Newmarket. The *chancel* was paid for by the rector the Revd Charles Phayre and the *nave* by the Marquess Townshend for £7,000 overall. A drawing by Robert Ladbrooke shows the original building as early *Perpendicular*, and the replacement is largely a copy; a rather wayward detail is the s. chancel *porch* converted into an organ chamber. Leaving aside the strong C19 character, there are a number of interesting things to seek out, and the most important is the large and extraordinarily lavish *Easter Sepulchre* in the chancel. This dates from 1499 and commemorates Sir Roger Townshend and his widow. She left money for the monument and directed that it be 'cunningly graven a Sepulchre for Easter Day'. The tomb chest, with its *Purbeck marble* slab, is panelled, with shields in ornate settings; there is a panelled recess below more traceried panel, and against the back wall, five stepped niches of very fine, partly pierced work contain fragments of the original statuettes. Overhead there is a carved stone funerary helme that was reinstated in the

1950s. In the s. wall opposite, to the e. of the *piscina* there is a recess on three re-used spiral-fluted *Norman* shafts, which appear to be upside down, carrying a stilted arch. The C15 font has an octagonal traceried stem, with roses in the bowl panels and traces of original paint. All the woodwork in the church is of 1868, with the exception of a fine chest dated 1602 which has the remains of marquetry scenes in perspective separated by fluted columns. A *brass* lies in the s. *aisle* floor for George Townshend who died as a boy around 1500, and the 15in. figure of Robert Godfrey, dressed in academicals, who died in 1522, can be found in the n. aisle. The 1852 monument to Lord Charles Vere Ferrars Townshend is a relief in white marble blessed with a pair of hefty angels, and the Royal Arms in wood are Hanoverian. The church has an excellent ring of 8 bells, tenor 9-3-5 cwt.

East Rudham, St Mary (E3): When the tower collapsed in 1876 it brought down most of the rest of the church and there was a general rebuilding that re-used a lot of the original material. The s. *porch*, for example, has a large *boss* of the *Trinity* (minus the Dove), and the early-C14 doorway was retained with its fine pair of King and Queen *headstops*. The interior is wide, open, and rather bare, with a clear view into the *chancel*. When the church was restored, fragments of a C15 alabaster *reredos* were found embedded in the n. wall of the sanctuary, and they are now in a glass case at the w. end; the Coronation of the Virgin is virtually complete, and there are sections of the Crucifixion and Entombment; the bottom half of St *Anthony* can be identified by the pig with a bell round its neck. A C13 coffin lid lies underneath – found e. of the chancel and probably connected with nearby Coxford Priory. The s. *transept* was also rebuilt but retains its *trefoil piscina* and blocked *low side window*. The restored round window in the w. wall is said to have been given by Sir Aylmer de Mordaunt as a thank offering for a safe return from the Holy Land during the Crusades. There is an interesting *Norman* pillar piscina in the chancel – only 18in. tall, with a plaited design round the rim. The trefoil-headed recess behind it was perhaps a *credence*. Outside again, note the fine floriated cross on the transept with two dragon heads on the shaft; rather large for the gable, it may have been a wayside cross originally.

East Ruston, St Mary (J3): Standing close by the road that runs due north from Stalham up to Walcott, St Mary's dominates the ridge just in from the coast, and on a winter's day the wind from whatever quarter cuts like a knife. Don't be deterred, because this is a church well worth a visit. It became redundant in 1977 and came into the care of the *Churches Conservation Trust* four years later. A circuit round this largely C14 building reveals some interesting points, and although all its windows have been either filled-in or boarded-up, the mid-C14 tower is sturdy and uncompromising. Its n. side is intriguing, because at ground level there are remains of a single-story extension, and in the corner a little *squinch* might be all that survives of an entrance into the main body of the church. In 1513 John Hunston was the rector and his will specified burial in the new Lady Chapel 'edified and builded in the churchyard' which, despite its unusual position, might have been here. By the late C18 the church was in a sad state, with a ruinous spire and holes in the roof, and three of the bells were sold to pay for the demolition of the n. *aisle* and re-roofing. A new n. wall of red brick was built for the *nave*, with ponderous buttresses and the restored *Perpendicular* windows were reset. The C14 *chancel* lost one of its windows on the n. side early on, the second was filled in with brick later, and there is the outline of a small blocked door between them. The 5-*light* e. window with its high sill has intersecting *cusped tracery*, and the stonework was renewed in the C19. On the s. side *Decorated* windows with triple chamfered arches flank a *priest's door*, and although three of the s. aisle windows are C15 replacements, the fourth dates from the original C14 building (its wooden tracery is an example of C19 penny-pinching). There is Decorated tracery in the aisle w. window but it was bricked up long since. The C15 porch is tall and slim and its image niche above the entrance has nicely pierced tracery. In the floor at your feet are the remains of two C14 grave slabs, and low on a buttress to the e. there is a *mass dial*. The inner door has been repaired more than once over the years, but its original wrought strap hinges are intact across the whole face, and note how they lift over each board moulding. To the right, the base of a *holy water stoup* is partly submerged in the wall. The interior is rather barn-like, a feeling enhanced by the blank w. wall pierced only by a small doorway into the tower; the door itself is medieval and still has its strap hinges and the backing plate of a closing ring. The octagonal font has the *Evangelistic Symbols* in four of its panels and varying heads in the others – in the e. panel is the bust of of a man

with his hair brushed out at each side which is very odd; there are demi-angels under the bowl and devil faces round the base, but much of this may have been part of an 1882 restoration recorded on a brass plate on the shaft. The remaining C14 arcade between nave and aisle has five bays with octagonal pillars, bases and *capitals*. As part of the C18 rebuilding the nave was given a curved plaster ceiling which has been restored recently and it is thought that lamps originally hung from the two centre roundels. A plain C19 *bier* stands in the s. aisle, and in the sanctuary there is a *piscina* to the right and to the left is the lower section of the stairs that once led to the *rood loft*. The theme of the glass in the aisle e. window is Christ's Presentation in the Temple, with figures of the Blessed Virgin, Simeon holding the Babe, and St Joesph, with a quote from the Nunc Dimittis above – conventionally heavy and rather uninspired work by A.L. & C.E.Moore. There is another C14 priest's grave slab in front of the sanctuary step and between aisle and nave have a look at the large and very worn slab. Judging by the indent it must have carried a magnificent sepulchral *brass* before the *Reformation*. Just beyond is a small brass c.1534 for Roger and Margaret Skynner. Quite the best thing in the church is the late – C15 *rood screen*. It rises to the old loft level, and although all the tracery has been lost from the upper lights the double ranks of delicate pierced cusping that enriched it have largely survived. The uprights are beautifully painted to their full height on both sides with leaf trails in three colours, and the exceptionally wide entrance has a most unusual feature unmatched anywhere in East Anglia. On each side, a heavily moulded and buttressed shaft is topped at dado level by a seated lion facing boldly down the nave, its mane and tail gilded. There are four painted panels on either side in the base of the screen, and the style of painting dates them between 1490 and 1510. From the n. the figures are: *Saints Matthew, Mark, Luke, and John*. They are matched on the s. side by the *Four Latin Doctors – Saints Gregory, Augustine, Ambrose* and *Jerome*. All the tracery and moulding carries painted decoration and even the e. side of the screen has the remains of large painted diapers. This is one of the best examples in the area and it was expertly conserved in 1990 by Pauline Plummer. The chancel was restored by the Ecclesiastical Commissioners in 1887 when they renewed half of the roof, leaving two of the original archbraced bays with pierced carving in the *spandrels* to the w. In the sanctuary the plain piscina lacks its drain and is flanked by dropped-sill *sedilia*. The two head *corbels* high in the chancel walls may possibly have supported a *Lenten Veil*.

East Tuddenham, All Saints (G4): A splendid avenue of limes and pantiled *lychgate* lead to this good-looking church. A simple, battlemented tower of mainly C13 date contrasts with the striking *porch*, which is *Perpendicular* and of two storeys; and with surprisingly grand Perpendicular windows in *nave* and *chancel*, focussed by a superb four-*light* example at the centre of the 'picture'. The finely proportioned porch is a feast of *knapped flint, flushwork* and decoration: pinnacles at the gable ends; a handsome figure niche, with filled in windows to either side; below, a frieze of opulent, crowned letters in stone set in flint, spelling out 'Gloria Tibi TR' – Glory to Thee Trinitas. Below again, an excellent arch with a square hood, and in the *spandrels*, a particularly good carved *Annunciation* – Mary on one side, with traditional vase and lily (for virginity), and the Dove (the Holy Spirit) descending in a blaze of sunrays; on the other, an athletic, winged Gabriel, bringing her The Good News on a swirling banner, like celebratory ticker-tape. Inside the porch, a s. doorway, which is the oldest part of the church – *Early English*, and pointed, but so *Norman* in its loyalties, with its criss-cross carving round the arch and a *hood mould* of stonily stiff leaves, and mounted on trim little round pillars and slightly less-self-conscious leafy *capitals*. Before going inside, a walk round the outside, clockwise, is rewarding: in s. face of tower, a tiny *lancet* opening, filled over with a filigree tracery which is almost Eastern; in the nave w. end, a 'Y' tracery window of about 1300 which matches the bell openings in the tower; but above and to its right is a filled-in, traceried window whose existence, as we'll see when we go inside, begs interesting questions; nave n.e. (*Tudor*) window set into a large arch outline, which presumably led into a now vanished chapel; at this point, the steps and staircase to the old *rood loft* are clearly visible; on the chancel n. side, a lovely 'flowing' *Decorated* window; and adjacent, a modern vestry where enormous trouble was evidently taken to give character to doorway and window – notice especially the window *corbels*, left, a funny grotesque eating its own tail, and right, a charming nut-eating squirrel. Inside the church now, to slight disappointment after the exterior display. Everything is plastered over, including the plain rounded ceiling of the enormously wide (34ft.) nave. This was created

at some earlier period by tearing out the s. *arcade* and joining nave and aisle into one great 'hall' – thus that filled in w. window noted from the outside. The font is early-C13, large, round, robustly carved. A *brass* on the w. wall shows a civilian and two wives, about 1500. Adjacent, tucked away in the corner, is a stone knight of the late C13, in full armour, his feet on a dog: and between his hands he holds his heart (see also Wickhampton). High up on the w. wall, the faded *Royal Arms* of Charles II; by the door, a fine *Stuart* table of about the same date. Some nice old *poppy-head* benchends, including a quite extraordinary one – the head of the poppy is a very lugubrious face on one side and an upside-down naked figure on the other, hands clasped round thighs, with the 'lobes' of the poppy carved with caricature heads, so positive you feel they must be wicked portraits. In the chancel, the Victorian reproduction poppy-heads are carved, on the n. side, with '18' and 'B', on the s. with 'V' and '55' – Blessed Virgin, 1855 – a lovely idea.

East Walton, St Mary (D4): The round tower has two *lancets* in the w. face, the lower one very small, and is likely to be *Norman* rather than *Saxon*. There are double lancet bell openings, and a later ring of battlements which have been recently restored. The s. side of *nave* and *chancel* is divided by a buttress, and a *rood stair* turret takes up the angles on either side of it, with corner arches just above ground level. The outer arch of the C14 *porch* is 'on the sosh', as they say, and leans comfortably to the w. The nave has three grand *Perpendicular* windows each side, filled mainly with C18 clear glass, and the flood of light suits the quiet orderliness of the rearranged interior of that period. There are open benches at the back, then a range of *box pews,* and finally a *three-decker pulpit* set in the s.e. angle where the *rood stairs* used to be. The pulpit has simple decorative beads on panels, back and *tester,* there are built-in seats at all levels, and the *parish clerk's* portion has its own door. All the wood-work is pine. Other C18 alterations are not so happy; the C14 chancel arch has a beautiful pierced band of foliage in the mouldings of both faces, but only tantalising fragments are visible because a piece of infilling has masked it, and a miserable quasi-classical arch now forms the entrance to the chancel. The chancel was not arranged for worship when visited, but there is a very pretty gable over the inside of the *priest's door* – a six-leafed roundel with a rose in the middle. Back in the nave, the late-C14 octagonal font has plain *quatrefoils* in the bowl panels, with a very deep mould beneath and a panelled shaft. The *wall posts* of the old roof rested on stone *corbels* and they each display a finely carved head. On the w. wall, a good set of Georgian *Royal Arms* on canvas – undated, but painted before the union with Ireland.

East Winch, All Saints (C4): A favourite tower which is always a welcome sight to the traveller coming home from the w., with the broad acres of Norfolk stretching out beyond it. Mainly of *carstone*, it has a distinctive stair turret built as a buttress on the s.w. corner, which rises to a pinnacle above the parapet. The *sanctus bell turret* is equally memorable and was luckily found and replaced during a C19 restoration. The n. doorway is blocked and entry is by a charming s. *porch*, all in craggy *Tudor* red brick, including the finely moulded entrance arch and traceried windows. There was a big restoration by *Sir Gilbert Scott* in 1875, and in 1913 *Sir Ninian Comper* designed a lovely cover for the font. Small by his standards, it matches a 1380s original given by the Howard family and illustrated in Weever's 'Memorials'; in dark blue with *crockets* and mouldings picked out in dull gold, it has panels with lots of heraldry (details on the wall nearby). The sides of the early-C15 font itself are carved with the Howard arms and big floral motifs, and there are traces of paint below them. Look up and you will see that the ringing chamber floor rests on *arch-braced tie-beams*, and the stone *corbels* have fine carved heads; also above is a very good set of George III *Royal Arms* of 1774 painted on board. Back at floor level, one of the smallest chests to be found anywhere – C14, banded with iron and with a coved lid, it is only 3ft. 3in. long and 18in. high. The *nave* and *aisles* are C15 and between the *clerestory* windows, very thin shafts rise to the corbels of the roof *wall posts*. The s. aisle *arch-braced roof* has excellent tracery in the *spandrels*, and below it is a range of small battered C15 benches; there are more in the n. aisle but the rest of the pews are plain and seemly C19 pine. At the e. end of the n. aisle lie two C13 coffin lids, one with the double Omega sign, the other with a cross within an embattled edge. Beyond them, a substantial *Norman pillar piscina* with spiral carving on the shaft, and three panels saved from a C15 *screen*. Unlike the nave, the C15 *chancel* has its original roof and the entrance arches to earlier side chapels can be seen just beyond the chancel arch. The n. has disappeared, but the s. has been rebuilt and houses the organ. If you can squeeze through by the side, there is a plate in the e. wall which

records the burial there of Howards in the C14 and C15, for this was the cradle of that great and powerful clan who, as *Dukes of Norfolk*, punctuate the pages of the country's history. Having got that far, pause to read the epitaph of William Barnes who retired and died in 1657, having:

> for many years with great prudence & fidelity serve his KING & CUNTRY. Such was the iniquity of ye tymes that LOYALTY was esteemed a crime; whene no allurements or threats from him who usurped ye Highest power could seduce him from his constant adhereance to his abandoned Prince and ye persecuted CHURCH OF ENGLAND.

East with West Beckham, St Helen & All Saints (H2): Both Beckham parishes had their own churches, but St Helen's in East Beckham had long been ruined and All Saints' West Beckham was used by both until 1890. It was then decided to start afresh on a new site midway between the two and All Saints' was pulled down and its stones, together with the remains of St Helen's, were used to build the new church. The architects were Habershon & Faulkner of London and the foundation stone laid by the wife of the local MP is set in the w. wall below a large rose window. The walls are entirely faced with uncut flint pebbles taken from the beach, laid closely and regularly. The outer arch of the *porch* was constructed almost entirely from stone salvaged from St Helen's. Within, the real surprise is that, like the outside, the walls are entirely faced with uncut flint pebbles, relieved only by thin courses of brick. Many churches in other parts of the country have stripped stone interiors, but this is the only example in East Anglian flint country of this finish, and it imparts a much warmer feel than the normal lime wash. To offset that, the 'cathedral' glass in all but one of the windows has the usual lowering effect. The exception in the n. wall has a *Trinity* emblem at the top and is a memorial to a curate of the parish who died in 1857 so that it must have been transferred from the old All Saints. Framed on the s. wall there is an interesting display of Ladbroke lithoghraphs and early photographs of the two former churches. The C14 *chancel* arch with its chamfered *piers* came almost entirely from St Helen's. In the short chancel the communion rail features sliding brass extensions to close the entrance to the sanctuary – a favourite Victorian device, and the *decalogue boards* on the e. wall are rather nice. Their Gothic lettering takes its inspiration from medieval illuminated manuscripts, and was the first choice in the 1890s for such things as Sunday School certificates, peal books and boards like these.

East Wretham, St Ethelbert (F6): The tower has a *Perpendicular* w. window, but underneath a stone inscription records that the children of Wyrley and Katherine Birch rebuilt the church in 1865, and they did it comprehensively. Nevertheless, parts of the old *Norman* s. doorway were kept – two ranges of zigzag in the arch, and the columns. The main structure of the tower was undisturbed and the C14 *arch* to the *nave* has a single chamfer that fades into the walls. Beneath it, a memorial to William Grigson which 'was removed from the dilapidated *chancel* of West Wretham church' in 1794. The 1883 font cover is a superb essay in Perpendicular style, echoing the one at Elsing; tall, intricately canopied and *crocketted*, with standing figures. The font itself is Victorian and so is the *angle piscina* in the chancel, but there is a very nice pierced vine trail over the latter carved in stone. Nave and chancel have an excellent range of wrought iron candelabra and the whole interior is most attractive. The churchyard was being grazed by sheep to the e. and geese to the w. – a delightful and perambulating mixed metaphor – on the day of my visit.

Easton, St Peter (H4): Time has not treated this little church well. Its tower fell in the late C18 and was not replaced; its *nave* and n. *aisle* (*Perpendicular* in fabric as in character) have been most heavily restored, with a cement coating applied to the s. outer wall which is far from pretty; and even less harmonious is the red brick restoration at the w. end – though the lace-patterned window placed there is a most creditable reproduction of C14 *reticulated*. The *chancel*, trim and flint speckled, is a Victorian rebuild of 1883. But there is nonetheless much of interest here to make a 'church-crawling' stop wholly worthwhile. The charmingly rustic *porch* first, very tall for its tiny ground base – presumably it had an upper room at one time. Structurally it is a mixture of flint and mellow pink brick – most pleasing – and has a sun dial, dated 1694, set into its gable end, and a rough brick hood over its ancient outer arch. But it is what the porch hides which is the surprise: an excellent s. doorway, late *Norman* in date, and wholly Norman in its rich carving and sturdy

character, but with a pointed arch which must surely have been adapted just a little later, as *Early English* gothic made its debut, while re-using the materials and decorative carvings of the original round arch. An ancient door, with heavy, unsophisticated ironwork, leads into a most pleasing interior, brilliantly light, the sun reflecting off the white-washed walls, and surprisingly spacious. Immediately facing is an intriguing filled in arch, pointed but of obvious Norman materials – an adaptation like the arch of the s. door. Judging by its position, it led through to a now vanished n. w. tower – in addition to the later w. tower, lost 200 years ago. The nave roof is the simplest of *arch-braced* types, with 'fretwork' *bosses*, the plainest of *wall plates*, and *wall posts* sitting on chunky wooden *corbels*. A four-window *clerestory*, half filled in at the bases but with naive and pretty Perpendicular tracery, tops a delightfully rustic two-bay *arcade* of the C13, with octagonal pillars and roughly rounded *capitals*, whose very poorness of workmanship gives a special charm. C13 too is the font of *Purbeck marble*, octagonal and very plain, with typical shallow arcading carved round the bowl. Most attractive pulpit, panelled in *linen-fold* and neatly traceried and flower-carved, and standing on a central pillar and eight little *baluster* legs. It was brought here from the redundant church of St Mary Coslany in Norwich. In the chancel, some nice old *poppy-heads* re-used; a *piscina* and *dropped sill sedilia* and (n. side) an *aumbry*, all totally remodelled. The tunnel-like passageway between the e. end of the n. aisle and the chancel was in fact a kind of *squint* – for it gave sight of the high altar, and access too, from the side-altar in the aisle.

Eaton, St Andrew (I5): Most of the old village of Eaton has fallen victim to the pressure of urban Norwich and cowers below the new bypass, but the church is set apart sufficiently to retain its attraction. Coming in by way of an avenue of close set limes, one has a good view of the only thatched roof left on a Norwich church – a long swathe over both *nave* and *chancel* with a n. *porch* to match. The C15 tower has *flushwork* battlements and a curious *quatrefoil* pattern on the n. side which may have been a true *soundhole* originally. There is a large belfry window at the same level on the w. side and nothing e. and s. The tower was so well restored after a lightning strike in 1930 that there is no trace of it, but a photograph inside shows the extent of the damage. By the long line of small *lancets* along both nave and chancel one can assume that the main building was done in the C13, but a hefty restoration in 1860 tidied everything up, and a new flat-roofed vestry in good flint and stone was added to the s. in the 1950s. Inside, everything is very tidy with a solid range of pews to match the neo-classical *screen* designed by Fletcher & Watson in 1958. This, with the pulpit-cum-reading desk forms a seemly composition of just the right weight for the continuous run of nave and chancel. Apart from the lancet windows, the C13 *pillar piscina* is a reminder of the building's age. The column has been restored but the carving under the bowl is good, with large bulbous leaves. Midway down the nave are two C13 *consecration crosses*, and there are little *holy water stoups* on either side of the n. door. The font came from Sandringham in 1896 and is so drastically recut that it no longer looks or feels medieval – in the floor of the tower lie John and Mary White. Southey had appreciated the genius of their poet son Henry Kirk White before his early death in 1806. One of his verses is the parents' memorial. It was unfortunate, to say the least, that when *Thomas Jekyll* did some work here in 1861, he destroyed some C15 frescoes that included a rare *Thomas of Canterbury* (Beckett) martyrdom on the s. wall. In 1996 the church was transformed by a substantial extension on the s. side. Leaving the rather dark nave, one passes through a glass door opposite the entrance into a beautifully light and airy space where four wooden columns support sturdy arches under a canted roof. Ahead, the sanctuary *apse* is lit by high-level stepped windows, and both angled side *aisles* are backed by a window up to full height with stepped glazing bars. Vestry and cloakrooms have been neatly fitted in, and gently curved beams over the entrance support a *gallery* which has a small *Royal Arms* of George III framed on the ledge. Outside, the architect Nigel Sunter has bodly marked the angles of the building with faceted columns up to the eves.

Eccles, St Mary (G7): It sits quietly in a wood, approached by a long grassy track closely bounded by trees (planted to celebrate the Festival of Britain in 1951). The round tower is *Norman*, with later belfry openings and battlements; the body of the church is dominated by large *Perpendicular* windows; the e. window's ambitiously decorative tracery is deceptive – it dates from the late C19 when the window, blocked off for many years, was opened up. But basically this is a much older building, the *chancel* being of *Early English*

origin, as the shape of the *priest's door* on the s. side indicates. At one time there was a C14 *Decorated s. aisle*; but this was demolished in the C18, leaving only the outlines of its arches and pillars, both inside the church and on the exterior. The top parts of the arches are now filled by unfortunate misted glass. The Decorated s. doorway is the original one – it was moved to its present line when the aisle was demolished. The entrance to the *rood stair* is also visible from outside, with the stair intact through to the interior. Now blocked off is the C15 n. *porch*: its outer arch is very attractive, being supported on trim round pillars with leaf-carved *capitals*, and both inner and outer surfaces and the *jambs* decorated with carved floral motifs. The church interior is uncluttered, with a big plain roof over the *nave*, modern and *tie-beamed*. Dominating all is a modern *rood* and beam, in the traditional position across the chancel arch. The C15 arch itself is beautiful, being studded on the nave side with floral motifs, leaves and tiny faces, both human and grotesque – look for the one behind the pulpit, devilish and with tongue out. To either side are figure niches, that on the left being particularly attractive, with a *cusped* and *crocketted ogee* arch under a square hood, with traceries in the *spandrels* and miniature battlements over the top. On the opposite side, the niche is half filled in, vertically, for some reason. Above it, the old *rood loft* entrance, and above the chancel arch, an e. window – built to rise above an earlier roof than the present modern one in the chancel. The immediate feature of the chancel is the magnificent *double piscina*, with recessed arches, and round capitals and pillars, all under a square hood, and with interesting *trefoil* shapes, ornamented with tiny crockets, deeply carved into the spandrels. Equally notable is the altar, which has the original C15 *mensa slab* – an unusually huge one, nearly 10ft. long by $3^1/_2$ft. wide – which is clearly marked with its five *consecration crosses*. It was discovered outside in the churchyard as recently as 1947, and restored to its rightful place after just 400 years. The panelled pulpit is *Jacobean*; the plain octagonal font, with embattled rim, C14; on the w. wall, *Royal Arms* of George II.

Edgefield, St Peter & St Paul (G2): Except that the tower is placed very oddly at the n.e. corner, this church looks like an average medieval building in remarkably good condition. But appearances are deceptive. What we see is the result of virtually one man's vision, enthusiasm, and sheer hard work over many years. That man was Canon Walter Marcon. He was born in the rectory in 1850, came back on the death of his father to follow him as rector in 1876, and died in the same room in which he was born in 1936 – a record scarcely to be equalled and unlikely to be surpassed. At first it seemed to him 'a moral wilderness', and he found the absence of music particularly hard to bear, 'a sort of slow starvation'. Nonetheless, he drew the village to him, and among many other things, determined to do something about the church. It had been isolated since the *Black Death*, far from the present centre of the village, and was in a sorry state of decay, and so – he moved it! It took ten years to raise the £2000 needed and a further two years to complete the building. Apart from the tall octagonal tower still to be found along the road to Hunworth, and the s. *porch*, the church was dismantled stone by stone and moved to the new site. Some re-arrangements were made, so that the old e. window is now at the w. end, there is no chancel arch, and the chancel is all new work. Consecrated in 1885, the church was completed by having its tower added in 1908. The main *screen* combines C15 painted and gilded sections with new work very effectively, and the small *parclose screen* to the s. *aisle* chapel is dated 1526. It has two wide painted panels, with group portraits of the donors, William Harstrong, his wife and family. Defaced though they are, it is good that they too moved with the living church and keep company with the man behind it all – Walter Hubert Marcon.

Edingthorpe, All Saints (J2): An enchanting little church, as picturesque inside as out. Round *Norman* tower, distinctly narrowing to its octagonal top of about 1400 with bell openings filled with agreeable *Decorated* tracery. Attractive *porch*, with a pretty figure niche over its outer arch; and a late-C12 inner doorway of beautifully simple lines, with one kingly head remaining as a *corbel*. The *nave* and *chancel* windows are a real pleasure of diverse Decorated designs, from Y-tracery to geometrical (*Appendix 2 – Styles of Architecture*): all different on s. side, a lovely e. window (*reticulated*) and, on n. side, three with *cusped* tracery. On n. side also, an ancient doorway, late-C12, with rough-hewn *jambs* and arch stones. Inside, the church is a delight of rural character. A modern, white painted match-boarding roof to the nave looks charmingly in keeping. On the n. there are some fine remnants of wall paintings, with a very good St *Christopher* (against which is a figure niche) and towards the chancel a splendidly

carved and painted statue niche with traceried head over the old *rood stair* entrance. Upon a battered reading desk, facing the stair, is carved the date 1587. The nave has some very apprentice-like bench ends, flat cut-outs rather than carved; a restrained octagonal *Perpendicular* font; a C17 pulpit and, beside its steps, a little *brass* inscription in Latin, undated, invoking prayers for one Raffe Spor. The chancel arch has the slots which once supported *rood beam* and loft. Below it is the church's treasure, a lovely old *rood screen*, with an upper part C14 having two carved wheels with intricate tracery. The panels below have six painted saints, with symbols: *Bartholomew*, knife; *Paul*, bible and sword; *Catherine* (?), bible and palm frond; *James the Great*, staff and *scallop-shell*; *Andrew*, cross; *Peter*, keys.

Ellingham, St Mary (J6): Another *isolated church*. Coming s. from the main road the battlements just peep over the trees in the big churchyard beyond the long defunct railway line. The plain C14 tower had those elaborate stepped and *flushwork* battlements added later, and in the C18/C19 a massive and ugly brick stairway was clapped on to the s. side. At about that time the e. end of the *chancel* was rebuilt in brick. The n. door *hood mould* has a worn pair of heads and the arch of the main entrance s. *porch* is decorated with floral motifs in the moulding, and traceried *spandrels* enclose shields. Inside, a number of mysteries. The n. wall of the *nave* has remains of C13 *arcading* and the middle an *Early English* shaft with a highly unusual carving over it – a curly tailed dragon head down, and two little heads in the curve either side. Above that is the head of a bishop wearing the flattish mitre of the period. Now, was this the *arcade* of an earlier n. *aisle* and if so, why was it replaced by a s. aisle? The fragmentary arcade appears again on the n. side of the chancel, but at least in the s. chancel wall there is an unequivocal C13 window of high quality – slim shafting and stiff-leaf *headstops* to the *hood mould*. The second query is the s. aisle arcade. The two e. bays were restored in 1853 to match the one in the vestry, but the arches at the w. end are barely more than holes cut in the wall. Why and when? An *arch-braced roof* with renewed *bosses* runs the length of the aisle and in the vestry (formerly a chapel) there is a bracket canopy for a statue in the corner and a very worn C16 memorial below the s. window. The font follows the pattern found in a number of churches locally – eight columns attached to the shaft, and roses alternating with shields around the bowl, this time backed by varied tracery. The late-C17 *communion rails* have a square and heavy top rail, almost too much for the slim barley sugar *balusters*. The *box pews* are more difficult to date – they could be C17 or anything up to 1800, but interesting; made in pine and grained to look like oak, they include a square squire's pew still graced with cushions on the n. side, and a range of open high-backed pews at the w. end for the less fortunate. There is a good set of George I *Royal Arms* on canvas, and don't overlook an 1880s window in the chancel by *Ward and Hughes*, with the stylised figures of Ruth and Naomi in rich colour.

Elsing, St Mary (G4): The church stands on a little eminence, and its battlements peep over low hills when seen from a distance. There is something comfortable about a church that was all built at one time, and there is no need to puzzle out the sequence of operations here. There was a previous church, but Sir Hugh Hastyngs and his wife Margery built afresh in about 1330, and this is one of the best copybook examples of the *Decorated* style. The *nave* windows are large, with an elaborate tracery that does not sit too happily within the frames, but the five-*light* e. window is a beauty. The outer arches of both *porches* are unusually bold *trefoils* and the inner n. doorway has a multi-*cusped ogee arch*. Inside, there are no *aisles* and acres of space. This holds the record at 39ft. 6in. for the widest pillarless nave in East Anglia – perhaps in all England. The low pitch-pine pews seem to hug the floor and it is a good 8yds from the last pew to the font. The great width of the nave emphasises the narrowness of the tall tower arch and sets off the superb 8ft. font canopy. This probably dates from the time the church was built, and its tabernacle work has been dexterously restored and recoloured. New figures of the *Evangelists* have been placed in the niches to the e. side, but the w. side has been left alone so that you may judge between what has been restored and what has not. The C14 font makes a nice change from the common East Anglian form. The shallow octagonal bowl has a trail of trefoils, and rests on a deep concave base and stub shaft. In the n. w. corner, an old Norfolk plough complete with road trolley and set of whippletrees (to which the traces are fixed); and over the s. door, the *Royal Arms* of George II dated 1794. Just below stands an example of Victorian design that would have been quite at home in the Great Exhibition of 1851 – an oil stove craftily concealed in a miniature pavilion

Elsing, St Mary: font cover

of cast iron filigree panels. The base of the *rood screen* has ogee arches and crisp carving in the *spandrels*. The paintings are defaced and very faded but the one to the left of the opening looks like St *Anne* teaching the Virgin to read. There has been a great change in the *chancel*. The Victorian stalls have gone, and in the centre, raised on a plinth that is angled inwards at the base, the Hastyngs *brass* is encased. This memorial is of European importance and it is right that it should be protected – particularly as portions of it have been stolen over the years. But it is both helpful and thoughtful of the church to provide an excellent full-scale replica on top of the case so that it can be studied at any time. The brass dates from 1347, and the design was taken from the Earl of Pembroke's tomb in Westminster Abbey. The armoured knight carries his shield, and his pillow is born up by angels at each side. Above his head, a miniature of angels receiving his soul, and a St *George* roundel in the apex of the canopy arch. His comrades in the battles of the Hundred Years' war line each side like a roll call of the age of Chivalry – King Edward III, Thomas de Beauchamp, Earl of Warwick, Roger Lord Grey of Ruthin, Henry Plantaganet Earl of Lancaster, Ralph Lord Stafford and Almeric St Armand. At the top is the Coronation of the Virgin flanking Sir Hugh's crest. This brass has always been famous and was in fact cited and meticulously described in a case brought before the Court of Chivalry in 1408. The *piscina* and *sedilia* have bold trefoils that match the porch arches, and the *communion rails* are a nicely restrained mahogony set in the Gothic style, either late-C18 or early-C19. The e. window was blown in by a gale in 1781, and parts of the medieval glass were placed in the s. *chancel* windows in 1901. There is a murky figure of the Blessed Virgin on the left, a *censing* angel, fragments of a *Trinity*, and much restored figures of St *Matthew*, St *Jude* and St *Philip*.

Emneth, St Edmund (A5): A tall, well balanced church which presents a most interesting composition as you approach from Outwell. It is predominantly a *Perpendicular* building as we see it today, but the tall and slim *chancel* is late-C13 *Early English* – its e. window of three grouped and spartan *lancets* contrasts sharply with the Perpendicular expanses of *aisles* and *clerestory*. Lofty tower, battlemented in brick and with a little lead spirelet on top (possibly an C18 addition) but otherwise sturdily plain, leaving its big windows (to n. and s., unusually, as well as to w., at first stage level) to give it its character. Before going into the church, note the neat old *sanctus bell cote* on the *nave* e. gable. The formerly two-storey Perpendicular *porch* has a good figure niche over its outer arch, nicely *cusped* under a much-worn *finial*. Loftiness and light are the instant impressions inside this building, accentuated by the considerable height of the *chancel* and its arch in relation to its width. Very fine roof to nave, *tie-beams* and *arch-braces* alternating with angels at the terminations of arch-braces, giving a *hammer-beam* look. Bold battlemented moulding on the tie-beams with angels and traceried *spandrels* above, and deep *wall posts* below on which are carved apostolic figures. From below each of the apostles runs a slim shaft down to the intersection of the *arcade*

arch immediately below, a stylish detail. The six bay *arcades* (Perpendicular again) are interesting in that their pillars each have four concave sides, separated by pencil shafts running directly up into those descending from the wall posts. Contemporary with the arcade are the great tower and chancel arches which both, in lieu of *capitals*, have charming half-figures of angels. Abutting the chancel arch, on the n. side, is another unusual interior feature – a turret to enclose the *rood stair*. It has an embattled top studded with jolly little animal head *corbels* and, in the corner of the n. aisle, a gorgeous little stair doorway under a very pronounced *hood mould* whose sturdy *headstops* are not so much heads as busts – for they sweep back to shoulders streamlined for flight. Solid old *arch-braced roofs* to n. and s. aisles. Notice that both roofs, on the sides abutting the arcades, are supported by a whole range of rough little stone corbels – some 16 each side as very practical *corbel tables*. In the n. aisle, n. side, the roof's corbels to its wall posts number two very large and weird stone faces. Yet more weird, and with a touch of the pagan, are the faces carved into the pedestals set in the *pier* and window *jambs* respectively at the e. end of the s. aisle. The one in the window is a maniacal mask with its tongue sticking out. Below it is a plain *piscina* under a *Tudor* arch. Tall plain chancel *screen* with pretty tracery and remnants of original colour; unfortunately the panels in the lower section have gone. The chancel here is a beauty – sublimely simple C12 and C13 work. To each side, low two-bay arcades with round arches on bluff round pillars are late-C12, late *Norman* work. On the n. side notice the dog-like corbel carving between the two bays. Above the n. arcade is a deeply splayed lancet window, open through to the later aisle. The e. window has slim, ringed shafts separating its three lancets, the two centre shafts are sitting on protruding, triangular footings. Reconstructed piscina and plain *sedilia* under an arch set flush into the wall. In the chancel s. chapel are two notable and notably colourful tombs. Under a great canopy, like a four-poster bed, lies Sir Thomas Hewer, 1631, curiously described as 'eqves avratvs' – 'Golden horseman'? Beside him is his wife Emma, she richly robed, he in armour and a ruff and noble of face and in the e. wall at their feet, in an ornamented recess, lies the image of their infant son. This tomb was made by *Nicholas Stone*, greatest sculptor of his century. Opposite is the tomb of an earlier Sir Thomas Hewer and his lady, 1586, without effigies but much embellished.

Erpingham, St Mary (H2): Standing away from the village in a big churchyard, mainly late-C14 with a fine C15 tower. This has ERPINGHAM picked out round the battlements, the letters interspersed with crowned 'M's for the dedication. The w. door has been well restored and has unusual brackets for figures in the centre panels. There are little figures too in niches on either side of the door as part of the *base course*. Note the *sanctus bell turret* on the gable of the *nave*. The interior has a spacious feel about it emphasised by the sparkling white walls, plain brick floor, and general air of cleanliness and care. By the door is the font which came from the bombed Norwich church of St *Benedict*. The figures round the bowl have been recut and given new heads in some cases. Still at the door, look for the large *squint* to the right of the *chancel* arch. Through it one can see the *aumbry* (where the Sacrament is reserved) which is offset to the left so that it is in line with the door. At the e. end of the s. *aisle* is a big *brass* of Sir John de Erpingham who died in 1370, although the brass dates from 1415. He was the father of Shakespeare's 'Old Sir Thomas' of Agincourt fame, who may well have built the tower and aisle here. The e. window contains a beautiful assembly of German and French C16 glass from Steinfeld monastery in Germany (more from the same source is in the Victoria and Albert Museum). The Adoration with the shepherds in the bottom left panel is particularly fine. Much of the statuary in the church is good modern work as is the charming head of the Virgin in the window by the font. The church has a good ring of 6 bells, tenor 9-2-0 cwt.

Fakenham, St Peter & St Paul (F3): From a distance, especially from the n. and w., the 115ft. tower stands beautifully above the town and one almost seems to see the base, but in reality buildings cluster close to the church and the way up to the s. *porch* is by snug little lanes under deep brick arches. The big n. graveyard has been transformed into a broad and pleasant park and from there one can take in the fine proportions of the C15 tower, with its double *base course* and panelled buttresses. The square *sound-holes* are filled with a net of lozenge tracery and above them, great three-*light transomed* bell openings. Until 1828 the top was plain, and here is a case where C19 battlements and pinnacles greatly improve the whole. The town fire engine was once kept under the tower but now there is a modern glass panelled w. door; deep canopied

niches either side and a frieze of shields over, with crowned 'P's for the dedication. Entry is by the late-C15 porch which once had an upper room, and then into the great *nave* with its C14 *arcades*. A massive restoration in 1864, when roofs, windows, pews, and much else were replaced seems to have robbed the building of a certain quality, but now that the obscured glass has largely been replaced with clear panes the effect is light and open. Note the imaginative modern roundels with symbols that connect with their individual donors (see the card at the back of the church for details). Good C15 font with crowned 'P's in the shaft panels and, round the bowl, *Symbols of the Evangelists* with, w., *Instruments of the Passion*, s.w. *Royal Arms*, and n. the *Trinity* emblem. Also at the w. end, a pedestal poorbox dated 1665 which disappeared and came back to the church only in 1888. A generously proportioned nave altar is now used for most services and behind it the C14 *rood screen* has turned pillars between uprights, *ogee arches* and good tracery; much restored, its cornice is all C19 and the improvers cut away the base panels and inserted *trefoil* arches. On the n. wall, a fine portrait in oils of C18 rector Dr John Hacket who was Vice-Master of Trinity College Cambridge, the Patrons of the living. By Joseph Highmore, it was purchased for the church in 1941. The *chancel* is spacious, with a big C14 e. window of five lights with flowing tracery – C19 stained glass. The C14 *sedilia* and *piscina* are on a large scale and very like those at North Creake; fine but rather stiff design in which *crocketted* pinnacles rise from each intersection of the *ogee arches* which are themselves crocketted; fore edges of the pillars are 'V' shaped and battlemented. A good modern set of *communion rails* with turned *balusters*, and within the sanctuary, four small *brasses* have been fixed to a board – one to Richard Betteson has the date 1497 in arable numerals rather than the more usual Roman. 2005 saw the begining of another restoration and improvement, with pews replaced by chairs; a new vestry, choir stalls and lighting are planned, and the n. aisle arcade will be glazed to provide a community room. The church has a good ring of 8 bells, tenor 19-3-0 cwt.

Felbrigg, St Margaret (I2): Now that the estate has passed to the National Trust, Felbrigg is much more accessible and the church, lying some distance across the park from the house, should not be missed. It has a magnificent series of *brasses*, and of them, the one commemorating

Felbrigg, St Margaret: Sir Simon de Felbrigg's brass

Sir Simon de Felbrigg and his wife is one of the finest in England. It is in the *aisle* between the foremost pews, and is over 9ft. long and 4ft. wide, with two figures under an elaborate and graceful double canopy. Sir Simon was standard-bearer to Richard II, and his wife Margaret was the Queen's cousin and her maid of honour. This is one of only five old brasses remaining in the country to Knights of the Garter. The *chancel* has a fine e. window and an early-C15 *piscina* – ruined by having the sculptor *Joseph Nollekens'* monument to William Windham, of Felbrigg Hall (d.1813) jammed into it. Other windows in the chancel were blocked up to house an astonishing array of Windham monuments, and one to another William (1686) is by *Grinling Gibbons*, having typical swags of flowers and fruit. The two convex tablets close by are beautiful examples of C17 lettering and design. *Box pews* and a series of *hatchments* add to the delights of this church.

Felmingham, St Andrew (I3): The bulky C15 tower has a distinctive look from a distance because there is no parapet and it seems to bulge. There is quite elaborate *flushwork* around the w. door and the *sound-holes* are traceried. When the remainder of the church was rebuilt in brick in 1742 the good windows on the s. side with *reticulated* tracery were re-used. The roof is mean

matchboarding on stark braces and there is no *chancel* arch. The C19 pulpit has some old tracery incorporated in it which may have come from the *rood screen*; a *griffin, woodwose*, hawk, and dragon can be seen carved in the little *spandrels*. The local style of C14 font shaft with eight attached columns supports the familiar type of C13 *Purbeck marble* bowl. The church has an excellent ring of 9 bells, tenor 15-3-26 cwt.

Felthorpe, St Margaret (H4): Attractive churchyard with Scots pines standing above pond. Peculiar, oblong tower with large buttresses. Church almost entirely rebuilt in 1846, and a cramped narrow s. *aisle* added. Variety of windows, C14 to C15. Inside, a curiosity is a glass frame of photos of World War One servicemen – number roughly tallies with the Roll of Honour. A good *Jacobean* chest, nicely carved with *scallop* frieze, inscribed I.T.F. The C19 stained glass is by *Ward & Hughes*.

Feltwell, St Mary (D6): From the n., the *nave* is overshadowed by a large *aisle* and *chancel* chapel built in the 1860s, but attention really focusses on the splendid *Perpendicular* tower. The stepped battlements are pierced and chamfered, with a line of small shields within *cusped* squares; each of the *crocketted* corner pinnacles has a little weathervane and the whole effect is very decorative. The mid-C14 chancel has a wide e. window, with *reticulated* tracery in the side windows, and see how one on the s. side is cut short to accommodate the *sedilia* you will find within. Large Perpendicular windows in the s. aisle have stepped embattled *transoms* and entry is by way of the s. *porch*. The s. *arcade*, like the chancel, is *Decorated*, with miniature shafts between the main lobes of the *quatrefoil piers*. In contrast to the narrow s. aisle, the n. aisle is as wide as the nave, and the Victorian architect indulged himself with the arcade details, particularly in the e. chapel. The whole of the nave is filled with lovely C15 benches, with every top rail carved and varied pierced work in the backs. Most of the figures on the arms are mutilated but there is a sentry box group (Mercy ministering to prisoners) on the s. side at the w. end, similar to the one at nearby Wilton; opposite, a priest, with acolytes carrying the *censer* and candle, stands over a shrouded corpse. The chancel *screen* is handsome, but more replacement than original, and the stalls beyond have remarkably large *poppy-heads*. The *piscina* and stepped sedilia are set within large five-leafed *ogee arches* cut square at the top with very little elaboration, and there you will find a *brass* to Margaret Mundford (1520) – an 18in. figure in *kennel head-dress* with a heavy rosary and girdle. A little to the w., a brass for Francis Hetht (1479) in armour, and two wall monuments for Moundefords – they both have small kneeling figures and Francis (1590) is by the screen, while Osbert (1580) and his two wives are above the Hetht brass. On the chancel n. wall, a large and elaborate example of a Victorian Gothic Revival brass for the Rev William Newecombe (1846). The chancel windows are filled with remarkably good C19 glass signed by Didron (1862) and Eugene Oudinot (1859), both of Paris. A coherent series of vignettes in the style of medieval manuscripts is displayed in roundels set against intricately patterned backgrounds, and creates an impression of richness combined with sparkling clarity.

Feltwell, St Nicholas (D6): Vested in the *Churches Conservation Trust* in 1975 and still used for occasional services. It stands high by the road in from Methwold Hythe and has an oddly truncated silhouette because the *chancel* was demolished in 1862, and then the tower collapsed in 1898 while repairs were under way. It was a round *Norman* tower built of *carstone*, with a lining of clunch (the hard chalk sometimes used as building stone in the eastern counties) and the bottom section of the drum remains, with a hollow half shell rising to the gable of the *nave*. The n. *aisle* wall was rebuilt in brick in 1830 with re-used *Perpendicular* windows but to the s., a pleasant *porch* in *Tudor* brick. There are tall Perpendicular *clerestory* windows, and between those on the s. side, six striking *flushwork* panels with crowned initials on four and a chequerboard design on another. Inside, the Norman tower arch is massive and almost overpowers what is now a small church. The C13 s. *arcade* has *quatrefoil piers* with well moulded *capitals*, and opposite is a C15 variation on the same theme. In the s. *aisle*, a C13 *piscina* within a five-leafed arch, and on the floor below, fragments of what may have been a medieval *mensa* which was used for many years as a doorstep. When the n. wall was rebuilt, the workmen found a stone coffin complete with its lid and this now lies at the w. end. Its tapered shape was not in vogue after 1270 and so it is likely to be earlier and was probably used for a priest. Another fragment of the church's Norman origins can be seen in the n. e. angle of the sanctuary – a single column decorated with zigzag, but not necessarily in its original position.

During the 1940s there were prisoners of war in the area and they used this church for services. In gratitude, one of them, Ernst Bojahr, carved the crucifix on the altar, and in the best tradition of such men, he used only a penknife to do it. By the tower arch hang three bell clappers, and there is a nicely lettered verse from the pen of Feltwell's own historian A.J. Orange to say why:

> Five of us used to speak to you
> Two hundred years and more;
> We called you from your cottages
> And from the old fen shore.
> With lofty tower one morn we fell
> In Eighteen Ninety Eight,
> No more we'll call you to your prayers
> For silence is our fate.

Fersfield, St Andrew (G7): The remarkably small-based tower – barely 14ft. square outside – with its cap and weathercock, somehow gives this attractive little church a look which is almost Continental. The tower's date is uncertain. The fabric of the *nave* is earlier, as indicated by the graceful s. door of about 1300, but the church's general character as we see it now is *Perpendicular*. The *chancel* is a Victorian rebuild of 1844. Notice that the point of the gable of the charming litttle *porch* has been rudely hacked away to accommodate a sundial and give it a 'truer' angle to the sun. This porch, which has its original timber roof, can be fairly accurately dated, because in 1493 Jeffery Ellingham died in Fersfield, leaving in his Will four marks to build the porch; as well as his lands in the parish from which the yearly profits should be 'laid out in repairing, beautifying and adorning this Parish Church FOREVER' (see inscription below w. window). The church is spacious and uncluttered, and though its roofs and furnishings throughout may be modern and of no special virtue, it has a lovely atmosphere. High two-bay *arcade* between nave and s. *aisle*, with a further small arch at the e. end which presumably led to an enclosed chapel (see *squint* through to the high altar); in the aisle e. end a simple *piscina*, deeply inset into the wall; and beside it, the particular treasure of this church, lying in an arched recess under a window, a splendid wooden effigy of a knight. He is said to be Sir Robert du Bois, who died in 1311, and is credited with having refounded this church. The effigy, with much colour of indeterminate date, shows him in his armour, helmeted head resting on two cushions, sword at side, hands in prayer, and his feet resting on a buck deer. His legs are uncrossed – exceptional in the C14. On the wall of the s. aisle, the *Royal Arms* of Queen Anne, dated 1703. To the right, by the door, an oval memorial tablet, with Arms above it, to members of the Blomefield family, and nearby, in the floor, small memorial tablets to yet more. In the s. e. corner of the chancel, lies the *ledger-stone* to the most illustrious of them, *Francis Blomefield*, Rector of Fersfield:

> and author of the History of Norfolk, a work which had he lived to have completed, would have conveyed a lasting obligation on his native county; and on himself the merit of Extensive powers, successfully Exerted. To the grief of his Family and Friends and the regret of Learning, he was snatched away in the midst of his Labors, at the age of 47, on the 16th of January 1752.

In this otherwise Victorian chancel, the fine *Jacobean* panelling round the sanctuary is notable and of special interest, under an arched recess in the n. wall, is the stone effigy of a C13 priest, plainly severe. As you turn to leave, notice the tremendously tall tower arch; and above it, a *sanctus bell opening*. The bowl of the font at the w. end is *Norman*, its stem somewhat later, perhaps C13.

Field Dalling, St Andrew (G2): A handsome church, the outside beautifully cared for, the fine C14 *Decorated* tower (which boasts excellent bell-opening tracery) was restored and repointed in 1977. The windows here are a graphic object lesson of the leap from ambitious late Decorated to *Perpendicular*. The first is seen in the fine *chancel*, all of a piece, including its lofty arch, about 1370 (the *hammer-beam roof* is modern). Secondly, the large and imposing Perpendicular *nave* windows on the s. side, in the tracery of which are some good remnants of C15 glass. The nave *arcade*, with its slender columns, is C15, like the excellent *arch-braced roof* with elegant *bosses* at the main beam intersections, carved with *Tudor roses*. In the s.e. corner is the old *rood stair* entrance (outside the spiral stair juts out, with its tiled cap). Good C15 octagonal font, carved with the *Instruments of the Passion*. In the chancel, a little *angle piscina*; *dropped sill sedilia* adjoining. The filled-in arch opposite led to a chapel whose remains can be seen outside. In n. aisle, an unusual lozenge-shaped *Royal Arms* for the Hanoverian Georges; undated, but pre-1801. There are some old C18 *box pews* here, now serving the purpose of 'play

squares' for the children. In this *aisle*, and in the nave, a lot of medieval *poppy-heads*, very simple, complete with their C15 benches. On leaving, note the *corbels* supporting the outer arch of the *porch*, carved with shields showing the Cross of Christ on one side, and that of St *Andrew*, on the other. By the gate is the stump of the ancient *preaching cross*.

Filby, All Saints (K4): Tall tower with prominent stepped and panelled battlements and figures of the *Four Latin Doctors* of the Church at the corners. All the windows have been re-worked in the course of restoration except the diminutive *clerestory* circles and *quatrefoils*. The font is C13 *Purbeck marble*, made to look like new. Near it, the tower stairs door is heavily banded with iron and with a profusion of locks; it may be a re-used medieval chest top deployed to safeguard parish valuables in the tower. The recently restored base of the *rood screen* is very good. Virtually no defacement mars the painted figures, and much of the minor decoration survives.l to right St *Cecilia*, St *George*, St *Catherine of Alexandria*, St *Peter*, St *Paul*, St *Margaret of Antioch*, St *Michael*, St *Barbara*. In the *chancel*, the 'Lucas Angel' monument is a fine piece by Hermann of Dresden. Three *ledger-stones* witness 140 years of continuous ministry by successive rectors, 1681-1820.

Fincham, St Martin (C5): Large and handsome in the centre of the village. Almost totally rebuilt in the mid-C15, it is a coherent expression of the *Perpendicular* style in full flower. The tower is well proportioned and has excellent detailing – a *base course* of recessed panels with *trefoil* heads, angle buttresses with carved panels on the upper stages of crowned 'M's, *IHS* monograms, and traceried battlements. The deeply moulded arch of the w. door terminates in profiled lions, and above the tall w. window there are big three-*light* bell openings. Most of the windows of the church have stepped *transoms*, and the (renewed) e. window is a huge five-light expanse of glass. On the n. side of the *chancel* is a two-storied vestry built by Sir Nicholas Fincham on older foundations in 1503; it had space for an *anchorite* (which may explain the small blocked door) and the first floor room was used as a school at one time. This is a church that puts its best face to the street, for the n. side parapets are plain and the *clerestory* windows are of two lights only, while on the s. side, the *aisle* has elaborate *flushwork* battlements punctuated by tall *crocketted* pinnacles, and the clerestory windows have three lights. Have a close look at the big *gargoyles* on this side – a double-headed figure, and a woman with a devil swinging a rosary on her shoulder. The s. *porch* is in keeping but plainly dated 1852, although it must have replaced something similar – see the remains of a *holy water stoup* near the door. True to its period, the church is light and spacious, with a tall tower arch and five-bay *arcades* with lozenge shaped pillars. The *nave* roof is alternate *hammer-beam* and *arch-braced* construction, with recumbent figures of angels and grotesques on all the principals; some are repaired but the high quality carving reminds one of the n. aisle at Mildenhall, Suffolk. The font is an astounding *Norman* example and can be classed with Burnham Deepdale for quality and interest. It came from Fincham's other church (St Michael's, ruined and demolished in the 1740s) and stood in the rectory garden from 1807 until 1842 before being moved here. Square, with a band of ornament above and below triple arcades on each face, it has a unique sequence of scenes: n., the Garden of Eden with the (restored) Tree of Knowledge between Adam and Eve; e., the Magi, each with his gift; s., the Nativity – the Babe in a manger, attendant cattle, and a huge star overhead, with the Blessed Virgin and St *Joseph* alongside; w., the baptism of Christ, St *John the Baptist* pointing to Our Lord and the dove descending, with a Bishop holding a crozier. Close by is the iron banded parish chest, and on the s. side a C16 table with carved and turned legs and a carved top rail – no doubt an altar table at one time. The inlaid side table in the s. aisle is actually part of the old pulpit *tester*, made and given by one Gregory Watson in 1604. The pine benches were installed in 1847, but note that many of the oak *poppy-heads* were saved, and some have double eagles carved on them. In the aisles, an interesting and unusual set of boards painted with the Lord's Prayer, the creed, and some texts which seem to hark back to the C17, despite the fact that that one is dated 1717. There is a long *squint* through the masonry of the chancel arch to give a view of the high altar from the n. aisle chapel, and the *rood stair* rises from the s. side. The *screen* is very tall, and the centre arch has a double row of delicate *cusping* – partly broken but still beautiful; the slender subdivisions of the lights have been renewed in pine, but above the transoms are crocketted pinnacles in threes within the tracery – a very lively conceit. Quite a lot of original colour remains, and the panels below are painted dull red, with a vine and flower

repeat design in each. On the n. wall of the chancel, in incredibly convoluted Latin, the epitaph of Joseph Forby, last rector of St Michael's and last vicar of St Martin's before it became a consolidated living. His great nephew Robert Forby was rector for a quarter of a century until 1825, and is remembered now as the author of 'The Vocabulary of East Anglia' – the first systematic survey of our dialect. As you leave, note the shaft and base of a *preaching cross* to the s. of the church – it is another relic of St Michael's and was moved here in 1905.

Fishley, St Mary (J4): This little church is so closely guarded by a thick grove of pines, oaks, and limes, that were it not for the tower one would take it for a copse in the middle of open fields. Less than a mile from the w. outskirts of Acle, its isolation seems absolute. Even after the narrow byroad, there is a long path between high hedges before one reaches the churchyard, and from the e. end the open country drops away to the marshes and the river. The round *Norman* tower has a later top of narrow red bricks with early-C14 bell openings. The s. door is also simple Norman work with a *billet* frieze, but drastically re-cut in the 1861 restoration. Everything was rebuilt then and calls for little comment. There is a pretty little C18 chamber organ at the w. end.

Flitcham, St Mary (D3): It is said that this is where St *Felix* built a church in the C7, and the core of the present building is undoubtedly *Norman*. The massive tower has C14 bell openings, but below them is a band of large Norman blank *arcades* in *carstone*. This was a *crossing tower*, but the *chancel* has disappeared except for the raised mound of its foundations, and only the ruins of a late-C13 *transept* survive to indicate the original *cruciform* shape. The *nave* has traces of two Norman windows but all the existing windows are C19 and early-C20 renewals. The C14 s. *porch* originally had a *groined* ceiling and the worn *corbel* heads are still to be seen in the corners. It is a plain interior, with a panelled barrel roof and a *clerestory* on the s. side only, over the C15 *arcade*. The base of the tower now serves as a chancel and the plain arch to the nave has been restored. There is a deep *lancet* to the n. and the outline of a Norman *transeptal* arch to the s. In the nave, a *brass* inscription for Edward Runthwite who died in 1614 aged 82 – a long way from his native Yorkshire.

Flordon, St Michael (H6): Like most of the village, the church is perched comfortably on the side of a hill and a path climbs up through a little avenue of limes to the s. *porch*. Its round tower fell down in 1774, but tucked in by the eve of the porch there is a double splay *Saxon* window and another on the n. side that confirms a pre-Conquest foundation. There are C13 *lancets* in the *nave*, and the *chancel* windows have pretty *Decorated* tracery. For a small church, the porch has a generous width and the pale pink brick floor set *herring-bone* fashion is most attractive. The C13 doorway is set within the outline of an *arcade* arch – one of a number in the nave walls that suggest that the church once had *aisles*; so the s. door must have been re-set quite early on. By the rudimentary chancel arch is a substantial staircase in the n. wall, complete with little window, that led to the *rood loft*. The present *rood* has remarkably small figures – only 12in. tall. Above the arch, a dark set of Hanoverian *Royal Arms* in a curly gilt frame. The pulpit is late-C16 but has the look of having been cut down and put on a fresh base. One of the sides has four panels decorated with shallow chip carving and all has been given a coat of shiny varnish over very dark stain. The lectern and reading desk match it, and have initials and the date 1575 (both bases look younger than this). The tracery at the head of the e. window has managed to retain its original C14 glass with canopy designs in each *light*, and in the centre there is a C17 St *Peter* wielding a large key.

Fordham, St Mary (C6): A small and humble building mainly of *carstone*, by the roadside in this little by-passed hamlet. The *chancel* dates from the late C13 but now has no e. window and the side windows are renewed. There was a tower once but all trace has now gone and the *nave* collapsed in about 1730. It was rebuilt in *Decorated* style and there must have been a s. *aisle* originally because you will see the outline of the *arcade* from the outside. One of the n. nave windows is larger than the rest, with *ogee* shapes in the tracery and appears to have been undisturbed. Most of the old *headstops* survive outside too. A plain and simple interior, with Decorated chancel arch offset. The chancel has been plastered out and given a coved ceiling but on the n. wall there is a very faint outline of an ogee canopy which possibly covered a tomb or *Easter Sepulchre*. The simple *arch-braced roof* has *tie-beams* and there is a plain octagonal C14 font on an equally plain shaft. No surprises here save that this tiny church has survived tenaciously.

Forncett St Peter, St Peter (H6): Altogether a picture postcard church, rich in character and its *Saxon* tower alone is worth coming far to see. Complete right to the top, save for the battlements, it has two-*light* belfry openings with typical triangular shaped heads, supported on slabs and with a central shaft; slit windows at two levels; and round, deeply splayed ones at two further levels, eleven in all. The body of the church is *Perpendicular*, though the fabric is much older. In the walls of the *chancel* can be seen *herring-bone* work, which is typically Saxon. Curious, and very puzzling, on the s. side, is the outline of a large opening, long since filled in, set some six feet above the ground, with round, rough head of Saxon character. Much too big for a window of the period, illogical as a door – yet there it is: so what was its function? Beneath it is a small *priest's door*, which appears *Early English*. Entry to the church is by a lovely n. *porch*, which has a square hood over its outer arch, and in the *spandrels*, the keys of St *Peter* and crossed swords of St *Paul*; above, a long inscription which begins 'St Peter and St Paul, patrons of this place'; above again, a panel with the sacred monogram, *IHS*. Inside, the church has a fine C15 *arch-braced roof*, with 'embattled' *tie-beams*, and deep *wall posts* resting on 'embattled' *corbels*. The C14 three-bay *arcade* has deeply splayed, two-light *clerestory* windows above which have interlacing tracery, possibly contemporary with the roof. The w. wall retains its tall, slim Saxon arch to the tower, showing the massive thickness of the tower walls. Across the step between tower and *nave*, a *mensa slab* is placed, with at least two of its original five carved *consecration crosses* surviving. Below the step, *brasses* to Thomas Baxter, 1535 (left) and Richard Baxter, 1485, the latter's Latin inscription including the curious 'ignave vulneratus' – 'cowardly wounded' – was he murdered? Note close by the two pew-end bird carvings, including a splendid *pelican* in her piety. At the opposite end of the nave the two-sided pulpit is *Jacobean*, finely carved, was evidently assembled from something else. The C15 bench ends in the nave have exceptionally good figures on the elbows above squared columns. Look particularly for the huntsman with his falcon and the miser with his coin box. In 1857 *Thomas Jekyll* had the benches repaired and added some new ones with *poppyheads* in the centre aisle. In the s. e. corner of the s. *aisle*, set about 4ft. from the ground, is the doorway to the old *rood stair*, which emerges in the nave. In the sanctuary is a heavily carved *reredos* behind the altar, said to be part of the vanished *rood screen*. Also here, a tablet on the s. wall commemorates Anna Cookson, who died, aged eight, in 1804 – her cousin was William Wordsworth, the poet, whose equally celebrated sister Dorothy stayed here in Forncett for several years. In the n. aisle, under the e. window, is a charming and unusual C15 alabaster table tomb to Thomas & Elizabeth Drake, whose portraits are incised into the slab – he dressed in an ermine cape, she in a *kennel head-dress* and with lovely ruffed cuffs to her sleeves. The C15 font is very simple, octagonal and unadorned – except that underneath the bowl, modestly hidden away, are a couple of faces, *Tudor roses* and other floral decorations. By the n. door is a *holy water stoup*, with a fine flowing *trefoil* head, topped by a *crocket* flower. The church has a good ring of 6 bells, tenor 13-0-12 cwt.

Foulden, All Saints (D6): Very much a unified C13 and C14 building is the impression given, despite the intrusion of a later *Tudor* window in the *chancel*, as you view it from a distance. The tower collapsed in the C18: now a little *bell cote* on the w. gable must serve. Closer to, the detail of the church becomes yet more interesting. The C14 *Decorated* traceries in the *aisle* windows – flowing forms of confident vitality – are very good indeed. At the end of the s. aisle another fine window (*quatrefoil, trefoil* and *mouchette* patterns) was rudely eaten into to build a stair turret up to the *rood loft*. The Tudor imprint on what is in fact a Decorated chancel is almost complete, and great windows under flattened arches do look rather grand. In the s. aisle wall is a big, *cusped* tomb recess which could be that of the C14 founder of the church, Sir John de Crake. Excellent little s. *porch* – C13 outer arch and pillars with ring *capitals* and a C14 window with *reticulated* tracery in the e. wall. Inside, under a modern ugly timbered roof, are a vast chancel arch and tall, powerful C14 *arcades* of four bays. Plain C15 octagonal font on an attractively moulded and fluted stem. Some good C15 *poppyhead* benchends, with a variety of birds and beasts and grotesques carved in the elbows; C15 too the pulpit. Only the base of the ancient *screen* remains, though it still has its doors (not a common survival), on one of which two painted saints can be seen, one with a happy looking little bearded devil at his feet, the other with a crowned angel above his shoulder. On the other door the two figures there have been brutally defaced, though one is said to represent *Henry VI*. The *box pews* in the aisles are C18 Georgian. In the s.e.

corner of the n. aisle the little *Tudor* doorway to the *rood stair* still retains its original door. Immediately above, and on the corresponding arch opposite, see where the stonework was hacked away to slot in the *rood beam*, and in the capitals to each side the indentations where the loft itself was supported. In the base of the two pillars at this point, on the n. side, enormous slots were cut out to take what must have been a pretty hefty *parclose screen*. Plain timbered and attractive C15 *arch-braced roof* to the chancel; Decorated *piscina* under an *ogee* arch adjoining plain *dropped sill sedilia*; C17 carved panelling against the e. wall, and a sturdy mid-C17 altar table. The clergy desk appears to have re-used a couple of old poppyheads. On the n. wall, a pompous wall monument to Robert Longe, 1656, all classical columns, scrollery, shields and skulls in black and white marble.

Foulsham, The Holy Innocents (G3): The late-C15 tower is very handsome. It has *flushwork* around the door and in the *base course*, and the shields in the doorway *spandrels* have the arms of England and Lord Morely. The *sound-holes* have a honeycomb pattern of lozenges and the stepped battlements are a rich mixture of *cusped* panels and 'M's. To the n.w. of the tower is a table tomb with decorative panels and groups of crowned letters. They spell 'Robert Colles, Cecily his wife' – Foulsham people in 1500. Apart from the mainly Victorian e. window with its glass by Charles Gibbs and the roof, the *chancel* is C14 and this is the date of the lavish *sedilia* and *piscina*, although C19 restoration has overlaid them heavily. The *priest's door* is tucked away behind the chancel arch on the n. side and its position is curiously improbable. It lies at an angle within the corner formed by the chancel and the n. *aisle*, and the internal arch shows that this was intentional. There seems no reason why a conventional placing should not have been chosen further along the wall. The *nave* still retains three circular *piers* on the n. side from the earlier C13 building, but the most noticeable thing here is the plaster ceiling – it looks sadly out of place, and its incongruity is emphasised by its immensity. The village was devastated by fire in 1770 and this ceiling is the most permanent reminder. So much of the church was damaged by the fire that few of the original fittings remain, but one might assume that the font did – until the eye lights on an account written in 1846: 'The font consists of a circular marble basin placed on a modern stone pedestal'. The present one is a very good C19 reproduction of what one would have expected to find here. One of the survivors of the fire is a fine wall monument in the chancel to Sir Thomas Hunt (d.1616). He kneels in company with his three wives (he always married widows, it seems) under triple arches, his coloured coat of arms above: behind him, resting against the wall, is his sword – not in alabaster, but the real thing. A *brass* which also survived is by the lectern…a cautionary example of 'you can't take it with you':

> Of all I had this only now I have
> Nyne akers, wch unto ye poore I gave
> Richard Fenn who died March 6, 1565.

Foxley, St Thomas (G3): Some of the *quoins* and the coursed flintwork below the windows on the s. side point to an early original, but the present *chancel* dates from the late C13 and the tower followed about a century later. The late-C15 *porch* has a nice outer arch with a niche, a shield in one *spandrel* and a ragged staff in the other, a possible reference to the builder's heraldic badge. The inner door is older and may be C14. The plain C14 font has a pleasing C18 candle-snuffer cover topped by a gilded dove, and over it is a *Regency gallery*. The bench ends have *poppy-heads* of varying naive designs, with a mask on one and the initials 'R.W.' on another. There are plain C18 *box pews* at the front (there were some in the chancel with curtains in the C19), and a matching pulpit. It is a two-decker but the reading desk panelling looks earlier. Behind it there is a patch of colour on the wall with no discernable design, and it possibly marks the position of a *guild altar*. The late-C15 *screen* has an unusual and most interesting reminder of how parishes reacted to royal commands. The top was dutifully sawn off for Edward VI but was obviously not destroyed; the advent of Mary gave the village a chance to put it back – and so it remains, held on with iron straps. Presumably when Elizabeth came to the throne the *rood loft* had to go, but the doors survive with paintings of the *Four Latin Doctors – Jerome* holds an open missal with staves of music visible, and below there are fine portraits of the donors John Baymont and his wife.

Framingham Earl, St Andrew (I5): An unpretentious, pretty little church. The hand of restoration has marked it heavily, but still there is much of its ancient heritage to see. The slim round tower is *Norman*. Basically Norman too is the *nave* (notice its massive flint quoins at the w.

end), despite the appearances made by changes over the years – including the unfortunate 'faked Norman' windows. Earlier still is the *chancel*, its deeply splayed, small round windows to n. and s. pointing to *Anglo-Saxon* construction; the slim *lancet* windows here are C13 *Early English*. Norman again is the s. doorway – small and slim, but ornately and surprisingly delicately carved on arch and *capitals*; Norman too is the n. door, but of much simpler cut, complementing inside the plain but massive arch between tower and nave. The real surprise is the chancel arch – more solid Norman work, large-scale, enduring, and embellished with zig-zag and other carved ornamentation. To each side are later openings, now much altered, which serve as *squints*, to give a view of the high altar. There is a homely little w. end *gallery* for the organ, modern roofs and furnishings (except for the handsome *Jacobean* pulpit which came from Sotterley, in Suffolk); and in the chancel, the old *piscina* niche was given a rather good modern carved head, with an *ogee* arch and lots of *cusps* in 1925. In the nave n. window, notice the St *Catherine* in C15 glass – crowned, with her wheel and sword to hand, and set against a dark blue background contained in a gold medallion.

Freethorpe, All Saints (K5): This beautifully kept little church stands in a great churchyard, and the truncated round *Norman* tower has a conical tile roof topped by a jolly gilt weathercock. The two-bay *arcades* are C13 but C19 restoration has effectively confused most of the rest, so that dating is problematical. Except, that is, a big *Early English lancet* in the s. wall of the *chancel* which has shafts on either side of a deep interior splay, and outside, the hood has delicious little curlicue leaf stops. The plain octagonal font stands on a heavy shaft which is reeded to look rather like *linen-fold panelling*. A cadet branch of the Walpole family (see Wickmere) were Lords of the Manor here, and there are a number of tablets in the chancel, including that of Robert, grandson of the first Lord Walpole of Wolterton. In the C19 they built a little manorial pew opening off the chancel; it has its own cast iron corner fireplace and prominent chimney, and the family arms are emblazoned in the window.

Frenze, St Andrew (H7): A church that has to be sought out, but worth the effort. A by-road off the Diss-Scole road leads past a business centre to the drive of Frenze Hall, and after half a mile of fields and copses, one finds a farmyard with the Hall on one side and the church on the other. It is now in the care of the *Churches Conservation Trust*. There is no tower – merely a *bell cote* on the *nave* roof, and the ruined *chancel* was pulled down in the early C19, with the e. window re-set. The C15 *Tudor* brick *porch* is charming – an outer arch that is pinched at the foot, and a C13 priest's slab carved with a double omega in two separate pieces in the floor. Above the inner doorway are remains of niches. The interior is calm and simple. The C14 font on a high step has a reeded shaft and the bowl panels are like a window mason's pattern book – take your pick of 'Y', *reticulated*, or *lancet*. Beyond the few rows of chairs are two pieces of *Jacobean* furnishing in lovely untreated oak, faded to the palest cream. On the s. wall, an oblong pulpit with plain panels bearing split bobbin cylinders in the centres, with a range of shallow carving in panels under the rim; the *tester* has turned pendants at the angles and in the centre. Opposite, a family pew, obviously by the same man, but this time the carving in the panels is a little more elaborate, and there is a pretty range of little *balusters* around the top. During a restoration, the old stone *mensa* was found under the floor and brought back into use. Its slightly bowed and polished surface is incised with five roughly cut *consecration crosses*. Frenze escaped the wholesale destruction of *brasses* and has a fine collection. By the n. door is the effigy of Dame Joan Braham (d. 1519), a *vowess* shown wearing cloak over her gown and a girdle with long tassles. The Blennerhassets flourished in this place for centuries, and young Sir John Paston made fun of the name in a letter of 1473 – 'Raff Blaundrehasset wer a name to styrte an hare.' In front of the sanctuary s. side lies Jane (d.1521), wearing a *kennel head-dress*, with a long chain pendant from her embroidered girdle. By her side to the n. is John her husband (d.1510), with bobbed hair and in armour with his sword hung centrally. Half of Anne Duke's effigy remains in the n.e. corner of the sanctuary but her husband George's has gone. The earliest brass here is Ralph Blennerhasset's (d.1475), his mailed figure lying in front of the altar, and to the right there is Mary Bacon's (d.1587). Above, on the e. wall, Sir Thomas Blennerhasset (d.1531) is shown wearing a tabard that was enamelled originally. On the wall to the left of the altar is Thomas and Margaret Blennerhasset's brass and close by on the n. wall is an inscription for Thomasin Platers. Lastly, by the pulpit is a little *shroud brass* for

Frenze, St Andrew: pulpit

Thomas Hobson (d.c.1520). The *Royal Arms* of James I hang above the n. door.

Frettenham, St Swithin (I4): On its own, half a mile n. of the village. Apart from the 1869 *chancel*, the church is C14 throughout, with little *quatrefoil*, *clerestory* windows above graceful *arcades* which match the s. *porch* doorway. The C13 *Purbeck marble* font stands on a new base. In the *sedilia* wall are *brasses*. One figure, to Margaret Whyte (1435), and a label to Richard Woodes: 'Master of Artes who dyed Ano 1620 haveing continued a paynefull and profitable minister of God unto this Pish 48 yeares'. ('Paynefull' in C17 meant one who took pains in his vocation.) On the n. side of the chancel is another small figure brass to Alys Burnham (1430).

Fring, All Saints (D2): A church of delightful completeness in its unpretentious, early-C14 lines, it sits on a little hill high above an enormous farmyard. Very slim tower with a later, flat parapet in alternating red brick and flint; big, plain 'Y' traceried windows to the belfry; and a fascinating w. window with a diamond-shaped frame containing flower-like tracery in four big, balanced outlines – lovely. Every window in the body of the church, with one exception, is of a piece, two-*light*, *cusped* 'Y' traceries, of the very early C14. The e. window is a small modern replacement, set within the original big arch and *jambs*. Under the head of this arch, however, fragments remain to show that originally it was filled with *reticulated* tracery. Small *priest's door* on the *chancel* s. side, and to its left, a tiny, filled in, *low side window*. Inside the church one could well feel that time stopped here a hundred years ago, when the Victorians put the plain deal pews in the *nave* and cleared the chancel. Barnlike roofs, hanging oil lanterns, and two on iron brackets in the sanctuary. All the walls throughout the church are faintly tinged with the blush of ancient colour, creating a memorable atmosphere. There is a huge, faint St *Christopher* in a painted frame on the n. wall, and faint figures on each wall in the s.e. corner of the nave, all of about 1330. In this corner too is a tall niche with a fine, multi-cusped, *ogee* head. Immediately above, and on the opposite side of the C14 chancel arch, are the wooden stumps of the *rood loft* supports, and a stone *corbel*, presumably for the same purpose, in the e. *jamb* of the s.e. window. The entrance to the *rood stair* is behind the pulpit. In the sanctuary is a lovely *trefoil* headed *piscina* under an *ogee arch*, complete with stone *credence shelf*. Adjoining are unadorned *dropped sill sedilia* on two levels. The *communion rails*, barbarously varnished, appear to have incorporated bits of tracery from the old *rood screen*. The massively severe font bowl is C13, in *Purbeck marble*, with typical *blank arcading* round its eight sides. Nearby there is a scrubbed and worn *Stuart* table. Beyond, the lozenge window in the tower sits in a deep embrasure of the oddest shape, which catches the light and reflects it glowingly into the church – memorably so at sundown.

Fritton, St Catherine (I6): A grassy track leads off the road up to a big churchyard where there seems always to be either jays or pheasant or both. Despite its C15 octagonal top, the round tower is *Norman* and has a tall plain arch to the nave. The blocked n. door-way is also Norman, but the one by which you enter is C14 and has worn male and female *headstops*. On the door itself, look at the centre rail – it has the initials of the churchwardens of 1619 carved on it. The C15 font belongs to the local group which all have lions round the shaft and angels alternating with lions in the bowl panels. But the variant here is that the shaft is square, and what is more, everybody smiles – all the angels, all the lions. In fact, the ones round the shaft positively laugh! Above, on the n. wall, a faded and flaking St *Christopher* is hardly recognisable – a great pity

because one can pick out the last traces of an inscription at the bottom which said once that John Alward gave the painting and was buried in the *porch* in 1506. Further along the n. wall, a big St *George* and the Dragon has been over-restored, but at least the whole of the legend can be seen and understood now. There is a *consecration cross* near the *rood stairs*, and above that is the partial figure of a bishop in a low C13 mitre – it could be Archbishop Rich (later canonised as St *Edmund Rich*). A C19 restoration programme changed many of the windows, but the *lancets* are probably as they always were. You will see that there is a *low side window* incorporated in the pair on the n. side of the chancel. For once, a chance to see what the old *rood screens* and lofts looked like, because Fritton has a new *rood* and a proper loft, fitted in the early 1900s, so that the stairs in the wall lead somewhere – as they were intended to. All that it lacks in comparison with the original is colour, but the early-C16 base shows how rich and brilliant the whole must have been. The heavily *cusped* tracery has gilt and multicoloured decoration, carvings of St George and the Dragon, and a pair of unicorns in the *spandrels* by the chancel entrance. The donor John Bacon and his wife have excellent portraits in the two left hand panels, she with three daughters, he with eleven sons. Next come the *Four Latin Doctors*. On the s. side, St *Simon* with a fish and St *Jude* with a boat. As you go back down the path, look for the consecration crosses on the *jamb* of the priest's door, still visible after 600 years.

Fritton, St Edmund (K5): Nowadays many people come to Fritton to enjoy the delights of the Country Park established round the long lake in its beautiful setting. That they can also call in to see the church is an advantage not to be missed for this is one of the most fascinating that the county has to offer. Until 1974 it lay within Suffolk's boundary but now Norfolk has within a few miles a trinity of churches with the rare *Norman apsidal* e. end surviving. Like Hales and Heckingham, Fritton is thatched, with a round tower that has courses of Roman tiles at its base. Walk round the outside first to see the C11 flat buttresses on the *apse*, and the little trapdoor under the eaves on the s. side of the *chancel* that tradition calls the Smugglers' Loft – brandy for the parson and baccy for the squire. The inside of the church is an object lesson in survival. Against all the odds, the tiny Norman chancel is intact in its essentials – the *vaulted roof*, the sanctuary arch and the tiny *lancet* windows.

The e. window surround is original with single flanking columns, decorated *capitals* and a zig zag arch, framing a little portrait of St *Edmund* and his wolf in bright stained glass of about 1875. The two other lancets have replica arches to match, and the two side windows under wide timber lintels were cut through walls and vaulting in the C15. The glass in the n. lancets, with its pleasant range of delicate colours, was fiited in the early years of the C20 and has affinities with J.C. Buckley's work at Burgh Castle. In 1967 came the revelation that under the whitewash of 400 years lay a painting of the martyrdom of the patron saint. Centrally, St *Edmund* wears a crown, the arrows have pierced his body, and on the left his faithful servant who found the body after the wolf below had appeared with the head in his jaws. To right and left are the Danish bowmen loosing their arrows to complete the scene. Round this theme are four other subjects: two upper panels representing, on the left, Mother Church – crowned and holding the pastoral staff and chalice; on the right, Pagan religion – her crown falling off, her staff broken and her pitcher draining away. Two more figures (possibly the donor on the left and St *Peter* on the right) fill the bottom corner panels. Expert opinion believes that these paintings are more or less contemporary with the C12 apse, and are thus among the earliest figure paintings to be found in any church. This beautifully intimate chancel also has a C13 *pillar piscina* and a lovely little set of C16 choir stalls – very plain with nobbly flowers, the wide oak plank tops having worn so smooth that the grain of the wood stands up like ripples on a drying beach. When the *nave* was widened in the C14 it had its own scheme of decoration and a lot has been uncovered. A big St *Christopher* faces you as you enter. The Christ child has a halo and raises his right hand in blessing; the saint wears a green tunic and although his staff doesn't sprout leaves as in some other examples, it forks at the bottom. As usual, fish sport around and there is a pretty vine trail border in red and green. There was probably an altar dedicated to St *John* where the pulpit now is (making use of the extra width provided by the rebuilding) because a painting of the saint has been uncovered in the e. *jamb* of the nearby window. The whole wall surface must have had scroll painting like the fragments to be seen in the n.e. and s.e. corners, and the vivid lozenge/band decoration of the chancel arch was designed to match. The screen has no doors but it must have come from the same workshop

as the one at neighbouring Belton – the same turned columns, with roundels springing from them, all under a flat cornice. Over the arch is a fine and large set of George II *Royal Arms* on wood and dated 1749 (though you need binoculars to check that!) In place of the pre-*Reformation* altar stands a plain mid-C17 *three-decker pulpit*, with *parish clerk's* desk and reading pew side by side, leading along to the pulpit, angled slightly in the s.e. corner of the nave. Fat little *finials* at the corners of each frame fit the hand snugly and are its only embellishment. The Victorians ordered a font suitable for a Norman church and may themselves have been faintly surprised at the result.

Fundenhall, St Nicholas (H6): This sturdy building comprises *nave*, central tower and *chancel*, and a widely spaced screen of Scots pine sets it off very well. When it was restored in 1869 all the windows were re-done except the two small *lancets* in the base of the *Norman* tower. The s. doorway is Norman and has single shafts with simple *capitals*. The C13 n. doorway is only 3ft. wide and has a good arch with fine mouldings. The interior is a little barren, giving the impression that it is rather a struggle against the odds. There are settlement cracks in the Norman w. arch of the tower, and a vista through to a glum Victorian gothic stone *reredos* of the commandments, creed and Lord's Prayer. The work of 1869 cleared away the massive *rood screen*, but a remnant has been put back and whereas bottom panels are the most usual survivors, here it is the underside of the loft. It is complete from wall to wall and there are shadows of painting in the panels. Those over the wide centre arch were coats of arms. If by some remote chance you favour the pulpit, a framed drawing tells you that it was designed by the architect R.M. Phipson in 1869.

Garboldisham, St John the Baptist (G7): A quiet village since the busy main road was moved away. And comfortably within it, this good-looking church with its handsome *Perpendicular* tower. A pity, as you approach it from the lower end of the village, that the *chancel* should have quite so dull and lifeless an e. window, with replacement tracery (1887) of *quatrefoils* and *trefoils*. The tower rising beyond, however, is excellent – a piece of C15 elegance of line and style. The parapet is richly ornamented, with *crocketted* pinnacles at the corners; a carved angel standing at the centre of each side of the embattled parapet; the parapets themselves lushly embellished with *flushwork* panels, the *IHS* and crowned initials of saints. The angle buttresses are decorated in like manner, including wheel motifs and panels of diamond-studded flushwork; and a good panelled *base course* with roundels, flowers and shields – one of the latter with scratched graffiti giving one 'James Taylor, 1787' a minor line in history's margin. Somewhat more evident a place is given William Pece, who gave the *porch* in about 1500 – it is on the n. side now, but was originally a *galilee porch* on the w. face of the tower, where you can see its old outline, before being moved brick by brick. It has a handsome outer arch, with floral motifs and angels with shields carved round its moulding; finely canopied figure niches to each side and good flushwork. But what distinguishes it are its enormous stone-carved inscriptions, with letters nigh-on a foot high. That above the arch commemorates 'Galielmi Pece cappell' – William Pece, chaplain here. All round the base of the porch is an invocation in Latin to Christ, *John the Baptist, Zacharias* and *Elizabeth* and *John the Divine*. Inside, the porch has its original *arch-braced roof*, with well-carved *wall plates*. The n. and s. aisles are C14 *Decorated*, the windows having good *cusped* and intersecting tracery of the period; Perpendicular *clerestory*, with four pretty two-*light*, square-topped windows each side, and the remains of a *sanctus bell turret* on the e. gable. The chancel is largely Victorian. The interior of the church has an air of richness about it, being both architecturally imposing, and glowing with the colours of a gilded modern *rood*, abundant stained glass by *Powell & Sons*, beautifully vested high and side altars. Good *arch-braced* and *tie-beamed* roof to the *nave*; soaringly tall tower arch with a tiny quatrefoil *sanctus bell open*ing high above it; fine four-bay *arcade* of about 1300, two pillars being round, the rest octagonal. Mostly modern furnishings, but with some old *poppy-heads* re-used in the aisles; and at the w. end, a nice *Jacobean* chest and a sweet little churchwarden's desk, shaped like an old-fashioned child's school desk, but built to take a man of substance. Late-C13 octagonal font bowl, completely plain on a modern stem. Over the s. door, a good set of *Royal Arms* for Queen Anne, carved in wood. Big plain *piscina* in corner of s. aisle. Opposite, in n. aisle, the well-preserved entrance to the old *rood stair*. The base of an ancient *screen* has been placed here, with excellent Victorian upper section, made by a village craftsman. The base, of about 1500, is said to have come from the now-ruinous neighbouring church of All Saints. It has four

painted panels, much defaced and faded, but still showing workmanship of high quality, both in the one remaining set of tracery, and in the painted figures: St *Germanus*, seen as a bishop carrying a crozier; *William of York*, as a bishop but carrying a processional cross; *Mary Magdalene*; and *Agnes*. Just behind the screen, another piscina, with a crisply cut trefoil arch; it was moved to its present position during Victorian restorations, but originally served the n. aisle chapel of the Bois family, further along where the organ now stands. Across the chancel arch is the C15 base of this church's own original screen, with no colour and only basic tracery carvings. It was put back in its old place after the last war, having been removed and forgotten for an unknown number of years – being at last retrieved from the Rectory piggeries! The chancel retains an enormous and rather fine late-C13 *double piscina*, under one big arch with a mass of *cusping*. Dropped sill *sedilia* adjoin it. The church has a good ring of 6 bells, tenor 11-1-21 cwt.

Garveston, St Margaret (G5): A handsome C14 *Perpendicular* tower, the battlements ornamented with *flushwork* and shields; big belfry windows with boldly *cusped* tracery; *sound-holes* on three sides, that on the s. having pretty *quatrefoil* tracery – and the general effect is splendid as you approach up the hill from the direction of Hardingham. The body of the church is largely *Decorated*, though the s. *aisle* and *nave* windows are all Perpendicular / *Tudor*. The *chancel* window tracery (excepting the big replacement Perpendicular-styled e. window) is Decorated, with early 'Y' tracery seen on the n. side. There appears to have been a nave e. window over the *chancel* arch before the chancel was raised to its present height. After collecting the foot-long key from the Post Office abutting the churchyard, you enter to find a plain and unadorned interior. Look to the e. and see how the chancel *weeps* to the s. The four-bay *arcade* with its octagonal pillars, between nave and s. aisle, is early-C14 Decorated, as is the chancel arch with its slim rounded 'shaft' pillars. The s. aisle has shallow 'blind' wall arches over the s. side and w. end windows, and over the s. door – a decorative feature presumably, and not indicating further, now vanished, buildings beyond. The simple font, with blank shields carved round its octagonal bowl, is C16. In the chancel, the *piscina* by the altar has had its headstone replaced by a ponderous piece of moulded masonry. Beside it *dropped sill sedilia* remain, though the window above has long since been blocked. The church has a good ring of 6 bells, tenor 10-2-0 cwt.

Gateley, St Helen (F3): An unpretentious church, mainly C15, but the doors are of about 1300 and the *chancel* was entirely rebuilt in 1866. The tower has buttresses to the w. and *Perpendicular* bell openings. On the s.w. buttress of the *nave* there are the arms of Thorpe quartering Baynard and Northwood, and the buttress itself half covers the outline of an earlier door in *carstone*. Through the *Tudor porch* to an interior with some surprises. The monument by *Robert Page* to Mrs Elizabeth Segrave is nowhere to be seen, but the inscription slab stands in the n. w. corner and says that, 'she was a Person of good understanding and Just Principle but in Conjugal Life not so happy as Deserving'; one wonders whether Mr Segrave or his wife composed that careful distinction. On the n. wall, a *consecration cross* and beyond, Robert Sharbrook (1803) has a large heart-shaped memorial held aloft by three cherubs. Some of the front benches have traceried backs, and although most of the figures on the bench ends are mutilated, there are two fine monsters on the s. side. The C15 *screen* is excellent, with a lot of original colour; it has lost its vaulting but the painted panels are in reasonable state, albeit decayed at the bottom in places. There are four figures each side; from left to right: St *Audrey*, St *Elizabeth*, the Blessed Virgin, St *Puella Ridebourne* (the only known painting of her), St *Louis*, *Henry VI*, St *Augustine*, and *Sir John Schorne* holding a little boot with the devil peeping out. The chancel retains its solid set of late-C17 *communion rails*, and on the s. wall of the nave, there is a most interesting set of Charles I *Royal Arms* in pale colours, painted on board. The frame is inscribed 'Custos utruisque tabulae' which Stanley Wearing translated as 'Guardian of each table of the law' and believed that it was evidence that arms and commandment boards were set up together.

Gayton, St Nicholas (D4): A building mainly of the C14, with a very leggy tower. The buttresses reach only to 12ft, and above the *quatrefoil sound-holes* there are two ranges of bell openings, the first with 'Y' tracery and then a further stage with *Decorated* tracery; the battlements have the *Symbols of the Evangelists* at the corners and the whole is crowned by a vaulted dome. The *clerestory* has alternating circular and two-*light* windows, and the *aisles* and chancel windows have variations on the 'Y'

theme – all, that is, except the 1850s e. window with glass by George Hedgeland, whose great window dominates the w. end of Norwich Cathedral. There was a vestry to the n. of the chancel (see the foundation mound and the blocked door) and there is an *Early English priest's door* on the s. side. Although the n. door is now the main entrance there is a *porch* on the s. side, with a sundial over the depressed outer arch and an Early English doorway within. The *nave* roof has been altered twice – outside there is the line of a steep gable on the tower and a blocked *sanctus window*, and inside you will see the line of an earlier roof that was much lower. The tall C14 *arcades* have octagonal *piers* and there are plain boarded ceilings to the aisles, with a C19 nave roof. Note that neither the chancel arch nor the tower arch of the earlier church are quite in line with the later rebuilding of the nave and aisles. The C14 font has a deep bowl with quatrefoils, standing on a short panelled shaft, and there is a simple *trefoil piscina* in the s. aisle chapel. The chancel piscina and *sedilia* are grouped under a square label, and the door to the old vestry has thick rosettes as stops for the *hood mould*. Epitaphs fascinate many of us, and here are two with an agreeable contrast: on the s. wall of the chancel we find that the Rev. Ligonier Tredway 'was suddenly summoned to appear

Gateley, St Helen:
rood screen panel of St Puella Ridebourne

before his Judge' in 1830, while on a ledger slab before the chancel step there is a Latin elegy to William Tyler who died in 1657. It translates:

This tomb is index of his dear dust, of his death, of the man; not of his soul, life history, virtue; those the stone, and marble page, these heavens and the book of life declare. The rest is grievous and should not be told, whether you would take warning or find fault; for he lived well, superior to description or detraction. His wife Mary placed this here.

Gayton Thorpe, St Mary (D4): A little church in a very pretty situation, perched on a mound just off the by-road. The pre-Conquest tower is oval rather than round, there are two *lancets* to the w. (the upper one with a very deep splay), and large boulders are embedded in the lower walls. The C12 top has two-*light Norman* bell openings, columns each side and a sturdy one in the middle, with zig-zag in the arches and down the sides. The e. window has intersected tracery and the other windows there have 'Y' tracery and so the *chancel* probably dates from about 1300. There are *Perpendicular nave* windows under very long labels and the entrance doorway within the diminutive *porch* is *Early English*. The interior is plain, with pitchpine pews, pulpit and stalls. The C15 *hammer-beam* and *arch-braced roof* must have started to spread at some stage because *tie-beams* have been inserted under the hammers. Most of the fonts in this area are rather plain but this one has the *Seven Sacraments* illustrated in the bowl panels, and there are thick, rounded ribs running down the stem. The design differs from others in the county by having the eighth panel carved with a crowned Virgin and Child. All the detail is very mutilated, but clockwise from the e. the sequence is: extreme unction, ordination, matrimony, confirmation, confession, mass and baptism. The chancel arch has a pair of small late-C13 *headstops* and note that it was morticed both for the *rood screen* and for a *tympanum* to fill the space above. In the chancel is a simple *piscina*, and the *dropped sill sedilia* are separated by armrests. On the s. wall of the chancel, a chaste, well designed tablet with an urn on the *pediment*, in grey, tan and white marble, it is for Martin Coulcher (1818) who was both rector and Master of the Grammar School at Lynn.

Gaywood, St Faith (C3): Close by one of the busy roads into King's Lynn, but well back in a pleasant churchyard. After many vicissitudes this brick church was rebuilt and enlarged – *chancel* in 1909, *nave* in 1926, and the work was well done. Walking round, one can recognise many features of its predecessors that have been incorporated; the outer arch of the *porch* is *Norman*, with zig-zag decoration, the *transepts* have 'Y' tracery windows although much of the fabric there is C17, and the new chancel retained the C14 e. window. The handsome brick tower is basically C14, with *cusped* 'Y' tracery in the bell openings, and narrow slits for *sound-holes*. The interior, neat as a pin, has some very good things. Firstly, the octagonal font by the tall brick tower arch; it is heavy and squat with a panelled shaft, and has three C17 Latin inscriptions from the New Testament, together with one in English on the s. side – 'I am thy God and the God of thy seede'. In the s. *aisle*, a pair of fascinating C17 painted panels; one shows Queen Elizabeth at Tilbury in 1588 after the defeat of the Armada, with a vignette of the battle in the background and the Queen at prayer above; the companion piece is inscribed, 'In memory of the Gunpowder Treason Plot', with the king at the top, his parliament in session, and below that, Guy Fawkes creeps in led by a devil with a flaming torch while guards search. These panels were given by the rector Thomas Hares who died in 1634, 'wearied and wasted in constant paines in the ministry' – as a *brass* on the chancel s. wall puts it. The modern joinery and carving in the church is excellent, particularly the choir stalls, the five-sided pulpit with its 2ft. figures, and the *reredos* Virgin and Child by Norman Hitch. The church has an excellent ring of 6 bells, tenor 12-0-16 cwt.

Geldeston, St Michael (J6): The church is on the main road away from the village and there is a handy car park so that you can avoid the perils of parking on the sharp bends. Big cedars frame the w. end very attractively and the churchyard has more than the average number of readable inscriptions. Look for George Holland's stone s. w. of the tower, with its finely cut lettering and 'The night is past, the Stars remain'. In 1864 the *chancel* was rebuilt, the n. *transept* added, and in 1886 the *Norman* round tower was re-faced and given a new top. The *Perpendicular* s. *porch* entrance has shields in the *spandrels* (emblems of the *Trinity* and the *Instruments of the Passion*), They are carved as though they hung from pegs but diagonally, and happily deny the force of gravity. There is a niche above with new pinnacles and worn *headstops* of a king and queen. The

C15 font has a slim square column set lozenge fashion on a base which is inscribed with the donors' names, the Garneys; tall smiling lions under a bowl which has two forms of the *Tudor rose* and a variety of shields. The s. wall of the *nave* was apparently not much altered by the restorers and they uncovered the staircase to the old *rood loft*. Opposite, the n. transept has an elaborate double arch with a highly polished marble centre column. The chancel has a set of *corbels* and *capitals* that defy classification. They sprout and gambol unrestrainedly and in one (n. side, w. end), the serpent tries the fruit itself. The e. window glass is by Leonard Walker – a central Christ with multi-coloured swirls left and right against a background of tinted panes; of 1957, it is not his best work.

Gillingham, St Mary (K6): At one time Gillingham had four parishes and still has evidence of two. To the left of the Hall drive stands the tower of All Saints, open to the sky and mantled with ivy. The rest was knocked down in 1748 and used to make a new road near the church, but there were still burials around it as late as 1918. St Mary's to the right well illustrates the panache and self-confidence of Victorian churchmen – they inherited a church essentially *Norman* and employed Penrice of Lowestoft in the 1850s and 1860s to improve it in consistent style. The old *nave* was cut down to the size of a large *porch* with the doors re-set, and a new nave, *aisles* and *apse* built e. of what was a central tower. The tower was not altered a great deal and has slim columns set in the corners up to the belfry where two-*light* bell openings are contained in larger arches and flanked by blank *arcades*, providing a continuous scheme of ornament all round. The w. and n. doorways have a proportion of original material in them and it is likely that their designs were followed when they were re-used. Entry from the n. door is into a w. porch with plenty of space round the C19 font. Then comes the old tower – four deep arches with minimal decoration on the two e. and w., and two original *lancets*. Beyond, the Victorian version of no-expense-spared Norman, with everything hard, smooth and overdone. The *wall plate*, and braces of the roof with little perching angels, look as if they were saved from the old nave w. of the tower and used again, like the *sanctus bell turret* on the gable outside. The *chancel* step has a re-set *brass* inscription to John Everard and his wife (1553) and in the s. w. corner by the font is a big wall tablet to the lord of the manor Nicholas Bacon

(1666) – grey marble medallion with heavy mantling set between *Corinthian columns*. The three coats of arms are topped by the wild boar family crest. On the opposite wall there are two panels from the C15 *rood screen*, having against all the odds survived incorporation into the squire's pew and the wholesale rebuilding. The rail has an inscription for the Corder family as donors, and the panels show how varied medieval colour schemes were. The w. window is a memorial to a rector's widow and her daughter who were drowned on their way to Australia in 1895 and the figures of the Virgin and St *John* are by *Kempe*. Rector John Lewis's memorial is unremarkable but he apparently was not – a lifelong horseman who, when he could no longer stand in the pulpit, had his old saddle installed and preached from there. Did he ever use Psalm 68 as a text, 'magnify him that rideth upon the heavens, as it were upon an horse'?

Gimingham, All Saints (I2): A church which greatly rewards some time carefully spent here. Seen from n., it looks rather dull. Look from the s. and it's very different; a good *porch*, embellished, panelled and battlemented like a miniature abbey gateway. There are three grouped windows over the entrance arch, but as the central one has a 'foot' projecting underneath, it was probably a figure niche. To the right, elegant *Tudor* windows in the *nave*, finished off with rose-red brick toppings. Unusually, the nave buttresses are capped with slate. Inside the church, all is white and simple and beautifully cared for, the light streaming in through the clear glass. Small, *Decorated chancel* with agreeable tracery in e. window. A feature not to be missed is the s. windows – they have delicate, fragile *jamb-shafts*, with tiny, exquisite foliage *capitals*, framing the window splays. Date about 1300. At the n.w. corner of the nave, a later craftsman has used the same pattern – but his work lacks the airy lightness of the original. Prayer desk in chancel is made up of two old medieval bench ends with funny little animals carved on them. The font is *Perpendicular*. As you leave, note in w. face of the flint tower (with nicely contrasting *knapped* battlements) a defaced coat of arms set in a tiny, square-headed opening. Nice to muse fancifully that it might have been the arms of John of Gaunt, whose palace was just up the road from here and who would have been but recently dead (1399) when the tower was built. The church has an excellent ring of 5 bells, tenor 8-1-25.

Gissing, St Mary (H7): One of the best round towers, with very regular flint-work in bands, and three *Saxon* round windows halfway up. The little two-*light* w. window is *Norman*, with elementary zigzag surround, and Norman too the bell openings which have centre shafts and simply carved *capitals*. Both doorways into the church are Norman, and the one on the s. is the more elaborate, possibly indicating that it was then the principal entrance. The double *chevron* and *billet* carving of its arch is topped by the menacing head of a beast wearing a bridle – it must have had some deep significance for the man who carved it. By the C15, the n. side was favoured, and the big two storey *porch* was put there. There are crowns and floral motifs in the moulding of the outer arch, rosettes in the *spandrels*, and wide canopied niches either side. The whole n. face is decorated with *flushwork*, and the upper room has a two-light window under a deep hood. Inside, the real surprise is that such a small church should boast a superb double *hammer-beam roof*. If possible, pick a bright sunny day for your visit, because the obscured glass in the *nave* windows cuts down the light, and the detail of the dark roof is difficult to see. This is a lovely construction – *tie-beams* link the top hammers, with *king posts* in the ridge, and there are angels at both levels bearing shields. The *wall posts* terminate in canopied niches carved in the solid wall, which have figures in them (note that four were cut through when the windows were altered later). The early-C15 font has a plain octagonal bowl, with half round columns at the angles, and a shaft in which there are deep empty niches under canopies. The *chancel* s. chapel was rebuilt in 1879 and houses the organ, although its simple double arch and octagonal *pier* is early-C13. The n. chapel probably matched it originally but that now has a single arch, and was altered to become the chapel of the Kemp family. Separated from the chancel by a *Jacobean* half *screen*, the chapel has a flat *arch-braced roof* with tracery in the diminutive *spandrels*. Interesting to see that the two easternmost rafters have been carved with floral motifs as a *canopy-of-honour* for the altar below. The Kemp memorials are nicely varied. In the n.e. corner, Robert (1612) 'sometime officer to K. Edward VI & Q. Mary in theire Custome house at London' – a black marble tablet within an alabaster arch, jolly armorials above and a swag of bursting pomegranates below. A helm, fragile with rust, hangs on a bracket close by. In the n. w. corner, is *Edward Stanton's* memorial to Sir Robert Kemp (1734)

– flamboyant and a bit fussy, in grey veined and white marble; two *putti* sit on the flat cornice, the tablet is flanked by *Corinthian* columns and framed in acanthus, and a small coat of arms below is almost overwhelmed by the mantling of the helm and the associated drapery. Of his two wives it says, 'Both these ladyes were very prudent and pious, few exceeded ye former, scarce any the Latter.' Make of that what you will! Below all this dazzle, a long *bier* with folding handles dated 1700 that speaks for the more mundane practicalities of death. On the s. wall of the sanctuary there is an omnibus memorial to four Kemps on a tablet by *Charles Regnart* – a big flat urn with drapery oozing over the plinth. The yards of tightly packed text includes a copy of the Westminster Abbey epitaph to Sir John Kemp: 'A Youth who to a graceful Person added such purity of Manners' plus an abundance of other virtues. Further w., a big tablet to Robert Kemp that is remarkable only for the cherub perched in acute discomfort on the very tip of the *pediment*.

Glandford, St Martin (G1): The original church was already in ruins by the early C18, and when Sir Alfred Jodrell of Bayfield Hall built the village he decided to provide a new church in memory of his mother Mrs Adela Jodrell who died in 1896. Between 1889 and 1896 the architects Hicks & Charlewood used material from the old building to create a medieval replica. It has a very convincing exterior, standing proudly as it does on the little hill above the village. Mrs Jodrell's monument is a white angel sculpted by Pietro Bazzani of Florence, of the type seen in quantity in Paris at the Père Lachaise or in Italy at the Cimitero of Staglieno. Inside the church the is a *Perpendicular*-style arcade with octagonal *piers* and double-chamfered arches, and the font is a copy in marble of Walsoken's *seven sacrament* example. The *chancel* is generously appointed with a *hammer-beam* roof, lavishly *traceried screens* and lots of fine panelling. There is glass by *Kempe* in the e. windows of chancel and the rest of the glass in the church is by Herbert Bryans who had been a pupil with *Clayton &* Bell but whose work was very much in Kempe's style. The pews, pulpit and roofs were the work of Walter Thompson and Franck McGinnity, and although the interior is faintly overpowering, the whole building is a perfect example of what C19 craftsmen could achieve in the tradition of their C15 predecessors.

Gooderstone, St George (D5): The tower appears to be *Norman* in foundation (see the slit window in the lower s. face) with *Decorated* additions – in particular, the lovely w. window with its tracery of flowing *mouchettes*. The *nave* and *clerestory* are *Perpendicular*, the nave n. side being something of a *Tudor* showpiece, with noble windows under 'basket' arches. The *chancel* is C13, with single *lancets* each side and a group of three at the e. end. The s. *aisle* is C14, with a superb e. window – whirling mouchettes so light and vital that they seem in motion. C14 s. *porch*, with linked *trefoils* in the tracery of the most unusual circular windows. What takes the eye almost before anything else inside the church is the superbly complete set of C15 benches, all with pierced backs carved in a variety of lively traceries, the seats themselves being roughly adzed timbers warmly smoothed by 500 years of use. There are *poppy-heads* on the ends, but sadly, every last one of the carved elbow rests has been sawn off. A very satisfying *arch-braced roof* and neat little C14 *arcade*, with chancel arch of the same date. Plain *Jacobean* two-decker pulpit and in the s. aisle, a most opulent *piscina/credence shelf* arrangement. The piscina sits on a little pillar set into the wall while above, a large niche is divided into four by a central *mullion* and solid *credence shelf*. The whole thing is under *cusped, ogee arches* and a triangular hood filled with deeply carved mouchettes. This richness is explained by the fact that this was the site of the pre-*Reformation* chapel of the local St George's *Guild*. Next to it, plain *dropped sill sedilia*. The *rood screen*, with traces of original colour, is something rather special and is one of the most remarkable in the country. It is very tall (16ft.), with beautiful and delicate mullions and tracery. But most notable is the rare survival of one complete carved bracket, and the stubs of several others, which were most probably used to support tiny statuettes, directly below the *rood loft*. In the lower part of the screen are well preserved and finely painted panels showing the Apostles with their emblems. Above each saint is a gorgeous half-figure of an angel, richly robed and gilded, and, barely decipherable now, the saints' names. They themselves carry labels with key words from the creed. left to right we have *Peter, Andrew, James the Great, John, Thomas, James the Less, Philip, Bartholomew, Simon, Jude, Matthew*. The last must be *Matthias*, although the set-square (?) he carries is puzzling. The screen doors carry paintings of the *Four Latin Doctors*, savagely defaced. The interior of the e. window presents a lovely *Early English* ensemble, each of the three lancets being defined by slim shafts with ring *capitals*. On the s. side, a beautiful C13 double piscina under

cusped and moulded heads. Forming a square hood over it is a raised freize moulding which continues right round the chancel, taking in the *priest's door* and the sill of the westernmost lancet on the s. side – probably a *low side window*, and an *aumbry*. As you leave, mark the ancient poorman's box at the w. end, roughly formed out of a solid chunk of wood.

Gorleston, St Andrew (L5): Standing high enough above the town to be a mark for seamen, a big church made bigger by a recent vestry and meeting room extension on the n. side. The origins of the present building are C13 – see the *lancet* windows in the lower stages of the tower, but when walking round the outside, the work of the 1872 restoration is the most obvious thing. That was when the *nave/chancel* and both *aisles* received their steep tiled roofs, and the completely renewed e. end has three gables side by side. The n. wall was rebuilt and so was the s. *porch*. The tower was extended upwards in the C15 and has tall, handsome bell openings with their *drip moulds* reaching well down in *Tudor* style. A bold staircase on the s. side reaches to the stepped and panelled battlements and the heavy diagonal buttresses run to the second stage. It was restored in the C20 as a memorial to the men of Gorleston who lost their lives at sea manning the town's lifeboats. The churchyard is well over three acres but was cleared of the old gravestones in 1800. The vicar of the day claimed the use of all those more than 35 years old, and they do say that one was sold to a baker who floored his oven with it. As a result some of his loaves bore the impress 'aged 75 years'. Well, it is a nice story isn't it! Inside, the church is wide and open. The eight-bay early-C14 *arcades* run through to the e. end, and there is a single foliage *capital* to be found at the e. end on the n. side. Nave and aisle roofs are *scissors-braced* pine, and the chancel has a panelled barrel roof fronted by a big wooden *trefoil* arch on stubby pillars (all 1870s work). With no *clerestory* this makes for a faintly lowering effect, but good flood-lighting and immaculate housekeeping stave off the encircling gloom. *William Dowsing*, that scourge of Suffolk churches in the early 1640s, wreaked havoc here as well. Armed with parliamentary authority, his journal records:

...we did deface the font... we took up 13 superstitious *brasses* and ordered Moses and his rod and Aaron with his mitre to be taken down and 19 pictures on the windows. The organ I broke and I gave orders to break in pieces the carved work which I have seen done...

Looking at the noble ruin of the *seven sacrament font* you can still see how beautiful it must have been, with figures in niches against the stem and the scenes in the bowl panels contained under deep *ogee arches* that were themselves decorated. By a remarkable chance, one of the brasses that Dowsing attacked has come back. Sir John Bacon was Lord of one of Gorleston's two manors in the late C13 and the family chapel was on the s. side of the church. His brass effigy disappeared for nearly 200 years and was rediscovered in a private collection in 1830. It was purchased and restored to the church – this time re-fixed to the original slab and set in the n. wall of the n. *aisle* at the e. end (one of the darker corners). This is no ordinary brass – it is one of only five in the whole country that have the figure cross-legged, and the armour belongs to that interesting period when chain mail was giving way to plate armour – note the little leather wings with crosses on them that project above the shoulders. The legs below the knee are missing and so is the wild boar family emblem at the foot, as well as the canopy, but it's well worth studying. When the n. aisle wall was rebuilt, the C14 *Easter Sepulchre* was reset – a rich *Decorated* ogee arch with heavy *crockets* climbing the rim to burst in a flourish at the top. Flanked by pinnacles it is boldly *cusped*, and it now serves as the entrance arch to the new suite of vestry, octagonal meeting room and youth club. From within the church the effect is not happy. There are good wrought iron gates set within the arch itself, but beyond them, a vestibule of emulsioned breeze blocks and plywood doors top-lit from a sky light betray a paucity of inspiration and lack of material quality that do less than justice to an imaginative idea. The n. chapel has a very good early-C14 *piscina* s. of the altar. Its five-leafed ogee arch is topped with a crocket and the hood *mould* has a delicate male and female head as stops. While here, note the low barrel topped C14 chest, and on the other side of the vestry entrance a fascinating C19 Table of Fees painted on a big board. Every contingency catered for – even the cost of a corpse dying *in* and carried *out* of the parish. Moving back down the n. aisle there is a group of good tablets on the wall, particularly the little one to Mary Custins (d.1817) by local masons Croskill & Logdon of Yarmouth. There are flat cupid heads in a scroll frame at the top, an open book with gilt edges set in a spray of foliage below,

and delicate pendants on the flanking *pilasters*. A pretty composition. The church has a ring of 8 bells, tenor 10-2-0 cwt.

Great Bircham, St Mary (D2): Because there is no *clerestory*, a building of this size has a curiously shuttered look, particularly when set in a large churchyard. The early-C14 tower is unusually placed at the w. end of the s. *aisle* and this provided an opportunity for the C15 builders to insert a grand w. window in the *nave*. At the other end of the building the equally large e. window dates from 1850 but it probably copies what was there before. The *chancel* itself is early-C14, as is the majority of the building but the n. *porch* is C15, and its square-headed windows are complemented within by *blank arcading* and a frieze of small shields. The early-C14 n. doorway with its double columns was part of the main building programme and inside, the graceful *arcade* with stone seats at the base of the slim clustered columns is the same age. Straight ahead, a C13 *Purbeck* font with the familiar blank arcading on its bowl; the pretty little cover is embellished with a gilded dove and was given in 1962. Beyond, the tower has a most interesting doorway – it is late-C12, and when it was re-used the masons changed the shape from semi-circular to pointed to match the current style. That it is there at all is a strong indication that a *Norman* church preceded this one. The C19 nave *box pews* with their odd *poppyheads* are from the same hand as those at Bircham Newton. The aisle e. windows have very pleasing *Decorated* tracery and in the s.e. corner is a small *piscina* with a five-leafed *ogee* arch and three image brackets close by. A substantial *rood loft stair* on the n. side of the chancel arch has an attractive doorway and the big C15 square-headed *screen* has a pattern of roses and fleur de lys on the panels, although most of the right hand side is masked by the stairs to the pulpit – C17 with crude cherub heads above blind arcaded panels; the base is renewed. Nearby, look for the pre-*Reformation mensa*, now laid in the floor – two of the five *consecration crosses* can still be seen. The chancel is wide, short, and full of light, with a blocked *priest's door* on the n. and an unpretentious, solid C14 piscina and *sedilia* to the s. The Clare family were patrons here in the C14 and their arms are featured in the top of the 'Y' tracery s. window. The communion table is a lovely piece, exaggeratedly Elizabethan with great bulbous 'melon' legs; a case of time-lag in the style because the top rail shows that it was given by 'G.Y.' in 1640. Behind it, a very effective modern 'Christ in Majesty'. In all, an interesting church, beautifully maintained. The church has a good ring of 5 bells, tenor 9-0-17 cwt.

Great Cressingham, St Michael (E5): A handsome church from any angle, but particularly so from the w. The C15 tower is well proportioned and the battlements and pinnacles added in 1898 complement the rest. Between the tall w. window and the door, a strong band of foiled circles carved with alternating shields and crowned 'M's. The latter reappear in the *base course* of the *porch*, together with the sword of St *Michael* outlined in *flushwork*. The *Perpendicular* e. window of the *chancel*, with its stepped, embattled *transoms* nearly fills the wall, and the corner buttresses rise to rugged late-C13 pinnacles. The chancel side windows have attractive tracery and are slightly later, and there is a blocked *low side window* on the s. side. Entry by the s. porch (the worn original figure in the niche overhead may have been the patron saint), to a spacious interior with C15 *arcades* and *clerestory*. The two easternmost pillars have image brackets and are possible sites for *guild altars*. The *nave* roof *hammer-beams* are carved as big horizontal figures and they alternate with *tie-beams*; below, demi-figures jut from the bases of the long *wall posts*. The plain font has a conical *Jacobean* cover with a line of decoration on the spines and a deeply carved classical *capital* under a ball on top. Nearby is a simple waggon chest and, high above the tall tower arch, a tiny *sanctus bell window*. There is C15 glass in the n. *aisle* window tracery. Note that the sill of the e. window in that aisle is dropped – a sign that it was planned to contain the *reredos* for an altar. To the right, the blocked door of the *rood loft stairs*. Go past the C19 pulpit and screen and see that it emerged on the e. side of the chancel arch, with a large head carved below the sill. The late-C13 chancel is most impressive, with a three-bay arcade of arches each side that reach the roof, resting on solid round shafts. Only the *responds* at the w. end of the nave give the clue that this style of arch was used originally throughout. Low stone seats line the chancel walls, and the *piscina* has a very pretty five-leafed arch. On the n. side, a pair of flat *cartouches* for Elizabeth and Sarah Lobb (1725, 1728). On a wall they would excite little comment, but here they are applied like shields to the arcade columns and look decidedly strange. There are a number of *brasses* to be found, and the earliest lies in front of the screen: Richard Rysle with Thomasine his wife (1497); he wears armour with his sword slung before him and she has a *kennel head-dress*. By the reading desk, the 3ft. figure of William Eyre (1509). This is a beautifully engraved example – note the *IHS* at his throat; most of the inscription remains, but not his wife's effigy. In front of the pulpit is the brass of John Abarfield (1518) who was rector here, and lastly, at the e. end of the n. aisle, only the lower half of twice married Elizabeth Fludd (1538) – one of life's, and death's little indignities.

Great Dunham, St Andrew (E4): There is a real element of surprise here in finding oneself suddenly in a *Saxon* church. Both central tower and *nave* of this fascinating little place are pre-Conquest (or just post-Conquest). The squat, powerful tower has massively splayed windows, those at belfry level being of two *lights* and supported on muscular, jutting *capitals*, each with a thrusting *abacus*. On w. and e. sides there are small round openings typical of the Saxon period. Notice here and all around the church that red Roman tiles have been freely used. Down the corners of the tower, and at the w. end of the nave, is *long and short work* which is clear example of its period. At the w. end too, equally typical, is a massive triangular headed doorway, now filled in. The window above it, in interlacing tracery, is an insertion of about 1300. Some decades earlier, and most interesting, is the window in the nave s. side: very early *Decorated*, with a pierced *quatrefoil* in solid *plate tracery*. Both chancel and *porch* are *Perpendicular*, the latter with a quite fine outer arch under a square label, and supported by slim attached columns with tiny embattled capitals. Through the C13 doorway into a high, supremely simple interior which remains staunchly Saxo-Norman despite its big Perpendicular windows. Round-headed *blind arcading* on both walls, with some carving remaining at *impost* level; big plain arch into tower, with carved imposts; and a chancel arch with imposts boldly carved in typical rope motif and a couple of plain bands above them. Serene chancel, with a lovely *piscina* – five-leaf head under a square hood, and birds beautifully carved in the *spandrels*. In the chancel floor, a *brass* inscription with coat-of-arms to 'Henry Bastard Gentleman: Lord of the Manor' who died 'aged 62 yeares II moneths' on 23rd August, 1624. The octagonal font is C14, its bowl very battered, but still recognisable are the *Evangelistic Symbols*, punctuated by shields.

Great Ellingham, St James (G6): A strikingly attractive church in outline, character and decoration. Almost all of C14 date, it has a decorative quality which especially draws the attention. The *clerestory* range of *nave* and *chancel* is boldly worked in large chequer-work squares of dark and light flints and the light squares are flecked with red brick. More of the same on the front of the *porch* (sunk at one corner and delightfully lopsided), and small chequerwork round the battlements of the tower, with its lead-covered wooden spire topped by a gleaming weathercock. The tower has large two-*light* belfry windows with *Decorated geometrical* tracery, with a later *Perpendicular* w. window with an embattled *transom* right across its three lights. Below the window, still more chequerwork. The windows in the chancel have gorgeous 'flowing' tracery, showing Decorated in its fresh-found confidence – note the e. window especially. A curious feature of the clerestory is that the westernmost windows are cut in half where they meet the tower; the work can hardly be earlier than the tower. On the n. side of the n. *aisle*, notice the tiny filled-in doorway with three varieties of floral motifs carved into its arch. The porch is lovely, with a *trefoil*-headed niche over the outer arch, neatly restored on one side with red slates, and containing a modern figure of St *James the Great*; a large recessed arch takes up the whole of the w. wall, with a *holy water stoup* at one side, and a pretty little window at centre with trefoil-*cusped* arches. And what pleasures await inside this church! The continuous C15 roof is *arch-braced* and *tie-beamed* over the nave, with replaced timbering over the chancel, done some 200 years ago. There being no chancel arch, a *screen* divided nave and chancel; only fragments remain, but the four panels show its most elaborate Perpendicular tracery. Note that the *rood stair* and its upper doorway are in the wall on the n. aisle – indicating that the screen stretched right across the church – as at Attleborough. Immediately below the *rood stair* is the door-way giving access to the chapel which was here before the *Reformation*, when two *chantries* and two *guilds* were established in this church. Still in the e. wall is a footing for a statue of the Virgin, to whom the chapel was dedicated. There are remnants of the *parclose screens* which enclosed it. Halfway down the n. aisle there is a chain fixed to the wall – possibly for a chained bible. Look to the w. at the charming little musicians' *gallery* on its stumpy columns – a happy memento from the C17. Below, a C14 font with shields in the panels and floral motifs under the bowl. The s. aisle chapel still has the traceried

and coloured bases of its original parclose screens; there is a tall *piscina* niche with a handsome arch; beside, a second piscina set into the side of *dropped sill sedilia*. In the window above, a fine 1920s St James complete with the little ship that took him to Compostella, though this one, contrary to the legend, has a sail. To the right, a large niche still showing traces of its former splendours of richly carved and *crocketted* canopy and glowing colours, with painted angels discernible in the corners. To the left of the adjoining window, note the faded outline of another angel; below and to the right, two *consecration crosses*, and by the s. door, a remnant of wall painting showing a turbaned figure with a staff, beside a *preaching cross*. This may be a detail from a scene showing pilgrims on their way to St James's shrine at Compostella. The chancel, illuminated by its great plain glass windows is surprisingly sparse. It has large dropped sill sedilia with an elaborately carved piscina drain set into the seat, a placement not seen anywhere else in Norfolk or Suffolk. At each end are stumps of columns showing that it was once arched and canopied. The *Jacobean* communion table stands upon the medieval *mensa slab*. On the n. side, a good *brass* to Anne Coniers, about 1500, showing her wearing a stylish head-dress and flowing gown. The church has a good ring of 6 bells, tenor 8-3-7 cwt.

Great Fransham, All Saints (E4): The church was badly damaged by a flying bomb during the war, but skilful work and the passage of time have smoothed the evidence away. The early-C14 tower has *quatrefoil sound-holes*, 'Y' tracery in the bell openings, a brick parapet, and an attractive little recessed spire sheathed in lead. Through the small n. *porch* and *Early English* doorway to the *nave*, where the pitchpine pews and pulpit do not have the usual coat of heavy varnish and look quite distinguished in consequence. The original font had been missing for many years but in the 1970s a C15 example from St *Etheldreda's*, Norwich was installed as a memorial; pointed quatrefoils in the bowl panels, with half-angels at the angles, and a panelled shaft. All trace of a former s. *aisle* had disappeared by 1800, except the *arcade*, and that still stands just within the restored s. wall – C13 round *piers* with later *Perpendicular* arches and bases. The n. nave windows are also Perpendicular with very long labels, but in the *chancel* there is just the gawky Victorian e. window. Below it on the n. side is a good early London *brass* that can be classed with the

Erpingham and Felbrigg examples. It commemorates Galfridus Fransham (1414) and his tall figure wears full armour and a lion crouches under his feet; above his head, a richly *cusped* and *crocketted ogee* canopy with slender pinnacles either side and two shields; most of the inscription set in the border of the stone survives. Beneath the tower arch lies another brass, a curiously attenuated figure in a shroud; inscription and scroll are missing but it is known to be John Legge's wife Cicely who died about 1495.

Great Hockham, The Holy Trinity (F6): Approached up its long lane, the church is set in an unspoiled parklike and wooded landscape. The tower has long since been replaced by an unfortunate *bell turret*, but otherwise a most interesting building, with some fine and varied window traceries to greet the eye. Not least the e. window of the tall *chancel*, with its elegant *reticulated* tracery of the first half of the C14, as too are the s.e. window of the s. *aisle* (unusual and lovely, with its multiple *cusps*) and the e. window of the s. aisle. There are earlier *lancet* outlines of the C13, though with later tracery – that on the s. side of the chancel having, below a heavy transom, a *low side window*, various other *Decorated* forms and both pointed and square headed *Perpendicular* examples: of the latter, that over the *priest's door* on the s. side of the chancel is characterised by delicate shafts on the *jambs* and down the centre mullion – a C13/C14 device on a C16 window. The *clerestory* too appears to be Perpendicular, though it could be earlier. The interior of this church is a real pleasure, a feast of details over which the visitor definitely should not hurry. Light and serene, it is a perfectly lit setting for the notable wall painting over the chancel arch, which has been dated at about 1450; at top centre, God with the emblems of the *Holy Trinity*; to left of arch, the *Blessed Virgin*; to right, the angel Gabriel, joined in a representation of the *Annunciation*. On the n. wall, in the aisle, are more fragments, dated about a century earlier: the subject of the easternmost one has not been identified, but that at the w. end is thought to show Herod receiving the head of *John the Baptist*. The fabric of the church is Decorated and earlier, the little three-arch *arcades* and the chancel arch being C13. In the s. aisle, in the angle of the two reticulated windows, is an impressive *angle piscina*, richly carved with cusps, flowers and *crockets*, abutting onto the *dropped sill sedilia*. Opposite, an *aumbry* recess, with its old latch-mark deep in the stone.

The *Royal Arms* of Victoria are on the s. wall; nearby is a simple C14 font, carved with outlines which mirror the window tracery which is such a feature here. In the *nave* are some good C16 *poppy-head* bench ends, some eccentrically carved – don't miss the mermaid with a mirror, a contortionist praying figure with the back of his head on his feet, two little bears clinging to a post and a couple of weird gnome-like figures similarly engaged. To either side of the chancel arch there is a *squint*, and the massive shape of the vanished *rood stair*. The modern pulpit incorporates ancient panels, a little seat inside and handsome brass candelabra on top. In the chancel, note that the e. window has delicate shafts down its jambs, and compare it with the decoration on the exterior of the window over the priest's door. The low side window on the s. side has one hinge bracket remaining on the left and on the right the latch-mark in the stone. There is a splendid and elaborate double piscina, with *trefoil* arches and crocketted pinnacles; it adjoins dropped sill sedilia on two levels, separated by a simple stone armrest (as at nearby Larling). On n. wall a monument – crowned with an urn and heroic fire and by two skulls, and supported by a gold-winged cherub – tells in Latin of Robert Baldock, killed in 1673, aged 18, in a naval battle against the Belgians, 'It is uncertain whether the Earth or the Sea has his body.'

Great Massingham, St Mary (D3): Beautiful position by one of the largest village greens in the county. The C15 tower is perfectly proportioned, topped by panelled battlements and *crocketted* pinnacles; the angle buttresses have two pairs of panels between each *set-off*, and the white flints are recessed within the stonework. The *chancel*, though restored, is essentially C13, with a typical wrap-round buttress at the s.e. corner; the e. window is probably original and has five *trefoil*-headed *lancets* under one arch. The church has a splendid s. *porch* (C13 but rebuilt by Penning in 1863) which has tall *arcades* each side of six arches arranged in groups of three, with slim pairs of pillars supporting the deep five-leafed mouldings. The outer arch is flanked by polygonal buttresses which rise to pinnacles and the inner C13 doorway has two ranges of *dog-tooth* in the arch; the door itself is medieval with remains of tracery at the edge. Within, C13 chancel arch and arcades, but see how the bases of the *piers* on the n. side were re-modelled later in *Perpendicular* style. The C15 tower arch is exceptionally tall, rising to the very roof, and there are big Perpendicular windows in the *clerestory*. Below them on the s. side, two ancient painted shields of arms – Despencer to the e., Warren to the w. Although the *nave* roof is a restoration, the early Perpendicular n. *aisle* has original *arched braces* with tracery in the *spandrels*. The C14 font is a big, solid octagon, with shallow arches under crocketted gables on each face of the bowl. An interesting range of C15 benches at the w. end, all with pierced and traceried backs; the ends have tracery, and although the *poppy-heads* have gone and most of the figures on the arms, on the s. side there is a dour cowled figure saying his rosary. The last bench on the n. side also has carved panels at the base, with a woman holding a dog by the tail as a centrepiece. In the chancel, the *ogee arch* of the *piscina* has the look of having been cut down to rest on the side shafts; next door, plain *sedilia* under five-leafed arches. Above, C15 glass in the top *lights* – the remains of an Apostles sequence that will have fitted neatly into the three side windows. All but one of the figures have lost their heads, but it is possible to name most by their symbols: from e. to w. they are: Saints *Peter* (?), *James the Less, Bartholomew, Matthias, Simon, Jude, Matthew*. Turning w., look high up to the n. of the chancel arch – stairs to the *rood* seldom had doors at the top but this one still has, even though the bottom access has disappeared. The church has a good ring of 4 bells, tenor 9-4-1 cwt.

Great Melton, All Saints (H5): Beside the ruined tower of St Mary's, once its 'sister church', stands All Saints itself in virtual collapse until it was restored, rebuilt and enlarged in the 1880s. So only the tower is original, its plain parapet nicely decorated with *flushwork* panels of flint alternating with stone shields set in roundels; neat two-*light* belfry openings; a bold five leaf *sound-hole* in the w. face, placed in a square frame with a square-moulded hood; and an attractive geometrically styled w. window. The interior is not of great interest. But there is a restored *holy water stoup* by the s. door; an enormous square-headed *piscina* in the sanctuary with angel-head *corbels* to its square hood, beside small *sedilia* framed by a rather lovely modern *ogee arch* and *hood mould*, with carved corbel heads at the ends and a big flowery *crocket* at the top. The *Early English lancet* window opposite is said to have come from St Mary's next door. As you leave, notice in the *porch* the two ancient coffin lids of very early date, carved with 'Celtic' crosses; and on either side, benches with time-ravaged medieval *poppy-head* ends.

Great Plumstead, St Mary (J5): In 1711 a new tower was build on the foundations of a medieval predecessor (although an inscription inside says it was 'restored'). It has clasping *pilasters*, arched bell openings, and battlements that are prettily faced with brick and flint in a chequer pattern. The *chancel* is all Victorian – there was a restoration in 1875, but the e. wall has a renewed *Perpendicular* window, and on each side of it, close to the corners, there are two blocked *lancets*. They point to an *Early English* predecessor to the existing chancel, and the C13 shafts to be found inside confirm this. The arrangement is reminiscent of Acle and one wonders whether there were three or five windows in the wall. The *nave* is C19 and is lit by three-*light* Perpendicular windows that match the e. window.

Great Ryburgh, St Andrew (F3): Undoubtedly a Saxo-Norman round tower (opinions differ), its construction materials include a deal of *carstone* blocks for the first 12ft. or so, often a *Saxon* component. It is worth noting too that the carstone extends around the n.w. corner of the *nave*, not in *long and short work* but in massive alternate slabs. The tower's attractive octagonal top is an early-C14 addition, with 'Y' traceried belfry windows and a neatly-finished flat parapet set with flints. The body of the church is largely *Perpendicular*, though from the mid-C14 come the lovely *reticulated* traceries to the n. and s. of the surprisingly long *transepts*. Before going into the church via the Victorian *porch*, take in also on the outside the ancient gable cross on the e. gable of the nave; and below the e. window a low arch – perhapes a tomb recess – which has been filled in with heavy chunks of carstone. Intriguing are the tiny filled-in, square headed windows in the e. gable of the nave, n. side, and just round the corner in the n. wall – probably inserted to light the *rood*. The interior of the church has a quiet dignity and beauty which is memorable. Below a high w. *gallery*, on which a little pipe organ stands, is a sturdy tower – plain round arch, *imposts* and *piers*. Around the modern font below the arch, the floor is laid with numerous C14 tiles. The *chancel* roof is *arch-braced*, plaster-panelled, white painted overall, with raised wreaths cast in the panels, winged angels against the *wall plates*; and high in the ridge, little embattled collars to the arches. All this dates from 1910, and is the work of *Sir Ninian Comper*, who thoroughly re-stored the church at that time and placed the tiles around the font, having collected them from around the church. On the chancel n. wall are the remnants of a grand stone tomb, with five nobly carved coats-of-arms above it, a massive stone coffin, and pieces from a second monument. The lower part is thought to be the tomb of Thomas Buttes, who died in 1592. It is his family's coat-of-arms which is seen on a panel above the w. door on the outside of the tower. The imposing *ledger slab* in the floor immediately below, with its huge coat-of-arms, is to members of the great Norfolk family of Bacon, the premier baronets of England – Sir Robert, 1655, and his wife Dame Anne, 1640. Further along on the n. wall is a tiny, plain arched *aumbry*; and opposite, a simple *piscina* and adjoining *dropped sill sedilia*. The chancel arch is C14 Decorated, but the arches of the n. and s. transepts are restorations. Interestingly, one can see above the *capitals* of the chancel arch where pieces of masonry have been let in to fill the holes left by the removal of the old *rood loft*. Below the s. transept arch is a handsome painted *screen*, erected to commemorate the fallen in the first world war. In the transept, one can appreciate the rich detail of the *reticulated* s. window, with its additional cusping within the main panels. The other windows here replacements. There is a C14 piscina, and under plain arches, an aumbry and a tomb recess. The church has a good ring of 6 bells, tenor 12-0-16 cwt.

Great Snoring, St Mary (F2): The general impression is of a rather fine, late-C15 *Perpendicular* building, with its tall, square tower (two storeys of which were once used as living accommodation by the priest, complete with fireplace and privy) and noble *nave* n. windows. But there is much more to this splendid church – the great e. window, with its confident *reticulated* tracery of the C13, and the elegant *priest's door* of the same date. Inside it is very fine and spacious. A plain, braced roof, the wood turned silvery with age. Attractive four-bay s. *arcade* on its round pillars, *Transitional* C13. A wide, C15 Perpendicular *chancel* arch, and below it a tall *screen*, of similar date, long ago hacked about and daubed with varnish, but with one panel uncovered to reveal the remains of a *Trinity*. Below the dominating chancel e. window is a most unusual frieze of carved heraldic shields (with modern colouring) of local families. Formerly behind the altar was the large C16 *decalogue board*, but now on wall of nave. To left of altar, remnants of a *brass* to Sir Ralph Shelton and wife, 1453 – he built the handsome *Tudor* rectory next door. Probably from there

came the C17 *communion rails*, sturdy and unpretentious. Very battered C14 *Decorated angle piscina* and graduated *sedilia*, carved with foliage, flowers and *crockets*. There is a fine alabaster memorial on n. wall, dated 1610 and with 1728-29 graffiti scraped on it. Across the chancel, a poignant memorial to a young priest in his prime, 1710, who, like his two brothers, fell 'to the same shaft from the quiver, namely smallpox'. Nice early-C14 angle piscina in s. *aisle*, and *dropped sill sedilia* alongside. Good selection of *poppy-heads* and benches in nave. C13 font in *Purbeck marble*. As you leave, note the *Royal Arms* of James II, dated 1688 – having been updated from James I just by changing the date – painted unusually onto the box-porch built around the door.

Great Walsingham, St Peter (F2): A beautiful church, with the singular advantage of being virtually all of one period, the late C14: the windows have a common theme of delicate, lace-like tracery. The *chancel* has gone, and so the e. end is rather abrupt. But within, attention focuses elsewhere – under an *arch-braced roof*, there is a complete set of C15 benches, despite wear, worming and mutilation; *linen-fold panelling* along the front row and the ends have a great variety of figures, animals and foliage. Some of the original wall panelling survives, and so do the floor sills, designed to keep in the straw for warming the parishioners' feet – a general habit which lingered on in some churches until the C18. In 1967 the *nave* benches were restored with the help of the Pilgrim Trust. That same body, in the spring of 1980, paid for restoring the 20 original *aisle* benches. Fittingly, the work was done by local craftsmen, successors to those local men who created the benches 500 years ago. The pulpit, on a new base and steps and crudely grained in brown paint, is dated 1613, but parts of it are earlier. Close by, in the aisle wall, is an *aumbry*, which still has its original door, hinges and locks – a rare and unusual survival. On the s. aisle wall is a *consecration cross*. In the nave aisle are two thoughtful inscriptions: Jane Golding (d.1632) is remembered as

> Sober, Meek, Patient, Modest, Constant
> Harted,
> Here soule remains in blysse, in peace
> departed.

Elizabeth Alee (d.1641) was surely happily married:

Great Witchingham, The Assumption of the Blessed Virgin: Mary Peterson's memorial, 1748

Heaven hath her soule, this earth her earth,
Her love her husband keeps,
The ods twixt him and her is breth,
Which gon all flesh thus sleeps.

By the font sleeps 'Joseph Wilson (d.1790) late of the Black Lion Little Walsingham', and one feels there should be faint odours of beer both strong and small.

Great Witchingham, The Assumption of the Blessed Virgin (H3): Beautiful setting in a large well kept churchyard. The big C14 tower has very sturdy buttresses, a *flushwork base course*, and two *ogee* headed niches flanking the w. window. The C15 *clerestory* has eight windows a side, or rather seven (note that the westernmost pair are flushwork dummies), and there is a pretty lozenge pattern in brick on the s. side but not the n. It is worth the stroll round the outside here, not only to appreciate the overall quality of the church, but for the little things of interest. On the outside w. wall of the *porch* is a rare thing – a gravestone with a portrait. Richard Sendall (d.1745) has his likeness carved in a roundel at the top, flanked by cherubs' heads, and at the bottom there is a skull in a half-roundel – a

feature that turns up on two other tablets on the e. wall of the s. *transept*. These, and the lettering on all the stones, show that they all came from the same mason's shop. On the e. wall, flanking the lovely late-C13 window, are two exceptionally good matching tablets – and again, a portrait! This time, the quality is higher, and the head, quarter turned and carved in deep relief is probably a good likeness of Mary Peterson (d.1748). Husband James (d.1772) and his second wife share the other memorial – but no likenesses this time. Two little stone *corbels* on the outside of the *chancel* n. wall once supported the roof of a *sacristy* (confirmed by a blocked doorway inside). The rich C15 porch has two flushwork friezes with crowned 'M's for Mary, and the arch *spandrels* have beautiful carvings of the *Annunciation*. On the left the Virgin kneels at a desk with her emblem of a lily in a vase, and faint traces of lettering can still be seen on the scroll behind her. On the right the archangel Gabriel has two sets of wings and holds a sceptre. The porch has a fine pair of Victorian wooden gates which repeat the 'M' theme in a band of pierced tracery. Inside, C14 *arcades* and a good *arch-braced roof* with *wall posts* resting on stone corbels carved with heads and angels bearing shields. A traceried cornice runs the whole length and the eastern bay is panelled, forming a *celure* for the *rood*. That and the loft have gone, 'pluked down' in 1561. The late-C15 *seven sacrament font* is a beautiful example and remarkable for the amount of colour that remains – more than on any other. The panels have alternating backgrounds of red and green, and the sequence is reversed in the corona below. The priest's stole in the baptism panel is red, and the service book in the server's hand still has some of its lettering. In the corona there are angels bearing scrolls with the names of the Evangelists and the *Four Latin Doctors* (anti-clockwise from the s.) *SS Gregory, Matthew, Augustine of Hippo, Luke, Jerome, Ambrose,* and *Mark*. The demi-figures of kings at the angles of the bowl have gilt crowns and ermine robes. The bowl panels are (anti-clockwise from s.) baptism, confirmation, penance (a red, horned devil leaves by the door), marriage, extreme unction, the *Assumption of the Virgin* (the figure backed by a glory of lovely coloured rays; very rare to find this subject on a font – the only other known example is at Bridgham in the s.w. of the county), mass (note the lighted candle and gilt chalice), ordination. The church has two chests – late-C16 Italian in the s. *aisle*, and a German leatherbound travelling trunk banded with iron, dated 1654 and with G.W. for the parish on the lid in the n. aisle. The Charles II *Royal Arms* over the s. door were given by Oliver le Neve at the *Restoration* in 1660.

Great Yarmouth, St Nicholas (L5): A phenomenon is this great town church. It is, to begin with, the largest parish church in England, with an area of more than 23,000 sq ft, including the widest *aisles* (wider than either *nave* in the kingdom too. Secondly, it may be said to have almost 'died' twice. By the C18 (having been dogmatically and brutally divided in the preceding century into three different places of worship by the Puritans) it was in a sorry state of repair. By the early 1800s, having been stripped of its finery, the situation was serious. Then a great restoration took place, and mighty St Nicholas again displayed its medieval majesty of proportions. Forward almost a century, to the night of 24th June 1942, and German incendiary bombs gutted the place from end to end, leaving standing only the walls – and the great central tower, built in 1101 by the church's *Norman* founder, Herbert de Losinga, Bishop of Norwich. On 8th May 1961 the totally restored church was rededicated. So what we see today is in effect a great rebuild and remodelling, reproducing much of the form of the original, but with the architect, Stephen Dykes-Bower, introducing a lot of his own neo-Gothic ideas. It is all vastly impressive in an impersonally grand sort of way, with its styles encompassing ranges of windows, pillars and arches, its boldly painted ceilings and majestic prospects. Yet the visitor may feel unmoved and untouched by the whole. Nevertheless, examine the font, with its curious and attractive Norman bowl on its C13 base, which came from the deserted village of Highway, Wiltshire; the beautiful Georgian pulpit, of 1715, which came from nearby St George's, which also provided the railing now enclosing the lectern; the pulpit's *tester* now provides a canopy to the font; the many coats-of-arms around the walls of the church, to which there is a guide on the w. wall of the s. aisle; the two tombs, richly rebuilt in 1959, set into the walls on either side of the church: that on the s. is said to be to Sir John Fastolf, who built Caister Castle: that on the opposite side, to an early-C14 Prior of the pre-*Reformation* monastery here. To the e. of the Fastolf tomb, a double *piscina* and an *aumbry* which would have served one of the 18 side-chapels which at one time existed here. In the *chancel*, specially note the *sedilia*, with

an unusual five seats. The St Andrew's Chapel is notable for its splendid modern wrought-iron work by a local craftsman; note also its triple sedilia, with a piscina under the same pattern of arches. In the south *transept*, the Colman window – a dazzling display by Brian Thomas, 1959-60, who also created the e. window. It shows Yarmouth harbour; steam drifters and their catch; full-rigged sailing craft; a Norfolk *wherry* and the Fisherman Apostles – *Peter* with his key, *Andrew* with his cross, *James* with his sword, *John* with his cup and dragon. In the tracery, Broadland birds, angels, the Arms of Norfolk and those of Yarmouth. The church has an excellent ring of 13 bells, tenor 30-2-4 cwt.

Gresham, All Saints (H2): Up on its hillside above the village, and set off by its trim, sturdy round flint tower, this is a charming place. The tower is *Norman* at the base, C13 above, with early-C14 bell openings in the simplest *Decorated* style. The top used to be octagonal, but was rebuilt in 1886-7 during an enthusiastic restoration. The two-storey *porch*, nicely *flint-knapped*, adds a touch of pretention to an otherwise simple little church. On the s.e. *jamb* of its stonework, the porch has traces of two *mass dials*. The *nave* windows are all *Perpendicular*, yet contrasted with the centre, square-headed window – those to left and right of it have a look of harking back to Decorated. *Chancel* is early-C14, with attractive flowing tracery in the e. window. Inside, a treasure awaits: one of the finest *seven sacrament fonts* in Norfolk, 500 years old and perfectly preserved. There's a jolly little pipe organ, dated 1893; and in the chancel a severely simple *piscina*, which had been plastered over and forgotten until it was discovered in the C19 by the rector. Note the Batt family memorials of military and civil loss. The blocked doorway in the n.e. corner of the nave formerly led to the *rood loft*.

Gressenhall, St Mary (F4): Set all alone amid rolling countryside, this is a big confident church on the *cruciform* plan – a central tower with *nave*, *chancel* and *transepts*. On first appearance it has the look of a rich *Perpendicular* building, but in fact it is *Norman* at its heart, as a closer look at the tower indicates, for on n. and s. sides are typical Norman double window openings, that on the s. with central mullion and carved *capital* beautifully preserved. The top of the tower is C15. Walk round and admire the church's splendid display of subtly varied Perpendicular windows; the jaunty gable end of the *porch* with a couple of very homely dogs (much ravaged by weather) perched atop the buttresses; and the fine *Decorated* w. window, with its excellent and unusual flowing tracery of big *mouchettes*. As you go in through the s. porch, notice the medieval door, massive in proportion and finely traceried, under its elegantly Decorated doorway. Inside, a light, spacious church with that unmistakeable air of care. The feeling of space is accentuated by the tall, clean-lined Decorated *arcade* of three bays and the later *clerestory* windows. Very striking is the old Norman double window in the w. face of the tower, carved with a bold zig-zag decoration, and with a slim central *mullion* and plain capital. The chancel – wonderfully light and lofty with its great windows – has notable late Perpendicular triple *sedilia* and *piscina*, all under a continuous hood, with variety of carving above the sedilia arches and down the *jambs* of its pillars, as well as in the canopies and on the back walls. Set into the window sill above is a small stone carving which, though mutilated, still clearly illustrates the stoning of St *Stephen*. Opposite, note the (filled in) doorway, its arch and shafts surprisingly richly carved with a crown and mitre, floral motifs and tiny shields. A *ledger-stone* in the chancel floor has this:

> Here resteth the Body of Robert Halcot of Gressenhall, Yemon, hooe departed this life the 2. daye of November Anno Dom 1640 Him have wee for a time lost who bilt this galerey att his oune cost.

Yeoman Robert presumably built a w. *gallery*, now gone. The Hastings Chapel in the early-C16 s. transept has a colourfully restored roof, all gilt and angels and *Tudor* roses; a charming little Tudor door to the tower; an ancient piscina; and incised into a stone floor slab, of about 1350, the figures of a knight and his lady whose unusual, original features of brass faces and hands have now been replaced. Nearby, a poor remnant of the old *rood screen*, with four brutally defaced panels showing SS *Leonard*, *Margaret*, *Anthony* and – just discernible – an angel treading down a dragon (*Michael?*). There is a Victorian *Royal Arms* and a big plain C14 font. The church has an excellent ring of 8 bells, tenor 9-2-13 cwt.

Grimston, St Botolph (D3): Caught within a bend of the village street, this church stands well and has a mini-avenue of limes leading to the s. *porch*. The C15 tower has big three-*light*

bell openings and deep panelled battlements with corner pinnacles; it looks best from the n. and w. – the s. side has an uncompromising square stair turret that goes all the way up. The s. *aisle* dates from about 1230, and the *transepts* and *chancel* followed some hundred years later. The *Decorated* tracery in the windows at this end is varied and good, and the Victorian replacement e. window harmonises well. In walking round, do not be misled by the stone in the C19 n. vestry wall dated 1631 – that refers to the little school room that was there before. Continuing round, you will find a *holy water stoup* outside the n. door, and to the s.w. of the tower, a most unusual memorial – a small and ancient anvil without inscription that marks the grave of a village blacksmith. Entry is through the C15 porch and handsome C13 s. doorway rather like Great Massingham's with double *dog-tooth* decoration in the arch and pairs of columns each side. The C13 *nave arcades* have *quatrefoil piers* in which the shafts almost stand free, and the variation in the *capitals* shows that the n. side and the e. bay of the s. side date from the end of the C13. The tower arch reaches to the nave roof which, like that of the chancel, was restored in the late C19. Although the s. aisle windows are later, their inner shafts and arches are C13 and the inside of the s. door has leaf stops to the *hood mould* of the same period; a *consecration cross* also survives further along. The arches between aisles and transepts rest on half-figure *corbels*, and in the n. transept you will find the blocked doorway that led to the *rood stair*. The whole of the top of the *screen* is C19 but the C15 panels are painted in a red and green simple floral design. Behind the screen are six stalls with wrap-round backs and small carvings on the arms worn smooth by countless hands; there are five original *misericords*, and if you lift them the newcomer is easy to spot – they have roughly carved heads with acanthus leaf supporters. The w. range of choir stalls is original – wide book rests, *poppy-heads*, and figures on the front buttresses, including a lion, a mermaid, and a poor soul clutching an all-enveloping blanket. The companion set of stalls are good C19. The C14 *piscina* and *sedilia* had their *trefoil* arches, *crockets* and pinnacles sharply restored, and so did the tall *ogee*-headed niches either side of the e. window. Back at the w. end, the C13 font is a very plain square with the corners sliced off, standing on five slim shafts. The C15 benches nearby have grotesques on the arms (look for the dog and goose), and over by the n. door, a man sits in the stocks with an animal or a carcase tied to his back (the thief with his booty, possibly). The church has an excellent ring of 6 bells, tenor 7-1-16 cwt.

Griston, St Peter & St Paul (F6): A close-set avenue of limes leads to the tall plain *porch*, but one should circle the church first to admire the handsome tower. Although there was a rebuilding in 1477, the tower is C14 and has two-*light* bell openings with attractive *Decorated* tracery. The angled buttresses are finished with *flushwork* to the top, and both battlements and *base course* are embellished with the keys of St Peter and the crossed swords for St Paul. The *chancel* too has early-C14 work – e. window and one with 'Y' tracery on the s. side. The outline of a *lancet* in the n. wall suggests an even earlier date for this end of the church. A simple *sanctus bell turret* crowns the *nave* gable, and although nothing can be seen inside, note the *rood staircase* tucked into the angle between chancel and nave on the n. side. The plain C14 font would pass without comment except that for some extraordinary reason it was chosen to record a C16 restoration of the top of the tower – on the e. face there is a 'black letter' inscription: 'A' o D'm 1568 was thys Steple tope newe set up to the great cost of landed me (n)'. An elegant little set of *Royal Arms* – either cast or plaster, is mounted on a *Jacobean* panel in front of the ringing *gallery*, and below, part of the *Stuart communion rails* have been re-used. They are worth remembering because they have exactly the same peculiar top rail as those at nearby Thompson. The door to the tower stair, with its roughly chamfered boards is original, and by the arch stands a worn angel figure that must have come from the original nave roof. The square-headed *screen* is handsome late-C14 work with exceptionally nice net tracery above the *ogee* centre arch. To the right a fine pulpit – late-C16 or early-C17. The blank *arcaded* panels have pairs of richly carved semi-round pillars between them at the angles, and the wide bookshelf has decorated supports. The backboard is lavishly panelled and the *tester* has a deep canopy that matches the reading pew opposite. By the pulpit, a plain C15 *piscina*. At the 1885 restoration, some medieval glass was put in the top of two windows on the s. side of the nave and, apart from two feathery yellow angels, there is a good figure of St *Catherine*, and what could be a set of the *Four Latin Doctors* with scrolls. In the chancel there is Jacobean panelling at the back of the choir stalls which are, in the main, old benches. Take a look at the first *poppy-head*

on the n. side – it has a pair of eyes looking slyly each way. The sanctuary has a sill piscina and *dropped sill sedilia*, and three of the church's old *mensa* slabs are embedded in the floor. *Consecration crosses* still show on the one on the n. side, and the other two were rescued from ignominious use as a doorstep and a churchyard stile. The church has a ring of 6 bells, tenor 7-0-10 cwt.

Guestwick, St Peter (G3): One might almost call this the church that moved next door. The tower abuts the n. wall of the *chancel* and was once the centre of a former *nave*-tower-chancel arrangement. It dates from the late-C11 and the old nave and chancel arches are still there in the walls. The arch to the e. has a triple half-roll moulding – an unmistakeable *Saxon* motif. Most of the rest of the building is C15, although the nave roof is a good 1851 reproduction. The C15 font has the *Emblems of the Trinity*, St *James the Great*, St *Paul*, St *Andrew*, St *George*, St *Peter*, and *Instruments of the Passion*. The *rood loft* stairs at the end of the n. *aisle* are unusual – they are set on the old tower wall and are open to the church except for a solid balustrade. The chancel *angle piscina* has a pretty combination of decorative carvings under an *ogee* arch. In front of the late-C17 *communion rails* is a pair of interesting oatmeal-coloured *ledger slabs*. To the s., Edward Bulwer (d.1626); standing figure in cloak and knee breeches with arms, crests and inscription in Roman capitals. To the n., his wife Anne (d.1604). She stands on a pedestal with her family kneeling below – nine daughters on one side, four sons on the other, the inscription in gothic 'Black Letter'. Both are incised in the fashion of portrait *brasses* and as such are most unusual. A 12in. brass to Richard Athylle (d.1505) by the harmonium is recessed and is consequently in fine condition, as is another to James Athylle (c.1500) in the n. aisle. The remains of the church's C15 glass have been collected in the s. aisle windows. There is a good figure of St *Catherine* in the eastern window with her wheel beside her, and at the bottom of the window, a fragment of a St *Lucy* – just the neck with the identifying dagger plunged into it.

Guist, St Andrew (F3): The whole building had declined into decay by the 1850s, and this is why much of the church is more C19 than anything else. The C14 tower has a remodelled C15 upper stage, and within the *porch* the original C13 door has a *mass dial* in the top of the arch. This is a most unusual position and may be unique in the county. The door itself is largely original and has massive hinges across its entire width. With the exception of the windows in the *nave* s. wall, all else is solid Victorian non-inspirational. The *chancel* was rebuilt in 1881 and the nave in 1889. The mean-looking n. *aisle* goes with the nave. In mitigation, some of the fittings are very good. Look at the crisp carving on the pulpit, especially the little ornamentations below the rim – one of them is a *Green Man's* head. The font is a good copy of a C16 design and looks quite at home. There is also a parish chest decorated with simple chip carving scrolls dated 1636. The memorials to the Wiggett family in the chancel are good. Robert and his wife (1697 & 1722) with an English epitaph on the n. wall, and Richard (1749) with a Latin epitaph on the s. wall. William Morris the younger (1818) has a plain tablet with an urn on the n. wall, and there is a moth delicately carved on the surface of the marble above. In the nave floor by the chancel step there is a small plain coffin-shaped slab to a child who died in 1736, Boley Rice Wickes. It says nothing more and does not need to.

Gunthorpe, St Mary (G2): The neat, late *Decorated* C15 tower immediately attracts the eye – bell openings with good, elegant tracery, topped by alternate flint and brick finishings (as is the w. window) and with a nice chequered parapet, evidently the work of a mason who liked to add his individual touch. The *porch*, like the tower and most of the church, is Decorated and has a lovely modern double figure niche over its arch. Inside the church, two things strike at once; the proverbial new-pin cleanliness of the place (always a pleasure to encounter); and the fine C15 font, with seated figures around the bowl, and carvings of Arms of local gentry punctuating the *Symbols of the Evangelists*. Nearby on the n. wall, note John Towne's bounty in 1777 – 25 shillings a year for blankets for the poor of the parish 'observing that no Person shall have the Benefit, two years immediately following'. Now to the *chancel*, rebuilt by Canon Sparke in 1863-64 – a rush of Victoriana, all alabaster, tiles, marble flutery and powerfully coloured glass. As you are about to leave, appreciate the delicate moulding of the C15 tower arch; and note the doorway out to the porch, and the corresponding one, now blocked – these are the oldest parts of the church, both of around 1300. Don't miss the gravestones just outside the porch, carved with bits and bones and most lugubrious skulls.

Gunton, St Andrew

Gunton, St Andrew (I2): This is the one building in the whole of Norfolk designed by Robert Adam and it is well worth the trek along the road through the 1000 acre park to see it. Sir William Harbord commissioned it in 1769 to complement his new house rather as a garden temple would. Although close to the house, it was intended to be almost hidden by trees and when one comes across it suddenly, the effect of the classical portico on six great Grecian columns is dramatic. It is severely simple in grey brick, with high windows in the side walls only. Inside, calm simplicity is the keynote again but with richness added. The original plaster ceiling fell in 1976 but has been faithfully restored – a large oval design with centre-piece of feathers and acanthus leaves. Both the *reredos* and the w. *gallery* are in dark oak with *Corinthian* columns, and on either side of the tall entrance doors the family pews are raised above the others. They have brass candle sconces and a fine set of 1764 Cambridge prayer books. The beautifully tooled bindings have centre labels 'Gunton Chapel 1769' and are faded, but if you turn them over the brilliance of the green and crimson inlays shines again. The church is now in the care of the *Churches Conservation Trust* and still used for occasional services. Long may it be so.

Hackford, St Mary (G5): Tucked away in a side lane in its quiet rural hamlet, the church stands on a slope, tower at the top, and gives the impression of descending with the lay of the land, an engaging optical illusion. A mixture of late *Decorated* and *Perpendicular*, with a good, plain, battlemented tower, which has a fine big Perpendicular w. window and complementing door below it. Its curiosity is its *sound-holes* – tiny 'Y' traceried openings each cut from a solid chunk of stone: they must have been notable anachronisms when the tower was built, if they are original that is, as this church was thoroughly repaired about 1830 and again restored in 1886. The Perpendicular *porch* is very good, the whole w. gable end being covered in silvery-grey, square-*knapped flint*; excellent *flushwork* in stone and flint round the base; angle buttresses boldly *aracaded* in stone and again flint covered; a good outer arch having slim round pillars with little battlemented *capitals*; a square hood over the arch with tracery and floral motifs carved in the *spandrels*; and above, the prettiest of figure niches, with a little canopy above, tiny shafts down the sides topped by diminutive angel heads; and a projecting foot carved with more angelic heads – all, alas, nearly crumbled away to nothing. Inside the porch is a quite outstanding *holy water stoup*, mounted on a pedestal and with a panelled bowl – like a miniature font – carved with large and confident flowers; and above, a plain recessed canopy. There is an unadorned n. door, and a *nave* n. window of Decorated intersecting tracery. The two-*light* Perpendicular windows on the nave's s. side are distinctively different, and could well be separated in date by up to a century, the easternmost one, with its flattened *Tudor* arch, being the later of the two. The early-C14 *chancel* has lovely 'Y' traceried and flowing window designs, the e. window being particularly attractive with its interlacing lines and large, gentle *cusps*. The church interior is appealing, with yellow-washed walls whose discolouration and cracking somehow adds to the 'sepia' atmosphere. The old *Norman* n. doorway serves as a cupboard, with a big, ugly, varnished deal cover over it. Next to it, of equal size, is a huge 'alcove' recessed into the wall, with a pointed arch. The C15 octagonal font has shields around its bowl, mostly carved with large-toothed crossed keys; and one with three *chalices* with the *host* above. The real curiosity is at the nave's e. end. The *rood stair* is gouged deeply into the n. wall-and still has, on a plain *corbel*, a 3ft. remnant of a carved wooden *wall post*. This was possibly a part of the *rood loft* supports. Above

and opposite are further small remnants of the same variety. Then, between the stairs and the chancel arch, and in the e. wall on the opposite side of the arch, are no less than five figure niches, three of them beautifully cusped. Before the *Reformation*, there must have been some busy *guild* or *chantry* altars here. In the sanctuary is a large *angle piscina* – with an enormous, rather ungainly, single foiled arch. Adjoining, *dropped sill sedilia*, with a strange indentation in the w. *jamb*, very tall and narrow and with a small, plain projecting foot. In the top of the e. window, C19 glass by *Powell & Sons* shows the sacred monogram *IHS*, the *pelican* feeding her young with her own blood; and the Lamb of God.

Haddiscoe, St Mary (K6): A lovely church in a dramatic setting, particularly from the s. w. where the land falls sharply away. The late *Saxon* round tower has a subtle variation in its outline that, with the deep C15 chequer-work battlements, makes it unmistakeable. The two-*light* bell openings have Saxon triangular heads but there is *Norman billet* decoration and so a likely date is C11. Inside, apart from the ground floor arch to the tower, there is another doorway high in the wall – a feature often found in the county's Saxon towers and probably evidence that they were used as places of refuge in time of trouble. The C15 *porch* leads to an elaborate Norman doorway which has concentric bands of zigzags and *scallops*, the arch resting on decorated *capitals*. Above it, a rare piece of Norman sculpture – a vested priest seated with hands raised and what may be a dove overhead. The door itself is covered with splendidly barbaric ironwork of an early date. The C15 font with its angels and *Symbols of the Evangelists* round the bowl, upheld by lions round the stem, is a good example of a type common to Norfolk (much of the carving appears to have been recut). When the n. *aisle* was added, an *arcade* was formed by punching holes through the old n. wall, and the variations in the *imposts* and arches set a pretty problem in deciding just when it was done – you will see that they vary a good deal. The easternmost is Norman, but the aisle as a whole was probably built in the C14 when the *clerestory* windows were added and when the old Norman n. doorway was re-set in the outer wall. Another puzzle is the blocked circular windows in the *chancel*. They could have been an C18 elaboration that C19 restorers disliked. While in the chancel, look for the two *corbels* just w. of the sanctuary that once supported the *Lenten Veil*. Haddiscoe

Haddiscoe, St Mary: Norman s. doorway

Hales, St Margaret

church figured often in the paintings of Sir John Arnsby Brown (1866-1955), and a simple bronze plaque to his memory is on the s. wall. Above it, a pretty window by Martin Travers to Mia Arnsby Brown, 'a painter of flowers and children', 1931; the Virgin and Child with *John the Baptist* in the foreground and this church beyond. Above that strange arcade opposite, there are remnants of medieval decoration. There is a well restored head of St *Christopher* with the Child grasping his cap, and traces of a *Three Living and Three Dead* sequence. Halfway down the *nave* a small black slab recalls the great changes wrought in this area by the Dutch drainage experts. It is to Bele, the wife of Peter, son of Peter the Dykegraaf (master of the dykes), who died in 1525. As you leave, don't fail to go in search of the splendid memorial on the outside of the s. wall of the churchyard (if you can get through the overgrown vegetation) to William Salter, 'Yarmouth Stage Coach-Man, Died October the 9th 1776 Aged 59 Years'. It reads:

> Here lies Will Salter honest man
> Deny it Envy if you can
> True to his business and his trust
> Always punctual always just
> His horses could they speak would tell
> They loved their good old master well
> His up hill work is chiefly done
> His Stage is ended Race is Run
> One journey is remaining still
> To climb up Sions holy hill
> And now his faults are all forgiv'n
> Elija like drive up to Heaven
> Take the Reward of all his Pains
> And leave to other hands the Reins.

The church has an excellent ring of 5 bells, tenor 5-2-24

Hales, St Margaret (J6): The village is a mile away, and the *Black Death* could have occasioned this isolation although the original settlement may have been scattered round the large common pasture that was Hales Green. There have not been regular services here since 1967, and when the parish was united with nearby Heckingham in 1973, St Margaret's became redundant. It is our good fortune that it was placed under the protection of the *Churches Conservation Trust* the following year and they have had the thatch beautifully renewed since then. With its plain round tower, *nave* and eastern *apse* it is Norfolk's best example of a C12 *Norman* church essentially in its original form. The plan hasn't altered, even to the extent of having a *porch* added, and this accentuates the extraordinary richness of the main n. doorway. The arch is a great fan of wheels, zigzags and bobbins, each separated by bands of decoration. The door is often open in summer, framing the view of the late-C15 font – deep octagonal bowl with alternating angels and roses and the ubiquitous East Anglian lions squatting under more angels with outspread wings. Beyond the font is a large C15 St *Christopher* painting. At the time of writing not much more than the head is discernible but there are plans to uncover and restore the remainder. More unusual is the C14

Hales, St Margaret: Scratch or Mass dials

figure of St *James the Great*, with his staff and wallet, in the window embrasure by the pulpit, and above it there is a band of C13 decoration reminiscent of Fritton near Gorleston. The stairs for the *rood loft* are on the s. side but only the lower half of the *screen* survives. Note that the painting in its panels on the n. side stops short – a sign that an altar probably stood there. The present altar is a simple modern oblong of brick but the old stone *mensa* which had been embedded in the floor has been restored to its rightful place, and you can trace the *consecration crosses* at the corners. Over the e. window more traces of C14 wall decoration and on either side niches – perhaps for figures of the Virgin and St *Margaret*. The large *aumbry* in the n. wall has lost its door but the original shelf for the Holy Oils is there and it has been suggested that a windlass for raising and lowering the *pyx* over the altar was housed in the front. Hales is such a peaceful and beautiful place that the temptation to wander in the churchyard should never be resisted. The line of the original Norman windows round the apse has been interrupted by later insertions but the general effect is still charming, and the s. wall has not only another Norman doorway and window, but a grand total of six *mass dials* – three on the s.e. corner, one on each side of the door and one at the s. w. corner.

Halvergate, St Peter & St Paul (K5): From the s.w. the lovely C15 tower has a perfect setting, with its stepped battlements rising among the trees. It has deep *arcading* in *flushwork* as a *base course*, and a most unusual double range of *sound-holes*. They are exceptionally small for a tower of this size, and the upper ones have a pretty wheel design. There were figures of the *Four Latin Doctors* on the corner pinnacles until the C19, but they were replaced by others in 'rustic C19 folk-art' style, and three of them now stand rather disconsolately around the s. *porch*, as though craving admittance or pondering upon a summary ejection. The s. door is the best individual feature here, and its *crocketted*, *ogee* arch flanked by shafts is excellent. The church was heavily restored in 1874 when the exterior of the *chancel* was completely refaced and the windows renewed. There are rubbings of an interesting *palimpsest brass* in the chancel – the head of a Yarmouth Franciscan monk (c.1440) on one side, and the bust of Robert Swanes' wife (c.1540) on the other. The brass itself is kept safely in the vestry. The church has a ring of 6 bells, tenor 11 cwt.

Hanworth, St Bartholomew (I2): Driving through Hanworth village, with its protected Common Land, and on through the park-like landscape to the church on its knoll, is a pleasing excursion into old England, especially when you enter a churchyard elegant as a gentleman's garden – then turn to get a fine view of the splendid *William & Mary* hall across the fields. First appearances are against the church at close view – a 'blind' n. wall and *nave* and *porch* faced with crumbling plasterwork. But this is a place which repays a little time and attention. The tall, flint *Perpendicular* tower is fine, topped by very odd little red-brick pinnacles, with angle buttresses and a hefty tower stair. On the s. side of the church, between modern vestry and end of s. *aisle*, an interesting case of an 'adapted' window, with *Decorated* tracery most coarsely filled in. The s. aisle has very simple Perpendicular windows, with a nice arch to a small door. High on the side of the *chancel*, note a curious little *trefoil* opening, blocked in to make way for window below. The e. window has lovely, flowing tracery. Inside, the charm of the little *clerestory* windows, with rather flattened arches, at once impresses – and unusually, there are double the number of windows as arches in the Perpendicular *arcade* below. There are many details of interest in this church: the crude and battered chancel arch shows the shapes and indentations of the fittings of the *rood loft*; the heavy pew now at the back of the s. aisle was the old hall pew in more hierarchical days; the *Royal Arms* hanging over the chancel arch are Queen Anne, 1702-14; hanging either side of the arch are two Elizabethan helmets – they were found in the lake in the grounds of the nearby hall some years ago; the little organ is an original by *'Father' Willis* and built in 1865 for £70. The Barclays at the hall seem good at finding things. Apart from those helmets, a great find in the 1890s was the massive *mensa slab*, discovered buried in the churchyard. It was put back in its place, and encased in the present wooden altar.

Happisburgh, St Mary (J2): It stands gauntly sentinel, between village and sea, the great 110ft. *Perpendicular* tower being truly striking on approach from Walcott. It is of four stages, supported by powerful buttresses which extend right up to the *flushwork* and panelled battlements; there are great three-*light* bell openings, large square *sound-holes* in the third stage with delightfully lacy tracery, an enormous and noble Perpendicular w. window and below it, all of a piece, a fine doorway decorated with shields. The tower has a particularly fine *base course* with deep *arcading*. From the s. the prospect is equally grand, the *clerestory*, *aisle* and two-storey *porch*, all Perpendicular, having identical panelled battlements with the tower. The C14 *Decorated chancel* is part of an earlier church, largely replaced in the C15 rebuilding; its n. side facing the sea is much restored, all the windows, including what must have been a delightful little clerestory, being filled in. The e. window is good Perpendicular with two kingly *corbel* heads to its *dripstone*. The s. chancel windows have beautiful Decorated tracery, but look like replacements. At this point also can be seen the outline of a two-bay chapel, said to have been demolished during the C15 rebuilding. What is less easy to understand is the roof-ridge outline at the w. end of the s. aisle: if it was a chapel, it was in a very unusual position, although nearby East Ruston poses a similar question. Entering through the handsome two-storey Perpendicular porch, we come to a grand and spacious interior. What takes the eye at once is the magnificent C15 font, its superb carvings in an astonishingly fine state of preservation, having the *Symbols of the Evangelists* around the bowl, alternating with angels playing musical instruments; with round the stem alternating lions and *woodwoses* all looking wonderfully benign. Modern pews and *arch-braced roof*; a C15 *screen*, but much restored and altered; C15 five-bay *arcade* (Note at e. end, on n. side, there is a cut-away pillar, indicating a lower arcade in the earlier church). In the s. aisle there is a *piscina*, and nearby a big oblong niche with the remnants of what must have been a splendid stone canopy. The chancel has a piscina, contemporary with the C14 fabric, with a rich, *crocketted* arch; the arcade outline on the s. wall of the disappeared chapel; some good re-used medieval *poppy-heads*; and, high upon each wall a single, very small stone *corbel*, possible used as a *lenten veil*. The church has an excellent ring of 8 bells, tenor 10-0-22 cwt.

Hapton, St Margaret (H6): A very neat and pleasant churchyard here, fringed by mature trees. The tower is all Victorian – before 1848 there was nothing but a bell hung in a frame on the ground. All the windows of the *chancel* and the *priest's door* are *Perpendicular* and there is a blocked C13 n. door. *Nave* and *porch* C14, and *quatrefoils* with centre flowers decorate the buttress plinths and the entrance. A *mass dial* can just be traced on the s. e, corner of the porch

and the medieval door, with its wide chamfered boards has a C13 closing ring fixed to a foliated lozenge plate. The C15 font is very plain and the rim and centre post of its *Jacobean* cover have been augmented by modern scrolls which are nicely done. The C14 triple columns of the chancel arch have caps composed of knobbly foliage and the head of a *woodwose* peers out on the n. side. Four sections of tracery (probably from the head of a screen) have been put together to form a back for the *sedilia*, and two more sections have been worked up into a *credence shelf* on the n. side of the sanctuary. The early-C20 (?) oak altar has panels in the front recessed behind tracery hoods – a Holy Family group which is quite Mannerist in form, and two attendant angels. In front of the nave pews is a C15 chest with sloped lid and plenty of heavy iron straps and hasps.

Hardingham, St George (G5): In a perfect English rural setting, perched on a knoll in deep, rolling countryside, with only a gracious old rectory for company. The tall, slim C13 tower (unfortunately with brick parapets) has bold *quatrefoils* and crisp tracery in its belfry windows; in the next stage down, neat quatrefoil *sound-holes*; lower still, *lancet* windows – and enormous splayed buttresses which frame the entrance *porch* under the base of the tower. The rest of the church is largely in C14-C15 *Decorated* and *Perpendicular*, with much variation in style. At the *nave* w. end, s. side, a large, earlier lancet of the C13; e. window, a *reticulated* tracery; the n. and s. sides are Perpendicular. Perpendicular also in the *chancel*. Under the tower, the inner doorway has slim *Early English* shafts. Inside, the church is rather gloomy. Modern *arch-braced roof* to nave. In nave s.e. corner, a tiny *piscina* with a drain running backwards into the wall rather than the usual vertical into the ground. Nearby, another arched opening, with raised crosses carved in its base The large, octagonal font is C13 and unusual, with carved *trefoil*-headed arches round its bowl and standing on eight rounded legs. On the n. wall, the *Royal Arms* of George III. Opposite, a large wallboard commemorates the building of a *gallery* here in 1843, providing 143 seats – all to be free, compared with a previous arrangement of 200 seats of which only 31 were free. The gallery has gone – and so has the whole system of pew rents. In the chancel the choir-stalls have some old *poppy-heads*. In the sanctuary, we come to the best feature of the church – a C13 Early English double piscina, with crossed and interlacing pointed arches; adjoining two single-seat *sedilia*, one wider than the other, with separate arches resting on a slim *quatrefoil* pillar. A frieze carried right round the sanctuary harmonises these with, on the opposite side, a generously large niche with a plain trefoil arch.

Hardley, St Margaret (J5): Many of the churches round here perch on the edge of the marshes, and we are not far from the ancient Hardley Cross that marked the boundary between the jurisdictions of Norwich and Great Yarmouth on the river Yare. The round tower is *Norman*, but the windows of the *nave* are *Perpendicular* and there are simple *arch-braced roofs*. The pews are interesting because the old C15 bench ends were encased later in natural unvarnished pine that has aged very agreeably and provided plenty of scope for idle boys to scratch outlines of the craft that worked the river. The back pews are angled to give space round a fine chunky font. Angels alternate with the *Evangelistic Symbols*, and two of them squat like Buddhas on piles of crimped drapery – looking for all the world as though they were prone to chronic dyspepsia. Opposite the door there is a big St *Christopher*, and the orb held by the Child sports a little pennant. A crane (or is it a heron?) looks up at Him, and fishes swim between the giant's legs. Just beyond the scrolly border is a smaller figure of St *Catherine* – crowned and holding her wheel emblem. The flat panels of the *Jacobean* pulpit are shallow carved with lozenges and half-roundels, and the old *rood stairs* are set in the s. wall behind. Only remnants of the C15 *screen* survive but in the sanctuary there is a *piscina* of the same period – an unusually late example with a wide arch on columns which have leaf *capitals*. Look at the C18 *communion rails* – they have delicate *balusters* grouped in threes and cry out to be rubbed down and painted again. But with sad evidence of damp and structural decay on the n. side they can hardly demand priority.

Hardwick, St Margaret (I6): A storm in 1770 caused the downfall of the round tower, but both the *Norman* doorways remain – the n. very simple and the s. a late-C12 example with a line of *billet* moulding over the pointed arch, plain columns and scored *capitals*. It was probably altered in the C13 and the battered head to the right probably came from the apex of the arch. The font has simple tracery in the panels of the bowl and shaft, and on the n. step a very odd series of notched grooves. What were they for?

A guess is that the stone was used to put an edge on hedging tools. By the door, a good and complete example of a *Jacobean tester* pew, few of which escaped the C19 restorers. It started life in the *chancel* as the squire's pew, was then used by the rector's family, and finally came to rest as a diminutive vestry. It has a complete top like a fourposter bed, the original latch is on the door, and it is good to see the old paint being stripped off the oak panels. A fine and solid single roof over *nave* and chancel has deep *arch-braces* on the walls between the main timbers and the *rood stair* is cleverly arranged in a n. side window, with a small arch set in the wall. The *screen* was quite opulent and had a double range of light filigree tracery – fragments of delicate *crocketting* show round the entrance arch. Two of the panels have most of their tracery left and some faded colouring to show what it must once have been like; the top, however, is a rustic botch by Messrs John Ebbes and Joseph Cock, the churchwardens of 1661. They thought well enough of the effort to put their names to it. At the step, a small *brass* to George Bacon with the familiar wild boars of the Bacon arms. There is a C14 *angle piscina* in the sanctuary, an early smiling head set in the wall above it, and Jacobean *communion rails* with flat *balusters* and modern top rails. Thomas Gleane (1666) lies under a big tomb in the chancel – three alabaster shields in flattish relief, and to the e. is the table tomb of Sir Peter Gleane (1683) and Dame Penelope. Their fallen fortune caused them to be buried in the churchyard, but this is a splendid monument – and an epitaph which opens a window on their history:

He served Charles the 1st in all the civil wars, raised, and armed two foot companies at his own charge. He served the Crown faithfully above 40 yeares in military offices (and as MP and Deputy Lieutenant for Norwich) in which several services for his king and country he spent his strength and weakened his fortunes, and the wounds which that received were not healed in this year 1683.

Now that is mighty odd, because Dame Penelope did not die until 1689, nor Sir Peter until 1695, so this gloss on the injustice of it all must have come from his pen twelve years before he died. His son was in the Fleet Prison for debt in 1698 'in great misery and want and almost naked', so who, one wonders, paid for the monument?

Hargham, All Saints (G6): Part of the tower of this lonely little church collapsed during the C18 and in falling, demolished most of the *nave*. And so it remains now – a separate ruined tower, and a truncated nave attached to its *chancel*, all looking very picturesque against a frieze of trees. The chancel is *Perpendicular*, with nicely renewed windows, though the fabric is earlier, as indicated by the small and graceful *priest's door*, which is C13 *Early English*. To left of the door there is a *low side window*; and to the right a singular curiosity – a narrow, round *squint*, about four inches across on the outside, looking directly through to the altar. Or rather, where the altar was, for the church is stripped and deserted – but not forgotten, for though it is no longer used as a parish church, caring people are looking after the building, which is now safely vested in the *Norfolk Churches Trust*. There is a story here worth telling; of how Attleborough builder Clifford Amos and his wife Jacqueline fell in love with this place when it was a hopelessly overgrown, decaying ruin. Not only did they personally clear the rampant vegetation (the building was strangled by ivy and creeper, and the churchyard a jungle), but also replaced the roof at their own expense. Inside, though all is sadly bare, the echoes of the church's former charm are clear. Notice especially the really lovely *angle piscina* in the sanctuary, both angles being beautifully arched, traceried and *cusped* under square hoods. Adjoining it are *dropped sill sedilia* – in the w. corner of which the squint, already noted, emerges through a tiny pointed arch which mirrors in miniature the adjacent priest's door. The s. window of the truncated nave has a figure niche set into its e. *jamb* – it has a plainly moulded, single-leaf arch, and an odd rounded *hood mould* which has tiny, carved-leaf *stops* at its ends. Below, on the edge of the window sill, is a *corbel* piscina, on the base of which are traces of original medieval colour. Almost every available foot of floor space throughout the church is taken up by a surprisingly rich collection of *ledger-stones*, the majority scripted in very wordy Latin, and almost all to the Hare family. The font is totally plain, an octagonal bowl on round stem, without a hint of decoration. But at the end of May in 1982 it had its day again: at the first Christening under All Saints' roof for many years, Mr and Mrs Amos had their daughter, Marina Charlotte, baptised here. What could be more fitting?

Harpley, St Lawrence (D3): A fine church standing a little above the village, but partly hidden by the big trees that surround it. The patron saint's gridiron emblem shines as a weathervane on the early-C14 s.w. tower and is seen again on the s. *aisle* battlements. John de Gourney was both patron and rector from 1294 to 1332 and he rebuilt not only the tower, but also the s. aisle and the lovely *chancel* with its enterprising variety of *Decorated* window tracery. Remember when you go in to look for his grave slab in the chancel – the indent of the vanished *brass* figure and the inscription are both clear. A hundred years later, the rector John Drew and patron Sir Robert Knollys made big changes by adding an ambitious *clerestory* and new roof, the mighty w. window, s. *porch*, and the frieze of battlements on the s. aisle. The porch leads to a very good early-C15 door with canopied figures in the surround and a wicket carved with the emblems of St *Luke* and St *John*. Above the C14 *arcade*, the C15 *arch-braced roof* has a deep *wall plate* studded with angels and, unlike any other in the county, there are more small angels spaced out lengthwise along a panel in the ridge. John Martin gave the *nave* benches in 1638 and his name is carved on the one at the front on the n. side; they have pierced and traceried backs, and some on the n. side have tall, roughly cut figures, including a bishop. The s. aisle has surprisingly elaborate *piscina* and *sedilia*; the double piscina marks it as dating from the early years of the C14, and the five-leafed arches of the stepped sedilia have stiff-leaf *stops*. The tracery of the big C15 *rood screen* is excellent, but the repainting of the figures in the panels has all but destroyed their original character. A big internal *rood stair* rises on the n. side, and the stones at the bottom would seem to be fragments of the original *Norman* font. In the chancel, the side windows have nice *headstops* and the *jambs* of the original e. window survive in the corners and show that it was very big – probably a range of five or even seven *lancets*. The *priest's door* has beautiful arches, both outside and within, and there is an equally fine arch opposite, with openwork *spandrels*, that leads to a vestry. To the right, an *Easter Sepulchre* under a *Tudor* arch. The *chancel* had an elaborate piscina/sedilia suite but most of the detail has been hacked away, leaving only fragments of the background diaper work. Going back down the nave is perhaps the best time to study the medieval glass in the w. window – but remember to have your binoculars with you. Right at the top is the kneeling donor in a dark red robe; below him, the two figures of the *Annunciation*, with the Blessed Virgin in a choir stall complete with missal; below again, the two royal saints, *Edmund* with his arrow and *Edward the Confessor*. Round the edge, a very individual selection of saints: from bottom left to bottom right: St *Wilfrid*, St *Lawrence*, St *Vincent*, St *Ledger*, St *Thomas of Canterbury*, St *Martin*, St *Stephen*, St *Blaise*. In the tracery below the *transom* there are members of the hierarchy of angels – the *Nine Orders of Angels*. In such a vast window, the figures are no more than flashes of colour, but they do repay a closer look.

Hassingham, St Mary (J5): This small church stands beautifully on a hillock above a quiet lane that leads through a grove of sallows to the marshes. The round *Norman* tower has a later octagonal battlemented top, and the *chancel* roof is higher than the *nave*, imparting a distinctive profile to the building. Entry is by way of a simple Norman doorway, and once inside, the whole impression is one of clean austerity – white walls, glazed brick floors in grey and russet; beech interlocking chairs, beech reading desk and altar, all upholstery in black fabric. A gift for a flower arranger. Much of this came about because of a fire in 1971 which gutted the building – although the nice C17 chest escaped damage. Altogether a good example of sensible and sympathetic restoration. Note that the new floor level in the chancel has left the *piscina* high and dry, and also the very narrow *banner-stave locker* in the n. wall of the nave. By the gate there is that lovely admonition which ends:

> O gently, gently shoulds't thou speak,
> And softly, softly tread,
> Where in the church's peaceful shade,
> With solemn words the dead are laid
> In their last lowly bed.

Haveringland, St Peter (H3): One of Norfolk's many wartime airfields transformed this parish for a while with runways and buildings breaking up the old pattern of lanes and hedges. Now, a turkey farm and open fields have changed the scene again, leaving St Peter's in a sort of no man's land, approached by one of the wartime concrete tracks. The round *Norman* tower has a C14 square headed window at ground floor level which matches one at the w. end of the n. aisle. Apart from that and the C15 font, virtually everything else was rebuilt in 1858. All good solid stuff but not too interesting.

Heacham, St Mary (C2): A big church with a late-C13 *nave* and *crossing tower* that has unusual and distinctive round *sound-holes*; a walk round reveals that it was once even bigger, with *transepts* and a longer *chancel* – the latter virtually rebuilt in the C19. Enormous buttresses were applied to the tower in 1800, and the one on the n. side has a strange cluster of openings at the top like little windows. The local *carstone* has been used in abundance but there is a great variety of flint, tiles, brick and even glacier stones as well. The C15 *porch* once had an upper room – see the stumps of the vaulting and the entrance door inside, and it leads to a good C13 doorway with free-standing shafts and foliage *capitals*. The C13 nave *arcade* pillars have stone seats around each base and this arrangement crops up in other churches locally. Overhead, the circular *clerestory* windows echo those in the tower but are early-C15, as is the fine w. window. In 1712 the chancel arch was filled in down to the level of the *screen* and at the sides, and in 1800 a flat false ceiling cut off the view of the flowing tracery at the w. end; that is why the C19 chancel window was designed to match. In 1928 the chancel arch was unblocked and the early *Perpendicular* screen was skilfully extended to its original width. At the same time, the ceilings came out, and the *Royal Arms* moved from above the screen to the only space big enough to take them; they are difficult to see but interesting because although they are of George III after the union with Ireland, the 'R' is floriated and they could be a *Stuart* set overpainted. At the w. end, a plain and rather unusual C15 font, and on the w. wall an anonymous *brass* of a knight dating from 1485. Six *hatchments* of the Rolfe family hang above the nave *arcades*, and at the e. end of the n. *aisle* is a reminder of the romantic story of John Rolfe and the Red Indian princess who came as his bride to Heacham in 1616; it is an alabaster bas-relief of Matoaka Rebecka Pocahontas, sculpted by Otillea Wallace – sad that she survived but another year to die of consumption at Gravesend. The story is told in David Garnett's *Pocahontas, or, the nonpareil of Virginia*, Chatto & Windus, 1933. Opposite on the n. wall, a large monument to Robert Redmayne 1625, once mayor of Lynn; a plain chest, inscription between two black *Doric* columns and a coloured coat of arms above. Close by, a group of Victorian Rolfe inscriptions framed in garish colours. A compact Virgin and Child with original colour is set in a carved wooden frame above the pulpit – C16 Italian? Above the s. door there is a touching inscription which tells of the five men and four women 'who went in a Boat from this shore on a Party of Pleasure' and were unfortunately drowned one Sunday in 1799, and further e. a telling verse in memory of a Coldstreamer who fell in 1916. Beyond, a memorial to a casualty of the next war whose peaceful habit had been to study the mysteries of whales in the Southern Ocean.

Heckingham, St Gregory (J6): Now in the care of the *Churches Conservation Trust*. The approach is a stony track down to the nearby farm, and you then climb onto the little churchyard hill where the wind often sweeps across from the river valley to flatten the grass. The original *Norman* base of the tower had an octagonal top added later but the simple *nave* with its steep *arch-braced roof*, and the *apsidal chancel* are a pure Norman outline – if one sets aside the more recent n. aisle. The *apse* has typical flat buttresses outside and the early form of the windows is still to be seen inside at the e. end. All the thatch has recently been beautifully renewed by the same craftsmen who dealt with Hales. The s. doorway is the main attraction and must surely be the product of the same mason who worked at Hales. The fantastic series of Norman motifs – zig zags, bobbins and wedges in the arch – is completed by a hoop of the wheel pattern. All the four shafts on either side have decorated *capitals* and even the space between the two of them is filled with a pattern rather like scooped-out orange segments. The bobbins and wedges are covered with incised dots, and the whole effect is quite overpowering inside the small *porch*. The font is Norman too – a plain cube of stone set on a centre shaft with four sturdy columns at the corners. There is no cover now but a C19 engraving nearby shows 'a cumbrous and tasteless cover of the C17 which is now decayed and unfit for use.' We would probably have found some virtue in it, had it survived, and in the range of *box pews* and two-decker pulpit that were discarded a little later. Here as at Haddiscoe, openings were roughly cut in the n. wall to make a simple arcade for the aisle in the C13.

Hedenham, St Peter (J6): Prettily placed on a little hill at the end of the street, with views across pleasant countryside. The tower is slim and unbuttressed with stepped *flushwork* battlements. The w. buttresses of the *nave* have *trefoiled* gables, there are C13 *lancets* in the w. wall of the nave, signs of early-C14 work in both nave and *chancel*, but the wholesale restoration of the 1860s has overlaid everything. Inside, this is markedly so, particularly in the chancel. Here we have uninhibited Victorian '*Camden Society* Gothic' by E. J. Tarver, with harsh glass by *Hardman* in the e. window and by *Clayton & Bell* on the s. side. The roof is *arch-braced* and panelled in lowering fashion, upheld by big standing angels with gilded wings. The *piscina* and *sedilia* are backed by red and green tiles with coats of arms applied. The C18 *communion rails* with close-set *balusters* have been re-used as a chancel *screen*, and beyond them the nave is quite calm by contrast. The simple *arch-braced roof* has lateral braces between the *wall posts*, and plenty of plain glass in the windows lets in the light. What coloured glass there is is interesting. A little coat of arms of the Garneys family in the middle lancet on the n. side has a mermaid crest (which explains the pub sign on the main road to Bungay) and next to it is a pastiche of *Pre-Raphaelite* Holman Hunt's 'The Light of the World'. In the opposite window, a beautifully delicate set of Victorian *Royal Arms* in pale colours surrounded by strapwork and sprays of berries. The C15 font is one of the local group which all have eight columns round the shaft, with roses and shields set in *cusped* panels on the bowl. Against the tower arch are two interesting oddities. There is a gilded bust of St *Peter* and some acanthus *arcading* which came from an early-C18 *reredos*, and above that, part of a screen. Rescued from the rectory summerhouse in 1902, it looks like C16 work, and has a centre panel with three figures depicting Christ at Emmaus, with angels on either side. It may well have formed part of an earlier reredos. The church is well blessed with memorials to the Garneys and Bedingfields; at the w. end 'Clere Garneys late of London, merchant' has a coarse rococo drapery tablet with a *putto* blowing a trumpet over it and two more heads in the folds. Back in the chancel there is a big monument to Philip Bedingfield who died in 1621 at 28. His is a free-standing kneeling figure in armour and ruff, and the whole feeling is Elizabethan rather than *Stuart*. Next to him, Robert Bedingfield's epitaph of 1594 runs to sixteen lines but is worth the reading. He died young.

Helhoughton, All Saints (E3): The early-C14 tower has lost its bell stage and two of the old *sound-holes* were converted to serve as oblong bell openings. At the same level on the e. face, the original height of the *nave* is marked and there will have been *clerestory* windows before the n. and s. *aisles* were demolished in the 1780s.

The showy tower w. doorway has niches with shields in the *reveals* plus *ball flowers* and *fleurons* in the arch mouldings. Having removed the aisles, the parish used the stone to build a new nave, inserting windows with wooden frames and hexagonal panes; those on the s. side were restored without alteration in 1990 as part of a restoration programme that began a few years earlier in which the e. gable was stabilised, the roofs re-tiled, and many other defects dealt with. Entry is through the tower and the two steps up into the nave show how the floor level was raised in the C18 rebuilding. All is bright and fresh within and there are now recessed lights in the gently curved plaster ceiling. The octagonal font is an oddity, with triangular rounded spurs on four of the faces. It rests on sturdy columns and although it has the feel of C14 work, the components may have been salvaged from the old s. aisle *arcade*. Six oil lamps from an earlier era are now on standards fixed to the C19 pine benches, and four boldly-lettered C18 *ledger-stones* were re-laid in the floor, together with one earlier slab that once carried a *brass* inscription. The set of James I *Royal Arms* that hangs on the *chancel* s. wall has (as usual) the motto 'Exurgat Deus dissipentur imici', but economy prompted the C18 wardens to paint 'A1705R' for Queen Anne in the *pediment*, to bring it up to date. A neat little Bryerson chamber organ of 1852 was acquired in 1890 and stands opposite. On a large tapering ledger-stone in front of the sanctuary step there is one of the county's finest *heart brasses* dating from the mid-C14 for William Stapliton and his wife. Sections of the scroll inscriptions survive, translating: 'I believe' (on the heart), 'Jesus is my redeemer', 'I sleep but will rise from the ground' and 'I entrust myself to my Saviour'. In the sanctuary, the revised floor levels have made the *piscina* sit very low in the wall.

Hellesdon, St Mary (I4): The good people of Hoxne in Suffolk will insist that St *Edmund* was martyred there, but it all depends on the old name 'Haegelisdun', and those who know about these things favour Hellesdon as the place where the Danes caught and killed the East Anglian king in 869. No clue to be found at the church, though, nor of the bitter fight between the *Pastons* and the Duke of Suffolk in the 1460s, when the Duke's men ravaged the church, stole all its valuables, and turned the parson out of doors. It is small but tall for its size, and has a distinctive *bellcote* topped by a leaded spirelet. The walls of the *nave* and *chancel* are *Saxon*, but the n. *aisle* is C14 and so is the tall *porch*. This has

a *groined* ceiling and the ribs drop down to low pillars in the corners – an angel *boss* with the three crowns of Ely on a shield in the centre, two leaf *bosses* and a single head by the outer arch. The whole church was heavily restored in 1869 and most of the windows renewed. The n. aisle *arcade* is C14 and so is the font – simple *quatrefoil* panels, and eight attached columns round the shaft. During the same period, a *chantry chapel* was built n. of the chancel and the blank arch is pierced midway by a later square-headed *screen* – something not often seen in Norfolk churches. Just inside the door from the chancel is a *piscina* which matches the one for the high altar – that one is a double, with one drain blocked and a stone *credence shelf*. Half of the chantry chapel now houses the organ, and the modern lattice screen to the w. has a fluid and sinuous sculptured design of Christ displaying His wounds, with all Creation reaching up from below – imaginative and lively. In the chancel, look for the *low side window* with the shutter hinges still there, and by the pulpit, the epitaph to Robert Marsh (1762):

> The toils of Life and Pangs of Death are o'er,
> And Friends, nor Foes, can ever Vex me more.

Perhaps they were relieved too! There is a good example of the plain C14 style of dress to be seen on a *brass* in the n. aisle floor – the half-figures of Richard de Heylesdone and his wife (c.1370), and a fine 2ft. 6in. brass to rector Richard Thaseburgh (1389) has been mounted on the wall further e.. The small, almost square *Jacobean* table at the w. end was originally an altar and would look nicer if the dark streaky varnish could be removed.

Hellington, St John the Baptist (J5): On its little hilltop, with views of rolling countryside around, this church is in the care of the *Churches Conservation Trust*. The round tower is *Norman* (with later parapet), but the big two-*light* belfry openings are early *Decorated*, with massive tracery which is only just moving from '*plate*' to '*bar*'. The unusual C13 *porch* – much battered now by time and elements, but it must have been very grand in its prime – has a lovely outer arch and pillars, and the remains of a large figure niche over it. The angle buttresses have very large figure niches, and there are three deeply splayed windows to each side of the porch. The inner doorway is a bigger surprise: a superb and very tall Norman piece, with recessed arches having six different kinds of decorative carvings, and more carvings still on the *capitals*. There is a Norman n. door also, but much plainer. Walking round, the windows of *nave* and *chancel* (square headed late *Perpendicular*; chancel e. window renewed in Decorated style; s. side, a range of five splendid Decorated windows, all different, in flowing and geometrical tracery patterns, complete with lively corbels showing faces and foliage). Inside, the church is very spartan, but note the heavy rounded arch from the tower, a beautiful Decorated chancel arch, with leafy carvings round the capitals, and on the chancel side, a raised *hood mould* finished with two corbel heads. In fact corbels abound all over the church and many of the windows have slim fluted shafts down the *jambs*, with delicate little leafy or rounded capitals. The chancel s. windows are all unusual in being recessed into the wall, and all lowered to form *dropped sill sedilia*. Beside the altar is a big plain double *piscina* with only one drain, contemporary with the C14 windows. On the floor in front of it, a rather poor attempt at a *brass*, with inscription and shield, dated 1642, by which time *brasses* were no longer fashionable. It is for Sir Anthony Gaudy, Knight, in verse which if not great poetry, is worth reading:

> Vertve, Ivstice Goodnes Race
> Are all interd wthin this place
> With this good Knight so good whose fame
> That now in Heaven most glorious in his
>   name
> Wheather hee is gon to Christ his rocke
> To singe Hailviahs with His celestial flocke.

Hemblington, All Saints (J4): Remote in the deep countryside and interesting in outline. It has a round *Norman* tower with very basic bell openings and, atop the tower, an odd little 'cap'. *Nave* predominantly early-C14, most windows having attractive *Decorated* flowing tracery, and one *Perpendicular*. The *chancel* windows are Y-tracery of about 1300; but the e. window is a poor modern replacement. The early-C16 entrance *porch* has a charming brick outer arch and *hood mould* with simple crosses in *knapped flint* set flush into the walls on both sides and above. The inner arch is C14 Decorated. Inside, a feast of curiosities awaits. One is arrested at once by the enormous St *Christopher* on the facing wall, which was discovered in 1937 under layers of plaster. St Christopher is in the centre astride a rushing stream with the Christ-child on his shoulder. On the left bank were representations of

incidents in his life before his conversion, but most of these are gone; on the right however there are than ten episodes after his conversion. To right of the mural, a precarious open staircase, set into the window embrasure, led to the *rood loft*. Just to its right there is a tall canopied niche in the nave e. wall, with some original colouring; on the opposite side, a coarsely constructed double recess, again with colour; adjacent, in n. wall behind the pulpit, a plain, deep niche connected by a tiny passage to a crude *piscina*; and built onto the sill of the immediately adjoining window, a square plain pedestal. There were *guild altars* in these two corners of the nave before the *Reformation* and 'lights' were maintained in this church to three saints. The pulpit is C18, neatly panelled, with backboard and *tester*. Several good benches with *poppy-heads*, some with attractive animal carvings. To left of s. entrance door, an incised C14 stone coffin-lid is placed against the wall. Some seven *brass* inscriptions, from 1480 to 1630, are set into the nave pavements. The roof overhead has its original C15 *arch-brace* beams and simply carved *wall posts*. No chancel arch as such, but a massive cross-beam with vertical timbers and plaster above. The simple, white-painted chancel has a modern barrel roof, very agreeable; one window embrasure drops to form *dropped sill sedilia*; beside it, a large, plain angle piscina. Finally, the church's beautiful medieval octagonal font, whose carvings (with most subtle modern colouring) are very unusual. It has seated figures set into each face of the bowl, and eight standing figures in niches around the stem. Above, starting from w., God as *Holy Trinity*, SS *Augustine of Hippo*, *Edmund the Confessor*, *Barbara*, *Agatha* and an apostle. Around stem: SS *Leonard*, *Catherine*, *Stephen*, *Citha*, *Lawrence* and *Margaret of Antioch*; a monk, and a gowned figure.

Hempnall, St Margaret (I6): Go round to the n. side of the tower and you will see, in the corner between n. *aisle* and tower, a line of *quoins* in the wall that are *Saxon long and short* work – the only evidence left of the earliest period of the church's history, and which shows that it had a sizeable tower. The present tower is basically C14 with later additions, and has an odd placing of two *sound-holes* under the clock, while on top a handsome gilded weather-vane is dated 1727. Inside, the round pillars of the n. *arcade* are C13 while the s. range are C14 octagons. The church was badly damaged by fire in 1390, which may account for this change in style. The *chancel* was burnt down in the late C17, and in the 1850s *Thomas Jekyll* rebuilt much of the church – walls and roofs replaced, eighteen new windows, e. end enlarged, a stub chancel added, plus a *bell turret* on the tower. Jeckyll's benches were removed in 1986 and the internal tower space has been cleverly adapted. The arch has been glazed at first floor level to enclose a meeting room, reached via a handsome wooden spiral staircase and *gallery*. Soldiers of the Earl of Manchester were billeted in the village during the Civil War, and it was they who defaced the font – what is left shows that it was well above average quality. William Barwick the vicar was a doughty Royalist, calling Parliament 'a company of factious fellows' and was not to be intimidated: 'If there be any disturbance in the county I have a gun at home, and powder and bullets, and will defend myself as well as I can.' He was understandably ejected from the living in 1644. The s. aisle altar is *Jacobean* – nice and solid with heavy stretc.hers and strapwork decoration along the top rail. In front of it, a heartfelt and moving epitaph to Susanna Stone who died in 1784, aged 24:

No sculptur'd Tomb, or storied urn,
Decks the lone, simple, Village Grave;
Yet here unseen, soft Virtues mourn
Her, whom nor Art, nor Vows could save.
'Farewell!' a weeping Husband cries,
'All cold my Love, thy gentle Heart;
'Farewell! till Heav'n shall bid thee rise,
Then: Once more given: no more to part.

Hempstead (near Holt), All Saints (H2): A pretty little church, set well back from the village street in a well-kept churchyard. As you approach, the tiny little rounded *chancel* catches the eye, in neat flint and with a fussily detailed thatched roof as whimsical as a ginger-bread house from 'Hansel and Gretel'. This part was built in 1925. At the opposite end of the church, there's a solid, stumpy little red brick tower – rebuilt, in 1744, more for form than appearance. Inside, the church is charmingly simple. It has little to show of its ancient past: a severely simple round-headed archway into the vestry, wholly without ornament; a w. window with simple *plate tracery* of the C13; and a much-battered bench bend, on the *nave* n. side, with mutilated *poppy-heads*. The nave windows are probably C17, the stained glass Victorian. The little west *gallery*, complete with tiny organ and choir-boy graffiti on the book rests, is delightful. Don't miss the *brass* memorial wall tablet in the n.e. corner of the nave to 'Edmund Hunt of the gentry' (that he was descended from Thos. Hunt, soap boiler, of London, is tactfully overlooked) who, 'having lived long in service of his King and country', finally 'climbed to the stars of the sky' in February 1610.

Hempstead (near Stalham), St Andrew (K3): A pretty, quiet church in quiet countryside, its plain C15 tower having a very good w. window with agreeable tracery and 'battlemented' *transoms*, all recently most skilfully restored. The big *Perpendicular* windows to n. and s. of the *nave* have the same curious *corbels* to their *dripstones* as seem at Swafield, not far away. At the w. end of the nave, each side of the tower, are *Decorated* windows, one filled in – indicating former *aisles*, which were taken in to make the present unusually wide nave. Look for the C13 *lancets* on n. and s. of *chancel*, and on s. a little *Early English priest's door*. Possibly original Y-traceried window to right (about 1300), as might be the e. window with three stepped lancets under one arch. The neat C15 *porch*, with flush-panelled battlements, formerly had an upper room lit by a two-*light* window separated by a figure niche; but these are now filled in and the porch open to its roof. Inside, a plain modern *arch-braced roof* spans the spacious nave and frames a rather coarse chancel arch – below which is an immensely pleasing C15 *screen*, battered but beautiful, with a fine display of painted saints. There were 16 originally but not all are intact. Recognisable (from left) are *Juliana, Theobald,* a rare *John of Bridlington, Dionysius (Denys), George, Stephen, Lawrence,* and a rare *Eligius*. A quartet of old *poppy-heads* adorns the front pews; there is a gorgeous *Jacobean* pulpit on legs; behind it, the *rood stair*; opposite, a *piscina* with handsome Perpendicular canopy and inside it, on the right, an inner recess for the cruets used in the Eucharist. The plain chancel has a nicely arched C14 piscina with a flower drain; and little *dropped sill sedilia*. A *low side window* and a splendid Jacobean reading desk. The C15 font in honey-coloured stone, with roses and plain shields around the bowl, and funny woolly lions on sentry duty round the stem is most attractive.

Hempton, Holy Trinity (F3): Partially hidden by trees on a small common, this little church is well worth a visit. The village was blessed with two medieval churches, but a new start was made in 1855 when John Henry Hakewell was comissioned to design the replacement. He was one of the consulting architects for the Incorporated Church Building Society and built dozens of churches, parsonages and schools, and here he limited himself to a small and simple hall building which served until 1952 when it became the *chancel* of an enlarged church. J.P.Chaplin designed the extension which consists of a *nave* roughly as long as the chancel and two stub *transepts*, with a white louvred lantern over the *crossing*. Walking round you will see a large bronze Calvary high on the s. transept wall. Entrance is by way of a s. vestibule into the compact squarish nave. The n. transept has been blanked off to house the organ and a small cast-iron coloured set of *Royal Arms* hangs on the wall. The 1950s extension made good use of masonry from the bombed church of St Michael at Thorn in Norwich, and the altar in the s. transept is formed from it. Its *reredos* is a montage of the burning of the city church – a lively composition taking in Ber St, the *Mother Julian* shrine, and the railway station. On the w. wall is a dark painting of the Holy Family by J.P.Chaplin reminiscent of 1930s work by Eric Ravilious. Nearby, the C19 pen drawing of the Hakewill chancel is a useful reminder of what the first stage of the present building looked like. There is a striking elongated wooden figure on both of the vestibule doors, and the *Stations of the Cross* are excellent – small, grey *cruciform* plaques with the figures highlighted in red. The altar and reading desk in the sanctuary are surely those installed in 1855.

Hemsby, St Mary (K4): Large and spacious interior with *nave* and *chancel* under one roof. The s. *porch* has an upper room and is vaulted with a series of *bosses* – unusual in a village church. They depict: God the Father, the Resurrection, *Assumption*, Ascension, *Annunciation* and Nativity. Close by the *screen* in the s. wall of the nave is a *piscina* which has a surprise inside – the drain is set within a lion's mask. In the chancel s. wall, a 1908 window has good glass by W. Aikman; showing St *George*, and a woman knitting. Further along, armorial glass of the Ferrier family. The church has been heavily restored and most of the fittings are modern, but a print of 1840 shows it with *Jacobean* screen, *three-decker pulpit* and *box pews*. The base of an ancient *sanctuary cross* is by the churchyard gate, and around are many good C18 and C19 headstones.

Hethel, All Saints (H5): Go down the winding cul-de-sac of a lane and you could be a hundred miles from anywhere – that ancient tree, the Hethel Thorn in the next field has been there for over 700 years and timelessness pervades the place. The square unbuttressed tower is probably *Norman*, with its small pebble flints in regular lines and the outline of an original w. door (pinnacles and battlements are much later). Worthwhile here to walk round and see how the Branthwaite family converted the n. chapel into a mausoleum and rebuilt the *chancel* about 1730. The n. facade is red brick with heavy *quoins*, and blank arches filled with a darker brick. The parapet echoes this motif and then continues in plainer style around the rest of the chancel. Odd to think that after all that trouble and expense only two of the family were buried in it. Through the plastered s. *porch* under a crow stepped gable and into an interior that has positively ugly flat ceilings. But ample compensation lies in the study of the tomb in the chancel. Myles Branthwaite (1612) lies stiffly on his side, robed with narrow ruffs at neck and wrist. His wife Mary rests more comfortably below and wears a deep hood, full ruff, and boasts a line of bows down the centre of her stomacher and skirt. With their brother, her two little girls kneel in front of the tomb and have their own bows, but in their hair. The main figures are hardly damaged at all and are carved in a delectable pink tinged alabaster. The Branthwaite arms have lion heads attached to scrolls for supporters, and the coffered arch is full of sprightly scroll work with a lot of colour. This is one of the best in the county for its period. High on the chancel s. wall is the epitaph of Mrs Anna Bettina Finch (1780) – pure *Regency* in feeling and sentiment:

> Thus adorned with the finer and more elegant accomplishments both of body and mind, she easily acquired what she so justly merited during the term of a short life, a conspicuous station amongst ye most distinguished and most amiable of her sex.

A *Norfolk Churches Trust* working party has recently completely redecorated the interior after extensive repairs.

Hethersett, St Remigius (H5): The sunken line of the old turnpike curves round between the present road and the church which has a most unusual profile. The *chancel* had been in ruins since the *Reformation*, and when it was rebuilt in 1898, the *nave* roof was partially reconstructed so that half of it has a steeper pitch and an extra gable, and this gives the impression of two chancels one in front of the other. Most of the windows were re-done then, but the main fabric is C14. The tower with its small spire is both sturdy and finely proportioned. The buttresses have seven *set-offs*, pretty *ogee*-headed niches set in the w. pair, and a matching niche over the w. window. The C15 *porch* has a lavish *groined* ceiling with a big centre boss of the Coronation of the Virgin, and the ribs swoop down to *corbels* with little grotesque heads; there is an upper room but apparently no stairway any more. Inside, the fine C14 *arcades* rest on *quatrefoil piers* and the C19 'text and transfer' decoration seems to bring out their quality. The bowl of the big C14 font has shallow tracery panels and rests on eight plain columns round a centre shaft. The monument in the s. *aisle* to Isaac Motham (d.1704) and his wife by *William Stanton* is excellent; *Corinthian* columns support a broken *pediment* and coat of arms, two cherub heads below – all crisply executed in white and grey veined marble. There are only five churches in all England dedicated to St *Remigius* and he is hard to find in medieval art. By way of compensation, Hethersett has a modern bronze statuette of the bishop, dove in one hand and holy oil flask in the other. See also Dunston. The church has an excellent ring of 8 bells, 9-2-21 cwt.

Hevingham, St Mary the Virgin & St Botolph (I3): Stands well away from the centre of the village on the road to Aylsham. It is a big church, and even from a distance the lacy tracery in the s. *transept* window, the *Decorated* butterfly motifs in the s. *nave* windows, and the massive s. *porch* catch the eye. The great chestnut tree in front was planted in 1610, and you might like to check to see if it really does measure 19ft. round. There was a thorough-going restoration here in the late C19 which introduced a lot of new work, but the *angle piscina* shows that the *chancel* must have been built around 1300. The C15 porch has an elaborate window for the upper room – two canopied niches one above the other, flanked by traceried windows – but the room itself has lost its floor, so that its little staircase leads nowhere now. In 1642, this upper room was used to store gunpowder, bullets, pickaxes and other martial material for the Hundred of S. Erpingham. Nearly all Norfolk fonts are octagonal but here we have a hexagon, and quite unlike its brethren in design. The traceried top panels are largely C19 restoration but the bottom half is C14, and has clustered columns at the angles. The figures in the deep

niches are very worn and mutilated although the Crucifixion at the w. is easily recognisable. The most memorable thing in the church is the set of four benches in the chancel. They are low, with broad tops and were patently designed for school use. The fronts and end have *blank arcading* – *cusped* arches between half-round columns with varied carving in the *spandrels*; and all in oak which has gone silvery with age in a way no restorer can imitate (compare the two original tops with the two replacements). These marvellously solid pieces are said to have been used in the porch chamber when it was a schoolroom, but their length makes this questionable if you look at the access stair. Still, they predate the porch and could conceivably have been put in during building, and then lowered when the floor was taken out. The chancel has another choice item. When St George's at Gt. Yarmouth was restored in 1882, the superb 20-branch candelabrum, given to the church by its Warden Thomas Grimston in 1741, was sold. Hevingham's rector bought it for £4 and here it still is, in a setting worthy of its quality. Perhaps it was then that the remarkable foreign glass in one of the nave windows came in. High up on either side of the chancel arch, note the four stone brackets which carried the *rood*, showing that it spanned the whole church here and not just the arch. The big blank arch on the n. side is all that remains of a n. transept, and a big village *tithe* map of 1838 now hangs there. The s. transept arch has been filled with a glazed screen to form a self-contained Lady chapel. Furnished and carpeted in simple style, it is a sensible arrangement for a country parish with a small population and huge church. The church has a ring of 5 bells, tenor 12 cwt.

Heydon, St Peter & St Paul (H3): A blissfully peaceful place, and one of Norfolk's most attractive villages, but particularly in summer when sheep sometimes crop the grass in the churchyard and loll against the gravestones like superannuated clubmen after a good lunch. The C15 tower has bold *string courses*, a staircase turret that reaches the battlements, and *sound-holes* with inset shields. The dressed flints are packed round with little shards of the same stone – a feature known as 'galletting' often used on Norfolk churches and a marvellous defence against frost and damp. The w. doors are original, with excellent tracery – a trail of *quatrefoils* round the edge and two stools for images like the ones at Erpingham. The tower was part of a great modernisation in the C15, when the walls of

Heydon, St Peter & St Paul

the *nave* were raised, the *aisles* rebuilt, and the *porches* added. The s. porch has a vault with a 'Lord in Glory' centre-boss, and the upper room doorway to the church is high in the wall, which means that it was probably used as a treasury. The late-C14 *arcades* and the windows at the w. end of the *aisle* were kept, but the *clerestory* of alternating two-*light* and quatrefoil windows may be either all C15, or a mixture of old and new. Surviving from an even earlier church is the C13 font – a big rounded tub with smooth roll mouldings, looking itself as chubby as a well nourished baby. Repairs in 1970 brought to light a most remarkable series of C14 paintings. On the n. aisle wall we can now see part of a *Three Living and Three Dead* sequence – one of the ways that the church in the middle ages used to point out the transience of earthly things. The 'dead' are three skeletons (the skulls are visible), and the 'living' are three kings. The 8ft. figures of two of them are beautifully clear, one with a hawk at his wrist and one with a sceptre. The n.e. chapel was dedicated to St *John the Baptist*, and fragments of a series of illustrating his life and death have been uncovered. In the s. aisle Lady chapel, two other sequences have come to light. High in the s.e. corner there is an exquisite head and shoulders of a crowned woman (as yet unidentified) which really merits study through binoculars. On the n. side of the altar, a sequence dating from the late C14 has two kings in ermine robes bearing gifts; they stand behind a kneeling figure and may have been part of a nativity scene. Another survivor from the earlier church is the C13 *sacristy* door in the n, wall of the chancel – look at the bottom and you can see where the original floor level was. There is a very plain *Easter Sepulchre* recess beside it which has just a trace of colour. The fittings in the church are more than usually interesting because a number of them can be dated. The tall *rood screen* was given by John Dynne in 1480 according to the inscription on the rail, and the panels still have coloured diaper decoration. The 1930s restoration was a bit cavalier and there is no coving or *loft*. The pulpit, a lovely solid piece on a wine glass stem, was given in 1470. The C17 backboard has an inset Flemish carving of the Last Supper dating from the 1640s, and the C19 stairs incorporated *balusters* from the old *communion rails*. The big manorial *box pew* built on to the w. side of the chancel screen is very good joinery of 1696, and has its own bible box on the wall. All monuments in the church pale before the majesty of a 12ft. x 6ft. black slab at the e. end of the n. aisle. They say it broke three bridges on the way to Heydon and the back of one of the men who laid it. It is guarded by a tall and very spiky wrought iron screen, and under it lies Erasmus Earle – M.P. in the Long Paliament from 1640 and Sergeant at Law to Cromwell, who doubtless worshipped here when he stayed at the Hall. Earle passed Christmas Day 1648 sentencing to death the men who raided the Norwich powder magazine which blew up and left St Peter Mancroft windowless. The family of Heydon moved to settle in Baconsthorpe in 1447, but a unique reminder of their presence hangs on a pillar at the w. end by the font. It is a green painted wooden shield, with the cross of St George and the family name crowned at the top. It may well have been carried in procession – perhaps once only at the funeral of a Heydon returned from the Crusades, in the way that *hatchments* were used in a later age. This church is not only full of interest, it is full of information. The captions and displays for the benefit of visitors are first class. The church has a ring of 6 bells, tenor 6-1-6 cwt.

Hickling, St Mary (K3): One of the best w. tower elevations in the area, with door, window, niche and sound-hole, all melded into one harmonious composition: a pity that the buttresses stop short at the bell stage and spoil the total effect. Rigorous and repeated C19 restoration has left the church interior rather harsh. Good wall monument in *chancel* to John Calthrop (d.1688). The tomb chest in the n.e. corner of the n. *aisle* is covered with C17 graffiti, including *Nine Men's Morris* frames and 'Roundeheade 1645'. Nearby is a very rich C13 coffin lid, with a floriated cross and a border inscription in *Lombardic capitals*. The 'melon-legged' communion table is *Jacobean*. The church has a ring of 5 bells, tenor 20-2-0 cwt.

Hilborough, All Saints (E5): Down a long tree-lined track to a tree-studded, English park setting you go to find this marvellous surprise of a church. What confronts you, very suddenly, is a tall and elegant *Perpendicular* tower, a *clerestory* of four beautiful *Tudor* three-*light* windows, and a s. *aisle* which half overlaps the *chancel* with three rather grand Tudor windows. Contrastingly plain chancel of around 1300, with windows to s. and e. of interlacing tracery. But back to the tower, which is made especially striking by a magnificent pierced stone parapet, richly carved and ornamented with shields, with *crocketted* pinnacles at the corners. The w. face is excellent, with *string courses* springing both from the *drip mould* over the belfry window, from its sill, and from the *dripstone* over the big w. window. Below, a frieze of shields centred on the coat of arms of the de Cliftons, who acquired the Manor in the mid-C14. The fine w. door, deeply moulded and ornamented, has intriguing figures carved in the *spandrels* – on the right a bearded man holds aloft a severed head, on the left is a trim and fashionably dressed young nobleman whose extended arm is missing. To each side are tall canopied niches bounded by *flushwork* panels with a big *trefoil* above, that on the right being ingeniously pierced to light the tower stair. The Perpendicular s. *porch* is a beauty. Like the lower s. face of the tower and the s. aisle, it is faced with a chequerwork of stone and flint and has a canopied figure niche over the outer arch, and a *base course* of flushwork, crowned Ms for Mary alternating with crowned swords for St *Michael*. Lovely calm interior, with a *hammer-beam* and *arch-braced roof* to the *nave*. It has moulded collars, floral *bosses*, angels on the hammers and deep *wall posts* with angel *corbels*. Nice C14 *arcade* on *quatrefoil* pillars, Perpendicular chancel arch, and the *rood stair's* top door just visible to the left. Plain arch-braced roof to the chancel with wooden corbels below short *wall posts*. Gnarled C15 benches in the nave with solid *poppy-heads*; massive octagonal font. In the chancel are a double *piscina* and *sedilia* under triangular hoods with 'portrait' heads at the intersections. Opposite, a plain *aumbry* whose hood looks as if it once had carved ornamentation. The e. window is most unfortunately outlined in strips of awful gaudy glass. In leaving, note the *Royal Arms* on the s. door of James I, dated 1611, carrying his initials and motto – 'Let God arise and let his enemies be scattered'. This church has close connections with two of England's heroes, *Nelson* and Wellington. Every rector between 1734 and 1816 was a Nelson except one – and he wisely married a Nelson. The Admiral's father was rector here before he moved to Burnham Thorpe. The Duke of Wellington lived for a time at the hall across the park and worshipped here.

Hilgay, All Saints (C6): A lovely narrow avenue of limes up to the church from the n., with an oaken *lych-gate* at each end – the only pair that comes to mind in the county. The tower of grey brick, with its heavy w. buttresses, dates from 1794 (see the roundel over the n. door) and in the 1860s *George E. Street* carried out a massive restoration which raised the ridge of the *nave* roof almost to the top of the tower, and he built a totally new *chancel* in place of the long lost original. Two bays of the C14 s. *arcade* remain at the e. end and the taller bays to the w. are C15. The s. *aisle* retains its original *arch-braced roof*, and at the e. end there is a restored *parclose screen* which incorporates much of the C16 tracery. Within the s. chapel, a *trefoil*-headed *piscina*, a small *aumbry* in the e. wall nearby and on the left, a large image bracket. Above the piscina, an alabaster tablet for Henry Hawe (d.1592) and his two wives; the little figures kneel demurely under a shallow arch. Between the chapel and the low stone chancel screen stands an extraordinarily large wooden eagle lectern, and beyond it, an ornate High Victorian stone pulpit probably designed by Street. For those with an interest in Norfolk's maritime history, Hilgay has a special appeal. Captain George William Manby was born in Denver in 1765, was briefly *Nelson's* school-fellow, and went on to be the inventor of the lifesaving rocket line which he first used successfully in 1808 at Great Yarmouth, saving the crew of the brig 'Elizabeth' when all seemed lost. Eccentric and undervalued, he died in poverty here in 1854 and was buried in a coffin of his own making. There is a tablet in the s. chapel which recalls 'a name to be remembered as long as there can be a stranded ship', and the 1863 inscription bitterly concludes, 'the public should have paid this tribute'. An advertisement for Manby's 'Portable Life Apparatus' – 6 guineas from Samuel Moore of Great Yarmouth, is framed at the w. end of the church, and his gravestone carved with little reliefs of a mortar, a ship and an anchor stands just outside the wall of the s. chapel. If you walk round to see it, don't miss John Whittome's headstone of 1891 s. of the church – it has a lively roundel of a tower mill with a tumbril and two men delivering corn.

Hillington, St Mary (D3): The C15 tower has bell openings which are filled up with honeycombs of red brick, a brick parapet, and a little *flushwork* on the buttresses. The *chancel* is also C15, with blocked windows and *priest's door* on the s. side, and a C19 e. window with a little niche below it. The old *nave* and s. *aisle* were demolished in 1824 and rebuilt as a wider nave, with cast iron *Perpendicular*-style windows. *Cautley* could not abide them but the mullions are slim in section and look very acceptable painted pale grey – at least there is no maintenance problem! Entry is by the w. door, under a garish 1840s window by William Oliphant, into a plain white interior with a flat ceiling. The chancel arch is Victorian, and below is a most convincing fake C15 font made in 1822. The n. *transept* was unsympathetically restored in 1892 and contains three big table tombs of the ffolkes family. Its entrance is taken up by a large 1756 Snetzler chamber organ in a very nice mahogany case with restrained gilt embellishments and brightly decorated pipes; made for the Duke of Bedford's music gallery originally, it finally found its way here in 1857. There is a C15 *piscina* in the chancel s. wall and another opposite which probably migrated from the old s. aisle. On the n. wall, the 1653 Hovel monument is very compact, and shows how the Elizabethan style of ruffs and farthingales lingered on into the Commonwealth period; Richard and Frances and their children face each other over prayer desks below a pair of panelled arches. Opposite, nearly the whole wall is taken up by a pair of pale grey marble slabs, with side *pilasters* and unmatched *pediments*. They commemorate Sir William and Mary, Lady Browne (1774); he was President of the Royal College of Physicians and there is an excellent bas-relief portrait of him in a roundel signed by Joseph Wilton, the sculptor who carved that quality bust of Richard Gipps at West Harling. The wife's epitaph is in Latin (repeated in Greek and English just to make sure) and inconsequentially remarks that a grandson was currently in the 3rd form at Eton. By the pulpit is the memorial to Lucretia, Lady Browne West (1828) by Humphrey Hopper, and reminiscent of Flaxman; she leans disconsolate over a sarcophagus, cradling a dead child in her arms.

Hindolveston, St George (G3): On a Sunday in 1892 the tower collapsed (providentially between services), and although the *chancel* survived until 1933, that too had to be pulled down. A year before that, the present church had been completed, designed by the Diocesan architect H.J.Green and making extensive use of material salvaged from its predecessor. There are short n. & s. *transepts*, and all the windows are brick *lancets* except the round one in the w. wall below the bell-cote. A statue of the church's patron saint in a niche high on the outside of the e. wall takes the place of a window, and four of the lancets are carried above the wall line to create dormers. It is good to see that one of the medieval doors of the old church has been re-used for the entrance to the n. *porch*, and on the wall beyond the vestibule there are four *brass* inscriptions that have been similarly translated. The lower pair commemorating John Mair (1531) and Joan Wood (1491) are typical pre-*Reformation* requests for prayers, while Beatrice Bullye's (1621) at the top records her legacies for the repair of the church and the renewal of the stock held for the relief of the poor. On the opposite wall there is a fine brass set in its original frame for Edmund Hunt (1558) and his wife Margaret (1568). Richly dressed, they kneel with their ten sons behind him and four daughters behind her, and there is a helpful transcription of the long 'black letter' inscription. Just to the left a little *rib*-vaulted niche with angels in the *spandrels* has been re-sited in the wall. The tall C15 font is a handsome piece, despite the mutilation suffered by the bowl panels; their subjects are: the *Evangelistic Symbols*, a *Trinity* shield, a shield of *Passion Emblems*, St George's cross, and a Crucifixion that has only the bare outline of the cross remaining; crowned 'M's and 'T's decorate the panels of the shaft. As a gesture of support for the new church, the deans and chapters of Canterbury and Norwich Cathedrals gave fragments of stone from their buildings and they have been mounted in the walls at the w. end of the *nave*. Octagonal *piers* from the old nave have been re-used and half-round *piers* from the former chancel flank the sanctuary. Bench ends with varying *poppy-heads* have been incorporated in new seating in the chancel, and beyond the altar a *rood* group with excellent 1930s figures by Lillian Dagless stands under a *canopy-of-honour*. To the right, the shaft, drain and part of the arch of an early-C14 *piscina* have been brought back into use. There is another piscina in the s. transept, and to the left stands a chest of 1681 with a chip-carved front, with a smaller, much older example alongside. There is a fine example of a C20 brass on the n. chancel wall for two schoolfellow victims of the Boer War – Cpl. Edward Watson fell at Belmont, while Sgt. Arthur Sayer survived the siege of Ladysmith only to die in hospital at Woolwich.

Hindringham, St Martin: C12 chest

Hindringham, St Martin (F2): To find so large and fine a church in this tiny village comes as something of a surprise: approaching from the e. end, the visitor's pleasure is redoubled at sight of the magnificent *Decorated* e. window (though the *chancel* itself was partly rebuilt in 1870). Move round to the s. and the impression becomes still grander – the tall, slim, beautifully proportioned Decorated tower, with lovely detailed tracery in the bell openings; and the stately *Perpendicular aisle* windows, finely balanced by the later Perpendicular *clerestory* windows. The interior proportions are splendid, with the chancel *weeping* heavily to the s. The five-bay *arcades* of the *nave* are C14 Decorated, as is the chancel arch and the two-bay chancel arcade; though the tower arch and the good w. window are later, and Perpendicular. The splendid C15 font deserves close attention – octagonal, richly carved with the Crucifixion, the Arms of England quartering France, the *Emblems of the Trinity* and the *Instruments of the Passion*. Hindringham's greatest treasure is the remarkable chest which is probably the earliest of its kind in England which stands in the chancel. In the 'History of Oak Furniture' (The Connoisseur, 1920) Fred Roe says, 'It can hardly have emanated from a later period than the last quarter of the C12', and he places it at about 1175. There is a huge former *squint* on the s. side of the nave, and an *angle piscina* – indicating the presence of an altar here. Note either side of the n. *pier* of the chancel arch the remains of the *rood stairs*. Restoration lies heavily upon the chancel itself, including the massively reconstructed triple *sedilia*, and a blocked-in *priest's door*.

Hingham, St Andrew (G5): A large and grand 'town church', sitting securely amidst its neighbourly cluster of elegant old houses. It is a notable building in that it is virtually all of one construction, having been built in the later years of the life of Remigius of Hethersett, who was rector here from 1319 to 1359. It is almost all of the *Decorated* period – but almost certainly late, coming after the *Black Death* of 1349-50 when generally the Decorated style had already given way to *Perpendicular*. The enormous tower is very fine, with great windows of eloquent flowing and geometrical tracery. The w. face is imposing: it has huge windows at three levels, plus a complementing w. door with an *ogee* hood decorated with ample *crockets*. A massive turret, 'disguised' by right-angled buttresses, supports the s. w. corner: its lowest *light* at the s. w. angle is interesting – a single block of stone into which has been cut a roundel with a tracery outline in a pattern of *mouchettes*. On the body of the church, interesting detail is provided by a frieze of *ballflower* ornamentation to *clerestory* and *aisles* on both sides, and to the *porch*. Especially glorious are the window traceries at the e. ends of the n. and s. aisles (made especially large to honour the chapels, dedicated to the *Holy Trinity* and the Virgin Mary respectively – there were no less than eight *guilds* that met in the church). The vast seven-light e. window has been re-modelled in tracery of remarkable ugliness – so as to contain ancient glass of considerable beauty. The interior is truly striking, the soaring *nave* being crowned by a modern (1872) but very good *hammer-beamed* and *arch-braced roof* (modern too are those in the aisles with their winged and happy-looking angels hovering on the hammers), with five large two-light clerestory windows each side placed above the *spandrels*, rather than directly over the tops of the arches. Below, the elegant six-bay *arcades* stand on *quatrefoil* pillars. Majestic chancel and tower arches, of tremendous height, with high over the latter a *sanctus bell window*. In the s. aisle, an enormous *piscina*, with an eight-leaf drain. In the n. aisle (passing en route the excellent Victorian wood-carved pulpit, with a quintet of swooping angels around its base) is the striking bust of Abraham Lincoln, whose ancestors for many generations lived here in Hingham. It was given by American citizens, and expresses in its inscription the hope that between America and Britain and all lands there shall be 'Malice towards None with Charity for All'. Into the hugely spacious chancel now, with attention first on the magnificent e. window glass. It is all German, of about 1500, and was brought here from abroad in 1813 by Lord Wodehouse, who is said to have bought it from a nunnery in the Netherlands. To do it full justice it needs a numbered diagram to point all its details; enough here to indicate a saint in the centre (*Andrew* or *Matthias*), with below him St *Anne* holding the Virgin and Child; to his left the Crucifixion; to his right, the Ascension; to St *Anne's* left, the Deposition; to her right, the Resurrection. To the right of the high altar is a mutilated piscina and *triple sedilia* which once must have been very fine. A curiosity in the sanctuary is a cast-iron 'pan', dated 1677, of considerable weight, which was formerly chained in an open place in the village for the use of parishioners as a 'Winchester bushel measure' – a standard measure used from 800 AD to 1824. There are said to be only four of these measures in existence, of which three are in Norfolk. Finally, on the n. side of the chancel, we come to the astonishing monument to Thomas, Lord Morley, Marshal of Ireland, died 1435, and his wife, one of the most impressive wall monuments of the C15 in the whole of England. Carved in red stone, it looks like a cathedral w. end in miniature, or, more closely, the Erpingham Gate into the Cathedral Close in Norwich, if its soaring height to the very top of the chancel wall can properly be described as 'miniature'. It stands under a canopied arch, replete with figures including Christ, Lord and Lady Morley, kneeling on the massive tomb chest – undoubtedly used as an *Easter Sepulchre* – overall are masses of shields. The church has a good ring of 8 bells, tenor 16-1-0 cwt.

Hockering, St Michael (G4): A trim *Perpendicular* tower, battlements with *flushwork* and blank shields and *crocketted* pinnacles at the corners; angle buttresses neatly chequerworked all the way down; w. window and bell openings nicely topped with contrasting pink *Tudor* brick and flints. The body of the church is much older, though there are Tudor windows in the *nave* s. side, and slightly earlier Perpendicular examples on the n. with bold *quatrefoils* in the heads. The fabric is C13, see the 'Y' tracery *chancel* windows and the simple *priest's door*; on the n., by the *lancet* window; and by the uncomplicated interlacing tracery of the e. window, whose lower third has been filled in – and once inside the church you see why, because the space is occupied by an enormous and ornate Victorian *reredos*, which is as overstated as the adjacent *piscina* and double *sedilia*, under the same *hood mould* and carved in a profusion of leaves and birds; even more startling is the chancel arch, a froth of carving in an exceedingly fussy Victorian

interpretation of *Early English*. Of special interest in the chancel are the *low side window* and, in the sanctuary, a C13 coffin lid with an ornamented cross. Above them, a rustic *arch-braced roof*, its rough dark timbers contrasting with the white plaster ceiling and providing a link (having passed through the severely restrained C19 *screen*) into the nave, which is as charming, unspoiled and unsophisticated a little country place as one could hope to find. Under a C15 roof, with plain *wall plates* and *wall posts*, is a C14 *arcade* with quatrefoil pillars. The pulpit is C16-17. There is a delightful *gallery* at the w. end, with a splendid carved and gilded *Royal Arms* of the Hanoverian Georges, boldly at its centre. Below it, a modern font bowl is mounted on a finely carved stem: under a frieze of eight angels is a set of figures under individual little arches – clockwise from the e. face: St *George*, St *Christopher*, the Virgin and Child, St *Margaret of Antioch*, St *Catherine*, St *Andrew*, St *Peter*, and a fork-bearded figure with a book. Nearby are some miniscule bench pews with old *poppy-heads*; in nave and *aisle* a lot more good poppy-heads, one with a noble head (nave, s, side); and in chancel, some bench ends with *talbots*, antlered deer and family crests (including, I think, the bear-in-harness of the Brereton family – see Briningham).

Hockwold, St Peter (D7): There is a tastefully lettered roundel designed by David Holgate over the *porch* entrance that will remind you that this church is vested in the *Churches Conservation Trust*, and it is still used on occasion. A circuit of the churchyard first: to look at the C14 s.w. tower with its small *Decorated* w. window and matching bell openings, the n. side with enormous sloping brick buttresses by the door and very tall and thin *Perpendicular* windows, a small *priest's door* tucked in by a *chancel* buttress, and a Decorated s. *aisle* with one Perpendicular window inserted later. Don't overlook John Woolsey's epitaph w. of the tower – 1858 but C18 in quality, beginning: 'What does each sudden dissolution say'. Inside, a C15 roof well restored by the Friends of Friendless Churches. Lit by *clerestory* windows on the s. wide it has, like Methwold, *arch-braced tie-beams* alternating with *hammer-beams* and the same style of recumbent angels – and looks particularly fine from the chancel. The C14 *arcades* have octagonal *piers* and the tower arch matches, except that its plinths are fluted and are said to be *Saxon* – which seems an extraordinary survival. A large square area over the n. door is painted with a

C14 mock masonry pattern stippled with flower shapes, with an earlier deep red leaf trail at the top, and you will see fragments of later Black Letter texts in the upper corner. In the s. *aisle*, a sturdy C14 *piscina* with foliated *cusps* in the *ogee* arch, a *crocket* at the top and a pair of very worn *headstops*. The chancel arch is perhaps part of the heavy restoration of 1857, and there is the line of a much larger arch around it. In the chancel, parts of the stalls are medieval and there is a large *aumbry* in the n. wall of the sanctuary. Neither of the monuments on the e. wall has the mark of quality, although they do try – especially John Hungerford's (1719). It is by Robert Singleton of Bury St Edmund's, who did excellent work elsewhere, notably at West Dereham; the two portrait busts look ill matched below a riot of musical instruments, flanked by fluted columns and standing *putti*. On the other side Cyril Wyche (1780) is commemorated by a sadly overweight putto holding a wreath and wiping tears away with the corner of a drape; surprising that this was a collaboration between *John Ivory* and his apprentice John de Carle – both with much better work elsewhere.

Hoe, St Andrew (F4): Lovely chestnut trees arch over the road outside, and a thick wall of evergreen fronts the e. end of the churchyard – which is a good place to explore if you collect C19 epitaphs, like George Back's (1861) on the n. side: 'Happy in affliction while on earth he lived, And safe in Christ he died'. The church was rebuilt from the ground in 1794 and only the tower was untouched. There had been *aisles* originally, but no trace of them now, and although the tower had a belfry stage in the early C19, it was reduced to the level of the *nave* roof later on, perhaps when the *porch* was added in 1833. The n. porch is original, with a weathered C14 outer arch, and both n. and s. doors are medieval. Inside, the church is very bare, with plain white walls, pitchpine pulpit and pews. There is a small set of Hanoverian *Royal Arms* in the blocked tower arch and below, a good C15 font. This has varied and well carved roses in the bowl panels, and pairs of shields; below, the shaft is decorated with columns of *quatrefoils*. The memorial to Roger L' Estrange (1706) by the pulpit makes effective use of gilt lettering on black *touchstone*, and the coat of arms beneath is a very pretty combination of white marble and heraldic colour. The C17 *communion rails* are simple turnery, and the wide altar frontal conceals a plain *Stuart* table.

Holkham, St Withburga (E1): The church has its own entrance from the coast road some distance w. of the main entrance to the Hall. Standing on a great *Saxon* burial mound, with woodpeckers drumming in the surrounding trees and pheasants exploding all around, it broods romantically and would be a fine setting for a tale to be told late at night. Some people count the dedication as unique – true for medieval churches now but East Dereham was another originally, before St *Nicholas* became so popular. The present building was so thoroughly restored and rebuilt by James Coling in 1868-9 that one might pass it by, but there is much of interest. Entry by way of the tower on the s. side – early-C13 with bell openings of a century later, but like the rest, rebuilt. Foundations of a much older tower were found in 1869 in the w. bay of the *nave*, so there was doubtless a Saxon church on top of the pagan burial mound. Look at the s. side of the nave *arcade* and you will see foliage *capitals* on one of the bays showing that there was a C13 s. *transept*. Now there are two *chancel* chapels with modern *parclose screens*. The whole of the e. end was rebuilt and it is odd that Coling did not disturb the extraordinary architectural tangle on the n. side of the C14 chancel arch. The *pier* cuts right through one of the arches of the early-C14 arcade. In the s. chapel a panel of heraldic glass in crude orange and bright blue says that in 1767-8 the Dowager Countess of Leicester beautified the church at her sole expense. Nearby, two fine monuments by *Nicholas Stone* – both of 1639; on the s. wall, Miles Armiger – a large kneeling figure with a skull for company, set in an arch with coloured coat of arms above; on the e. wall, a combined effort for three couples (two Wheatleys and a Coke); they face each other across prayer desks and the women have an interesting variety of head-dresses; below kneel fifteen children, with the odd one or two distracted by something so that they turn and smile and that lights up the whole ensemble. In the n. chapel lies Juliana Countess of Leicester (she who paid £10,000 for the 1868 restoration); a fine, calm, recumbant figure in white marble, with the head a little to one side. The sculptor was Sir Joseph Edgar Boehm whose lovely mother and child group now stands in the grounds of the old Norfolk and Norwich Hospital. The church has an excellent ring of 6 bells, tenor 19-1-1 cwt.

Holme Hale, St Andrew (E5): A big church wrapped around by its small village, dominated by a massive four-stage tower, and predominantly *Perpendicular* in character. The tower deserves particular attention, for though the mass of it was built in the 1430s the lower part is much older. Inside will be seen a stolid, bricked-up *Norman* window which looked through to the *nave*. But both outside and inside, what is intriguing is that on all four sides are roof-ridge outlines of thin red brick and flint, that on the n. side being somewhat higher than the others. So was there formerly a *cruciform* church here around a stumpy Norman square tower? Or was there a processional way below the tower? Notice in passing that on each side of the tower, even in the buttresses, are surprisingly large numbers of *put-log holes*. Inside the church there is a fine C15 roof, with alternating *arch-braces* and *hammer-beams,* the hammers carved with winged angels. Bold *clerestory* to n. side, complementing the big *Tudor* windows to the s.; also a big three-*light* window over the elegant *chancel* arch. Four-bay *arcade* of the C13, with delicate, flower-carved *stops* to its arches – except for one at the e. end, which is a most curious snouted creature with its tongue out! The tower arch looks later, C14 *Decorated.* In the n. *aisle* good stone *corbels,* deeply and richly carved with foliage, support the *wall posts.* Good range of C16 bench ends, all carved with animals, figures and grotesques – on the n. side particularly, pick out the grinning devil with his tail wrapped over his arm, an elephant-and-castle, a haltered bear and the *pelican in her piety. Rood stair* and *loft exit* in s.e. corner of the chancel. Fine Perpendicular *screen* with most beautiful, advanced tracery, including two intricate wheel designs. Nicely panelled *Jacobean* pulpit. In the chancel there are figure niches on the *jambs* of the n. (filled in) and s. windows; recessed *sedilia* with an unexplained, small square cavity in the e. jamb; and a C13 *angle piscina* with an endearing bungle – its angle pillar, a bit of re-used *Norman* work, was put in upside down. As you leave, note the *holy water stoup* by the n. door – with a demonic face set into the wall below it. The church has a good ring of 6 bells, tenor 15 cwt.

Holme-next-the-Sea, St Mary (D1): Though the body of the church is a very sparse C18 rebuild, the individuality of the *Perpendicular* tower more than compensates. It is *flint-knapped* overall, save for red-brick battlements and pinnacles (possibly part of the 1778 reconstruction); enormous belfry windows. A large and splendid *sound-hole* on the s. side with honeycomb tracery; and below, a most distinctive feature: a s. window with the oddest of concave-sided *hood moulds* and topped by a stone cross set flush into the wall. Below again, a well-proportioned arch below a square hood, with tracery and shields in the *spandrels,* leads into the *porch* under the tower; here there is a good vaulted roof with carved *bosses* and shields at the intersections. Over the s. door is a figure niche; and to its right, the indications of a *holy water stoup* having been savagely hacked away. Plain interior, but several reminders of the original church are of interest, including the retention of the late-C14 *chancel* arch – complete with the coarse indentations where the *rood loft* was secured. In the sanctuary, simple triple *sedilia,* under separate solid arches set into the wall; and a pretty, very small double-arched opening in the e. wall – presumably an *aumbry.* Here also are two Hanoverian *Royal Arms,* one carved in wood (very stylish), the other elegantly painted on panels and dated 1779. Nearby, mounted on the s. wall, are the remnants of a great alabaster monument (14 figures and two small black obelisks) to Richard Stone, 1607, with an inscription both in English and Latin. Richard and his wife Clemens were married 64 years and had seven sons and six daughters, who in turn between them produced 72 children 'which the sayd Richard & Clemens to their greate comforte did behoulde'. Richard died on 5th October 1607, aged 87, but the gaps left for his wife's death date and age were never filled in. In the corner of the *nave,* on the s. side of the chancel arch, is mounted on the wall the two-figure *brass* to Herry Notingham, (died 1413), and his wife, he shown in his robes as a Judge of Assize in the reign of Henry IV. The inscription bears repetition:

Herry Notingham and hys wyffe lyne here
Yat maden thys chirche stepull and quere,
Two vestments and belles they made alsoe
Crist yem save therfor fro wo
Ande to bringe ther saules to blis at heven
Sayth Pater and Ave with mylde Steven.

Below is a brass inscription (a *palimpsest*) to Barbara Strickland, 1582. The church has a ring of 5 bells, tenor 7-3-2 cwt.

Holt, St Andrew (G2): Ravaged by fire in 1708 when the whole town was burned. Money was still being raised for rebuilding in 1723. Heavy-handed restorations in the C19 have left rather a dull building. Without its spire, the tower sits heavily and the southern vestry extension is quite nasty. Still a nice little *sanctus bell cote*. Interior *arcades* and *chancel* arch all of the early C14 and so is the s. *aisle piscina*, which has a large *consecration cross* within. The double *piscina* and *sedilia* in the chancel are *Decorated* with large *headstops*. Monument to Edmund Hobart (d.1666) in the chancel by *Linton of Norwich* records that he:

> escaped the malice of the Usurper
> who...sought after his life...but his Loyalty
> carried him steadfast through Ye storms
> of that Unnatural Rebellion & here at last
> he found rest.

The church has an excellent ring of 8 bells, tenor 7-0-8 cwt.

Honing, St Peter & St Paul (J3): Sitting handsomely on raised ground above the village, the church has a fine, slim and lofty *Perpendicular* tower, with a good w. window divided by a central *transom*; below the window was a fine doorway, now it is filled in by a window with woefully out-of-place intersecting tracery and with red brick. This 'addition' presumably dates from the 1795 reconstruction which provided the church with its eccentric body. The *chancel* was cut down to form a mere alcove, and the *aisle* walls rebuilt and given the same drear tracery as in the tower insertion. Inside one finds that the aisles are no more than passage-ways, and it has been generally assumed that they were narrowed down to this width when the walls were rebuilt. But as *Pevsner* has logically pointed out, the C15 Perpendicular *porch* is intact, and unless it was rebuilt stone by stone – a most unlikely possibility – it must therefore indicate the original building line. Rather gaunt inside, with those passage-way aisles, the coarse, heavy *arcade* pillars and arches (of about 1500), the earlier, graceful chancel arch and the 'indent' chancel, oddly combining. But at least, it is different – especially with the C18 roof, a sensible, barn-like construction, sitting right across the *nave*, *arcades* and aisles in one span. *Rood stair* and loft entrance in the tiny chancel interestingly give a better idea than most of how the *rood loft* would have 'sat'. Between the choir stalls is an attractive little *brass* to Nicholas Parker, 1496, he in armour and his hair flowing full and free. The time-weathered C13 octagonal font bowl, of the common variety, carved with shallow arcading, stands on a later and more richly carved Perpendicular stem. Two *hatchments* hang on the n. wall.

Honingham, St Andrew (H4): It stands all alone, a good half mile from its village, and separated still further by the big dividing line of the A47. Yet obviously not left alone, for the churchyard is a model of orderliness, and the handsome church has a well-maintained look about it. Mainly *Decorated* in character, except for the battlements and w. window of the tower, and the little *porch*, which are *Perpendicular* in style and date. The high battlements, adorned with flush-work, have battlemented pinnacles at each corner on which sit the Four Evangelists. Each holds a shield, blank now, but perhaps they once bore their *Evangelistic Symbols*. The belfry openings, with 'Y' tracery, indicate a date of about 1300, earlier than the rest of the church, where rich *cusping* of otherwise simple interlacing Decorated tracery suggests a couple of decades later. Interesting too, to find such uniformity of window design throughout one building. The s. door, inside the porch, has a Decorated arch, and beside it, a very good *holy water stoup* on a little sculpted pillar. Inside, the church is rather austere under the sturdy, *arch-braced* modern roof of the *nave* and pannelled barrel roof of the *chancel*. Note the fluted pillars and battlemented *capitals* of the tower arch – and the massive interior angle buttresses to either side – a sign that the tower is earlier than the nave. The C14 Decorated octagonal font has bold *quatrefoils* around the bowl and little pillars around the base. Some pleasant old *poppy-heads* enhance the modern deal pews. Modern too is the *screen* (1927) and very well done, in particular the cusped traceries of the lower panels, with their complement of carved flowers and leaves. To either side, however, one can see in the stone-work of the chancel arch where the original screen and *rood beam* were roughly taken out. There are a couple of splendid *ledger-stones* in the chancel floor, with deeply incised and vibrant coats-of-arms – wild rampant horses support the arms, and a braying unicorn crowns the crest – to members of the Richardson family, 1674 and 1701 respectively. To an earlier member of the same family, Thomas, died 1642, there is on the s. wall fine monument in black and white marble and alabaster, with a half-figure portrait of Thomas, looking very like the famous one of Shakespeare at Stratford in pose, save that Sir Thomas, Master of Cramond (to give him his full title) holds a militaristic baton and wears a shoulder-hung sword. Extremely dyspeptic looking lion heads serve as *corbels* to support the framing pillars of this aggressively confident piece. The church has a ring of 6 bells, tenor 7-1-25 cwt.

Horning, St Benedict (J4): Before going in, note the C13 *priest's door* on the s. side of the *chancel*, which has *dog-tooth* decoration round the arch. There was formerly a n. *aisle* of the same date, but only the *arcade* remains, embodied in the *nave* wall. The tower, which has figures rather than pinnacles, the s. *arcade*, and the w. window of the s. aisle are all C14. In the s. *porch* is a very decayed C13 chest still held together by fine ironwork. A tiny *squint* in the n. wall of the chancel is a reminder that there was once a chapel where the vestry now is. The benchends in the chancel have panels of crude carving below the *poppy-heads*, and pierced buttresses on which sit grotesques. One panel on the n. side shows the earliest version of the arms of St Benet's Abbey (whose ruins are a few miles away near Ludham, on the bank of the River Bure). The church has a pottery alms dish, with a *wherry boat* design in the centre– a nice idea.

Horningtoft, St Edmund (F3): A neat little country church of just *nave* and *chancel*, it long ago in the 1790s having lost its tower. Not until nearly a century on did the Victorians replace the tower with a bell-cote. The church is almost wholly C13 *Early English* work, as most of the windows indicate – narrow *slit lancets* and two-*light* lancets; also the contemporary doorways to n. and s. of the nave and the *priest's door* on the chancel s. side. This latter is very small and charming in its simplicity, with a single, bold *dog-tooth* moulding at each side of the arch, in lieu of *capitals*. The *Perpendicular* e. window is the only later addition. Inside, the church is cool and serene, with immaculate white walls, polished wood, scrubbed brick-tile floors, crisp curtains to sanctuary and screen, and faultless sanctuary and chancel carpeting. In such a setting one can appreciate at its best the essential simplicity of the architecture, and the effect of the furnishings within it: the wine-glass pulpit, slightly startling with its modern painted adornments; and the even more colourful, repainted screen, both of which are matched by the modern altar-frontal panels and the delightful little restored reading desk in the chancel. On the n. side of the sanctuary is a large *aumbry* opening. The font is a good C15 octagonal example, deeply carved with angels and lions around the bowl, and wide-eyed little lions around the stem, and standing on a modern base in the shape of a Maltese cross.

Horsey, All Saints (K3): The round *Norman* tower has a C15 octagonal top, the haunt of owls and harriers, and the whole church is thatched. The interior, with its simple roof exposing the underside of the reeds, imparts the homely feeling of a *tithe barn*. There is a simple square-headed *screen* with *ogee arches*, and the sanctuary boasts three little *aumbries* all in a row. A window in the *chancel* to Miss Catherine Ursula Rising (d.1890) is a good period portrait of the lady herself, posed as an artist before an easel.

Horsford, All Saints (H4): A pleasant thatched church, with a C15 tower (about 1456). *Early English chancel*, with original triple-*lancet* e. window; *Decorated nave* with square-headed windows; n. *aisle* built in 1869 when the first of two heavy restorations took place, which manage to make the whole church look Victorian. Square late *Norman* font of *Purbeck marble*. There's a nice plain C16 *screen* with good tracery; also a *Stuart* table and a *low side window* in the chancel containing armorial glass to the ancient Barrett-Lennard family, who held the manor and estate of Horsford by direct family descent from the time of the Conqueror until 1973 when the 35th Lord of the Manor, Sir Richard, sold up to Norwich Corporation to make way for improvements to Norwich aiport. The pews in the church came from St Mary's, Tunstead. The *communion rails* were made from *balusters* of the staircase at Didlington Hall, deep in the Brecklands of south Norfolk, now demolished. Note two poignant commentaries on their times; a stained glass memorial by Zettler of Munich to three consumptive sisters who died, 1891-93, in Davos and Cairo; and outside, a headstone near the path to eleven years old John Pirsins, who died serving on a man o' war in the battle of Camperdown, 11th October , 1797 (in which the Dutch were defeated by a British fleet under Admiral Lord Duncan).

Horsham St Faith, Blessed Virgin & St Andrew (I4): An imposing church with a *Decorated* tower, the rest *Perpendicular*, as in the arch between tower and *nave*, but excepting the original *Early English* e. wall of the *chancel*, with distinctive *lancet* windows. Exterior wall has fine flint and stone chequer pattern. The two-storied s. *porch* has a *groined* roof with – most unusual – a figure of St *Andrew* bound to the cross. Inside, well carved octagonal font of about 1450, with fine *Jacobean* cover; C15 nave *arcades*; a *rood screen* with painted panels, dated 1528 and with names of the donors; C14 oak lectern; a set of medieval stalls, three each side, with *misericords* with good small heads; a few old *poppy-head* benches in n. *aisle*. Most interesting pulpit, dated 1480, with painted panels, recently restored, of unusual saints, St *Faith*, and St *Wandregisil*. In chancel, there is a head bracket on one wall from which was suspended the *Lenten Veil*. On n. wall, *brass* to Geoffrey Langeley, 1437, Prior of Horsham St Faith (remains of the priory, whose monks are said to have built this church, are now part of nearby Abbey Farm). The church has a ring of 6 bells, tenor 8 cwt.

Horstead, All Saints (I4): Apart from the C13 tower and the pleasing C14 doorway, the whole church is a re-building of 1879. There is some good stained glass. In the s. *aisle*, a *William Morris* window has two brilliant figures, Courage and Humility, designed by *Sir Edward Burne-Jones*. The *chancel* e. window is by *Kempe & Tower* – separate wreaths for all the virtues hang in heavy foliage in the top. Below, are four large figures of some interest: Bishop Herbert de Losinga with Norwich Cathedral – the building which he began in 1096; The Virgin Crowned; St *Nicholas of Myra*; and *Mother Julian of Norwich*. The *nave* monument to John Langley Watts (d.1774) is a very nicely balanced composition in various marbles. The *Royal Arms* of Anne are decidedly murky.

Houghton, St Giles (F2): Rebuilt in the 1870s, but a lot of the original materials re-used. The C15 *screen* is back in place and although, as so often, the faces of the saints are mutilated, much of their original colour remains. From left to right they are: *Emeria, Mary Salome* with her sons, *Elizabeth* with her son, *Anne, Gregory, Jerome, Ambrose, Augustine of Hippo, Silvester* and *Clement*. The stencil decoration on the back of the screen can still be seen. The *Stuart communion rails* have simple, homely turning.

Houghton, St Martin (D3): Gloriously situated in the park within sight of the great house. The church marks the site of the old village before Sir Robert Walpole transplanted his tenants to new cottages outside the gates in 1729. He it was who built the tower with its very brisk set-off to the top stage. Most of the rest of the building is C19, although the n. *aisle* is early-C16 and the windows have not been altered there. Inside, *box pews* fill the aisles and the early-C19 pulpit matches the delicate w. *gallery* which rests on slim *quatrefoil* wooden pillars. At the e. end of the *nave* is a most impressive life-size effigy of a priest, fully vested, with a dragon

at his feet and his scarred, tonsured head lying within a deep, *crocketted ogee* canopy. He was a prior of Cokesford and the stone was moved to Houghton in 1522. The early-C17 *chancel* stalls have simple shallow carving on their backs, rough *poppy-heads*, and naive figures on the arms. There is an excellent array of *hatchments*, including a recent addition for the 5th Marquess of Cholmondeley who died in 1969. Sir Robert Walpole, England's first Prime Minister (d.1745) and Horace Walpole of Strawberry Hill fame (d.1797) both lie in the vault here. Unlike so many lesser men, they have no grandiloquent monument above their graves. Indeed, Horace wrote to the Countess of Ossory just before he died: 'I shall be quite content with a sprig of rosemary thrown after me, when the parson of the parish commits my dust to dust.'

Houghton-on-the-Hill, St Mary (E5): This isolated little church is to be found at the end of a half-mile of track leading from one of the lanes between North and South Pickenham, and enquiries about access are advised before visiting. That should not be allowed to deter anyone because this is one of the most interesting and, in one respect at least, most important of the county's small churches. That it is still there at all is due to the indefatigable enthusiasm and energy of Mr Bob Davey, a local churchwarden and retired engineer. By chance in 1992, he discovered what was then an ivy-covered and roofless ruin in a jungle of undergrowth on rising ground in open country, with a single farmhouse close by. It had never been deconsecrated and he single-handedly set about restoring it to use. Within two years he had enlisted the support of the county and district councils, English Heritage, the *Churches Conservation Trust* and the *Norfolk Churches Trust*, and work began on restoration. This was so successful that the building received a national Heritage Award (keeping company with Windsor Castle in that year's awards). Even to visit the churchyard is worth the effort just to enjoy the flowers and shrubs that bloom throughout the year – again as a result of Mr Davey's hard work. There was once a village of some size here, but only humps in the neighbouring fields to the n. and e. remain as witnesses, and although the last cottages did not succumb until 1994, St Mary's was abandoned in the 1940s. There has been a church here since before the Norman Conquest, and when the *nave* floor was relaid recently, a building line and post-holes were discovered on the n. side – firm evidence that the first *Saxon* building was wooden. This was followed by a simple nave and *chancel* with an *apsidal* e. end in the late C10/early C11, and in the C12 a s. *aisle* was added. In the C15 a larger, rectangular chancel replaced the original and the tower was built. By the 1760s the chancel had become a ruin, and the remains having been levelled, a tiny rectangular extension with a hipped roof was put in its place. Walking round the outside is a good way to make sense of this progression through the years. The unbuttressed C14 tower is largely brick and has a substantial stair turret on the s. side; many thin Roman bricks were re-used, together with a few *long & short quoins* from the Saxon building. In October 1916 a German Zeppelin unloaded its bombs haphazardly over the countryside and one fell close by, doing considerable damage to the tower. Its condition deteriorated over time into an ivy-clad ruin, but it has now been restored to its full height, floors have been inserted, and a new interior door fitted to the stair (which is virtually all brick, including the treads and risers). Work just outside the w. end revealed that there was a round tower in the first instance, and the footings show that it was probably as large as East Lexham's, for which a C10 date has been suggested. The n. door was inserted in the mid-C12 but was closed later, although one slim shaft survives topped by a diminutive *Romanesque capital*, and a change in the masonry at high level shows clearly where the walls were raised at that time to support a new roof. The one Saxon *lancet* on this side was blocked up in 1895, embedding and hiding the original wooden frame, and the window with *Decorated* tracery further along is a very good example of modern quality masonry that follows the design of the original. The stub chancel has a new window too, echoing its C18 predecessor. Beyond the e. end, flints mark out the apsidal end of the first chancel and also the rectangular outline of its much larger successor which survived long enought to be described in *Blomefield's History of Norfolk*. A fragment of masonry at ground level by the n.e. corner of the building shows that the C14 chancel was only a little narrower than the nave; a wooden cross has been laid on the site of its high altar. The C12 rebuilding included a s. aisle, and the footings of its walls having been determined, they too are marked with flints. In the C14, the aisle was demolished and a new nave s. wall made by filling in the two-bay *arcade*, leaving the outline

of its arches showing and moving two lancets inwards from the old aisle wall. The outline of the w. lancet shows plainly, and the other was restored and glazed in the C19 when the large rectangular window (recently restored) was inserted further along. The s. dooway was re-used in the same way, although the replacement door was cut square rather than bother with the arch shape. Moving in through the tower w. door one comes to a substantial display of photographs concerned with the progress of restoration, and opposite is an excellent parish chest in pine dated 1724 and carved with the names of the rector and churchwardens of the day. In company with the altar, it managed to survive the funeral pyre of the church's furniture which took place in the churchyard supervised by the rector in the 1940s. Above the C14 tower arch to the nave one can trace the outline of the massive semi-circular arch that linked the original round tower with the rest of the building. At this point in the church's renaissance, the inside is a little harsh to the eye, mainly because work is still progressing on the walls. Half of the font has been rescued from its use as birdbath in a neighbouring garden and re-set on its original shaft. Its smooth rounded shape and complete lack of decoration point to a very early date – possibly C10. A *holy water stoup* has been set in the wall by the n. door and, like the outside view, the arches of the C12 arcade are clear in the s. wall. Having been removed to what was thought a place of safety, the flooring of the nave was inadvertently sold and could not be replaced, but the red *pamments* are a sound and acceptable alternative. Work on the churchyard has resulted in a number of discoveries, and one of the most important was the uncovering of the church's original stone *mensa*. It had been hidden by adherants to the old Catholic faith at the *Reformation* in the belief that one day they might restore it to its rightful place. One hopes that their souls are gladdened by its resurrection and replacement in the church they knew – not to the high altar admittedly, but to a side altar in the nave. The chancel arch is unadorned *Norman* in style, but when the surrounding wall was examined there was evidence that it had been larger, ballooning out slightly at the top. The exisiting arch is built entirely of thin tile-like Roman bricks and is flanked by two large niches associated with nave altars. Remains of lath and plaster in their back walls show that, although they were sealed off in the C18, they were open to the chancel originally. The reason why this diminutive church has assumed such importance and considerable publicity is that during the course of restoration and renovation, remains of extensive wall paintings were discovered which are of national significance. They survive in fragments on all four walls, with the largest on the e. wall above and on both sides of the chancel arch. There are at least three layers of work, and the earliest has been dated around the beginning of the C11. Above the arch, within a lobed *mandorla*, is a huge *Holy Trinity* group – God the Father enthroned (with a small *quatrefoil* on his right knee), Christ on the cross in the centre, and the dove of the Holy Spirit just above. This is the earliest known example in Europe of a wall painting showing the Trinity in this fashion. Beyond the edge of the mandorla, haloed heads of the blessed gaze upward, and above the top of the arch runs a frieze of roundels, each containing a bust-length saint with a scroll. They can perhaps be interpreted as the Apostles (In Luke 22:30 Christ promises his disciples that they shall judge the twelve tribes of Israel – there is a Christ figure in the centre, and all the figures are young and beardless.); or they could be a series of Old Testament prophets. On the n. side of the arch there is a Resurrection of the Dead scene, where an impressive angel with elegant wings blows the Last Trump, and little naked figures leave their graves beyond him.Turning away from this vision of Heaven and Judgement to the e., the congregation would have faced the prospect of an alternative pictured on the w. wall – a Harrowing of Hell. On the n. wall, between the *lancet* and the Decorated window, there is a fragment of a scene rarely depicted – God the Father creating Eve, with the Tree of the Knowledge of Good and Evil to the right The supreme importance of these paintings in the history of church art has prompted a study in depth by experts in the relevant disciplines, and the photographs on display in the tower record some of their findings. The work of interpretation continues, but meanwhile the visitor must be content to concentrate on what is immediately accessible to the eye. The fact that work of two later periods which must not be destroyed overlays the earliest, means that this is not easy. No electricity supply rules out artificial lighting at the moment and, for the time being, take a torch or pick a sunny day for your visit. St Mary's is now a chapel of ease within the parish of South Pickenham, and as well as regular parochial services it attracts groups from far and wide to worship or meditate. Its future is secure.

Hoveton, St John (J4): A *Norman* or earlier church stood here, witness the *carstone* corner *quoins* of the n.e. corner of the *nave*, visible from the path. The tower is rustic red brick of 1765. There has been much restoration inside, and the modest C15 *screen* is painted brown. In the heads of the plumply *Perpendicular* n. windows there are fragments of good medieval glass, including a figure of St *John* with the devil peeping from his chalice. A tablet on the *chancel* s. wall, with an urn fronting crossed sword and musket, records that John Spencer Blofeld of the 5th Madras Infantry, 'fell a Victim to his Exertions in camp near Hyderabad' in 1803. Above are five *hatchments*. Outside, below the e. window it is recorded that George Brown died at 73 in 1757, having been 'an useful, honest and faithful servant to Thomas Blofeld' for 37 years. The sequence of adjectives is revealing. An oddity by the path to the gate – an oaken memorial slab set upright in a wrought iron decorative frame, to Amos Thrower (d.1882), which is just legible after 100 years.

Hoveton, St Peter (J4): This small church is down a lane off to the w. of the Wroxham-Stalham road, about a mile n. of Hoveton St John. A simple, neat building of red brick, with a thatched roof, little *bell cote*, and crow-stepped gables, it carries its date of 1624 above the arch of the *porch*. Behind it, open fields stretch away to Hoveton Hall. The set of *Stuart* arms above the w. window are nicely carved in relief against a painted background, and have been re-gilded. The pulpit is of the same period as the building, and there is a series of seven *hatchments* hung around the walls. On the monument to Mrs Aufrere (d.1750) and her daughter, the lettering is cleverly cut over the folds of marble drapery held by a *putto*.

Howe, St Mary (I5): Here we are in deep rural England – a picturesque little church, with a stubby, sturdy *Saxon* tower, in a serene setting closely protected by high trees. The tower, now capped with a conical tile cap, has deeply splayed round windows at one level, coarse round-headed ones at another; inside the church, there was another opening, now blocked up, over the massive rounded tower arch, looking down into the *nave*. That blank eye looks down now on a very plain and over-modernised interior, with largely modern roofs and furnishings throughout, and a replacement e. window, in the *Decorated* geometrical style, containing modern stained glass by *Heaton, Butler & Bayne*. The nave roof retains its original C15 principal beams, with very long *wall posts*, six completed with praying angels as *corbels*, and two with regal heads, one male in a crown, the other female in a dashing head-dress which was high fashion around 1450 – a close cap on the skull with enormous Bunny-Girl 'ears' on each side of the head. The *rood stairs* are in the s.e. corner of the nave. On the n. side is a deeply splayed, round headed window, possibly of Saxon origin; and set into deep blank arches, very low down, two tiny 'Y' traceried windows: the overall effect is most pleasing, set off by the white walls of this punctiliously cared for little place. In the *chancel*, there is an *Early English lancet* on the n. side, Decorated windows on the s.; also a neat *trefoil*-arched *piscina*; an oblong niche in the wall on the opposite side was an *aumbry*, perhaps; and above it, an undated brass inscription plate setting out the hopes and wishes of the patron of the church, the Rt. Hon. Lady Elizabeth Hastings, on the duties and calling of the priest, trusting, not least, that he 'would be much in Conversation with his People and would inform himself of the Spiritual Condition, the respective wants and Occasions of their souls' and would 'turn the Stream of their Affections from the momentary and vain Enjoyments of this world, to the Everlasting Riches and only solid Pleasures of the Next'. We do hope he did. As you leave, note the outline of the C11 s. door.

Hunstanton, St Edmund (C1): When Henry Le Strange decided to create a new holiday resort in the mid-C19, he not only planned the layout, the houses, the hotel, and ensured that there was a rail link to Kings Lynn, but he determined that the town should have a church to match. After his early death in 1862 his son Hamon put the work in hand and the *chancel* was ready for use by 1866, with completion of the whole in 1872. The architect was Hamon's cousin Frederick Preedy who had previously carried out the restoration of St Mary's in the old village. A tower had been intended but it was never built, leaving the building with a slightly stolid look, but the brick and flint mixture enlivened by *carstone* banding is in tune with the general character of the town. The original entrance was via a w. door, but a s. *porch* was added in 1934 and it opens on to a spacious interior. *Pevsner* complains that the removal of the furniture in 1962 has taken away its character, but although the low, plain pews impart a rather flat feel in such a broad setting, the general impression if one of understated Anglo-Catholic richness. Above the old w. door the 1962 glass in the 3-*light* window is by John Lawson and Vera Flint – figures of SS. *Francis, Christopher, & Nicholas*, with three themes in the bottom frieze – wild life, period motor cars & planes, and a variety of sea-going craft. To the right is a chapel dedicated to Our Lady of Walsingham created in 1982. The C15 font is by far the oldest object in the church, having come from the chapel of St *Giles* at Fressingfield in Suffolk. Scenes from the life of St *Edmund* fill the *aisle* windows with bright, clear colour and are extremely attractive. Installed between 1937 and 1966, apart from one, they are the work of William Lawson and John L. Lawson with those by the latter displaying the greater vitality. The exception is the window furthest e. in the s. aisle which came in 1911 from the studio of *Sir Ninian Comper* and is signed with his strawberry emblem at the bottom. Despite his high reputation it has to be said that the design and colouring is decidedly thin. The broad chancel arch has triple shafts whose rings are studded with *ball-flowers* and *capitals* thick with seaweed, with the *rood* reaching to the apex. Ritual emphasis is given to the sanctuary by using first four steps and then six to reach it via a wide and stately chancel. The sanctuary s. window glass illustrates the raising of *Lazarus* and is by Frederick Preedy the architect of the building; it has much in common with his work at St Mary's, particularly the pink and mauve tones. The e. window is unmistakedly by Charles Eamer *Kempe* – lush, dense designs – the centre filled with a Crucifixion above a Nativity, flanked by the *Evangelists*, 2 bishops and 2 female saints. After all this richness it is quite a shock to turn and face plain glass in the large w. *lancets*.

Hunstanton, St Mary (C1): Standing in a quiet retreat below the former home of the ancient Le Strange family and beside a duck-thronged pool, this is a handsome church in a setting to remember. Though in essence an early-C14 building, it was decisively restored in 1853 and 1865 by Frederick Preedy for his cousin Henry Le Strange. All the windows were renewed and the 5-*light* e. window has a quite extraordinary tracery pattern. The *Decorated* s. *porch* is beautiful, with large open-work *cusps* set under the outer arch above slim pillars, and the matching niche displays a modern Madonna and Child; the circular side windows are filled with whirling tracery of great vitality. The interior of the church is spacious and the roof of the *nave*, designed by Thomas Earp in the 1850s, employs every concievable type of brace. It rises from enormous *corbels* carved with life-size demi-figures of the Apostles. At the w. end there are *Royal Arms* of William IV, and the big square *Norman* font stands on chunky little legs. Nearby, find a good *brass* marking the 1480 grave of Edmund Grene and his fashionably dressed wife. The soaring five-bay *arcades* are early-C14, with a mixture of round and octagonal *piers*, and all have stone seats around their bases. Filled-in slots in those at the e. end show where *parclose screens* were once fitted, and note the remnants of original zig-zag decoration on the last one on the n. side. In the corner here is the great table tomb of Sir Roger Le Strange, 1506, with its fine brass. He is shown under a resplendent canopy and helm, wearing armour and an heraldic tabard. Nearby is another tomb whose carved decoration suggests a late-C13 date. The panels of the early-C16 *rood screen* are painted with the figures of the Apostles, and they form an artistic group with those at North Elmham and Norwich St James and St Mary Magdalene. The upper part of the screen was restored and given new coving by G.F.Bodley in 1892, and the understated choir stalls were designed by Sir Walter Tapper in 1928. The *chancel*, however, is dominated by the massive arched and canopied tomb of Sir Henry Le Strange (1485) which has been heavily restored. Its tomb chest was designed for use as an *Easter Sepulchre*, and was modelled on the one at Hingham as directed by Sir Henry's will. There is a plain *angle piscina* alongside *dropped sill sedilia* in the sanctuary, and the e. window glass of 1867, with its 15 scenes of the life of Christ, is quite the best example of Frederick Preedy's work. A few years earlier he had made the glass in the s. *aisle* e. window – a *Jesse Tree* designed by Sir Henry Le Strange.

Hunworth, St Lawrence (G2): One of the starkest of interiors in the county, but not uncomfortably so. In fact, the church has an almost Scandinavian simplicity about it. Tall whitewashed walls reach up to *arch-braced roofs*, with no memorial tablets to distract the eye save one – the record of the six men of Hunworth who did not return in 1918. The one spot of colour in the *nave* comes from a diminutive modern statue of St *Lawrence*. Holding his gridiron like a shield at rest, he stands in a pretty little 12in. niche cut on the angle of the C14 window embrasure on the n. side. A Lady chapel opens off the nave to the s. and has fine, big C15 windows and a *piscina* in the corner. A pity

that the main fuse box overshadows it, and that this little *transept* is crammed with pews. The *chancel* is an 1850s rebuild which fits the church well, and in it hangs a Turkish sanctuary lamp in bronze filigree, said to have belonged to Florence Nightingale. Clues to the real age of the building are outside. A little *Saxon* window was revealed on the s. side during a restoration in 1960, and the tower dates from the C12, although it's disguised a little by western buttresses. These had decorative panels under the *set-offs* and one remains on the s.w. – a *cusped* Star of David, set in a circle of shallow carving, St Lawrence has the last word – look down as you leave the *porch* and you will see his initial and his gridiron picked out in *flushwork* at the base.

Ickburgh, St Peter (E6): Almost the last stop down a long village cul-de-sac is Ickburgh's little church. Last stop appears to be a line of Victorian almshouses for the elderly which in large letters across the gables reminds its residents, with singular lack of tact, one might think 'it is towards evening, the day is far spent'. No such thought was in the minds of the industrious Victorians who, 20 years before the almshouses were erected, entirely rebuilt the body of the church in 1865-66 and endowed it with windows in exaggerated *Decorated* style which fairly shout Nineteenth Century. The simple, battlemented tower, however, is original late-C14 work, with Decorated and *Perpendicular* forms still not entirely reconciled. The Victorian timber and stained glass n. *porch* is most attractive. Worth a close look all round are the grotesque *gargoyles*, and the pretty stops – floral and 'portrait' heads – to the *drip moulds* of all the windows. Best of all are the stops to the n. door – chained and haltered bears against backgrounds of oak leaves and acorns. The interior of the church is in its own way something of a collector's piece, the rebuilders having taken endless trouble to ensure a 'medieval' look. Nice *arch-braced roof*, with big carved angels, all carrying musical instruments, on the *wall plates*, *arcade* with quite splendid *corbel* carvings at each end, a lovely nativity scene at the w. and the Adoration of the Kings at the e. A stone pulpit has more carved biblical scenes in high relief, adjoining a low stone *screen* set with scroll-bearing angels. Full suite of double *piscina*, arched *aumbry* and triple *sedilia* in the *chancel*. At the opposite end of the building, at the back of the nave, there are even mini-benches for the children. Those Victorians thought of everything!

Illington, St Andrew (F6): Now leased to the *Norfolk Churches Trust*, and although easily spotted from the East Wretham – Larling road, you need to take the drive down to Park Farm as far as a bridleway which strikes off to the right just before the farm buildings; after 300 yds of stiffish going the church is gained, set in a roughly mown churchyard surrounded by farming in high-tech polythene mode. The distinctive *Perpendicular* tower, recently rescued from decay, has strong diagonal buttresses, each chequered and with three gabled *set-offs*. Bold *dripstones* drop diagonally back to the walls and small image niches, with nodding *ogee heads*, flank the w. door. In the stage above the w. window there are splendid *sound-holes* – quatrefoils within quatrefoils, and the bell openings are variously shuttered. The tower's parapet echoes the *flushwork* of the buttresses in a running lozenge pattern, and a sturdy stone stair-turret rises to the ringing chamber against the s. wall. The fabric of the *nave* is *Norman* – look for a typically narrow *lancet* in both the n. and s. walls, and the n. door which became a half-length window in the C19. In the s. wall the outlines of two widely-spaced arches are all that remain of an *arcade* that linked the nave to a vanished s. *aisle*. One of these arches was later used to house a window using sections of C13 'Y' tracery, and that in its turn was truncated to a C19 half-length. The n. wall has flints set in regular courses typical of the Norman period and alongside there is a single *Decorated* two-*light* window with inward-turning *headstops*. The *chancel* is almost as wide as the nave and its Perpendicular e. window has an angular head with a little C19 glass in the tracery. Round the corner, windows of the same period flank a slim *priest's door*. The s. *porch* overlays one of the old arcade arches, and one enters a clean and decent interior via a narrow C13 dooway. At the time of my visit the Trust was about to lime-wash the interior and re-lay the floor. The arch of the tower fades into *imposts* at high level, and below there is a plain octagonal font both deep and heavy. C19 pine benches in the nave, enlivened by excellent *poppy-heads,* match the pulpit on its coved stem, and the pine *communion rails* are crisply carved in medieval style. The church's *mensa* was not destroyed at the *Reformation* but lies snugly in the n.e. corner of the sanctuary. The churchyard on a summer's day could well be a place to linger – an old crabapple tree close to the church's s. wall shelters some good C18 stones, and there is at least one tombstone oddity. William Doe has lain a few paces from the porch since 1888 'Gone but not forgotten'; truly, because his stone can be picked out at 100yds. for, above the inscription there is a startlingly white bas-relief head of Christ in a roundel with a curlicue frame, and it is quite unweathered. Was it always thus?

Ingham, Holy Trinity (J3): A grand church, with a noble four-stage tower with stepped, pinnacled and panelled buttresses, large bell openings (though tracery and mouldings have gone), a magnificent w. window with composite door below, richly ornamented in *spandrels* and above with shields and coats-of-arms; and a fine *flush-panelled base course*. There are two n. doors, one (*Decorated*) in the usual w. end position; another (*Perpendicular*) in the centre– for this led to the priory whose conventual church this was. In 1355 Sir Miles Stapleton obtained a licence from the Pope to rebuild the existing parish church and to establish a priory of Trinitarian Canons, dedicated to ransoming captives of war. Just a few ruins of the priory may be seen beyond this door, including the *rood stair* and, in a dark corner, what was presumably a *holy water stoup* for the monks on entering the church. Moving on, the n. *chancel* window is Decorated, in a lovely *reticulated* style, and the e. window a complex and beautiful pattern of later Decorated craftsmanship; above it is a curious little outline, bricked in, with a *trefoil* head. The large three-*light* s. chancel windows are Perpendicular, two with very rich tracery; likewise the *aisle* windows, in two of which the tracery is still strongly of Decorated character. The *clerestory* is unusual – round windows with complex flower-like tracery. The Perpendicular C15 *porch* is splendid and very rare in having three storeys. In the upper two, lived the parish priest who was also sacrist of the priory. The entrance has a fine, unadorned *groined* roof, A spacious and fine interior to the church, with a handsome modern *nave* roof which combines *arch-braces* with *hammer-beams*, and cross beams with *king posts*, and is adorned with colourful shields. The five-bay C14 *arcade* is beautiful, with its clustered columns and elegant *capitals*, and is complemented by the later, soaring tower arch. The nave and n. aisle have numerous old *poppy-head* bench ends. The C13 font is octagonal, with the simple double-arcading round its bowl excellently preserved; it stands on an unfortunate modern stem and shafts of coloured marble. At the e. end of the s. aisle is a fine late-C15 table-tomb on which lie effigies of Sir Roger de Bois and his wife Margaret, she, slim and wearing a demure head-dress, he bluff and armoured with his feet on a dog. Nearby is a *brass* to a knight and his lady which, until as recently as the 1930s, included a named brass to their dog Jakke – but this has since disappeared, leaving one at Deerhurst in Gloucestershire as the only 'dog brass' in England. In the chancel (beyond the remains of the stone *screen*, which divided the monks from the laity) are the remnants of two once great *brasses*, one on the s. side to Sir Miles Stapleton (founder of the priory), 1364, and his wife Joan, and on the n. to a knight, 1410. Then there is the tomb to Sir Oliver de Ingham, 1344, who lies in an acutely uncomfortable posture on a bed of cobbles (see also, Reepham Church), under the remnants of what must have been a most opulent canopy. Opposite, there are lovely graduated *piscina* and *sedilia* – C15, though Victorian restored – arched, pinnacled and canopied.

Ingoldisthorpe, St Michael (C2): Snugly set at the end of a sinuous little tree-lined drive, a church of the early C14 (with late-C14 *clerestory* and *chancel*), which was enthusiastically restored in the 1850s. The base of a *preaching cross* stands by the s. *porch* and inside, one of the first things to be seen is a square *Norman* font which was roughly cut down to an octagon – in the C15, judging by the shaft and base; remains of the original decoration survive on four sides of the bowl. The tower arch has been recently blocked up, but venture into the gloom to find a late (1608) *brass* on the w. wall for Agnes Bigge and her parents, the Rector Thomas Rogerson and his wife; three separate figures (one damaged and loose) and interesting because *brasses* of post-*Reformation* clergy are not common, and also because the women wear broad-brimmed high-crowned hats like trilbys. The brightly painted demi-figures of saints and prophets below the roof *corbels* look like C19 work and the flatter line of the previous roof can be seen clearly on the tower wall. The *rood screen* has *ogee arches* which have lost most of their *cusping*, but the tracery above is excellent and the cresting complete – a pity that it is still smothered in dark brown paint. The chancel arch responds are slightly concave on three faces, with small *trefoils* at the top – a delicate touch that is used on a large scale at Dersingham and Narborough. Most of the stained glass is 1850s by the *O'Conners* and unremarkable, but look at the panels in the head of the n. chancel window – they are like early tinted photographs; Thomas Becket died young in the woods of 'New

Brunswick, British America' in 1863, and he is seen seated it a study table and lying prone beneath a tree with his gun. The rector's two young children are shown in the same style in the opposite window.

Ingworth, St Lawrence (H3): A delicious little church perched prettily on a mound above the village street and thatched throughout. Its round *Norman* tower fell in 1822 and the remains have been skilfully recapped with a thatched half-cone to provide a small raised vestry within. The *nave* was of the same period but was rebuilt in the late C14 when the s. *porch* was added. This has an attractive crowstepped gable in red brick and there is a big *mass dial* high on the wall. The interior has a 'busy' feeling, as though everything has been fitted in – just. A diminutive organ, for example, is cleverly housed in a *gallery* tucked into the n.w. corner. The C15 font looks as though it once had the *Seven Sacrament* scenes round the bowl, but they have been completely chiselled away. The base of the *screen* is C15, with a lanky *Jacobean* top said to have come from Aylsham – all painted brown and quite unattractive. The cut-down pulpit portion of a *three-decker* has an *hour-glass* stand complete with glass, and it fronts a range of C18 pine *box pews* on the n. side. Opposite, extraordinarily coarse deal pews have been fitted on to the old oak sills and cut-down ends of the originals. At the w. end above the tower arch is a very fine example of the *Royal Arms* of William III in carved and gilded wood and mounted in a frame on a deep red background. Quite different, but just as nice in its way is the floor of plain salmon pink bricks.

Intwood, All Saints (H5): This little church sits picturesquely on its mound above the crossroads with a thatched cottage for company, and it is a shock to recall that in the C16 it was a neglected ruin used as a sheepcote. When Sir Henry Hobart bought the manor, he lived here while Blickling was being built, and at the same time he pulled down nearby Keswick church to restore Intwood. Apart from the octagonal top and a C13 *lancet*, the round tower is undisturbed *Saxon*, and you can see the outline of the original doorway in the w. face and, now that the old organ has gone, the tall plain arch into the *nave*. There are *quoins* of *carstone* and thin tile at the e. end of the nave that must be *Norman* or earlier. The C14 *porch* has a little lancet over the arch which shows that it had an upper room, but the 1852 restoration has left no trace of it. The outer arch has large *headstops* of a queen and a bishop – possibly in honour of Edward III's Philippa and Bishop Bateman. Inside, a short nave and *chancel*, a low w. *gallery* and a very good set of early-C19 pews all combine to give a cosy domestic feeling of quality and comfort. The *poppy-heads* in the chancel are very good for the period – one has a profusion of acorns with a coat of arms hung from a branch and a grasshopper perched above. Nearby, shades of our Imperial past: Lieut. Clement William Onley Unthank, 3rd King's Own Hussars, died aged 25 at Lucknow in 1900 'from the effects of a fall at polo'. The church has an excellent ring of 5 bells, tenor 5-2-18 cwt.

Irstead, St Michael (J3): To be found in a most picturesque setting at the end of a tree-lined, narrow lane, close to the River Ant. The C14 church is thatched, and this shows through between the rafters in a diagonal pattern. There are remains of *Norman* work in the heads of both the n. and s. doorways, and the C15 s. *aisle* is separated from the *nave* by a very rudimentary *arcade*. The C14 font is unusual in having the Head of Christ in two of the panels, and the Hand of God in another. The pulpit has unremarkable C16 *linen-fold panelling*, but has part of a C13 stall attached to it as a handrail. With a small carved head and stiffleaf foliage it is a most interesting survival and, like many oddments in this area, it is said to have come from St Benet's Abbey, whose ruins are not far away near Ludham, on the bank of the River Bure. The base of the *rood screen* has large panels with paintings of the Apostles, three to each panel, apparently painted over earlier work. There is a tiny *rood loft* staircase set in the n. wall. The oak *chancel* rails of 1852 have varied tracery roundels and are rather good. They were a memorial to Lady Palgrave, whose husband Sir Francis, of 'Golden Treasury' fame lies buried at the e. end of the churchyard. There is a modern statue of the church's dedicatory saint, St *Michael*, wrestling with a very sinuous serpent in the niche above the s. door.

Itteringham, St Mary (H2): Plain unbuttressed tower, simple *nave* and *chancel*, dating principally from the C14. The e. end shows clearly that there was a larger window before the C19 restoration when the present one was put in. Entering by the s. *porch* it is a pleasant surprise to find that a new n. door has been fitted with leaded *light*s in the top half so that you have a view across the

churchyard as a bonus to the additional light inside. The chest by the door looks late-C16 or early-C17, but is dated 1716 – a good example of time-lag in country craft styles. The *box pews* have *poppy-head* bench ends that seem to be of the same vintage, which is rather an odd mixture. The sanctuary has big C17 panels of some quality. They have perspective arches, and are set in later woodwork to form a seemly *reredos*. Interesting also to see in the chancel a large engraving of Goetze's painting 'Despised and rejected of men' – an Edwardian allegory that spells everything out.

Kelling, St Mary (G1): Mainly *Perpendicular* in style, although there are two blocked windows above the n. door which look *Norman*. There is a n. *transept* and the ruins of its opposite number to the s. The diminutive C15 *porch* is charming, with a well-proportioned arch outside and sheltering the C14 doorway. Two things invite attention here: the C15 font, with an inscription round its rim seeking prayers for the De Kelling donor and his wife Beatrice: and the *Easter Sepulchre*, which as usual is in the n.e. corner of the *chancel*: although the later raising of the floor obscures its base, it is a well-nigh perfect example. *Royal Arms* over the door illustrate the way these are often re-used: the initials are G.R. but the motto ('Semper Eadem') is Queen Anne's.

Kenninghall, St Mary (G7): A big, good looking 'town church', with a sturdy, squat tower, impressive in its plainness of roughly chequerworked flint and stone – it is C15 *Perpendicular,* with small red brick battlements, simple two-*light* belfry openings, and a big w. window with rather weird *corbel* heads to its *drip mould*. All round it has a fine *base course* of large, stone-carved panels in a variety of designs. That on the s. w. buttress has a crumbled shield in a multi-spiked surround or 'bordure'; at the end of the C19, apparently, the arms on the shield were still visible and were confirmed by one authority then as those of Thomas, *Duke of Norfolk*, who built the tower. He intended to add a spire but, we are quaintly informed, he was 'attainted for alleged treason ere his design was completed' (Henry VIII conveniently died on the eve of the day Norfolk was to be executed: so the Duke escaped with his head; freedom from the Tower took a bit longer but Kenninghall never got its spire). As you approach the church from the road, the s. aspect of the *nave* is very striking, with its large and elegant Perpendicular windows, and above them, a neat *clerestory* range – an unusual element, since there never was an *aisle* on this side. Perpendicular too, and lit by fine windows of the period, is the n. aisle, with a pretty little door at its e. end which gave access in former days to a *chantry chapel* Its arch is slightly flattened under a square hood, and the initials WB are carved in the *spandrels*. The *chancel* is older, of about 1300, with a lovely e. window of *cusped, intersecting* tracery. A neat contemporary *priest's door* on the s. has a heavy drip mould with correspondingly huge corbel heads. The window to its left, with its *mullioned* lower panels, was a *low side window*. The squat Perpendicular *porch* protects a *Norman* s. doorway, characterised not only by unusual mouldings to its arch and *capitals*, but by a lively carving of a horse on the l. hand *jamb*, and of a lion low on the right. The *mass dial* on this side obviously preceded the C15 porch. The horse carving, according to Prof. Peter Lasko dates from about 1300 or a little earlier, judging by its kirb bit and decorated trappings. Through the heavy timber door now (stenciled 1752 on the inside) into a bright and spacious interior. Substantial *tie-beamed* roof to nave, with *king posts* and copious open carvings over two of the ties; C14 n. *arcade* of five bays; cusped *holy water stoup* by s. door; and half way down the s. side – an odd position – a curiously ungainly *angle piscina*, with a *cusped, ogee* arch. To its left, a painted *consecration cross*; and left again, mounted on the wall, a couple of remnants of an ancient *brass,* dated about 1500 and showing two kneeling groups of children; also set into the wall, two stone footings, one moulded, the other carved with floral motifs, to hold saints' effigies. Footings for figures are also set into the pillars of the chancel arch (which is contemporary with the arcade), one carved with oak leaf and acorn, the other with a female head. The chancel has a tie-beamed roof; a very plain arched piscina and equally plain *sedilia*, recessed into the wall under a low, flattened arch; an old low, long bench with *poppy-heads,* one additionally with a carved beast; and a particular curiosity, a small remnant of a table tomb, its brass effigy and shields long since ripped from the top, but stone carved shields and tracery intact around the chest. Dominating the n. aisle is a splendidly lively and very unsophisticated *Royal Arms* of Elizabeth I, obviously made to fit the chancel arch (as generally directed by Her Majesty), and now sitting on a moulded and embattled beam over the n. aisle chapel. At the opposite end of the aisle, another Royal Arms, for Charles I, this

one in a square frame. A severely plain C14 octagonal font, with what must once have been a glorious steeple canopy, nearly 10ft. high. It is C15 Perpendicular, and much-faded and ill-used by time and circumstance. In this aisle, and at the w. end of nave, some good poppy-head benchends; also at nave's w. end, a plain pillar poorman's box; over the s. door, an intricately carved remnant of the ancient *rood screen*. And finally, a modern stained glass window by Paul Jefferies, on the nave's s. side, dated 1966, showing St *Felix* and Norfolk's own St *Walstan* in colours and style which are essentially 20th century, yet which manage to contain a medieval spirit. Before you leave the churchyard, take a look at the baroque carving on the little gravestone by the s.w. buttress of the tower – dated 1770, most intricately sculpted with cherub head, swags of cloth, skulls, crossbones, hour-glasses and scrollery. The church has an excellent ring of 8 bells, tenor 15-2-3 cwt.

Keswick, All Saints (I5): From the w., the fields sweep gently up to the church with its slim round tower set romantically within a dark copse, reminiscent of a James Stark engraving. When Sir Henry Hobart bought the two manors in 1598, he raided Keswick church for materials to rebuild Intwood, and Keswick remained a ruin until 1893. Then, John Henry Gurney built a private mortuary chapel here, and it came back to use as a church in 1922. A long grassy track leads to the thick grove of trees, and within an iron fence there is a neat graveyard. The *Saxon* tower of regularly banded flint has one bell opening in medieval brick (the others are modern), and until 1893 there was a gaping hole in the e. face. This was repaired with a brick arch to the *nave* but the inside of the tower and the wall to the nave remain undressed flint. To call it a nave overstates the case a little, for it is all of 6yds long and 7yds wide, with a diminutive *apse* added in 1954. There are some small C15 painted angels set on the *wall plates* which must have come from another church – which one? Over the apse, a 1922 window from the *William Morris* workshops, with a figure holding an anchor, against a romantic landscape with sea birds overhead. This is pleasing but owes no allegiance to the Arts and Crafts movement. Outside, beyond the apse, are the ivy-clad ruins of the *chancel* – only 4yds long, so the original church was pocket size like its successor.

Ketteringham, St Peter (H5): A church which is tucked away, and reached by a road that leads only to a few houses and the Hall – once stately home, USAAF HQ, school, and now part of the Lotus organisation. It is a picturesque setting, with thatched cottages, cypresses, and great sweet chestnuts looming at the e. end. There are two blocked *Norman lancets* in the *nave* s, wall, and beyond a blocked *priest's door*, single and double C13 lancets in the *chancel*. Both doorways are simple C13, and the tower was rebuilt in 1609, with further restoration and embellishment in the 1870s by *Jekyll* (the curious corner pinnacle figures were carved by James Minns of Heigham). The font of about 1500 has shields on the tall step, floral motifs in the deep shaft recesses, and a pretty vine trail under the bowl retains traces of colour. The C13 *piscina* has a *trefoil* arch with a simple chamfer, and columns with ring *capitals*. In the back of the fine table tomb beside it, a beautiful pair of *brasses* (1499) both gilded and enamelled; Thomas Hevenyngham, fully accoutred with heavy sword and spurs, has an heraldic tabard on his left shoulder and his five sons kneel with him; his wife Anne wears a rich red gown with lace at wrists, backed by their five daughters. Two scrolls curl upwards from their lips. Spare a moment for the medieval glass in the e. window – there is a range of saints minus their heads in the top tracery, the arms and part of the figure of C15 Sir Henry Grey at the bottom, and some interesting roundels; a St *Christopher* in the top row, a hen with 'rey' on a scroll (*rebus* for Henry) 2nd from left in the 2nd row, and a pale and beautiful figure playing a psaltery at the far right of the bottom row. Ketteringham fascinates mainly because of the people who lived here. Sir William Heveningham was one of those who sat in judgement on Charles I and, although he did not put his hand to the death warrant, he was convicted of high treason and deprived of his wealth when Charles II came in. But his resourceful and influential wife Mary managed to put things right. Even so, the large monument she placed at the n. e. corner of the sanctuary manages to avoid mentioning his name and he was laid beneath a plain black slab in the floor. Strange, too, that the kneeling figures and prayer desk at the bottom successfully obscure much of his epitaph; he lived and died under something of a cloud, but admire the floating angel that holds a *chrysom child*. Just to the w. of this is Harriet Peach's memorial (1825) – a typical *Flaxman* design in which smooth white angels bear the lady up. Opposite is work by *Robert Page*, an omnibus remembrancer for a series of Atkyns in a nicely balanced variety of

marble with a big sarcophagus in front. Edward Atkyns died in 1750 and set it all up, 'in memory of his Ancestors who have so Honorably presided in the courts of Justice in Westminster Hall' – three Barons of the Exchequer whose service spanned half of the C17 and part of the next. If you have read E. Tisdall's 'Mrs Pimpernel Atkyns' you will know all about Charlotte, who brought her family to ruin by her extraordinary devotion to Marie Antoinette. It was the nearest thing in real life to the Scarlet Pimpernel, and is a tale of mystery, romance and eccentricity exceptional even by C18 standards. She died in Paris in 1836 and lies in an unknown grave; in 1907 a belated tribute was raised on the n. wall here, to the ex-Drury Lane actress, lady of the manor, and cloak and dagger eccentric, by 'a few who sympathised with her wish to rest in this church'. Across the w. *gallery* run the words, 'erected September 26th 1841 by Sir John Boileau Bart'. At once, we hear the echoes of a feud between parson and squire that rankled in the parish for 30 years. Sir John's memorial in dull brass is in the chancel, and the Revd. William Wayte Andrew's memorial on the nave s. wall is as stiff, spiky and uncomfortable as the rector himself Seek out Owen Chadwick's book, 'Victorian Miniature' and savour the whole story – guaranteed to bring you back again to Ketteringham. The church has a good ring of 6 bells, tenor 8-1-20 cwt.

Kettlestone, All Saints (F2): A late-C13 or early-C14 octagonal tower (there are only six like it in the county) which has a curious succession of openings. The middle stage has a little door on the s. side, above it the belfry windows, and above them small *quatrefoil* openings. Before the Victorian restoration it was even higher, and some suggest that it may have been used by Lord of the Manor Sir Thomas de Hauville, Keeper of the King's Hawks, to watch his charges at work. The s. *porch* and the *chancel* are C19 and they blend in well. There are fragments of *Norman* stonework above the porch doorway and the stump of a *churchyard cross* stands by. The e. window is C14, and in the top, the excellent tracery forms the shape of a butterfly with outspread wings. A good heraldic C15 font under the tower, with the *Royal Arms* (i.e. England quartering France), arms of the Diocese (with a sprightly crozier added), and emblems of St *Paul*, St *Peter*, St *George*, and the *Trinity*. All are in high relief and set in panels round the octagonal bowl. By the chancel steps is a

Lilliputian organ. Although C19, its pipes are all exposed in the modern fashion, and it measures a mere 5ft. x 2ft. 4in. In the chancel there is a big *ledger slab* to a vicar, William (Gulielmus) Young (d.1667) with italic lettering of very high quality, and by the s. door a wall tablet to a local boy who did not forget his native village: William Newman was reared by the Parish, and the Wardens apprenticed him to a tailor in 1738. He went on to make his fortune in London, and when he died in 1787 'He gave by his will the interest of five hundred pounds in the four per cent to the poor of the parish of Kettlestone for ever.' The spacious churchyard is a pleasant place in which to stroll, and it is worth looking round the corner at the e. end just to see the two enormous headstones to James Cory, Rector, and his family (1793). 5ft. high and 3ft. 6in. wide, they have at the head a charming *Adam style* decoration of shell and acanthus leaves. James and his son (also James) had the living for almost a hundred years from 1766 onwards, and their descendants gave the *lych-gate* in 1907. Damaged by enemy action during the war, it was restored in 1955.

Kilverstone, St Andrew (E7): A long green lane leads down to a charming 1907 *lych-gate* and the little church lies snug within surrounding paddocks. The round tower is broad and rather squat, and although the bell openings and midway *lancets* are *Norman*, the coarse banded flint may be pre-Conquest. A singularly unconvincing w. window in Victorian/Norman style was added in 1857 when *nave* and *chancel* were restored – so much so that it is difficult to identify anything that is original. The exceptions are the Norman s. doorway with single shafts and zigzag moulding, and a five-leaf *piscina* on the outside of the n. wall of the nave. This proves that there must have been a n. *aisle* at one time. Inside, a rather odd C19 font – Norman *dog-tooth* decoration on the stem and broad lily leaves as a base. The *Royal Arms* on the tower wall are a very good set but rather hard to see; the intricate plaster relief work is coloured, gilded and framed, and carries the inscription 'Ex dono Charles Wright 1716'. The memorial to Thomas Wright (d.1775) on the n. wall has a quotation from Gray's 'Elegy written in a country churchyard' which shows how popular the poem had become since it was written in 1750. The *ledger-stone* of Ann Wright is at the e. end of the nave; she died at 41 in 1691 and there is a long inscription with nicely cut capitals ending:

Since then she loved this Sacred Place so
    well,
Tis very meet that here her name should
    dwell.

The chancel seems to have been virtually rebuilt in the C19 but there is a large and deep *ogee*-headed recess in the n. wall that looks original. The stone *reredos* has a rather good mosaic roundel portrait of Christ the Shepherd, and in the s. wall of the nave, an excellent memorial window of 1908 probably by Leonard Walker with plenty of character about it. Something not seen elsewhere are the long kneelers in the pews – they rest on hinged brackets and fold away neatly.

Kimberley, St Peter (G5): Attractive thatched cottages grouped round a green, and then the church just by the lodge and gates to the park. The tower was rebuilt from the ground in the 1530s, with a generous *Tudor* w. window and delicate *flushwork* on the buttresses. Above the first stage, the texture changes completely to a mixture of undressed flint and brick, and this was a rebuilding of a hundred years later, proudly marked in large initials on the four faces T.W. B.W. ANNO DOMM 1631'. (Sir Thomas and Lady Blanche Wodehouse). There is a window of about 1300 on the n. side of the *nave* and the rest are C14, with Victorian work in the *chancel*. A particularly massive *hammer-beam roof* was constructed in 1904 when the chancel arch was rebuilt and the mock-medieval *screen* installed. Opposite the door is a beautiful set of *Royal Arms* in wood, cut to the outline of the design. Apart from its high intrinsic quality, it is the only one in Norfolk that bears the *Stuart* motto used by James I – 'Beati Pacifici' (Blessed are the peacemakers.) when he was hoping for true union between England and Scotland. The C15 archway decorated with floral motifs behind the pulpit lead to the *rood stairs*, and there is a figure niche on the other side of the chancel arch. The whole church bears the impress of the powerful and influential Wodehouse family, and in the sanctuary is the *brass* of John Wodehouse; he coined the family motto Trappe fort' (Strike hard!) at Agincourt, 'spiriting up the English that were inclined to stand'. He died in 1465, but the effigies were not made until seventy years later – the dress betrays this. Next door is the *ledger slab* of the Sir Thomas who completed the tower. The roundel of his arms encloses a delightfully rustic pair of *woodwose* supporters, but what a pity the wooden dais obscures half

Kimberley. St Peter:
E. Window detail – C14 St Margaret

of his epitaph which begins: 'God's mercy and Christ's meritts make me trust To ryse from Sleeping in my Sinful dust'. His daughter Dame Elizabeth Strutt (1651) has her monument on the wall above, and one is sorry that she has to kneel facing e. For this is a charming portrait figure in fashionable alabaster, set within a miniature arch, flanked by pink columns, with little skulls and coat of arms on the *pediment*. Kimberley chancel has a fine variety of medieval glass and binoculars will help you to appreciate it and sort out the various fragments. At the very top of the e. window is an early-C14 head of Christ – now dark and brown, and the sun and moon on either side have faces. Just below, there is a Christ displaying His wounds and a Crucifixion, and below them, a bishop, St *James*, apostles and angels. In the 2nd from left of the large panels, an exceptionally fine St *Margaret of Antioch* which dates from the last quarter of the C14. To the right there is an early-C16 German figure of a weeping woman, and the angels in the bottom corners are also German and of the same period. In the s. chancel window, the two bottom panels are C16 from the German monastery at Steinfeld – Christ expelling the money changers on the left, the General Resurrection on the right. One of the most pleasing things here is the simple black slab in the centre of the chancel. On it reads:

Under this stone Rare Jenkins lie,
The Master of the Musick Art.
Whome from ye Earth the God on High
Call'd unto Him to bear his part.
Ag'd eighty six: October twenty Seven
In Anno sev'nty eight he went to Heav'n.

John Jenkins was a talented musician who spent most of his life as instructor and guest, first with the Le Stranges, then with the Norths and finally with the Wodehouses, and died – if his obituary verse does not make it clear – in 1678. Roger North remarked that he had:

a very good sort of wit which served him in his address and conversation, wherein he did not please less than in compositions. And his way took with the age he lived in, which was a great happiness to him, but he lived so long that he saw himself outrun and antiquated.

No matter; he was appreciated here.

Kings Lynn, All Saints (C3): After all the attention lavished on St Margaret's and St

Nicholas, All Saints – wrapped tightly about by a huge modern housing development around its tree-shaded churchyard – is eminently worth a visit, with masses of interest, structurally and historically. In addition to which, it lays claim to being the oldest building in Lynn. First impression, and one most pleasing to the eye, is its lovely constructional jumble of colours and textures and patterns, of stone and flint, ancient pink brick and yet older dark brown *carstone.* This is all set off by a frieze around the roof line of the *nave*, with crosses in stone, set in flint, above a big *clerestory* range, the walls being partly faced in a bold chequerwork pattern composed, higgledy-piggledy, of the mixture mentioned above. Tower long since gone – it collapsed in 1763 – and replaced by a rebuilt w. end in unfortunate yellow brick, crowned by a sturdy bellcote. On the opposite, e. gable is a C15 *sanctus bell turret.* The nave and *aisles* are otherwise *Perpendicular*, the big *transepts* C13 but with late Perpendicular window insertions. The *chancel* was rebuilt and lengthened in the C15 and is strongly Perpendicular in character. Move round now however to the chancel s. side for an initially puzzling building pattern. The small vestry-like, brick addition here is C15 – and a very rare survival, having been an anker-hold or *anchorite's cell.* To its left the battered chancel s. wall shows various signs of now disappeared additions – a roof line; below it, the remnants of a rather castle-like frieze, a typically *Norman, C12 corbel table,* indicating the interior roof line; below again, the outline of a big arch. Low down on the wall to the left is the top of one pillar and part of an arch, again Norman. The surmise – and one must stress that it is surmise – is that these disappeared buildings were the 'service accommodation' for the anker-hold. Inside, this church is tremendously spacious: but with ingenuity, taste and not a little courage, it has been divided up for more comfortable use and worship. A solid wall *screen* encloses the chancel to form The Chapel of St Michael, where colour, simplicity and care combine with tranquility to produce a lovely atmosphere. White walls, a *crocketted* Victorian *reredos* reproducing medieval spirit and colour – and the same inspiration in recolouring the simply arched and *cusped* C15 *piscina* and triple *sedilia.* Look closely at that piscina and draw aside its interior hanging to disclose that it goes right through the wall to the anker-hold, thus doing dual purpose both as piscina, and as access for the *anchoress* to receive communion. In agreeable contrast with the colours of paintwork, furniture

and soft furnishings here is the lovely scrubbed look of the clean-lined, *poppyheaded* choir stalls. The nave retains its original massive *tie-beams* and *queen posts* in its roof, with completely original roofs in the *aisles*, adorned with *bosses;* one in the s. aisle is especially good, being a *Trinity* representation of God with the Crucifix between his feet (best viewed through binoculars). Lofty, late-C14 four-bay *arcade*, with a corresponding and noble chancel arch over which is a deeply-set opening: not a filled-in window but (note the hinge marks in the stone on its l. *jamb*) an access door to a roof loft; to left and right in the clerestory walls are corresponding doorways. Opened up on the n. side is the *rood loft* exit. Pretty *cusped* figure niches now look down onto a nave altar, which has a lushly coloured modern reredos in designs and hues borrowed from a *Saxon* manuscript. In the s. aisle, the South Chapel is beautifully appointed (with something of an Italianate look about it) and has brought back into use its plain, ancient piscina. Notice to the left of the altar the scrap of moulded Saxon stonework incorporated into the wall. Placed at the w. end of the s. aisle is a sorry remnant, much abused by time and bigots, of six slim panels of the old *rood screen*, painted with saints with their respective symbols: *Bartholomew, Matthew, Philip, Thomas, James,* and *Peter.* The font, necessarily much restored after spending a century on someone's rockery, is C14. The imposing screen under the w. *gallery* is C17 and came from West Lynn.

Kings Lynn, St Margaret (C3): Known conveniently as 'St Margaret's' but its full dedication is 'The Priory church of St Margaret with St Mary Magdalen and all the Virgin Saints', an appropriately resounding title for the great limestone church of an ancient and historic town. Founded in 1101 by the same Bishop Losinga who began building Norwich Cathedral in 1096, it soon had two w. towers added, and the outside of the lower stage of the s.w. tower shows what the *Norman* work was like-interlaced *arcading* between square, densely moulded buttresses. As the work progressed the style changed, and a line of small *Transitional trefoil* arches appears. Come the C13, and the original church made way for a new and larger building and the s.w. tower again shows the shift in style – the second stage has *plate tracery* in the windows with blind replicas on the buttresses, and the bell openings above move on to *bar tracery* of the C14. By the mid-C15 the

Kings Lynn, St Margaret

foundations of the n. w. tower had weakened and a whole new tower was built in *Perpendicular* style and thirty years later an octagonal central lantern was added, rather like the one on Ely Cathedral. A tall spire then completed the s.w. tower and (apart from the dissolution of the priory) there things stood until 1741. At noon on 8th September of that year a great storm brought the spire tumbling down onto the church, but within five years a new 'Gothick' *nave* designed by Matthew Brettingham linked once again the w. towers with the rest of the church – by which time the wooden lantern on the *crossing* had been dismantled. A building, then, with a history of change on a large scale, and entering by the n. *porch* you will see the strange blank arch on its e. wall showing where the market place moved in on an outer *aisle* after the great C18 storm. Inside the porch, rich and swirling colour in the modern w. window by Geoffrey Clarke, and a novel listing of the church's priests on a rotating block of slate designed by John Skelton. Within the *nave*, look w. at the massive Norman tower bases and see how the foundation problem is betrayed by the leaning stonework. Above the crossing arch, a fine set of Charles II *Royal Arms* (Lynn was staunchly Royalist and in 1643 the Roundheads had shattered the great w. window with a 16 lb shot from across the river). Against a pillar on the n. side of the nave, a magnificent early

Georgian pulpit with rich *rococo* carving framing marquetry panels, the heavy base moulding worked with a vine and wheat design. After being discarded for years the inlaid *tester* is back in place. A new and starkly simple nave altar of aluminium designed by Colin Shewring stands within a central sanctuary of dull blue brick and teak which leads as a raised walkway to the teak throne installed when the first suffragan bishop of Lynn was appointed in 1963. To the n., the *chancel screen* of 1584 has been re-sited with the centre doorway moved to the w. end; it was raised on extra panelling in so doing – spoiling its proportions. although they were copied in the replica opposite. There are two rows of open arches and the *pilasters* at the left hand end of the lower level carry the royal initials and the date. The top cornice has a *Jacobean* inscription of 1621 when it was' new beautified'. Behind it is a Snetzler organ installed when author Fanny Burney's father was organist here in 1754. We are now in that part of the C13 church which survived the fall of the spire and the *piers* of the crossing and the chancel *arcades* are subtly varied in design and have beautiful stiff leaf foliage around their *capitals*. The transepts have large Perpendicular windows and the chancel was given a new C15 *clerestory* – but note that there is a passage in front of the windows and that the capitals of the previous early-C13 clerestory were re-used. In the arcades below, a lovely range of C14 oak screens with varying tracery and heavy *crockets* – the earliest is at the s.w. corner and at the e. end on that side, a section of a C15 screen with a beautiful doorway, its richly carved and crocketted arch rising to a pinnacle. A brass lectern stands before the high altar and probably came from the same late-C15 East Anglian workshop that provided others for Redenhall and Clare in Suffolk. Fragments of an original rose e. window were found in the C19 but the present form does not, apparently, reproduce it. Below, the solid mass of G.F. Bodley's 1899 *reredos* rises in tiers of muted red and gold, with large figures of the *Four Latin Doctors* of the church flanking the risen Christ and a Crucifixion panel beneath. In the n. chancel chapel, a C19 Oberammergau reredos and an *aumbry* for the reserved Sacrament in the n. wall which has a cast aluminium door bearing an abstract design. Before leaving the chancel, study the fine range of *misericords* dating from 1370 – sixteen in all plus carved heads on the arms of the stalls. On the s. side from the centre, the head of Bishop Spencer (Bishop of Norwich 1370-1407), the Black Prince with his badge of ostrich plumes hung beside him, and Edward III. Round the corner is a *Green Man* and on the n. side, the head of Queen Phillipa, Edward III's wife; beyond the *scallop-shell* shield there are two particularly fine heads with foreshortened arms and shoulders bearing the ledge above. An interesting detail can be seen in the angle of the front of the stalls on the s. side – a canopied gateway complete with portcullis. In the s. chancel aisle there are two *brasses* which are the largest in England (about 9ft. long and 5ft. wide) which are the only surviving examples of Flemish work brought into the country. Approaching from the w., the first is for Robert Braunche (1364) and his two wives; he has an eagle and a wild man under his feet and both women have cheeky little dogs with bell collars. Over fifty tiny figures fill the upper canopy niches and across the bottom is the famous peacock feast scene, believed to recall the entertainment given by Braunche as mayor to Edward III when he came to the town in 1349. Beyond, the second brass is for Adam de Walsokne (1349), another prosperous merchant mayor and his wife – simply portrayed but set in an intricate frame with myriads of figures in the niches and a very worn but lively rural scene along the bottom; there is a post mill on the left, and a jibe against Norfolk would have us believe that the man on horseback is carrying his sack of corn on his back to save the horse. As you leave, pause outside to admire the moon clock on the s.w. tower, given by a C17 churchwarden and clockmaker mayor Thomas Tue. Beautifully restored, it reveals not only the phases of the moon but St *Margaret's* dragon points to the times of high tide at Kings Lynn (midday at the top and midnight at the bottom). The church has an excellent ring of 10 bells, tenor 29-2-2 cvt.

Kings Lynn, St Nicholas (C3): A C12 bishop of Norwich enlarged the town to the n. and a new community was formed around the Tuesday market place, but it was and is still part of St Margaret's parish and so St Nicholas' is a chapel of ease and not a parish church proper. Happily, this glorious building is in the care of the *Churches Conservation Trust* and continues to be the setting for concerts during the Kings Lynn Festival. The first C12 church was rebuilt around 1200 and the tower was added some 25 years later. Inside you will see three tall *lancets* on its e. side that probably formed the w. wall of the old church. The tower lies lower than the rest of the building and the tall arches of the lower stage enclose two-*light* windows with plate *tracery quatrefoils*, the bell openings above having plain *bar tracery*. The same storm of 1741 that felled St Margaret's spire brought this one down as well and a replica was put back by *Sir Gilbert Scott* in the C19. The rest of the church was rebuilt in its entirety in the early C15 and was completed by 1429. The w. front of the *nave* is all but filled with a stupendous eleven-light window, and the frame of the double doorway is stepped into it, with a fragmentary statue of St *Nicholas* in the centre. The side buttresses have tall niches with *ogee* canopies crowned with large crested helms and the w. doors retain their original tracery. The s. *porch* is tall and splendid; there are shields with *Emblems of the Trinity* and *Instruments of the Passion* in the *spandrels* of the entrance arch and a line of niches with intricate canopies covers the whole width above; three larger niches are set in the upper story and the space between them is filled with delicate small scale panelling. The vault within has been beautifully restored, the gilded *bosses* of Christ in Majesty and His angels set off by cream and tawny ribs against a rose coloured background. The vault and door arches rest on very large civilian head *corbels* – the men have a nice line in hats. The s. door is C15 and look for the tiny figures that crouch on the ogee *arch* of the little *postern doors* by which you enter. Within the church, a marvellous uninterrupted vista with space and light in abundance. The *rood screen*

Kings Lynn, St Nicholas

and *loft* were removed in 1559 and there is now no division between nave and *chancel*. Over both, a lovely single roof of *tie-beams* on slender traceried *arch-braces*, with more tracery above them as far as the arched *queen posts*. Between the tie-beams there are angels with spread wings and the *wall posts* rest on small *corbel* heads with a tall niche each side, vaulted, canopied and with dainty *crocketted* pinnacles. The amount of clear glass and the number of windows accentuates the odd angularity of the tracery. The theme is uniform and lively but arch shapes and tracery lines produce unexpected combinations that surprise the eye. Equally individual are the doorways on the n. side – arches composed of half octagons with *cusping* added. The centre of the chancel has been recently rearranged and now a free standing nave altar is set within a spacious, raised paved area. In the n.w. corner of the n. *aisle* is an interesting little enclosure that was made in 1617 to accommodate the ecclesiastical consistory court when it was held in the w. of the county. The heavy *Jacobean* front rails with their turned *balusters* are like *communion rails* of the period – as they may well have been, for the table in the centre is the old altar cut down in size for its new use. There was an undercurrent of discord between the mother church and the chapel over some matters, and although papal permission for baptisms was secured as early as

1378 it was not until 1627 that St Margaret's objections were finally overruled and a font installed. To make sure that everyone knew their rights it was inscribed: 'This Funt was granted by Samuel Harsnett Bishop of Norwich', and apart from the intrinsic interest of the unusually late design, a small *brass* plate in the floor at the e. end of the n. aisle records the first baptism:

> Here resteth Anne daughter to Joseph and Isabell Raylie She was the first God gave unto her parents and the first Baptized in the Funt of this Chappell and died the tenth of March 1627 aged 24 dayes.

Daniel Defoe died in 1731 and the adventures of the real Robinson Crusoe were in 1704 but strangely enough you will find s. of the font a *ledger-stone* for a Robinson Cruso, son of Robinson and Alice Cruso, who died aged 10 in 1773. Nearby on a wooden base is a lovely *holy water stoup* almost as big as a font, with *quatrefoils* in the panels and one figure jutting out bearing a scroll. The late-C15 brass lectern with smooth lion feet and a big upstanding eagle is from an East Anglian workshop that supplied not only Billingford, Peterborough Cathedral and Christ's College, Cambridge, but St Mark's, Venice as well. The old benches with their carved ends and *misericords* were sadly removed in 1852 and two of the best ends are now in the Victoria and Albert museum, but two C15 stalls remain in the high altar sanctuary. The *poppy-heads* enclose roundels, and on the n. side there is a man riding a horse backwards, a seated bishop, and a figure rising from a whorled whelk shell with attendant fish. This nautical theme is echoed on the s. side where one of the roundels is carved with Our Lady, Star of the sea enthroned on the crescent moon. On one of the arms of this stall is a beautiful carving of a creature with a coronet collar and long horns that curve back along its neck. This may well represent the ibex which, in the bestiaries, is said to throw itself over precipices and land safely on its horns. The mutilated remains of large *sedilia* are on this side and by the vestry door opposite there is an unusual stone bookrest set in the wall with a half-angel over it. All the monuments in the church have been beautifully and meticulously restored and there are four which merit special attention. In the s. aisle e. end, the large figures of Thomas Greene (1675) and his wife kneel on cushions above a neat tableau of four sons and five daughters and the work may have been by Henry Bell, architect of the nearby Customs House. On the e. wall nearby, an omnibus

Kings Lynn, St Nicholas: Thomas Greene's monument

memorial for the Clarke family but principally for Matthew (1623) kneeling with his second wife above the recumbent body of his first choice. It also records that 'the aged Richard Clarck (1602):

> Who ser'd Late Queen Eliza Thirty Yeares
> As searcher and Collector in this Porte
> And who besides (as in record appeares)
> Was sometime Alderman Justice of Peace
> And Maior here his Travayles all did cease...

The family history continues in similar vein and uncertain metre. Across on the n. aisle wall, a companion piece for Matthew Clarke's son-in-law Thomas Snelling (1623). Below the parents are two sons and a daughter kneeling with their baby brother in a cradle alongside. Just in front is a superb marble memorial urn on a square plinth designed by *Robert Adam* for Sir Benjamin Keene (1757), sent as ambassador to the court of Spain by Sir Robert Walpole and brought back here for burial. There is a portrait roundel on the e. side and a fine has relief of a ship being loaded on the w. panel. As you leave, don't overlook the fine wrought iron gates at

the s.w. corner of the churchyard – initials and the date 1714 in the scroll work at the top. The church has a ring of 8 bells, tenor 19 cwt.

Kirby Bedon, St Andrew (I5): Virtually entirely rebuilt in the late Victorian period – the tower in 1883, *porch* in 1885, and earlier, in the mid-1870s, a total 'restoration' of *chancel* and *nave*. The s. doorway, however, is original *Norman*, plain, solid and unpretentious, with neat little flower mouldings on one *capital*. Norman too, and therefore of very special note, is the door itself, complete with its honest blacksmith's ironwork. The interior, accepting its architectural blandness, is charming, and like everything about this church, beautifully maintained. Handsome eight-branch candelabra hang from the sprucely timbered roofs; there's a neat C15 octagonal font with simple *arcading* carved round bowl and stem; a deep *holy water stoup* recess by the door (matching the one immediately adjacent in the porch); a plainly panelled, mellow pulpit; beside it, two old *brass* inscriptions, and a *shroud brass* – two dead figures, shown in their winding sheets – to William Dussyng and wife, 1505. Another Dussyng brass has disappeared from its tomb slab just in front of the sanctuary steps, leaving only the outline and, carved in the stone, 'Here lyeth Dvssing'. In the sanctuary is an unusual brass of c.1450 in the shape of a heart, with Latin scrolls above it, name and date have long since gone. Several handsome C18 and C19 wall monuments and *ledger slabs* adorn the chancel; but from an earlier date comes the alabaster memorial on the n. wall with its coats of arms and two richly clothed kneeling figures, to Robert Sheppard and wife, 1600. Note the unusual form of the *piscina* opposite, set into the side of the *dropped sill sedilia*. The lovely, plumply sturdy *communion rails* are late-C17.

Kirby Cane, All Saints (J6): Great cedars in the churchyard and the big house for company just the other side of a long wall in pale rose brick. The round tower pre-dates the *Norman* Conquest – look for the 4ft. high *pilaster* strips around its base to confirm this, and then the Normans added a fine s. doorway. An animal's head is set barbarically above the arch which has an outer ring of decoration which doesn't figure in the other Norman doorways in this part of Norfolk – little flowers with bulbous centres like gaillardias. Big zigzags inside this, with more on the inner surfaces of the entrance. The inventive designer varied the pattern on the flanking columns and gave them fearsome masks as *capitals* – one is only a decayed honeycomb, but the other still bares its teeth convincingly. The two little windows high in the s. wall of the *chancel* could also be Norman, though the rest have variations of 'Y' tracery dating from around 1300. The font is one of a little local family in style (eight columns attached to the shaft and alternate shields on the bowl), but here there is deep tracery in the bowl panels and the alternate male and female heads beneath are virtually unscathed – a little gallery of hairstyles of the late C14. The n. *aisle* has a hipped roof with sloping ends and a plaster ceiling of the 1750s and it looks as though they re-used the C13 windows. The chancel plaster ceiling has been colour washed in blue and the rest of the church in cream as part of an ambitious programme of regeneration for a most attractive church. There is a simple early-C17 pulpit which has a variety of shallow carved patterns and beside it, stairs to the *rood loft* which are a little out of the ordinary – window embrasures were often used to get into the wall, but this one has a nicely moulded archway cut in the e. side from which the steps rise to the upper level. The sanctuary is graced by a very good set of late-C17 *communion rails*, and is paved with great grey *ledger slabs* of the Catelyn family. They were the squires and built the Hall next door. Although Cromwell rested there on his way to deal with Yarmouth, they were firm royalists as Mary Catelyn's epitaph shows. It tells of her eldest son Thomas:

> a man of Great hopes, att one and twenty Yeares of age was Captaine of a Troope of horse for the service of King Charles the first in his English wars and was Slaine by the Rebels at the Second Neubery fight in the Yeare of our Lord 1644.

So was it royalist or roundhead interloper who cut '1644' among the graffiti on the door? Above the tower arch are two *hatchments*: one to Lord Berners, the other to Raymond John Crisp, C20 squire and churchwarden for 30 years – a welcome revival of the practice.

Kirstead, St Margaret (I6): At first glance this smart little village church looks like straightforward Victorian gothic construction. It is in fact of ancient foundation – but the *chancel* and tower were rebuilt in 1864 during a 'restoration' vigorous even by Victorian standards, at which time the *nave* windows were also renewed. However, there is a very pretty s. doorway of about 1190, when the *Early English* period was asserting itself with its gracious

Knapton, St Peter & St Paul: C18 font cover

pointed arches, while still retaining, in delicately slimmed-down form, the spirit of the *capitals* and columns of its *Norman* predecessors. Inside, a pleasingly comfortable and welcoming little place, with lots of colour in decoration and furnishing, not least in the blue, white and gilt of the tiny *apsidal* chancel with its 'Victorian Early English' arches and pillars; and with a whole range of handsome wall monuments, almost all to members of the Kerrison family, through nearly 200 years. Behind the organ hangs a large framed *hatchment* – presumably that of Sir Roger Kerrison, died 1808, remembered on the s. wall of the nave, as the coats-of-arms match.

Knapton, St Peter & St Paul (J2): A handsome, mostly C14 church, up on its mound, its largely early-C14 tower with its shoulder to our 'lazy' east coast winds – note that it's slightly offset from the *nave*. On top is a weather-vane (cockerel and flag-piece) made from a drawing by the famous artist of the Norwich School of painting, John Sell Cotman, early in the C19 – it is said he did it while giving a drawing lesson at Knapton House. A fine *porch*, with a treble niche above the entrance arch – but filled-in in ugly cement. The *chancel* has a pretty *Perpendicular* porch, with trim pillars, over the *priest's door*. A local feature this – don't miss the one nearby at Trunch, where a buttress actually goes up from the top of the porch. Enter the church now – and stop in your tracks to gasp with wonder and delight. For we have here one of the best roofs in Norfolk, a glorious double *hammer-beam* carpenter's masterpiece, an amazing 70ft. x 30ft. 6in. wide, thronging with 138 angels – not all original, the lower ones definitely modern. This wonderful roof can be definitely dated to 1504, when it was given by John Smithe, rector here 1471-1518. Also fine are the font and its cover: the first, C13, in *Purbeck marble*, resting on shafts, and the whole on three confident steps. The cover, dated 1704, is a jolly piece – like a miniature seaside bandstand. The inscription upon it, in Greek, translates: 'Wash my sins and not my face only'. It's a palindrome – ie, it reads the same backwards as forwards; this one is said to have been composed originally by the Greek Emperor Leo (880-911). Victorian pulpit; a good C15 *screen*; *rood stair* entrance in s.e. corner of nave; the *corbels* which supported the *rood loft* can still be seen on either side of the chancel arch; in n.e. corner of nave, a double niche, which no doubt once had statues of the church's two dedicatory saints; behind organ, an odd little arch, built into the window, and a rough *piscina* (which probably served a *guild altar* of one of the numerous medieval guilds known to have been connected with this church). In chancel, a reader's desk made up of medieval and *Jacobean* bits and pieces – a happy botched-up job of charm and character; a very attractive C14 *piscina*; opposite, a recess which probably once contained an *Easter Sepulchre*. The church has an excellent ring of 6 bells, tenor 5-2-10 cwt.

Lakenham, St John the Baptist & All Saints (I5): The church sits happily in its wooded, well-kept churchyard, between the old village below, and the new suburbia crowding around it. Heavily restored and altered, with a trim and battlemented tower of C14 origin: slightly earlier is the fabric of the body of the church, as indicated by the late-C13 *cusped*, intersecting tracery of the e. window. The n. doorway (now leading into a modern vestry) would appear to be of this period. An interior of pleasing simplicity, with the stamp of loving care. *Nave* and *chancel* are in one uninterrupted 'hall', with a modern brick-built s. *aisle*. Against white walls

and ceilings, the simple timbering of the roofs, picked out in black, looks cottagey and homely. Some of the roof timbers – simple *arch-braces* and sections of *wall plates* on the n. side, look original. The rest, like the plain oak pews, is modern. There is a rather imposing wall monument on the sanctuary n. wall to William Crowe, 1778, with a couple of endearingly chubby carved cherub heads: but note that on the right hand of the two urns which top the monument, the sculptor, M. Crowe, has none too subtly added his signature; not that it helped his advertising, for this piece of work, it seems, is all that history knows of him. In the s.e. corner, across the angle of the walls, a charming *piscina* niche, with a *trefoiled* head. In the s. aisle is an oval monumental plaque to James Crowe, 1807, once Sheriff of Norwich and twice Mayor:

> His excellent understanding and penetrating Judgment applied to the study of Mankind & of History confirmed him in principles truly worthy of a Briton and a Man the same talents applied to the study of Nature most especially of Botany were ever devoted to practical utility.

The treasure of this church is the C15 *Perpendicular* octagonal font, richly carved round the bowl and stem. Clockwise, beginning with the w. face: winged Man with the *Evangelistic Symbols*, the *Instruments of the Passion* surrounded by angelic faces; and The Virgin, in a very full and distinctively medieval gown.

Lammas, St Andrew (I3): A most attractive setting in a broad meadow on the banks of the river Bure. Apart from the slim early-C15 tower, most of what you see is C19 rebuilding using old materials in some places. The *chancel* was entirely replaced, but on the old foundations, so that it still *weeps* about 6ft. to the n. to make use of firmer ground. There is a big *mass dial* on the easternmost buttress of the nave, and on the s. chancel wall outside there is a 1741 memorial to the young sons of Henry and Alice Utting. It is worth studying for the charm of the unsophisticated lettering. Within, an early-C16 font with fat *Tudor* roses and shields in the panels, and beyond it, behind the organ is a *consecration cross* uncovered in the 1887 restoration. The lid of the parish chest was cut from a solid trunk and probably dates from the C14, although the ends and base are later replacements. Walter Rye, one of Norfolk's most assiduous antiquaries, lived for a time in

Lammas, and gave the heraldic roundels in the n. window which display the arms of various Lords of the manor. The 'Sable a turnip proper' of the Damant family in the right hand corner is good C18 Norfolk eccentricity, and Rye's own memorial below has a touch of it too – 'an antiquary and athlete'. He linked his own arms with those of the Thames Hare and Hounds Club. The church has a good ring of 5 bells, tenor 8-2-17 cwt.

Langham, St Andrew & St Mary (G1): With its turret staircase thrusting up above the battlements of the high, handsome tower, the church provides a distinctive feature in the landscape. On closer acquaintance, note the finely decorated *base course* all round the tower and extending across the end of the s. *aisle*, with *flint-knapped flushwork* set into the panelling. The three-*light sound-holes* in the belfry stage are unusual. Like the tower, the body of the church is largely C15. Inside, it is immaculately decorated and beautifully looked after. There is a striking *Decorated* C14 *arcade* of four bays – very elegant, and a lovely *chancel* arch, complemented by the contemporary and beautiful tower arch at the opposite end. Well preserved *rood stairs* and loft entrance. Nice C13 octagonal font – the e. face has the inscription, 'Alice Nettleton baptised the 14th day of April 1692'. Roofs and benches modern throughout, though a few old *poppy-heads* have been re-used. Heavily restored chancel, with a *piscina* niche and *dropped sill sedilia* on s. side. In the s. aisle are *Royal Arms*, dated 1740, altered from 1712 – but that's an alteration too; for though it may have the initials AR for Anne, the motto marks it as Carolean. Good stained glass in the tower by *Kempe & Tower*; and from a little earlier, a bold one behind the pulpit by *Sir Edward Burne-Jones* from the *William Morris* workshops – Faith and Hope vigorously treading underfoot Unbelief and Despair. Spare a moment too for the tablet to Captain Marryat – who lies in the churchyard outside under the trees – and his son Frederick, who went down with his ship a year before his father's death. Captain Marryat was the author of those staples of childhood literature until not so long ago, 'Children of the New Forest', 'Masterman Ready' and others. He lived for some years at Langham Manor and farmed there: but his house has long since disappeared.

Langley, St Michael (J5): In a very gracious setting next to a farm and reached by a path across the paddock. The C14 tower has the line

Langham, St Andrew and St Mary: William Morris window

of an earlier and steeper roof on its e. face. The *arch-braced* successor is fine – wide and rather flat, with heavily moulded main timbers and a line of square-cut flowers at the ridge. The C14 font has three heads (one a bishop) and shield in the bowl panels with roses in the other four. The *nave* has C19 wooden framed windows which followed the *chancel's* conversion to 'gothick' in 1803. This has a flat plaster ceiling which until recently had the painted arms of the Beauchamp family and there was a set of Hanoverian *Royal Arms* in the *tympanum*. Not only have these gone but the *box pews* in the nave (which were seen with contemporary name-cards in 1964) and the *three-decker pulpit* have also been removed. In their place is a range of deadly dull C19/C20 oakpews and a cumbrous pulpit of the same vintage which is positively ugly. A poor exchange, but admittedly more convenient for services with 200 boys present from the nearby school. By way of relief the chancel has, like neighbouring Chedgrave, C16 glass from Rouen Cathedral, brought here by the Dowager Lady Beauchamp during the French Revolution. The family (which confusingly veers from Beauchamp to Beauchamp-Proctor to Proctor) lived at Langley Hall. Some fine monuments in white marble – Sir Thomas Beauchamp Proctor rises from the tomb to touch finger tips with an angel on the s. side, and on the opposite wall two excellent portraits of Emma and Julia who died young in the 1820s. Close by, an affecting epitaph to Elizabetha Columbine who died in childbirth in 1766. The enigma of the church is the shallow blanked-off recess high in the s. wall of the nave. It has a C14 *hood mould* with good *headstops* and is fitted with an iron grill. Was there once a chamber beyond it?

Larling, St Ethelbert (F7): Fronted by fields, with a backcloth of woodland, and set a good half mile from its village down a long track, this handsome church has a big, plain *Perpendicular* tower; s. *aisle* of about 1300 with big eight-leaf traceries in the heads of its s. windows and an eloquently simple e. window; *chancel* of similar date, with contemporary 'Y' tracery to n. and s. and a replacement e. window in a stolid geometrical pattern. *Early English nave*, but with inserted Perpendicular windows; Victorian rebuilt porch. Inside the porch, a splendid and opulent *Norman* s. doorway, under a square hood; it is richly carved and ornamented, with double shafts, boldly carved *capitals* and, half way up the shaft on the l.h. side, a tiny *mass dial*. Its corresponding doorway on the n. side of the church is interesting; into an earlier arch is set a later doorway whose style indicates a date of about 1300. A delightful church inside, all painted in white – even the stubby, plain C12 font – and lovingly looked after. Fine hanging

oil lamps and a pretty little organ add to the general character. Modern roofs and furnishings throughout. Lovely little three-bay *arcade* of very early-C14 date, with octagonal pillars; and a graceful chancel arch of extreme simplicity. Beside the s. door, a very good *holy water stoup*. At the e. end of the s. aisle is a large C14 *angle piscina* under a big *trefoil* head and a triangular *hood mould*, the latter completed with little carved *corbel* heads. Adjoining, three-seat graduated *sedilia*, set into the sill below a window, each seat divided from the next by little stone arm rests – an unusual detail, seen also at nearby Great Hockham. The large pedestal built into the wall below the aisle's e. window would have held a saint's effigy, probably the Virgin, to whom a pre-*Reformation* altar was dedicated. Opposite are the stairs and entrance to the *rood loft*. The *chancel* is beautiful in its simplicity: it has a good early-C14 piscina, notable for having re-used as its central pillar a piece of C12 masonry; adjoining are *dropped sill sedilia*. Restored to its old position on the altar is the medieval *mensa*, rediscovered in 1867. It is very large, and retains its five *consecration crosses*, all elaborately carved.

Lessingham, All Saints (J3): A tiny, unpretentious little church, marooned in fields up a narrow lane. The neat tower has an early *Perpendicular* upper stage, but the lower half is early *Decorated* with a w. window whose Y-tracery just might be original. The *nave* windows are all Victorian replacements, put in when the nave walls were rebuilt in 1893. The simple Decorated tracery of one n. window looks original, as is the Decorated n. doorway. There is no *chancel*: it became ruinous some time in the C20 and was walled off. Inside, the nave has a handsome modern panelled roof, with *arch-braces* and 'battlemented' cross beams and *wall plates*. The C13, octagonal font, standing on a modern base, has faint double-arcading round the bowl, a common feature. Unusually on the n. side of the sanctuary are C19 *dropped sill sedilia*, adjoining the narrow entrance to the *rood stair* (the turret can be seen outside). On s. side, a simple *piscina*. The little *Jacobean* pulpit, of about 1650, with its tiny backboard, and a *tester* with hanging pendants, is charming. There are remnants of *brass* inscriptions, one dated 1505, in front of the altar.

Letheringsett, St Andrew (G2): An attractive, compact church, set off by its round *Norman* tower. This has a C14 top with neat *Decorated* two-*light* bell openings. The *nave* and *clerestory*

Letheringsett, St Andrew: C15 Norwich glass

windows are simple *Perpendicular*, and those of the *chancel* have most attractive Decorated geometrical tracery. The s. *porch* was added in 1875. Inside, there is no chancel arch and the continuous roof is modern, enhanced by the 1979 re-decoration of the church. Impressive display of candelabra, seven hanging, eight wall mounted. Like those at nearby Glandford, they were brought back from Italy at the end of the C19 by Sir Alfred Jodrell, of Bayfield Hall. The nave has lovely *Early English*, C13 *arcades* with, unusually, full columns and *capitals* offset from the *aisle* e. walls. At w. end of arcade, notice the *corbel* heads – one a flat-faced visage like a 'bruiser', the other a weird grotesque with arms and legs growing from its massive head. The little C13 font is octagonal, in *Purbeck marble*. Interesting early Victorian *barrel organ*, originally at Hindringham Church, then in a private house at Holt, and installed here in 1956. In n. aisle, a *piscina*, and entrance to the *rood stair*; also an *aumbry* installed in the 1950s. In both n. and s. aisle windows there are good examples of stained glass *Kempe*. The s. aisle has a nice C14 piscina with a modern bowl; a lovely little C17 communion table was brought here from North Barningham church in 1957; a wall tablet to William Hardy, (d.1842), aged 72, 'zealous promoter of gospel truth...impartial magistrate...upright landlord' (The Hardys were squires here, living at the hall immediately next

door, until not many years ago); and in s.w. corner, the death mask of Johnson Jex (d.1852), the village's celebrated blacksmith, inventor, watchsmith and self-taught scholar. Sadly, in the past few years the face of his tombstone has flaked away, destroying a splendid epitaph that ended with the lines, 'Insensible to the voice of fame, he lived and died a scientific *anchorite*.' The chancel is early-C14 *Decorated*, with some good remnants of C15 *Norwich glass* in s. window. Magnificent Victorian *reredos* in alabaster, erected to the memory of Adela Monckton Jodrell by her three children – the same lady for whom her son Sir Alfred rebuilt Glandford Church. Plain C14 *angle piscina* and *dropped sill sedilia*. A tiny filled-in doorway on n. side is only about 4ft. high – the chancel floor was originally much lower.

Limpenhoe, St Botolph (J5): A restoration in 1880 which was virtually a rebuilding. There is a blocked *Norman* s. doorway, and the typical zigzag and scallop mouldings can be seen from the outside. The base of the C15 tower is more or less as it was, although an early-C19 engraving shows that there was then a big square window in the w. face and a tiled pyramidal roof. The font is C13 *Purbeck*, its canted sides having shallow arcading, and resting on eight columns and a centre shaft. A fine Flemish tapestry of the Sacrifice of Isaac is framed on the s. wall and came from the nearby ruined church of St Edmund's, Southwood.

Lingwood, St Peter (J5): The base of the tower is C13 but its upper stage, with the *porch* and *chancel*, is early-C14. There is a big *mass dial* on the e. side of the porch entrance, and although the *headstops* of the arch are very worn, you can see that one was a figure holding a battle axe. On the n. side of the *nave*, a patch of brickwork shows were the *rood stair* was sited. Inside, the nave has an *arch-braced roof* which, with no intervening chancel arch, comes to an abrupt junction with the ugly flat ceiling of the chancel. Above the tower arch the *Royal Arms* of George IV are cut to outline and there is the head and shoulders of a big St *Christopher* on the n. wall which must have been rather fine in its entirety. There are two bench ends in the chancel with figures on the arms, and a set of simple but robust C17 *communion rails*. The *piscina* is a shallow *trefoil*-headed recess which has had the projecting section of its bowl chopped away. The nave n. door now leads to a little suite of rooms for parish use – all in seemly flint and stone under a tiled roof that matches the chancel.

Litcham, All Saints (E4): Litcham's red brick tower is something of an acquired taste – first impression is of ugliness, then it grows on you. It's older too than you might think – it was built by Matthew Halcot a few years before his death in 1675. The *nave* is *Perpendicular*, the *chancel* windows are a replacement of about 1800. The same style, but original this time, of about 1300, is seen inside the church in a big, three-*light* window in the nave w. wall, filled in but not covered over when Matthew Halcot built his tower. The interior is plain, with a tall, four-bay Perpendicular *arcade*. The eastern-most arches are fluted into the chancel arch – a lovely composition – with at every arch intersection a bearded and formidable head. From the arcade arches hang handsome wrought iron lampholders. Plain octagonal Perpendicular font under a w. *gallery*; a remnant of a *holy water stoup* by s. door; a prettily restored *piscina* in s. *aisle*; solid and good looking 'wine glass' pulpit, panelled and traceried, of about 1500. The splendid C15 *screen* has been tactfully recoloured, while leaving untouched its 22 panels, each containing a saint. This includes six panels in the doors, though these paintings have been so brutally hacked out that the subjects are hardly distinguishable. Just recognisable are three money-bags hanging from a belt, which could indicate St *Nicholas*. Not all the figures on the screen are identifiable, and some are open to question, but tentatively they are: A nun; *Cecilia* or *Margaret*, *Dorothy* (?), *Juliana* (?), *Agnes*, *Petronella, Helena, Ursula, Gregory, Edmund, Armel* (very rare, this one), *Geron* (rare), *Walstan of Bawburgh, Hubert, William of Norwich, Louis of France* (rare). In the chancel (which *weeps* to the s.) is a massive C14 Flemish chest; a couple of ancient *misericords* – notice the *squint* from the chapel (now a vestry) behind them; and C17 *communion rails*. Back in the nave, there are deep slots in the bases of the first pillars westward from the chancel arch. These held the *parclose screens* which enclosed side chapels. On the middle pillar, s. side, at about eye level, is amost interesting survival – The Litcham Cryptogram. Scratched into the stonework, it is said to be a prayer, carved by a pilgrim on his way to Walsingham: one suggestion is 'Save (my soul) Jesus Mary & Joseph' and the name of the pleader, Wyke Bamburgh. The church has a ring of 6 bells, tenor 9 cwt.

Little Barningham, St Andrew (H2): Very prettily placed on a green mound above the village street, with a broad grassy path leading up to the gate. Subjected to extensive restoration in the C19, much of the exterior is in dressed flint. Inside, all is starkly simple, the *chancel* in duck-egg blue and no mural tablets at all. What does catch the eye is the panelled pew at the front of the *nave* on the l. dated 1640; it had an 18in. carved skeleton standing upright on the outer corner of the panelling, wearing a shroud and holding scythe and hour-glass. Two inscriptions are carved below in curious conjunction:

> For couples joynd in wedlock and my
> freinds that stranger is. this seat did I
> intend, built at the cost and charge of
> Steven Crosbee.

> All you that doe this pace pass by
> As you are nowe even so was I
> Remember death for you must dye
> And as I am soe shall you be
> Prepare therefore to follow me.

What one might call friend Crosbee's version of the 'skeleton at the (marriage) feast'. The skeleton carving was stolen in the 1980s.

Little Cressingham, St Andrew (E5): The s.w. tower fell sometime before 1781, and by that time much of the church was in decay. Then, a faculty was granted to build a new w. wall and repair the e. end of the church, so that there is now a short *nave* and *aisles* of two bays and a *chancel* of roughly the same length. In its ruin, the w. end is rather beautiful, with parts of the *arcade* and *clerestory* rising from the grassy enclosure approached through the archway of the ruined tower. From the w. the frontage is still impressive; a deep *base course* of chequered flint spans nave and n. aisle and the outline of a big w. window had a smaller one inserted within it. There was a w. window to the n. aisle originally, but it is strange that it was carefully filled with *flushwork* as though it were a dummy. Inside, the *piers* of the C15 *arcades* have bold mouldings n. and s. which run without interruption to the heads of the arches, and the generous *Perpendicular* windows of the s. side lie within *blind arcading*. Between them, a large mural monument to William Henry Fortescue, Viscount Clermont. It is by Robert De Carle of Bury St Edmund's, and has stylish lettering on white marble, with *pilasters* and *pediment* outlined against a darker background. The early-C14 chancel's s. windows are blocked and the e. window was reduced in size in the C18. When it was restored, the flowing tracery appears to have been eccentrically re-arranged in the process. The tall *piscina* niche has a prettily *cusped trefoil* arch and the *communion rails* are an ingenious Victorian design – a cylindrical brass top rail extends like a telescope from both sides to lock in the centre and thus form a solid barrier.

Little Dunham, St Margaret (E4): Tucked away down a farm drive is this serene little church to which the centuries have been kind. At heart it is a C13 *Early English* building, with C14 and C15 additions and alterations. The simple tower, for example, is late-C14 – very attractive are its *quatrefoil sound-holes* in square frames. The *porch* is *Perpendicular* too, but later, possibly C16, by the look of its arch (above which, set into the gable wall at an angle, is a big slate sun dial). A walk around the church testifies to three centuries of gentle change: simple *lancet* windows, including a big bold triple set under a single arch at the e. end of the n. *aisle*, through to Perpendicular. The porch shelters an attractive C13 doorway, the well-moulded arch resting on ring *capitals* and single slim shafts. Inside, all is rustic simplicity, with a lovely C13 *arcade* on clustered pillars running the length of the church – three bays for the *nave*, and three slightly lower ones for the *chancel*, though only one of the latter is open. The other two have long since been filled in, leaving outlined arches and clustered pillars which probably led to a chapel. There are traces of original colour on the arches of the chancel arcade, and a painted *consecration cross* on one of the pillars. Opposite is a most unusual C13 *angle piscina*, with *sedilia* complete with stone elbow rest slotted into it. Another curiosity is the enormous *corbel* head supporting the westernmost arch of the chancel arcade. The head sprouts leaves – and horns! At the w. end is a fragment of the stem of a *Saxon* cross, on which some carving is still discernible.

Little Ellingham, St Peter (G6): A neat little village church, with its ancient tower offset to the s. of the rebuilt *nave* and *chancel* – a reconstruction necessary after a disastrous fire in 1867. The tower, with modern parapet, attractive two-*light* bell openings and *quatrefoil sound-holes*, is probably early *Decorated*. The base of the tower serves as a *porch*, entered through an archway on the s. side over which is a pretty figure niche. The church interior is simple and charming, with details where possible preserved or reproduced from the original building – like the arched tomb recess on the n. side of the nave, and the *piscina* opposite. In the sanctuary, s. side, a little stone

shelf has been set into the wall, supported by three re-used carved *corbel* heads – a lovely idea. Immediately below in the floor, an incised *Norman* stone slab, with zig-zag and circular designs. The glossy marbled-brown font is Victorian, and made of porphyry.

Little Fransham, St Mary (F4): Not far to the n. of the busy main road but peacefully secluded. The tower fell down at the end of the C17 and a plain mullioned window was set in the w. wall. In 1743 a second storey in brick was built on the *porch* to house the remaining bell and the date appears on the ends of the iron tie bars. The *nave* has tall late-C13 windows with *cusped* 'Y' tracery and all the *chancel* windows display that early-C14 *reticulated* tracery that encloses another reticulation. A very light interior, with white walls and light-coloured roofs. The *hammer-beam* and *arch-braced roof* of the nave was repaired and restored in 1909 and has distinctive tracery in the *spandrels*. The C13 square font stands obliquely on four sturdy columns, and three of its sides have an interesting succession of *blind arcades* which illustrate the transition from *Norman* to *Early English*, with a roughly cut flower decoration on the remaining face. The George III *Royal Arms* over the blocked n. door are well painted – a full achievement on canvas, with a wreath of roses and thistles at the bottom. There are two pews with traceried backs at the w. end and the same designs recur in the chancel stalls and reading desks, with the addition of roughly carved grotesques on the bench brackets. The *piscina* has a simple *trefoil* arch and the *dropped sill sedilia* have been fitted with a back made up from early-C17 panelling.

Little Massingham, St Andrew (D3): The C14 tower has a *Decorated* w. window, two-*light* bell openings, and the w. buttresses have gables to the bottom *set-offs*; a strong stair turret on the s. side is handsomely patterned in C16/C17 narrow red bricks and there are later brick battlements. There is a *clerestory* on the s. side only, and the *Perpendicular* square-headed windows are set in a wall which is a fetching mixture of salmon pink brick and flint. There are floriated crosses on the *nave* and *chancel* gables, and a nice variety of Decorated tracery in the chancel windows and at the e. end of the s. *aisle*. The C15 s. *porch* is strong and has pinnacles, a gable cross, and small *flushwork* panels either side of the arch. Its roof is a good example of quality modern work in oak using traditional forms. The early-C14 doorway has large mutilated *headstops* and, within, there are C14 *arcades* and chancel arch. There is an *angle piscina* in the chancel with a small niche close to it in the e. wall, and in the s. aisle chapel, another *piscina* – this time with an *ogee* arch. A *squint* links this chapel with the chancel and above it, a tablet with coats of arms above and below for Sir Charles Mordaunt (1648). The 1857 stone pulpit is by *Thomas Jekyll* and there seems little hope that it will age gracefully, but his choir stalls are rather good.

Little Melton, St Mary & All Saints (H5): A most attractive church, in a beautifully wooded churchyard. Largely C14 *Decorated*, but with additions and insertions up to the very early-C16, it still has a sense of unity which adds to its beauty. The tower is sturdy and simple, with a little battlemented parapet, and belfry windows with 'Y' tracery, of around 1300: its large w. window is late-C14/early-C15 *Perpendicular*. All around the body of the church 'Y' traceries are repeated, together with several *lancets* (the long one on the *chancel* s. side is a *low side window*) including miniscule ones in the *porch*. The e. window has a modern *ogee* head and tracery, but this is wholly in sympathy. For the rest, the old masons chose a pleasantly simple, two-*light* design, very lightly *cusped* under a flattened arch. Before going in, notice the *corbel* heads to either side of the entrance. Inside, the church is a delight, and packed with interest. Modern roofs, save for the silvery timbers of 1508 in the n. aisle. Early-C14 *arcades*, with delicate, leafy *capitals* at the ends of both arcades. Several very faded wall paintings: on n. wall, possibly a St *Christopher*; to right, a 'gossip group' of two women though the usual accompanying devil has gone; more fragments in the n. aisle, part of a painted canopy round the chapel altar; and to either side of the chancel e. window, angels with musical instruments. The C13 font, octagonal and very large, with plain arcading round its bowl and standing on stumpy little round pillars. Lovely late-C15 *screen* with richly ornamented ogee arches and a great deal of original tracery colour, but with blank panels. To its left is the loft-level exit of the *rood stair*, entered from the n. aisle: notice here the beautiful *piscina*, set into the end pillar of the arcade. Across this arch would have been a *parclose screen*: the lovely pulpit and *communion rails* were apparently made from pieces of this screen, together with sections in the prayer desks and stalls in the chancel. The wooden lectern is much later, but a beautiful piece, with under the bookrest a richly carved

central capital which appears to have drawn its inspiration from the carvings at the ends of the arcades. In front of the pulpit, a brass inscription to Dorothy Angwish and her son Robert; he died 2nd June 1604 and his mother just six weeks later on 19th July – the arms of this ancient Norfolk family are shown below the inscription. In the chancel, a remodelled double piscina, and two *sedilia*, inset quite separately into the wall, under plain arches. The *Norman mensa* slab has been restored to its place on the high altar, and stands upon a *Stuart* table. Its original stone supports, badly broken, are beside the chapel altar in the n. aisle. Spare a moment for the 1968 stained glass by Paul Jefferies in the e. window of the s. aisle. It shows St *Francis* with a profusion of flora and fauna. It's in memory of Mildred and Arthur Pratt, who lived in the village. Immediately outside this window, on the s.e. *jamb* of the aisle, may be seen as you walk down the path a carved *mass dial*, set unusually high up.

Little Plumstead, St Protase & St Gervase (J4): A dedication unique in England, to twin brothers martyred in Milan in Nero's time. The church is tucked away in the grounds of a large hospital, centred on the old hall. A small, round flint tower, narrowing towards the top; almost certainly *Saxo-Norman*; it has plain, modern bell openings and a brick parapet. The body of the church, very heavily restored, is *Perpendicular* in character, though the fabric is obviously much older – a fascinating patchwork of flint and stone and of bricks of many hues and sizes. Standing, fittingly, outside the *porch* – for it looks more like a garden ornament than a piece of church furniture – is a fluted C18 font. The porch itself is predominantly brick, and rather pleasing, especially its outer arch, which looks C16 (similar to the one at Hemblington, nearby). The inner arch is very plain *Norman*, with a coarse *billet* moulding over the top. Inside, starkly plain, with spartan modern pews; and the roof is modern also. But a round-headed n. doorway, and a massively thick wall-arch into the tower, speak of antiquity. Three *hatchments* hang on the *nave* walls. At head of nave, s. side, is a remounted *brass* to Sir Edward Warner, 1565 – very good, showing fine Elizabethan armour. In the chancel, a grandly pompous monument, something of an C18 throwback, to Thomas Penrice, of Yarmouth, 1816, and his wife Hannah, 1829, complete with funerary urn on top and coat-of-arms underneath the inscription.

Little Snoring, St Andrew (F2): At first sight across the fields the tower looks like a very large pigeon-cote, with its conical cap (added about 1800), weather vane and tiny dormer-like openings. This sits on top of a *Saco-Norman* round tower, with the remains of arch and facia, which led formerly into the *nave* of a now disappeared church. The tower stands about 6ft. clear of the present church, and a walk around its exterior reveals windows which form a text-book in stone of 400 years of architectural styles. On *chancel* s.e. window a *mass dial*. On n. side, a little *Early English* filled-in doorway, with an an odd little inset above it. Entering the church through the *Decorated porch*, with its rudely carved outer arch, we are confronted by a fascinating curiosity. This is the inner doorway, where a *Norman* arch, with bold zig-zag ornament, was crammed into Gothic, pointed conformity. The carved *capitals* are Early English, but each keeping its Norman *abacus*. Supremely plain and uncluttered inside, with nave roof of barn-like simplicity. Westernmost n. and s. windows, like castle arrow slits, are *Norman*, as is the font, round and richly carved. Note splendid and rare *Royal Arms* of James II, dated 1686, above s. door. Pulpit, neatly panelled in mahogany into a corner, is handsome C18. Through the wide Early English arch into the chancel, brilliantly light – a real pleasure with its deeply set, separated lancets forming the e. window, each marked with slim shafts; and square headed *Tudor* windows, to each side, that on the s. having *dropped sill sedilia* below it adjoining a C13 *angle piscina*. Note the *ledger slab* – s. side between the pews – to a parish priest 'as good perhaps as ever lived'.

Little Walsingham, Anglican Shrine of Our Lady (F2): Traditionally it is believed that in 1061 the lady Richeldis de Faverche had a vision in which the Virgin Mary asked her to build a replica of the Holy House in Nazareth, which she did at Walsingham. An Augustinian priory was founded here in 1153 and the village became the premier place of pilgrimage in England. All changed at the *Reformation* when the shrine was destroyed by Henry VIII's commissioners and it was not until the 1890s that the Slipper Chapel outside the village was restored by the Roman Catholic church as a place of pilgrimage. Anglican interest in the tradition was aroused by Fr Hope Patten in the 1920s and in the following decade the new Holy House was established on the present site, with the enlarged building completed in 1938 and designed by Sir William Milner, one of the shrine's great benefactors, and Romilly Craze. The site did not allow a conventional e – w alignment and the slim brick campanile topped with a gilded angel stands at the far end of the building which is largely of brick under pantile roofs, with lime-washed walls and an Italiante portico fronting the street. On entering one is faced immediately with an altar backed by a large bas relief *reredos* in clear white and blue of the *Annunciation*. Just to the left, steps lead down to a medieval well uncovered during the building of the shrine, from which water is drawn for sacramental and devotional use. The Holy House itself was an entity from the begining, the rest of the shrine having been built around it, and its walls are studded with fragments of stone from monasteries that were destroyed at the *Reformation*. The altar within is the focus of pilgrims' Marian devotions and its reredos and frontal were both designed by *Sir Ninian Comper*. Beyond the Holy House the *nave* is comparatively narrow, with *arcades* of chamfered brick *piers* and sharply pointed arches, its soft shadows broken only by the flickering lights of myriad candles. It is here that the unique atmosphere of the Shrine is strongest – a calm silence and the elusive hint of incense. Ranged on each side of the *chancel* are the stalls of the College of Guardians formed in 1931 as the body of trustees of the Shrine. The eye moves naturally past them to the splendour of the high altar with its six mighty candlesticks and cross, and the five panels above and beyond them illustrating the life of the Virgin which were painted by Enid Chadwick, the artist whose murals can be seen elsewhere in the Shrine; above and softly lit there is a glowing *mandorla* of Christ and the Blessed Virgin. The side *aisles* with their large windows form part of an ambulatory round the whole building which provides sites for fifteen subsidiary chapels, each with its own devotional theme and all richly furnished. The Chapel of the Ascension beyond the high altar is notable for the painting of the Virgin and the Christ Child by Il Sodoma (Giovanni Antonio Bazzi) a leading Sienese artist of the early C16. Since its inception, the Shrine has steadily developed as a place of pilgrimage and a college, refectory, pilgrim hall and other facilities are grouped around it in the grounds.

Little Walsingham, St Mary (F2): This fine church was gutted by fire on the night of 14th-15th July, 1961, leaving only the tower with its pretty lead covered steeple, and the s. *porch* intact.

Little Witchingham, St Faith

A very beautiful and effective rebuilding, of great care and taste, has been achieved, all colour and light – and giving an impression of what many medieval churches would probably have looked like in their original state. A treasure saved from the fire was the *seven sacrament font*, described by *Pevsner* as 'Almost the perfect Norfolk font – it would be, if it were better preserved.' This splendid C15 piece, beautifully carved with the seven sacraments and the Crucifixion, with round the shaft the four Evangelists and the *Four Latin Doctors*, stands on three traceried steps in the shape of a Maltese cross. Sir Henry Sidney and his lady have a fine alabaster monument, 1612: their figures have been remounted 'step fashion' under the w. window in the n. *aisle*, with Arms below. He was Lord Chamberlain to Elizabeth I, and cousin to Sir Philip Sidney, Elizabeth's celebrated courtier. On n. wall of *chancel* is an interesting little *Jacobean* tablet, showing the front of a four-poster bed with the curtains drawn, and announcing simply: 'Dormitorium Edwardi de Fotherbye – 1632'. 'Here sleeps'. Another monument worth noting is the *cartouche* on the s. aisle wall to Robert Anguish, with its cleverly compact wording and dating – 'E.R. 1590 XXXII': ie the 32nd year of Elizabeth Regina's reign. The church has an excellent ring of 6 bells, 19-1-23 cwt.

Little Witchingham, St Faith (H3): You might say that St Faith's has drawn back from the grave. *Cautley* described it as 'disused', and *Pevsner* as 'disused and ruinous' – and so it was until 1972. The problem is that, although there are a handful of houses nearby, the focus of the village has now shifted down to the valley, and thus the odds against the building surviving were high. But help came just in time from the *Norfolk*

Churches Trust, through whose financial aid roofs, windows and floors were repaired and replaced. Now in the care of the *Churches Conservation Trust*, the unbuttressed tower, with its frieze of *flushwork* below the battlements, has been repointed and has new louvres in the bell openings; here are new fall pipes from the gutters; the walls have a deep gravel-filled trench against them, and all the windows have been reglazed with clear glass in oblong leaded *lights*. More than that: inside, the remnants of a complete scheme of medieval paintings have been uncovered, and their reclamation by Mrs Eve Baker in 1975 won the church an award during European Architectural Heritage Year. All the designs are in a dark red, and a pattern of foliage scrolls reaches up 8ft. from the floor. Above that, there are traces of figure groups and one is tolerably clear on the n. wall. The *arcade* arches between *nave* and *aisle* have a zig-zag pattern painted on the outer chamfer, and in the *spandrels* on the s. side there are two fine and very large roundels-one with the lion of St *Mark*, the other of St *Matthew*, both with lettered scrolls. A most exciting discovery. There is now a font again, a spiky brass lectern of the 1860s, a ringable bell, and a vested altar, but it is heartening to see the march of decay halted. In your circuit of the outside, don't overlook the fragment from a *preaching cross* with a Crucifixion carved on it, which is set in the s. wall of the *chancel*. Near it, John Mountain's epitaph (1773):

We daily see Death spares no Sex nor Age,
Sooner or later All do quit the Stage;
The Old, the Young, the Strong, the Rich & Wise,
Must All to Him become a Sacrifice.

Loddon, Holy Trinity (J6): St *Felix* brought the faith to East Anglia in the C7 and one of the churches he founded was here in Loddon. The *Normans* built another and then, just before he became Henry VII's Attorney General in 1486, Sir James Hobart cleared the site and began again. A church, then, which is a guide in itself to the full flowering of the *Perpendicular* style (despite wholesale restoration work in the C19). The sturdy tower has plenty of *flushwork* decoration in both the *base course* and battlements, and the s. *porch* is one of the best examples of the attention that builders of the period lavished on the main entrance. It has its own substantial turret stair to an upper chamber above the vaulted ceiling enriched with *bosses*; the s. face is

Loddon, Holy Trinity: Lady Dame Dyonis Williamson's memorial by Joshua Marshall

a lovely composition of flushwork panelling and battlements, enriched buttresses, and carving applied both to the base course and above the *spandrels* of the entrance. The focal point is a carving of the *Trinity* set in a canopied niche between the upper windows. Inside, the tall lozenge-shaped pillars of the *arcade* march under a great range of 30 *clerestory* windows towards the e. window, which, with its great arch anticipates the final *Tudor* phase of the pre-*Reformation* building styles. All is light and height and vista. The dull 'ecclesiastical' glass in the *aisle* windows serves to emphasise the rather dull stereotype of the tracery pattern, but the rich dark *hammer-beam* and *arch-braced roof* of the *nave* is compensation enough. In its youth the *seven sacrament font* must have outshone all its fellows locally; set on three deep ranges of panelled steps formed as a Maltese cross at the top, its shaft and bowl are all encrusted with carving that still bears traces of original colour. After 160 years came the Commonwealth and Puritan reaction in the person of a Mr Rochester of Beccles – a glazier who was perhaps brought in to deal with the painted pictures in the windows. For 6 shillings he so successfully defaced the font that not one figure or scene can now be recognised. The C15 *rood screen* has been cut down so that only the bottom half remains in place, but that has a most arresting series of panel paintings. Instead of the usual single figures of saints or angels there are complete scenes. Most of them are easily recognisable as episodes in the life of Christ – the *Annunciation*, Nativity, Circumcision, the visit of the Magi and the Ascension – but the one on the left of the choir stalls is quite different. It shows a small boy spread-eagled on a rough frame, to which one hand and one foot are tied, the others nailed. His side has been pierced and one of the attendant figures holds a basin to catch the blood. The faded lettering below confirms that this is the story of St *William of Norwich*, the child whom the Jews were accused of murdering in Holy Week 1144. The *Jacobean* pulpit partially hides the last panel of the screen – a big affair with a ponderous convex cornice, it stands on a C19 base banded with quite nasty glazed black bricks. At the e. end of the n. aisle is the memorable tomb of the Lady Dame Dyonis Williamson sculpted by *Joshua Marshall* (the only example of his work in Norfolk). There is no

Loddon, Holy Trinity

attempt to deceive here, no concession to convention – simply the eloquent portrait of an old lady whose £2000 was the biggest single contribution to the rebuilding of St Paul's after the Great Fire of London. Another £2000 went to St Mary-le-Bow, and £4000 to St Dunstan-in-the-East. This monument may have been originally destined for the latter, but how good to have it here – close to her childhood home with the Hobarts of Hales Hall. A remarkable confirmation of the present building's genesis is to be seen in the painting on the wall of the s. aisle. It shows Sir James and Lady Hobart, he in armour and she in a heavy cloak lined with ermine. They kneel before open missals with their coats of arms between, and in the top corners are pictures of his church and her bridge at St Olave's. There are two good Hobart *brasses* as well – one at the e. end of the n. aisle and the other in the sanctuary (both on top of table tombs). By the door, an ancient iron banded poor box survives from a former church. Standing in a great churchyard giving onto open meadows beyond, this building has much to offer. The living church in Loddon is remarkable too. Anglicans and Methodists have achieved a quiet unity and sharing worship here that is an inspiration in itself. The church has an excellent ring of 8 bells, tenor 11 cwt.

Long Stratton, St Mary (H6): The round *Norman* tower has a little lead covered spike on top, and the church itself is spacious, with a range of seven *clerestory* windows over the C14 *arcades*. The n. arcade, with its *quatrefoil piers* dates from 1330, when Sir Roger de Bourne built the *nave* and the n. *aisle*. His brother Richard was rector at the same time and built the *chancel*, and another C14 rector Robert de Swaffham Bulbeck lies under the mutilated slab on the n. side of it. In the sanctuary lie Sir Edmund Reeve and his wife Mary – in some considerable state. He was appointed a judge of Common pleas in 1639 and lies stiffly on his side in the full panoply of red furlined robe and black tricorne cap. Fat of face, with goatee and moustaches, he smiles faintly. Lady Reeve is sober in black, with a wide Puritan collar, and lies below him on her back looking a deal less pompous but much more comfortable. The pulpit is *Jacobean* on a new base, and has wide strapwork (interlaced bands), blank arches with curly *capitals*, and deep acanthus-framed panels above. The font by the s. door has a cover of the same period which is beautifully light and elegant. Four tall columns support an octagonal top which bears the text from St John's Gospel, 'Except a man be borne of water & of the Spirit...'. Above that, delicate scroll brackets rise to support a tall decorative *finial*. Near it, you can see remnants of C16 black letter text on the s. aisle wall, and a little patch of C15 mural decoration just to the w. The thing Long Stratton is famous for is the Sexton's wheel – now beautifully displayed in a glass case in the n. aisle. In the C14 and C15 when veneration of the Blessed Virgin was at its height, penitents would sometimes be directed or would choose to observe the Lady Fast – either one day a week for seven years, or 365 days continuously on bread and water. If they chose the latter, they would come to the Sexton to determine the day on which to begin. There are six days in the church's calendar set aside for the honour of Our Lady, and six long threads were tied through the holes in the rim, each one identified for a particular feast. The Sexton would spin the wheel, and the devotee would grasp a thread at random to decide when the fast should start. There must have been hundreds of these wheels, particularly in churches dedicated to the Virgin, but only two have survived – one here and one at Yaxley in Suffolk. The church has a good ring of 6 bells, tenor 10-0-10 cwt.

Longham, St Andrew & St Peter (F4): The C15 tower has an oblong look because the e.

Ludham, St Catherine: Tympanum Rood group painting

buttresses are at right angles and a bulky stair turret goes up behind the one on the s. side. The tower was reduced in 1778 and the present shallow top was added around 1900. With *chancel* totally rebuilt in 1867, and *nave* re-roofed and thoroughly re-stored in 1898, the outside is neat rather than interesting. The s. *porch* exterior arch has the look of being cobbled together and does not match the *jambs*. Through the *Early English* doorway, with original closing ring on the door itself, to a modest interior. The C15 font has a plain bowl with floral motifs underneath, resting on a panelled shaft. The *rood screen* has been sympathetically restored, picked out in gilt and colour; above its *ogee arches* there is a delicate web of *Perpendicular* tracery and it is altogether very attractive. There is a good stair to the *rood*, set in the s.e. corner of the nave, and just below the sill of the upper door, a stone bracket is set in the window embrasure close by, with another in the same position on the n. side. It seems certain that these carried the original front beam of the loft, well forward of the chancel arch. That being so, the present screen must have come in from elsewhere as a replacement. The stretchers and top of the early-C17 altar have been renewed but the legs and rails are original.

Ludham, St Catherine (J4): The village's connection with St Benet's Abbey – whose ruins are nearby on the bank of the River Bure – goes back to before the Conquest, and successive Bishops of Norwich spent much of their time here. Partly because of this no doubt, the church is large and fine, with ample C15 *arcades* and a range of *clerestory* windows to match, leading the eye forward to a great e. window, the head full of *reticulated* tracery. The wheel emblem of the patron saint can be seen in the *spandrels* of the *hammer-beam* and *arch-braced roof*. The C15 font is unusually enriched by having two ranks of figures below the bowl, and there are two lions, a wild man with shield, and a wild woman, standing round the stem. The *piscina* and *sedilia* form a very rich composition of profusely *crocketted, ogee arches*, and on the other side of the *chancel* hangs a good C17 *decalogue board* painted in oil and tempera on canvas. The *tympanum* filling the chancel arch is of exceptional interest. It lay hidden for many years in the blocked-up *rood stair*, and was discovered in 1879 by an Archaeological Society outing, (on which they dined-out for years no doubt!) On the w. side is a roughly painted *rood*, with two angels flanking St *John*, the Virgin, and two soldiers. This was probably a makeshift alternative put up in the short reign of Mary Tudor, to replace the original. The whole was then reversed, and the arms of Queen Elizabeth substituted. These now appear on the e. side, inscribed, 'Non me pudet evangelium Christi' ('I am not ashamed of the Gospel of Christ'). Below there is one of the best *screens* remaining in the county. The middle rail has a diagonally folded label that gives the names of John Salman and his wife Sicilie who gave £14 in 1493 for its construction. Below, in intricately decorated panels are fine paintings of (from left to right) *Mary Magdalene, St Stephen, St Edmund, Henry VI, the Four Latin*

Doctors, Edward the Confessor, St *Walstan,* St *Laurence, and* St *Appolonia.* Delicate detached buttresses grace the front of the *screen.* Restoration of both screen and *tympanum* was completed by Miss Plummer in 1972. Note a labeled *brass* to Christopher White (d.1652) which is brief and to the point: 'Hodie mihi, eras tibi' ('Today for me, tomorrow for you'). The church has a ring of 5 bells, tenor 18-0-19 cwt.

Lyng, St Margaret (G4): Well guarded by houses in the bend of the village street, the approach is either from the pub yard, or by a gravelled loke between the cottages to a churchyard that was being grazed by goats that eat banana skins with avidity, and utter plangent cries, when first I was there in the 1970s. The C13 tower has tiny 'Y' tracery bell openings and a plain parapet with corner pinnacles. A stroll round will reveal a blocked n. doorway and the base of an outside *rood stair* turret at the e. end of the *nave,* plus a good view of the outsize *Perpendicular* windows – ogee tracery arches and stepped horizontals. The C15 *porch* is tall and dignified, albeit battered by age. The C17 brick gable is worn and pitted, and the three-*light* window is blocked nearly to the top. The outer arch is angular, and its shape is echoed by the *holy water stoup* to the right; as you go in, you will see that the upper room has gone. Note also that there were two entrances to it – odd, that. An explanation may be that the original staircase was on the w. side. That got in the way when the big window was inserted, so it was filled in and a new one cut through from the e. side. When the room itself was gutted, staircase No. 2 was also redundant – hence the blocked doorway inside the church. The main doors are a fine C15 pair, with traceried panels and a heavy border of *quatrefoils.* The interior poses a puzzle in itself. The *chancel* was rebuilt from the ground in 1912 but the foundations were not altered, and it is offset to the s. On the left of the chancel arch there is a fairly narrow blocked window, and the 27 ft. wide nave has no *aisles.* Tower and chancel were sometimes built separately and then joined up piecemeal, and this could account for the lack of alignment, but one is still left with the blocked window to explain. It may follow that there was a n. aisle originally, and when the suite of big C15 windows went in, the n. wall was moved inwards to accommodate their height and bring everything under one roof. Behind the organ, incidentally, you can just see part of the Elizabethan 'black letter' text. The worn C13 *Purbeck* font has the customary *arcade*

of pointed arches round the bowl – the columns are replacements, the cover modern. There is a glass case on the w. wall which contains an altar cloth made up from C15 vestments – two copes and chasuble in red, blue and amber velvet, stiff with intricate embroidery and the figures of saints and angels. The chancel e. window was fitted with clear glass in 1968, and a large figure of St *Margaret* by Farrar Bell is set in the centre *light.* She looks pensively down at the fierce green dragon that encircles her feet and flashes its red tongue – a fine sight from the w. end of the church. The church has a good ring of 5 bells, tenor 9 cwt.

Marham, Holy Trinity (D5): The village once had two churches but St Andrew's was ruinous by 1500, leaving *Holy Trinity* to serve for all. Its *Norman* origin can be seen on the n. side where the doorway has a *tympanum* carved with a chequer pattern – the only other example of this in Norfolk is above the door that leads out of the n. *transept* of the cathedral. The bold early-C15 tower has *quatrefoil sound-holes,* big three-*light* bell openings and, like many another in the county, it was once crowned by a spire. Through the C14 *porch* to see the font of the same period. This has variegated tracery in the bowl panels and, interestingly, the sides of the shaft are carved with complete miniature window patterns which take in most of the designs current in the first half of the C14. The s. *arcade* has an early *Perpendicular* character and there is no arch to separate *nave* and *chancel.* All the roofs were replaced in 1844 and new seating was provided in 1875, though fortunately at least some of the C15 benches were saved. These are on the s. side of the nave and have very attractive pierced and traceried backs, with a line of carving along the top rail. On the n. wall of the tower is a fine and large set of James I *Royal Arms* dated 1619; an achievement in pale colours set within curtains and columns like a theatre proscenium, with the royal motto in strapwork below. Also at the w. end, a splendid honey coloured Elizabethan altar over 7 ft. long, with six bulbous legs and carved rails. The s. *aisle* chapel is nearly filled by the tomb chest of John Steward and his wife (1604). The heavy *tester* is supported on pillars sheathed at the bottom with leaves, and a coat of arms with innumerable quarterings is surrounded by pierced strapwork on top. The effigies are apparently carved in clunch – the hard chalk sometimes used as building stone in the eastern counties – and the colouring has been restored overall. His head rests on a silver helm, hers on a crimson cushion, and a small but peevish lion crouches at their feet. Behind the harsh stone pulpit is a memorial for Henry Villebois (1847). Two angels bend over an altar on which stand a cross and bible, and the comment that the sculptor was in general 'competent but uninspired' seems apt.

Marlingford, The Blessed Virgin Mary (H5): The early-C14 unbuttressed tower has plain 'Y' tracery in the lower window but slightly later *Decorated* bell openings. Within the wooden 1880s *porch* is the only sign of an earlier building – a *Norman* doorway which has zig-zag down the outside of the plain columns and plain incised rings on two faces of the arch. Just inside is a pretty *holy water stoup* with a tiny head set at the top of the *trefoil* arch. The font is C13 *Purbeck marble* with typical shallow arches on the bowl – the columns have been renewed round the shaft. Look out for an interesting C19 coloured set of commandments in the tower. The C19 changed the look of the church quite a bit – the ruined n. *aisle* was completely rebuilt, the *chancel* encased in brick, new roofs and windows put in, and the *priest's door* blocked. The monstrous stone pulpit was another addition and you have to peer behind it to see a tiny *piscina* on the s. wall. The old place for the pulpit was on the n. side, and the *hour-glass stand* now looks stranded and forlorn with nothing below to give it meaning, In the centre of the chancel floor is a great black slab commemorating physician Richard Clarke. The long Latin epitaph is finely cut and tells us that he was the friend of another and more illustrious Norwich medical man – *Sir Thomas Browne*. His coat of arms is so deeply recessed that it must be a constant snare to the cassocked! The *lancets* on the s. side contain an attractive 'Faith, Hope and Charity' set, and one commemorates a submariner lost in 1905. Back in the *nave*, two wall tablets have outsize lettering (Life [1763] and Rant [1779]) – were they *ledger stones* originally?

Marsham, All Saints (H3): Entry is by a tall, thin s. *porch*, which now has a jolly red and olive-green ceiling. The C14 *hammer-beam roof* is a very nice piece of work, although the picture is confused by heavy transverse beams. These were inserted after a great gale in the C18 which caused the s. wall to move, and the *arcade* on that side still has a distinct list. The *seven sacrament font* is very good, and can be dated c.1460 by the ladies' head-dresses. Clockwise from the e., the panels

are baptism, confirmation, extreme unction, the Last Judgement, penance, matrimony, ordination, and mass. The *rood screen* has 14 painted saints in the panels, most of whom can be identified by their attributes, although all the heads are defaced. From left to right they are: SS. *Faith, James the less, Thomas, James the Great, John, Andrew, Peter, Paul, Philip,* four saints without emblems, and a bishop. The *gesso* work is reminiscent of Aylsham and Cawston, and the screen probably dates from about 1500. There is an interesting framed pastel on the n. sanctuary wall, showing the e. end in 1842 – classical *reredos, Laudian* rails, and two statues – now all gone. In the centre *aisle* floor, the epitaph of Mrs Margarett (d.1698) admits defeat: 'whose worth & goodnesse cannot be expressed within the limits of a gravestone'. Close by is an uncompromising piece of honesty: Sarah Bear (d.1757) aged 58:

> To die I must
> To stay I'd rather
> To go I must
> I know not whither.

The Rev. Samuel Oates, sometime rector here in the C17 has a place in history at one remove, so to speak. His son Titus Oates was the notorious conspirator and perjurer who took Anglican orders like his father, but was soon dismissed from his curacy for misconduct. His feigned Catholicism was followed in 1677 by his giving endless spurious details about the so-called 'Popish Plot' that was aimed at Charles II, which caused widespread panic; over 30 innocent people were tried and executed on his evidence. Two years later he was found guilty of perjury, was flogged and then imprisoned for life. The Revolution of 1788 set him free, and was even granted a pension which the odious man enjoyed until his death in 1705. The church has a good ring of 8 bells, tenor 7-3-15 cwt.

Martham, St Mary (K4): Large enough to have been dubbed 'the cathedral of the Fleggs' (the name of this part of Norfolk). the C15 church has a great west tower topped by a spirelet. The s. *porch* has two storeys and a *groined* roof, and much of the carving of the lovely doors is original. Beyond them is an enormous tower arch and a *seven sacrament font*, mutilated but understandable: clockwise, starting from the e. face – extreme unction, mass, matrimony, the baptism of Christ, ordination, penance, confirmation, baptism. At the w. end also, a *bier* of 1908 – good honest workmanship, carefully restored. The s. *aisle* chapel is dedicated to St *Blide* (who is said to be buried here at Martham), mother of St *Walstan*, the Norfolk patron saint of farm workers whose shrine was at Bawburgh, just west of Norwich. The remaining medieval glass is set in the e. windows of the aisles, with a particularly nice figure of Eve with her distaff, in a green meadow (s. aisle, bottom pane). Between 1855 and 1861, Mrs Alice Langley decided to honour the memory of the Rev. Jonathan Dawson by financing a new chancel. *Pevsner* aptly described the operation as one in which 'neither money nor inventiveness were spared. The e. window is a splash (probably by *Powell & Sons*) and the chancel arch even more so. The monument to Mr Dawson, in the form of a traditional *Easter Sepulchre*, the arcading of the e. wall, the *sedilia*, and the pulpit are all in keeping'. The wrought iron *rood screen* was part of the same scheme, and the architect chosen by Mrs Langley was Philip Boyce of Cheltenham. An article in *The Builder,* 1861, says that he built the arcades in the parish church there, but over the rest of his career history draws a veil. The same source identifies the carving at Martham as the work of M. Earp, but neither architect nor mason feature anywhere else in East Anglia as far as I know. The church has an excellent ring of 6 bells, tenor 12-2-8 cwt.

Matlask, St Peter (H2): To drive through this pretty village on a sunny day and come suddenly upon the church with its rough, round tower, is a pleasure. The tower is *Norman* (part of the original church, built between 1066 and 1189) with traces of Roman tiles here and there. The octagonal top is C14 *Decorated*, with window-openings of text-book tracery. The n. *porch* has a mellow Decorated arch; nice square-headed *Perpendicular* windows in *nave*; the pretty s. porch has been blocked off to serve as a vestry. No *chancel*: on the morning of 19th March 1726, while the rector was celebrating Holy Communion, it suddenly collapsed – but outwards, so no-one was hurt. Inside, this little church is a pleasure of light, calm and simplicity, where colours of masonry and walls combine in harmony. The modern roof is supported on medieval *corbels* carved with faces: so distinctive they are, that it would be agreeable to think that they are portraits of the masons who built the church. Simple C15 font; carved cover of same date; massive C14 chest under tower; good benches and *poppy-heads* in nave; *Royal Arms* of George III, restored in 1969 by local artist Mary l'Anson. *Jacobean* table in *aisle* was formerly the

altar. Two *hatchments* at the w. end – both of the Gunton family, of Matlask Hall, dated 1794 and 1804.

Mattishall, All Saints (G4): A large, impressive church with a most distinctive silhouette as you approach from the direction of Honingham, and set within a circle of old houses of elegant line. The church is almost wholly *Perpendicular* and much restored. Dominating all is the massive, buttressed tower, topped with a trim lead-and-tiled cupola, one of whose beams bears the date 1640. The s. *porch* is C19 and is rather fun, with its ridiculous minarets. They were, together with the gable cross, personally made in 1887 by the Revd. Thomas Jennings Cooper, who was curate of Mattishall Burgh nearby and something of an enthusiast about architecture. The n. porch, now a vestry, has a Perpendicular outer arch, with three fine figure niches above, and in the *spandrels* the *Annunciation*, with the Angel Gabriel appearing to the Virgin. The *capitals* of the arches are minutely carved: on the left, with a couple of dragons; on the right, birds. Inside, this church is spacious early-C15, with slim pillars and lofty arches to its four-bay *arcade*. Above, a Perpendicular *clerestory*. The splendid C15 roof, *arch-braced* and with 24 *hammer-beams* carved with angels and other figures, has much original colouring, including two painted *celure* panels above the *rood*. Lower down, there are *tie-beams,*; on one of them are initials and the date 1617. The n. aisle roof matches, but the *wall posts* here have been defaced. The s. aisle roof is a good Victorian replacement and retains the original *wall post* figures. Modern pews, but with old *poppy-head* benchends at front – two jolly duck-looking birds, in pelican postures. Under the tower, is a plan of the old arrangement of *box pews* which formerly crammed the nave right up to the *rood screen* in the C19. The tower has a ringing *gallery*, the carved front of which possibly came from the rood loft. Octagonal C15 font, notable in that its eight sides are concave. Handsome *Jacobean* pulpit – though its 'wineglass' stem was for a long time stored out of sight and its *tester* used as a table for vestry meetings, in 1856 it was brought all together again. In the centre nave floor is a tiny *brass* to William Brabant, 1480 – but his wife, and their inscription, are long gone; eastward, another William Brabant, Vicar here, 1688, is remembered on a palimpsest brass showing a civilian and his wife, she wearing a *butterfly head-dress*; they are thought to be Robert Foster, 1507, and his lady, by whose bounty was built the Lady Chapel south of the chancel. In n. aisle, a brass and inscription to Geoffrey Dene, 1510. Over s. door, *Royal Arms* of George II, dated 1745. Only the lower part of the C15 screen remains, look for the tiny carvings in the *spandrels*; s. side, a greyhound and an antlered deer with a 'T' below for Thomas; St *George*; and a defaced *Annunciation*: n. side, lions and hunters with an 'M' for Mary at the centre. On the panels: the 12 apostles – brought to light in 1856 by Cooke, the curate. The C14 screen of the adjoining Lady Chapel has tiny faces and flowers in the *ogee* centre arch. The chancel has a whole range of fine *ledger-stones* and memorials. On the s. wall, the Rev. Thomas Bodham is remembered – he lived at South Green House, now known at Mattishall Hall, and was a great friend of *Parson Woodforde*. Big *piscina* with replaced arch and attractive colour details in the back and sides; spacious *dropped sill sedilia* adjoining. Every *Rogation* Sunday, the Parker Sermon is preached here, recalling the great Elizabethan Archbishop who married a Mattishall girl. The church has a ring of 6 bells, tenor 14 cwt.

Mattishall Burgh, St Peter (G4): A really pretty little church, settled on a slope on the edge of its hamlet, and so clearly cherished and cared for and welcoming that a visit becomes a double pleasure. It has a trim C13 to C14 tower, its belfry windows displaying both 'Y' and *cusped* tracery of about 1300, and little *quatrefoil sound-holes* on two sides. A staircase turret adjoins the little *porch*, whose outer arch is topped off with alternating pink brick and flint with above, a figure niche filled in with *Tudor* bricks. On the e. gable end of the church, a *sanctus bell cote*. The layout of the church looks puzzling, until one realises that there is a large n. *transept* – of the same date as the tower. Inside, the church is as pretty as the outside suggests. The timbers of the *chancel* roof look as if they've been freshly scrubbed, and stand out against white-painted plaster. Below, plain choir stalls and *communion rails*. In the corner of the sanctuary, a little C15 *angle piscina*, with at the angle a short pillar carved like a miniature arcade column; adjoining, *dropped sill sedilia*. In the centre of the e. window, an oblong of good modern glass by Kingston with the Dove of the Holy Spirit above a *chalice* and *host*. The C15 *screen* has the *IHS* stencilled on its panels. The C13 font is a typical octagonal example, with shallow arches carved round its bowl. Nearby, a plain-panelled *barrel organ*, in full working order. On the s. wall, an

unsophisticated memorial to Elizabeth Inyon, 1706, with well-fed cherub faces, wings and gilding. The n. transept has a two-bay arcade with a quatrefoil centre-pillar. Below the transept's e. window is a simple *ogee*-arched piscina. As you leave, take a look at the loose-flint damp course right the way round the church. Nothing unusual there. Except that the building used to be very damp – so four pensioners from the congregation laboured lovingly and voluntarily for 18 months, digging a 3ft. wide by 3ft. deep trench, plus large soakaways at four points of the compass, then barrowed away the gritty soil – and barrowed back 50 tons of clean flints. The church is now sweet and dry. Of such is the nature of true parochial caring.

Mautby, St Peter & St Paul (K4): The round *Norman* tower has a C15 octagonal top like many others in the county, and a long thatched roof covers both *nave* and the early-C14 *chancel*. When the nave was restored in 1884 and new windows inserted, the *arcade* in the s. wall was uncovered and it is the only trace left of a C13 south *aisle*. A pity, because Margaret Paston (of the famous *Paston Letters*) directed that her body be buried, 'in the ele of that cherch at Mauteby, byefore the ymage of Our Lady there, in which ele reste the bodies of divers myn auncestres'. She was at Mautby before her marriage and came back here after her husband's death in 1456, writing many of the letters from her childhood home. The tomb of one of her forebears – probably Sir Walter (c.1248) is now in the s. wall within the easternmost arcade, having been moved there when the aisle was demolished after the *Reformation*. Under a fragmented canopy is a monolithic figure of a *Knight Templar* in square-topped helm and chainmail, with sword and shield. The cross-legged effigy has been harshly treated and only the little paws show that a dog or lion once lay at his feet. The old Crusader's bones were actually handled by an antiquary in 1822 and are still there in the stone coffin. The C15 *screen* has good tracery, and when it was restored in 1906 the *rood* was added. It has a *squint* cut in one of the panels, which indicates that a nave altar stood on the s. side – the *piscina* for it is in the wall by the chancel arch. In the chancel itself, the pleasing *cinquefoil* arches over the *sedilia* and piscina have small animal heads as stops to the *hood moulds*. Note that the piscina has two drains. This was general practice 1250-1350, when the priest's hands as well as the *chalice* were washed there. On the opposite wall, an excellent architectural tablet to Richard Gay Lucas

Melton Constable, St Peter: Reredos

(d.1771). It has a coat of arms over it, lively swags of flowers, a cherub's head below, and is a subtle exercise in varying the planes to take full advantage of shadow. C15 font of good proportions, with slim traceried panels between the shaft columns. Only the *crocketted* ribs of the candle-snuffer cover are original but they show that it was made at the same time.

Melton Constable, St Peter (G2): By the e. lodge of the disused hall, trees on one side and a great vista of open fields on the other. This is a small but fascinating church. The central *Norman* tower retains its big undecorated arch to the *nave*, and above it, set within an outline replica of the arch below, a double arch separated by a massive round pillar. Beyond is a very short C15 *chancel* which has big figures as roof *corbels* in the corners – one of the Virgin crowned. The whole is oddly reminiscent of an opera set, an impression heightened by the Hastings pew in its own s. *transept* approached by a staircase. The altar *reredos* is a Flemish triptych (Gethsemane, the Crucifixion, the Deposition) brought into the church during the C20, which everybody is careful to describe as 'attributed to Rubens'. But the chancel's unique contribution is the *low side window*. The lower half is still unglazed and there

is a stone bookrest and hollowed-out seat beside it; this is the clearest indication anywhere of the true purpose of these windows – to enable the sacristan to ring the *sanctus bell* at the elevation of the *host*. To the s. of the chancel arch is an elaborate recess with a large *ogee* arch where there was once a nave altar. There are still traces of colour in the mouldings and there was much more before the war memorial was set in the back. On that, the list is headed by the squire's son (writ twice as large), which brings us back to the Hastings pew. The short flight of stairs (steps would be too flimsy a word) is dated 1636 on the newel (post) and leads up to the white panelled front of a *gallery*. Twin doors, each emblazoned with a coat of arms, are topped by crimson plush-padded canted sills matching the rest of the frontage, on which lie folio 1721 Prayer Books bound in sheep skin, each labelled 'Melton Constable Chapel'. The gallery is large enough to take four carved walnut upholstered carvers and a dozen gilt and cane occasional chairs without overcrowding. Behind a low screen there is an area for the servants with its own door to the outside world. The white wainscot panels have upwards of forty numbered coats of arms emblazoned in miniature, with genealogical notes in careful gilt of the ramifications of the Astley/Hastings family. Above them, a splendid array of marble

Melton Constable, St Mary: low side window

tablets. Portrait medallions adorn the memorial to Sir Philip Astley (d.1779) and his wife by *Robert Page*. There is a lovely baroque *cartouche* in the corner to Isabella (1741) – all shells, scrolls and undulations. On the e. wall, Anna Maria Astley (d.1768) has asymmetrical rococo striving rather too hard, while Lucy and Judith's epitaphs have a curtained canopy supported by *putti*. The two recent additions to the collection are beautifully executed, and look like well-moulded plastic pastiches of their C18 neighbours. In the silence, the weight of an ancient family obsessed by lineage is almost oppressive. I'm not sure what they would have made of the use to which their splendid pew has been put – a carpeted space for coffee and chat tricked out with urn, stacking chairs and portable heater. I'm sure they would have had something pertinent to say, especially that valiant old Royalist Sir Jacob Astley – the victor of Edgehill: 'O Lord! thou knowest how busy I must be this day: if I forget thee, do not thou forget me'. No noble family in the great house now, but plenty of memories here.

Merton, St Peter (F6): A small but most interesting church prettily set within the park. The round tower has renewed *Norman* bell openings but the *jambs* are flint, and above the plain arch inside there is a *lancet* with a deep splay, and so the beginnings were probably pre-

Conquest (flint *quoins* at the n.w. corner of the *nave* and a thin n. wall support this view). Nave and *chancel* are mainly early-C14 and have a wonderful series of windows. There are tall double lancets with *cusped* 'Y' tracery in the n. nave wall, and the three-*light* windows of the chancel have a most unusual variation of *plate tracery* which is cusped and intersected. Within and without, the windows have delicate shafts and a fine variety of *headstops* – those on the s. side outside are all smiling. The s. *aisle* windows are slightly later, but again exhibit a refreshing originality in the intersected tracery. The *Perpendicular* n. *porch* (re-roofed in the C19) has a deep *holy water stoup* outside, and an ancient *corbel* remains above the inner doorway. The nave was heightened in the C15 and given a single-sided *clerestory*, but the C14 *arcade* and chancel arch were left alone. All the roofs are C19 renewals. The C15 font is the only six-sided example hereabouts, and there are mutilated angels below the bowl whose wings sweep up to support large blank shields in the panels; lions once sat on the rings of stools around the shaft and fragments of a paw still adhere on the s. side. The tall cover was originally raised and lowered from the wooden bracket above, and parts of it are C15, although the majority is competent C19 replacement. The s. aisle chapel is enclosed as a family pew by plain *Jacobean* panelling which has pierced *finials*. Within, a large *piscina*, and a long *squint* cut through to the chancel, with an image bracket above, supported by a good carved head. Under the carpet is the *brass* of Thomas de Grey (1562) in armour which, like the Hobart brass at Loddon by the same hand, shows the Norwich craft in decline. A C19 rector noted that the *Tudor Royal Arms* in the chapel e. window are C16 and were bought in London to be inserted here in 1880, but Mr David King judged it to be all C19. Across the nave is a Jacobean two-decker pulpit with flat, shallow carving in the upper panels, a tall canted book ledge supported by scrolled brackets, and a very large *hour-glass* stand on a bracket nearby. On the wall to the left, an excellent brass – William de Grey (1495) with his wives Mary and Grace; he kneels in full armour with his helm before him, and wears an heraldic tabard; there are five sons grouped behind him and five daughters kneel behind their respective mothers. The stairs to the *rood loft* are behind the pulpit and the *screen* itself is as individual as the rest of the C14 work in the church. Little attention was paid to the rough panels (but note the *elevation squints* bored in them, including a *quatrefoil* to the right of the

entrance) and simple stencilled decoration was used there and on the uprights. The tracery with its faded colour, however, is remarkably rich; the *ogee* centre arch is cusped and sub-cusped, with two tracery wheels in the *spandrels*, and there is more variety above the flattened ogees of the two-light divisions each side, with every outline barbed and crisp. In the chancel, the design of the early-C14 double piscina matches the tracery of the side windows, and the pattern is extended to the sharply stepped *sedilia* separated by slender shafts (The piscina drain patterns vary – individuality again!). The late-C17 *communion rails* have barley sugar twist *balusters*, with a heavily moulded top rail, one of only three sets remaining in Norfolk which enclose the altar on three sides. This was a C17 arrangement which became particularly fashionable after the *Restoration* in 1660. The n.e. window still has some of its original glass dating from about 1320, with a lovely figure of St *Margaret* in the centre with a glowing red dragon, and although the saint to the right now carries St *John's* emblem, it may have been St *Catherine* before the C19 heads were inserted. Most of the canopy work above the figures is original too. The figures in the other windows are interesting only because they were an 1830s attempt to match the style of the real thing. Before leaving, seek out the lozenge of C17 glass in the s. aisle which has an oblong sundial with a motto and, at the top, a lifesize spider and fly.

Methwold, St George (D6): Opinions vary about the practice of clearing churchyards of headstones, but it does provide a very gracious setting for a church such as this. There is the shaft of a *preaching cross* e. of the *chancel*, and it is a good place for a first look at the building. The tower, with its small bell openings would be unremarkable were it not for the beautiful C15 octagon and spire. The drum is recessed behind the parapet and has two ranges of *blind arcading* which rise to a pinnacled and pierced crown, and the slender crocketted spire provides an elegant landmark for miles. *Sanctus bell cotes* are normally sited at the apex of the *nave* but here there is one on the s.e corner of the roof, built mainly of thin brick. A line on the e. wall below it shows that the chancel roof was once higher than it is now, and the long labels over the *clerestory* windows have excellent *headstops* with a great variety of hats and hairstyles. Apart from the flowing tracery of the *Decorated* e. window, the style of the whole building is

Methwold, St George

Perpendicular and the outside was well restored in 1977. Before entering, note the *holy water stoup* and the 1721 sundial overhead carved with the church-wardens' names. The tower clock is older still, and for over 300 years the visitor has been braced by the admonition over it, 'Man know thyself.' Inside, fine C15 *arcades*, with half-angels and heads carved on the *capitals* matching those at the spring of the tall tower arch. Unusually large three-*light* clerestory windows light a beautiful roof; *arch-braced tie-beams*, with *queen posts* alternate with *hammer-beams* carved as recumbent angels – and see how the easternmost pair hold the nails of the Crucifixion and the crown of thorns. The plain C15 font in the s. *aisle* has a cover given in 1905 and beyond it, a C14 iron bound chest with two locks and three hasps. This stands on a 1737 *bier* which not only has a warden's name carved on it but also that of the maker: 'MAd By ME WILAYARS'. Four C17 bells lie on the floor nearby and provide a rare chance to study the inscriptions normally seen only in the gloom and dust of a bell chamber. St George's is well blessed with chests – there is a plain late-C16 example by the s. door, and another (probably a little older) by the tower which has naive carving on the front panels and rails, with a scalloped skirt – a nice piece. Mounted on a board in the n. aisle is a fine and important early *brass* from

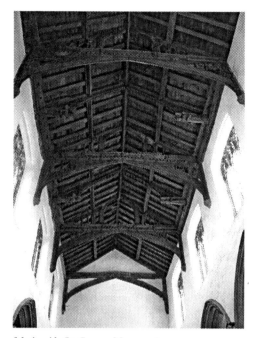

Methwold, St George: Nave roof

the London workshops. Dating from the 1360s, it is the life size effigy of Sir Adam de Clyfton, and although parts are missing, it is a wonder that it is here at all. Originally in the chancel, it was sold in 1680 to a tinker and broken down for melting. The 130 pieces were recovered by the parish and lay in the chest until 1888 when they were pieced together and put on show. Further along, lovely stained glass by *Henry Holiday* of 1866; there are scenes of the Ascension, Martha and Mary, feeding the multitude, and the healing at Capernaum; the treatment of clothes and faces is typically *Pre-Raphaelite*. At the e. end of this aisle, a *pillar piscina*, and in front of the *screen*, a lovely solid *Stuart* table with shallow carving and a pendant on the front rail. The screen is a good C19 reproduction, and for once, the old stairs lead to a real loft in front of the *rood* – as they were meant to do. In the chancel, the painted barrel roof rests on half-angel *corbels* (mainly original) and there is a plain *piscina* under an *ogee* arch. The 1850s glass by Sutton Brothers is an attempt to match C14 style in rather harsh colours, and on the e. wall, a restrained tablet to Henry Partridge (1803) by John Athow of Norwich. On the n. wall, another of the same name of 1793, with a rare use of the black portrait silhouette so popular in drawing rooms of the

period – but as a lawyer it looks as if he was pursy and persuasive rather than dominating.

Metton, St Andrew (H2): The C14 tower has a processional way (n. to s.) beneath it, and the scaffolding *put-log holes* are open all the way up. Inside, the church is homely with boarded ceilings. There are some *brasses*, including a good one of Robert Doughty and his wife dated 1483. The *chancel* e. window contains roundels of Flemish glass, and close by is a *piscina* with the unusual addition of a grotesque head to support the bowl. The small C19 organ has a nice classical mahogany case, although the attached striplight is a pity. By the door is a dumpy Parish Constable's staff of the 1830s.

Middleton, St Mary (C4): Traffic thunders by on the bend of the A47, but this *carstone* church has the imperishable look of something that will not be moved. The *Perpendicular* tower has a strong stair turret right to the top like a backbone in the n.w. corner, and inside, its elongated arch is flanked by massive buttresses. The *aisles* wrap round it and it has the unusual distinction of additional arches n. and s. The 1857 glass in the w. window by *Clayton & Bell* is very decorative – a nativity scene with a luscious red background. There are fragments of Elizabethan 'comfortable and profitable sentences' on the n. *pier* of the tower arch and more traces will be found above the lectern. C15 *arcades* with octagonal piers and no *capitals* reach up to a modest *clerestory* and a good *arch-braced roof*. The Lady chapel in the s. aisle has a small *piscina* with a stone *credence shelf* and half the bowl sliced away, while on the left there is a *squint* reaching through to the *chancel*. A very strange pedestal is built into the corner here which looks earlier than the chancel arch next door; there are some medieval tiles set in its front face and it probably served as the base for a statue of the Virgin. Traces of the old stair to the *rood* can be found to the n. of the chancel arch, and before leaving the body of the church have a look at the glass in two of the aisle windows – pastiches by *Powell & Sons* in medieval style of Christ in the Temple and the visit of the Magi – inserted in 1926 and 1931 respectively. The chancel is *Early English*, with *plate tracery* in the side windows and an unusual and very decorative band of carved foliage running round the walls at sill height. It is interrupted by clumsy Victorian *sedilia* but fits happily with the exceptionally pretty double piscina. The arch of this has a semi-circular roll

Middleton, St Mary: Lectern by Robert Thompson

moulding which is pierced and carved with berried holly and the centre s*pandrel* carries the Virgin's lily emblem. Two panels are all that remain of the *rood screen*, and they are mounted by the organ; the heavily overpainted figures are, from left to right: St *Jude*, St *James the Great*, St *Anthony* (or St *Philip*) and St *Thomas*. There is more C19 glass here – the 1865 n. side window is signed by H. Hughes and the e. window crucifixion might well be his work too. A former vicar was a Yorkshireman and perhaps that is why we find work by *Robert Thompson* of Kilburn – the only examples in Norfolk. *Communion rails*, table, prayer desks and a particularly fine eagle lectern – all have the 'mouse' signature, and the distinctive adze finish is clearly seen on the rails and lectern. Two memorials of interest in the chancel – s. wall, Major Everard-Hutton, one of the 'gallant Six Hundred' of the famous Light Brigade, and a plain *ledger slab* in the n.e. corner of the sanctuary to Dr Robert

Barker, who bequeathed a superb collection of early medical books to Kings Lynn in 1717. As you leave, see the little poor man's box fixed to an old bench end near the door, and in the churchyard on the n. side, the shaft of an old *preaching cross.*

Mileham, St John the Baptist (F4): The first thing to catch the eye is the shaft and base of an early medieval *churchyard cross* which was later mounted very effectively on a C15 table tomb by the path. Circle the church and see how the s. side has large additional buttresses which blend very well with the old work yet mask reinforced concrete beams, inserted to check the subsidence that has been a worry for years. The blocked *priest's door* in the s. *chancel* wall has *Norman* pillars and *capitals*, but the arch is *Early English* in shape – either a *Transitional* form or a C13 remodelling at the time when the *aisles* were added. The early-C14 tower abuts the n. aisle and has 'Y' tracery bell openings and a good range of *flushwork* battlements, with seated figures at the corners and large *gargoyles*. It also serves as the entrance *porch*, and the measured thud of the clock pendulum reverberates above as you go in. Upright by the door is a coffin lid with a very decorative foliated cross, and another by the s. door has the double omega sign – both found at Mileham Hall. The n. *arcade* was formed by simply cutting arches through the nave wall, but on the s. side there are two stocky pillars, one round and one octagonal, which lean alarmingly outward and show the extent of the subsidence and the size of the rescue operation thankfully completed in 1982. Both aisle roofs are original and have pretty tracery in the *spandrels*. The C15 font is placed on a high step, with varied tracery on the slim shaft and a heavy mould beneath the pointed *quatrefoils* in the bowl panels. The poor man's box at the w. end has the customary three hasps and is clearly dated 1639, and the C15 pulpit stands on its original stem, with modern stairs and additional carving at top and bottom. The tall niches either side the e. window have had their canopies hacked off, but it must have been an impressive arrangement with, presumably, a *reredos* in the three recessed stone panels behind the altar. There is an *aumbry* low in the n. wall of the sanctuary, and before the floor levels were raised, the plain embrasures on the s. side would have been useable as *sedilia*. While in the chancel, look in front of the rails on the n. side for the *ledger-stones* of Samuel Pepys' Norfolk cousins John and Fermor, who died in 1658 and 1660. Fermor's epitaph is well worth reading, and so, on the opposite side of the chancel, is that for the four young children of Thomas and Elizabeth Browne who died between 1676 and 1680. There is a London-made *brass* of 1526 at the e. end of the s. aisle for Christopher Crow and his wife: 18in. figures, inscription, and a small separate brass for the five daughters, with the sons' plate missing. The three-*light* w. window with its *Decorated* tracery is remarkable because its C14 stained glass is virtually intact, rich in yellows, browns and greens, with miniature coloured windows enclosed within the elaborate canopies. From left to right, the three large figures are St *Catherine, St John the Baptist* and St *Margaret;* below them, three more have been moved in from other windows: a C14 St *John the Evangelist* (holding a book) in the centre, with a C15 St *Barbara* to the left and a C15 St *Margaret* to the right This is a most satisfying window to study so take your binoculars. In the top of the e. window are three more figures: another C14 St John the Evangelist, with a bishop below him and, to the left, a C15 St *Agatha* with a name scroll. Lastly, in the corner of a s. chancel window, a fascinating C15 fragment which shows a pedlar with his wife and two pack horses.

Morley St Botolph, St Botolph (G5): A disastrous fire on 8th May 1959 gutted *nave* and tower, leaving only their walls standing – though the Victorian *chancel* was left almost untouched. For some time the church lay ruinous, until at last a decision was made to restore it, and with energy and enthusiasm, the parish gave action to the word. The job was done by J. Fletcher Watson, the architect who was responsible for the enchanting rebuilding at Bawdeswell in 1950 and St Botolph's reopened on 3rd October 1964. What we see now is a very big, square tower, looking as solidly *Perpendicular* in spirit as when it was first built; the nave restored to its Perpendicular lines; and the chancel as the Victorians left it. Also intact is the most attractive n. doorway, in typical *Tudor* shape and style and dressed with red bricks. Inside the church there is therefore an impression – light, refreshing and welcoming – of total newness. The nave has been given a plainly plastered barrel roof, painted in palest blue, above the walls colour-washed in pristine cream. Fitting perfectly into this setting are the light, clean-lined pews, specially designed by Fletcher Watson. Later two very light-weight pulpits were added – not so successful: they have a cheap plywood look about them – one to serve as a lectern, thus underlining the dual importance of Sermon and Bible. There is a tiny plain *piscina* niche in the nave s.e. corner; another in the chancel, with adjoining it, *dropped sill sedilia* which have been neatly panelled and seated. The chancel is characterised by a roof in a freely interpreted Victorian version of *hammer-beamed* and *arch-braced* construction – which in the 1964 restoration had its timbers painted in alternate light and dark blue and the wingless angels on the hammers coloured and gilded. Not the best of aesthetic taste, perhaps – but very agreeable and fun.

Morley, St Peter (G6): This little church stands quietly remote on a sharp bend of a minor road, and almost looks as though it grew there. The low squat tower is unbuttressed and has a pyramidal roof with a jaunty copper weathercock on top. There is a stair turret in brick on the n. side, and two brick niches flank the small w. window. Inside the s. *porch*, the C13 doorway is a plain chamfered *lancet* only 3ft. wide. The inside is very plain with modern roofs, no nonsense pine pews, and a good brick floor to the *nave*. The C16 font under the tower has a quite unusual shape. The octagonal bowl has simple carving in the top half of the panels, and then they curve inwards halfway down to rest on a slim square shaft, chamfered at the corners. On the n. wall of the nave, a monument to Martin Sedley (1609) whose epitaph pays due attention to his adventitious and extremely practical marriages – first an alliance with the Sheltons of Shelton, and then as second wife, Abigail Knyvett of the wealthy Ashwellthorpe clan. His son went on to claim Sir John Pettus of Norwich for a father-in-law; plain black marble with alabaster surround and a coat of arms on top, picked out in colour. In front of the nicely carved and finished modern oak *screen* there is a *ledger slab* over the Graver-Browne vault. This has traces of colour and the motto 'Sur Esperance', but can be no earlier than C19 because the arms include the label of Bishop Bathurst – for the family connection see the brass plate for Frances Graver-Browne on the s. wall. In the *chancel* on the s. wall, a pretty monument to John Turner Graver-Browne (1861) by Gaffin of London. It shows none of the decline in taste that the date might otherwise suggest. The e. window is modern, by A.L. Wilkinson, a centre panel of the Virgin and Child, marking the coronations of George VI and Elizabeth II. There is just the vestige of a *piscina* in a tiny oblong recess.

Morningthorpe, St John the Baptist (I6): In a village with a surprising number of fine old houses for so small a place, stands this lovely little church against a frieze of huge trees. Its *Saxo-Norman* round tower has a massive arch inside the building that suggests a pre-Conquest date. The tower has C14 belfry windows and a *Perpendicular* w. window of late-C14/early-C15 origin, contemporary with the general character of the rest of the church though the fabric is largely early-C14. The n.w. *Tudor nave* window has a filled-in doorway immediately below it. The inner archway of the s. porch is *Decorated*, and very good. Inside, the church is beautifully appointed, with a surprisingly spacious *chancel*. The roofs are Victorian, and excellent. There are painted *Royal Arms* of George III over the s. door; and over the tower arch, another set for the same monarch, this time handsomely and massively carved from a solid block of oak. Below is the briskly carved C15 font, with lions alternating with angels – two male, two female, all with opulent hair-dos, and one of the 'ladies' wears a bonnet of C15 fashion. Below, little lions support the base. To the left of the chancel arch is the entrance to the *rood stair*; to the right, a tiny *piscina* arch, indicating the presence of a pre-*Reformation* side altar. There are everal handsome C18 and C19 wall monuments in the chancel. The C15 *piscina* is extravagantly carved, its canopy lushly decorated with leafy *crockets*. Opposite, the fine Elizabethan altar-tomb is richly carved and adorned, but with no effigy or inscription. It could commemorate Richard Garneys, who bought nearby Boyland Hall in 1571. Immediately adjoining is an C18 wall monument to another member of the Garneys family, and also to Sir William Costlin, Alderman & Sheriff of the City of London; as well as several fine *ledger stones* to Garneys in the chancel floor.

Morston, All Saints (G1): The church stands castle-like on a knoll, no trees or vegetation around to soften its lines. A chunky, square tower, largely C13, but part rebuilt in red brick when it was struck by lightning in 1743. Interesting and unusual *clerestory*, with little *quatrefoil* windows, perhaps as early as C12; above, partly battlemented. The window tracery all round is specially interesting and attractive, for here we have C13 *Early English* in transition on the edge of early-C14 *Decorated*. The *chancel*, s. side, has one window with Y-tracery extended to three *lights*, of about 1300. Look closely at the tracery in the s. *aisle* windows

– this is *plate tracery*. Entering through the C15 s. *porch*, we find ourselves in a light, white, refreshing interior, with a simple C13 *arcade* with its slim round pillars. The arcade has *corbels* carved with individual faces – gossip with tongue out, a bulbous-nosed boozer or a half-wit and a moustached gent. Above the C13 chancel arch are the *Royal Arms*, 1823, *decalogue*, and *tympanum*. Below, the 1480 *rood screen* has well preserved figures – on the left, the four Evangelists, on the right, the *Four Latin Doctors*. Above the paintings on the screen are carvings of small figures: a *pelican*, feathered angels, a bird with a crest and a dragon. The chancel has a coarse *angle piscina* and *dropped sill sedilia*; opposite, an *aumbry*, now adapted with a modern tracery head. Under the altar – to where it was moved for safe keeping a few years ago – is a fine *brass* to Richard Makynges, 1596, rector here for 40 years – a rarity, for there are few *brasses* to Elizabethan clergy, and this is the only one in Norfolk. The *Evangelistic Symbols* are also carved on the C15 font, where they alternate round the octagonal bowl with four seated saints.

Morton on the Hill, St Margaret (H4): Turn off the Ringland-Weston Longville road, down the long drive to Morton Hall, and you will find this little church secreted among the trees close by the house. The *Saxon* round tower collapsed into the *nave* in 1959, and 27 years later the church was declared redundant. That might have been the end of the story but for the determined enthusiasm of Lady Prince-Smith, supported by the *Norfolk Churches Trust* and others. The remains of the tower, the s. *porch*, and the western half of the nave are open to the sky, but a new gable and a tall glass screen have been inserted to enclose the e. end, so that we now find a short nave/*chancel* linked by a two-bay *arcade* to a n. chapel. 'Y' tracery of about 1300 and a *lancet* in the nave, and a Victorian '*Decorated*' e. window in the chapel – through which there is a delectable view clear across the valley (and how sensible to have plate glass instead of small panes here). As with many of our Saxo-*Norman* churches there is plenty of *carstone* in the walls, and there is evidence of a Saxon double-splay window in the tower on the nave side. Pottering round, have a look at the *holy water stoup* in the s. porch, with its own little brick arch, and also at the original door with good tracery. That will pose a problem if it is to be protected from the weather. The font has been skilfully dismantled and re-erected inside (the base locked together like a jigsaw), and it has shallow shields in the bowl and a panelled shaft. The main sanctuary has the base of the old *rood screen* lining the walls, and a set of robust early-C17 *communion rails*. In the centre of the nave is the grave of Katherine Awdley. She was the daughter of Sir Richard Southwell (see Wood Rising) and 'she lyved 45 yeares a widdow. She kept good hospitality. She was charitable to the poore'. Her brother Thomas (1609) lies in the tomb chest set in the n. wall of the chapel. The polished black slab records that he:

> lived unmaried with the good love and reputation of all men untill the age of three score yeares & so departed this life...being Lord of this Manner and bewlder of the capitall mantion house there upon.

In those days they were not content to assume that you had noticed little things like that! Although St Margaret's is now a private chapel, it is still used regularly for the public services.

Moulton St Mary, St Mary (K5): An attractive setting, well back from the road, and lying by the side of the manor house and farm. Approached across a broad meadow, the generous churchyard is neatly kept – as one has come to expect with a church that is secure in the hands of the *Churches Conservation Trust*. The round tower is probably *Norman* and, with its later conical cap, it just tops the ridge of the deep *nave* roof. Walking round, you will see the shapes of square *put-log holes* on the s. side which were probably inserted for scaffolding used in medieval repairs or alterations. The C15 w. window has been blocked and so has the small square bell-chamber window on the n. side, and they possibly date from the 1520s when the nave was partially rebuilt and had its roof replaced. Probably as part of the same programme, three-*light Perpendicular* windows were set in each wall. Both nave and *chancel* date originally from the C13 with typical Y tracery in three of the windows. The chancel e. wall was rebuilt in 1877 using red brick, and when the window was renewed in 1901 the intersecting tracery was carried out in wood rather the more expensive stone – an economy practiced when the smaller windows on the s. side were dealt with. There is a large *priest's door* in the chancel s. wall but the main entrance is via the homely *Tudor* s. porch in worn red brick, with an empty niche over the outer arch and the remains of shields in the *spandrels*. The good *mass dial* set high on the s.w. corner is slightly unusual in having the hour

markings incised around the edge. Its predecessor is just to the right of the inner door and was made redundant when the porch was built. The medieval entrance door still has its original ironwork – wrought hinge straps across its whole width, clamped around the outer edge, and the pierced plate that backed the missing closing ring. A step down into the nave with to the right, a *holy water stoup*, and ahead an early – C13 octagonal font of Purbeck marble (one of a number in the county); the pairs of shallow arches on each face of the bowl are typical and it is supported on eight columns with a centre shaft. The walls in the base of the tower have been newly boarded out, and the plain chamfered arch comes down to *corbels* lightly decorated with paterae. The church's large C17 *decalogue board* has been moved to the wall above the tower arch and although it is high up and unlit, the design is interesting. At the top a tasselled drape backs an *IHS* in a roundel, and the commandements are flanked by the Lord's Prayer and the creed which have small painted panels above them – Noah's Ark balanced on the top of Mt. Ararat to the left. The chest by the door is precisely dated 4th April 1694, and in the n.w. corner lies a C13 or C14 open stone coffin with faint traces of the base of a cross on its lid. The bonus that awaits the visitor here is to find an excellent range of wall paintings, with a huge early-C14 St *Christopher* facing the entrance door. Against a dark red background he stands bearing on his left arm the haloed Christ Child with arm raised in blessing, and the saint's robe is lifted and draped over the arm that grasps a tall staff. With patience, one can pick out fragments of attendant figures, buildings, the traditional hermit, and fishes in the waters of the river; to the left there there are remains of beautiful scroll work worked round a shaft down to a worm-like creature at the base. Even better, and of unusual interest is the range of painted panels high on the nave s. wall, stretching from the s.w. corner, over the doorway and (broken into by the C13 window) continuing to the Perpendicular window embrasure. Here we have a *Seven Works of Mercy* sequence of around 1360 which is the work of the same artists that produced the set at Wickhampton only a few miles away. Perspective is attempted in the angular canopies over the figures and a good deal of the text on the scrolls is still readable. The subject in four of the panels can be easily recognised – from the e., Feeding the Hungry (or Receiving the Stranger), Clothing the Naked, Christ blessing (within a looped scroll) and

Burial of the Dead. A bright day and a pair of binoculars are a great help here. The nave was re-roofed in 1901 and the pitch-pine pews were put in at the same time. There are four small medieval *brasses* in the floor of the nave – from the w. end: for Anne Underwode (1535), for John Holler and his wife Catherine (1505), and in front of the chancel step for Henry Palmer (1525). Just to the s. of the latter is the 7in. effigy of Thomasine Palmer (1544) wearing a *kennel head-dress* and kneeling at prayer. Once lost, this has recently been returned to the church and is a *palimpset brass*, having been cut from a Flemish brass produced some fifty years earlier. The stained glass window in the n. wall was installed in 1915 – Via Dolorosa, Crucifixion and Deposition groups against plain glass under pale and elaborate canopies. No arch divides the chancel from the nave, and access to the vanished *rood screen* was from the window embrasure in the s. wall where the lower brick steps of the stair have been re-pointed. Beneath them, the remains of a *piscina* suggest that it was used in conjunction with an altar on the *rood loft* itself. On the n. side is a *Jacobean* pulpit with large centre lozenges in its panels; the backboard is flanked with cut-out scrollery and the *tester* had turned *finials* at the angles. After Bishop Scambler's visitation in 1593, the parish was admonished for not having a pulpit and it would be nice to think that this was the response, although its matching prayer desk in the chancel is dated 1619 which seems a mite tardy. The chancel roof was masked with a plaster ceiling in the C18 and has since been renewed with plasterboard. Medieval benches from the nave have been moved into the chancel and their substantial ends have nicely scrolled tops and small *poppy-heads*; small carved sections that match the reading desk have been inserted in their modern fronts. The early-C17 *communion rails* have simply turned *balusters* and the sanctuary boasts a fine early-C14 double piscina. By that time the ritual of the Mass involved the washing of the priest's hands as well as the chalice and this prompted the provision of two drains. The nicely compact design has a centre shaft with a pierced star within the roundel above; to the right, a dropped-sill *sedilia*. The church as a whole has few wall monuments, but don't miss the one above the piscina – in fine alabaster and *touchstone*, it commemorates Edmund Anguish who died in 1616, his son Richard and his grandchildren. At the top is a frontal bust of Edmund holding a skull while below, the figures of his son and daughter-in-law face each

other across a prayer-desk with their children ranged behind them. Armorials decorate the pediment, and it was all provided by Anguish's nephew in 1628 'in tokene of his love'. The arms of an C18 descendant, Thomas Anguish, are featured in a small oval set in the e. window, and over on the n. side of the chancel a C14 priest's grave slab, partially hidden and sunk below the wall, is probably the earliest monument in the church.

Moulton, St Michael (H6): Moulton is one of those Norfolk villages that go to ground when you try to find them, and the church is more easily seen from a distance than close to. It is near the railway line and the approach is by way of a winding green lane shaded by trees from the gate on the road. There were two drastic C19 restorations, and the one in 1887 virtually replaced the tower and rebuilt the n. *aisle*. Walk along the s. side however, and there is the outline of a *Norman* window to be seen in the *nave* wall and another in the *chancel*, and the latter has a later *lancet* set in the s. wall. There is a *low side window* w. of the *priest's door* which has a *mass dial* on the e. *jamb* and there is another on the sill of the nave window. The C15 *porch* has *flushwork* on the face and fine carvings in the *spandrels* of the entrance arch – a leaf in one and a *Green Man* in the other. It has an *arch-braced roof* and shelters a s. door that has floral motifs in the *hood mould* which rests on *corbels* carved as angels carrying shields of St George. The original door still has its big closing ring. Inside, there is a faintly roseate glow from the tinted glass, but it is very dark, particularly at the w. end. There, tall *decalogue boards* hang on either side of the Norman arch to the tower. On canvas, they have paintings of Moses and Aaron at the top, but this will have to be taken on trust unless the lights are on or you have a torch. The C15 font has roses, angels and lions in the bowl panels and the original lions round the shaft have been replaced by plaster copies. The n. *arcade* was entirely re-done in 1887 but the C15 chancel arch was left alone and is unusually handsome. In the w. moulding there is a series of small heads, and the range continues with floral motifs over the arch; the moulding on the e. side has flowers all round. Over the arch, a scene of St *Michael* overcoming the Devil painted in 1909, and the whole chancel is covered with C19 stencil designs. In the sanctuary to the right of the altar stands a Norman *pillar piscina*, with a spiral *capital* and a heavy knob halfway up the shaft decorated with rosettes. Local tradition has it that this came from Moulton's other church – All Saints which was demolished in 1570. There are two sets of *Royal Arms* here and those of James I over the n. door have not worn well. Over the s. door, those for George III dated 1762 with the churchwardens' names – a good set but the canvas is going at the bottom.

Mulbarton, St Mary Magdalene (H5): There is a wide prospect of the 45 acre common from the churchyard, across to the roofs of the new village beyond. The slim tower with buttresses to the w. was rebuilt, along with the *nave*, by Sir William de Hoo at the end of the C14, and the *chancel* is a later *Perpendicular* rebuilding. S. *porch* and n. *aisle* date from a heavy handed restoration of 1875. There is a large blocked arch over the s. door, and although there is some conjecture about a previous porch having an upper room, it looks too large an opening and was more likely to have been an extra window to give more light at the w. end. The door sill has been described as a re-used altar slab, but the mark of a brass inscription plate effectively denies this. The 1870s work destroyed the old *rood loft* stairs to the n. of the chancel arch, and in building the vestry the line of the sanctuary was altered so that the new *communion rails* were set in what were the *sedilia* on the s. side. The *piscina* escaped and has a *quatrefoil* drain under a five-leaf arch. Slightly odd that the *credence shelf* was taken out to make way for a little memorial plaque to Richard Spurgeon who died aged 12 in 1814. There is another piscina tucked behind the pulpit for use with a nave altar, and this is later – square headed with a fluted drain. Nearby to the w., an arched recess that could be the resting place of the builder of the nave. At the w, end, two big mural monuments: on the w. wall, to Sir Edwin Rich (1675), a long inscription which has all the marks of the careful lawyer:

And though I cannot skill in rymes yet
    knowe it
In my lyfe I was my own Deathes Poett,
For he whoe leaves his work to others
    truste
Maybe deceived when he lyes in the dust

The voice of experience! On the s. wall, an omnibus memorial to others of the Rich family (but specifically for Robert who died in 1651) which was rather knocked about when it was moved from the old n. wall in the 1870s. The real surprise for addicts of the epitaph lies hidden behind the *chancel* arch on the s. side. Resting on a replica bible, with the back realistically

painted in red and gold, are two heavy copper plates which open like a book. On one page, the epitaph of 'the most Religious Mrs Sarah Scargill. The wife of Mr Daniel Scargill rectr. of this Parish with whom she lived in all conjugal vertue near 7 years; and then Death divorced them upon the 22th day of August 1680 in the 30th yeare of her Age...'. The second page has a hand engraved at the top, as if from Heaven, with the words 'Come, Pilgrim, to thy home'. Below, one of the most poignantly beautiful farewells recorded of any husband:

Dear Love, one Feather'd minute and I come
To lye down in thy darke Retireing Roome
And mingle Dust with thine...
... More Swift than Wind
Or Flying Hind
I come, I come away.

But life has a habit of going on, and his 'Feather'd minute' stretched to 41 years, and he so far relented of his passion to marry again. Not only that, the burial register entry for his second wife in 1718 was annotated by him in slipshod Latin 'nulla secunda'! Scargill was once a Fellow of Corpus Christi Cambridge, and was suspended in 1668 for 'several impious and atheistical tenets'. Read all about it in Charles Linnell's 'Some East Anglian Clergy' (Faith Press, 1961). Mulbarton has some most interesting early glass, and as so often happens in our churches, it is here by chance. In the early C19 a curate at Martham obtained the living here, and managed to bring some of the painted glass from the s. aisle of his old church with him. It was an Old Testament series and, having left 'Eve spinning' behind, he installed three of the panels in the e. window of his new chancel. In the centre there is a fine figure of Adam at work with a spade; to the left Adam and Eve are sadly leaving the Garden of Eden clad in fig leaves; to the right, one of the Orders of the Heavenly Hierarchy – 'Powers' (you can read his label 'Potestates'). He is crowned, with a beast under his feet leashed on a golden chain. (See glossary, *Nine Orders of Angels*, for more about the winged hierarchy). The faces, particularly Adam's, are beautifully expressive, and the technique links this work with the Passion scenes in the great e. window of St Peter Mancroft in Norwich dating from around 1460. There is more medieval glass in a chancel s. window; in one panel, a figure of St *Anne* teaching the Blessed Virgin to read has been given the bearded head of a patriarch, in the other, a king (possibly Solomon) holding the model of a church.

Above, two angels from different schemes play lute and harp; at the bottom, two panels of C17 foreign glass – a monk and nun kneeling. The church has a ring of 6 bells, tenor 8-1-0 cwt.

Mundesley, All Saints (J2): A complete rebuild, between 1899 and 1914, of what for a century had been a deserted ruin – and most successful it is. Every remnant still in situ, or discovered in the churchyard and round about, appears to have been re-used with imagination and affection: note diagonal buttress of *nave* (to l. of *porch*) with pleasant old *Tudor roses*; nave and *chancel* window tracery, using as far as possible the original materials; the attractive buttress at s.e. angle of chancel, with its *Decorated* statue niche. Inside there is a real air of antiquity, accentuated by the fine 1904 *rood screen* below the reconstructed C15 chancel arch and, to left, the *rood loft* entrance. Facing as one enters by the s. porch is a tiny *Norman* slit window – probably the oldest visible part of the fabric – but with a pointed head. There's a nice *Jacobean* pulpit with *tester*, which came from Sprowston, near Norwich; a massive plain C14 font, and the arms of Queen Victoria.

Mundford, St Leonard (E6): A jaunty little saddle-backed tower, topped by a tiny fleche, is what catches the eye from the main road. It is in fact a mid-Victorian rebuild, set off from the *nave* to the s.w. The Victorians also replaced the *chancel* windows to the s., most unsuccessfully. Fortunately they left intact the plain triple *lancet* in the e. wall, which points to the *Early English* origin of this part of the building. The nave is later and *Decorated* and has much of its original tracery (lively and attractive in *mouchette* and *quatrefoil* patterns) to n. and s., some of it having been replaced, but in faithful copy of the original. Pretty n. *porch* finished in pink brick round outer arch and windows and down the corners – C16? The s. doorway is small-scale and rather elegant Decorated. The interior has quite a dramatic surprise in store, an early-C20 coup devised by *Sir Ninian Comper* – an organ *gallery* cum *rood loft* across the chancel arch, with six large wood-carved figures of apostles across the front, all under *crocketted* canopies and standing on rich pedestals, with a Crucified Christ at centre, again under a canopy. Above, the carved case of the organ occupies the centre of the gallery with a flourish of opulent gilding. The *screen* below the gallery has some medieval components in it, but much spirited carving of Sir Ninian's time of angels and cherubs, shields and crests. To

the right, a big oblong *piscina* has been gilded and coloured and re-used as a figure niche. Sir Ninian also transformed the chancel and it is lush to a point: richly painted roof, adorned with shields; *jambs* to the e. window similarly beautified; hanging brass candelabra; and quietly dignified choir and clergy stalls with large-winged *griffens* at the bench ends. The font at the w. end is interesting and unusual; its octagonal bowl, with the simplest of carved panels, is ordinary enough; but from under the bowl and the fluted stem spring upwards and outwards three chunky angel figures (the one to the w. is missing, that to the e. has lost its head) which assuredly are set for take-off, rocket style. The church has an excellent ring of 6 bells, tenor 6-0-3 cwt.

Mundham, St Peter (J6): In this rural nook of Norfolk, only a couple of fields separate Mundham and Seething churches. This one is a good looking building, with a *Perpendicular* tower topped by *flushwork* battlements, Perpendicular *nave* and *porch*, modern n. *transept* and *Decorated chancel*. The latter has most attractive geometrically styled Decorated windows to n. and s., and the e. window handsomely re-modelled in lace-patterned tracery. The surprise is the s. doorway – rich, large-scale *Norman*, with two 'rolled' arches punctuating four powerfully carved varieties of decorative motifs; and *capitals* and columns no less grandly sculpted, the latter including leaves, flowers and shells – a very fine piece altogether. The n. doorway is similar, but plain in construction and decoration. A tall, narrow interior, without chancel arch, carries the eye most agreeably, and accentuates the fact that the chancel *weeps* to the n. Simple raftered roof in the nave, but with much older *wall plates* showing medieval colouring. The chancel roof is *arch-braced*, with massive *wall posts* and quite enormous wall plates. An indistinct St *Christopher* faces the s. door (unfortunately with an early-C19 monument slapped on top of it), with its floral 'frame' down each side intact. To its left, on the w. wall, is a painted *consecration cross*. To its right, framed *Royal Arms* for George II, dated 1743. The modern font under the tower is undistinguished – but in a corner are the broken remains of a square Norman font of *Purbeck marble*; in the s. wall of the tower, a brick-faced *wafer oven* has been exposed. By the s. door, a large and equally rough *holy water stoup*. The simple C15 chancel *screen*, square headed between its uprights, is stripped of all its medieval colour; attached to it is an *hour-glass stand*; to its right, a rustic indentation in the wall shows where the *rood stair* was torn out. In the chancel, from whose roof hangs a fine candelabra, there is a C15 *piscina*, with an *ogee hood mould* with *corbel* heads of children's faces, and a wooden *credence shelf*, notched to hold draining *chalices* and a deep, six-leaf drain below to catch the drips. It adjoins *dropped sill sedilia* with pretty little *cusped* arches to left and right in the *jambs* of the window.

Narborough, All Saints (D4): An attractive setting in the centre of the village. The late-C13 s.w. tower has a tall w. *lancet* and 'y' tracery bell openings (except to the e. where there is an unusually fine C15 replacement). A puzzling feature is the faint outline of a large window surrounding each *sound-hole* and it is possible that the original tower was much lower before a *Perpendicular* top stage was added which re-used three of the bell openings. A small spire came down in 1679 and this may be why the *nave* was shortened and a new w. wall built. There is evidence of an even earlier building to be seen outside to the w. of the n. *aisle* – a blocked *Norman* window, and you will see a blocked *Early English* door on that side further along. Through a good s. doorway with floral motifs in the arch to the interior. Here, the C14 *arcades* illustrate an odd building sequence; the w. bay and pillar of the s. arcade belongs to the period of the tower, then comes the n. arcade with its *quatrefoil* pillars, and then the completion of the s. range with concave-faced *Decorated* pillars like those at Dersingham and the *chancel* arch at Snettisham. The Perpendicular chancel boasts a wide and handsome e. window and, with no chancel arch, the centre of the church is open and spacious. The 1865 restoration roofs are frankly ugly. Just inside the door, a bench is carved with the Spelman arms, and mementoes of that powerful legal family abound here. Beyond the Victorian font is the shallow tomb chest of John Spelman (1662); it bears two shields, and above it, a black marble tablet has an alabaster surround decorated with stiff swags of fruit, topped by a broken *pediment*, two skulls and another shield. While at the w. end, you will find a good 1759 *Royal Arms* of George III in the tower and two large *hatchments*. On the wall of the n. aisle are two brass reliefs of the Adoration of the Shepherds and The Descent from the Cross – fine C18 French and Italian work. Narborough has a magnificent array of *brasses* in the chancel, and in chronological order they are – sanctuary floor n. side: Henry Spelman (1496) and his wife – he was Recorder of Norwich and wears his civic mantle, while she wears a *kennel head-dress* and

Narborough, All Saints:
Spelman monument by Cibber

has a rosary on her girdle; sanctuary floor s. side; John Spelman (1545) in full armour with a long inscription; sanctuary wall n. side; Sir John Spelman (1545) and his wife. This is the finest and most interesting brass in the church, and shows him kneeling in his judge's robes (recessed to take colour), while she wears a mantle bearing coats of arms. The prayer scrolls rise to a plate which is engraved with the Resurrection scene, and the slab bearing the brasses is enclosed by a stone frame decorated with floral motifs and resting on a wide ledge. It is likely that this tomb was designed (like that of Lady Townshend at East Raynham) to serve as an *Easter Sepulchre*. As Justice of the King's Bench, Sir John took part in the trial of Sir Thomas More and prepared the indictment against Anne

Boleyn that led to her execution. Sanctuary wall s. side; John Eyer (1561) and his wife Margaret, kneeling with prayer scrolls and a coat of arms; chancel floor centre: John Spelman (1581) in full armour with a helm behind his head, finely engraved. In 1982, much careful restoration and repair work was carried out by an expert in conservation, Mr William Lack. In doing so, he found a number of *palimpsests*, and these are all fully described and illustrated at the w. end of the church, with resin replicas for brass rubbers. The chancel has two excellent Spelman monuments in contrasting styles. On the n. wall, Sir Clement Spelman (1607) and his wife lie one above the other in that uncomfortable position that was the convention of the time (Did some unfortunate ever have to model while lying on his side propped up, throttled by a ruff and wearing full armour?); she wears a farthingale and the same style of large hood seen on Mary Branthwaite at Hethel. Above them, a child kneels and a baby peeps from an upright cradle. Opposite – that same baby has become a man, the fine figure of Clement Spelman (1672), proudly upright on a pedestal in full wig and Recorder's robe, carved in pink-veined alabaster by *Caius Gabriel Cibber*. Originally the body of this proud lawyer was coffined upright within an 8ft. pedestal, but when the church was restored in 1865 he was removed and his effigy lowered to a more reasonable height. In the n.e. corner of the sanctuary is the church's oldest monument; Lady Alethea de Narborough (1293) directed that her heart be buried here, and the *wimpled* half-figure lies in a niche with a heart held to the breast. Before leaving this fascinating place, have a look at the late-C13 double *piscina* and, especially, at the glass in the chancel n. window. There are very decorative Spelman arms dated 1578 in roundels, and above them, three C15 angels (one with a birch and a chained devil) and a vested figure in white to the right who encircles three enchanting and tiny medieval figures with his left hand (binoculars are well worth taking).

Narford, St Mary (D4): The church is in a delectable setting between the Hall and the extensive lake that lies beyond; the access track runs alongside the w. boundary fence. Before the *Reformation* it served a sizeable village but now, apart from the Hall, there are only a few houses in the parish. There was a major restoration in 1857 but by the end of the century things had regressed and services were suspended in 1890. Once again, it was repaired, but in the C20 it fell on hard times, and although never de-consecrated, it was effectively out of use for nearly forty years. Happily, circumstances changed with the beginning of a new century and restoration began once more, backed by grants from the *Norfolk Churches Trust* and English Heritage. Services are now held at least three times a year, and the work of improvement goes on steadily. The church's history reaches back to the C13, but of the early years very little remains, following the extensive C19 work. As part of that exercise, a wooden spire was removed and the whole tower was rebuilt with corner pinnacles, and it has a pierced parapet which is a memorial for Catherine Fountaine, the squire's wife. There is a centre panel on each side – three of them bear scriptural testimonies of faith and the fourth has a Latin inscription which translates, 'To his wife, Caroline, most holy and beautiful, this monument is dedicated by Andrew Fountaine, 1858'. Walking round, note that the n. doorway has been blocked and the *aisle* windows repeat the original *Decorated* design, and although the aisles' e. windows have been blocked, they retain the original 'Y' tracery of the early C14; the two *clerestory* windows closest to the tower are C14 and the rest were made to match in the C19. The n.e. angle between aisle and *chancel* is taken up by a massive hump in the ground covering the Fountaine family mausoleum, established in 1830 and guarded by substantial iron railings. The chancel of 1902 has a *priest's door* in the s. wall, and beyond it, there is the outline of what was a *low side* window before the rebuilding. Brig Fountaine died in 1746 and his substantial table tomb with a good roundel of arms on the end is tucked into the angle below. The *scratch dial* incised in a *quoin* on the s.e. corner of the s. aisle may have been sited closer to one of the doorways originally. Entry is by a low, mainly brick, porch with a small image niche above the outer arch. The inner doorway is original and the door itself is dated 1787 – the accompanying initials are probably those of the churchwarden of the day. At the time of my visit, the interior walls were still heavily soiled with green damp stains, but now that effective measures have been taken to make everything well drained and weather-proof, one can confidently look forward to a cleansing coat of lime-wash throughout.When the church was enlarged in the early C14, aisles were added – probably financed by Petronilla de Narford, the wealthy widow of Sir William de Narford and Lady of the Manor. The C14 two-bay *arcades* have octagonal *piers* with double-hollow-chamfered arches, and both the tall tower arch and the chancel arch are of the same period. The faint marks on the *capitals* of the latter mark the position of the medieval *rood loft*. The plain octagonal font is enlivened a little by a *Jacobean* cover which has turned shafts and pendant knobs below a pyramid topped with a hefty *finial*. A waggon-type parish chest stands under the tower and, above the arch, the old *sanctus bell window* was blanked off in one of the C19 restorations with a bizarre pierced stone panel. Don't miss the delightful little memorial for Catherine Brown to the left of the arch – set within a delicate *rococo* frame, it mourns her loss in 1742, just as she came of age: 'Life how short. Eternity how long.' In the s. aisle there are much grander affairs, starting with the largest which takes up the whole of the w. wall. Designed by John Powley, it is the only example of his work listed by the relevant authorities. Behind quite ferocious railings, the plinth is fronted by a curving white marble panel to carry an epitaph of unusual brevity, in lettering fine and large, for the Sir Andrew Fountaine who died in 1753. A contemporary of Holkham's Thomas Coke, Earl of Leicester he was, like him, an assiduous and discerning collector – the Narford majolica was famous for its quality. An obelisk with curved sides topped with a massive ball provides a backdrop for an excellent bust of him which may or may not be by Powley. It is based on a terracotta by *Roubiliac* which was once in the Hall but has since passed to the nation in lieu of tax. In the centre of the s. wall, and a little too high to read all of the inscription, is the handsome marble *cartouche* for the Andrew Fountaine who bought Narford in 1690, began the Hall in 1702, and died in 1706, leaving his son (whose massive memorial I have just described) to finish it. The tomb on the s. aisle e. wall completes the trilogy of that generation – Sarah, Sir Andrew's mother and Elizabeth his sister, plus a niece who died in 1740. The inscription is well cut on the plinth and the black sarcophagus rests on heavy claw feet; there are three coloured armorials – Fountaine (three elephant heads), Fountaine impaling Chicheley, and Clent impaling Fountaine. The family motto (lifted from Ovid) 'Vix ea nostra voco' translates as 'I scarce call these things our own' referring, one assumes, not to elephants but to blue-blooded lineage. Entry to the medieval rood was via a stair, and the blocked doorway can be seen to the left of the monument. Floors here are mainly brick and there are a number of good *ledger-stones* in the nave and aisles. One in the nave at the w. end

(early-C17?) is very worn and the inscription almost gone, but the outline of a skull can just be made out. In the n. aisle Jeffery Browne has lain since 1740 under a large *touchstone* slab which is decorated at the head with 'Remember Death' on a label, plus emblems of mortality in the form of crossed bones, a winged hour-glass, and a flaming torch; the lettering is particularly good, and the sentiment both emollient and inevitable: 'A good companion and an honest friend, Rare virtues in this age, and here they end'. Three Fountaine *hatchments* have been excellently restored and now hang in the n. aisle. They were used at the funerals of two Andrew Fountaines (1835 and 1874) and the Caroline Fountaine for whom the tower parapet was added. Remembering the blocked window noted outside, look for the image niche to the left and the faint outline of a *piscina* arch to the right that both related to a side altar here. The six-sided *Jacobean* pulpit rests on a centre pedestal, and its carved panels are typical of the period. In place of a *screen* the sanctuary rails have been moved forward, and like other woodwork in the church they have been painted a dull red which does nothing to enhance their good 'barley-sugar' *balusters*. The only thing that survives from the C13 in the church is in the chancel and can be easily missed because it is so small. It is the arm-rest with its terminal knobs that divides the dropped-sill *sedilia*. Beyond it the piscina has a *sexfoil* drain, and in the n. wall there is a square *aumbry* recess. Close by, the arch of a large C14 recess rests on stubby cylindrical columns with round caps and bases. Below, lies a C13 tomb slab, bearing a floriated cross that marks the tomb of a priest of the period. The position of the recess would have made it suitable for use as an *Easter Sepulchre* later, bearing in mind that the floor levels have been raised significantly. As you leave, take the opportunity to examine more closely than is normally possible, the C14 gable cross that has been brought inside from the chancel roof and now lies in pieces by the font.

Neatishead, St Peter (J3): Over the w. door a tablet in the head of a medieval niche states that the church was rebuilt in 1790. What is left is basically the *chancel* of a much larger church. The w. face also has three little kneeling figures, flanked by shields, which may have come from the original *porch*. Further work in 1870 re-arranged the windows. The C14 font has shallow panelling reminiscent of window tracery, and there is a good *piscina*.

Necton, All Saints (E5): Necton's excellent tower, topped by a chirpy lantern like those at Shipdham and Mattishall thrusts upward from a luxuriant fringe of trees in faultless *Perpendicular* lines. It has huge, traceried, belfry windows, an equally good w. window above a traceried frieze with shields, setting off an elegant w. door and a chequerworked *base course* – and all this was built in 1865, a remarkable achievement in gothic revival. The body of the church is a progression from *Decorated* into Perpendicular. From the outside the latter style is dominant, not least in the large, impressive *clerestory* range. In the e. gable of the *nave*, the outline of a very large window, blocked in to make way for a higher *chancel*; and above it, a small *sanctus bell turret*. Inside the church, the four-bay *arcade* of clustered pillars reasserts the Decorated style. The real glory here is the roof, of which a thorough restoration was completed in late 1982. With alternate *hammer-beams* and simple *arch-braces*, it is a gentle harmony of original colour, with lushly carved decorative devices, angels on the hammer-beams, and *wall posts* thrusting down between the *clerestory* windows, each with a carved and painted figure on a pedestal – Christ, the Virgin and the Apostles. There is rich carving in the deep-set *jambs* of the clerestory and, on each side of the arcade, are beautifully carved *headstops* to the arches. In the recess of the filled-in window over the chancel arch are more carved and painted figures. The pulpit is a fine piece, dated 1636, complete with backboard and fine *tester*. Nearby, in the s. *aisle* chapel, is a C14 Decorated *angle piscina*. The chancel, wide and plain with its plastered ceiling, is dominated by a huge *reredos* installed by a C19 squire, with a central painting of the Raising of *Lazarus*. The e. window glass, vibrant with colour (1844) is by de la Roche of Paris. Through the two-bay Decorated arcade into the n. chapel, now a vestry, which could be the oldest part of the church. Here is a *consecration cross* scratched into the wall; a plain piscina; and two of the church's eight *brasses*: Phillipa de Beauchamp, 1384, robed as a *vowess*; and Mary Rust, 1596, showing how brasses had developed by this time in texture, shading and sophistication of design. The other six brasses are: in the chancel pavement, John Bacon, 1528; in the nave, proceeding westward, William and Alice Curteys, 1499; Robert Goodwyn and wife, 1532; and Ismayne de Wyston, 1375.

Needham, St Peter (I7): Round *Norman* tower, with C15 octagonal belfry stage. The jolly red brick *porch* is C15 too and is quite enterprising. There are *quatrefoils* in carved brick round the arch, with another line of them under the stepped battlements; a band of *trefoils* half way up the corner pillars, and a little *base course* of quatrefoils and *lancets* has an incised inscription on a panel in the w. face. Inside, a fine *arch-braced roof* in faded honey-coloured oak, with a deep moulded *wall plate* and longtitudinal braces under the ridge. Heavy *tie-beams* were added later. The squat font has the *Evangelistic Symbols* and *Tudor roses* in the bowl panels, with decorative carving on the mouldings, angels, and lions minus most of their heads around the shaft. In a varied set of a dozen medieval bench ends, one is richly panelled and ten have carvings on the chamfers. The back of the fifth pew from the front on the s. side has a little inscription with the initials of the donor: 'Use well thy tyme for dethe is comyng M / The sentence of God Almighty is everlasting E'. The *Jacobean* pulpit has disappeared, but some of its strapwork panels have been used to line the wall by the remains of the *rood stairs* on the n. side, and the doors of *box pews* have served a similar purpose in the tower vestry. An early restoration of 1735 included a rebuilding of the *chancel* by the vicar William Freston. He died in 1746, and his stiff architectural monument is on the s. wall; a Latin epitaph records that his wife Margaret died two years later 'indulging grief too much'. There is a crude chest at the w. end, and by it a lovely little door to the tower stair.

New Buckenham, St Martin (G6): A grand 'town church', originally built in 1246 by Sir Robert de Tateshale, where one needs to spend almost as much time looking at the outside as enjoying the inside. For the exterior is unexpectedly splendid in decoration and detail. The imposing *Perpendicular* tower is massively planned: huge corner pinnacles, encrusted with *crocketting*; great battlements picked out in a kingsize chequerwork of flint and stone; three-*light* belfry windows with flattened *Tudor* arches – and above them, *gargoyles*; lower down, square *sound-holes* with lacy tracery, that on the w. surmounted by a stone shield; a composite w. window and door, with shields in the *spandrels*, and another eight shields and six *quatrefoil* motifs in a frieze over it, plus *flushwork* either side. The angle buttresses are picked out in flushwork, including the crowned initials of St *Mary* and St *Martin* – leading down to a *base course* of carved panels and flushwork which extends not only right round the tower, but across the w. end of the s. *aisle*, right round the *porch* and all the way round the aisle itself to its e. end. The porch is battlemented, with *griffins* on the pinnacle corners. Over the outer arch, a canopied and crocketted figure niche. The porch buttresses have footings, half way up, for statues. The splendid range of *clerestory* windows, ten each side, are closely set together and patterned in smaller form on the Perpendicular aisle windows, and topped with red brick and flint; between them, more delicate flushwork. The exterior of the C13 *chancel* is in squared stone and flint. After all this opulence, the n. side of the church is plain. Through the porch and the inner C13 doorway, and we are in a nobly proportioned though rather austere building. The *nave* is tall in relation to its width, and has a plain C15 *arch-braced* and *hammer-beamed* roof, its *wall posts* supported on boldly carved heads depicting the 12 Apostles, David the psalmist, the four archangels and several lesser angels. In the angle of the roof, high in the w. wall, above the tower arch, there is a *sanctus bell opening*. Below, the font is dated 1st February 1619 and bears the names of the churchwardens of the time; it stands on a C15 base, around which is a curious assemblage of elongated lions, alternating with long, thin, hairy *woodwoses*. Beyond the elegant *Decorated*-into-Perpendicular nave *arcades* (that on the s. is the earlier of the two) the aisles have C15, *arch-braced roofs*, with shields and fretwork in the spandrels. The s. aisle has its Lady Chapel restored, the late-C15 *piscina* and Elizabethan altar table, with an inscription along the sill of the adjoining window: 'Remember here Hugh Whitwham, Priest-Vicar of this Parish 1959-77 Who restored this Chapel of the Blessed Virgin Mary for worship after 400 years of disuse'. In the n. aisle's e. end is the opening to the *rood stair*. The wide chancel has a tomb-cum-*Easter Sepulchre* on the n. side, set below a *Tudor* window. The tomb may be that of the church's founder, Sir Robert de Tateshale; the carved canopy over it dates from the early C16, when the missing *brass* figure, whose outline is on the back of the tomb, would have been erected, possibly to Lady Muriel Knyvett, a benefactor of the church who was buried behind the founder. Opposite, a C13 piscina, with an eight-leaf drainhole; adjoining *dropped sill sedilia*. Several fine *ledger stones* lie in the chancel floor. The church has an excellent ring of 8 bells, tenor 11-0-7 cwt.

Newton-by-Castle Acre, All Saints (E4): This little gem of a place presents a lovely outline as you approach it, for its sturdy, centrally placed

Saxon tower is crowned by a conical, tiled roof. Below are coarse, triangular headed belfry windows of two *lights*, with little central pillars and lower down, round headed slits roughly finished in stone and brick. The considerable quantity of brick scattered through the building may well be re-used Roman materials, though the fabric is basically Saxon. The windows are later insertions – square headed *Perpendicular* to s. of *nave*, and e. and w. windows in the simplest *Decorated reticulated* forms. This was formerly a *cruciform* church. But the transepts became ruinous and were demolished in the C18, leaving only their rubble outlines as a reminder. If you like small, intimate church interiors, then this one will be a joy. There isn't a straight line or a level surface in the place; the rough old walls are white and the pews are basic, but there's a touch of restrained style in the modern pulpit and prayer desk, where plain deal alternates with blue stripes spiked with gold stars. From the nave, you move under the tower (basic pointed arch to the w., the original round Saxon arch sitting on plain *imposts*, to the e.) into the atmospheric little *chancel*. Under the tower, there's a little iron-bound chest, and the entrance to the *rood stair*. The latter emerges high in the nave, where a door is now fitted, with alongside it one of the *corbels* which supported the *rood beam*. At the top of the ridge is a big, triangular headed opening, contemporary with the tower. Below it, the *Royal Arms* of George III, painted with a lack of sophistication which perfectly complements this little church. There's a minute fragment of medieval painting on the s. wall; and a severe C14 font.

Newton Flotman, St Mary the Virgin (I6): A steep little climb from the busy main road to reach the churchyard. A thoroughgoing restoration in the 1890s renewed almost everything, but the consistent style of the building is *Perpendicular*, and we know that there was a rebuilding in 1385. The stepped and panelled battlements carry an inscription on the e. face (visible with the help of binoculars) to Ralph Blundeville dated 1503, so the upper stage, with its bell openings under typical arches of the period no doubt dates from then. The brick s. *porch* has been recently restored and just inside there is a C15 font with shields hung in the shallow tracery of the bowl panels. In the *chancel*, a tall and obtrusive C19 *reredos* partially obscures the *Kempe* glass there, but his w. window is in full view, and very beautiful it is. Inscribed to the memory of the rector's 21 year old son who died in the South African war, the three main panels figure Christ the king flanked by Gabriel and St *George* – all in glowing jewel-like colour. The Blundevilles were lords of the manor from 1294 to 1721 and Thomas de Blundeville was Bishop of Norwich in the early C13. A later Thomas, in Elizabeth's reign, was the family's most famous son. He was a prolific author and ranged over astronomy, logic, horsemanship, navigation, and how to write history books with equal facility. Best known for his 'Mr Blundeville his Exercises' – a collection of treatises on astronomy and navigation which ran to at least seven editions. His family tomb in the n. chancel wall is a fascinating illustration of the sort of man he was. In the centre panel he kneels in armour, his helm on the prayer desk by him, while to his left his two wives Elizabeth and Patience kneel dressed in gowns with big ruffs and *Tudor* bonnets. In the right hand panel is a *brass* dedicated to his forbears. Three of them kneel in armour – great-grandfather Richard, grandfather Ralph and father Edward:

> Heare lyes in grave nowe thre tymes done,
> The Grandsyr, Father, and the Sone,
> Theyr names, theyr age and when they dyed,
> Above ther headds ys specyfyed.
> Theyr shyeld of Arms dothe eke declare
> The stocke wyth whom they maryed ware
> They lyved well and dyed as well
> And nowe wyth god in heaven they dwell,
> And theare do prayse his holy name,
> God graunt that we may do the same.

North Barningham, St Peter (H2): A church without a village, by the side of the road that runs from Gresham to Baconsthorpe, it is now in the care of the *Churches Conservation Trust*. Heavily damaged in 1714 and restored in 1893, it has again been put in order and contains a number of good things. The early-C14 *piscina* and *sedilia* are badly damaged, but were unusually rich and have inlays in the buttresses and arches. In the n.e. corner of the sanctuary is a tomb chest to John Palgrave (d.1611) with a number of shields, and three small alabaster figures representing Justice, Toil and Peace, which are fine despite their loss of heads. Nearby is the elaborate wall monument to Margaret Pope, who died on Christmas Day, 1624. She kneels beneath a canopy and between 2 angels, and of her it is said:

> The most of her life she past in Virginitie,
> But alwayes had care to serve well ye Trinitie,

Her that so ernestlie servd God on earth,
Christ tooke into Heaven the day of his
birth.

In the n.e. corner of the n. *aisle* is a splendid monument to Sir Austin and Lady Elizabeth Palgrave (1639). Within an elaborate surround, rich in heraldry, are two marble busts. He is bearded and faintly quizzical; she will brook no nonsense. Her double chin rests nicely upon a massive ruff, and is smooth to the touch. In front of this monument is a *brass* to Henry Palgrave (d.1516) and his wife – elegant figures with two groups of children below. The four shields are modern replicas. The enigma of the church is the circular design in brick and stone set in the *nave* floor e. of the font, reminiscent of a rose window. There has been no convincing explanation offered and it may have been purely decorative in origin.

North Barsham, All Saints (F2): A little church – just *chancel* and *nave*, of mainly *Decorated* work, standing high and windy in a meadow. During restoration in 1897-8, the *rood loft stairs* were exposed: you can see them set in the exterior buttress on the s. side. Note head and base of C14 niche re-set over w. door outside. Three of the four nave windows and the e. window are restored; one square-headed brick *mullion* window in s. wall of chancel is original. Inside, there's a C13 *Purbeck marble* font (only the bowl is original) and the C17 pulpit, into which you have to climb to read the lovely wording of the monument to Philip Russell, who 'spunne out his thred of time, in ye dimention of 66 years' etc. and whose 'exanimated body' (sic) went to 'ye common mother of us all' in December 1617.

North Creake, St Mary (E2): The buttressed tower of this big, stately church rears up from the roadside in soaring *Perpendicular* lines, up to a parapet set with *flushwork* and shields. The s. face of the church is very striking indeed, for though there is a *clerestory*, there is no *aisle* below it, so that one is confronted by a huge wall pierced by two rows of great *Perpendicular* windows. The *chancel* adds to the picture in no small measure, its unusual length being punctuated by large Perpendicular and *Decorated* windows and a neat *priest's door* with a flattened arch. Perpendicular lines in windows restored 'to their right proportions' by the Victorians dominate the n. aisle and clerestory, with muscular Decorated forms giving character to the chancel. At the e. end is Victorian tracery which, by all accounts, most faithfully echoes the original very early-C14 stonework which it replaced during a considerable restoration at the end of the C19. Through a C13 s. *porch* of notable simplicity, and a s. door of the same period, we enter an interior which has a touch of uncluttered grandeur, accentuated by the splendid *hammer-beam* and *arch-braced roof*. This has fine flower *bosses* along the central ridge; tiny winged angels carrying shields at the *purlin* intersections; more winged angels together with lush open carving along the whole length of the *wall plates* to each side; large priestly figures on the hammers bearing musical instruments, crowns royal and papal, a chalice, a cross etc.; and deep *wall posts* thrusting down between the Perpendicular windows of the clerestory to embattled stone *corbels* carved with shields. In contrast is the simplicity of the original arch-braced roof over the n. aisle. The four-bay *arcade* is C14 Decorated, as is the tall, beautifully balanced chancel arch – with its rather weird and nightmarish *headstops* to what is left of its *hood mould* (Possibly the moulding was removed when a *tympanum* was placed there after the *Reformation*). To its right is one of the stone corbels which supported the *rood loft*; to its left, the loft exit from the *rood stair*, which has its entrance in the n. chapel. Above the chancel arch, notice the merest vestiges of a large medieval wall painting – perhaps, say the experts, a 'Doom' representation. The chancel *screen* is Victorian, and most successful in its generously carved detail. In the *nave* s. wall, e. end, is a Perpendicular *piscina* and beside it, a plain C15 tomb recess under a pointed arch. In the chancel is another hammer-beam and arch-braced roof, though on a slightly reduced scale from that in the nave. It has apostles and winged angels on the hammers, and more figures on the wall plates and standing on the corbels which support the *wall posts*. Equally notable here is the C14 piscina and triple *sedilia*, under one grand 'label', and opposite, an *Easter Sepulchre,* all alike in the sumptuous quality and abundance of their carving, decoration and detail. On the right hand side of the *cusped* and *crocketted* arch of the Sepulchre is a little iron hook, set into the stone, which may well have been used to hang across the tomb a *Lenten Veil*. In the centre of the sanctuary floor is a very good *brass* of about 1500, more than 3ft. in length, showing a figure with hands joined in prayer and a church balanced on his right arm. This is said to be Sir William Calthorpe, 'second founder' of this church in the C15. Two more details as you leave: the finely

worked *Royal Arms* of Charles I, dated 1635, in their classical frame over the n. door; and the circular font bowl (said to be *Norman,* though caution is necessary) under a most attractive Victorian tabernacle cover. The church has a ring of 6 bells, tenor 12 cwt.

North Elmham, St Mary (F3): This was the centre of the first diocese of East Anglia, and a visit can take in both the church and the ruins of the late *Saxon* cathedral nearby. Having begun the new cathedral in Norwich in 1096, Bishop Losinga built the first parish church here, and the connection persisted – which is no doubt why the village came to have such a fine church. The late-C14 tower is very distinctive – the pairs of right-angled buttresses stop short under steep gables below the belfry stage, and sandwiched between two of them is a shallow western *galilee porch*. Its roof has its own *gargoyles* and there are pedestals at the centre which may have supported a Calvary (Crucifixion) group. Inside the porch see how two small dragons writhe in the mouldings of the inner door. The tower second stage has elaborate (blocked) belfry windows – *transomed*, with a line of *quatrefoils* under the square heads. The bell stage is later than the rest and is complemented by *flushwork* battlements and corner pinnacles. The s. porch has a good range of stone *corbels* (see the one in the corner pulling his mouth open), but the best entry is from the w. – because the *nave* is four steps down from the tower and this gives a fine view of the interior, Under the ringing *gallery* there is a tall, very robust C17 *screen* complete with gate – just one of the excellent pieces of joinery made by Francis Floyd – *parish clerk* and village carpenter. The nave, with its alternating round and octagonal *piers* was rebuilt in the C13, but at that time the arches were lower. A century later the roof was raised, and one can see how larger blocks of stone were used to heighten the pillars. Yet another extension upwards came at the end of the C15 when the present *clerestory* and roof were added. The bench ends in the nave are a delight; the chamfers are carved with a great variety of designs, and the arms sport a whole family of animals, birds and mythical beasts. Look specially for the muzzled dog (5th from e., n. side), the eagle that has a platypus beak (7th from e., s. side), and a *griffin* with a man's head in its beak, (2nd from w., s. side). The pulpit is Francis Floyd's work, and the backboard (now in vestry) is dated 1626. They say it took him 12 years on and off to carve, and it is a lovely piece. The carving is naive but lively – pairs of fluted *Corinthian* columns at the angles, *blank arcading* in the panels and above them, national emblems in honour of the recent union of the crowns of England and Scotland. It was discarded in 1852 but thankfully came back to the church in 1882. The *rood screen* was banished somewhat earlier and was found under the pew floors in the C19 restorations. Although incomplete, it has an excellent array of painted figures, including some of the lesser known saints. From left to right they are: St *Benedict*, an abbot (perhap St *Augustine*), St *Thomas*, St *Giles*, St *Jude*, St *James the Less*, St *Philip*, St *John*, St *Paul*, St *Barbara*, St *Cecilia*, St *Dorothea*, St *Zita*, St *Juliana*, St *Petroneila*, St *Agnes*, St *Christina*. Most of the panels have *cusped* and *crocketted ogee arches* set in the frames, and there is rich carving in the *spandrels*; left to right: rose, a headless man in a cloak riding a pig, lilies, two men fighting, two angels, and half of a St *George* and the dragon. It is in the *chancel* that evidence of the *Norman* building is plain. The arches there are C12, and the first chancel must have been e. of them. There was a rebuilding at the end of the C13, and by the time the nave was heightened in the C14, the division between nave and chancel had moved w., so the piers at the e. end were left alone. Note the Norman window that remains high in the wall on the s. side. The original *priest's door* now leads into the vestry, and when that chapel was built in the early C16, a new door was made further e.. For some reason, it comes in at an angle, with a little tunnel through the wall by the sanctuary steps – very strange, but there must have been a good reason for it. The e. end has one of those chilling Victorian *reredoses* – all hard and spiky, but in front, Francis Floyd's altar is left uncovered so that one can admire it. Dated 1622, it has turned and reeded legs, with carved *capitals*, and a vine trail under the rim; on a centre shield, a sun in splendour round the words 'Vera Vitis Chrs' – 'Christ, the true vine'. A splendid memorial to the craftsman who was parish clerk for 46 years. The monument to Richard Warner (1757) on the n. wall makes lavish use of coloured marble, and has a stiff cherub's head below the *pediment* and a *cartouche* of arms at the bottom; the epitaph is excessive by any standard. Facing it is an example of the reaction to such exuberance – Richard Mills' (1820) tablet by Henry Westmacott (his competent but not brilliant work can be found all over the country, and he contributed to *Nelson*'s tomb in St Paul's). This design is totally chaste, but if fashion ruled out pretention there were other means to impress, and the world

was reminded that the deceased's wife's grandfather was none other than the famous Bishop Tanner. Well, well! The church has some interesting C14 glass in the tracery of the aisle windows with a very nice figure of an angel to be seen playing a psaltery at the w. end of the n. aisle. The *hatchment* nearby was made for the funeral of Lord Sondes of Elmham Hall. The church has a ring of 8 bells, tenor 14-0-1 cwt.

North Lopham, St Nicholas (G7): Within sight of splendid South Lopham, but a very different building. This time we have a big, sturdy late-C15/early-C16 *Perpendicular* tower, with *flushwork* and crowned initials of saints in the faces of the buttresses, and a flushwork *base course*. Thomas Gentre left money to build the tower in 1479 and nine other bequests followed. Some of the donors' initials appear on the s. face of the tower, and there is an inscription across the full width asking us to pray for the souls of John and Alice Barker – he left money for the tower in 1486, but the work was not finished until 1526. The church is of varying periods; the s. *aisle*, with its most attractive window traceries, is C14 *Decorated*; likewise the rustic *porch*, with its tough little irregular battlements (picked out in chequerwork stone and flint) and, inside, a sweet little *cusped* figure niche over the s. door. The *nave* is Perpendicular; and the *chancel* an *Early English*, Decorated and Perpendicular combination. The e. window is a very good replacement in the *reticulated* style of the Decorated period – does this date from a chancel restoration recorded in 1862? Notice that one of the *corbel* heads of the window's *drip mould* seems to be original, while the other has a markedly C18 look about it – a gentleman with side-rolled wig and a high stock up to his chin. The church's interior is of immensely pleasing simplicity, under plain modern roofs – the plaster between the timbers of the nave roof (an 1879 replacement) is painted a pale turquoise; in the chancel, a pale beige; pale blue in the heads of the nave windows (which sit in deep, irregularly shaped embrasures which catch and reflect the light); a denser blue for the embrasures of the chancel and tower w. windows; and ochre in the nave's filled-in n. doorway. The simple *arcade* of four bays is of C14 date, as are the tower and chancel arches. In the easternmost pillar of the arcade, note how the stone of the *capital* is cut away – the fitting point, no doubt, of a *parclose screen* enclosing a *guild chapel* in pre-*Reformation* days (It is recorded that two guilds met here, dedicated to St Peter and St John).

The font – octagonal, with sloping panels delicately carved with tracery and similar to that at South Lopham just down the road – is C14. The cover, again like that at South Lopham, looks C17. Nearby, a massive chest, iron-banded and with three locks, does duty as a money-box – of no mean capacity. In the embrasure of the centre nave window, a wall pedestal, neatly carved with miniature 'battlements', holds a modern Madonna & Child. In the s. aisle, *Royal Arms* of George III; also three benches with re-used medieval bench ends, once carved with figures and grotesques, but now sadly mutilated. In the chancel, a big, boldly simple *piscina*, with a single-leaf arch, its interior painted by this colour conscious congregation, in the same rich ochre as the filled-in n. doorway in the nave. Adjacent are plain *dropped sill sedilia*. The altar table, of dignified simplicity, is *Stuart*. Before you leave, look at the list on the nave n. wall of those of this tiny parish who gave their lives in the two World Wars, 15 in the First, five in the Second – five from one family in 1914-18, and the same name recurring once more in 1939-'45. Here indeed one may honour Rupert Brooke's companions who 'poured out the red sweet wine of youth'. The church has an excellent ring of 8 bells, tenor 10-2-0 cwt.

North Pickenham, St Andrew (E5): In 1863 this little church was designed by architect D.Male and largely rebuilt, with only the tower and n. *transept* with its large *Perpendicular* windows surviving from the earlier building. That was probably the original style but Male's window designs follow *Decorated* forms. Within, it is notable that the door to the tower stairs is only 53 in. high, and a *sanctus bell* window can be seen higher up. Standing below is a chest dated 1724 which also carries the churchwardens' names. In the *chancel*, the *reredos* set in the wall behind the altar comprises glass mosaic panels of 1863 by Antonio Salvati, the Venetian artist who founded the Museo Vetrario in the 1860s and whose work attracted great attention in the Paris 1864 Exhibition. *Powell & Sons* provided the glass in the w. window in 1864, and used excellent cartoons by *Henry Holiday* medallions – Baptism, the Good Samaritan, the Sacrifice of Isaac and Moses and the Serpent; these are fine and important examples of Holiday's early work, although the glass is rather dark for a light background. There is more good glass of the period in the chancel and transept windows – this time by *M. & A.O'Connor* who provided strong Gethsemane, Crucifixion and Deposition

North Runcton, All Saints: By Henry Bell, 1713

scenes for the chancel and angel medallions in the transept.

North Runcton, All Saints (C4): Medieval churches are an essential element in the Norfolk landscape, but only two early-C18 buildings come to mind – St George's at Great Yarmouth (redundant) and North Runcton. In 1701 the steeple of the old church collapsed into the *nave* and all was 'beaten down flat to the ground'. By great good chance, the architect of King's Lynn's Customs House, Henry Bell, lived at the Hall nearby and he not only designed the new church but contributed generously to its cost. Completed in 1713, it is a compact, gracious building, standing above the gentle rise of the village green. Dark cypresses line the path and a delicate white painted lantern sets off the cool severity of the tower. Nave and tower are plastered and the *chancel* is a soft-toned mixture of red brick and *carstone*. Entering by the w. door, note first an interesting set of Georgian *Royal Arms* over the vestry door, with painted cut-out angels surrounding the frame. There is a Gurney *hatchment* opposite, and higher up on the w. wall, the arms of Edward Rudd, inducted as rector in 1719 – but they are almost too dark to see. On then, into the square nave, which has the characteristic C18 air of quiet and seemly order. Resting on four plain classical columns with high plinths, the centre vault is dominant, and from it hangs a handsome contemporary chandelier. A *screen* of three arches divides chancel from nave, resting again on.pairs of classical columns, and although the chancel originally had a large round-headed e. window, this was blanked off and made rather dark by a huge *reredos* that fills the whole wall. By an apt coincidence it, too, was designed by Henry Bell in 1684 for St Margaret's, Kings Lynn, and between the sombre *Corinthian pilasters* picked out in gilt, there are large paintings of Christ and the Evangelists that came from Florence in 1901. Matching *communion rails* complete the composition. The nave pews are in oak with gently curved tops to the panelled ends – part of a sympathetic restoration in 1887, and the grey marble *baluster* font came in 1907 – again from St Margaret's. There is a happy balance between clear and stained glass, and in the St *Catherine* window on the n. side the church tower itself is in the background, outlined against a lowering sky.

North Tuddenham, St Mary (G4): The busy A47 is only minutes away, yet this handsome church, distanced from its village, is serenely alone – save for a dignified old rectory next door and its resident, and vocal peacocks – amid peaceful fields. The tower is C14 *Decorated* (rather late, of about 1360) with corner pinnacles, parapets with excellent brick and flint *flushwork*, and crisply distinctive *quatrefoil* traceries in the bell openings. The rest of the church is wholly *Perpendicular* in character. The e. window is very good, with three levels of battlemented *transoms*, and at the ends of its *dripstone*, elegant *corbel* heads – contrasting somewhat with the weird ones on the *chancel's* n. and s. sides, who are close cousins of the fierce *gargoyles* up above. Around the roof, lintels of *nave* and chancel have a frieze of little stone-carved decorations – flowers of various kinds, and odd little animal faces. There is a *mass dial* on the s. side of the nave, on the buttress immediately to right of the s. door, about 5ft. from the ground. Two-storey Perpendicular n. *porch*, much restored, with a pretty figure niche over the outer arch containing a modern statue of The Virgin; inside the porch, the indentation of a *holy water stoup*. Rather startling, on entering the church, is the Victorian imprint on the place – maroon and green *encaustic tiles* of about 1880 all around the nave walls and window sills, and equally in the chancel, complemented by masses of 'mock medieval' wall colouring. Good modern roofs. The C15 font has plain shields

round its octagonal bowl, and flowers and 'lionish' heads around the base. A curiosity, hung up nearby on the tower arch, is an Elizabethan collecting shoe, or rather, shovel. Dated 1580, it has on one side the inscription: 'Let not thine hand be open when ye shouldest receive nor shut when ye shouldest give'. On the other side: 'Ye that giveth unto the poore lendeth unto the Lord. And look what ye layeth out. It shall be payed hym agayne' (Ecclesiasticus 4, v. 31, and Proverbs 19, v. 17). The painted panels in the little *screen* across the tower arch were given to a former rector by a friend who 'bought them out of a lumber shop after they had been discarded by a church unknown'. They are late-C14 English work – l., *Matthew* and *Mark*; r., *Gregory* and *Augustine*. Two ancient chests stand at the w. end – the larger is C15, the smaller one may be C13. In the s.e. corner of the nave is a Perpendicular *piscina*. The chancel screen is C15 and good. Its painted saints are, n. to s.: *Agnes*; *Gregory*; *Dorothy*; the rarely represented *Geron*; *Catherine*; *Edmund*, or possibly *Sebastian*; *Etheldreda*; and a rare representation, *Roche*. In the chancel, the choir stalls are raised on stone sounding-boxes, to give more resonance. Impressive monuments in the sanctuary include a big tomb chest with shields; above it, a large, black and white marble monument to Katherine Skippe, 1629, erected by her husband, 'Thomas Skippe, of North Tuddenham, one of the Gentlemen of His Majesties Privie Chamber'. To left, a portrait head in an oval recess framed by some 27 carved books, and bearing this inscription:

What stronger circle can art magick find
Where a schollers spyrit can bee confind
Than this of bookes! Note how he spent
  his time
Scorneinge earths drosse to thinke on
  things sublime
So longe thy love to learninge shall be read
Whilst fame shall last: or statues for the
  dead.

Now to North Tuddenham's important collection of medieval glass. The Rev. Robert Barry, rector from 1851 to 1904, bought it in nearby Dereham for ten shillings and sixpence, where it was lying in a builder's yard, its origin before that being less than clear. The best of what is on view now is in the lower section of the tower w. window: a pair of binoculars is essential to view them best. Two panels show scenes from the life of St *Margaret*, the third of *Saint George*. The lower left panel shows Margaret

North Tuddenham, St Mary

sitting spinning, being approached by the squire of the Provost of Antioch (they have 'speech banners' above them). In the centre panel, she is in the Provost's presence, he wearing rich red cloak, she a blue robe with white mantle – and the Provost is clutching at her mantle in his eagerness. It is at this point that she repudiates him, affirms her Christianity, and upbraids him for his paganism. R. h. panel: two distinct scenes from the adventures of St George, first rescuing a maiden and then mauling the dragon – marvellous colour and detail. In the tracery of the chancel s.e. window are angels playing lutes to each side; a bishop; and an archbishop. In the s.w. window: St *Leonard*; a fragmentary figure of a saint with a scroll; St *Edmund*; and a crowned abbess who is possibly St *Etheldreda*. Nave s. side: e. end window – censing angels to each side, Christ in Majesty, and possibly St *Gregory*; in the top, the head of God. The arms in the centre main light are those of the Wotton family, dated 1527. C. window – St *Lawrence* ('Definitely the chief treasure of the collection'); *Matthias* (labelled, and with a quote from the *Apostles'* creed); top, a horse's head fragment. W. window, s. side, a St George; possibly one of the *Four Latin Doctors*, but he's been given Christ's head

and the scroll of *Edmund Rich*; a group, possibly the parable of the Unjust Steward; possibly a *Trinity*, but badly diffused. Nave n. side, e. end: *John the Baptist*; decapitation of St George; a female saint, possibly *Clare*, but with a male's head on her; Christ with the woman at the well; c. window – the Provost with his squire, from the St Margaret series; Christ with Nicodemus and inscription; a naked female figure, possibly St Margaret; her flagellation. Nave n.w. window: a Deity, but named for St *Thomas*; a figure of Moses with *horns of light* coming from his ears; *James the Great*, but with an angel's head and St John's scroll. C. *light* of this window is the earliest coat-of-arms in the church, 1468, for the Brampton family. In the *porch*: in the e. window is, l. panel, a bishop with St *Martin* inscribed below him; r., various fragments. W. window: St *James the Great*, labelled; liveried horses and dogs, possibly from the St Margaret series; and various other fragments.

North Walsham, St Nicholas (I2): A grand town church, packed with much of interest. The ruinous tower used to be 147ft. high – but on 16th May 1724, the s. and w. sides fell, bringing down the steeple too 'and no-one getting any mischief. Thanks be to God'. 100 years went by before the next collapse, in a storm in February 1836. Rebuilding plans have come and gone – save for the vestry built into the base. Move on to the magnificent late-C14 *porch*, luxuriously carved, decorated and pinnacled, with three figure niches containing modern figures of St *Benet*, the Virgin & Child, and St *Nicholas*. In the *spandrels* of the outer arch are the contemporary arms of Edward III (right), 1322-77, and his son, John of Gaunt (d.1399), who owned great Norfolk estates. Inside the lofty porch the roof beams have fine *bosses*; set into the walls below are, again, the arms of John of Gaunt, and opposite, of St Benet's Abbey, once patron of the living. Inside, the church is one vast hall, the noble seven-bay *arcade* of clustered columns and eloquent pointed arches hardly seeming to interrupt it, and light streaming in from the great *aisle* windows. The e. windows are Victorian. C15 painted cover over the font, soaring up to its original suspension beam; nearby, a couple of old *misericords*, with *woodwoses*; in s.w, corner, a huge C15 iron bound chest, with seven locks; over the tower door, another rarity – *Royal Arms* with Charles II on one side and Cromwell's Commonwealth on the other; at w. end of n. aisle, a C13 *lancet* window; in n. aisle pavement, a *chalice brass* to Sir Edmund Ward, Vicar, 1519; nearby, an inscription to Dame Margaret Hettercete, 1397. At e. end of s. aisle, brass to Robert Raunt, 1625, with arms of the Grocers' Company; a few feet away, an inscription to John Page, 1627, by which time brasses were almost out of fashion. Further e. in aisle chapel, another chalice brass, this one to Sir Robert Wythe, Chaplain, 1515, next door to an inscription to William Rous, 1404; the chapel's altar, with an inscription taken from the Edward VI prayer book, 1549-1552. All that remains of the mighty *screen* which would have extended between the two *rood loft* entrances in the two aisles is the lower part. It once displayed twenty saints – one has gone and two are hidden but one can still find figures of the Apostles, SS *Catherine* and *Barbara*. The darkly impressive pulpit is pre-*Reformation*. Laid against the wall in the n. and s. chancel aisles are pieces of another screen, probably C14, the panels blanked but with excellent carving in the *spandrels*. In the sanctuary: handsome *piscina* and triple *sedilia*; and opposite, the ornate tomb of Sir William Paston, 1608, founder of the local grammar school, Sir William reposing full length in armour, comfortably propped on an elbow. A meticulous man, he erected this extravaganza himself before he died.

Northrepps, St Mary (I2): Although there are traces of earlier work in the *chancel lancet* windows and the C14 *arcades*, the rest of the church is C15 in style, with a good deal of C19 restoration. The tower is a compact design with good detail. The C15 *rood screen* was rescued from a barn and eventually restored to its proper place: although much of it is new work, it does have the original inscription mentioning its donor, John Playford and his wife. The C16 benchends are conventional except that the western-most *poppy-heads* are halved and squared-off intentionally – unusual. Under the tower a 'Gallas' plough: these were famous throughout C19 Norfolk, and were made at the local foundry here. The church has a good ring of 8 bells, tenor 11-1-10 cwt.

Northwold, St Andrew (D6): Seen from the main road, from half a mile or so away, the tower is very eye-catching, with its veritable coronet of pinnacles. It is a very tall, *Perpendicular* construction of four stages, with a handsome parapet set with *flushwork* – and with eight *crocketted* pinnacles. More flushwork too down the angle buttresses and round the *base course*. In a frieze between w. window and w. door are flush-panelled letters signifying the names of saints. The body of the church is a mixture of Perpendicular and *Decorated* forms. The *clerestory* is very striking, each side having four big *Tudor* windows under flattened arches, set off with brick and flint 'eyebrows', and between the windows, square headed 'false' window outlines, mullioned and *cusped,* and panelled in with flushwork. Over the westernmost window, s. side, notice the stone-carved panel invoking prayers for 'the sowle of John Starlyng'; and at the opposite end, two most peculiar grotesque heads set side by side into the *quoin* stones, with no apparent reason for their presence save as a whim of the mason. Very fine Decorated *chancel*, despite the intrusion of the big Perpendicular window on the s. side. On the n. side, and notably in the superb five-*light* e, window, the contemporary *reticulated* tracery survives. The Decorated vestry on the n. side of the chancel was originally of two storeys. Set into the outer wall on its w. side is a most extraordinary carved head which would be more at home in an Aztec temple. The church's interior is made impressive by a beautiful painted *nave* roof and by *arcades* equal in beauty. The roof, of *arch-braces* alternating with *hammer-beams,* has richly gilded *bosses* at ridge and *purlin* intersections, and gilded and painted angels and shields on the hammers and *wall posts*. The latter sit on massive stone *corbels* carved with angels and animals, though with no great expertise. The four-bay arcade below is C13; it has clustered *quatrefoil pillars*, with *capitals* alternating between plain rings and pronounced foliage carving. Notice that they change again at the w. end – a Perpendicular addition when the tower was added. There are faint traces of medieval painting on the n. wall. Over the chancel arch, the *Royal Arms* of George II. In the spacious chancel is the church's most remarkable possession, a large *Easter Sepulchre*, still resplendent despite its mutilations, and probably late-C14. It has a big tomb chest under carved canopies, and a back wall incised with deep arcading. On the front of the chest a group of 'Roman' soldiers guarding the sepulchre (actually in the uniforms of Richard II's reign) look thoroughly agitated and are apparently writhing about in a forest of cabbage-like miniature trees. Their discomfort has nothing to do with their aggressively armoured-in wedding ring waists, which are enough to knock the breath out of any man; but rather their reasonable reaction to Christ's resurrection. This parish seemingly abounded in people of quite remarkable goodness, charity, liberality, simplicity, piety, etc. see the *ledger-stone* and wall monuments in the chancel; another to the left of the tower arch, and to the right, a curious painted memorial on wood, done in the form of an opulent C18 *cartouche*. This last one was set up in 1727 to recall a worthy of the previous century and a time of grievous troubles for England. It makes fascinating reading.

Norton Subcourse, St Mary (K6): The big round tower may well be *Saxon* in origin, but the tall bell openings are C13, and the body of the church was rebuilt in the 1380s when a College of Secular Priests transferred here from nearby Raveningham. The mesh of *reticulated* tracery in the C14 e. window is particularly attractive from outside, and so are the *headstops* of nearly all the windows. They are a mixture of human and animal faces and can be found inside as well, varying surprisingly in size. The interior has a plain plastered ceiling, the vista broken only by an C18 *tiebeam* placed where the *rood* once was – see the stair in the n. wall. The C14 *double piscina* and stepped *sedilia* under *ogee* arches, with two large *corbel* heads, is an excellent composition; on the other side of the *chancel* there is a tomb recess (partly behind the organ) with a very flat ogee arch topped by a *crocket*. The C13 *Purbeck marble* font has the *blank*

arcading seen so frequently in the county; above it on the w. wall, the *Royal Arms* of George IV in good condition. There was evidently an altar by the *rood screen* because the piscina is still there on the s. side, and the three oddly shaped niches in the n. wall of the nave, with one in the window embrasure opposite, point to the existence of others. The church has an excellent ring of 6 bells, tenor 10-1-15 cwt.

Norwich, St Andrew (I5): The church is high above the street on its n. side, and can be seen from a distance, but otherwise buildings and alleys hug it closely. The arms of William Appleyard can be found in the range of shields (re-set from an earlier church) below the outside of the e. window. He was the first mayor of Norwich in the early C15 and lived close by, in what is now the Bridewell museum. The tower dates from 1478, and onto it was built this example of the full flowering of the *Perpendicular* style of architecture, the ultimate expression of medieval practice. The team of designer/craftsmen who had just then completed Shelton church moved here, and finished the work in 1506. Inside, one sees the principles of the style fully extended. A cambered *tie-beam* roof bears straight down, without any lateral thrust, on a structure that is almost skeletal. A great range of eleven closely spaced *clerestory* windows stretches from end to end, and below, ashlar panelling fills all the space above elegant arches and *piers* of the slenderest proportions. Without a *chancel* arch, and with large *aisle* windows reaching to within a bay of the e. end, everything is light and space. There is a C16 *brass* in the s.e. corner of the sanctuary, thought to be that of Robert Gardiner and his wife. He was mayor of Norwich in 1490, 1499 and 1506, and wears his civic robes; she has a *kennel head-dress* and around her waist, a buckled belt with a tail reaching nearly to the ground carries a purse and rosary. The *sedilia* canopy is largely Victorian, but fragments of the original indicate that it is probably a faithful reproduction. The *reredos*, low *screen*, pulpit and font are all exuberant Victoriana, and the last is very well done. It carries a stylish cover dated 1637 – restored from fragments found in the belfry. The solid C19 pews have that period trade-mark – hinged brass rails and drip-trays for umbrellas! In the n. aisle chapel is a fine assembly of late-C16 and early-C17 monuments. The largest and grandest is to Sir John Suckling (d.1613) and his wife Martha. He was James I's treasurer and uncle of the poet of the same name. They lie stiff and uncomfortable – he in armour and ruff, she in stomacher, full skirt and a great spreading collar. Boys in rich, well detailed costume kneel at head and foot, and the black marble couch rests on skulls over a shrouded, coffined corpse. Three daughters, graded in size, kneel along the front, and symbols and epigrams abound. On the e. wall is the tomb of Sir John's father, Robert (d.1611). This has the conventional couple facing each other in prayer with attendant figures, but the life-size flanking skulls rest most oddly on openwork baskets of fruit. Next door is a well-restored plain memorial (1607):

A Senator of Senators renowned race,
Was Francis Rugg now entombed in this
place,
He was thrice Mayor in 72 years life,
Ann, being by birth an Aldrich late his wife,
In love hath reared this memorial
To celebrate his worthy name withal.

Reformation followed hard on the heels of the building here, and there are two framed canvasses at the w. end of the s. aisle which highlight the strongly Protestant temper of the city:

This church was builded of timber, stone
and Bricks,
In the year of Our Lord God XV hundred
and six
And lately translated from extreme Idolatry
A thousand five hundred and seven and
fortie
And in the first year of our noble King
Edward
The Gospel in Parliament was mightily set
forward
Thanks be to God Anno Dom 1547
Decemb

As the good king Josiah being tender of
Age
Purged his realm of all Idolatry
Even so our noble Queen and Counsell
sage
Set up the Gospel and banisht Popery
At twenty fower years began she her Reign
And about forti foure did it Mayntain,
Glory be given to God.

Ironically, Bishop Underwood, that hot persecutor of local protestants in the intervening Mary Tudor's reign, was buried in the *nave* here. There are panels of medieval glass in the s. aisle windows, and the westernmost is an interesting extract from a *Dance of Death* sequence, showing 'Death and the Bishop'.

Among the many C18 and C19 wall tablets, the one to John Custance at the e. end of the s. aisle is particularly good. It shows a cleverly restrained use of coloured marble and gilt embellishment, with unusually crisp detailing.

Norwich, St Augustine (I5): Parishioners here were dubbed 'Red Steeplers' because the late-C17 brick tower is the only one of its kind in Norwich. The battlements were added in the C19, along with the s. *porch* as part of a major restoration, but the *gargoyles* and *sound-holes* survive from the original. Now in the care of the *Churches Conservation Trust*, the building has an odd profile. A high *nave*, with only four *clerestory* windows each side, is no longer than the *chancel*, and this has a steep tiled roof dropping to *aisle* leads which are all but flat. The body of the church is square, and what was described as 'a wilderness of horse-*box pews*' gave way to the late Victorian furnishings of little merit. One panel of the original *rood screen* has been framed on the w. wall of the n. aisle, and has a faded figure of St *Appolonia* holding outsize pincers with a tooth to match; her long wavy hair reaches to the waist. Tucked away in the vestry is a plain marble tablet to Matthew Brettingham:

of this city, Architect who departed this
earthly residence Aug 19 1769. As a man
his integrity, liberal Spirit and benevolence
of Mind endeared him to all that knew his
Virtues and his Talents as an Architect, to
the Patronage and esteem of the Nobility
the most distinguish'd for their love of
Palladian Architecture.

Holkham Hall, on the n. Norfolk coast, is his true memorial. The harshness and degradation of C19 industry was not absolute. On the s. aisle wall is a plain tablet of 1858:

Erected to the memory of Thomas
Clabburn, Manufacturer, by upwards of
six hundred of the Weavers of Norwich
and assistants in his establishment as a
mark of esteem for his many Virtues as an
employer and a kind, good man.

Clabburn died at the age of 70 in 1858.

Norwich, St Clement (I5): Four hundred years ago there were six churches in Magdalen Street and now there is one – St Saviour's – and that is redundant. St Clement's is really in Colegate but its churchyard opens onto Fye Bridge Street, and it too was declared redundant in 1975. But one man, the Rev. Jack Burton – Methodist Minister with a difference – would not let it happen. A bus driver during the working week, and a man of vision and energy, he was convinced that there must be at least one church in the area open for prayer and meditation, and he fought to keep St Clement's alive. When it passed into the hands of the Norwich Historic Churches Trust in 1978, he rented it, and has managed to keep it open so far against great odds. It is neither a parish church nor a non-conformist chapel but simply a place for prayer. For one man and his small band of supporters the financial commitment is frightening, and it is sad that he has to use a milk churn to collect donations because the alms boxes were all stolen. But there it is – a heart-warming example of faith. There has been a church here since before the Conquest, and it may even be the oldest in the city, but the present building is mainly *Perpendicular* in style. A simple building – tower, short *aisle*less *nave*, low *chancel*, standing in a churchyard almost bare of gravestones, so that the rebuilt tomb of *Archbishop Parker's* parents on the s. side is easy to find. One of Norwich's most famous sons, he is remembered by an annual sermon in the Cathedral and another here in the evening of the same Sunday. He asked that a prayer be said for the souls of his parents by their tomb on that day, and so it is still. The church has two good C18 wall monuments inside to Jeremiah Ives (d.1741) and John Harvey (d.1742), facing each other across the nave. Don't miss the *brass* to Margaret Pettwode (d.1514) at the e. end of the nave. Worn butter-smooth by countless feet, the figure turns slightly to the left instead of taking the usual stiff frontal position, and her *kennel head-dress* as well as parts of her gown were recessed to take coloured enamels. That embellishment has gone but it's a brass worth looking at.

Norwich, St George Colegate (I5): Built on a rising tide of the city's prosperity between 1459 and 1513, with an interior reflecting the wealth of the C18 cloth masters. The tower is tall enough for its richly decorated battlements to be seen from a distance over the roof-tops, and the whole church is compact and chunky. Stonework of the w. door-way and its surrounds is badly decayed, but in the left *spandrel* of the s. *porch* doorway there is an engaging carving of St *George* being dressed in his armour by attendant angels. The other spandrel has a defaced *Annunciation*. This is the one Norwich church where virtually all the C18

furnishings have been left undisturbed and they are very good. The *reredos* with its Grecian columns is splendidly classical, with an effect of rich simplicity harking back to the Wren period. The pulpit is an outstanding piece with a big inlaid *tester* and backboard like that at St George Tombland. The front panel is shaped and deeply moulded, with the *IHS* sacred monogram framed by delicate swags of flowers. The body of the church is filled with solid panelled dark oak pews which have an elegant range of *balusters* at the e. end and a seven-foot *screen* with curved ends at the w. The little organ of 1802 is topped by a diminutive gilt Apollo and sits comfortably on a substantial w. *gallery* which has a St George and Dragon weathervane mounted on the front. The n. *aisle* chapel was built by William Norwich, mayor in 1461, and there is there a big worn bracket *brass* (i.e. the figures stand on a decorative bracket) to him and his wife Alicia. By its side is the fine *Renaissance* tomb chest of another mayor, Robert Jannys. Dating from 1534, the tomb has his merchant's mark (he was a wealthy grocer) supported by angels in two of the panels, and in two others are seated cowled figures. The monument on the e. wall by *John Bacon* to 'honest John Herring', mayor in 1799 is a most uncomfortable composition. A mourning lady perches precariously in what looks acute discomfort. Much better is *Thomas Rawlins'* monument in the s. aisle to Timothy Balderston (d.1764). Cleverly framed within the C16 *blank arcading*, a *putto* points to a list of virtues on a scroll, with the mayoral mace and beaver hat behind him. John Crome, famous founder of the Norwich School of painting lived and died in the parish and lies buried in the s. aisle chapel. His name is added at the foot of a large *ledger-stone* of the Lubbock family, and an 1868 tablet with a medallion portrait is on the wall above. Good tablets and interesting epitaphs abound in this church, including one at the w. end to Bryant Lewis – murdered on Thetford Heath in 1698. The church has an excellent ring of 6 bells, tenor 9-2-24 cwt.

Norwich, St George Tombland (I5): One of the most attractive of the city churches, small in scale and beautifully placed. The tower is exceptionally good, and has angle buttresses with chequer-board facings, and well defined *string courses*. The stair projects on the n. side to the top, and adds a pleasing variation to that facade. The s. *porch* has a *boss* of St *George* in the centre of the vaulting, but entry is now by the *priest's door*. The *arcades* are squat and heavy, with widely spaced *clerestory* windows above. A good *arch-braced roof* rests on long *wall posts*, and those in the *chancel* have angels at the foot looking curiously like perching birds. The early-C18 oak *reredos* is a nice piece. Two blank arches, flanked by *Corinthian* columns, have a large broken *pediment* over, and the panelling extends round the walls to enclose the sanctuary. In front, a good set of *communion rails* with barley-sugar *balusters*. The pulpit is of the same period and is of very high quality. The front has a marquetry 'sun in splendour' in ivory around the *IHS* sacred monogram, and even the tiny beaded edge of the panel is inlaid to match. The backboard, the great *tester*, and charming miniature stairway complete the unit and one can only mourn the loss of the matching *box pews* that were removed in the C19. The C13 *Purbeck marble* font had the ring of eight pillars added in the 1870s. Its C17 cover has a baroque gilded St George and dragon on top, and on the w. wall on the n. *aisle* is another St George – a C16 bas relief, possibly German. Hidden away by the organ is a monument by *Nicholas Stone* to Alderman Anguish (d.1617). He and his wife face each other across a desk, and their attendant children each carry a skull. Even the two little *chrysom babes* rest their heads on skulls! Perhaps because he was Mayor, the coloured figures are in no way mutilated. There are two high quality C18 tablets in the chancel. At the w. end is the monument to John Symonds (d.1609), 'who has given by his last testament unto ye pore of this parish two shillings a week to continue for ever'. In front, the stone slab on a plinth may have been a dole table, from which alms were distributed, but it is traditionally known as the 'bread table', and may have been used for preparing the *holy loaf*.

Norwich, St Giles (I5): St Giles stands on an eminence above the valley, which would be enough to make it prominent even if it did not have the loftiest tower in Norwich at 113ft. high, plus the 1737 cupola on top. This is largely a *Perpendicular* building which was dated C14 at one time, but the more probable date is 1420-30 (and there was a bequest of £5 towards the tower in 1424). The *chancel* is wholly Victorian, of 1866. The tower has *flushwork* battlements, huge four-*light* belfry windows; big three-light ones at the belfry stage, blocked in with flint, save for the centre lower lights; and an enormous five-light w. window. Below the latter, the w. door has traceried figure niches to either side. As one walks around the outside of the

building, the massive grotesque *gargoyles* form a common linking theme. The C15 two-storey porch is excellent. It has a square hood over its outer arch, with shields in the *spandrels*, and the niche above contains a modern St *Giles*, with arrows, deer and crozier. Overhead is a little *Tudor* window, with canopied figure niches to either side. But the distinguishing feature of the porch is a splendid frieze of carved shields contained in crowned 'Gs' for Giles, and linked by a flowing vine; and on the top, a lovely ornamented cresting. Inside the porch, the *fan-vaulted* roof is the only one of its kind in Norwich. Entering through a w. door, we come to a noble interior, lofty, spacious, handsomely appointed and ornamented, yet with not the least feeling of being cluttered or over-furnished. The *nave*, bounded by soaring chancel and tower arches, has elegant *arcades* of five bays on slim, clustered pillars. There are big three-light *clerestory* windows, a tiny e. window above the chancel arch containing a modern figure of the patron saint; and above the tower arch a little group of four *quatrefoil* openings serving as a *sanctus bell window*. The fine C15 roof is *arch-braced* and *hammer-beamed*, with large, winged angels on the hammers, each bearing a coat-of-arms (England, France and Castile). See how the arches of the arch-braces start from the *wall posts*, a curve beginning right from the *corbels* and carrying the eye effortlessly up to the central ridge. In early C19 this roof was in such bad condition that parishioners sat under umbrellas to protect themselves from the weather. The panelled arch-brace outline between the wall posts and over the clerestory windows is not really successful. To either side of the chancel arch, there are carved figure niches, three each side, with a modern St *Giles* and a Madonna in the lower ones. The church had to wait three centuries before the arch was opened up and a new chancel built in 1866-67. And well done it was, being completed with an *arch-braced* roof. St Giles has two brass eagle lecterns – as with the effigies of saints at the w. end (*Gregory* and *Laurence*), they are the product of several city parishes being merged and their treasures brought here. One of the lecterns is C19; the other, which came from St Gregory's Church, is medieval. It is East Anglian, possibly made here in Norwich and is of the same type as that at Oxborough. It is dated 1493 and asks for prayers for William Westbrook and his wives Rose and Joan. With the congregation providing the City with a number of its mayors, there is a fine collection of sword and mace rests down each side of the nave, inscribed with a roll call of names from the C18 and C19. Only the bowl of the font is original, C15, neatly carved with shields and flowers; the stem is C19. Fine monuments and *ledger stones* abound. Several good *brasses* too, including a *chalice brass* to John Smyth, 1499, in front of the s. chapel altar. A rubbing of one, hanging on the tower arch, is on view, being the oldest of the collection, to Robert Baxter, 1432, seen in his mayoral robes, and his wife. Both his brass, and one to Richard Purdaunce and wife, 1436, are in the nave central pavement and are 'uncommonly good'; the inscription brass in front of the n. chapel altar to Elizabetha Bedingfold, 1637 reads:

> My name speakes what I was and am and have
> A Bedding Field a peece of earth a grave
> Where I expect vntill my sovle shall bring
> Vnto the field an everlasting spring
> For rayse and rayse ovt of the earth & slime
> God did the first and will the second time
> obiit Die Maii 1637.

In the s. *aisle* is the splendid wall monument by *Thomas Rawlins*, to Sir Thomas Churchman, who died in 1781 and was Sheriff of Norwich in 1757, Mayor in 1761, and who left considerable monies to local charities in his Will. His portrait bust is set above a richly carved, classical chest with a scene of angels in relief. Over the adjacent altar is a superb 16-branch brass candelabra, with a crowned Madonna and Child in the centre. At the opposite end of the aisle, in a carved and elegant frame, with coat-of-arms above and a trio of chubby-faced cherub heads below, is a memorial for Thomas Churchman, 1742, and his wife Deborah. By *Sir Henry Cheere*, it is a rare example of his work in E. Anglia. Immediately to the right is an excellent set of Queen Anne *Royal Arms*, 1708. Below the memorial, a curiosity is the cage, which in 1549 was installed on the top of St Giles' tower, to contain a beacon fire – this was the year of the Norfolk Rising and Kett's Rebellion and was no doubt a warning beacon. Immediately opposite, in the n. aisle, is the wordy monument to Adrian Payne, 1686, who left £120:

> for ye Clothing of poore men & women, in Gownes, once every yeare, in the moneth of November, as farre as ye annuall profits of the Said Sume would Extend.

At the e. end of this aisle is the rococo memorial of William Offley M.D., 1767, with an oval tablet, set askew, surrounded by pediments, carved books and cherubs. The church has a good ring of 8 bells, tenor 13-3-21 cwt.

Norwich, St Helen (I5): The Great Hospital, where this church will be found, in Bishopgate, had its beginnings in 1249 when its founder Bishop Suffield willed that a Master and four chaplains should pray for his soul, and minister to indigent clergy, the aged sick and seven poor scholars. It was a long *aisled* infirmary and *chancel*, with a tower (c.1375) at the s.w. corner, a great s. *porch* of three vaulted bays with an upper chamber, and a s. *transept*. The chancel was built by *Bishop Despenser* around 1380, and Bishop Goldwell rebuilt the remainder (except for the porch) in the late C15. From the beginning the building served as a parish church and it still does. Came the *Reformation*, and ownership of the Hospital passed to the city. Some years later the w. end of the *nave* and the chancel were partitioned to become wards, leaving the centre section to continue in service as a church. Entered now from the charming little C15 cloister on the n. side, the interior is sparkling white, and immediately the colour of the s. transept vault catches the eye. This gorgeous stone web, with its 41 *bosses* (by the same masons who worked on the cathedral nave) has been beautifully restored. The bosses are recoloured, the ribs lined with gold, the background a rich blue. Around a central Coronation of the Virgin are the *Annunciation*, Resurrection, Ascension, and Nativity – the latter the only representation in England of a midwife at the birth of Christ, and featured on a Christmas stamp in 1974. Other bosses have *Apostles*, saints, and a wide selection of kings and queens – all clearly marked on a chart below which is a great help to the visitor. The bench end on the s. side of the nave at the e. end has a fine figure of St *Margaret* and her dragon. She is crowned, with hands joined in prayer, and the beast arches up his head to her shoulder. The 'hec' below the figure stands for Hecker – Master of the Hospital 1519-32. Across the e. end there is a beautiful range of *box pews* in honey-coloured oak, enclosing a two-decker pulpit. The door knobs are brass and it speaks of an age when quality was taken for granted. Matching sets of pews fill the aisles and face inward. In the transept, William Ivory had his own – 'to be convenient for his family and servants', and it's a solid two-level essay in Gothick joinery, neatly inscribed with his and his wife's names on little labels along the front panels. His arms are on the door, dated 1780. The transept has a good *Stuart* altar table with a carved frieze along the top rail, and behind it a large and elegant painted *reredos* carries the Lord's Prayer, *decalogue* and creed below a pretty *tympanum* with the sacred monogram, *IHS*. To one side, a Master is recorded as having died of the stone – painfully in 1675; and at the w. end one finds a neat tablet to Jonathan Ward who retired suffering from 'gout & other informities' after 16 years as Master in 1765.

Norwich, St John Baptist & the Holy Sepulchre (I5): Commonly called St John de Sepulchre, it is now used by the Orthodox Church under the name of St John the Theologian. The church dates from 1472, and has one of the most beautiful towers in Norwich. It stands high on the Ber Street ridge, and visitors drawing into Thorpe Station often see it dramatically outlined against an evening sky. The tower has the C15 Norwich characteristic of angle buttresses faced closely with ashlar and dressed flint, imparting a chequer pattern all the way up, and the parapet is dressed with lozenges and *flushwork* battlements. The elaborate two-storied *porch* has a stone and flint panelled double frieze above the door, with a very tall canopied niche over it. The *chancel* has only one angle buttress at the s.e. corner – the n.e. is bare and cut away at the base, presumably to allow a passage to run between the church and adjacent houses which have long since gone. The interior is curiously simple for so large a church, *aisleless* and broken only by the stub *transepts*. Bernard Church, whose memorial is here, was an influential member of Cromwell's second parliament and mayor of Norwich in 1651. There is an unusual *consecration cross* in the s.e. corner of the sanctuary – it has a Latin scroll which translates: 'I will worship in Thy Holy Temple'. Two interesting *brasses* are mounted on the e. wall of the n. transept. One is to John Browne and his sister Winifred. They stand in *Tudor* dress holding hands rather touchingly, and below is this inscription:

John Browne of Waltone Gentleman Philip
  Browne's Son and Heir
Brother unto Winifred, his only Sister deare
Forseeinge that mans life is fraile, and
  subject unto death
Hath chosen him this syllie shrine, to
  shreud his corps in earth
Yet hopes he for to rise againe, through
  faith in Christ Gods sone
Whoe for his soule elect to life, a glorious
  Crowne hath wone

This is his hoape this is his trust, faith is his
  onely sheilde
By which he over syn and death and Sathan
  wins the feeild.
Winifrid Browne the daughter of Phillip
  and Ann his wife
Under this stone incloesed is devoide of
  Breathed life
A virgin pure she livde and dide, God
  garnisht her with grace
And like a Christian in his feare she ran hir
  pilgrims race
A lowlie hart she ever had, Belovde of ritch
  and poore
In spirit & truth she dailie sought The Lord
  God to adore
But though this virtue virgin young unto ye
  world be dead
The lambe of God we hope in heaven wth
  glorie crounes her head.

('Syllie' in line 4 is the old usage for 'holy', as in 'silly Suffolk'.) The second brass, to a civilian and his wife c.1535, is not in itself remarkable, but when it was lifted from the floor a *palimpsest* was found on the underside for an *anchorite* of much earlier date. The man, with tonsured head like a monk, stands behind a grill, within a *cusped* and *crocketted ogee* arch. No other like it is known. There was a hermitage in the churchyard here, and another at Ber Street Gates in the Middle Ages, and this may have been the brass of one of the anchorites. A copy of the *palimpsest* is displayed alongside. The font has a deep octagonal bowl, with large upstanding lions alternating with angels around it, and more dumpy lions round the stem. There is a good set of George II *Royal Arms* over the door, and on the top of the tower *screen* is a weathercock of 1713. The word 'Pax', Peace, pierced in it commemorates the Treaty of Utrecht at the end of the war of the Spanish Succession. In the changeover, the *nave* pews have been replaced by chairs, and a low iconostasis now blocks off the chancel. A range of small icons is displayed along the walls below the window sills.

Norwich, St John Baptist Maddermarket (I5): This church is now in the care of the *Churches Conservation Trust*. The view from the n. side takes in an attractive piece of town-scape. Buildings crowd in on the church, and there is a charming variation of levels, angles, and surface textures. Narrow Maddermarket Alley passes under the lovely tower, which has a staircase nestling in the angle of one of the boldly patterned buttresses. The n. *porch* has a curious octagonal upper chamber which may have been intended as the base of a tower originally. The church is square in plan, with slender C15 *arcades* and a tall *clerestory*, but it has no *chancel*. The e. window has quite exuberant C14 tracery, and it has been suggested that there was once a chancel extending over the street outside, and that the window was re-used when the body of the church was rebuilt. The striking feature of the interior is the superb early Georgian *reredos*, with its canopy supported by massive *Corinthian* columns. With a very solid set of mahogany *communion rails* and a great *Antiphonal Lectern* to match, the sanctuary has unity and beauty. At the w. end there is a *Jacobean* style *screen* of 1912, and under the *gallery*, an outstanding collection of *brasses* have been mounted on the wall. They range from 1412 to the C18, and include the fine effigies of Robert Rugge and his wife. He was Mayor in 1545 and 1550, and his brother William was the last Abbot of St Benet at Holme. This brass has a figure of an early-C14 abbot on the reverse and may well have come from the abbey. The big brass on the left is that of John Terry (d.1524) and his wife. The two 25in. figures stand on brackets with their children grouped on two more, with the arms of the city and Rugge's merchant mark between. There are many other excellent monuments in the church, including three of the early C17 in the s. aisle. There, Nicholas and Agnes Sotherton kneel facing each other conventionally across a desk, under a classical *pediment*, and their faces are full of character – assertive and self-confident. Further to the e. is a larger version of the same theme – this time the family of 'worthy Thomas Sothertone', 'whose brest enclosed an humbell sperryt'. Possibly, but the Sothertons were the wealthy merchants who brought the 'strangers' from the Netherlands to make Norwich famous for its fabrics, and Thomas (as Mayor): 'Hir one yeares father Norwch chose him & wyshed then she myght never lose him'. Easily overlooked, above the nave n. arcade, is a belated C18 memorial to a great lady. In 1563, the Lady Margaret, Duchess of Norfolk died while staying at her husband's palace nearby and her body was brought here in great state to be buried. The massive tomb in Framlingham church in Suffolk carries her effigy and that of the first duchess. The space between them was never filled – the Duke lost his head for treason on Tower Hill. .

Norwich, St John Baptist Timberhill (I5): Once known as St John at the Castle Gates and

used as a burial place for prisoners in the gaol, this small C15 church had become very dilapidated before being comprehensively restored in the late C19. Its dormer windows and perky bellturret are a distinctive feature of the city scene. Chosen as the focus for the new Parmentergate parish, it re-opened in 1980, having been imaginatively replanned to accommodate a wide range of worship and activity. With *chancel screen* removed and floor levelled, it is bright and spacious, with everywhere the evidence of parishioners' hard work. The *Stations of the Cross* and the Oberammergau *Rood* group have been restored and recoloured by artists among the congregation. In the chancel is a fine German chandelier of about 1500. It has a central crowned Virgin with the Christ child, amid a profusion of delicate branches sporting vine leaves and bunches of grapes. In the n.e. corner of the sanctuary is the memorial to *Robert Page* (d.1778) by himself. Work by this gifted Norwich sculptor graces many a Norfolk church, and his own tablet has a characteristic elegance. A very good weeping *putto* stands above it, but it is a pity that one arm is missing. The epitaph – 'An honest man's the noblest work of God' seems entirely right for one who set out the final public comment on so many contemporary men of substance. Perhaps he smiled as he chose it! The stained glass panel of the Virgin (with pomegranate) and Child in a s. *aisle* window came from nearby All Saints, and is a charming piece of 1910 work by Martin Travers. John Corfield was buried at the w. end in 1791. Although his stone is cracked and split, his wishes have apparently been respected:

> Forbear rash mortal! as thou hope for rest
> When Death shall lodge thee in thy destin'd bed
> With ruthless spade unkindly to molest
> The peacefull slumbers of the silent dead.

Norwich, St Julian (I5): This is a place of pilgrimage, following the great resurgence of interest in the C14 mystic, *Mother Julian* and in her classic 'The Revelations of Divine Love' – the first known book written by an Englishwoman. She lived as an *anchoress* here, and no doubt took her name from the dedicatory Saint – probably *Julian the Hospitaller*, patron saint of ferrymen. In 1942, the church was destroyed in an air raid and was rebuilt under the direction of A.J. Chaplin in 1953. The skilful blending of old and new has produced a small church of rare distinction. It is calm and beautiful in its simplicity. Two circular *Saxon* windows were revealed in the n. wall during the reconstruction, and the stump of the round tower is of the same period. The window between Mother Julian's cell and the *chancel* is where the original would have been, but there would have been no door into the church. The present connecting *Norman* doorway was brought from nearby St Michael at Thorn, gutted in the same air raid. The early-C15 font is an incomer too, from the redundant All Saints, and is arguably the finest in the city. It is carved with stylised vine leaves and has standing figures in niches round the shaft, and a pair of figures is recessed into each face of the octagonal bowl. Anti-clockwise from the e. they are: Saints *Michael* & *George*, *Peter* & *Paul*, *John the Baptist* & *John the Evangelist*, *James the Great* & *James the Less*, *Andrew* & *John*, *Thomas* & *Matthew*, *Jude* & *Simon*, *Phillip* & *Matthias*. Against the stem are: Saints *Clement*, *Walstan*, *Clare*, *William of Norwich* (?), *Christopher* (?), *Lawrence*, *Catherine* (?), and *Vincent*. The High Altar *reredos* is an excellent 1930s piece from Oberammergau – conventionally gothic, but with good figures and predominantly in muted colours of rose and pale blue. Mother Julian's cell, with its small shrine, is starkly simple. Against a bare wall under a plain wooden ceiling, the large crucifix hangs behind an unadorned altar slab. It is both moving and tranquil.

Norwich, St Mary in the Marsh (I5): Parish mergers and redundant churches – familiar enough things these days – but a parish that has not had its own church since 1564, and yet is thriving – that is unique in Norfolk. An elegant terrace of late-C18 houses in the Cathedral Close is known as St Mary's Chant, almost a folk memory of the church that once stood there to serve the parish of St Mary in the Marsh. When the monastic Priory was founded in 1096, the people living and working in the Close needed their own parish church, and Bishop Herbert de Losinga built St Mary's for them. In 1538, Henry VIII's Dissolution of the Monasteries transformed the last Prior into the first Dean, and in 1564 the parish church was pulled down (and the materials sold by the Dean!). By way of compensation, the parish was allowed to use the s. *aisle* of the Cathedral for their own services. Thirty years later, the parishioners were on the move again – this time to St Luke's chapel (s. ambulatory), and their successors have been there ever since. Because the monastic Priory had

no font (nor any need of one), the parishioners took their old one with them, and after being moved around once or twice, it now stands in St Luke's Chapel. It is one of Norfolk's *seven sacrament fonts*, and although heavily defaced, it has that richness which they all share – for detailed description see the notice nearby. No need here to describe the beauties of the Cathedral – there are excellent guide-books available, but one thing at least makes St Luke's Chapel worth a special visit. The Despencer *reredos* or retable stands behind the altar, and was probably given as a thank-offering for the victory of the 'fighting bishop' *Henry Despencer* in the Peasants' Revolt of 1381. Upside down, it served as a table-top for many years before being rediscovered in 1847. Beautifully restored, the jewel-like quality of its painted panels distinguishes it as one of the finest examples of late-C14 art in the kingdom.

Norwich, St Peter Mancroft (I5): This great church dominates the market place, and although nearby buildings have been removed over the years and the new Forum is close by, it still forms a quiet but living centre to one of the busiest parts of the city. Built on the site of a previous church, the present building was completed in 25 years, between 1430 and 1455, and remains substantially unaltered. This combination of precise date and original form is seldom found in a medieval building. Most of the outer surfaces are faced with ashlar, and virtually the whole tower is covered with panelling, niches or *flushwork*. The effect is very rich, but not, perhaps, graceful. It certainly reflects the affluence of its builders. What the tower gains in strength and solidity is offset by the cake-icing effect of the parapet and corner pepperpots added by the Streets (father and son) in the 1880s, and the spirelet of 1895. Old pictures show that the former plain top with its centre spike was infinitely preferable. The buttresses along the *aisles* and *transepts* are beautiful. Each has a tall canopied niche at the middle stage, and then the design sweeps up in a graceful inward curve to little castellated pinnacles on the parapet. No church in the county has such a *clerestory* as this. Seventeen windows each side, stretching the entire length of *nave* and *chancel* and separated by the slimmest of pillars, form the nearest thing to a wall of glass produced in any epoch before the Crystal Palace. It catches the eye from all over the market place. Making a virtue of its steeply sloping site, the church has a three-storied sacristy and treasury at the e. end and a passage-way under the chancel. This, together with the fine open arches under the tower, forms a processional way that is all within consecrated ground. The interior is a delight. Even on the dullest day it is filled with light from aisles, clerestory and from the huge e. and w. windows. The tall *arcades* are carried on slender *piers* of clustered columns, and the absence of a chancel arch, plus the fact that the aisles are only one bay shorter than the nave/chancel, imparts a tremendous feeling of space. The impression would not have been so marked before the *Reformation*. A great *rood screen* stretched right across from wall to wall, and the stairs that served it are still to be seen in the walls by the transepts. The pulleys from which were suspended the lights before the *Rood* remain on the westernmost *boss* in the roof. There would have been less light too. Until a Civil War gunpowder explosion close by blew out all the windows, there was much more painted glass, and the place must have glowed with colour. The remnants were collected later into the e. window, which is probably the best single surviving example of the *Norwich school of glass-painters* of the C15 and C16. There are seven C19 panels in the centre *light* and bottom row, but the rest form a most beautiful series of New Testament themes, full of rich medieval detail. Binoculars are a must here if one is to appreciate the quality of the work. Portraits of the donors appear in the four outermost panels in the bottom row. The two armed figures in the l.h. panel are Edmund and Sir Christopher Garnysh, the latter having been given a Saint's head at some stage. He was knighted for his courage in the French wars. Next to the right is Thomas Elys, three times Mayor and Member of Parliament. In the l. hand panel of the second row, a picture of the *Annunciation* includes a most rare portrayal of the embryo Christ descending a shaft of light, cross on shoulder, preceded by a dove. Bishop Parkhurst specifically forbade this particular representation in the diocese in 1561, but luckily this tiny example escaped notice. Next to it is the *Visitation*. In what is possibly the most beautiful of all the panels, the Virgin wears a blue robe thrown back to reveal a sumptuous dress of gold. *Elizabeth* has a yellow-diapered white dress and a rich dark-red cloak, caught at the neck with a brooch. To the right of this, the shepherds visit the Babe. They make music while a nurse warms the swaddling clothes by a fire and Joseph (looking a little fed-up admittedly!) is huddled in a tub chair. An angel lifts the thatch to let the Star

Norwich, St Peter Mancroft

shine in. The panel on the extreme right of the second row is an arresting composition on the massacre of the Holy Innocents. The faces are calm but the action brutal. It may have been the artist's commentary on the contemporary affluence of the city when he chose to show all the subsidiary figures in the Passion story (third row from the bottom) as richly dressed civilians, The fourth row from the bottom is part of a life of St Peter, and his blue robe distinguishes all the panels. The lovely nave roof has its *hammer-beams* concealed behind vaulting springing from tall *wallposts* which rest on stone *corbels*, each with its differing head. Below the e. window, the great *reredos* is work of the 1880s, but *Sir Ninian Comper* added the seated Christ in Glory, and Saints *Augustine, Columba, Felix*, and *Alban* in 1930. The badly defaced *seven sacrament font* stands under a rare form of C15 canopy.

Only the posts are original, but on them can still be seen traces of the original decoration. The tapestry dated 1573, hanging on the wall behind the font, may possibly have been an Easter altar frontal. Note that it shows Christ appearing to Mary in the guise of a gardener. St Peter Mancroft has long been famous for its bells and ringers. The first true peal was rung in this tower by John Garthon and 'The Norwich Scholars' in 1715. The Articles of their Benefit Society hang near the font. In 1707 the renowned Renatus Harris installed an organ on a *gallery* at the w. end of the church, where it remained until 1866 before being moved to the e. end. In 1984, the installation of a new organ in the same position completely transformed the w. end. Built by Peter Collins, it has an entirely mechanical action (unlike most modern instruments) and is voiced and constructed in the baroque style of the C18. With a weight of ten tons, it is cantilevered out on a gallery, with the ranks of shining pipes in their handsome case rising in steps in front of the ringer's gallery. Happily, the new arrangement does not mask the glowing glass by Andrew Anderson in the top lights of the w. window on the theme of Bach's 'Sleepers awake!' in which angels bear down the tower's thirteen bells. *Sir Thomas Browne (d.1682)* the famous physician and author, was a parishioner and his memorial is on the s. wall of the sanctuary – a beautifully restrained design, with fine lettering and crisp detailing. Below, a stone marks the spot where his skull was re-interred in 1922, having been removed to the Norfolk and Norwich Hospital in 1840. His wife Dorothy outlived him three years only, and her body, 'the prison of a bright celestiall mind, too spacious to be longer here confin'd', lies opposite across the chancel, under a monument some few degrees less severe than his. The handsome oak early-C18 organ case at the e. end of the s. aisle was originally in front of the tower arch, but it was banished from the church in the C19. When it was rescued from a country house in 1911, a portrait of the then vicar's daughter in the guise of a cherub was substituted for the original clock. The painting was by the vicar's father-in-law, Sir William Richmond, who also produced the large and somewhat consumptive 'Moses on Pisgah' which hangs nearby. In 1982 the St Nicholas chapel in the n. transept was transformed into what is possibly the finest treasury in any parish church and contains riches from the heritage of the past that have for long been stored away and seldom seen. There is the magnificent C12

copy of St Paul's Epistles, probably illuminated by the monks of Durham, and the superb C16 cup given by Sir Peter Gleane in 1633. Paintings, books, alabaster, silver, but best of all perhaps among the many treasures, is the panel of C15 glass which was originally in the e. window but removed with six others to Felbrigg Hall in 1837. One of a series of the *Assumption of the Virgin*, it offers a rare opportunity to study the quality of medieval *Norwich glass* painting at close quarters. The church has an excellent ring of 14 bells, tenor 37-3-15 cwt.

Norwich, St Stephen (15): The C14 s. doorway and n. *porch* survive from an earlier building, and the porch has a *groined* roof with a good *boss* of the stoning of *Stephen*. Here too is the memorial to a long-serving *parish clerk*:

> Underneath this stone doth John
>   Rookwood lay
> Waiting the Mercy of the Judgement Day
> His Life was such that he deserves these
>   lines
> To recommend his Name to future times.

The tower is an unusual upward extension of the porch and is separated from the church above the level of the n. *aisle* roof. It was remodelled in 1601 and has handsome surface decoration of *flushwork* window shapes, roundels and diamonds. The rest of the church has a strong unity of design although the *chancel*, completed in 1522, was some thirty years in advance of the rest. The last of the great series of Norwich churches to be built, it is a self-confident restatement of the themes of *Perpendicular* architecture – post-*Reformation* in fact but pre-Reformation in spirit. From the w. end, the interior vista is untrammelled by *screens*. The heavily moulded arches stand on octagonal *piers* with deeply concave faces, and above them a mighty range of sixteen three-*light clerestory* windows stretches from end to end under a *hammer-beam* roof – everything combining to draw the eye forward. The e. window is a colourful but confused medley of stained glass. There are five large C16 panels from a German monastery – the second from the left is a fine St *Christopher*. For the rest, faces, figures, and animals jostle with each other with abandon. A Jew counts the thirty pieces of silver here, a man leads a packhorse there. Many of the windows were blown out during the war and some good modern glass has been put in. A Nativity in the n. *transept* and a Resurrection theme in the s. aisle are particularly good – both by Alfred Wilkinson. They contrast well with a *Kempe* window in the s. aisle of St *Stephen* wearing a splendid brocaded cloak. The great C16 rebuilding was largely the work of the vicar of the day, Dr Thomas Cappe (d.1545) and his *brass* is in the chancel. Brasses to members of the Brasyer family, bell-founders and mayors of the city are to be found both in the chancel and at the w. end of the church. The earliest and most interesting brass is hidden under a small trapdoor at the e. end of the n. aisle. It portrays the last prioress of Campsey in Suffolk, Elenor Buttry (d.1546), and at her feet crouch two delightful old bedesmen, clasping their crutches and saying their rosaries against a background of rough grass and flowers. There are many fine mural tablets but undoubtedly the best here – if not in the city – is to Charles and Mary Mackerell (1747) by *John Ivory* who worked with such good effect both in Norwich and the county. It is a beautifully proportioned essay in pale cream and grey marble; an elegantly lettered panel is framed with acanthus and egg-and-dart mouldings, with a broken *pediment* and the family arms complete with crossed mackerel crest. The three cherub heads below have features of decidedly Norfolk cast. Devotees of Coade stone may be dying to see the monument to Elizabeth Coppin (d.1872) in the s. aisle, but it's an unlovely mud-coloured thing. An awkward *putto* hides his face in a pudgy hand – and no wonder! The extensive development of the Chapelfield complex involved an access through St Stephen's churchyard and there were some plaintive cries from those who do not realise that thousands of our forbears lie strewn across the city under our feet. Nevertheless, it was an understandable reaction, but I think the church has quietly benefited. A path now passes directly under the w. face of the tower and, because the old w. entrance has been replaced with a splendid plate-glass door, passers-by cannot be unaware of the lovely things inside, even if they take no advantage of the opportunity to explore. There are plans to make the interior even more attractive and, as St Stephen's was the last of a great series of medieval churches to be built in the city, that is something everyone should welcome.

Old Buckenham, All Saints (G6): This quaint little church is distinguished by a completely octagonal tower and by thatched *nave* and *chancel*. The tower is C14 *Decorated*, with four sides at belfry level pierced by big plain openings, the others by *flushwork* window outlines in flint and stone, with 'Y' traceries. There is a later red-brick battlemented parapet; a large *cusped-lancet* shaped *sound-hole* in the w. face; a most attrative w. window with *reticulated* tracery, and all the way down the corners of the octagon are pretty little stone shafts punctuated by delicate shaft rings. The n. *aisle* has large *Perpendicular* windows all round: but also a simple *Norman* n. doorway, with carved mouldings to arch and *capitals*. Over the door, and on all the aisle buttresses, are carved shields, and crowned initials of saints. The chancel – of the Decorated period, like the tower – has 'Y' traceried windows to n. and s. The e. end is a complete (Victorian?) replacement in red brick with an e. window of unfortunate 'concrete stone' which nonetheless faithfully mirrors with its intersecting tracery the early-C14 spirit of the rest of the chancel. Notice, on the s. side, the *priest's door*, with its *drip mould* of pink *Tudor* bricks. An air of yellow-washed, Victorian calm pervades the interior. The nave roof is plain plastered, that of the chancel modern barrell-panelled; only the n. aisle has its original timbers – simple *arch-braced*, with pierced carvings in the *spandrels*, and 'battlemented' *wall plates*. The C15, octagonal font, in the aisle has shields and *quatrefoils* round the bowl, under which is an octet of remarkably ugly little carved faces, all looking mildly disgusted with their five-century lot. Nearby is a plain wooden *bier*, with drop arms, and dated 1666. At the e. end, the base of an old *screen* has been added to with no great flair, to form a partition for a vestry. Attractive late-C14 four-bay *arcade* with quatrefoil *pillars*. The filled in outline of the entrance to the *rood stair* is in the n.e. corner of the nave. The chancel, with its 'Y' traceried windows all around in their deep embrasures, has some notable benchends, carved with *poppy-heads* and a small crowd of seated humans, plus a *griffin* and what just could be a lion with a scroll. In the chancel s. wall by the priest's door, there is a little wall pedestal with a hole right through it which was used as a bracket to hold the *Lenten Veil*. The 1897 glass in the window behind the pulpit – St *James the Great*, St *Andrew* and the Virgin – is by *Kempe*. All the glass in the tracery above, and in the tracery of the window immediately to the right, is C15-C16 – a varied collection of angels, saints, heraldic shields and other remnants. Over the tower arch is a faded Hanoverian *Royal Arms*.

Ormsby, St Margaret (K4): The church has a good-looking tower with stepped battlements and a nice *base course*. There has been much heavy restoration, but the solid *Norman* doorway with its four friezes of *billets* and zig-zags indicates the building's true age. In the *chancel*'s. side the C14 *piscina* and *sedilia* group nicely under arches with fine *headstops*, and there is an ornate tomb of the same period on the n. side which doubtless served as an *Easter Sepulchre*. A similar recess was moved to the e. wall of the new n. *aisle* in 1867. There is a *brass* effigy of Sir Rober Clare (d.1529) on the n. side of the sanctuary, and another half figure of Alice Clare (d.1538) has now been laid in the floor of the *nave* at the s.e. corner. Parts of a brass to Robert Clare (d.1446) are mounted on a board in the chancel. Glass of the 1920s and 1930s in the chancel by *Hardman* and *Clayton & Bell* shows how style and taste were changing, moving towards the modernist interpretation in the n. aisle w. window by Stammers of York, 1964. The Lacon mausoleum n. of the church looms like a wartime bunker, surmounted by an uncompromising cross.

Ormsby, St Michael (K4): A small compact church, obviously cherished. The C14 tower and much of the rest of the exterior was restored not long ago, and most of the windows have been renewed. The thatched *nave* has a good *arch-braced roof*. The C13 octagonal font has a ring of *Purbeck marble* shafts. Recent additions include a thatched and glazed s. *porch* and the arms of Elizabeth II. The *chancel* windows have glass by *Henry Holiday* spanning 1898-1920 on the themes of Faith, Hope and Love, and are very pleasing. There are good wall tablets to members of the local Upcher family in the chancel: 'Memory... the most sacred tablet on which departed worth can be recorded'. Outside, don't miss the line of C18/early-C19 head-stones by the path to the *priest's door*. They have carved tops with cherubs and ships, and some affecting verses.

Oulton, St Peter & St Paul (H3): A quiet and isolated little church. It had n. and s. chapels halfway down the diminutive *nave*, but only the arches now remain. On the wall opposite the door, a cheeky-looking fish is all that remains of a St *Christopher* painting. As with many minor churches of little apparent interest, there is still something to catch one's eye; this time, it is a little *brass* in the nave floor:

Here laye Edmund Bell
An Katherin his wife
Who thirty six yeares
Did live man and wife

Thay had three sonns
An daughters three
Farwill our freinds all in
Heaven we hope to see (1636)

The church has an excellent ring of 6 bells, tenor 10-3-0 cwt.

Outwell, St Clement (B5): A large and impressive *Perpendicular* Fenland church, where the style overlays earlier work. The square tower, with plain parapet and *crocketted* corner pinnacles, is partly mid-C13 *Early English* (up to the height of the octagonal brick and stone turret stair tacked onto the s. side), with a C14 *Decorated* top, characterised by bell openings with *reticulated* tracery. Crowning all, an C18 pyramidal cap. The big w. window is a bold Perpendicular insert, and at one with the character of the rest of the building from the flamboyantly confident *clerestory* (huge *gargoyles*, and a range of five *Tudor* windows with a fine variety of *headstops* to the *drip moulds*); spacious n. *transept*; *nave aisles*; and *chancel* aisles and chancel, all with enormous e. windows, though that of the chancel is Victorian. There is a panelled *base course* all round aisles and chancel and their buttresses which adds a handsome finishing touch. Immediately w. of the s. *porch* is a good mid-C14 window with flowing tracery – a survivor from the earlier building. The two-storey porch is fairly plain, save that inside it has a *groined* roof, with brick vaulting. A spacious interior, flooded with light. Big, dark Perpendicular roof to the nave, with carved *tie-beams,* braces and *wall posts* (the latter sitting on excellent stone-carved *corbels*), with little spread-winged angels all along the tie-beams and *wall plates*. Early-C14 nave *arcade* of five bays. Very high up, just under the w. gable of the roof, look for the *sanctus bell opening*. Entry to the tower stair was formerly by a little doorway, now filled in, in the w. wall of the s. aisle. An exterior door in the stair turret outside the tower now serves – though the bells have long been unringable. In the corner of the s. aisle is a C17 poorman's box, big and square and mounted on a carved column of timber, like an old fashioned gaslamp, and with large 'bobbles' on the top. Dismal faces carved in relief on two sides have their mouths open, through which coins were dropped. Above, the aisle's small-scale *arch-braced* and *hammer-beamed roof* of the early C16, which has a gallery of faces carved on its hammers on the n. side, and an array of angels on the other. Sections of wall plate which have survived are lushly carved and there is a fiery sun with a face. In the s. chapel, a C14 tomb recess has beautiful stone carving – fronds, floral motifs and tiny faces adorning rich cusping. Here too is a handsome table tomb for Nycholas de Beaupre, 1511, who 'maried Margaret one of the davghters and Heires of Thomas Ffodryngaye Esqvier' – a marble tablet, opulently carved, is set into the back of the monument. Half a century later, Edmund, son of Nycholas and Margaret, died, and a very similar tablet was added on top of his parents' tomb. The elegant wrought iron gates to this chapel are C18. The n. chancel chapel, now a vestry, has a roof with densely moulded beams whose *wall posts* sit on corbels carved with angels – one of them with the arms of John Fincham, who built the chapel shortly before his death in 1527. Some good C15 glass here. There is a *piscina* in s.e. corner. Diagonally opposite, a *Tudor* doorway, with bold *headstops*. This leads though to the splendid little n. chapel, with its compact hammer-beamed and arch-braced roof, carved with angels on the hammers. The wall posts carry shields on which are carved the *Instruments of the Passion*. On the wall to the l. of the archway into this chapel is a *brass* to Richard Quadryng, 1511, who is shown in full armour. Fine brass eagle lectern on a wooden base, late-C15; and a big, plain C15 font.

Overstrand, St Martin (I1): A rather confused mixture of rebuilding and restoration. The roof of the original church collapsed in the C18 and the *nave* was partitioned, leaving the e. end and *chancel* to decay. Then in 1859 a small church (Christ Church) was built on the site, and this was in use until summer congregations outgrew it. In 1911 the old building was restored/rebuilt and enlarged. We now have the original C15 tower and nave; a new n. *aisle* and chancel; and the old n. *porch* moved over to the s. side. The original n. doorway remains in position and makes a nice surprise as you come across it. There is an old *wafer oven* in the base of the tower. Buried here is Sir Thomas Fowell Buxton, who composed the long verse epitaph for his son John (d.1830, aged 16) to be seen in the n. aisle.

Ovington, St John The Evangelist (F5): There is no *porch* to shield the *Norman* s. doorway from the elements and it is badly eroded. It has a small *holy water stoup* to one side, and a *mass dial* has been incised on the right hand *capital*. The *nave* has a mixture of window styles from small Norman *lancet* to *Perpendicular*, but the *chancel* has 'Y' tracery. Note that there is a break in the wall line half way along the chancel – so

there was probably a Norman *apse* before the rebuilding of about 1300. At one time, there was a series of plaster panels on the outside walls that carried *consecration crosses*, but now only two can be identified – one on the s. *chancel* wall and one below the w. window. The n. door is blocked, there was another on that side in the chancel, and there are traces of an exterior *rood stair* turret. The C14 font is a highly individual design, and was discarded from Watton for some reason when that church was enlarged. The bowl is carved from a single block of stone, and large *Symbols of the Evangelists* protrude on four sides. It has a reeded stem but no base, and the effect is top-heavy. The tall *arch-braced roof* is plastered down to the *wall plate* in between the principals. The sanctuary has been raised so that the simple *piscina* and *sedilia* are nearly at floor level. The e. wall has restored and re-coloured panels from a medieval *screen*, and the altar itself is enhanced by a small *reredos* excellently carved to match.

Oxborough, St John Evangelist (D5): The church is hard by Oxborough Hall, one of the most beautiful National Trust properties in the region and no excuse is needed to recommend a visit to both. Tragically, the tower with its lofty spire collapsed in 1948, bringing with it the *nave* roof and most of the s. side. Thus, the *chancel* became the church and is now prefaced by a grassy forecourt and ruins that have created their own particular beauty. The n. *aisle arch-braced roof* with traceried *spandrels* is intact, as are all the unglazed windows on that side, the n. *porch*, the n. *arcade*, and the s. aisle wall. New w. walls to the chancel and Bedingfeld chapel complete the picture. Apart from the slightly earlier porch and w. window of the n. aisle, the building was *Perpendicular*, and the *piscina* and *sedilia* are remarkably good. Floral motifs stud the square moulded frame and the piscina arch, and small half-angels range along the top – all with traces of colour; the backs of the sedilia are panelled with blind tracery under a shallow coving, and there is the stump of a stone *credence shelf*. The lectern now stands in the sanctuary and is outstanding. Made in East Anglia at the end of the C15, it was given by Rector Thomas Kyppyng, and the inscription on the flange halfway up the stems asks us to pray for his soul. The eagle has lost his claws (like the one at Snettisham), and the heavy turned base rests on three very squat lions who lift their heads enquiringly. The maker sent lecterns like this far afield – to Newcastle and to Urbino Cathedral in Italy. *Blomefield's* 'History of Norfolk' is the

Oxborough, St John Evangelist: Bedingfeld chapel

bedrock of local studies, but the honours should at least be shared with Charles Parkyn, whose memorial is on the n. wall. He died in 1765, having been rector here for forty years, and was responsible for more than half of the survey that Blomefield's early death left uncompleted. Opposite, a great terracotta tomb divides the chancel from the Bedingfeld chapel – which now has its own entrance in the courtyard (key from the Hall Administrator). Descendants of this great Catholic family still live at the Hall, and in her will of 1513, Margaret Bedingfeld directed that her body be buried before the image of the *Trinity*, 'where I will a chapel to be erected'. Two earlier windows were incorporated but the rest have the flattened arches of the late Perpendicular style, and virtually no tracery. The two terracotta tombs are the finest of their type in England, and Margaret's is combined with an arched entrance to form a western *screen*, while the other lies under a double-sided canopy betwixt chapel and chancel. The work is probably Flemish and wholly *Renaissance* in character; the tomb chests are decorated with *pilasters* and arched panels, and above the crested canopies triangular motifs are supported by crude but lively cherubs clasping dolphins; above, a series of heavily decorated bow-fronted drums rise as a superstructure. The e. window is all but blocked completely by the monument to Sir Henry Bedingfeld (1704) and his two wives – black *touchstone* within an alabaster acanthus leaf frame, with swags, scrolls, *pediment* and three shields; the winged skull below sports a bizarre wreath of bays. When the young Elizabeth was imprisoned by her step-sister Queen Mary during the short Catholic supremacy, Sir Henry Bedingfeld, as Governor of the Tower, was her jailer, and it is interesting that, when he died in 1583 a staunch Catholic, he was content to be buried here according to the Anglican rite. His memorial inscription is surrounded by large gilt fetterlocks (horse hobbles) – a badge used not only by the Bedingfelds but by the House of York. Opposite, yet more Henry Bedingfelds – of 1657 and 1684, combined in one memorial, erected in the early C18 when it was quite safe to be fulsome about their loyalty, virtues, and sufferings in the *Stuart* cause. As a footnote, if you are seeking the fine *rood screen* that used to stand in the chancel arch, it may be found in E. Dereham church.

Oxnead, St Michael (I3): The church is approached by an estate road and lies close to the last great house of the *Pastons*, Oxnead Hall. The *lancet* in the ruined n. chapel, the base of the tower and the s. door point to a C13 origin, but the building is now a hybrid, with late-C16 brick e. gable, n. *porch* and top of the tower. The C18 s. porch is also brick with cement rendering. The *chancel* holds all the fascination. Here are the *Paston* monuments – well restored under Stanley Wearing in 1956 with the aid of the Pilgrim Trust. Sir Clement Paston built Oxnead and died in 1597. His sumptuous alabaster tomb chest is in the n.e. corner; a calm bearded figure in full armour, resting upon a thick rush mat which is rolled to support his head. Except for the hands, the effigy is perfect and still has traces of colour. Below him, his wife Alice kneels. As befits a widow she was all in black and died in 1608. Her ruff frames a grave and lovely face with high cheekbones. The floor in front has her *brass* inscription, 'who for great hospitallitie and bountie to the poore was the honor of her country'. Sir Clement, whom 'Henry VIII called his champion, Protector Somerset his soldier, Queen Mary her seaman and Queen Elizabeth her father' has a long epitaph which is worth the reading. Forty years on we have Lady Katherine, daughter of the Earl of Lindsey and wife to the fourth Sir William Paston. A large monument by *Nicholas Stone* who, although he did much work for the *Pastons* as well as the Coke monuments at Tittleshall, is not at his best here. It is a rather characterless bust with little expression in the smooth face. Perhaps that was a true reading, but on twin tablets her husband extols her virtues in Latin and English in measured periods, 'that future Ages might from it collect / Her matchless merit and his true respect'.

Paston, St Margaret (J2): An almost exclusively C14 building, presenting a lovely range of windows in several *Decorated* period styles, from Y-tracery to a lovely four-*light* e. window. The *porch* is C15, and beyond it a rather gaunt interior, accentuated by the darkly discoloured roof of the *nave* with its C14 scissor-braced beams. On the n. wall are some contemporary wall paintings (uncovered in 1922) including a 12ft. tall St *Christopher*; further on, vague skeletons are all that remain of a *Three Living and Three Dead* sequence; and finally, remnants of what could be a Scourging of Christ. There's a *Royal Arms* of 1831, over the filled-in tower arch; a C14 battered, iron-bound chest; and an octagonal C14 font carved with plain arcading. By the organ stands a lovely old carved reading desk, topped with *poppy-heads*; the first pew on the s. side is splendidly carved with the *Paston Family* coat and crest; and on the n. side, sixth pew from the front, note the devil with his tongue out. The C15 *rood screen* has been much restored – and much varnished. Behind the pulpit the entrance to the *rood stair* is exposed. Paston family monuments dominate the *chancel*, notably the enormous confection (which cost at the time a staggering £340) in black, white and pink-flushed alabasters, with pillars, arches, a coroneted skull and mourning figures 'to the reviving memory' of Dame Katherine Paston, 1628: the Dame, sumptuously dressed, reclines with her right elbow propped on a tasselled cushion, looking composed and amiable and indeed, 'expecting a joyful resurrection'. Next to it, by the same sculptor, *Nicholas Stone*, is the monument to the Dame's widower, Sir Edmund Paston, 1632. There are two more tombs to Pastons, abutting into the sanctuary, one of them squeezed into the triple *sedilia*, adjoining which is a good *piscina*, with a *credence shelf* and its drain mounted onto a neat little pillar. In front of the altar, the figure of Erasmus Paston, 1538 (father of Sir William, founder of the grammar school at North Walsham) is all that remains of the *brass* to himself and his wife. Either side of the e. window, there are lovely slim *jamb* shafts topped by exquisite little C13 foliage *capitals*. The *communion rails*, with their little *balusters* and dumpy posts, were put together in 1843 from the staircase of a 'great house' somewhere in Norfolk. The church has a good ring of 6 bells, tenor 11-3-3 cwt.

Pentney, St Mary Magdalen (D4): *Carstone* is much in evidence here, particularly in the *chancel*, and under the eves on the n. side, a band of it with small stones embedded in the mortar. The tower has 'Y' tracery of about 1300 in the bell openings, big *gargoyles* under the parapet, and another moved down to jut out just above the *Perpendicular* w. window. The late-C13 chancel has a line of four *lancets* in the n. wall and a fine e. window with geometric tracery – not all that common in Norfolk. From the outside, one has the impression that this is a C13 church updated with later Perpendicular windows on the s. side, but once inside, the time-scale alters immediately. Parts of a *Norman* blank *arcade* are preserved in the walls of the *nave*, and to the left of the door there is a deeply splayed Norman lancet. Beyond it to the w., both nave walls break back and show where the w. end of the original

church lay. It will have been very small, and the arcading will have been within its chancel. A new long chancel was then added to the e. and the nave extended to meet the new tower. Another fragment of Norman work is the column now to be seen in the embrasure of the square-headed window in the s. wall. By the pulpit, a fine grotesque face under an image bracket, and note that the narrow Perpendicular window in the chancel has a very low *transom* – a sign that the bottom half is likely to have been used as a *low side window*. There is a big *piscina* niche under a *trefoil* arch, plain *dropped sill sedilia* alongside, and a large *aumbry* on the n. side of the sanctuary. By it, on the e. wall is a neat tablet under a broken *pediment,* by Eldridge of Kings Lynn, for Ann Lancaster. During a general redecoration in 1999, an important late-C13 or early-C14 wall decoration was uncovered on the e. wall. It darkened rapidly and by its nature it could not be preserved, however, details were recorded. Designs typical of the period in a band of deep crimson stretched across the entire width of the chancel. Two beautiful *consecration crosses* formed part of the whole, and because their outlines were scribed on the surface, they have been preserved; fragments of their dusky red and pale cream colour remain, set out with a compass in a familiar design based on a 12in. circle. The two crosses are exceptionally large, and a third in slightly poorer condition was uncovered on the chancel s. wall. For their period they are the best in the country. The churchyard is of no more than average interest until one remembers that here in 1980 a gravedigger uncovered what is known as the Pentney Hoard – six fabulous *Anglo-Saxon* brooches now to be seen in the British Museum.

Plumstead, St Michael (H2): Nice late-C15 *Decorated* tower, with neatly contrasted *flint-knapped* and panelled battlements, with badly eroded pinnacles and *gargoyles*. The only carving to be seen in this simple church, and very agreeable too, is the *flushwork* panelling at the base of the tower. Body of the church fairly shrieks 'over-restoration', with its ugly *nave* window tracery dating from a general restoration of 1873. A s. nave *aisle* became ruinous in the C18, was demolished and the line of the *arcade* filled in. But inside, the arcade is still there in outline, very simple *Perpendicular*. For some reason the *clerestory* above was blocked in too. Plain C14 font with good modern cover. Nearby, a *Stuart* table, formerly the altar. In the 1300 *chancel*, remnants of a small *Easter Sepulchre*, now crudely coloured; tiny coats of arms to either side are interesting – replicas of ones formerly in the church of the Plumstede family, Lords of the Manor here for 300 years up to the early C17. To right of altar, heavily restored *piscina* and outline of *dropped sill window*. There are C15 glass fragments from Norwich in the e. window, the best being lower centre, St *Agnes*; and C16 Dutch in s. windows, including a lovely smug angel, levitating.

Poringland, All Saints (I5): A distinctive church of instant character, not least in its e. gable end facing the busy main road, with its large figure niches, completed with beautifully *cusped* and carved heads, above and to either side of the lovely *Decorated* period window. Note too the strange little grotesque figures carved at the roof line on either side of the gable: one animal – with teeth!! – the other of human face. The *chancel* is all Decorated, though it has been suggested that the e. end was built before the horror of the *Black Death* of 1349 and the rest finished afterwards. In any event, it looks unified and good, with its confidently traceried n. and s. windows, all of a piece with their four-*quatrefoil* tracery heads. The *nave* is later and *Perpendicular*, with big plain windows, and the unusual element of a *clerestory* above without there ever having been *aisles* below. Moreover, these two-*light* windows, though dating from about 1400 or a little later, have simple 'Y' tracery, a style popular just a hundred years earlier. Expert opinion is that the use of brick, rather than stone, dictated this simple approach. Moving clockwise round the exterior of the church: Victorian red-brick *porch*; round tower with *Norman* base and C14 octagonal top (let into the lower w. face is a small window of C13 character); n. porch, cleverly converted to serve as a passage-way and cloakroom into a new vestry/meeting room extension in an octagonal shape. Inside the church, the wide *nave* is full of light, reflecting off the white walls and the pale, 'scrubbed look' timbers of the handsome medieval roof – *arch-braced* with *king posts*, plus carved *hammer-beams*, and *wall plates* with deep *wall posts* thrusting down between the clerestory windows. Modern pews, with some old *poppy-head* benchends re-used. Most interesting font, C14, early Perpendicular and octagonal in shape: carved in the panels of its bowl are, facing the tower, two angels with shields and, clockwise, a huge flower; *the Evangelistic Symbols* of Eagle (John), Lion (Mark) and Ox (Luke); another flower; and another winged lion, supplanting the fourth evangelistic symbol of winged Man (Matthew). The pedestal

of the font is supported by a quartet of remarkably smug-looking little lions. By the s. door, large plain niche of *holy water stoup*. Notice that the large s. window in the nave thrusts up into the clerestory – a later addition in a church which from mid-C14 to mid-C15 can hardly have been without building and changes going on. Now through to the chancel, with its lovely old 18-branch brass candelabra suspended at its centre, and a good *piscina* to right of altar. The focus of interest here however is the fine and ancient stained glass, particularly in the e. window: centre panel, a Risen Christ wearing a blue robe and showing His Wounds; to left the Virgin, bearing a scroll in Latin (Hail Mary full of Grace, the Lord be with you); and right *John the Baptist*, the two being set in canopies. In the tracery above are the various *Instruments of the Passion* – in the left quatrefoil, cross, spear, scourge, nail, sponge; right quatrefoil, Christ's tunic ringed with pieces of silver; and immediately above, the ladder and dice.

Postwick, All Saints (I5): *Chancel* of the C13; *nave* with *Decorated* and *Perpendicular* windows, but whose original fabric seems to be earlier; and a good Decorated tower with *flushwork* around both base and battlements, make up this calm, simple village church. Chief feature here is the windows of the nave: s. side has a lovely C14 Decorated example whose 'flowing' tracery, even if rather stiff (a local mason doing his best?) is most attractive, with next to it a super Perpendicular example with battlemented *transoms* dividing the tracery. This one is twinned by another opposite, where there is also another Decorated window with tracery of elegant *reticulated* shapes. Though the chancel fabric is C13 *Early English*, its side windows are later and the e., Perpendicular. Set into the base of the window at the s.w. corner is a *low side window*, complete with shutters. Inside the church, where all is beautifully cared for, the hand of a restoration of 1866 lies heavy, not least in the 'Victorian Early English' chancel arch and the 'false' tower arch, whose columns have been plonked straight onto *ledger-stones*, as has the C14 font (Decorated, octagonal, crisply carved). In chancel, a good double *piscina*, of text-book C13 pattern – though its authenticity is open to question; *aumbry* opposite with modern door. In nave, lavish Victorian stone pulpit inset with chips of coloured stone brought back from the Dead Sea by the rector of that time, Sir William Vincent. In tower, a stained glass window and enormous wall brass to the 4th Earl of Rosebery, (d.1868), whose family were closely associated with Postwick. The tower contains a most interesting clock mechanism, recently described by one expert as about 300 years old and similar in date and mechanism to one at Dover Castle.

Potter Heigham, St Nicholas (K4): One of the nicest Broadland churches. The C12 round tower has a C14 embattled octagonal top which is superior to most in the county. All the roofs are thatched, and the six late-C15 *clerestory* windows are sumptuous for a church of this size. The combination of flint and pale pink brick around them is strikingly good. Local bricks are very much a feature here; not only do they figure in the s. *porch*, but the C15 font is made of them. It stands solidly on two steps, and the rare roller pulley that used to support its cover can still be seen in the fine *hammer-beam roof* above. The *rood screen* is of high quality. Although the heads of the figures are defaced, the panels are rich in the original red and gold. The third panel from the right depicts St *Eligius*, patron saint of farriers, holding his claw-hammer emblem. Above, the *rood beam* survives, and behind the modern crucifix the outlines of the original rood group of figures can be seen. There are many traces of medieval wall paintings, but only the *Seven Works of Mercy* in the s. *aisle* can now be understood with any ease. The *chancel* has a well restored set of *Laudian communion rails*, and in the floor a stone recalls 17 members of the White family, 'lovers of ye church, Loyal to their Prince, True to their Words'.

Pulham Market, St Mary Magdalen (H7): A very good looking church in a big lime-bordered churchyard just beyond the village green. The four-stage C15 tower is well proportioned and has a particularly fine w. front – *flushwork base course* and buttresses, and a main door and window composition that is linked to the whole by a combined window label/*drip course*; each side of the door, small *crocketted* and pinnacled niches with that rarity – their original figures within. (Another example of this at Ditchingham, near Bungay.) The w. door has floral motifs and crowns in the *hood mould* and large *Tudor* roses in the *spandrels*. The n. *porch* lives up to this: the whole face is flushwork and there are three niches above the door, which again has a band of flowers. This porch can be accurately dated from the 1540s will of John Intewode who gave twenty shillings to the making of it, but notice that the upper room came a little later – the floor cuts into the tracery

of the lower windows and the upper surface decoration is less elaborate. Unusually, a n. *aisle* was then added, using the e. face of the porch as its w. wall. The s. aisle is earlier in date and this is borne out by the slight variations between the n. and s. *arcades*. The roofs of the aisles are of differing levels too, and they vary in design. That of the n. aisle has tracery in the spandrels of the arch-braces, and the s. aisle has big flowered *bosses* and angels above the arcades and aisle windows. The roof of the *nave* is big and impressive, with flat arch-braces and *collar beams*. At the e. end, a single-bay *canopy-of-honour* for the *rood* which stood below. All the colour was heavily overpainted in 1873 but it is a lovely design of feathery angels with trumpets and *censers*, 'M's and *IHS* sacred monograms. There was a big restoration here in 1873 and the *chancel* arch was heightened. The painting of the Ascension over it was done in 1895. In 1913 parts of the old *screen* were made up with much new work and set in the tower arch. Pulpit and font came in 1873 along with most of the windows; the chancel and sanctuary were raised, making the *piscina* a mite inconvenient for all but dwarfs. The new stalls in the chancel incorporate medieval bench ends with headless figures on the arms. The one on the right by the step looks as if it may have been a *chrysom child* laid on a stool for burial, and its counterpart is a penitent kneeling before a priest. Nice to see a pair of *Camden Society* candelabra in the sanctuary – in the reaction against the Victorians, thousands must have been turned out. The outstanding glass in the e. window was designed by *Henry Holiday*, and the womens' tresses show the beginning of the *Pre-Raphaelite* style that was to flower in the next decade. In the s. aisle e. window the 1890s glass is very individual – a restful blend of brown and olive shades with a grainy texture. Some medieval glass has been re-set in the n. aisle w. window; an early-C15 head of the Virgin or St *Catherine* on the left and to the right a good C14 head of the Virgin from an *Annunciation* scene; below, two C15 heads of saints and an 'M' for the patron saint. The 1873 work uncovered a *banner-stave locker* in the s.w. corner of the church and this now has a door and is in use again for housing the processional cross. The church has an excellent ring of 8 bells, tenor 13-1-22 cwt.

Pulham St Mary, St Mary the Virgin (I7): The big churchyard is somewhat higher than the village street behind a screen of trees, and the long approach gives an opportunity to

Pulham St Mary, St Mary: S. porch

Pulham St Mary, St Mary: C13 piscina

savour the quality of the C15 tower. Tall as it is, it once had a spire as well, but now the proportions seem to be just right. The big buttresses have six *set-offs*, and there is a niche set in the one at the s.w. corner. Take time to study the early-C15 *porch* before going in – it is one of the most lavish examples in Norfolk and the facade is a beauty. There is a deep *flushwork base course*, and over the double niches either side of the door, a dainty frieze of angels play trumpets and lutes. The *spandrels* are carved with the *Annunciation* scene and in the range of shields above, the two in the centre are held by angels – the *Trinity* emblem, and a clear representation of the *Instruments of the Passion*. There is a broad centre niche, and this has a pinnacled canopy, as do the windows and niches either side, making a complete range across the frontage. The cresting of the pierced and embellished *quatrefoils* is punctuated by shafts on which a fine variety of creatures sit – look particularly for the wolf guarding St *Edmund's* head on the w. side, and the *woodwose* sitting comfortably cross legged on the apex with a club on his shoulder. The side walls are finished in flushwork panelling and the buttresses have plinths for yet more figures on the *set-offs* – truly a porch that was meant to be noticed! Inside, an early-C15 *arcade* and a fine sturdy *arch-braced roof* to the s. *aisle*, with heavily moulded main beams, tracery in the *spandrels* and lacy

flower *bosses*. There was a full scale restoration in 1886 superintended by G.F. Bodley, and all the evidence is of work well done. The tower arch was opened, w. *gallery* removed, and the highly individual staircase to the ringing chamber was probably inserted then. The *nave* roof is largely original but a new vestry was supplied, plus oddments like pulpit and reading desk. More significantly, Bodley designed a fine altar frontal chest and a new top for the C15 *rood screen*, and this is first class. The double range of filigree *cusping* in the arches is reminiscent of the fragments at Attleborough and all the woodwork is picked out in pale red, green and gold. There were thirteen painted saints in the panels and some can still be recognised by their emblems: 3rd from left St *Jude*, 4th St *Simon*, 5th St *James the Great*; right of opening: 1st St *Andrew*, 2nd St *John*, 4th St *James the Less*. The *chancel* arch has two sets of mortices marking the original position of the *screen*. The C13 chancel has a lovely contemporary *piscina* – the triple roll mouldings of a semi-circular arch are neatly intersected by those of two half-arches, the whole resting on three slim columns. The chancel roof looks original and was effectively tricked out by Bodley in red, green and black. There is a double *aumbry* in the n. wall, and beyond that, there was once a chapel (see the piscina in the wall outside). A storm in 1817 blew out part of the e. window and it now has a range of C19 glass (by Burlison and Grylls?) which is rather pleasing – the colour restrained and confined mainly to the robes; the New Testament scenes are easily recognised and have a quite individual quality. In the nave, some interesting C14 glass in the head of the centre window on the n. side – two rows of *Apostles*; top row left to right: SS. *James the Great, John, Peter,* Andrew, *Thomas, James the Less* (who has a young head); 2nd row left to right: SS. *Philip, Bartholomew, Matthew, Jude, Simon* and *Matthias*. At the top of the window further e., a C14 figure of Christ with hand raised in blessing, and two angels in the side tracery. (For all this medieval glass, binoculars are a great help.) In front of the screen there is a most interesting wooden lectern, set on a modern shaft and base. Found in the porch chamber a few years ago, it is a post-*Reformation* eagle very like the one at Redenhall with the same scrolls running from the beak to the tips of the wings, but in this case gilded overall. The bench ends in the nave are an attractive design, with a cresting round the arm rests and flared buttresses – a pity that all but two of the carved figures have long gone. The

Ranworth, St Helen: Rood screen

panelled backs of the westernmost pews are the right size and shape to have come from the front of the *rood loft* gallery, bearing in mind that the benches were originally backless. The font is highly decorative and gives a very good idea of the richness of the medieval original. It is alleged to have been protected by plaster and that Bodley only restored it, but the sharpness and style of at least some of the carving speaks strongly of new work. If so, never mind – the work was well done. The church has a ring of 8 bells, tenor 14 cwt.

Quidenham, St Andrew (G7): A picturesque little church, in a variety of styles. The round tower is *Anglo-Saxon,* with blocked round windows half way up, and with a sparkling octagonal *Perpendicular* upper section, topped overall by a shingled spire of the same period. There's an early *Norman* n. doorway, plain save for some tiny floral motifs on the *capitals;* good *Decorated* window traceries in the *chancel* (the e. window has been remodelled) picked out on the s. with delicate fluted shafts on the window *jambs;* also on s. side, a C14 *priest's door*. The *porch* is C14 too, with a C13 inner doorway – as is the w. window in the Victorian s. *aisle*. The s. aisle buttresses are inset with emblems in *flushwork, IHS,* the *Instruments of the Passion*, and a crowned 'M' for the Virgin. Inside, rather dark with all the church's Victorian glass, but still inviting. The roofs are modern, the s. aisle and *arcade* Victorian. But both *chancel* and *nave* are mid-C14. The tower arch, tall and plain, is Norman.

Above it, a fine set of *Stuart Royal Arms*. The dark wooden *screen* is part of an Elizabethan chancel screen. Attached to one of the rear pews, an early-C17 Poorbox, with three locks, matching that at nearby Wilby. The chancel, with its beautiful *Early English* arch, is splendid, its windows delicately outlined by pencil-slim shafts down the jambs. A stone frieze at window-sill level takes in an unusual triangular hood over the *priest's door,* and tops the good-looking *piscina* and triple *sedilia,* which in turn match the large arched figure niches on either side of the e. window. Built into the n. wall of the sanctuary are three short Saxon pillars, said to have once supported a font. Adjacent is an *aumbry* recess, with a decorative head carved from one piece of stone. Some fine wall monuments of the C17 and C18. The church has a ring of 8 bells, tenor 15-0-14 cwt.

Rackheath, All Saints (I4): Leased to the *Norfolk Churches Trust*, this pretty church, all alone in the fields, is now cleaned up, alive again and open for occasional services, as a place of meditation and the venue for activities diverse as a Japanese tea ceremony and children's art exhibitions. Largely early-C14 *Decorated*. The *aisle* roof is pitched so that, oddly, it cuts in half the small *quatrefoil, clerestory* windows. Inside, a charming C13 *arcade*. Interesting memorials to Sir Horatio Pettus (1746) by the Norwich sculptor *J. C. Chapling*; and to another Sir Horatio (by *Thos. Rawlins,* of Norwich) who married the granddaughter of a famous Dean of Norwich, Dean Prideaux; the baronetcy died with him in 1772.

Ranworth, St Helen (J4): Although there was a previous church on this site (see the fragment of a *Norman* arch re-set in a buttress on the s. side), the present building dates from the late C14 – early C15. The tower has a chequered *base course*, *sound-holes*, panelled battlements, and a fine view of Ranworth Broad from the top. The church is justly famous for its *screen* of c.1450. A report of the Society of Antiquaries says:

> The magnificent painted *Rood Screen* and
> *reredoses* of the nave altars form a
> composition which is unequalled by any
> now existing in a district famous for its
> screens. As a whole, it may be said that
> there is nothing of the sort remaining to
> equal it in England.

The vaulting and base of the loft are in situ, and there are twelve panels with painted saints below. On either side, the nave altars have their own *reredoses* with saints, and there are side partitions, again with figures in the panels, surmounted by delicate flying buttresses. The quality of the work is not to be equalled in the county, and the restoration by Miss Plummer and her assistants (completed in 1975) has revealed even more. In particular, neither the debonair and fantastical St Michael nor the gorgeous embroidery of the female saints' dresses should be overlooked. A rare Cantor's desk stands before the screen, and may have been used in the *rood loft* itself. It has a versicle of plainsong painted on the front, and the eagle of St *John* on the back carries the first words of the Evangelist's Gospel on a scroll. Some of the stalls have simple *misericords*, and there are the remains of a wooden *Easter Sepulchre* on the n. side of the sanctuary. The C17 *communion rails* are tall and very pleasing. In a case by the door is the exquisite manuscript Antiphoner of 1400 (see *Antiphonal Lectern*). Illuminated by the monks of Langley Abbey, it disappeared in 1552, and by 1852 was part of the collection of Henry Huth (Victorian merchant banker and bibliophile). Recognised in a bookshop in 1912 as belonging to Ranworth, it was happily brought home, and here it is on view, a priceless treasure to delight the eye. The church has a good ring of 6 bells, tenor 12 cwt.

Raveningham, St Andrew (J6): The church lies well within the park, and a path between low iron railings curves round between the grazing pasture and the gardens, giving occasional views of the warm red brick frontage of the Hall. An

Raveningham, St Andrew:
S. door and Major Hodge's memorial

overall cement rendering has given the church a cold hard character even on a sunny day. The round *Norman* tower has an early-C14 octagonal belfry stage with a capping of quite elaborate battlements. Negotiate two sets of iron gates in the *porch* and one set of double doors and you come to a splendid main s. door with three great wrought iron C13 crosses on its outer face. Immediately to the left inside is a large cube monument in marble with an urn on top; it commemorates Major Edmund Hodge of the 7th Hussars who fell at Genappe in the battle of Waterloo. The font is in the familiar local style, with saints and *Evangelistic Symbols* alternating in the panels of the bowl, lions squatting round the stem. (Take care in proceeding up the *nave* – there is a deep step down that catches the unwary roof-gazer!) The *chancel* is most interesting. On the s. side there is a large early-C14 recess which might be the founder's tomb except that one would expect it to be on the other side. Its steep arch is so lavishly *cusped* and *crocketted* that the whole thing seems to writhe with foliage. This piece has been taken as a theme for the decoration of the rest of the chancel and a series of similar arches frame memorials to the Bacon family of Norfolk – the premier baronetcy of England – whose seat is nearby. Note, however, that there are differences. The demi-figures on the n. side are all fat-faced characters reminiscent of the cartoon figures of Rowlandson, and link up with the 1820 date of the earliest memorial there; those on the s. are stiff and sharp conventional Victoriana. There is a very good *brass* at the w. end of the chancel to Margaret Castyll (d.1483). Wife of one of Richard Ill's squires, she is shown with a dragon at her feet for her patron saint and a little dog with bells on its collar hides in the skirts of her gown. Just across from this stone is another which uses the local pronunciation for the village – 'Raningham' 1648, and there's another slab to look for in the n. *aisle*; 'Here lieth the body of William Pearse gent. Aged 34 years he Dyed on the 22nd of June 1681 And left 3 childering William, Edmund and Mary'. 'Childering' is a variant of the Middle English 'childer' and this is a very late example of its use. The church has a good ring of 5 bells, tenor 8 cwt.

Redenhall, The Assumption of the Blessed Virgin Mary (I7): The name of the parish is Redenhall with Harleston and Wortwell, and in terms of the everyday it is in quite the wrong order – Harleston the small town, Wortwell the growing village, Redenhall but a few scattered houses. When it comes to churches the sequence fits – big, small, none. Once the centre of the parish, with 600 communicants in the C16, Redenhall is certainly big. In a land of small and often hidden churches, its tower shows up from miles away and it is the tower that dominates. Come up the slope from the road, and it looms over you, magnificently assured in its solidity and lavish in its adornment. It is a measure of its quality and consequent cost that it took sixty years to finish, with completion marked on the s.e. pinnacle by the *rebus* of Richard Skelton, rector in 1518. The big '1616' on the n. face serves only to date the bracing that was put in when it was struck by lightning. The w. facade is completely covered with a pattern of *flushwork*, from the pinnacles and elaborate battlements down to the big *base course*, in which the rose badge of the Brothertons alternates with the leopard of John de la Pole of Wingfield Castle in Suffolk. There are big canopied niches either side of the w. doors, on which are carved horseshoes, a hammer and pincers – possible evidence that a farriers' *guild* gave them. The n. *porch* rivals the tower, with its whole face covered with flushwork. The centre niche has a neat pair of small windows each side, and *holy water stoups* flank the entrance. The *aisle* windows match the

Redenhall: The Assumption of the Blessed Virgin Mary

tower and so does the lovely *clerestory* – another of those 'glass walls' with eight close-set windows each side, and the gable is crowned with a tall *sanctus bell turret*. Both s. door and *chancel* remain from the earlier C14 building, and going inside you see that the *arcades* date from then too. After the outside, the interior is faintly lowering – perhaps because of the pale tan walls and because entry is underneath a heavy C19 w. organ *gallery*. The *hammer-beam roof* has tracery in the *spandrels* and rests on an interesting variety of *corbel* heads – some are angels and one is a double eagle. The font is a good C19 copy and on the w. wall by the gallery, a version of a common epitaph:

Death
Behold thy Selfe by me,
Such one was I as thou;
And thou in time shall be
Even dust as I am now.

This is intriguing, because the churchwardens' accounts of 1711 refer to re-framing the 'death sentence' and it hung near the chancel *screen* in those days with a skull overhead – obviously a local late survival of an ancient custom. The lectern of about 1500 catches the eye immediately, and what a beauty it is! Double headed eagles are rare, and this one probably came to the church from a college of priests, although there is an alternative tradition that it was dredged from the moat of Gawdy Hall not far away. It is 6ft. tall, standing on three Assyrian-looking lion feet, with that lovely buttery texture that brass acquires when it has been polished and scoured for centuries. The eagles' beaks are open and there is a blocked slot in the tail, which has prompted the suggestion that alms were collected in it. The church's other lectern is in the chancel and is equally interesting. This time of wood (*Cautley* describes it as 'post-*Reformation*', i.e. later than 1540), the flat eagle holds scrolls in his beak and stands on a big, turned shaft. The battered feet may have been toads – a common symbol of evil to be overcome by the Word. If you carefully lift the carpet by the lectern you will find the memorial of John Rand, his wife Anne and daughter Elizabeth. He died in 1659 and was the 'late painfull (i.e. painstaking) preacher of the gospel at Rednall cum Harleston':

> Three temples of the Holy ghost
> Ruin'd by death ly here as lost.
> St John's fell first, St Ann's next year,
> Then St Elizabeth fell here.
> Yet a few dayes and thes again,
> Christ will rebuild and in them Reigne.

The chancel was restored in 1864 and the *reredos* and panelling came in 1897. The whole of the screen was built afresh in 1920 to frame the panels of its medieval predecessor, but unfortunately the paintings of the *Apostles* were frantically overpainted and much of their original character blurred. They are, from right to left: St *Simon*, St *Matthew*, St *Philip*, St *Thomas*, St *James the Great*, St *John*, St *James the Less*, St *Andrew*, St *Paul*, St *Bartholomew*, St *Jude*, and St *Peter*. Between the chancel and the Gawdy chapel to the n. is the tomb of Sir Thomas Gawdy (1588), Justice of the Queen's Bench. Plain, with uncharged shields, it has a helm on a bracket above. The low modern screen of the Gawdy chapel has two very attractive tortoises (the family crest) carved on the posts, and close by is a very interesting Venetian chest. Supposed to have housed vestments at Gawdy Hall, it came here in 1922; cypress wood, with a rare painting inside the lid of two ships and two galliasses (galleon with sail and oars) with coloured flags and sails, plus two angels, and *IHS* sacred monogram, a dragon and a bird – a re-use of panels designed for something else. The front of the chest is covered with intricate chip carving. The chapel has much heraldic glass – also from the demolished Gawdy Hall, and a pallid reredos of 1788 by J. Francis Moore is a memorial to the

Wogan family. There is an excellent tablet by Thomas Singleton, of Bury St Edmund's, at the e. end of the s. aisle to Simon Kerrich (1748). The church has an excellent ring of 8 bells, tenor 22-2-20 cwt.

Reedham, St John Baptist (K5): On the 19th March, 1981, disaster struck this fine church and it was gutted by fire, leaving only the tower and the bare walls standing. Undeterred, and refusing to move to a new site in the village, the community rallied round to such effect that it was rebuilt and in use within just over a year – a magnificent example of dogged faith and purpose. The village has drawn away from the church much as the sea has retreated from the village. The Romans had a lighthouse here, and while walking round you will see masses of their tiles embedded in the walls – strong evidence that they were active here. St *Felix*, Bishop of Dunwich founded a church at Reedham in the C7 and so the village has one of the longest established Christian traditions in Norfolk. The main structure dates from c.1300, but the nicely proportioned tower was built in 1447 and Margaret Paston records in one of her letters (see *Paston Family* in glossary) that she had given 8s. 4d. in thankfulness for childhood memories of Reedham. Enter by the n. *porch* and just inside there is a plaque in memory of Peter Ashley Miller (d.1997), the churchwarden instrumental in the great rebuilding, and beyond the inner door one finds an almost dazzling interior, with limewashed walls and excellent new furniture designed by John Barnard of Norwich. It is curious at first sight because the *arcade* that once separated *nave* from s. *aisle* was taken out long ago, but the s. aisle chapel of St *Helen* remains, so that you see two big arches side by side under a single roof with, in effect, two *chancels* beyond. At the e. end of the nave n. wall a large section of the original wall has been stripped of plaster to reveal a great swathe of ancient tiles and bricks in *herring-bone* patterns dating from the early C11, and the half shape of an arch in brick suggests that there was a n. *transept* at one stage. The chancel proper has two bays of blank ardcading in the n. wall and beyond them, an early-C14 door to the vestry under an attractive *ogee* arch. New choir stalls and reading desks in ash match the low and comfortable benches in the nave. St Helen's chapel was enlarged (see the additional arch) to become the chapel of the Berney family, and although Elizabeth Berney's *brass* that lay in the sanctuary floor was a victim of the fire, Henry and Alice Berney's fine tomb survived against the s. wall, with its odd mixture of forms – a *Tudor* arch over the recess, flanked by classical columns and topped by shields of arms within a purely Gothic ogee frame. He died in 1584 and the family kneel conventionally in bas relief, five sons behind him and four daughters behind her. All the glass in the e. windows was designed and made by Sarah Bristow of Norwich in a combination of colours designed to link the twin themes of Christ and St *John the Baptist*. On closer inspection you will see that the lower section of each window displays an engraved map – the village and its locality in the chancel and the Holy Land in the chapel. The church's own font was lost in the fire and the replacement came from redundant St Michael-at-Coslany in Norwich – a compact and rather nice late-C14 piece with *quatrefoils* in the bowl panels and clustered columns round the shaft. Above the s. door hangs a pretty set of Hanoverian *Royal Arms*, and the rebuilding provided a chance to reinstate the s. porch in the form of a cloakroom and meeting room. All the woodwork at the w. end of the nave is in limed oak, and below the ringer's gallery within the tower there is now a village history display and a parish lending library. Before leaving, take time to find the mermaid *headstop* on the outside arch of the *priest's door* and the *mass dial* on one of the buttresses on that side. Lastly, go down the path towards the graveyard extension and find the grave of Richard Pottle on the left He lived out his 108 years here, dying in 1840, and the stone was 'erected by those who, knowing his worth, supported him in his declining years'. The church has a good ring of 6 bells, tenor 8 cwt.

Reepham & Whitwell, St Mary & St Michael (H3): There are a number of cases where two churches stand in one churchyard, but Reepham is unique in having three, although Hackford church has been ruined since the C16, and only a portion of wall remains. St Michael's, Whitwell, is westernmost, nearest the marketplace. It has a good C14 tower, with finely proportioned buttresses and a delicately traceried parapet. The rest of the exterior has been unsympathetically restored and the interior, with the exception of an outstanding C17 pulpit, has little of interest. The *chancel* of St Michael's joins on to the s.w. corner of St Mary's, Reepham, and there is a connecting door. Entrance is via a s. *porch* which stands rather eccentrically w. of the s. tower. At the w. end, a square C13 *Purbeck marble* font and nearby, a fragment of a *churchyard cross*, with figures set beneath the arms. The tower door

Reepham, St Mary & St Michael: Kerdiston tomb

has elaborate C15 ironwork, and by the door into St Michael's is a fine set of James I *Royal Arms* in carved relief. In the centre of the chancel is a large *brass* to Sir William Kerdiston (d.1391) and his wife. His effigy has lost one and a half legs and much of the canopy has gone, but what remains is of high quality. The memorable feature of this church, however, is the tomb of Sir Roger de Kerdiston (d.1337) in the n.e. corner of the chancel. The large mailed figure lies on a bed of cobbles, possibly of some allegorical significance. One hand is on his sword, and his feet rest on a very plump and very large lion. Apart from a chipped nose, the effigy is in near-perfect state, and is set beneath a tall and elaborate canopy. Below it, the eight small weepers still have nicely varied attitudes and dress despite their mutilation. This is a fitting memorial to one who, to judge by his church at Ewerby in Lincolnshire, was a distinguished patron of architects. The church has an excellent ring of 8 bells, tenor 8-3-22 cwt.

Repps, St Peter (K4): Originally the church had the more usual dedication to both St Peter and St Paul. The round *Norman* tower has a pleasing C13 octagonal top stage. The two-*light* bell openings are linked with bays of matching *blind arcading*. Apart from the C18 brick *chancel*, five restorations in the last twenty years of the C19 have left their mark and little else. One of them uncovered a *stoup* by the door and a pedestal and a niche by the *rood loft* stairs, but all is smoothed and cement rendered. At the w. end by the wall is a C11 or C12 coffin lid. The worn, slightly coved top has a large plain cross, with a shield beneath one of the arms, and traces of scroll work above. There are three C15 label *brasses* in the *nave*. The C15 font is octagonal with simple decoration, and parts of the *rood screen* remain. The stairs that led to the loft lie behind the deal door in the s. side.

Reymerston, St Peter (G5): A delight on a sunny summer morning to approach this attractive village church through its close passageway of trees leading to the gate, and to be greeted by doves cooing from the C13 tower – a dating underlined by the 'Y' traceried belfry windows, and by the *lancets* in the w. face. The parapet, with its red-brick insets, was added in 1714. The body of the church is largely *Perpendicular* in character – though notice the fine n. *aisle* e. window and its w. window, both being late-C13 *Early English* merging into *Decorated*, and also the flowing stonework in the *chancel* n. window, which suggests mid-Cl4 *reticulated*. The chancel e. window is unlovely Victorian, in a heavy-handed Decorated idiom. From earlier in the C13 comes the n. doorway, a *Transitional* example of *Norman* into Early English, with slim pillars, a barely pointed arch, and traditional zig-zag moulding. Inside, the church is spacious and light, the *nave* having a fine yet simple C15 *arch-braced roof*, framing a delightful little *clerestory* of the same date – see how the centre windows have been given an extra-wide *mullion* to make way for a *wall post*. The *aisles* have solidly honest roof timbers, with the centre wall post on the n. resting on a most oddly carved *corbel*, curiously childish and naive. The *nave arcades*, of four bays, are C13, but still present something of a puzzle. The pillars on the n. side are all round, with generously leaf-carved *capitals*; on the opposite side, only one pillar fits this description, another is octagonal, with a simple 'cushioned' capital, and another is round, with a totally plain capital. Good octagonal C15 font, the richly carved bowl showing the *Symbols of the Evangelists*, alternating with prophets, the latter with opulent hair-dos which wouldn't disgrace a *Restoration* fop; floral carvings around the stem of the font, but at its feet, only one of its four little guardian lions remaining and looking ever-so-important about it. Nearby, a neat *Jacobean* poorbox attached to one of the nave's solid, unpretentious pews with

their flat-carved *poppy-heads* – probably C17. In the aisles are rows of C18 *box pews*, complementing the imposing C17 *three-decker pulpit*, which is complete with its *tester* and backboard. The chancel is graced by *communion rails* of quite astonishing opulence, carved in wood with scenes and figures, flowers, fruit and frills, and even St *James's scallop-shell*. The rails are said to have come from a Flemish convent, and to date from about 1700. Also Flemish is the C16 glass above the e. window, bold in line and colour, and representing St *John the Evangelist* with chalice (but no dragon or serpent!), Christ, and St *Peter* with his keys. Above the sanctuary, a rather fine marble wall monument to Robert Long, 1688, with a wordy Latin epitaph. Nearby, irresistible Victorian 'Gothicky' choir stalls. The church has an excellent ring of 6 bells, tenor 7 cwt.

Riddlesworth, St Peter (F7): A fairly long approach drive to the Hall (now a school), and the church is just beyond on left. The C14 tower abuts the lane and because of this, it has two tall doorways n. and s. to allow processions to circle the church without leaving consecrated ground. There is a niche above one of them, and small *trefoil sound-holes* further up. From inside you will see that the present *nave* has taken in the old *chancel* half way along there is a break back in the line of the walls and the *rood stairs* is behind glass on the s. side. There was a full scale rebuilding in 1855 and the present chancel is all modern. The C14 font is a plain and massive octagon with slightly canted sides on a stubby shaft – the cover is *Jacobean*. On the w. wall, a set of *Royal Arms* that came from ruined Knettishall church in 1933 – a crude but lively piece of work, and the original 1632 for Charles I shows through the 1666 that was painted on for Charles II. Knettishall also provided the tall Jacobean pulpit, which has a range of *blind arcades* and a *tester* with turned pendants. There is a reading desk to match, and some panelling from the same source made up into pews. The two painted panels of St *Edmund* and St *Peter* which form part of the modern *reredos* apparently also came from Knettishall, but they have been so thoroughly repainted in a modern idiom that no one would identify them as medieval – except that a little cross-shaped *elevation squint* is cut in St Edmund's halo – a sure sign that they were once part of a chancel *screen*. A fine set of *communion rails* here, with wide moulded top rail and barley sugar *balusters*. While in the chancel, note the two modern *cartouches* on the n. wall –

the one for William Needham Longdon Champion (1939) has a horse's head and two sheep's heads in the scrolls. The slabs in the floor at the e. end of the nave tell the sad story of two ladies who were killed in bed by the collapse of a chimney stack in a storm of 1703. Dame Elinor Drury, and:

> the Pious and Virtuous Mrs Mary Fisher whose soul tooke her flight to heaven in ye Furious hurricane on November ye 27th 1703. This Monument is Dedicated by her true & Faithfull lover Anthony Drury of Mendham in Norfolk, Gent.

There is a little showpiece of a monument high on the n. wall of the nave. Sir Drue Drury died in 1617 at the age of 99, and had seen stirring times. As Governor of the Tower of London he had guarded Mary Queen of Scots before her execution in 1587, and he was Gentleman Usher to Queen Elizabeth. It is a very compact memorial – his armed figure kneels at a desk within a recess; there is a cherub head above him, and two lively and rather wayward looking angels draw back the curtains.

Ridlington, St Peter (J2): A good-looking early *Perpendicular* tower with a pronounced 'cobbly' look to its flint work; topping its corners, in place of pinnacles, are the four *Evangelistic Symbols*: but these, like the tracery of the bell openings, are much ravaged by wind and weather. Though the body of the church is mainly of C15 date, most of its windows are replacements, with plain intersecting tracery (wooden, and not pretty, in one n. window!), including of course the e. window where the whole end wall has been rebuilt in red brick. The n. door to *nave*, and nice *priest's door* on *chancels*, side, are both *Decorated*. On n. side of chancel, what looks like a *low side window*. Inside, a charmingly simple village church, with harmonium and gas lights; modern roof and fittings; upper entrance to *rood loft* outlined to left of small, trim chancel arch; C13 octagonal font of the local variety – arcading carved on bowl panels, with modern stem and cover. The chancel has an old and sturdy *arch-braced roof*; an attractively clumsy *piscina* and adjoining *dropped sill sedilia*. There is a particularly large *holy water stoup* by the main door.

Ringland, St Peter (H4): The setting is so attractive that *Munro Cautley* chose an Albert Ribbans watercolour of the church for the dust jacket of his 'Norfolk Churches' (1949). The

Ringland, St Peter: The musical centaur

tower is basically C13 but has early-C14 bell openings, and later *flushwork* battlements which are stepped and which once had pinnacles. The e. windows of the *aisles* are new work, and the e. window of the C14 *chancel* has been renewed. The whole front of the *porch* is faced with dressed white flints, there are angels in the outer arch *spandrels*, and a deep flushwork *base course*. Notice that the blocked window over the chancel arch is not like the *clerestory* windows – the tracery pattern is earlier and there is a single *quatrefoil* window by the n. door for no apparent reason. Put these facts together, and there is the possibility that the original clerestory was a range of quatrefoils, one of which was saved to use again. The temptation now is to rush in and admire the roof with binoculars – and why not, for this is one of the most perfect small-scale roofs anywhere. It could be called St Peter Mancroft's younger sister, for the construction is the same – *hammer-beams* that are concealed behind ribbed coving, with small demi-angels resting against them. The *wall posts* are long, and above, a deep cornice of double quatrefoils rises nearly half way up the *arch-braces*. At all the main timber intersections there are feathery flower *bosses*. Mancroft, with its magnificence and daring, commands our admiration, but Ringland roof – so small, so compact, is simply and inevitably beautiful. Above the C14 *arcades*, the clerestory windows fill all the space between the wall posts, and those on the n. side have panels of fine C15 glass, probably of the 1460s. Although they have been moved from other windows, it is not often that so many full-scale figures are found undisturbed in a Norfolk church. From w. to e.: two male and one female donors; the

Ringland, St Peter: Nave roof

Annunciation (Unfortunately the Virgin has a split across the face, but notice the pot for her lily emblem, and see how Gabriel next door has both blue and red wings, feathery armour, and wields a sceptre.); the *Trinity* (the face of God is missing, Christ on the Cross displaying His bleeding wounds, with the Dove of the Spirit above); a male donor in deep blue robe; the Virgin and Child, a female donor at her feet; St *John the Baptist*; two male donors. The detail everywhere is good, and the faces are full of character. Still on the subject of glass, cross to the s. *aisle* and admire the little roundel of a centaur playing a viol, with his tail sprouting leaves and his dog gambolling between the hooves, in the easternmost window. He might have sprung straight from the margin of a C14 manuscript. There are *hatchments* above the n. and s. doors, and access to the tower is via a small door – heavily banded with iron (perhaps it was used as a treasury). The C14 font has lions against the stem, and the *Evangelistic Symbols* interspersed with angels and rosettes in the panels of the bowl. The chancel arch has the look of a complete reconstruction, and after standing at the w. end for some years the base of the *rood screen* has now been returned to its original position. The painted panels have been defaced, but some of the saints can be identified; from l. to r.: St *Jude*, St *John* (?), St *Andrew*, St *Peter*, St *Barbara* (?), St *James the Great*, St *Thomas*, St *James the Less*. A further single panel hangs on the wall of the n. aisle and bears the figure of St *Philip*. Some original bench ends have been made up into choir stalls, and the early-C17 *communion rails*, with their big acorn finals now front the aisle pews. Look out for Isabella Le Neve's epitaph in the sanctuary floor (1759), and the stone to young Frances Haidy (1777) in the *nave*.

Ringstead, St Andrew (D1): A pretty church up on a knoll, surrounded by its village. The church is much restored. The tower, topped with a lead spirelet, looks to be C13/C14, but has been rebuilt on the w. and s. faces in red brick. The n. *aisle*, added in 1865, has a large and unattractive e. window. The n. door has good head *corbels*. *Put-log holes* are a feature in the wall here. The s. door is of about 1300. The interior is unpretentious; modern *nave* roof, chancel likewise but coloured most effectively. The tower arch is tall and slender, and behind the modern stone pulpit is a tall figure niche under a worn canopy with floral carvings; nearby, a deeply recessed *piscina*, with an eight-leaf drain. Through the C14 arch into the chancel, where

there is a sumptuous angle piscina, with *ogee arches*, floral *finials,* human *corbel* heads to each side. Adjoining are *dropped sill sedilia.* In the window above, the glass is by Frederick Preedy, with St *Andrew* holding this church in his left hand, and in his right the church of St Peter, Ringstead Magna, which was pulled down in 1771. (See Hunstanton, St Mary for more of his work). Opposite, a tiny and beautifully shaped C13 *priest's door*; and on the s. side, a *low side window*. In the centre of the chancel floor is a good *brass* to a priest, Roger Kegall, 1482, who, according to the inscription, 'wholly made to rise up' the chancel roof.

Rockland All Saints, All Saints (F6): Far from its village in a sea of arable fields, with only the fragmented skeleton of the tower of ruinous Rockland St *Andrew* church across the lane for company. Very plain late-C13 tower, with a C14 *Decorated* upper section; pretty little *sound-holes*; a large lancet w. window and – unusually for a smallish tower of this period – a w. door below (now blocked in). The e. window is C19. The *nave* and *chancel* windows may be C14/C15. Be that as it may, the foundation fabric of this church is *Anglo-Saxon*, notice the *long and short work* in the *quoins* of the nave at all four corners; and low in its s. wall, some *herring-bone* work in flints. The tiny C14 *porch* shelters a s. door within, both of utmost simplicity and grace, and with each side deep splays narrowing to miniscule *quatrefoil* windows. Notice too the ancient coffin slab under your feet as you go in. The interior, despite much restoration and renewal, has considerable charm and character. The church is lit throughout by splendid oil lamps suspended from the nave roof, by others fixed to the walls, and by candelabra in the chancel, on lectern and the 1903 pulpit – large, octagonal and well carved in natural oak. Furnishings are modern, with the exception of a few *poppy-heads*, the top rail of the *communion rails* and the chest by the chancel arch. The desk beside the chest is made up from discarded pew timbers. The e. window and its painted surround, the stone *reredos,* the *double piscina* and the chancel arch, are all C19, as is the little round window in the s. wall of sanctuary. The stained glass in the e. window is again Victorian, but well worth a close look – it is full of people of real character, clustered round a preaching Christ, with a beautiful landscape vista stretching away behind them: much more like an oil painting of the period than glass painting. 1880s font, but against the n. door is the square bowl of its *Norman* predecessor, which was found in a garden in the village. The Saxon sepulchral slab which lies against the chancel n. wall was found, in two separate pieces, during restoration work in 1860. When the two were brought together, it was found that they fitted, with circular crosses at each end, connected by plait-work carving. Except that now, it will be seen that the carving at the centre has been smoothed away to make room for the initials 'I.M.'. This important Saxon piece was re-used as a gravestone for J. Mansfield at a time when archaeology and historical awareness were less regarded than in our own time. The church has a good ring of 5 bells, tenor 6-3-0 cwt.

Rockland St Mary, St Mary (J5): A neat little place with its pencil-slim tower, set in a churchyard as orderly as a formal garden. Much restored and rebuilt, though its ancient origins may be seen clearly in details like the *lancet* window in the w. face of the tower, with a flowing *ogee* head which in turn has a *dripstone* finished at the top with a *crocket*. The s. doorway is *Decorated*. Inside, all is great simplicity and charm, with plenty of atmosphere. There is a *hatchment* over the tower arch; a Victorian *Royal Arms* under the tower; and a handsome C15 font, with angels with shields in its panels, thoroughly recut. In the sanctuary, a pair of neatly lettered early-C17 *brasses* tell a poignant story: the first is to Robert Cocke, who died, aged 22, on 23rd June, 1638; the second is to his son John, who followed his father four months later on 26th October, no age given, but he could only have been a babe.

Rockland St Peter, St Peter (F6): A picturesque church, in a serene rural setting, with thatched *nave* roof, and a *Norman* round tower with octagonal C14 top, where blank plain arches alternate with pretty two-*light Decorated* windows. Interestingly for a round tower, it has a staircase turret on its s.e. side. Note on the roof-level gable end of the nave a *Tudor rose* and a *scallop-shell* (?). The *porch* is a mixture of stone, flint and soft red brick, with lettered panels, set in the w. face, listing those who rebuilt it in 1624 (the substantial outer arch, late-C13/early-C14, was re-used). Tudor windows to n. and s. of nave. To n. and s. also, a hint of *transepts*, jutting outward only about 3ft, with windows of early Decorated character. On the s.w. *jamb* of the s. transept, at about head height, is a carved *mass dial*. The *chancel* of 1909 replaced one which was already in ruins in 1824. Go inside and stop on the threshold in simple pleasure at what greets

the eye. A tall and dominant *screen*; and down the nave, a lovely display of carved benchends, with *poppy-heads* and a veritable herd of odd animals – a bear wearing a head halter; on the front n. side pew, possibly a winged *griffin*. The screen was brought here in 1950 from Tottington, an abandoned village in the Battle Area. It has a traceried base with a lot of colour remaining, and in the *spandrels* various carved decorative devices: a white rose, a little lion, ferns, an angel, and a lovely bird with pink beak and legs. Above, simple lights with *ogee* arches and gilded *crockets*; and above again, more tracery, which formed the parapet of the *rood loft* to which were added effigies, in 1973, of Christ, the Virgin and St *John*, which came from St Sampson's Church in York. The plain panelled pulpit, which also came from Tottington, is *Jacobean*. The reading desk opposite, with its jolly little 'pony trap' seat – like a three-sided box – may well be comtemporary. In the tiny n. *transept* are the *rood stairs*, the only remaining remnant of which can be seen in the small screen under the tower arch. In the e. wall of the transept, two *piscinas*, one very low; the other with a plain, almost triangular opening. Back to the w. end, note the enormous draw-bar holes, set into the doorway; the massive C14 octagonal font, with traceried bowl and base; and the remains of the *holy water stoup* by the n. door.

Rollesby, St George (K4): The round *Norman* tower has two C14 upper stages rather than one, and the unused s. door of the same date has an exceptional, richly carved arch. A fine *chancel* was added in the C15 with corner pinnacles, topped by heraldic *talbots*. As you pass through the n. *porch*, look for the *Nine Men's Morris* frame incised on the left-hand bench. The *rood loft* stairs s. of the chancel arch have a blocked *squint* which used to pass right through them. In the s.e. corner of the sanctuary is a small arched enclosure which remains a mystery; it may well have housed relics originally. In the n.e. corner lies Rose Claxton, her effigy sumptuously dressed in Elizabethan ruff and embroidered gown, poses uncomfortably on its side. One hand supports her head precariously, the other clutched a prayer book until it was chopped off:

Know Freindly Passenger that this smale roome,
Rose Claxtons bodie onelye doth intombe
Her bewtye love & gracefull modestye
In her freinds hartes shall lyve etarnallye
Her soule redeemd from sinns captivitye
In Heaven lyves crownd wth immortallitye.

Opposite is a good alabaster monument to Leonard Mapes (d.1619) with 14 kneeling figures.

Rougham, St Mary (E3): A pretty situation at the edge of the park with an avenue of huge limes to the w. that led to the old house. The early-C14 tower has a *rood group* in a niche above the w. door – defaced but still beautiful; the deeply moulded *ogee* canopy has intricate *stops,* there are figures in the niches each side, and there is a vine trail within. The w. window has 'Y' tracery of about 1300 and the bell openings are a little later, with varied *Decorated* tracery. The *chancel*, restored in 1876, has a fine set of late *Perpendicular* windows and the n. *aisle*, ruinous by the C17, was entirely rebuilt in 1913. Inside the base of the tower, the original stone *mensa* (see the *consecration crosses*) is clamped against the n. wall and above it, a nicely preserved example of an early-C19 set of commandments, engraved and hand coloured. The *Royal Arms* above the w. door are a complete achievement dated 1739, but could conceivably be a *Stuart* set altered although it is too dark to be sure. By the C14 font is an interesting image bracket – see how the supporting angel holds a little kneeling figure representing the soul on folds of drapery. This is on one of the pillars of the early-C15 *arcade* – remarkably slim like those at Weasenham St Peter, but here there is a band of floral motifs and *ball flowers* round the *capitals* and the arcade runs through without interruption to the end of the chancel. Rougham has some good *brasses* and they display a whole range of costume: by the lectern, one of Edward IV's knights, William Yelverton and his wife Katherine (1481); their seven sons are shown on a separate plate and the inscription has migrated to the s. side of the sanctuary; n. of the altar is another Sir William and his wife Agnes – he was Justice of the King's Bench, executor of Sir John Fastolf, and died in 1472; to the right, a tiny and most interesting brass showing two *chrysom babes* framed in an ogee arch – John and Roger Yelverton who died in 1505 and 1510; on the s. side of the altar, yet another William Yelverton who died in 1586, flanked by his wives Anne and Jane with their children below. Set in the chancel s. wall is a fine C14 wooden panel that may have formed part of a *reredos*; six saints stand in niches, with five smaller figures under *ogee arches* between them. Although the figures have been defaced the work is of high quality. Nearby, the *ledger-stone* of Sir John Bladwell is engraved with the flattering epitaph he

Rougham, St Mary: Sir William Yelverton's brass

composed for himself; apparently the endowment of a vicarage was wishful thinking – it never happened! In the top of a *nave* window are two fine C15 figures, St *Catherine* on the left and St *James the Great* on the right Before leaving the churchyard, have a look at the tombstone s.w. of the tower. At a distance it looks like C18 but you will see that it has an aeroplane carved at the top and is for Thomas Keppel North who had a hand in the design of the machine used by Allcock and Brown in their epic transatlantic flight.

Roughton, St Mary (I2): Stands finely exposed on a ridge above the main road in a big rough grass churchyard. The *Anglo-Saxon* tower is an interesting example, with a lot of the red Norfolk *carstone* laid *herring-bone* fashion, and triangular heads to the belfry windows. The *clerestory* range is nice, with interior shafts rising from bases which have carved heads. There was a n. chapel – the arches can be seen outside in the *chancel* wall, and a plain square-headed *piscina* has been reset below them. The font is not the usual East Anglian type and a number of churches in this area were obviously supplied from the same source; it has eight attached shafts with tracery between and around the bowl, and dates from the late C14.

Roydon (near Diss), St Remigius (G7): A markedly trim and orderly church in an equally well-trimmed churchyard, with a neat line of sentinel conifers from the gate to the *porch*, and a fine old yew standing loftily guardian over the *chancel*. The conifers present a good frame in which to view the n. porch, which is notably embellished. Firstly, it has *flushwork* panelled gables and angle buttresses; an arch carved with floral motifs and standing on slimly elegant rounded pillars with embattled miniature *capitals*. But also it has no less than five figure niches, all with canopies handsomely carved with *crocketted* pinnacles – one over the arch; one to each side; and, most unusually, one in each of the *jambs* of the arch. Round *Norman* tower, the lower section having recently been faced with smooth grey cement, a necessary operation, no doubt, but one which makes it look like a fat industrial chimney. But in marked contrast is the tower's most attractive octagonal top section, with a delightful parapet, battlemented and ornamented with flushwork, *quatrefoils* and shields. Surprisingly it is Victorian – a print just inside the n. door, dated 1857, shows the original low round tower wearing just a conical cap. The aforementioned porch is *Perpendicular,* and the rest of the church of like character, though the general fabric is much earlier. The e. window is a C19 replacement. The s. side of the building looks odd until you realise that, when the Victorians rebuilt the s. *aisle* in 1864, they 'lifted' the pinnacled and crocketted s. porch, built just 24 years earlier, from its position at the w. end – and shifted it to the e. end and incorporated it into their new construction. The arrangement certainly provides an individual outline! The church has a calm, uncluttered interior, distinguished firstly by a beautifully simple, single *hammer-beamed roof*, whose effect is accentuated by the plastered panels between the struts and *purlins* being painted in the palest of blues; and secondly by an *arcade* of intriguing style and origin. The original fabric of this *nave* is Norman; the *arcade* is C13, with plain pointed wall arches and massive square pillars, chamfered off at the corners, each chamfer being topped by a funny little carved face, or with stylised foliage. The arches therefore were pushed through in the C13 for a new aisle – which survived until the Victorians replaced it. Set into the easternmost arcade pillar is a *piscina* with a tall, graceful arch which looks *Early English*. Opposite is the entrance to the old *rood stair*, with a rebuilt doorway. Above it, a beautiful little C15 Perpendicular window, set rather high, which it seems was inserted to light the *rood*. The dark, abundantly carved pulpit is *Jacobean*;

notice too the handsome brass *hour-glass stand* attached to it. The chancel, originally C14 *Decorated*, has been much altered, renewed and restored, but it retains its piscina – under a large, plain moulded arch; and adjoining it, *dropped sill sedilia*. Opposite, a wide, arched recess, low on the n. wall, which presumably once sheltered a tomb. Nearby, half hidden behind a choir stall, is an opening, diagonally into the wall, which looks like a *squint* – an exterior one, as there is no trace of there having been a chapel on that side. As you leave, notice the pretty little niche for a *holy water stoup* by the n. door and in the e. jamb of the door, a large hole in the stone-work for the draw-bar. Over the door, the *Royal Arms* of George I.

Roydon (near Kings Lynn), All Saints (D3):

George Edmund Street was one of the leading architects of the Victorian era, and seldom adopted the *Norman* style for a new building. Here in 1857, however, he chose to do so because there were two original Norman doorways making a peg, so to speak, on which to hang the rest of the design. He left the C14 tower alone save inserting a new 'Y' tracery window. The overall result is not inspiring, but those doorways were well worth preserving. They both have an order of *colonettes* and zig-zag decoration in the arch. Their *capitals* and *hood moulds* differ, and the n. doorway, at least, was entirely rebuilt. The *nave* was given shallow buttresses and round-headed windows, and there is chevron decoration in the arch of the s. *porch* which rests on 'waterleaf' *capitals* – all of 1857. Within, all the details carry through the scheme – *dog-tooth* and roll mouldings in the *chancel* arch, and round arches over the *piscina* and *sedilia*. The font is neo-Norman and so is the pulpit (which is seldom a good idea whoever the architect is). The 1859 glass in the w. window is in the style of *William Wailes* and is good for that date – figures of SS. Peter and John in C13 style; the three *lancets* in the chancel have *Clayton & Bell* glass of 1876 – Crucifixion, Transfiguration and Ascension scenes, with a Nativity above.

Runcton Holme, St James (C5):

An open lane leads down from the road and then a path, bordered by cypresses to the charming C16 red brick *porch* with an arch that leans gently inwards and where a small figure inhabits the niche overhead. The tower is late *Norman*, with small, deeply splayed *lancets* in the ground floor and two-*light* bell openings with centre columns and flanking shafts embellished with rings.

The brick upper stage is later. The *nave* is a mixture of *carstone* and red brick, the *chancel* all brick, and there the windows have been renewed. All the buttresses are brick and in the one by the blocked and formless n. doorway there is a stone *holy water stoup*. The s. entrance doorway, like the tower, is late *Norman* but inside you will see an earlier Norman window above the wide and low tower arch – an indication that the original building had a flat w. front and that the tower must have followed soon after. The chancel arch, too, has Norman responds on which a later arch has been superimposed and there is a blocked lancet of the same period in the nave s. wall. The church was re-roofed and re-pewed in 1842 and it may have been then that it acquired the large and handsome early-C17 pulpit (local tradition asserts that it came from elsewhere). Note that above its familiar blank arches the panels have an unusual interlaced thistle design and that below the *tester* the backboard has dolphin supporters. Through the mutilated and varnished C15 *screen* to a C14 chancel where the roof *corbels* are large and impressive heads, of both men and women. Small *ogee*-headed *piscina*, an *aumbry* in the n. wall, and similar *cartouches* for two C18 clerics, Robert and Henry Jenkin. Of the same period, an affecting epitaph on a *ledger slab* in the centre of the floor for Eleanor Berney, 'Safe from Life on that Eternal Shore'.

Runhall, All Saints (G5): Its ancient round tower, much patched but sturdy, seems to have grown out of its little hilltop at one end of this quiet, straggly village. Its lower part is *Norman* and the upper part *Early English*, raised in the C13. The *chancel* was destroyed by fire in the C16 and never rebuilt (the squire of the day was a Roman Catholic, and used the loss of the a chancel to avoid proscription). A short *nave* is all that is left, stubbled with lichen and ivy. The fabric here is C13, with a n. door-way and 'Y' traceried window of about 1300 Square topped *Tudor* windows on both sides came 200 years later. Over the window on the n. side, below a clumsy topping of brick, stone and flint, is a *dripstone*, hacked into a rough *billet* decoration, which is re-used Norman. The window on the s. side has had its tracery replaced in nasty red brick. Entering via the Early English s. doorway, we find an unchanged rural setting, and time seems to have stood still. The 1871 roof, with wooden pillars and heavy arches, looks like a timber copy of C19 wrought-iron work. The C14 font has its octagonal bowl carved with

quatrefoils and its stem with little quatrefoil arches. Behind it, a door with magnificent ironwork, probably all C13; the s. door, with its venerable old handle, is C13 or C14 too. The niche behind the pulpit, with little roses in the *spandrels* and much original colour was perhaps the *rood stair* entrance. Outside there are remains of a turret, but the two don't align, and the niche is very small for access to a loft. It may merely have been an image niche – there was an altar for St *Catherine* here, and two guilds met in the church.

Rushall, St Mary the Virgin (H7): There is a blocked circular window halfway up the w. face of the recently restored tower that may well point to *Saxon* origin rather than *Norman*. The octagonal top with its plain parapet is C15, and at that time the *nave* was given new windows and the *porch* was added. Going round the outside, you find *mass dials* on the e. *jamb* of the *priest's door* in the s. *chancel* wall and on one of the *quoins* at the s.e. corner. On the n. side there is a late-C14 or early-C15 blocked arch to what was a chapel dedicated to the *Holy Trinity*, and in 1878 there was still a niche in the wall there – possibly the *piscina*. When going in, have a look at the door – it is original and has floral motifs, mitres and 'M's for the dedication. On the jamb of the archway low down on the e. side there is one of those individual 'masons' marks' that medieval craftsmen used to cut on stone that they had shaped. The church has rather a bare interior conditioned by the 1878 restoration. That must not be regretted though, for 150 years earlier everything was in a 'nasty and ruinous condition'. The C13 chancel has two big *lancets* in deep splays where one would normally expect to see three, and there are pairs of lancets to match in the side walls. A plain and sturdy *Stuart* table is still in use as the altar, and to the left, an intriguing prayer desk. The open tracery of the front is beautiful and very lively, and though the shield under the rim bears arms that could be those of the local Groose family, one is inclined to agree with the view that it is Spanish work.

Rushford, St John the Evangelist (F7): Edmund Gonville, founder of Gonville & Caius college, Cambridge, established a College of Canons here in 1342 and built the church. Came the Dissolution (1538) and much of it was pulled down, and by 1600 the building was being used as a barn. Negotiate the undergrowth and you will find the raised hump of the old *chancel* at the e. end, and see the pillars of the original chancel arch either side of the pitiful little *apse* that was tacked on in the C19. After half a century of disuse, the C17 owners of the estate re-established it as a church, and the *porch* was rebuilt to a smaller scale using material from the ruins (There are *corbel* heads in the corners inside from which the original vaulted ceiling would have sprung, and three panels of worn lettering are set over the door). The old *nave* windows had *lancets* inserted with brick mullions at that time. Inside, instead of the expected tower arch to the nave there is only a small door. This has deep slots in the *jambs* and may therefore have been used as a treasury – the only windows are two narrow lancets in the w. face, apart from the *quatrefoil sound-holes* and the bell openings higher up. There was a much higher roof at one time, judging by the line on the tower e. face, and the present thatched roof gives promise of something nice inside. Alas, a heavy flat ceiling cuts into the blank *arcades* of the walls and into the spring of the old *transept* arches. This, with Victorian panelling and stencilling on the walls, and a tall, heavy *screen* of the same vintage imparts a dark brown feeling to everything. The C19 pulpit is sharp and stiff, but the font of the same period was on the way to being rather good – if only the designer had known the sweet virtue of restraint.

Ryston, St Michael (C5): A lovely situation just within the park, with views of the distant golfcourse and the trees that almost hide the Hall, home of the Pratt family since 1528. The top of the tower had been in ruins for 300 years before architect William Lawrie designed his own version in 1858, but the base is *Norman*, as you will see by the arch inside and the deep splays of the small *lancet* windows. A small niche over the outer arch of the C14 *porch* contains a lovely medieval figure of St *Michael* – winged and crowned with cross on breast and sword grounded before him, and below to the right there is a large *scratch dial*. Except for the C14 e. window with its flowing tracery, all the windows are *Perpendicular* – straight headed with varying designs, and the C19 restorations uncovered two *low side windows*, one with a *trefoil* head. At the same time, the porch windows were unblocked – square with pretty tracery and rather like the tower *sound-holes* so often seen further e. in the county. The building is nearly all *carstone* and inside this is emphasised in the window embrasures, where the plaster has been stripped off and the stone painted white. The plain octagonal font could be C14 but, if so, it has been comprehensively re-cut. In the chancel, the

design of the e. window is echoed in the tracery of the *angle piscina* and the sill of the nearby window is dropped to form *sedilia*. Naturally, Pratt family memorials abound and the most imposing is the white marble figure of the Lady Anne (1706) in the sanctuary. She wears an elegantly crumpled gown with lace at neck and cuffs and reclines, rather stiffly, propped on one elbow. Although she married again, she appears here under her first husband's name, although the memorial was provided by husband No. 2. This was perhaps because the earlier marriage was to a man quite famous in his day, the Sir Roger Pratt who lies beneath an austere slab of black marble close by. Architect, protégé of *Inigo Jones*, friend of the diarist John Evelyn, and collaborator with Sir Christopher Wren in the rebuilding of London after the Great Fire, he was knighted for his services by Charles II. He died in 1684 and his epitaph ends: 'Until the Resurrection of the Just, My Bones untoucht will rest I trust'. On the n. wall of the *nave*, a small scale memorial by that prolific sculptor the younger *John Bacon* for Pleasance Pratt (1807); above a rustic arch, graceful young mourners gather at the base of an urn. On the s. wall, a tablet to Col. Henry March Pratt (1919), veteran of the Indian Army, has replicas of his campaign medals including the Mutiny.

Saham Toney, St George (E5): A big, handsome church, largely of the *Decorated* and *Perpendicular* periods, with a tall and imposing Perpendicular tower which was completed in about 1497, after nearly 50 years of building. It has enormous three-*light* belfry windows; big *sound-holes* (four *quatrefoils*, each carved through solid stone and set in a square frame); a great w. window complementing a w. door below it in whose *spandrels* are lively carvings of the church's dedicatory saint; and a series of opulently carved *base course* panels which feature crowned Gs and Ms. On the n. side of the church are good Decorated *reticulated* windows, and above, a *clerestory* range which looks very early Decorated. On the s. the clerestory range provides an interesting contrast with the *plate tracery* of the two s. *aisle* windows; earlier again is the *Early English lancet* at the w. end of the aisle. The *chancel* was largely rebuilt in the mid-C19, but it retains its *priest's door – Norman/Transitional*. To its left is a small *low side window*. The two-story C15 s. *porch*, with inside, a restored canopy over, was a *holy water stoup*. Inside, one disappointment is the plaster *nave* roof on heavy plastered arches. The five-bay *arcades* on their slim round pillars are C13. There are some good old *poppy-head* bench ends, including some funny lion elbow rests. A modest C15 font, topped by a magnificent wooden cover, inscribed and dated 1632: it has eight classical columns supporting a dome, which in turn is crowned by a *pelican*, striking her breast. *Rood stair* entrance in the n. aisle and *rood loft* exit in corner of the nave; below, a C15 'wine glass' pulpit approached by steps whose rails are quite remarkable – 'For the rector to snake up and down', commented *Dr Pevsner* in a rare moment of wry levity. C15 *screen* of delicacy and beauty, regilded in the C19: in the spandrels of the lower panels, don't miss the tiny carvings, which include a bearded bishop, an equally hairy devil with his tongue out, an angel, an eagle, flowers and fronds. In the s. aisle is a C13 *piscina*, and in the adjoining window *jamb*, a beautiful figure niche, cusped and *crocketted*. More old bench ends in the chancel: but the main features here are the matching Perpendicular piscina on the s. and *Easter Sepulchre* on the n., each having elaborate canopies and raised arcading on the back walls. The church has a good ring of 6 bells, tenor 13-3-0 cwt.

Salhouse, All Saints (J4): It seems that a rebuilding was begun here but not completed. The low n. *arcade* has nicely carved *capitals*, of large foliage designs, except one that has heads. The later C15 tower was placed off-centre in anticipation presumably of a larger church, but it was never finished, and goes no higher than the *sound-holes*. The *rood screen* has been restored to the extent that most of it looks new, but judging by its position and method of hanging, the little *sanctus bell* on the top may be original. If so, it is a very rare survival. There is one *misericord* on the s. side of the *chancel*, with a large and fine bearded head, and an *hour-glass stand* is fixed to the pulpit. There are two C12 or C13 grave slabs set in inner w. wall of the tower.

Salle, St Peter & St Paul (H3): Standing almost in open fields, this is a mighty church which draws one back again and again, by virtue of its exceptional interest and great beauty. Historically, it is important because it can be dated very accurately. In the line of shields above the w. door, the third from the right carries the arms of Henry V as Prince of Wales, i.e. 1400-13, and the building of the *transepts* is documented as 1440-1444. The tower has a richly decorated w. door, and there are carved angels with *censers* in the *spandrels*. Above, there are big, intricate

Salle, St Peter & St Paul

sound-holes, and a beautifully traceried and battlemented parapet. Both *porches* have two storeys, individual stair turrets, and *groined* ceilings with *bosses*. The n. porch is particularly grand, and the chapel chamber above has a large window, a *piscina*, and a series of bosses which have been re-coloured. The upper door has a massive bar which drops into slots when turned by the centre handle. (Virtually all the doors in the church are original.) The main parish footpath passed close by, and records show that this porch was often used to transact parish business. Entered now by the great w. door, the interior has a memorable ambience of calm and peace. The slender clustered columns of the *arcades* rise to roofs that are superb. The *nave* roof is *arch-braced*, and has angels at all the intersections, while the rafters retain their decoration of sacred monograms and crowned 'M's. *Aisle* roofs have great traceried spandrels, and the *transept* roofs are beautifully panelled. The *chancel* roof of 1440-50 is outstanding, and it is calculated that of the original 276 angels, 159 still remain. Apart from huge flowers at the intersections of the panelling, a line of carvings representing the life of Christ are spaced along the ridge. These have the appearance of bosses, but are actually carved blocks hung from the roof by hooks. Binoculars are helpful here to appreciate the high quality of the wood sculpture. Over the chancel arch can be seen the *corbels* that carried the *rood beam*, and below, the bottom half of the *screen* remains. Figures of four *Apostles* flank the two doors, on which are the *Four Latin Doctors*. The other eight panels apparently carry their original priming paint, and it can be inferred that altars stood before them. The stalls in the chancel have a fine set of *misericords*, and minor carving on the arms is worth studying – animals and birds on the n.

Salle, St Peter & St Paul: Three-decker pulpit

and human heads on the s. The head on the stall nearest the screen doors could well be a portrait of the rector of that time, and certainly Thomas King (rector 1628-57) left his initials on the end of the desk. The pulpit retains the alternating red and green colour scheme common to the whole nave, and is interestingly combined with the *parish clerk's* pew, reading desk, and *tester* given by Lord Knivett in 1611, thus forming a *three-decker*. Under the tower is a ringers' *gallery* which supports a huge bracket, from which the tall font cover is suspended. The fact that the cover has lost the tracery between its sixteen slender buttresses gives it a lightness and delicacy that cannot have been intentional. The font stands on two steps, the lower inscribed:

> Pray for the souls of Thomas Line and...
> his wife and Robert their son chaplain
> and for those whom they are bound to
> pray who caused this font to be made.

The *seven sacraments* round the bowl have a unique addition. Under each can be seen the relevant symbol, carried by an angel. Of the many *brasses*, two at least should be seen: in the nave, that of Geoffrey and Alice Boleyn (1440), and

in the n. transept, that of Thomas Roos (or Rose) and his wife. They stand with their twelve children on a fine bracket which was once part of an elaborate design. Thomas was the donor of the transept in 1440, and his *rebus* (a 'T' enclosing a rose) can be seen in the roof bosses. Note that Thomas wears his hair short. Fashion changed, and his sons' hair is longer and brushed forward, a style that lasted until 1480. The church has a ring of 8 bells, tenor 18 cwt.

Salthouse, St Nicholas (G1): Standing high and grey on its hillside above the village, the church looks down to the open sea. It is a handsome example of late *Perpendicular*, having been built in Henry VII's reign, and completed in 1503, by Sir Henry Heydon (a member of a family powerful hereabouts for around a century, their seat being not far away at Baconsthorpe). The tower is from the earlier church, with *Decorated* bell openings. The *aisle* windows to n. and s. are very tall and narrow, with neat little tracery heads. Inside – light, lofty and impressive; a single 'hall' with no *chancel* arch, the whole under a fine C15 *arch-braced roof*, with handsomely carved and panelled *wall plates* and deep *wall posts* resting on *corbels*. The posts frame a range of eleven small *clerestory* windows, twice the number of *arcade* bays, with an extra one for the sanctuary. The aisle windows go down to serve as seats. Each aisle has a *piscina* at the e. end, indicating the former presence of chapels there. The door and arch in the n. aisle corner leads into the vestry which was rebuilt in the 1900s. The C15 font panels have *Symbols of the Evangelists*, *Instruments of the Passion*, and a *Tudor rose*. There is a sill piscina in the sacuary and another in the floor, which is most unusual. Nearby, a *chalice brass* to Robert Fevyr, 1519, the church's first rector. Traces of painted texts, dated 1638, above. Soon after Sir Henry Heydon built his church, a *rood screen* was erected across the first bay from the e., and *parclose screens* across the arches between chancel and aisles. All dismantled and cut up, a major portion is now at the back of the *nave*. One can make out St *James the Less* and St *Jude*. Another section, with St *Thaddaeus*, is behind the pulpit. More pieces make up the choir stalls, which have masses of graffiti and scratched-in ships, with yet more remnants behind them.

Sandringham, St Mary Magdalene (C3): King George V's 'dear old Sandringham' has become a magnet for thousands of tourists, and the church is so encrusted with royal associations that it is impossible to view it as one would any other parish church. It was transformed by rebuilding, first by *S.S. Teulon* in 1857 and then by *Sir Arthur Blomfield* in 1890; *transepts* and vestries were added and not much of the original C14 and C15 *carstone* fabric remained undisturbed. The tower has decorative square tracery panels in the bell openings and one *sound-hole* on the s. side. The C15 *porch* has a *Tudor* arch with a little *flushwork* on either side and a tall niche overhead containing a medieval figure that has sprouted wings. Inside, all is compacted magnificence; colours of the Norfolk Regiment hang above the pedestal font in the base of the tower, and there are *hatchments* used on the funeral trains of George VI and his father. The oak pulpit panelled in silver was designed by Walter Stoye, the gift of the American Mr Rodman Wanamaker to Queen Alexandra on her 80th birthday in 1924. His fervid admiration for Edward VII as a peacemaker had earlier prompted him to present a silver altar in 1911, and the matching *reredos* was designed by W.E. Tower in 1920. The tiny *chancel* is lush with gilded wood, and ranks of angels fill the niches that frame the e. window. There is a marvellously intricate Spanish C16 processional cross, and by the s. side of the chancel arch a lovely statuette of St *George* – the face and hands of ivory, the armour polished aluminium. A window in the *nave* and another in the n. *aisle* share a very interesting gallery of saints in the upper *lights*; this is C16 glass, probably from the Norwich workshops, and the series comprises: nave (e. to w.) St *Erasmus*, St *Agnes*, St *Stephen*, St *Francis* (unique in England), St *Giles*, St *Apollonia*; n. aisle (e. to w.) St *Leonard*, St *Vincent of Saragossa*, St *Margaret*, St *Bridget*, St *Ignatius of Antioch* (unique in England). Two more figures from the same group are now in the porch – St *Catherine* and St *Etheldreda*. Sandringham gardens are a joy in spring and summer, but the best time to visit the church is probably a wet morning in early February.

Santon, All Saints (E7): A tiny church tucked away deep in the forest but still only a stone's throw from a railway line. It is a quaint place with the little tower offset at the s.w. corner of the *nave* – a square base with an octagonal, battlemented top. On the s. side is a nice little 'Y' traceried window with *corbel* stops to its arch in the form of intricately carved balls of leaves – these are almost certainly medieval, and rescued from an earlier church here. In the C17, that church was already ruinous: then in 1628 along

came Thomas Bancroft, who set about a complete rebuilding. Since then the Victorians have had a go at it and replaced all the windows in Thomas's nave with *lancets*. In 1858 they added the doll's house *chancel*, using materials from a demolished *transept* at nearby West Tofts, in the Battle Area. The interior of the church is plain to the point of being spartan, but thoroughly Victorian. The nave is only about 17ft. across, the chancel a mere ten, with a pretty painted roof whose *wall posts* sit on *Early English* corbels. *Encaustic tiles* on the e. will serve as a *reredos* to the altar with its brief *communion rail*. To attend services here must have a special element of pleasure and communion.

Saxlingham, St Margaret (G2): Village, churchyard and church alike here have a pleasing air of being cared for. Plain C14 tower (the *plate tracery* of the bell openings suggest this date). The rest of the church in C15 *Perpendicular*. At the end of the C19 the church was in so delapidated a state that the architects recommended complete rebuilding. Sir Alfred Jodrell of nearby Bayfield Hall, undertook restoration and renewal in 1898, as at neighbouring Glandford a year later. Inside, the effect is of a pure C19 quality work. There is a simple C15 octagonal font. In a niche in an arch leading into the n. transept is a kneeling alabaster figure of Mirabel, who died in 1593, wife of Sir Christopher Heydon; in the e. wall of the opposite transept is a curious little bible, carved with a quotation from a pre-C17 translation of the Holy Bible. These two remnants are all that remain of a monument which Sir Christopher, a scholar and astrologer, erected to his lady. It was removed in 1789, on the grounds that it was 'delapidated and dangerous'. The church has a good ring of 8 bells, tenor 8-1-20 cwt.

Saxlingham Nethergate, St Mary the Virgin (I6): A beautiful setting beyond the little triangular green, with the Elizabethan Old Hall on one side and the pale grey elegance of Sir John Soane's 1784 rectory on the other. The *Perpendicular* tower has a deep range of brick and flint chequer battlements and a smartly restored single-hand clock and sundial. There was a heavy restoration here in 1867 when the n. *aisle* was added and many of the Perpendicular windows renewed or replaced, but the *lancet* on the s. side of the *chancel* is C14, and its lower half was a *low side window*. Note the *consecration cross* to the left of the s. door, and the two iron *quatrefoils* in the door itself like the one at Shotesham St Mary.

Inside, the mid-C15 *arcade* has slim lozenge-shaped pillars with broad continuous mouldings. The font is enough like Shotesham to have come from the same hand – chunky, and with the same self satisfied lions round the shaft. There is deep carving in the bowl panels with a band of floral motifs round the lions, every head is fine, and two of the angels are feathered all over. In the chancel, the altar is backed by a range of woodwork that was undoubtedly a squareheaded C15 *screen*. It is said to have come from Norwich Cathedral when *Anthony Salvin* was at work there, but there is apparently some doubt about this. On the s. side of the sanctuary, John Baron's monument is a very good example of Norwich mason *Francis Stafford's* work. In black and white marble, *Corinthian* columns flank a long Latin epitaph, with twin cherub heads and a *cartouche* of arms below with rococo urns on each side. Baron, who died in 1739, was rector here and Dean of Norwich for the last six years of his life. Saxlingham is memorable for its glass, although most of it has been moved and much came from elsewhere – possibly from the village's other church which was abandoned in 1688. The earliest glass identified in any Norfolk church is here in the s. chancel windows. In the easternmost there are four mid-C13 medallions: top left St *John* and St *James* with their names on a scroll; top right the beheading of a saint; bottom left the Martyrdom of St *Edmund*; bottom right St *Edmund* proffering the instruments of his martyrdom to heaven. In the next window to the w. at the top there are late-C14 figures of St *Philip* with his basket of loaves and St *James the Less* with his fuller's club. In the low side window further along, there is a roundel of about 1500 of the Virgin and Child with St *Anne* and remnants of Nativity and Resurrection scenes. In the e. window, look for the *Pentecost* (top left) showing the dove of the Holy Spirit hovering over the *Apostles*, and for the Ascension (top right) with the Lord's feet disappearing into the cloud. In the n. chancel window you can see half of a set of the *Four Latin Doctors* of the Church – St *Jerome* in his cardinal's hat and St *Ambrose* with a clear name scroll and an ink horn. More panels are to be found in the C19 north aisle e. window, including a particularly nice figure of *Edward the Confessor* at the bottom. A rich haul for lovers of medieval glass and not to be missed.

Saxthorpe, St Andrews (H2): The church stands high and handsome, with a solid outside stair turret, with *carstone quoins* on the s. side of the C14 tower; and with pretty *clerestory* windows with pointed heads. The *nave* and *aisles* were rebuilt in 1482 by the lord of the manor and his tenants, and the fine tall *arcades* rest on big octagonal pillars. The older *chancel* has a *low side window* with a long wall seat below it. The C14 font has a plain bowl, but the panels of the stem are delicately traceried. Its cover is a neat little *Jacobean* piece marked 'A.P. 1621'. The C15 *screen* has been badly defaced, but one can see that the original painted brocade patterns were rich in colour and design. Unlike the rest, the front bench on the n. side of the nave has a traceried back. An *Agnus Dei* is carved in the recess on the double width end, and this crest of the Page family can be seen on *ledger-stones* at both ends of the nave. A crowned 'P' is carved on the bench end opposite for Peter Page, vicar from 1482 to 1536, who lies buried e. of the font. The C17 *communion rails* are distinctly eccentric. The uprights have large turned balls at the top, and the heavy top rail curves down between them, with flat supports that look rather like chair splats. Under the tower is a most interesting combination of *Royal Arms* and *decalogue board*. Used originally as a *reredos*, it has the arms of Queen Anne flanked by the decalogue, Lord's Prayer and verses from the psalms – all of it on canvas and in a wooden frame. It is faded and sadly torn in places, but the design and execution are all exceptionally good. The church has an excellent ring of 6 bells, tenor 2-3-0 cwt.

Scarning, St Peter & St Paul (F4): A quiet village once again since the bypass was built across the fields – and the church benefits greatly from it. The whole of this trim building is of the C15, but in succeeding phases – *chancel, nave*, tower, in that order. The battlemented tower is topped with carved figures in lieu of pinnacles; it has big *sound-holes* with *cusped* St Andrew's crosses as tracery, *flushwork* buttresses and *base course*, and neat stone trimming throughout. The nave is dominated by big *Perpendicular* windows. Interesting here, on the n. side of the chancel, is a two-storey vestry. It was built, it seems, in 1576 by the curate, Michael Denby, who lived in the upper room: but only seven years later he moved to more spacious accommodation, when he was promoted to the rectory. To the w. of his vestry is the *priest's door*, a neat little example of *Decorated* lines. Inside, the broad, spacious nave is spanned by a ponderous modern timber roof. Specially notable is the late-C12 font – a massive, square bowl sitting squally on four corner pillars and an octagonal central stem, stem to pillars being bridged by what look like tiny flying buttresses. The font is topped by a conical *Jacobean* cover, whilst the little lions at its corners have a distinctly morning-after-the-night-before look about them; the whole thing is coloured and gilded. On the nave wall, don't miss the dynamic and quite dramatic *Royal Arms* of George III, dated 1813. Good modern lectern-*pelican*, rather than eagle, with bishops and priests around the stem and lion feet. The *screen*, regilded and coloured in 1962, is good C15 work; but its outstanding feature, on its e. side, is the survival of a tiny, attached *sanctus bell*. In the nave s.e. corner, behind the organ, are the *rood stairs*. In the chancel are nice fluted *jambs* to each side of the e. window; a *piscina* with a five-leaf, cusped head; and a mellow *Stuart* altar table. In the 1850s, *Thomas Jekyll* altered the pitch of the roof so that he could use slate instead of lead to save money and lowered the side walls 2ft. to take it. He rebuilt the chancel walls and renovated most of the windows, entirely replacing those on the n. to match the s. side. He renewed the chancel e. window and provided new nave benches, pulpit and choir stalls. The church has a good ring of 6 bells, tenor 14-2-18 cwt.

Scole, St Andrew (H8): In 1963 the major part of the building was destroyed by arson, leaving only the tower, the walls and the *aisle arcade* above the smoking ruins. But within two years another church had arisen that is an imaginative and sensitive blend of old and new. The early-C14 tower has simple 'Y' tracery bell openings and chequered battlements, and the new pantile roofs sweep down un-interruptedly over *nave*, *chancel*, vestry and meeting room, with chancel walls raised in brick to meet them. Inside, the feeling is light and comfortable and as you move to the centre there is a flash of colour from the e. window. Designed by Patrick Reyntienne who carried out John Piper's Baptistry window at Coventry, it is a tumultuous composition, with dark reds and greens predominating. It draws counterpoint themes from Old and New Testaments – the Brazen Serpent linked with the Crucifixion, Jonah with the Resurrection, and Elijah in his chariot as the pointer to the Ascension; at the top, the Apocalyptic Judgement of the Lamb. On the n. side, a deep recess houses the organ behind a slatted screen at high level – approached via a wooden open tread spiral stair. In the nave n. wall, the rebuilding revealed a

Norman window embrasure which still bears its dark red pattern of decoration. At the e. end of the *aisle* in its new position is the C15 font, happily undamaged. There are eager little lions at the base and angels with scrolls and shields in the bowl panels. Close by is a C14 *angle piscina* and the pillars of the *arcade* (also C14) have a whole range of medieval graffiti scratched on them. Look at the pillar to the left of the door as you enter, and low down on the n. side there is a head with a conical hat which was probably done by some idle youth not long after it was built. An extension on the n. side of the church was added in 1973 in which meeting rooms and kitchen are ingeniously combined. Architect Peter Codling, builders W.S. Lusher & Son and Scole itself have good reason to be proud of this phoenix among churches. The church has an excellent ring of 6 bells, tenor 4-1-8 cwt.

Scottow, All Saints (I3): This church is quite some way off the road and the approach is through a farmyard where hens forage unconcernedly in the churchyard under the limes. Here is an interesting mixture of styles. The *porch* – *groined* with a *Green Man* centre *boss* – has battlemented *capitals* on the outer arch which match the s. *arcade piers*, and the *aisle* itself goes with the tower – all *Perpendicular*. The n. aisle has rather later square headed windows, but the n. arcade rests on slim *quatrefoil Decorated* pillars contemporary with the *chancel*. The big e. window has flowing tracery, and a late elevation of the sanctuary on three steps has put the *piscina* at floor level. A pity, because it has pretty, open tracery in the arch and can no longer be used. By it, an old 3ft. x 2ft. *mensa* has been framed on a stand as a memorial, and not far away there is a small *chalice brass* to a priest, Nicholas Wethyley c.1520. On the n. side is a great grey and rather ugly obelisk to Davey Durrant (d.1757) by *George Storey* on one of his off days. There is no chancel arch, but the *rood beam* survives and the *rood stair* to the s. has remnants of the original wooden treads. The *nave* has a set of plain deal *box pews* and in front, a C17 double-sided oak lectern which swivels on a turned shaft. Carved overall, it even has an openwork door at one end and came from a London church in 1876. The organ case is clad in a rich array of carved *Renaissance* panels dated 1641 and 1649 which have also been brought in from elsewhere. The font cover is a jolly C17 affair of thin painted dolphins supporting a centre shaft. There are ten *hatchments* of the Durrant family, the *Royal Arms* of William and Mary on the s. aisle w. wall, and above the s. door, the arms of Elizabeth II. These are remarkably good and look more like C18 work – possibly an update. The church has a ring of 6 bells, tenor 10-2-14 cwt.

Scoulton, Holy Trinity (F5): The C14 tower has pretty tracery in the w. window, and the *broaches* below the bell stage could well have been designed to support a spire. As it is, the octagon top has the blunt look of a compromise that somehow nobody finished – many Norfolk towers are like that. The *nave* is thatched, and the *chancel* pantiles have recently been renewed. The 'Y' tracery windows are of about 1300, except the *Perpendicular* e. window – that has its original frame and *headstops*, and there is a small blocked niche above it. If you examine the outside of the chancel n. wall you will find a blocked narrow doorway and traces of the walls of a former chapel – bear these in mind when looking at the inside. The s. door with its roughly chamfered boards and closing ring plate is likely to be C14, and just inside, the multi-*cusped holy water stoup* has the rugged bowl of another standing in it. The C14 font has a deep bowl and is absolutely plain, with a simple *Jacobean* cover. There is Jacobean panelling in place of a *screen*, and a pulpit of the same period on the s. side, with a modern replica on the n. side, but without backboard or *tester*. The stairs to the *rood loft* rise from the e. end of the n. aisle. Under plastered ceilings, the *arcades* have headstops and there is a small set of George III *Royal Arms* on the n. side, plus a single *hatchment*. The puzzle in this church is hidden away behind the organ. It is a large C13 niche that is large enough to have been an *Easter Sepulchre*, but in the base there are five holes, 5in. across and 7in. deep; they are far too large to be *cressets* (each would have taken a pint of oil!), but what else could they have been used for? Furthermore, the niche lies across the line of the vanished n. chapel w. wall – a very odd placement. The handsome *trefoil piscina* is contemporary with the side windows, so perhaps the Easter Sepulchre was saved from an earlier building but not moved from its original position. Even so, what were those holes for?

Sculthorpe, All Saints (F2): In June 1381 Sir Robert Knollys became Lord of the Manor of Sculthorpe. Soon afterwards this swash-buckling Cheshire knight, who won fame with his foreign expeditions and campaigns, set about the rebuilding of ruined Sculthorpe

church. Six hundred years later to the day his descendant the Viscount Knollys attended a special service here and, with his family, planted three rose bushes of ancient variety in the churchyard to celebrate historical continuity. Inside the church that continuity is being expressed by the placing on the *nave* walls of the coats of arms of the Knollys family and their kin, specially worked in cotton on canvas. History's heaviest mark has been left by the restoring hand of the Victorians, though they did leave behind them a most attractive building. In 1860, Sir Willoughby Jones of Cranmer Hall commissioned *Thomas Jekyll* to carry out a full-scale make-over with no expense spared. The roof was rebuilt with a raised pitch, the w. wall was rebuilt and a *galilee porch* was added beyond a new w. arch with exuberant floral *capitals*; a new s. *aisle* has pierced ribs and tracered *spandrels* in its roof, while the *arcade* has heavy foliated capitals. The benches are like Jekyll's at West Runton – a simplification of the *Pugin* set at Wymeswold in Leicestershire. A stone pulpit and richly carved main doors were part of the total scheme. Of Sir Robert's church, only the *Perpendicular* tower and the n. aisle remain. Inside, the C19 additions and alterations sit happily with the original work – neat Perpendicular arcade on the n. side. Above the *screen* is the top door of the old *rood stair* – open down to the n. aisle. Under the arcade arch here is the church's enchanting little 1796 Snetzler organ, brought here from York's Assembly Rooms. In front of it, a *brass* to John and Elizabeth Humpton, 1521, with the couple's seven boys and one girl. Nearby is an inscription and shield to John and Margaret Stebyrd, undated. Opposite, a deeply incised (and probably re-stored) brass showing a kneeling knight in armour, dated 1470. The Latin reads: 'Here lies Henry Unton 'Gentilman' – a very early usage of 'Gentleman' in that context. In the chancel s. side, stained glass in two panels shows Christ on the waves, very positive and full of energy – from the *Morris* workshops with the figures designed by *Burne-Jones*. Also from Morris came the s. aisle e. window showing Faith, Hope and Charity. There are exceptionally good panels by Robert Bayne in a s. nave window – the story of Ruth in full High Victorian style and exhibited at the S. Kensington Museum Exhibition in 1862. Finally, Sculthorpe's fine *Norman* font. In beautifully preserved and crisp carving it shows, on the e. face the Adoration of the Magi in five separate panels, with elaborate patterns on the other sides. The church has a ring of 6 bells, tenor 8-0-10 cwt.

Sea Palling, St Margaret (K3): Early unbuttressed w. tower, and what was a C14 *nave*, *aisles* and *chancel* arrangement – the aisles have gone, leaving blocked windows to the west. C14 font with shallow tracery round the bowl like an exercise in window design. A large *banner-stave locker* hides behind the organ, and there are *rood loft* stairs with square-headed doorways and an associated *piscina*. A series of boards listing lifeboat rescues 1860-1929 are propped up behind the decayed remains of the *rood screen*. Most of the s. door is original C15.

Sedgeford, St Mary (D2): The village nestles in a fold of the little hills just inland from the sea and the church, despite its size, hides away in the valley bottom. The *Norman* round tower with octagonal top of 1300 is flanked by extensions to the *aisles*, and there is now a flat w. front. Successive building stages can be identified from the outside – two large matching C13 *porches* with small *trefoil* windows; *chancel* of about 1300 with a fine but oddly placed 2-*light* window on the n. side which has a centre shaft bearing a *capital* that combines foliage and masks. The chancel was shortened in 1770, and this has left the *priest's door* right in the s.e. corner. Of the two *transepts* planned, only the s. exists, with one *Decorated* window on the e. face retaining the *ogee* arch, and both having pretty foliated *cusps* to the tracery. The transept roof cuts into the last window of the *Perpendicular clerestory* and must have been a late-C15 replacement. Inside, the late-C13 *nave arcade* has an odd pair of octagonal pillars halfway along. There is a substantial inside turret for the *rood stairs* on the s. side of the chancel arch and note how the opposite side of the arch encroaches on that fine little chancel window, suggesting that it was built later. The s. transept roof is neat and good and again, look for the blocked clerestory window that helps to date it. Below, in the s.e. corner, an *angle piscina* with just a hint of the ogee shape over the trefoil on the w. face – probably mid-C14. C19 *screen*, with a small *rood group* of 1924, and the glass in the e. window looks like the work of *Powell & Sons*. On the s. aisle wall, traces of a large St Christopher (see his fingers curled round the Child), and a *consecration cross* on the far side of the window to the e. Within the vestry at the w. end of this aisle is a surprisingly large fire-place. The C13 *Purbeck* font is small and plain, and behind it, the tower arch

has a mass of C17 and C18 graffiti with a contribution from a *parish clerk* who obviously saw nothing wrong in it. By the n. door is a fine C16 Venetian chest with typical poker-work designs on the front – Bacchus in the centre flanked by military scenes, and a frieze of lions and unicorns above. Leaving or arriving, have a look at the unpretentious *carstone* gateway to the churchyard – it recalls that 150 villagers were struck down by typhus in 1852 and commemorates the 20 that died.

Seething, St Margaret & St Remigius (J6): Just across the fields from Mundham's tall square tower, this church has a stumpy round *Norman* tower, narrowing distinctly towards its added brick top. In its lower w. face is a C14 *Decorated* window – and below that a bricked-in shape which marks, it is said locally, a former *wafer oven*. *Nave* and *chancel* are principally of the Decorated period, though their interesting range of windows is from the C13 *lancet* and *cusped* 'Y' tracery of about 1300, through to good-looking *Perpendicular* examples (late-C14/early-C15) in the nave s. side. Perpendicular too is the *porch*, though heavily restored, with its jaunty little *arch-braced* and original roof. Inside, the church is unexpectedly spacious. Dominant at once are the C14 wall paintings, in particular the huge St *Christopher* facing the s. door; and to his left three noble young men and a skeleton in a *Three Living and Three Dead* representation. To the right are five panels, much defaced but discernibly showing (left to right) the *Annunciation* (Mary & Archangel Gabriel); Christmas (note ox and ass heads at top); Easter (Christ with angels); Ascension (feet disappearing skywards); and *Assumption* (crowned Virgin with angels). Over the pulpit, the large single figure, bearded and with a distinctively pointing finger, is *John the Baptist*. On opposite wall, a large painting illustrates a popular medieval 'horror theme' – a gleeful Satan (at top) ushers numerous sinful souls down to purgatory, where busy little devils are waiting to pull them in. To right is a smaller fragment – a figure (winged?) holding an implement like a hockey stick; is this St *James the Less* with his fuller's club? Returning to the architecture, note the massive Norman arch between nave and tower, resting on simple *imposts* rather than *capitals*; large *holy water stoup* by the door; *rood stair* in s.e. corner of nave including a rare curiosity, a little window at the turning point at top of the stair. The base of the C15 *rood screen* remains, with only traces of its original panel paintings. The seemingly battered chancel arch in fact shows where the *rood beam* was formerly set into it; below, on n. side, is a footed recess which was presumably a figure niche; on the s. side is another niche, much lower, whose position suggests that it was a *squint* (subsequently filled in). The plain chancel has a handsome 'triple tiara' hanging candelabra; a large and elegant *piscina*, unusually constructed within the embrasure of the window, which in turn has *dropped sill sedilia*. Finally, Seething's fine and well preserved *seven sacrament font*, which has been dated at 1485. Its carved panels, clockwise from the e. face, show: extreme unction (last rites), baptism of Jesus by total immersion, ordination, marriage (of very young folk, it seems), baptism, mass, confirmation (again with very young participants – and don't overlook the babe-in-arms) and penance, with a (now headless) feathered-all-over angel and a grinning little devil in attendance. Round the font's stem are carved the four *Evangelistic Symbols*; small figures under rich little canopies, and floral motifs; and under the bowl, angels with scrolls and shields. Before leaving, the church's s. door merits a closer look. It is largely C15, with *linen-fold panelling*, and the tracery in the head has angels with *censers* on each side of a window shape. It almost certainly predates the porch that shelters it and all the woodwork is very abraded, having been exposed to the elements in its youth.

Sharrington, All Saints (G2): The C14 tower has a curious set of small windows above the more conventional bell openings, and its bare parapet gives it a slightly gaunt look. Having been comprehensively repointed, however, it is in fine condition, as is the whole church after restoration. Entry is by way of the w. door of the tower and just inside there is a medieval iron-bound waggon chest. Through the very sturdy arch in the e. face of the tower one finds a light and uncomplicated interior, with no *chancel* arch to break the run on the roof through to the e. wall. The church once had *aisles* and *transepts*, but they were demolished in the late C18 or early C19 and the C14 *arcades* were filled in to form the present *nave* walls and windows of a generous size were inserted. In doing so, the arches and the pillars with their round caps and bases were left to show boldly inside. There were major restorations in 1880 and 1908, and in the first, the chancel and the n.e. vestry were rebuilt and the whole building was re-roofed. Thankfully, in doing so, the gargantuan *corbels* of the original roof were retained and they are a

remarkably fine set, with heads of devils, pigs and *Green Men* deeply carved. There is a set of Hanoverian *Royal Arms* painted on board above the tower arch, and *Cautley* thought the font which stands below was C15, but both its appearance and its character belong to the 1880s; the varied tracery in four of the bowl panels encloses shields carrying the *Evangelistic Symbols*. Although they have been reaved from their stones, the group of *brasses* mounted on the s. wall of the chancel are of great interest. On the left, the knight in armour commemorates John Daubeney who died in 1469 defending Caistor Castle for the *Pastons* against the *Duke of Norfolk*. To the right, two small figures, identified as Daubeneys by the shields above, the woman wearing a *kennel headress*; then there is an inscription of 1527 for Thomas and Anne Daubeney, and to the right the small figure of John Botolff wearing his vestments who was rector here 1458 – 1486. Lastly a long inscription in English for Christopher Daubeney (d. 1583), the last Daubeney Lord of Sharrington, and his family. Above it he and his wife kneel – he in armour and lacking his head, she in a Paris cap and a decorative petticoat showing under her gown; five sons kneel behind their father and their three sisters behind their mother. The C14 *angle piscina* in the corner of the sanctuary seems to have been given a new *ogee* arch in the C19, and the cap of the pillar has recently been renewed; *dropped sill* stepped *sedilia* are alongside.

Shelfanger, All Saints (H7): On the village street with a fine line of horse chestnuts down the n. side of the churchyard. The tower of about 1300 has a foiled circular *sound-hole* and 'Y' tracery in the belfry windows. There is a small later niche lower down, and the pyramidal roof over the chequered *flushwork* battlements is graced by a diminutive copper weathercock. Like Shimpling a few miles away, here is a lovely late-C15 or early-C16 timber *porch* in weathered oak, with infill panels of flint. It has a low *arch-braced roof* and there is a big *holy water stoup* to the right of the inner door. Inside, you will see that the tower is off centre, but whether there was ever a separate s. *aisle* is hard to say now. Certainly there was a chapel at the e. end on the s. side – a fine little *angle piscina* remains in the window embrasure, still with its wooden *credence shelf*, and a tall niche with *trefoil ogee* head is in the wall behind the pulpit. The late-C14 font is a heavy piece with varied tracery in the panels and the prominent initials of Adam Bosville the donor have his arms between. Under the tower, two

Shelton, St Mary

sections of the C14 *rood screen* have been re-used; there are variant patterns of lively tracery above multi-*cusped* arches. In the early-C14 *chancel* there is what is now the church's treasure. Restoration work was going on in 1966 when a workman realised that the wall in the s.e. corner of the sanctuary was hollow. Breaking through carefully, he found an older wall nine inches behind and, when it was fully revealed, a painting of the visit of the Magi. Miss Eve Baker, one of the country's leading authorities, dates it as late C13, and describes it as a beautiful example of the work of the East Anglian School of artists of that period. It is indeed of outstanding quality and the happy chance and nature of its concealment has preserved much more detail than is usual; the Virgin crowned and with long wavy fair hair, the Child with one hand raised in blessing and the apple of knowledge and humanity in the other; Balthazar is handing up the kingly ring of gold, and to the right and round the angle of the wall, the angel beckons to the shepherds. His head in particular is well nigh perfect. The whole painting is 5ft. high and 4ft. wide and has been meticulously restored. The church has a excellent ring of 6 bells, tenor 5-1-26 cwt.

Shelton, St Mary (I6): For all those who love churches, Shelton is a joy and a delight. A fascinating and beautiful building deep in quiet countryside, it was also briefly caught up in English history. Sir Ralph Shelton, knighted when he came of age by Henry VII, and High Sheriff of Norfolk in 1437, not only built himself a new moated Hall but a grand new church as well. Leaving only the simple early-C15 tower, he began again – this time in brick, and that is the clue to Shelton's beauty. See it in high summer or under a hard frost, and the pale rose red walls seem to glow and to pick up light from the sky. In his will of 1487, Sir Ralph directed that the work should go on, but as we shall see, this was not to be. His son Sir John married the aunt of Henry VIII's Anne Boleyn, and the strains of that tempestuous and uncertain court overrode the simple pleasures of country church building. When Anne Boleyn was put to the block in 1536, her daughter Elizabeth (the future Elizabeth I) found refuge here at Shelton with her great-uncle, and was even hidden in this very tower when the Hall was no longer safe. Now to the building itself. Apart from the stone facing of the *clerestory* range, the whole is in brick diapered with darker bricks – s. *porch*, *nave*, and two *aisles* of the same length

Shelton, St Mary: e. window donor figure

with no projecting *chancel*. Instead, at the e. end, and projecting a little beyond two big buttresses, there is a *sacristry* on the lines of the one at St Peter Mancroft, Norwich but here of one storey only. It has a window and two big niches, and you have a close-up of one of the church's gargantuan *gargoyles*. All the windows except one have flattened arches and prominent *transoms* over *ogee*-headed main *lights*, and the nine window clerestory forms a wall that is almost all glass. The porch facade is tall and very impressive – the image pillar of the central niche drops right down to the entrance arch, while the panel above it goes up to the parapet making, with the two windows, a completely unified design. Before going in, inspect the gargoyle on the e. side of the porch which is unlike the rest of the set – a winged devil riding another and pulling its mouth wide open. On the other side is the first sign of a change from the master builder's plan. Instead of having its own stair, the upper room of the porch was reached from the tower stair by a bridging arch and passage that cuts right across the early-C14 aisle window that had been left below. Inside the porch there are the stumps of an uncompleted *fan vault* and, above them, the joist sockets for the old floor. Going inside, you see a n. door fitted into the very corner and

awkwardly combined with the window above. It seems at least likely that a whole new tower was planned, and the aisles would then have been taken another bay w. to marry with it. When this did not happen, the second floor of the porch and the n. door were pragmatic compromises. Even on a dull day the interior is light, and has a feeling of uncluttered space. The *mullions* of the clerestory windows run down the intervening space to meet the top of the nave *arcades* – stretching without interruption to the e. end. Again, flat arches and slender lozenge-shaped columns mark the definitive and final stage of gothic style. Overhead, alas, only a flat plaster ceiling. The old roof was unceremoniously taken off in the C18 to use for a *tithe barn*, and only the stone *corbels* remain. They are in the form of angels holding shields with the Shelton arms (gold cross on a blue ground) and the founder's *rebus* – an 'R', a shell, and a barrel (tun was the old word for it). By the time you leave you will have seen this so many times that anything else by way of decoration comes as a surprise. The font was left over from the old building and is in the same style as neighbouring Fritton though it is not so fine. The e. window is peculiarly tall and thin for the wall it is set in, and again there is the thought that something grander was planned. This is certainly true of the founder's tomb just below to the left There are the beginnings of an elaborate canopy, but sadly it was never completed, and although his descendants' names figure on the sides, Sir Ralph's does not. Somebody made a mistake in the C19 over the tinctures of the family arms and repainted the shields green (or, more pedantically, 'vert' instead of 'azure'). The *rood screen* once stretched from the stair on the n. side right across to the s., but now only the base is left and even that has lost all but part of the background tracery. By it is a lectern which must be about the same age – an unusual survival. It is a curiously ungainly article – slab sides with wide and shallow mouldings, Shelton arms at the top and dumpy *poppy-heads*. In the s.e. corner is the tomb of Sir Robert Houghton (1623). His effigy in judge's robes has been repositioned with that of his son on a new top, and the women folk kneel in the arch behind; there is a lot of original colour. Shelton has a deal of fine glass in the e. windows. Considerable rearrangement has gone on, but look for the many small donor figures – the two males on the left carry the Shelton arms and the women on the right the bull of the Boleyns. Perhaps the best quality work is the C16 figures in the s. aisle e. window, which expert opinion suggests are of German origin. The shields they bear are insertions from earlier schemes. Turning back from the chancel, there is yet another treasure in view – the *Royal Arms* of William III above the tower arch. This is one of the best sets in the county and came by gift to the church in 1881, long after it was made. 6ft. x 8ft. and carved in gilded and painted oak, it has luxuriant mantling to the helm, and the bottom panel is full of vivacious fruit and flowers carved in the style of *Grinling Gibbons*. Thank goodness that valiant local effort and generous help from the Historic Churches Preservation Trust have combined to restore this wonderful building so that we may all continue to enjoy it.

Shereford, St Nicholas (E3): Stands in a neat and well kept churchyard, and the solid little *Saxon* tower has a most attractive leaded cap, shallow in pitch with a scalloped vallance over deep eves – very effective. Despite quite heavy C19 restorations, evidence of the church's early history is fairly easy to find. There is a late *Norman* s. doorway with roll mouldings and double shafts, and the n. doorway is a little later and has lost its columns. Early-C11 windows on the s. side are double splayed and there was a C13 n. *aisle* which can be traced by its *arcade* in the wall and a *piscina* which has survived intact on the outside, against the site of a vanished altar. The jumble of windows with deep embrasures on the s. side give a very pleasing effect and the *chancel* has a C14 e. window with splendid flowing tracery. Inside, the tower arch has been fitted with a handsome grill and by it, an impressive *Norman* font; the round bowl slopes in slightly to a double row of scallops and the shaft is almost square with slightly rounded planes between the corner columns. The chancel piscina looks as if it may have been re-used – possibly it was originally an *angle* piscina. A stone coffin lid opposite has the double Omega sign which can be seen at Holkham and elsewhere locally. As you leave, look by the *porch* for an imaginative memorial in the grass to a Rector whose name was Robin.

Shernborne, St Peter & St Paul (D2): There was a medieval tradition that St *Felix* built a wooden church here in the C7, but what you find now is a neat little building that was rebuilt on its old foundations in 1898 'chiefly through the gracious liberality of HRH Albert Edward Prince of Wales.' *Sir Arthur Blomfield* was consulted and although a lot of the old

Shernborne, St Peter & St Paul: Norman font

stonework was re-used, the only pieces easily recognised are the C13 bases of the *aisle arcade* and part of the arches above. The *chancel* was made as wide as the *nave* (it had been ruinous since 1530) and the church now has an open and rather bare look. Despite that, there is something that no one should pass by – one of the finest *Norman* fonts in England, encrusted with plaited designs that even sheath the miniature corner columns. The bowl is round, with a square, decorated rim, and low on each side is a mask. There are two figures on the w. face – one in a shoulder cape holding a trail from the interlacing design, and the other seems to be plucking a fruit – suggestive of an 'Adam and Eve' theme. A *ledger slab* set in the n. wall of the chancel has a fine *brass* of Thomas Shernborne and his wife. He was Chamberlain to *Henry VI's* wife, Margaret of Anjou, and his wife was a maid of honour; a lion lies at his feet and a tiny, rather peevish dog at hers – see how parts of both figures are inlaid with lead where there was once bright enamelled decoration.

Shimpling, St George (H7): This church is cared for by the *Churches Conservation Trust*. It is easily seen from the village street, but the way to it is via a farm entrance and then a long rutted track through the fields. The earliest evidence of the church's history can be seen in the *Norman* flint work of the n. wall and a splayed window opening inside on the s. wall w. of the pulpit. The late-C13 *chancel* with its simple 'Y' and intersected tracery has not been much disturbed and now has a new pantile roof. The *nave* was rebuilt and given new windows in heightened walls in the late C14 and the *arch-braced roof* in lovely silvery oak soon followed. The main timbers rest on *corbels* that once had heads, but they have all been chopped off – except the one that was overlooked in the s.w. corner. The Norman tower now has two iron bands round it for support, and the C15 octagonal top has two-*light* windows which alternate with *flushwork* dummies; on top, a recessed shingled spire added in 1863. If you like to seek out *mass dials* there is a large one here on the s. nave buttress. The n. *porch* is handsome and very like nearby Shelfanger's – timber framed, but here the infill is brick. It was built in the early C16 and restored with a lot of new brick in 1867. As you see, the wrought iron gate commemorates the present queen's coronation. The C15 font is in the familiar local pattern, and here the bowl carries *Symbols of the Evangelists* and *Instruments of the Passion* held by angels. Lions as usual guard the base. Its cover looks as though it formed either the base or the canopy of a more elaborate design – probably C17. Behind it, the tower arch has sections of the old *rood screen* reset, and under the tower there is a small *Stuart* table that was no doubt the C17 altar. Two chests here, a rustic 'hutch' with a barrel lid cut from half a tree trunk, and its successor – C17, well made and unpretentious with fluted stiles. There is a full range of C15 benches (two are copies), with *poppy-heads* and there were once figures on the castellated arms. There are traces of painted labels (see the fourth from the back on n. side) and they were readable in the C18 as names of the months and so the carved figures may have been a 'Labours of the months' sequence. There was here, as in most churches, much painted glass in the C14 and C15, but little remains. However, in the head of the easternmost s. nave window there are four fine angels, mainly in shades of yellow, playing lutes and harps. Under the Commonwealth, the purge of things superstitious was vigorous here and every angel's face has been carefully scratched away. It seems odd that they could apparently stomach the rest of the body.

Shipdham, All Saints (F5): A large, handsome church which would befit a prosperous market town, characterised by an extraordinary, irresistible touch of fancy which crowns the tower like a bit of 'Old Russia' – a wooden, two-domed cupola, intricately leafed over in lead. Its date? Its date is uncertain, though the C17 is a possibility. A pity that the C13 tower, with its elegant, C15 battlements, had to be cement-faced at some point – it is the one hard-edged, ugly element in an otherwise splendid building, standing proud in its beautifully kept churchyard. Generally the appearance of the church, including the two-storey *porch*, is *Perpendicular*, though the fabric is obviously much older than that – the *priest's door* on the s. side of the *chancel* has free-standing, sturdy little round columns, topped with leaf-carved *capitals*, heavy moulded arch and pointed door-way arch, which are all patently *Transitional-Norman* between 1170 and 1190. The big five-*light* e. window looks like mid-C14 *Decorated* from the churchyard gate, but close to, its date is questionable. *Sanctus bell turret* on the e. gable of the *nave*. Inside, the nave has a good Victorian roof; an early-C14 five-bay *arcade*; above, a neat *clerestory*; and on the w. wall, a good and very large *Royal Arms* for Charles I, 1630, updated for Charles II in 1661. It was taken down from the *tympanum* in the C19. The C15 font is Perpendicular, with a neat, restored *Jacobean* cover. There is a lovely Jacobean pulpit in silvery wood; above it, the outline of the *rood loft* entrance; and nearby, the church's particular treasure, an excellent double-sided wooden lectern of the very early-C16, with *Tudor roses* on the book-stand and three little lions at the feet. The n. aisle has an impressive C15 roof, with timber arch-braces which look far too big for the job, plus a fine set of *bosses*. On the wall, a very fine decalogue board – 'The X Commandements of Allmightie God'. Next, the church's 'second font' – a *Norman* piece, restored to the church about 30 years ago when it was removed from the Rectory garden; nearby, a medieval chest with five locks. The n. chapel has a modern roof, deal pews, and late-C17 *communion rails* with nicely-turned *balusters* which formerly stood before the high altar. A Perpendicular two-bay arcade leads into the chancel, where some re-used medieval *poppy-heads* and C17 panelling were combined with modern choir stalls. The communion rails, on two sides of the altar, are modern, installed in 1970. In the sanctuary, a good example of a *pillar piscina*, mounted on stocky little *jambs*, with *dropped sill sedilia* alongside. The church has an excellent ring of 6, tenor 10-0-4 cwt.

Shotesham, All Saints (I6): A most attractive setting on a hillock above a small open valley through which a stream meanders to a water splash. Until 1731, Shotesham had four parishes and of the four churches, two remain in use and two are ruined. All Saints has a plain C14 tower with buttresses to the w. and an unusual staircase on the s. face. In 1898 – 1901, much of the structure and the roofs were renewed and the ringing *gallery* was removed. The font was repositioned in the base of the tower and the exterior iron stair was added to maintain access to the ringing chamber (it was splendidly restored in 2003). The 'Y' tracery of the *chancel* windows means that the main building probably dates from about 1300. When it was restored, the stone eagle bearing the words 'Veni Emmanuel' was discovered and returned to its rightful place on the *sanctus bell turret*. As well as the main n. porch, the *priest's door* has one too – a most unusual feature. Inside the tower there is a tall *banner-stave locker* and near it, the font is a fine chunky specimen. There are Lions in the bowl panels as well as angels holding shields carved with the *Trinity, Passion Emblems,* three chalices, and the three crowns of Ely. Over the n. door is an excellent set of *Royal Arms* in gilded wood – very spirited carving in deep relief. They are inscribed 'William IV, 1833', but the quarterings of the shield show that they were originally Georgian. On the s. *nave* wall, an interesting wall painting of a poor bound soul lapped by flames in purgatory, and opposite on the n. wall, a figure which has been frantically over-restored. There is another fragment of painting further e. on the s. wall that looks like a St *George* with his sword raised above his head, and on the n. wall by the *screen* are traces of more decoration. Close to this is an odd oblong recess in the wall, and it has been suggested that it held a light to shine on the *rood.* Of the screen, only the tracery in the right hand panels is original. The *communion rails* are a good solid C17 set with sturdy close-set *balusters,* and in the s. chapel there is a simple *Jacobean* chest with chip carving decoration round the front panels. Two n. windows in the nave and one in the chancel s. chapel still have the kaleidoscopic glass installed in the C19. It was copied from windows in Milan Cathedral and is unique in this country – rather nice. The church has a good ring of 5 bells, tenor 10-3-8 cwt.

Shotesham, St Mary (I6): The second survivor of Shotesham's four churches and still in use, St Mary's stands on a hill away from the main village with a farm for a close neighbour. The ruins of St Martin's are just to the s. – ivy mantled tower and a big tree in what was once the *chancel.* By 1879, St Mary's was in poor state, but then it was given a new *nave* roof and windows, re-floored and re-pewed. The tower has *Tudor* brick bell openings and distinctive stump pinnacles – also in brick. The *sanctus bell turret* is remarkable for still having its bell, but this may not be the original. A Virginia creeper, obviously cherished in its eccentricity, rises from the e. of the *porch,* the thick stem ambles across the head of the arch, round the corner and then up the tower to clad the s. face. The door in its C13 arch is worth looking at. Made of big planks with broad chamfers, it is studded with massive nail heads, and has a ring handle that carries two lizards with long scaly tails – ancient emblems of good fortune. It also boasts an iron *quatrefoil* window complete with bars and a wooden sliding shutter inside. The e. window of the late-C13 chancel has three *lancets* within a single arch; below it, a stiff and spiky Last Supper *reredos* of the late C19. To the right, a *piscina* surrounded by grey brick panels carved with swan, lion, and double eagle – they look as though they were applied as an after-thought. In the centre of the chancel floor is a most interesting *brass* to Edward Whyte and his wife who both fell victim to the sweating sickness in 1528. He was a lawyer, but is here portrayed in full armour – a unique distinction. As far as is known, his wife Elizabeth's dress is the earliest example of the fashion that had the upper sleeves thrown back to reveal the tight slashed sleeve underneath. She wears a *kennel head-dress* and a big rosary hangs from her girdle. Bartholomew Whyte built the n. chapel in the late C15, and the window there has fragments of medieval glass – a crowned 'M' for the dedication, an angel playing a cittern, and some small heads. A section of the *Laudian communion rails* has survived to be used in two tiers to make an unusual lectern, and nearby is the old clock bell cast by Edward Tooke in 1675. The *Royal Arms* of William IV are excellent.

Shouldham, All Saints (C5): Prettily placed on a hill to the e. of the village, with a pleasant path across a meadow up to it. There is much *carstone* showing in the solid C14 tower and you will see more as you walk round. In doing so, look for a C13 grave slab by the s. chapel wall which, with other fragments, came from the nearby Gilbertine priory. There was a big restoration in 1871 and the *chancel* was entirely rebuilt to the designs of R.J. Withers. Just inside to the left, a *Jacobean* chest with the front panels carved with an interlacing roundel design, and on the wall, a large crucified Christ realistically carved in limewood which looks like Bavarian work. At the w. end of the *nave* several benches have square ends with tracery cut in the solid wood reminiscent of the west country rather than East Anglia. The nave roof is particularly fine – *hammer-beams* with carved figures, steep arch-braces rising to *collars* under the ridge; there is a broad coving along the *wall plate* and flower *bosses* stud the intersections of the main timbers. The small early-C16 s. chapel has a lean-to *arch-braced roof*, again with flower bosses and there is a large *aumbry* with shelf set in the s. wall. In the nave n. wall is an early-C14 tomb recess and nearby, a framed tapestry of Jesus and the woman at the well – possibly Flemish. In the Victorian chancel you will find Thomas Alien's memorial by *William Groves*. It was exhibited at the Royal Academy in 1842 and has a heavily draped life-size figure of Faith holding a wreath in one hand and a bible in the other.

Shouldham Thorpe, St Mary (C5): The tower collapsed in 1730 and the remainder of the church was rebuilt in 1858. Rather like Barton Bendish St Mary, the old *Norman* n. doorway was moved round to the w. end and used again. It has double columns and heavy bands of zig zag in the arch. The Victorian interior is very neat and the large octagonal C14 font has a variety of pretty tracery in the bowl panels with a panelled shaft. On the *nave* s. wall, a small monument that was moved at the rebuilding:

> In this channcel lyeth buried Jane, Ann and
> John, thre of the children of Thomas
> Steuarde of little Barton Suff. and Franceis
> his wife, eldest daughter of William Buttes
> of this Towne of Shouldham Thorpe.

They died in 1590, 1591 and 1602, and three grave little figures realistically painted kneel one behind the other above the inscription. There are classical columns each side and a large coat of arms set in strapwork above, with a stag for a crest. On the s. wall of the sanctuary there is a very unusual tablet for one of the childrens' relatives, Thomas Buttes (1600); a coat of arms, and a portrait of him kneeling at a desk faintly incised in panels of alabaster – both set in a small grey slab framed in alabaster. By the pond at the roadside you will see that the parish has adopted those three small Steward children for their village sign.

Shropham, St Peter (F6): A massive C16 tower dominates this fine church in its quiet setting.

The tower has a curious w. window, with very narrow *lights*, forcing the arch into a compressed shape. The church is largely *Perpendicular*, though the fabric is much older – see the fine early-C13 n. doorway, with *dog-tooth* moulding round its *hood mould*, and typical stiff-leafed *capitals* to its slim round pillars. Save for its w. window, the n. *aisle* has good Perpendicular windows. The *chancel* has Perpendicular examples, with a fine five-light e. window which takes up virtually the entire wall. In the angle between chancel and n. aisle, is the outline of the remains of a *sanctus bell turret*. From here there was a small *squint* to enable the ringer to see the high altar; inside the church, the end of the squint emerged into the w. *jamb* of the n. w. chancel window in a tiny *cusped* opening, still there but now glassed in. On the s. side of the chancel, the centre buttress has, very faintly, a *mass dial* carved on it about 3ft. from the ground. Inside, the church is spacious and light, with fine roofs in lovely pale timber – the *nave* roof is *arch-braced*, with *tie-beams* and *king posts* and battlemented *wall plates*; and with *wall posts* resting on *corbels*. Odd little *clerestory*, with round windows filled with cusping. C13 *Early English* four bay *arcade* with octagonal pillars. Set into the wall at w. end of the arcade is a square panel with tracery deeply cut, which looks like a re-used *sound-hole* from a tower. Opposite, in the n. aisle, a pretty two-light window with cusped tracery, looking through to the chancel, with a *piscina* set into the sill. Either side of the window are wall pedestals for figures of saints (a St *Catherine* on one now); this was probably an important *guild* or *chantry altar* before the *Reformation*. Above it, indentations in the wall mark the *rood loft* entrance. The font is *Jacobean* and the restored *screen* under the tower is C14. Beside the door is a massive old iron bound chest. There is asplendid piscina and triple *sedilia* in the chancel, richly cusped and *crocketted*, with a blank shield above the piscina. The church has a ring of 5 bells, tenor 11-2-0 cwt.

Sidestrand, St Michael & All Angels (I2): Clement Scott – best remembered as the fiery drama critic of the 'Daily Telegraph' in the 1860s, rather than as a commentator on rural byways – brought fame to this old churchyard by calling it 'the garden of sleep'. But the last of the old church which he knew slipped into the sea in 1916. The present building was erected in 1881 by Sir Samuel Hoare. He duplicated the former church and re-used much of its fabric. The winged angel above the s. doorway came from there, and so did the strange cross in the *nave* e. wall. The inscription refers to a man of the C15, but it looks much older. The organ case of mixed Georgian/Gothic design dates from 1800, and the war memorial set in the n. wall made use of a niche found in an antique shop. Headstones from the old churchyard line the wall by the road.

Sisland, St Mary (J6): Sisland Church was rebuilt in the mid-C18 when the old building was struck by lightning. The result, sitting in a park-like setting beside the partrician old rectory, is a charming little brick and thatch building, *nave* and *chancel* being in one 'hall', whitewashed outside with neatly pointed red-brick copings to windows and doors, and a pretty little weather-boarded *bell turret* perched on the w. gable end, and in turn topped by a perky spirelet and weather-cock. On the n. side, adjoining some of the 'lightning-struck' ruins, part of what appears to be the s. side of the old church has been 'built in', leaving open to the sky a filled in arch, a traceried *piscina* and what just might have been part of the old *rood stair*. At the w. end, under the bell turret, the little window with its 'Y' tracery just could be an original, re-used. The interior is a delight in small scale, with white painted walls and plaster ceiling, a w. *gallery* standing on slim iron rods, and holding a diminutive organ; simple deal pews, a triple chancel arch on 'Greek classical' columns; and in the chancel windows, fragments of old glass from the original church including, in the e. window, roundels showing St *Peter* (with key), *Paul* (with sword) and the Holy Spirit in the form of a dove emerging from the rays of the sun. The old font has been retained – it is of typical octagonal type, generously carved around the bowl with angels, lions and flowers; and supporting the stem, a quartet of the snootiest, nose-in-the-air little lions you ever saw.

Skeyton, All Saints (I3): On a windy upland with big fields all around and but one house for company. The *carstone quoins* in the s.w. corner point to an early date and although the *nave* windows are C15, the tower and blocked n. doorway are C13 and the foundations of a n. *aisle* were found in 1845. One of the old *lancet* windows is blocked up at the side of the *porch*, and the door you enter by is C15 and has a fine robust knocker. This was one of the first Norfolk churches to exchange its *box pews* for benches in 1846, and the font at that time was apparently a wooden affair painted red and yellow! The replacement is a stiff uncomfortable

Sloley, St Bartholomew: Seven sacrement font

piece with a shallow octagonal bowl. The cover is better – in the style of Salle with radiating fin buttresses and well proportioned. The little cast Victorian *Royal Arms* are painted and gilt and look well.

Sloley, St Batholomew (I3): The ground plan is a little unusual. The tower is offset to the n. and its base seems to be the same date as the *chancel*, which has a blocked n. window and *piscina* c.1300. There were extensions in the first half of the C14, and a late-C15 rebuilding produced the stately arches of the *arcades*. Above the matching chancel arch can be seen the line of its predecessor, offset to the n. – so everything had been pushed sideways. The outstanding thing here is the *seven sacrament font*. It is quite the best surviving example with very little damage to the panels. Clockwise from the e. they are: the baptism of Christ, ordination, matrimony, baptism, mass (one figure ringing the *sanctus bell*), confirmation (illustrating the common medieval practice of infant confirmation), penance (the devil of sin pushed away by an angel) and extreme unction. Angels display shields in the corona under the bowl, and shaft niches have standing figures, and the

Symbols of the Evangelists crouch at the foot. In the s. *aisle* chapel is the recessed table tomb of Oliver le Gros (d.1435). He was Lord of the manor and in one of the *spandrels* the arms are encircled by the *Collar of S's*, and all the achievements have been picked out in colour. The *nave* has a homely set of C18 *box pews* with a two-decker pulpit en suite – all grained light oak. Although this church is isolated and serves a tiny parish, it enjoys a delectable setting in a trim and open churchyard and is beautifully kept. No electricity means that oil lamps and candles are the alternative, and how charmed Sir John Betjeman would have been:

> Light's abode celestial Salem! lamps of
>   evening, smelling strong,
> Gleaming on the pitchpine, waiting, almost
>   empty evensong.

Smallburgh, St Peter (J3): St Peter's tower fell in 1677, taking with it the w. bay of the *nave*. This was replaced in 1902 when the *bell-cote* was added. The e. window is Victorian, but those in the nave are pleasing late-C14 work. The roof is a High Victorian version of *hammer-beam* with *tie-beams*. Painted red and cream, with a running text on the *wall plate*, it even has at its e. end a *celure* as in medieval times, although there is no *rood* to go with it. The bottom half of the C15 *screen* has a good deal of its original colour, but the saints in the panels are heavily defaced. Some can still be identified: far left St *Anthony*, left of the opening St *George*, right of opening St *Giles* and St *Lawrence*. The back has traces of a pretty brocaded design. The *piscina* is very decorative, with a *cusped* arch and pierced *quatrefoils*. On the n. side of the sanctuary is a very elegant memorial by *Thomas Rawlins* to Richard Oram (d.1762). The plain tablet has a curvaceous surround and top, with a cherub's head below. Before you leave to go down the attractive little avenue of sycamores, have a look at the door. It is C15 with remains of applied tracery at the head.

Snetterton, All Saints (F6): First made redundant and thus the prey of vandals, Snetterton Church is now officially under the guardianship of the *Norfolk Churches Trust*. Plain, battlemented tower of the C14, with belfry windows traceried in good, bold, geometrical style; *Perpendicular nave* and n. *aisle*, the latter with fine large windows, especially that at the e. end with its battlemented centre *transom*. *Decorated* period *chancel* though of still earlier fabric; and

C15 n. and s. *porches*, each with C13 inner doorways – though that on the n. has been appallingly vandalised. The nave and aisle roofs are simple but fine C15 *arch-brace* types, with superb *bosses* in feathery carving of high quality. Spacious and lofty Perpendicular *arcade* of the C15, of three enormous bays with narrow shafts and mouldings to the pillars. Big octagonal C15 font, with bold traceries and *quatrefoils* in the panels. The colourful *screen*, with its intricate and delicate traceries and canopy, was brightly painted in the C19; how much of the screen itself is original is uncertain. Above and to the left, the outline of the old *rood stair* exit at loft level. In the s.e. corner, a plain, remodelled *piscina* with a deeply carved, eight-leaf drain; and two plain figure niches set into the walls above. The n. aisle has a remodelled piscina, and a wall pedestal for an effigy carved most curiously – a markedly ample, fat-faced cherub head with an abundance of kiss-curled hair. The chancel is thoroughly Victorian – but it retains a very fine late-C13 double piscina under an opulent, open-carved head, its *hood mould* being completed by two good *corbels*. Adjoining are *dropped sill sedilia*, on three sharply dropped levels. The e. window has its original shafts with flat ringed *capitals* down the *jambs*; and also the corbels to its *hood mould*. The glass is probably by the O'Connors like that in the tower window; the easternmost s. nave window of 1884 is by Cox, Buckley & Son.

Snettisham, St Mary (C2): Of the few spires in Norfolk, Snettisham's is the biggest and best. Rebuilt in 1895, its 175ft. of stone, flying buttresses and two sets of windows provide a fitting crown for the C14 church beneath. You will find ruins of the original *chancel* beyond the present e. end, and the s. *transept* had its counterpart to the n. – although most of it was in ruins by 1600. Built about 1340, the church is the finest coherent example of the *Decorated* style in the county, and the climax is the first thing to be seen when coming up fom the village – a great w. window with a web of exuberant tracery that is a delight in itself, flanked by buttresses that merge into turrets topped with cones that match those at the corners of the tower. Below the window, a shallow *porch* three bays wide, with a tiny chamber above the *groined* ceiling. Entry via the n. door to an interior made memorable by the grace of the clustered columns which support the nave *arcade*. They have stone seats at the base as at Heacham and the *clerestory* has alternate circular windows with a variant of the standard *trefoil* tracery. An unusual feature in the general scheme is the use of half arches to link the *aisles* with the transepts. While at the w. end, look for these – a *brass* in the n.w. corner to John and Anne Cremer and family 1610; unusual because all the figures are separate and his inscriptions are in Latin while hers are in English. Then cross over to the s. aisle to see a *palimpsest brass* cleverly displayed in a frame jutting from the wall; on one side, a man of 1495 with his sons in front of him, on the other, the brass re-used for a lady of 1570. Close by is a very early long-waisted *sanctus bell* complete with headstock which may pre-date the present building. Also in this corner, the stair to the porch chamber with its very slim original door. The font was restored in 1856 but the bowl is C14 or early-C15. The pulpit has re-painted panels that may have come from a *screen* but most of the woodwork is C19. Not so the lectern – a fine early *Tudor* eagle (now minus its claws) with three lions at the base. In the n. aisle chapel is Wymond Carye's monument (1612), an alabaster effigy in half armour, rather knocked about in the feet and legs; triple inscription under a richly panelled arch, and the wrought iron railings are original. The s. transept is now a vestry, but venture in to look at the Styleman monuments – two of 1807/1819 on the e. wall are almost identical, and two of 1768/1803 on the w. wall illustrate the subtle shift of style in the late C18. On the back of the organ is a homely *gallery* of vicars dating back to 1815, and two medieval tiles from the nearby Bawsey factory. The *hatchments* are all of the Styleman family. No medieval glass here, but a window in the s. aisle designed by Paul Jefferies in 1969 is worth a mention, and although the 1846 glass by *Warrington* in the w. window has strident blue backgrounds, the Old Testament scenes are very lively – look out for Jonah and the whale. Nothing to do with architecture, but Snettisham rates an entry in the record books for being the first church in England to be bombed from the air – the e. window was blown in by a Zeppelin raid in January, 1915.

South Acre, St George (E4): Almost within sight of its grand neighbour up on the hill at Castle Acre is this inviting village church, whose small size is out of all proportion to the interest it contains. It is largely *Perpendicular*, though its C13 origins are clear to see. The tower is Perpendicular. Between label and w. window are inset shields carved with the Arms of Sir John

Harsyke and his family, who built the tower in the C15. Perpendicular window outlines and traceries can be seen all the way round the building. The *nave* n. door is simple C14 *Decorated*. The interior of the church is a delightful package of character and interest. *Hammer-beam* and *arch-braced roof* to nave, with bold floral *bosses*, and good arch-braced examples to *chancel* and *aisle*. Low late-C13 nave *arcade* (fragment of original colour on one *pier*); Decorated chancel arch; old pews with rough *poppy-heads* and animals on the elbows; paraffin lamps neatly converted to electricity. Massive *Norman* font on a central pillar big enough for an arcade; topping it, a restored C16 canopy which bears a Latin inscription commemorating Geoffrey Baker, rector here, who died in 1534. Under the tower are the remains of a once very fine C14 *screen*, with tracery in rich foliage forms and slim 'pillars' with ring *capitals*. In the n. aisle, which extends the whole length of nave and chancel, is a grave slab, carved with floriated crosses (there are more *ledger stones* in the pavement under the chancel arch). Next to it is the figure of a *Knight Templar*, fully armed, cross-legged, his feet upon a dog. It could be Sir Eudo Harsick, who went on crusade to the Holy Land. In the chancel chapel at the e. end of the aisle is a life-size *brass* for Sir John Harsick, 1384, and his wife, the couple shown holding hands. Adjacent, a grand and colourful alabaster monument to Sir Edward Barkham, 1623, a former Lord Mayor of London, and his wife. He and his lady lie on a tomb chest, he in armour with his civic robes over the top. Against the chest are their daughters and sons – separated by a collection of broken bones. Against the wall above are the Barkham Arms. On the opposite wall is a facsimile of Sir Edward's own helmet – it was given to the church in 1956 by the Tower of London in return for the permanent loan of the original. A large *squint* looks through to the high altar. Nearby is the entrance to the *rood loft*, which emerges in the corner of the nave. In the sanctuary is a C14 *piscina* with a stone *credence shelf* and *dropped sill sedilia*; and a tomb recess in which rests the barely recognisable remnant of a C14 wooden effigy, representing another member of the Harsyck family. Between the choir stalls is a little brass with the figure of Thomas Leman, a former rector who died in 1534; there is a fragment of a scroll above him, and a little plaque engraved with the Madonna and child. The modern choir stalls, carved by a C20 rector, have quirky elbow rests – frogs, snails, an otter and a fish.

South Creake, St Mary (E2): A large and grandly balanced church, with a squatly powerful *Decorated* tower. It did have a parapet originally, but this was removed long since – bits of it will be found built into the churchyard wall. Boldly *cusped* belfry windows and a quite magnificent w. window of four *lights* with fine *reticulated* tracery, give the tower extra character. The view of the church from the n. is a splendid one, taking in the tower, the dignified *Perpendicular clerestory* and n. *aisle* of the early C15, and the big late-C13 *chancel* (the oldest part of the church) with its contemporary richly cusped 'Y'-traceried windows and one confident *Tudor* insert. A walk around the church is in fact an object lesson in styles of fascinating variety – from the late-C13 interlacing tracery of the e. window across five lights, through the interesting form of the C15 vestry e. window, to the noble Perpendicular example placed high over the chancel in the *nave's* e. gable. The s. *porch* is C14 Decorated, with crowned Ms for the Virgin in *flushwork* over the outer arch flanking a prettily *cusped* little figure niche which now holds a modern Madonna and child. The interior of the church is wide, lofty and dazzlingly light, the spaciousness accentuated by the complete lack of fixed pews in nave and aisles. Handsome *hammer-beam* with *arch-braced roof* to nave, complete with 22 winged angels (freshly painted and at least some of the wings being replacements) on the hammers; big floral *bosses* at the ridge intersections; and deep *wall posts*. Good arch-braced roofs also in the aisles, with lovely carved ornamentation on the s. side, notably in the *spandrels* – a dragon, a unicorn and possibly a *pelican* with doves. Enormous and powerful Decorated tower arch; C15 nave *arcade* of five elegant bays, the columns having stone seats around their bases. The C15 *seven sacrament font*, which carries traces of original colour, has been so savagely defaced that the panel scenes are almost unidentifiable. The pretty C15 pulpit, on its wine-glass stem, was once coloured too, but little remains save a spot of gilding on its attractive raised traceries. All the colour has, with equal single-mindedness, been removed from the *screen* – though perhaps this accentuates the delicacy of its tracery, foliage and fragile upward lines. Look to the left, and original colour is in evidence in the head of a lovely little cusped, two-light window which looks through from the n. chapel. On this side it has a square hood, generously carved with floral motifs; on the chapel side, a *piscina* set into the wall below it. On the s. side is the *rood stair*, and to either side of the chancel arch (with

most distinctive *headstops*, surely portraits, to its *hood mould*) are the supports which held the *rood beam*. The long, stark chancel – with the ugliest of utilitarian roofs – contains a few old *poppy-head* benchends, placed against the walls; and a damaged but still splendid piscina and *sedilia*, the latter having a canopy formed by the sill of the window above it which is richly carved with angels. The totally plain recess in the n. wall was an *Easter Sepulchre*. In the windows of both aisles there is a profusion of fragments of ancient stained glass; and in the n. aisle also, a C17 *bier* with 'collapsible' arms; and a sadly broken and depleted *Royal Arms* of George II, painted on wood.

South Lopham, St Andrew (G7): South Lopham is a by-word among enthusiasts for Norfolk churches – for here is one of the grandest pieces of *Norman* architecture in the county. It has a central tower of five stages reaching to 100ft, which broods, hunch-shouldered, over its village. It is part of a church which William Bygod, Earl of Norfolk, gave to the monks of Thetford. Below strong belfry openings (the *flushworked* parapet is later, *Perpendicular*), it descends in rows of blind *arcades* to the lowest level, where on the s. side, there is a blocked-in doorway of about 1200, rather than the tower's building date of 1100-1120. The *clerestory* above the *nave* is Perpendicular, as is the *porch*. The s. *aisle* and *chancel* are Decorated (the e. window is a C19 replacement). Walk round the church and admire the nave's w. window – an enormous and splendid affair, of three *lights* and great height, divided into two by a heavy, battlemented *transom*. The n. door is Norman, with zigzag and other mouldings round its arch and simply sculptured *capitals*. High up on the n. wall's e. end is a small, Saxon round window, deeply splayed, of about 1010. This remnant shows that when the Normans built their tower, they attached it to an existing, lofty, Saxon church and used part of its fabric in their own rebuilding, before it too was overtaken by C15 alterations and enlargements. The interior of this building is a delight of light and shape, detail and style. At the centre is the *crossing* – big, entirely plain, fine *Norman* arches sitting on fat-cushioned capitals, the absence of any decorative carving accentuating the creamy texture of the stone. The nave has a *hammer-beamed roof*, with small collars and *king posts* at the top. The hammers, and the generous *wall plates*, are luxuriantly carved. Five windows in the Perpendicular clerestory sit over the four-bay, C14

s. *arcade* with its slim, clustered *quatrefoil* pillars. There are four clerestory windows on the n. side, though there has never been an aisle there. Below the w. window, stands the C14 font, octagonal, with sloping sides, and delicately carved around bowl and stem with tracery outlines; it has a rather jolly C17 cover. Nearby is a huge chest, made from a single tree trunk, and believed to be as old as the tower. In the s. aisle chapel is a little *angle piscina*, with adjoining plain *dropped sill sedilia*. Under the tower is a range of excellent C15 benchends, the complete ends carved with figures and traceries, and topped by figures and grotesques. One of them, e. end, n. side, is of an Elephant and Castle. In the s. side of the tower crossing is the outline of the *rood stair* entrance. The chancel is Decorated, built between 1361 and 1380 by the Rector, Nicholas de Horton. A solid, almost flat *tie-beamed* roof and a *low side window* on the s., complete with a modern door. In the sanctuary is an angle piscina and dropped sill sedilia. The church has an excellent ring of 6 bells, tenor 20-3-14 cwt.

South Pickenham, All Saints (E5): A little church of charm, in a pretty village. The round tower is *Norman* with a later octagonal top. The fabric of the body of the church is ancient, but changes through the centuries have further contributed to its character – a mixture of *Early English, Decorated* and *Perpendicular* styles. Especially good is the C14 e. window, under a flowing *ogee* arch. Below it, set into the wall, is a *trefoil*-headed figure niche. The odd circular buttress-like attachment on the n. side of the *chancel* is a chimney. Beside it is a *Tudor priest's door*, outlined in pink brick. Through a tiny *porch* into a pleasing interior. In 1604 the whole roof was carried away in a violent storm and the nave walls were raised by about three feet. The sturdy roof, with its carved and coloured *wall plates*, dates from 1737. The chancel barrel roof is dates from 1907. The C17 pulpit, which is carved and panelled, was originally installed in the private chapel of a West Country mansion and was presented to All Saints in 1973. On a *gallery* sits an excellent coloured and gilded organ designed by *Augustus Pugin*. Beside it on the s. wall is a faded St *Christopher*. Surviving, on either side at the e. end of the nave, are the carved *corbel* heads which supported the beam of the *rood loft*. In the chancel, a C14 *angle piscina* and adjoining *dropped sill sedilia*. To each side of the e. window are delicate jambs, slim and rounded, with C13 ring *capitals*. Supporting the side of the central

chancel window on the s. side is a re-used small pillar and capital, probably *Transitional Norman*. Under the w. gallery, a C14 font; and an ancient stone coffin with a fragment of the carved lid.

South Raynham, St Martin (E3): Church Lane winds up and away from the village street and at the end the church is prettily embowered among trees and evergreens. It is mainly C14 and the unbuttressed w. tower, with its two-*light Decorated* w. window and matching bell openings has recently been repointed. The main *nave* windows are square-headed *Perpendicular* but one on the s. side is early-C14 and is set within a blocked arch that will have led originally to a *transept*. There were restorations in 1810 and there are signs that the walls of nave and *chancel* were raised when the new roofs went in. The interior is very modest, with a plain octagonal font and 1880s glass in the e. window that glows with rich colour – scenes of the Shepherds, the Nativity, and the flight into Egypt. Beneath it is a real treasure – the original C13 *Norman mensa*, in use as an altar once again and standing on two plain supports. The whole of the edge of the six inch thick stone slab is deeply cut with a continuous square cross motif and there is not another like it, as far as is known. For years it was used as a step in the sanctuary, but now the corner *consecration crosses* are visible although the one in the middle has worn away,.

South Walsham, St Lawrence (J4): The church stands just beyond St Mary's in the same churchyard, and visitors may be forgiven for thinking that it is no longer in use, but that is far from the case. It was originally thatched, which was probably the source of a disastrous fire in 1827 which gutted the building. Five years later the *chancel* was restored and a new w. wall enclosed one bay of the *nave* to form a smaller useable building. Its fortunes fluctuated over the years and for a time it was used as a Sunday School. In the 1970s the remains of what had been a fine tower finally collapsed and St *Lawrence's* future seemed bleak. However, the village, led by a priest with vision, decided otherwise, and trustees were appointed to raise funds and administer the building. Restoration and renewal followed and now it enjoys facilities seldom found in a medieval church – underfloor heating and excellent cloakrooms among them. In the late C19 the floor of the ruined nave was used for a few burials but in the 1990s it became 'The Sacristan's Garden'. Entered through a pergola, and set with clumps of all the herbs with which a medieval sacristan would have been familiar, and with a seat snug against the base of the old tower, it tempts one to linger even on a winter's day. The most important point to be made about St *Lawrence*'s however, is that, unlike many churches in a similar situation, it has never been made redundant nor has it been de-consecrated; the Daily Office is said regularly and occasional services are held throughout the year. Run in conjunction with St Mary's, it is a splendid example of positive renewal.

South Walsham, St Mary (J4): The C15 tower and s. *porch* catch the eye for the unity of their design and the quality of their execution. The porch has a fine frontage, with the Virgin and the Angel of the *Annunciation* in the *spandrels* of the door. Over it, a lovely little niche contains a small sculptured group which probably represents the coronation of the Virgin, In the s.e. corner of the sanctuary is a large incised slab which was from the tomb of a C15 Abbot of St Benet's Abbey (whose ruins are on the banks of the River Bure, not far away from here near Ludham). After use as a doorstep in the palace in Norwich, long since disappeared, of the Dukes of Norfolk it came home to the abbot's birthplace in the 1940s. The C15 *rood screen* has the distinction of retaining its original door handles, and has a most interesting inscription in a mixture of Latin and English, 'Pray for the souls of John Galt and his wives the which have done painting this perke'. Galt was a serf who, having gained his freedom, had the screen painted in gratitude. The wall behind the pulpit shows how the decorative pattern of the screen was continued beyond it in paint. In a showcase in the n. aisle are photocopies and transcripts of the *Solemn League and Covenant* entries from the parish registers. South Walsham's are the only example left in Norfolk. The church has an excellent ring of 6 bells, tenor 7-3-4 cwt.

South Wootton, St Mary (C3): There was once a steeple on the C15 tower, but in 1881 lightning split the whole thing down the middle and it was rebuilt in brick and *carstone*. This was part of a big restoration completed in 1893. Stones set in the n.w. buttress and s. of the tower in the middle of the w. wall look like *Saxon long and short work*, and the *chancel* is early-C14 with a fine e. window – four *lights* with *cusped* 'Y' tracery and *trefoils* above. The two short *transepts* have windows of the same period and, although the angle of their w. walls is unusual, the window reveals inside and the mouldings where the

transepts meet the *nave* look undisturbed, so there seems little reason to call them C18 variations. The interior is plain and uncluttered, with a single tablet on the cream-washed walls (Rev. Hamond 1815, by William Eldridge of Kings Lynn), but the eye is immediately taken by the stupendous *Norman* font. It stands on eight columns round a centre shaft, and the carved bowl has a huge and fearsome mask at each corner. In the s. transept is a wonderful example of a C17 *bier*. It has drop handles and a semi-circular framework on top to support the pall. On this, and along the sides are four texts and a Latin inscription saying that it was given by Henry Kidson in 1611 after 41 years as rector. Close by, a trefoil-headed *piscina*, with a *credence shelf* and a pair of small but beautiful *headstops*. In the chancel, the tomb chest of Sir Thomas Winde (1603) is set in a n. wall recess; the *Purbeck marble* top is packed with fossils and the sides have the family coats of arms with much of their original colour. Opposite, a simple piscina and stepped *sedilia* with trefoil arches all contained under a single square label.

Southburgh, St Andrew (G5): Prominently sited on a hilltop in lush farming country, this church is a virtual Victorian rebuild. The battlemented tower with its little spire is a replacement in the *Decorated* style. At the same time, 1878-82, the *porch* was taken down and moved slightly to the right, so as to set it clear of the s.w. *nave* window. The *nave* and *chancel* windows have a mixture of tracery styles, with a four-*light* e. window of intersecting tracery. Difficult to know what is original and what is replacement. However the basic fabric of the chancel is late-C13, and that of the nave early-C14. In the *jamb* of the s.e. nave window is the entrance to the *rood stair*. The base of the *rood screen* remains, with some nicely gilded, carved *Tudor* flowers in the *spandrels* and the restored panels stippled with tiny flowerlets. In the sanctuary an e. wall *piscina* and an angle piscina have been remodelled; to the left of the altar, again in the e. wall, is a large square *aumbry*, also rebuilt, with a continuous freize round the chancel and sanctuary to blend them all together.

Southrepps, St James (I2): This is a big church which was even larger before the *aisles* were pulled down in 1791. The *arcades* can still be seen. The commanding 114ft. tower is beautifully proportioned and one of the best in Norfolk. The *base course* has the shell emblem of St *James*, and the large w. door is flanked by nice niches with shields and tracery above. The *sound-holes* have a delicate lattice design, and above the large three-*light* belfry windows is a fine parapet. Inside, the panels of the C15 *screen* have their original colouring – a diaper of crowned 'M's on alternate red and green grounds. The *priest's door* in the s. wall of the *chancel* has a lovely *hood mould* terminating in demi-figures of laymen with most expressive heads. The church has an excellent ring of 6 bells, tenor 12-2-12 cwt.

Sparham, St Mary the Virgin (G4): This is a church where rebuilding has resulted in some curious anomalies. The early-C14 *chancel weeps* slightly to the s. and must always have done so, because the two easternmost *arcades* of the *nave* match it in date. At that time there was a lower roof and the *clerestory* had small *quatrefoil* windows. Two of them can still be seen blocked up, above the arches at the e. end. The tracery of the window at the w. end of the n. *aisle* shows that it too was built at the same time. The present C15 tower has buttresses on the inside – a sure sign that it was free-standing when built, but when the nave arcade was extended to meet it the original setting-out proved to be faulty and the western-most bays had to be stretched to bridge the gap, and heavier pillars were used. The s. aisle was added in 1481, and the detailing of the s. *porch* matches the clerestory. A *scratch dial* on the left hand *jamb* of the inner door shows that it was in use before the porch was built. The tower is handsome and has an unusually rich niche over the w. door. Designed no doubt for a statue of the Virgin, it has a nodding *ogee* arch with canopy, and attendant lions on top of slim pillars. The C15 clerestory stops short one bay from the e. end and a big gable window was used to complete the top lighting. The *arch-braced roof* has little angels under the ridge bearing shields, looking for all the world like birds in flight. The chancel is now nicely open, with modern stalls incorporating old bench ends set well back. The original C15 *screen* is no longer there, but four of its panels have been framed and stand in the n. aisle. They are of quite exceptional interest and two of them are illustrations from the *Dance of Death* – a unique portrayal in screen painting. In one, a shrouded skeleton rises from a tomb by the font in a church, and the text on the scrolls is from the Book of Job, chapter 10: 'I should have been as though I had not been born'. In the other, a macabre pair of corpses are dressed in the fashionable clothes of Richard III's day, with another paraphrase from Job: 'Man that is born

Sparham, St Mary: C15 Dance of Death screen panels

of woman hath but a short time. Now he is. Now he is not'. The two other panels have St *Thomas of Canterbury*, and the local St *Walstan* of Bawburgh, who was believed to be of royal blood – witness the crown and sceptre. Just by these panels is a good *brass* to a rector, William Mustarder (c.1490) in mass vestments. While still in the n. aisle have a look at the lengths of carving on the e. window ledge. They probably came from the *wall plate* of the original roof. The C18 *Royal Arms* have been well restored and are now over the n. door.

Spixworth, St Peter (I4): The church presents an odd outline, with a tiny unbuttressed tower at the s.w. corner which was rebuilt in 1804. The *nave* and *chancel* are in one, separated from the s. *aisle* by an *arcade* set on thin octagonal columns. The e. window has a nice variation of tracery, with a spray of leaf forms springing from the centre above the panels, two of which have *ogee* heads. The C15 *piscina* and *sedilia* are grouped under a single square label. On the other side of the chancel is a splendid monument to William and Alice Peck (1635), by Edward Marshall. The two marble figures lie in shrouds, one above and behind the other, below a canopy. A helm is fixed to the wall above. There are verses below, one of which reads:

Tread soft, tis holy ground, the dust lyes heere
Was once pure flesh, the relique of a cleere
And noble soule, which because, free and rare
Heav'n did translat, and there it shines a starre,
But this sad earth's below, which being dust
Did heere fall downe & this kind ground in trust
Keepes till it starts refind; for then this clay
Shall ev'n a sunne appeare at that great day.

Sporle, St Mary (E4): The church sits on a slight rise, trees to either side, a great swathe of cleared green churchyard setting off the western aspect of the fine tower. Those crisp panelled battlements are a *Perpendicular* addition; but the rest of the tower is an interesting *Early English* into *Decorated Transitional* example – very elementary belfry window traceries; splendid w. door, deeply moulded, with triple detached pillars; above the door, a large and notable figure niche with *trefoil* tracery and a heavy triangular hood. Over the niche there is the outline of an old pitched roof line. This is a big church in a mixture of Early English, Decorated and Perpendicular styles, though inside, signs of earlier, *Norman* work have been identified. The C13 e. window is good – three big *lancets* below an eight-leaf opening in solid *plate tracery*, all contained under a simple arch standing on pencil-slim shafts with ring *capitals*. Within, an outstandingly good modern, *arch-braced roof* with excellent carved *wall plates*, is a *sanctus bell opening* high in the e. face of the tower, and a C13 *arcade* of four bays. This is not continuous, however, as there is a solidly walled section between the second and third arches from the e. – probably to enclose side chapels. On the pillars on both sides can clearly be seen the marks where the *parclose screens* were fitted; the *piscinas* are still there to see, and the s. back wall has traces of the original colour, complementing the remarkable adjoining range of 24 painted wall panels discovered in 1886 and late-C14/early-C15 in date, with scenes in the life of St *Catherine of Alexandria*. The *rood stair* entrance, in the s.e. corner of the nave, has been used to site a modern pulpit in stone. The simple chancel has a fine e. window, embellished on the inside, with miniature blank *arcades*, inset with solid *quatrefoils*. In the chancel n. *aisle* (now a vestry) is a sturdy C13 Early English angle piscina. Of the same period, a shallow octagonal font at the w. end stands on a central column with eight slimmer shafts around it, on a raised stone dais with a Maltese cross outline.

Sprowston, St Mary & St Margaret (I4): Almost entirely *Perpendicular*, though the tower is C18, and everything was heavily restored 1889-90. The *porch* has C18 sun dial and four *mass dials* on s.e. buttress. Inside, the *arcades* are C14, s. earlier than n. *Royal Arms* of George III on canvas. An attractive C15 *piscina* has, erected across it with scant regard, one of the unusual number of monuments here. This one is to Sir Thomas and Lady Adams, 1667 – he was Lord Mayor of London, an intimate friend of Charles II, and bought the Sprowston estate from the last Corbet baronet in 1645. The epitaph tells that Sir Thomas suffered from calculus and that, after death, a stone was taken from his body which weighed 25 ozs. The C19 was offended by 'this minutely indelicate catalogue of his ailments'. In contrast is the simplicity of the adjoining small tablet to Dame Anne Adams who, poor lady, had ten children and died in 1674 giving birth to the last of them, when only 33. In the n. chapel are the Corbets: John, 1559 – half his body missing, but four sons and six daughters still in attendance; Thomas, 1617 – High Sheriff and father of one of the regicides of Charles I; his son Miles, executed 1662 – a very good monument; and an earlier Miles, 1607. Also fine is a monument in the n. *aisle* to Christopher Knolles, 1610 – even though he, wife and nine offspring are all decapitated. The brown and white marble piece, for Nathaniel Micklethwaite, 1757, by *Robert Page* of Norwich, is excellent; and a piece by the younger *John Bacon* for Lady Maria Micklethwaite, 1805, symbolising her death in childbirth, is one of his best. As you leave the church, note the lovely group of yews to the e..

Stalham, St Mary the Virgin (J3): A big, *Perpendicular* town church with a massive, squat tower. An outline in stone indicates that the tower once had an enormous w. window, but there is now only a modest one in Perpendicular style. The s. *aisle* windows are impressive Perpendicular, but those on the n. side have Y-tracery, which if original puts them about a century earlier. While outside the n. aisle, note at the e. end the strange interlacing triple-head stone carving, sharing four eyes; and near it, on the *clerestory* corner, a carving of what looks like a lovable bear! The e. end windows of the two aisles have lovely flowing tracery of late *Decorated* style, which is reproduced in the *chancel*, which was rebuilt in 1827. Entering through the s. *porch* (a Victorian restoration) we find ourselves in a spacious, uncluttered interior. The eye is drawn at once to the fine octagonal C15 font, standing high on its three traceried steps, its rich carvings round bowl and stem magnificently intact – during the C19 it was found, partially buried and covered in plaster, thus its happy preservation. The bowl carving shows a lovely Baptism of Christ, God as *Trinity*, and pairs of saints, with more saints around the stem. The five-bay *arcade* and above, the clerestory with its deeply inset *quatrefoil* windows, are Decorated, as are the soaring tower and chancel arches. To either side of the latter are two enormous *squints*, but these no longer, as originally intended, look direct from the side chapels to the high altar – for the chancel has been stripped and cleared and the altar brought forward to the centre: it looks impressive, and admirably serves for today's family communion. In the s.e. corner is a splendidly pompous tomb, all swathes and cherubs, to Katherine Smyth, 1718. Mounted on the s. wall are five restored panels from the old *rood screen*, left to right, Saints *Andrew*, *Thomas of Canterbury*, *Edward the Confessor*, *Edmund* and *Roche*. The latter is a very rare representation; he draws aside his robe to display his particular and unpleasant symbol, plague spots on his left leg. The s. aisle has a beautiful *angle piscina* and a *dropped sill sedilia*. In front of the altar are two tiny figures from a C15 *brass*. Beside the n. aisle altar an *aumbry* shows hinge marks of its old door in the stone. As you leave, note by the s. door the remains, still opulent, of what must have been a remarkably grand *holy water stoup*.

Stanfield, St Margaret (F3): Hidden from the main road by surrounding trees, this C13 church has had few major alterations. The *chancel* has *lancets*, one shortened window above the *piscina* with 'Y' tracery, and an e. window of 1864 that suits exactly the period of the building. The tall C15 s. windows of the *nave* have unusual *moulds* – flat, and terminating in heads and figures in strange positions. The late-C13 tower has a plain parapet, 'Y' tracery bell openings and *trefoil sound-holes*, and there are headless kneeling figures at the corners of the *porch* gable. The nave is light and bare, with no tower arch, and an *arch-braced roof* which would appear to have been painted a light tan at some time. By the door, a plain font with a pretty *Jacobean* cover – a flat top with a centre shaft supported by scrolls and carried on *pilasters*. The nave pews stand on high sills and have *poppy-heads* and fairly rudimentary animals carved on the arms. The early-C17 pulpit has the familiar shallow carving in the form of blank arches with arabesque panels over them and, with its backboard and *tester*, was roughly converted into a two-decker later. The carving on the *communion rails* matches the pulpit and no doubt came from the same workshop. Beyond the C15 *screen*, the chancel shows more of its quality than can be seen outside. The windows have sturdy shafts and deeply moulded arches, and the late-C13 double piscina fits neatly into the design, with an *aumbry* to the right A *ledger slab* nearby for members of the Morris

family mentions Lieut. George Morris who fell at the siege of St Sebastian in 1813.

Stanhoe, All Saints (E2): A pleasant approach past thick and bushy yews to the *porch* in the base of the late-C13 tower, a simple unbuttressed affair which stands almost clear of the s. side of the church. The s. doorway is about the same age although its blocked counterpart on the n. side looks earlier. The s. *aisle* has a range of windows with pretty *Decorated* tracery, and in the *chancel* the 'Y' tracery windows are delicately shafted on the inside. The easternmost window was specifically designed shorter than the rest to fit above the fine Decorated *piscina* and stepped *sedilia*. These have *trefoiled ogee arches* and there are *headstops* above the intermediate detached columns. In contrast to the flood of light through the intersecting tracery of the C13 w. window, the Victorian e. window is full of excellent early *Kempe & Co.* glass of 1879; small figures of saints, prophets and martyrs in groups of two and three, about a vine that rises to a Christ in Majesty – a very rich composition, and the s. aisle e. window with its two resurrection scenes is by Kempe too. The chancel has a host of Hoste monuments, the local family which included Capt. Sir William Hoste – one of *Nelson*'s captains. His tablet is on the s. wall, although he has others in St Paul's and St Margaret's, Kings Lynn. Walking round the outside note the *scratch dials* on the s. porch and the s.e. buttress of the chancel and see how the *dripstone* follows the change of window level on the s. side of the chancel – all carefully planned.

Starston, St Margaret (I7): A lovely position on the steep little hill above the stream that meanders down to join the Waveney; a great cedar n. of the church and plenty of trees all round. There is some C12 stonework in the s. wall and blocked windows that might be earlier still, but the tower is of about 1300 with a later set of stepped battlements with *flushwork* chequer that is repeated along the top of the nave. Fine *gargoyles* here with one e. of the *porch* that looks more recent and quite different in character – a bearded man with a pitcher. Inside the porch with its embellished *Tudor* arch, four *corbels* have the *Symbols of the Four Evangelists* which are well and deeply carved. There was a restoration in 1858 and another big one in 1870 when the n. *aisle* was added. The font has *Tudor roses* and blank shields in the bowl panels, and lions round the shaft; the outline of the *rood* *stairs* doors shows in the wall s. of the *chancel* arch. In the n.e. corner of the sanctuary is the big monument to Bartholomew Cotton who was Clerk of Briefs in the Star Chamber. In his black robes and skull cap he seems a kneeling epitome of that fearsome tribunal. Below the *priest's door* on the s. side of the chancel, carefully lift the carpet to find the sad memorial to:

> Philip, the sonne of Francis Bacon Esq., and Dorothy his Wife, who died unweaned at Nurse, and was buried the 21st day of Nov. 1657. Death is the Sentence of the Lord over all flesh.

What a pity that we are too self-conscious and tightly regulated nowadays to leave such little illuminations of history behind us. Even the 1826 Gaffin tablet to rector William Whitear leaves out the most interesting titbit – that he was accidentally shot by one of his own parishioners while apprehending a thief. The church has a ring of 6 bells, tenor 8-2-0 cwt.

Stibbard, All Saints (F3): A pretty village church within a peaceful curtilage of trees, the lead cap on its stumpy, C14 and recently restored tower being visible above the foliage as you approach. The tower's red brick, Victorian buttresses surprisingly set it off rather well, even the one slapped over the w. window. The range of windows here is a good one – simple, attractive *Perpendicular* in *nave* s. wall; a curious pair in the n. *aisle*, one pointed, the other square headed; the irregular tracery over the aisle altar. In n. wall of *chancel*, a little *Decorated* window containing a lot of fragments of C14 glass, made up into a mosaic; and the best of them, the chancel e. window-five slim *lights* of interlacing tracery, but with a *quatrefoil* slipped in interestingly at the top. Within, the *rood beam* now bears a modern cross: above, fragments of original painting on the wall. Perpendicular *arcade*. Base of an old *screen* remains; some nice carving on the pulpit, which would be better without the paint; some lovely old C15 *poppy-head* bench ends, with assorted carved figures.

Stiffkey, St John Baptist (F1): Tucked away below the seaside ridge where this picturesque village clings, this church surprises with its impressive parapets to the *nave*, in chequerwork flint, punctuated by tiny pinnacle-columns rising from the buttresses; and by its handsome *porch*, with a *Decorated* outer arch with shields in the *spandrels*; above it, a figure niche and the upper gable end in chequered red brick

and flint. The upper room to the porch has gone but the octagonal turret at this corner was the stairway to it. A similar turret stands at the s. e. corner of the nave: this was a *rood turret* for the *rood loft*. Within, all is bright and light, the nave lit by large C15 windows, with fragments of ancient glass in the centre-s. window. The *chancel* arch has *corbel* portrait heads and interesting *capitals* – one is carved with floral motifs, but the other has heads of two women and a man in fashionable head-gear, the former in *butterfly head-dresses*. The chancel has a coarse *piscina* with a lop-sided arch; and nearby, three *misericords*, though the seats have gone. In front of the *communion rails*, only a small inscription remains of the *brass* to Margaret Branche, 1479. Opposite, set low in the n. wall, is a deep recess with a pointed arch – possibly an *Easter Sepulchre*. Nathaniel Bacon's large monument of 1615 is restrained, in black marble with coloured shields in alabaster (the monument was erected by Nathaniel before he died and the date added later). The chancel n. window is a good example of *plate tracery*. The e. window looks like a replacement.

Stockton, St Michael & All Angels (J6): The round *Norman* tower has a coating of plaster and is topped by an attractive miniature spire. The *nave* and *chancel* lie under one continuous roof of thatch, and inside this gives a pleasingly uncluttered vista of steep *arch-braces* springing from an embattled *wall plate*. Although there is one C13 *lancet* in the s. side, the rest of the windows are a mixture of *Decorated* and *Perpendicular* styles, and the *porch* was added in the C16. A fashionable Dutch gable was stitched on in 1683 and at some stage the huge timbers from the old bell frame were pressed into service as porch benches of a highly individual character. The dumpy C14 font is equally individual. From four of its eight sides project bulbous lion head symbols of St *Mark*, with shallow arcading on the other faces. The cover is one of the *Jacobean* candle-snuffer variety, with *crocketted* ribs and an interlacing strapwork pattern round the edge. The 1890s e. window by Suffling won't let you ignore it but there is quite a lot of medieval glass in the windows on the s. side. Look particularly for the Virgin and Child in the chancel, and for a shield of the *Passion Emblems* in the nave showing the pierced hands and feet. It is odd that the heavy C17 *communion rails* have had every other *baluster* carefully removed to leave neat stumps under the top rail. They certainly wouldn't deter the dogs now! In the corner of the sanctuary lies the Rev. Valentine Lumley Bernard. He died 'in the performance of his Duty on Sunday the 24th March 1816 aged 69 years.'

Stody, St Mary (G2): The church stands prettily on its small hill, approached by narrow winding lanes, with a house or two nearby. The round tower has C14 bell-openings but may well be *Saxon* in origin. The *chancel* windows have good and varied *Decorated* period tracery, while those in the *nave* are later. Best of all is the composition of *arch-braced roofs*, culminating in a timber *rib-vault* at the *crossing* of nave and *transepts* – most unusual in a church of this size. The remains of a St *Christopher* have been rather boldly re-coloured opposite the door and provided with a painted frame.

Stoke Holy Cross, The Holy Cross (I5): This little church on its steep knoll at the edge of the village is meticulously maintained. Between 1867 and 1872 the architect *Thomas Jekyll*, who was very active in Norfolk, wrought a wholesale restoration/rebuilding. The basic fabric is C13 but he replaced the small original windows in the *chancel* with *Early English style lancets,* reroofed the whole church, and added a new vestry and *porch*; new seating, *communion rails,* a reading desk and a renewed *piscina* completed the makeover. However, at the w. end of the *nave*, two attractive *poppy-head* bench-ends – a bear on one, and on the other an odd beast which just could be a monkey – which have been incorporated into a charming little bench seat. Modern font – the original one, inexplicably, is outside by the tower, discarded, though it is finely carved – visible are *Tudor roses* and two *Evangelistic Symbols* (Lion and Man). Under the tower, n. side, a deep, slim and very tall *banner-stave locker*. Over the s. door, Hanoverian *Royal Arms*. The best thing here is the memorial on the outside s. wall of the *nave* to the Revd. Thomas Havers, who died in 1719. This remarkable gentleman was, as the plummy Latin of his memorial declaims, Theologia, Medicina, Chyrurgia et Lythotamia, Doctus fuit et Expertus' (He was expert in theology, medicine, surgery and especially cutting for the stone.) and to prove it, he's surrounded by his instruments – scalpel, callipers, scissors and various other business-like medical tools of an age when surgery was nothing if not basic.

Stokesby, St Andrew (K4): A field path from the n. (where you can run your hands through the ears of corn in the summer), or a grassy track from the s. leads to the well kept churchyard lined with beech and lime. Altogether a delightful spot, and the church itself is very attractive. The roofs are thatch, the C13 tower has triple-stepped battlements of the C16, and there is a *porch* in warm red brick which sets off the white slatted outer door. The s. door proper has a C14 ring handle with long wrought iron decorated straps, and on its inside face, a most eccentric placement for the Victorian *Royal Arms* painted on a semi-circular board. The C14 *nave* has a *scissors-braced roof* left open to the thatch, but the *chancel* now has a coved ceiling in pale blue – that and its whitewashed walls mark it off clearly in the absence of the customary arch. At the w. end there is an interesting set of benches with *poppy-heads* and traceried backs; the ends, (one with initials 'E.W.') have big figures carved on the arms. There are dogs, a lion holding a shield blazoned with the arms of Berney, a *griffin*, a mighty odd eagle, and the best is a lady kneeling at a desk on which she has laid her rosary. On the chancel floor (s. side) a *brass* to Edmund Clere (d.1488) and his wife – he in armour with a fawning greyhound under his feet, she in a low cut dress with arms akimbo. The sanctuary now has a raised board floor and the brass to Anne Clere (d.1570) has been lifted and screwed to the wood (s. side). This is a very good figure in cloak, hood and ruff, with lots of character in the face. Her five sons and six daughters are grouped on two separate plates. At the sanctuary step look for the *ledger slab* of John Wace, rector here for 60 years while his brother James served nearby Filby for forty. On the e. wall is an interesting evasion of the low church prejudice against prayers for the dead – the Rev. William Taylor Worship's memorial: 'Reader, offer, if not a prayer, at least a kind wish for the welfare of his soul'. The enigma of the tall blue pole at the end of a front pew is solved if you know that it was put there recently to help a blind parishioner find his accustomed place.

Stow Bardolph, Holy Trinity (C5): Now that the main road skirts the village, the church is in a cul de sac and its broad graveyard is very peaceful. The sturdy *carstone* tower is *Norman* at the base with thin *lancet* windows n. and s., deeply splayed inside. The belfry stage is *Perpendicular* and there are heavy red brick diagonal buttresses to the w. The Hare family came to Stow Hall in 1553 and in 1624 John Hare built a brick mausoleum on the n. side of the *chancel* as 'a spacious dormitory for the interment of himself and his family'. The rest of the church was virtually rebuilt in 1850 and an organ chamber added to the s. in 1869. The architect was John Raphael Brandon and it is sad that in his enthusiasm for Gothic he swept away the *three-decker pulpit*, the *box pews* and a *Jacobean screen*. Nevertheless, the interior is fresh and well cared for and still has lots of interesting things. The massive Norman tower arch is very wide, and over the s. door hangs one of the best sets of *Royal Arms* in Norfolk – Charles II, painted and gilded and carved three dimensionally. Just within the chancel to right and left, look for two original *misericords*, two men trying to strangle each other with halters, and a cowled figure prising open the mouth of a dragon. There is an excellently carved C19 hare on the arm of the n. choir stall holding the Hare shield, and a hind opposite is for Samuel Hind, Bishop of Norwich. In the 1850 restoration a new arch was made between the chancel and mausoleum, and the Hare family pew was moved back so that it is now rather like a large theatre box. The mausoleum itself is light and cheerful, with large windows, and obviously well used as a Sunday school annexe. Do not pass it by on any account however, because it houses a marvellous – indeed an extraordinary collection of Hare memorials. To the right of the door, the tomb chest of Sir Ralph (1623) with a centre panel of *touchstone* with gilt lettering surrounded by painted alabaster decoration; *Corinthian* columns uphold a heavy cornice richly carved. Further e., the very large monument for Susanna (1741) is by Peter Scheemakers, well known for his statue of Shakespeare in Westminster Abbey, and this is his only work in Norfolk. On a 5ft. plinth she sits languidly, clad in loose crumpled drapery and gazing up rather sadly, with a pair of cherub's heads in clouds above her. Sir Thomas's (1834) memorial in the n.w. corner is a more restrained work by the younger William Theed; three small females, one with children, stand spaced before a plain tablet. On the w. wall, Nicholas (1597) has a beautifully lettered tablet within an alabaster frame carved with a delicate leaf design picked out in gilt and colour; mottled marble columns either side and a coat of arms on top. Against the n. wall the large and imposing figure of Sir Thomas (1693) reclines upon an altar tomb dressed in wig and Roman armour (the only example in Norfolk of this short-lived fashion). He was only 36, and his wife Elizabeth erected this memorial to one who was 'the treasure of her heart and the pleasure of her

eye', and came to lie beside him 56 years later. Their daughter Sarah had her own ideas about memorials, and when she died in 1744 her wishes were obeyed. Go to the mahogany case that looks like a wardrobe in the n.w. corner, open the half door, and you will see what they were. As it opens, a face appears behind a window and there is Sarah – or rather, a horrifyingly lifelike wax effigy clad in grubby bodice and scarlet hood peering out between the tattered curtains. Her glance is curiously sly, her hands are pudgy – and the effect is totally shattering. The legend that she pricked her finger while embroidering and died of blood poisoning at 18 is false – she was at least 51 when she died. How many nightmares, I wonder, have sprung unbidden from that innocuous mahogany case!

Stow Bedon, St Botolph (F6): Mid-way between the two halves of the village, and lonely on a windy little hilltop, the distinctive feature of this small church is the stone *bell cote* with its candle snuffer top. It is tacked on to the w. gable – over a *corbel* figure which looks medieval. Added in 1852, its design was taken from a Dorset example. At that time, the church was partially rebuilt and restored, and the w. porch was added in 1887. When *Blomefield* described the church in 1740, it had a square tower, but this had disappeared by 1820. The e. window has attractive *Decorated* tracery, but during the restoration two *lancets* were discovered in the *chancel* n. wall and so the foundation must date from the C13 or earlier. The *nave* windows are a mixture too – C14 on the n. and big, late-C15 on the s. Once again, a little parish church that reflects the will and the need to improve and replace over the centuries. In 1949, *Cautley* said that it had been terribly treated and was rapidly falling into ruins, following war damage, but thankfully it was restored once again. The inside has boarded ceilings, plain white walls and a homely tranquility. For its size it has a massive font – re-cut in the C19 but not offensively; the bowl panels have varied tracery patterns, with a narrow trail of carving above them and an embattled rim. The chancel *screen* has been called medieval but is wholly Victorian, as are the benches and pulpit. A very faded set of George III *Royal Arms* painted on board are dated 1785, and the church-wardens of the day added their names (as they did on the bell on the roof). In the very corner of the chancel is an interesting early-C13 bracket *piscina*, with nail-head decoration on the rim. The two drains slope,

Stow Bardolph, Holy Trinity: Susan Hare's effigy

and are very close together within a deep plain recess. The stone *mensa* has been found and put to its original use on the altar – incised with five *consecration crosses*, it is a massive four inches thick. No memorials of note here, but in the matted grass by the vestry door there are three hump-backed slabs in a line. They have worn floriated crosses and probably date from the C13 – anonymous, primeval, enduring.

Stradsett, St Mary (C5): An idyllic setting. The long avenue of chestnuts leads both to the Hall and to the church within its meticulously maintained graveyard and there are views of the lake beyond. The C13 tower is unbuttressed and when the belfry stage was rebuilt in the C15 the original central shafts of the bell openings were re-used. *Nave* and *chancel* lie under one continuous tiled roof and the whole building was extensively restored in 1891 when all the windows were replaced with the exception of the chancel e. window. The C13 s. doorway has large worn *headstops* and beyond the C19 font there is a pretty set of Victorian *Royal Arms* in gilt metal over the vestry door – mounted on a red shield beneath crossed flags. Further along, C18/C19 creed and *decalogue boards* have been resited on the n. wall. The chancel is full of

interest, and even from the w. end the glass in the e. window immediately catches the eye. The tracery is filled with small angel figures set in vivid blue glass and the three *lights* below contain a complete Adoration of the Magi scene; Blessed Virgin and Child to the left, a kneeling wise man in the centre dressed in a rich gold cloak with ermine cape, and his companions to the right; ox and ass watch on the left hand side, Joseph looks in through a window and the donor kneels in the right hand corner. The centre panel is dated 1540 and this magnificent array of German glass, made in Augsberg, was presented to the church by Thomas Philip Bagge in 1820. The family have been Lords of the manor since the C18 and of the many memorials, two are notable: Thomas Philip Bagge (1823) sanctuary n. side, by *Sir Richard Westmacott* has the seated figure of a mourning woman. Opposite, the tablet for Grace Bagge (1834) is surmounted by two female angels enfolded in each other's arms with heads together, their wings and drapery in a swirl of fluid movement. This is unsigned but Westmacott carved an identical piece at Berkswell in Warwickshire in 1818 and so we can assume that this is his too. Pretty *communion rails* in church-warden's gothick, and an excellent *brass* which is accessible under the choir stalls on the n. side – Thomas Lathe (1418), a 2ft. 2in. figure in full armour with a lion behind his feet, inscription below. Halfway down the nave there is the big tomb slab of Dame Emme de Montalt. This dates from the early C13, and although the brass inlays have gone, the indents of the marginal inscription in *Lombardic capitals* and the floriated cross are clear to see. Before going, look in the base of the tower for an early oak *bier* with turned legs and drop handles that has the unusual addition of extra folding handles at each side so that four men could carry it. More importantly, you can see another panel of the German C16 glass in the w. *lancet* – a small but beautifully detailed Crucifixion, with three angels holding chalices under Christ's wounds; vivid colours in robes and wings.

Stratton St Michael, St Michael (I6): The church lies with a scattering of houses just to the e. of the main road leading into Long Stratton. The unbuttressed tower rests on a foundation of boulders which can be seen at the w. corners. A line on the e. face shows where the old thatched roof lay, before the pantiles were put on, and it is highly likely that at one time the tower had a second belfry stage. Now it is topped by a little wooden turret and spire.

The *chancel* dates from the early C14 – e. window with *reticulated* tracery and slender shafts with little *headstops*. The fine *piscina* is from the same period – columns with ring *capitals* under a heavily moulded and multi-*foiled* arch. The later *aumbry* opposite is rebated and socketed, but no longer has its door. *Nave* and chancel are in one, but the roof line alters at the *screen*, and the chancel roof has little castellated *tie-beams* supporting short *king posts*. The *rood stair* is in the n. wall, with what looks like its original bottom door. Only very rudimentary remnants of the screen itself remain. There is something very satisfying about the simple country benches. The ends are 3in. thick, with the *poppy-heads* carved out of the solid – not carved and then applied as they often are. The backs are single massive planks 15in. deep and 7ft. long, with a simple moulding scratched along the top, and two of the ends have shallow panels containing seated figures – one of a bishop. The C15 font has the local pattern of alternating lions and angels with shields in the bowl panels, but the attendant lions round the circular shaft have been hacked away. What would have been the nicest thing in the church has been cruelly spoiled. A superb set of three-sided late-C17 *communion rails* have been sawn apart so that only the front range remains in place. The sides have gone to make fronts for the indifferent choir stalls. There are only three examples of this arrangement left in the county, at Thurning, Merton and West Dereham, and another of such high quality would have been very welcome.

Stratton Strawless, St Margaret (I3): The squat C15 tower was probably planned to go higher, but was finished off at an intermediate stage, and has seated figures at the corners, two of which have been recently renewed. The *aisle* was rebuilt in the C17, and is divided from the *nave* by a gothicky *screen* beneath the *arcade*. It houses the monuments of the Marsham family. At the e. end is Thomas Marsham (d.1638). His marble effigy reclines gracefully on a black sarcophagus, one hand negligently lifting aside the shroud, as the eyes look heavenward. A coat of arms is supported by improbable swags of fruit, and is flanked by trumpeting angels. Evidences of mortality peep out of the grill below. On the s. wall, the family of Henry Marsham kneels. Henry (d.1678) sports a full wig, son Henry is in long buttoned coat with stylish pockets, and wife Anne is demure, with a pearl necklace under a plain cap. They all kneel on cushions, but so shallow is the ledge that they are without benefit

of legs below the knee, and the effect is of a family of amputees. Baby Margaret in swaddling bands is upright on a pedestal. By the n. wall is the effigy of a late-C13 woman wearing a *wimple*, and in the heads of two of the n. windows there is some fine C15 glass. The easternmost window contains figures of the four Evangelists – note St *Luke* in his role as painter of the Virgin's portrait. The nave is dominated by a magnificent brass chandelier, with 25 branches in three tiers. It is said to have come from Russia, and looks to be late-C17 or early-C18. The church has a ring of 6 bells, tenor 10-3-0 cwt.

Strumpshaw, St Peter (J5): The continuous roof over *nave* and *chancel* has been lowered and flattened, to the extent that the outer line of the tower arch to the nave shows above it. This gives the C15 tower a remarkably gaunt look, particularly from the e. when the w. buttresses cannot be seen. It is handsome nonetheless, with stepped battlements bearing St Peter's initials and a flourish of eight pinnacles. The rest of the building is of the late C14 with Y-tracery in the chancel and later square-headed *Perpendicular* windows in the nave. The nave roof interior is moulded and painted, and there is no chancel arch. The bowl of the C15 font has alternating shields and roses in the panels and deeply overhangs the shaft, around which sit six lions. A fragment of a former C13 font sits at the bottom of the thin *banner-stave locker* e. of the n. door. The *rood screen* is good and has delicate tracery above the *crocketted* arches, with much of the colour remaining. The lower panels are painted in alternate red and green, patterned with ornament. That to the left of the opening incorporates little 'R's which may indicate that the nave altar on that side was dedicated to St *Edmund*, king and martyr. There are clear indications that additional sections projected westward to flank the altars, in the manner of the more famous screen at Ranworth. The *Early English* double *piscina* has beautiful *trefoiled* arches and an engaging dragon in the foliage of one of the stops.

Suffield, St Margaret (I2): A big church standing high and almost alone in gently rolling open country. The top of the C15 tower is severely plain like Cawston, but has very decorative *sound-holes* and a chequered *base course*. The C16 s. door is handsome with a succession of *cusped* panels round the edge. Inside, the *arcades* and *aisles* do not match – the n, side is in straight-forward *Perpendicular* style, but the s. side is coarser work, possibly late-C16. The late-C13 *chancel* has an unusually tall *lancet* where one would expect to see a *low side window*, and a *double piscina* with little arches springing from a *Purbeck* shaft. The early-C16 *screen* (only the lower part remains) has a fine variety of livestock in the *spandrels* of the panel tracery, including a pig playing the harp, eagle catching a rabbit, and an owl. Eight of the panels have painted figures: left of the opening, the *Four Latin Doctors*, to the right *St Luke*, *St John*, *Sir John Schorne*, *and St Heiron*. The rather battered tomb chest in the s. aisle is that of John Symonds (d.1504) and his coat of arms in colour on the front features a sprightly dolphin.

Surlingham, St Mary (J5): Prettily set on the edge of its quiet village, with the land dropping away to the e. to the placid river valley. Round *Norman* tower, much altered and restored over the years, with a C14 octagonal top faced plainly in flint and bell openings with the simplest of *cusped* 'Y' tracery. Restoration and change are yet more noticeable around the body of the church. *Chancel* rebuilt in red brick in the C18; a n. door in the same material and aping Norman lines. An unexplained oddity is the exterior walling of the n. e. corner of the n. *aisle* – big, ill-assorted blocks of grey stone, with flints rudely inserted to maintain the horizontal levels. Charming interior, despite so much restoration and renewal. All the roofs are plastered over, virtually all the window traceries are replacements, and all the furnishings are modern, but have a look at the lectern, in flecked grey wood, with an eagle of great liveliness and a lovely stoical owl between the feet. All is beautifully decorated and cared for that the place has a character and atmosphere of its own. The *nave* is C14, though the simple pointed arches of the three-bay n. *arcade* rest on round pillars with flat, moulded *capitals*. In the n. *aisle* are two C13 *lancet* windows. In the s.e. corner, the *rood stair* has been opened up through to the nave. Between the choir stalls is a good *brass* to John Alnwik, 1460, complete with inscription, and the figure in robe and shoulder mantle. Below the sanctuary step, is a tiny *chalice brass* with inscription to Richard Loupouwys, or possibly Lonhawkys, 1512. Upon the small w. *gallery* is a neat pipe organ. Below, a good traditional East Anglian octagonal font, well carved – in the panels, four lions alternate with angels carrying shields bearing *Trinity* symbols and *Instruments of the Passion*; under the bowl angel heads are in full flight; below them, butter-in-mouth little lions sit

guard. The church has an excellent ring of 6 bells, tenor 8 cwt.

Sustead, St Peter & St Paul (H2): W. of the village in an exposed position, with a single house for company. Round tower with a neat brick battlemented cap. The C14 *porch* is particularly pleasing, and has diagonal hooded buttresses, two large *flushwork* crosses, and an unusual decorative jeu d'esprit at the top of the arch. The outer *jambs* have C17 and C19 graffiti including a large hand-in-glove outline. The *chancel* s. windows are excellent – leaf terminations to the hoods outside, and inside, stiff-leaf foliage surmounting delicate shafts. Within, the *double piscina* has clustered shafts and steep arches, but the *sedilia* are oddly broken into by the window above. The C14 n. *transept* has gone, leaving a blank arch, and an *ogee*-headed doorway is also blocked. The C17 pulpit with little angel heads came from the redundant church at N. Barningham. The C15 font has a set of armorial shields round the bowl, including those of the Calthrop and Palgrave families. There are fragments of high quality medieval glass – in the head of one of the s. windows look for the angels playing instruments, particularly the bagpipe player, whose instrument has a lion's head at the junction of pipe and bag. There is a C15 exterior *rood loft stairs* in the s. side in red brick, with a little two-*light* window and decorative (diaper) patterning in flint.

Sutton, St Michael (J3): Much restored, but most attractive. Interesting range of windows: the three in the s. *aisle* have Y-tracery of around 1300 and at the w. end, a simple intersecting pattern. The C14 tower (with *Decorated* bell openings) has a neat *Perpendicular* w. window; also Perpendicular, but square headed, are the n. side windows. The e. window is C19. The attractive late Perpendicular *porch* is in red brick, notably the splendid outer arch, which is squared off with a hood; the porch formerly had an upper room, but is now open to the roof. Inside, the church is uncluttered, with whitewashed walls and gleaming woodwork. All the furnishings are modern, except the pulpit and combined reading desk below it, a simple *Jacobean* piece. An old wooden carved frieze, with tiny *Tudor* roses, plus two well-carved heads and *poppy-head* fragments, have been added to the low rail dividing the wide chancel from the nave and its C14 *arcade*. The C14 font – octagonal, on eight shafts – stands at the w. end.

Swaffham, St Peter & St Paul (E5):
Dominating with its huge tower this busy,
prosperous little market town is Swaffham's big
and strikingly self-assured 'town' church. It is
almost wholly in soaring *Perpendicular* lines,
though the lower fabric of the body of the
building is *Early English* in origin, the present
church being a complete rebuilding over a 40
year span in the second half of the C14. The
tower came slightly later, being completed in 1510
in creamy Barnack stone – a most effective
contrast with the flint and brick of the rest of
the building, and indeed something of a rarity
in this county of flint. Crowned by a splendid
wood and lead cupola (this one dates from 1897,
having replaced an C18 one) it has a richly open-
carved parapet – among whose adornments are
carved the words 'Petyr and Pawle' for the
church's dedicatory saints – and massive
crocketted corner pinnacles. There are enormous
three-*light* belfry windows, and a vast five-light
w. window with tall, finely canopied figure
niches in the *jambs*. Below, flanking the deeply
moulded w. door, are more figure niches, two
tall and canopied and two very plain ones under
the most simple of *ogee arches*. Completing this
magnificent structure is a fine carved *base course*,
with traceried panels containing shields, the
emblems of Peter (keys) and Paul (crossed
swords) and that curious whirling *mouchette*
motif in a circle. The n. side of the church, facing
the main road into the town, is a showpiece – a
terrific range of 13 three-light *clerestory* windows,
with flattened *Tudor* arches, and six enormous
four-light windows, splendidly traceried, to the
aisle below them. Eastward is a big two-storey
vestry, again Tudor, with carved figures on the
gables. Notice on the e. gable of the *nave* an
open-work *sanctus bell turret,* with an eagle open-
winged on top. The *chancel* e. window is a C19
replacement. On the s. side the clerestory is not
so prominent, being balanced by the s. *transept,*
by the projecting Chapel of the *Guild* of Corpus
Christi, and by the elegant s. *porch.* The transept
noted has an exquisitely traceried e. window in
delicately *cusped* mouchettes and *quatrefoils.* The
chapel displays a big Tudor window, three cusped
figure niches and a time-ravaged *talbot* on the
gable. And lastly the porch has crocketted
pinnacles at the corners, Tudor windows to each
side and a fine outer arch under a square hood.
Also, a dog on the ridge point of the gable – a
very special dog, whom we shall meet again
inside the church. One small survivor of the
Perpendicular rebuild is the trim three-light
window, with *reticulated* tracery of the first half

Swaffham, St Peter & St Paul: Pedlar bench end

of the C14, at the w. end of the s. aisle. A noble
interior, under a superlative nave roof on which
to feast the eyes: double *hammer-beams* with ornate
carving in the *spandrels,* collars with fine *bosses,*
luxuriantly carved *wall plates* and *wall posts* with a
heavenly host of angels, both 'in effigy' and in
relief on the wall plates, spread winged at every
conceivable point – a staggering total of 192 of
them. Marvellous and it all looks almost like
new, the whole carpenter's masterpiece being of
chestnut wood which, by all accounts, repels
cobwebs and dust! *Arcade* of six and a half bays
on beautiful clustered columns – the westernmost
bays abutting the lofty tower arch are cut into
just off the point of their arches, presumably
during readjustment when the tower was built
a couple of decades after the nave. Under the
tower are low vaults, with fluted stone carvings
at the corners like heavy *linen-fold,* and winged
angels spread languorously below. Half way
along the s. aisle is the former Chapel of Corpus
Christi, now a memorial chapel to the fallen of
two wars. The chapel (which has a fine
window from the *William Morris* workshop,
showing scenes inspired by the 1914 war)

would in former times have serveding a guild of which perhaps eight had their altars in this church before the *Reformation*. In the s. transept is an especially fine *piscina* (no doubt serving one of the guild altars) with a multi-cusped arch, and *crockets* and foliage in relief above, under a square hood. On the e. wall here is a striking monument to Katherine Steward, 1590, maternal grandmother of Oliver Cromwell: she is seen richly gowned and kneeling on a cushion in a marbled recess, with a profusion of coats-of-arms above and below. In the sanctuary, a table tomb under a canopy bears the stone effigy of John Botright,' Rector of Swaffham from 1435 to 1474, shown skull-capped, and robed as a Doctor of Divinity. John Botright earned his place of honour here: he it was who spearheaded the C15 rebuilding and himself paid for the new chancel. He was much aided by *John Chapman*, benefactor of the church and a warden at that time – but better known as The *Pedlar of Swaffham*. He was in fact a rich man and built the n. aisle. The Pedlar and his equally well-known dog (the one we met on the gable of the porch) are seen carved on the front nave bench ends and on the prayer desk on the chancel s. side, he with a pack on his back and his dog muzzled and chained. These details, and those on the opposite prayer desk of rosary-carrying shop-keepers looking out of their doors, are said to have come from the Chapman Family Pew. The church has a good ring of 8 bells, tenor 15-3-23 cwt.

Swafield, St Nicholas (I2): Standing clear above the village, a handsome small *Perpendicular* building with large windows. Those in the *nave* have carved *corbels* to their *dripstones*. The *priest's door* in chancel, s. side, and the blocked n. doorway have arch heads, cut from just two pieces of stone. The little *porch* has a lovely outer arch with an early coffin slab as door step. Massive inner door with original C14 ring and plate. Inside, spacious, wide nave with fine *arch-braced roof*, enormous *bosses* carved with portraits and *Tudor roses*, still showing hints of original colour; and deep *wall plates* and plain *wall posts*. The filled in n. doorway has had wooden steps added, as a war memorial. Nearby a crucifix, in sombre colour, hangs on the n. wall – it was found in separate pieces over a two week period in spring 1937 on Walcott beach, each piece being thickly caked with clay. It is thought it must have been buried, when or why unknown, in nearby cliffs which had collapsed in a storm shortly before the discoveries. Behind

the organ is the entrance to the *rood stair*. Attractive 1900 lectern: an angel bears the bible rest, which is convex in order to hold the book open. Plain chancel, a C15 *piscina* with Perpendicular head, and *dropped sill sedilia*. The base of the old *rood screen* remains, with some very good paintings of saints: *Andrew; Peter; Jude; Simon; James the Great; John; Thomas; James the Less.* The screen's central door posts still have their colouring of great beauty.

Swainsthorpe, St Peter (I5): Despite the C14 octagonal top, the round tower is probably *Saxon* and has a tall, plain arch into the *nave* rather like Intwood. The *arch-braced roofs* have been extensively restored but they rest on a fine series of brackets carved alternately with heads of men and animals. The big angels at the *purlin* intersections bear harps, chalices and crowns and although the wings have been replaced the bodies look original. The *chancel piscina* is C15, square headed with an *ogee trefoiled* arch in tracery and a stone *credence shelf*. Opposite, John Dearsley, Mayor of Norwich in 1764, is handsomely commemorated, 'who after indefatigable application to the Duty of His Public Offices retir'd to this village and dyd'. There is more in similar vein. He wife Elizabeth died the following year and her portion was but two lines and no eulogy. Seek relief from such injustice and read the small *brass* plate on the opposite wall:

> Here lieth the body of Gilbert Havers Esq. who served Quene Elizabeth. Captaine in Barwick, then in Scotland, after in Ireland, and last in the Netherlands 22 years. He maried Frances one of the daughters and heires of Tho. Nashe. He lyved 87 years and dyed the 5 of Maye 1628.

Memorials often seem to fit the men. At the w. end by the tower is an exceptionally good modern collage, mainly in gauze, of a figure at the foot of the Cross with the shadow of it falling across him – beautiful use of muted colours. As you go, look for the fragment of a *mass dial* on the w. *jamb* of the door – a reminder that there was no *porch* originally.

Swannington, St Margaret (H4): One of those churches where a series of rebuildings and adaptations over the centuries has produced an interesting mixture. The n. doorway is C13, as is the shallow *Purbeck* bowl of the font – now in the s. *aisle*. The nave *arcades* date from c.1300 and the *Perpendicular* tower was built into the existing church so that the aisles flank it. This gives a nice space at the w. end, with big double-depth arches on three sides. The late-C15 *porch* has a *base course* of crowned letters, and I.H.S. NAZARENES in matching *flushwork* above the door. The dragon from the legend of St *Margaret* crouches in one of the arch *spandrels*. The fine C14 *sedilia* in the *chancel* have *cinquefoil* arches with shallow carved vine, oak, and lily leaves in the spandrels – all neatly enclosed in an ornamented band. The surprise of the church is there too – a *Norman* pillar *piscina*. It had been hidden in the *rood loft* stairs and was discovered by the rector in 1917. Most piscinas of this type are plain, but this one has lovely little carvings on the cap – St *George* slaying the dragon, and a knight charging into battle with his lance and shield who might have stepped straight out of the Bayeaux tapestry. While in the chancel, look at the late Perpendicular roof – panelled overall, with carved flowers at all the intersections, and supported on massive cambered *tie-beams* which have tracery above them. The richly carved communion table came to the church in 1846. Although the top and stretchers are new, it is a fine piece, dated 1635. The sanctuary rails were given in 1912 and are excellent. They have heavy mouldings above and below, and the six-*baluster* clusters at the ends are an original touch. Below the n. aisle e. window there is a stone panel with traces of colour, and this would seem to be the original *reredos* for an altar, although it looks as though it was used subsequently for a mural monument. A plan of the church in 1892 shows how times change – then there were 'raised seats for the band' below the tower. (see *galleries*). Things are still changing, and the w. end has recently been divided off from the body of the church by tall panelled *screens*, each with a solid door. This is well done and has created a useful meeting area. Full marks too for the modern kitchen/cloakroom built onto the side of the church, with access via the old n. door.

Swanton Abbot, St Michael & All Angels (I3): The C14 tower has angle buttresses and a square outside stair turret reaching to the top. The rest is C15 rebuilding and the 29ft. wide *nave* proved too much for the *arch-braced roof* – it had to be completely reconstructed in 1953. The s. door is medieval but is probably not as old as the ring and plate which may be C13. The C14 font has a thick panelled stem with heavy mouldings and heads at the angles under the bowl. The *screen* is rather extraordinary. Between 1906 and 1913 the octagenarian Rector rebuilt it, and the majority

is 'his unaided work'. Very competent too, but for some unknown reason he reversed the panels and the faded paintings of the saints now face the altar. From left to right they are: Saints *Andrew, Peter, John, James the Great, Jude, Simon, James the Less, Philip, Anthony* and *Thomas*. In the *chancel* there is a good *brass* to Rector Stephen Multon (d.1477). 18in. long, it shows him robed for the Eucharist. The sanctuary has been raised and clad in *encaustic tiles* – a Victorian blunder that reduced the *piscina* to floor level and made it quite unusable.

Swanton Morley, All Saints (G4): From the churchyard, the land drops away sharply to the e. and n. so that there are pretty views over the Wensum valley, and the great tower is a landmark for miles. Work on the *nave* and n. *aisle* may have started before the *Black Death* in 1349, but the main building operation was between 1360 and 1440, and the style is *Perpendicular*. The tower has massive octagonal *piers* at the base, and from these spring rectangular buttresses which change to diagonal further up. Because the aisles embrace the tower there is a continuous w. front, and a lush *base course* stretches right across. The w. window is not really big enough to counter-balance the door below, and the eye is drawn upwards to the extraordinary bell openings. They are huge – so tall and wide that they are quite out of proportion, but they are the very thing that makes the tower memorable. The aisle windows have a pretty sequence of *quatrefoils* below the *transoms*, and everywhere the tracery is handsome. In walking round the e. end, note a narrow slit below the e. window and an iron grill low in the *chancel* s. wall. These allow a glimpse into a large chamber below the sanctuary that must have been an ossuary (charnel house for bones) originally, but was at one time used as a vestry before the stairway was removed and new accommodation built in 1879. The s. *porch* is fairly plain, but there are two excellent wooden *corbels* inside, and the inner doorway (like its opposite number on the n. side) has two ranges of floral motifs in the mouldings. On going in, the first view is of the mighty pillars of the tower, and one of the bases is extended to take the plain font. The nave *arcades* are very tall and the tiny *quatrefoil clerestory* windows seem almost an afterthought – although there is a window with elaborate tracery over the chancel arch. With such an expanse of glass in the aisles, the church is flooded with light even on a cloudy day. The Victorian pulpit has an ugly stone base, but the woodwork is good and is picked out effectively in gilt. Looking back down the nave, you will see one of the smallest *sanctus bell windows* to be found anywhere – an opening only 4in. across high in the tower wall. The s. aisle chapel has a small *piscina*, and the altar table there is early-C17 (raised on blocks for convenience and thus effectively spoiling its proportions). The chancel was the last part of the church to be built and has a good *hammer-beam roof*, not easy to see because it is so dark, but the *wall posts* have some interesting carvings – s. side, second from e. end, a *rebus* on the village name 'Swan-Tun', and n. side easternmost, a rather nice hedgehog. The e. window was reglazed in 1944 with a series of heraldic roundels – for more information, see the chart on the n. wall by the vestry door. There are two original stalls with lions (now gilded) on the arms, and it would seem that two medieval *screen* panels have been built into the desk fronts. Retracing your steps, see the *Royal Arms* over the s. door – attractive pale colours, and a slip of the pen (or brush) in the motto. They are dated and initialled for Queen Anne, but the style of the mantling and motto suggest that is is a set of Charles II brought up to date in 1711. The church has an excellent ring of 6 bells, tenor 8-2-22 cwt.

Swanton Novers, St Edmund (G2): Remote from its tiny village, peacefully surrounded by forest and farmland, with Barney Church visible a couple of miles away across the fields – a beautiful spot. A very heavily restored church – the tower was rebuilt in 1821 and, by 1960, it was again in such bad condition, it was said in the village that 'one good hard kick' would have sent it tumbling. In fact the whole church was so bad that the question of abandoning it and building elsewhere was examined. Happily, the parishioners refused to take that course and faced up to the considerable restoration task before them. The job was done and today St Edmund's is beautifully cared for. Old materials were re-used in the tower rebuilding, including the *Decorated* bell openings and the w. window, with a nice old statue niche below it. The n. *aisle* and the s. *porch* were added in the 1880s, and the *chancel* is a C19 rebuild too. On the outside wall of the *nave* you can make out the outline of a round-headed doorway, long since blocked. The masonry is probably *Norman*. Inside the church, the effects of successive restorations are severe, but there is a curiously carved, *ogee*-headed *piscina* in the chancel, with a 'W carved on each side, each surrounded by a circle studded with *Tudor roses*. Those same 'W carvings appear on the

C15 font, where they occur on shields surrounded by thorns, punctuating other panels bearing the *Symbols of the Evangelists*.

Swardeston, St Mary the Virgin (H5): The early-C15 tower has a stairway on the s. side which reaches almost to the *flushwork* battlements, and the long leaded roof stretches over *nave* and *chancel* without interruption. Although the nave and chancel windows are a mixture of styles and periods there are two *lancets* (one with a double splay on the n. side) which shows that the origins are *Saxo-Norman*. The main entrance used to be the n. door for the people while the s. door was reserved for the squire. This has a lovely *Tudor* brick arch, and when the *porch* was restored in the 1960s Tudor tiles were obtained for the roof. Much work has been done recently and the cream lime-washed walls inside still have a pleasant freshness. The roof has *king posts* resting on *tie-beams* which were obviously logs chosen for their natural curve and only roughly trimmed. Note that although the *rood* itself has gone, the beam over it was specially decorated as a form of *celure*. The base of the *screen* is modern but the late-C14 top with its *cusped* and *crocketted ogee arches* is fine and was repainted sympathetically in the 1950s. As you can see from the *piscina* in the s. wall there was a nave altar nearby – probably for a *guild*. In the sanctuary there is a fragment of a pillar piscina set in the wall, and e. of the one that succeeded it there is an *aumbry*. The C17 *communion rails* are a very plain set with turned *balusters* – interesting that the style of the turning points to the same man having worked on the font cover. That is a sturdy piece with eight columns set in a top frame from which spring ogee braces up to a centre post. The font itself is an absolutely plain early-C14 deep octagon on a heavy shaft. There are some old *poppy-heads* set on new benches in the *chancel* and under the organ is a very nice set of old pews. The seats have been renewed but the bench ends have floral motifs carved on the bevel and the bottom frame is original. For all its intrinsic beauty, Swardeston church might go unremarked were it not that *Nurse Edith Cavell* was born in the village and grew up here as a daughter of the vicarage. She lies in the shadow of the cathedral but it is here that the poignancy of her story is felt. There are two large pictures of her, and in a glass case, the shaft of the cross that marked her first grave. In the memorial e. window by E. Heasman she kneels in her nurse's uniform attended by little figures of Florence Nightingale and St Joan of Arc.

Syderstone, St Mary (E2): A beautifully maintained church in a neat churchyard that rises from the head of the village street. Round *Norman* tower with a C12 doorway which has a C14 niche over it in which a lion now squats; the bell openings are C13. The *nave* was remodelled in 1785 but the walls tell a most interesting story. This was originally a *Norman cruciform* church, and the clue lies in the outlines of round arches – one behind the organ and the other opposite. They led to *transepts* and match the s. *arcade,* with its round pillars and extraordinarily large *capitals* – now embedded in the s. wall. There was a contemporary s. *aisle* (demolished in 1784), and in the C14 a n. arcade and aisle were added. This was removed in the C16 when new windows were inserted and the n. door re-set – only to be blocked up some 200 years later. Beyond the C15 *chancel* arch, the C14 e. window has superb flowing tracery and the glass by *Joan Howson* is most attractive; placed there as a thank offering for peace in 1948, it features a jolly garland of angels below a nativity group in the tracery. Rector George Hall's tomb of 1605 has a terse biography in black letter, to which is added a sober reflection from the Book of Job.

Tacolneston, All Saints (H6): An attractive building standing in a tight loop of the main Norwich road, and far from its village. Largely *Perpendicular,* the tower was rebuilt in 1509. Its one *sound-hole,* on the s. side, is a *lancet* shaped slit, with a pretty little *cusped* arch under a square hood. The e. window is a replacement in over-stated geometrical mode; and the rest is Perpendicular, save for a C13 lancet at the w. end of the s. *aisle.* There is a *Tudor* window immediately to the right of the *porch,* the tracery, arch, *drip mould* and *mullion* all being in mellow pink brick. The interior is unexpectedly spacious, under a continuous C15 *arch-braced* roof, with a wide and high s. aisle (*arcade* and aisle are C15). A broken remnant of the *rood screen* stands against the aisle wall, with good carvings. Another section is placed against the organ, with two panels having remains of gilt and colour, and defaced painted scenes. They show, from l., the *Annunciation,* and The Temptation of St *Anthony* – unusual scenes, which were copied from engravings by Lucas van Leyden (1494-1533). In the s.e. corner of the aisle is a plain *piscina* niche and wooden *credence shelf,* for an altar here dedicated to St *Nicholas.* Near it, a very large wall niche. The s. aisle chapel has a good *Jacobean* altar, and the pulpit, with at each angle, double *pilasters,* is from the same period; in the

panels, big perspective Romanesque arches. The chancel has a piscina complete with stone credence shelf and adjoining *dropped sill sedilia.* Opposite is a painted *consecration cross. Hatchments* hang on the nave arcade and the s. wall; there is a plain C15 font, with a variety of simple carvings round its bowl, including a Sacred Heart. Above, over the tower arch, a silvery and blue *Royal Arms* initialled for Charles I – but set in a splendid wooden frame, topped by a triangular gable, which is dated 1610 for James I. The church has a ring of 6 bells, tenor 8-1-10 cwt.

Tasburgh, St Mary (I6): Set high above its village, this is an attractive church with a venerable round tower, which is undoubtedly *Saxon.* Note the 'blind' *arcades,* seven at one level and lighter outlines of others above them; the latter were obviously disturbed and cut into when the tower was altered and raised in about 1400. The fabric of the body of the church is C13, but the *nave* windows are *Perpendicular,* as are those in the *chancel.* The s. and e. windows are replacements. The meeting room to the s., beyond the old s. *porch,* has been most tastefully and sympathetically achieved. The church's interior is a real pleasure, where the ancient and modern, the original and the restored, the expected and the surprising, meet together in happily. Modern roofs to nave and chancel. White painted walls throughout, with 'comfortable words' painted in bold black lettering set on the nave walls. In the nave s.e. corner, a *piscina* niche has been high-lighted by painting over and round it a decorative frame. Below, two stone-carved coats-of-arms are set into the wall. Modern furnishings in the nave, save for half a dozen *poppy-heads* at the w. end. Octagonal C15 font, with big flower motifs in the panels, and more rich flower carvings round the stem. On top is a simple, *Jacobean* cover, completed with a 'cut-out' pinnacle. Above, the *Royal Arms* of George III, 1818, and above that, a *lancet* which occupies a much older, Saxon round arch. Under the renewed chancel arch, parts of the *screen* have been combined with tracery, like miniature windows, and roughly prepared timbers, to create a reading desk. Two more poppy-head bench ends have been re-used to form a seat. The tiny *priest's door* on the n. side has a C13 pointed doorway set into it, with the ancient door and its massive lock slotting directly into the wall. Opposite, a fine Elizabethan table tomb set into the wall in the base of the window, with seven coats-of-arms under a hood incorporated into the window sill. Adjoining is a handsome C14 piscina with a *trefoil* head. The tiny memorial *brass* in front of the sanctuary steps, dated 1586, is elegantly lettered and carries two of the same shields as on the table tomb. The pink alabaster monument on the n. wall, still bearing traces of original paintwork, and is for Thos. Newec and Margarita, his wife, 1629 and 1632. The church has a good ring of 5 bells, tenor 9-1-17 cwt.

Tattersett, All Saints (E3): Look carefully at the map and then persevere along the half mile of rough track to find this little church, alone in the fields above the valley of the river Tat. A C13 building with no buttresses, save the one in brick on the s. side of the *chancel*. The tower has two *lancets* and brick-filled bell openings, with brick battlements. A small and plain C13 n. door is blocked, and to the e. is the shadow of another with a *Norman* outline. The outer arch of the s. *porch* rests on massive round columns and leads to a beautifully simple doorway and restored medieval door. Just inside is an untouched *holy water stoup* with an *aumbry* next to it. The windows are *Perpendicular* and one was changed again for a square-headed *Tudor* design. The chancel arch *responds* match those at the s. porch entrance, and the doorway to the *rood stairs* in the n. wall has a good moulded frame. The small lancet niches either side of the chancel arch will have been above the *rood loft*. The chancel has an unusually late *piscina* and *sedilia*, all carried out in Tudor red brick, and the C14 font is a plain octagon. This is a church that is memorable for its isolation, for the fact that it is cared for and used, and for the quiet triumph of its survival.

Taverham, St Edmund (H4): Up to 1970, both *nave* and *chancel* were thatched, but in that year the nave roof was tiled. It is on record that the nave was destroyed by lightning in 1459, which dates the present one accurately: but a *Norman* doorway of the same period as the base of the round tower (the octagonal top was added in the C15) remains on the n. side. The chancel is *Decorated* in style. The church was heavily restored in 1861-62 by *Thomas Jekyll* when the *porch* and s. *aisle* were rebuilt. Inside there is a fine C15 *Perpendicular* font, with exceptionally good figures round it (Saints *Edmund*, *Lambert*, *Giles* with doe, *Margaret*, *Anne*, *James the Less*, *Agnes* and *Leonard*); a nice C15 *screen*; a *Jacobean* chest; and – one of the best things in the church – some lovely fragments of a C14 screen, probably from some other church, formed into an altar rail. Unfortunate that the modern rail above this

delicate filigree tracery does not do it justice. A fragment of the *sedilia*, and *piscina* of the same date, remain in the chancel.

Terrington St Clement, St Clement (B3): A number of Norfolk churches have attracted popular titles and 'cathedral of the Marshes' seems not unreasonable for this great church of Barnack stone set in the level expanse of the huge northernmost parish of the Hundred of Freebridge Marshland. *Norman* work was found at the w. end in the C19 and there is even a fragment of *Saxon* interlace carving embedded inside the *chancel*, but this building is mainly *Perpendicular*, with late-C13 work to be seen in the chancel. The w. front is memorable, with a five-*light* window flanked by tall niches under pierced canopies, and turrets at the *nave* corners that rise to *crocketted* pinnacles. The *aisle* corners have turrets too, like graceful stone spires in miniature rising to the height of the nave roof. A *crossing tower* was planned, but whether because of unsure foundations or lack of money it was never built and instead, a C15 bell tower rose so close to the n. aisle that one can only just squeeze through between the buttresses. It has a *quatrefoil base course*, large three-light bell openings and stepped, panelled battlements crowned with eight pinnacles. There is a w. door and large belfry window flanked by pedestals but the rest of the walls are smooth and featureless. The nave *clerestory*, with its 14 three-light windows a side is almost a wall of glass and the chancel has its own clerestory – this time in *Tudor* brick. The e. wall of the s. *transept* shows a change in building plans, for there the *rood stair* turret cuts into one of the high windows and there are exposed sections of others. There is good reason to believe that longer transepts and wider aisles were intended when the effects of the *Black Death* called for a less ambitious conclusion. The *porch* has a quatrefoil base course like the tower and there is fine panelling on the s. face and on the buttresses, with a sundial over the arch. Inside, in the enclosure to the left of the door, are damaged but most interesting stone figures of St *Clement* and St *Christopher* with Christ on his shoulder. They were found when two strengthening buttresses were removed from the w. end in the C19 and are thought to have come from the niches either side of the w. window. The w. end of the nave is divided from the rest of the church by a tall and solid oak *screen* with plain panelling of 1788. It has centre half doors, full doors into the aisles, and a centre *gallery* resting on cast iron pillars – with no access now

Terrington, St Clement

that the stairs have been removed. On the n. wall, a fine example of Queen Anne's *Royal Arms* painted on canvas and just through the screen, a simple C15 font with an extraordinarily interesting cover. The lower section is octagonal and two sections hinge outwards to reveal Flemish paintings on thin boards within. In the centre is the Baptism of Christ and either side there are scenes from the Temptation in which the Devil wears a red robe and golden crown; strange beasts including an elephant lurk in the landscape and the four *Evangelists* float on clouds in the sky. The outside of the case is classical in style, with clusters of *Jacobean* columns painted to look like marble, but the tall tabernacled pinnacle, with miniature vault inside studded with rose *bosses,* is pure Gothic, and one wonders whether the bottom half was redesigned in the early C17 to accommodate the new paintings from overseas. The nave *arcades* have plain octagonal *piers* and the roof was replaced in 1829, with old plaster *bosses* applied to the panelling. There is an impressive arrangement of graduated niches under the apex of the roof at the e. end, and below the plain boarded ceiling of the *crossing* you will see the

corner bases from which the vaulting for a centre tower would have sprung. In the w. walls of the transepts the beginnings of Perpendicular piers can be seen, showing that w. aisles were intended and the shortened s. transept was given a neat arrangement of windows in three tiers. In the floor below the crossing there are no less than three *mensa* displaying their *consecration crosses* and there is yet another under the high altar. The two large boards on the e. walls of the transepts are inscribed with the creed and the Lord's Prayer and are without doubt the finest examples of their period in the county if not in England. Dated 1635, they are over 9ft. across and have elaborate strapwork designs incorporating human heads, animals and birds; the lettering is all Old English except, strangely enough, the last sentence of the Lord's Prayer. The chancel has an e. window that matches its counterpart at the w. end and the altar was raised rather eccentrically in the C19 to accommodate a vault beneath, leaving cul de sacs either side. In the one on the s. can be seen a good late-C13 *double piscina* and *sedilia* with *trefoil* arches and *dog-tooth* decoration – uncovered in the wall during restoration. On the n. side is the fragment of Saxon carving mentioned earlier and a small C13 slab with a cross on the top which is likely to

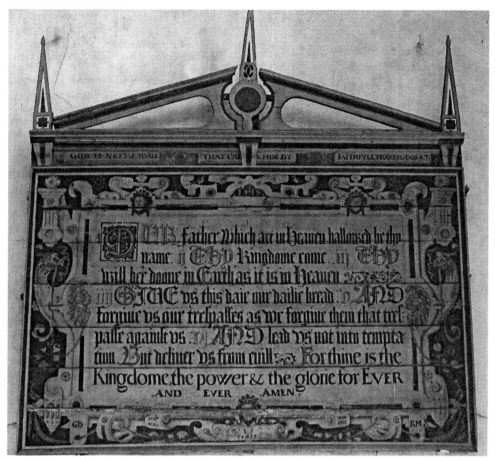

OUR, Father Which art in Heaven hallowed be thy name. i] THY Kingdome come. ii] THY will bee doone in Earth as it is in Heaven. iii] GIVE vs this daie our dailie bread. iiii] AND forgiue vs our trespasses as we forgiue them that trespasse againste vs. v] AND lead vs not into temptation. But deliuer vs from euill. For thine is the Kingdome,the power & the glorie for EVER AND EVER AMEN.

Terrington, St Clement: 1635 Lord's Prayer board

have been an exterior consecration cross. The church has not many memorials but there are two pretty *cartouches* on the n. wall of the chancel and opposite, a tablet for Mary Anne Morphew who died at 15 in 1843; figures of Faith and Hope flank the inscription and it is signed by Thomas Denman – *John Flaxman's* brother-in-law who was not ashamed to copy his designs.

Terrington St John, St John (B4): Until the C19 this was a daughter church of Terrington St Clement's and was served from there. That, plus the fact that travel was difficult in the fens, may have been the reason for the extraordinary 'priest's house' that links the tower with the s. *aisle*. The tower at its base seems to be late-C13, although the top with octagonal corner pinnacles is C15. The rest of the church is a rebuilding of the early C14 with later *Perpendicular* w. front, aisle windows, *chancel* and s. *porch*. The 'priest's

house' is brick and may have been added after the main rebuilding was complete. It has rooms at ground and first floor level, with passages overhead that lead to the tower and the roofs. Altogether an oddity. Circle the church to have a look at the C15 w. front and at the chancel; there, *priest's door* and e. window have large matching *headstops* and, unusually, there are blocked *low side windows* on both n. and s. sides; blocked up windows and a door show that there was a chapel on the n. side of the chancel. Inside, the *nave* and aisles are so wide that they make the chancel look shorter than it is, and the chancel arch is an eccentric restoration with pointed arch and square classical *responds*. The nave roof is nearly flat and the *wall plates* are carved with the names of the 'carpender' and 'plumar' who worked on it in 1668. The vicar and churchwardens of 1932 carried on the tradition on a *tie-beam* further e. Near the s. door, on an *arcade* pillar, is a glass case containing a beautiful 2ft. wooden figure of a woman; her dainty head

Terrington, St Clement:
The 'Dorcas' window in the chancel

with its thick ringlets inclines forward, and both her face and her pregnant figure are so remarkably like the woman in Van Eyck's 'Arnolfini and his wife' that the work must date from the 1430s and is probably Flemish. There are not many C17 fonts about but St John's is dated 1632 – big, with a shallow bowl carved with strapwork and standing on a broad octagonal plinth with three steps. C18 oak *box pews* at the back of the nave, with a C19 set in front of them, and above you will see a pretty arrangement in the *clerestory,* where *quatrefoiled* circles alternate with two-*light* windows; above that odd chancel arch, two square domestic windows were inserted, probably at the time of the restoration. At the e. end of the s. aisle there is a small *trefoil*-headed *piscina,* and the door to the *rood stair* hides behind the organ on the n. side. The *screen* has gone, and there is not even a step now between nave and chancel. The pair of

low side windows have wide embrasures inside and, strangely, there are two matching *priest's doors* as well. Above the vestry screen at the w. end, the *Royal Arms* of George III – large and dark.

Tharston, St Mary (H6): It stands clear on a slight eminence, in open, rolling countryside, and looks good as you approach it, the eye being caught by its trim *Decorated* tower topped with perky pinnacles. The tower's w. face is very good – a smart *Tudor* window with below it a door with a squared hood and bold *Tudor roses* carved in the *spandrels.* The door itself, long since sealed, has had two jolly little windows cut into it. The *chancel* is Decorated, with a contemporary *priest's door* of charming simplicity, but the rest heavily restored, the e. window being a sad replacement. *Perpendicular nave* and n, *porch,* the latter faced with sturdily-done *flushwork,* and flints too filling in the pretty little figure niche over the outer arch. Simple, homely interior, with modern roofs and largely modern furnishings. Some good old *poppy-head* bench ends have been re-used, however, three very good ones at the e. end of the nave having excellent carvings set into the bench ends themselves – one figure wears a kingly crown but carries a bishop's crozier; next to him a crowned and winged lady with attendant angels (the church's dedicatory St Mary?) and opposite, an angel holding the scales of judgement, in one being a little devil (on the up side!) and in the other a (presumably) repentant sinner. Nearby is a restrained, panelled *Jacobean* reading desk. More old poppy-heads in the chancel, where there is also a large *piscina,* with a handsomely carved and *crocketted* head. At the w. end notice the big, chunky 'country house bannister' railing, dated 1707, across the ringing platform. Good font, with some curiosity in the carving: one *evangelistic symbol* (lion) is repeated twice; there are four Tudor roses; and two angels, one of whom has rather crudely carved C15 headgear, the other wears a hat which is positively Napoleonic. Some handsome monuments adorn the church – in the nave n.e. corner is one to Robert Woode, 1623, the said gentleman is depicted as a very lean skeleton, reclining on a divan. To his left, less exuberant, an alabaster memorial to John Woolmer, died 1598, and his wife Alice, died 1610, though the monument is dated 1617 (notice that their coat-of-arms includes the crusading *scallop-shell*). Opposite, a deep indentation in the s. wall shows position of the old *rood stair.* The church has a good ring of 5 bells, tenor 10-0-6 cwt.

Thelveton, St Andrew (H7): A sylvan spot within the park and ringed around with oaks, beeches and a mighty Wellingtonia pine on the s. side of the *chancel*. Treated to lavish restoration by the Mann family from 1872 onwards, a blocked n. door of simple outline shows that the church was originally *Norman*, although most of the existing fabric is C14. The tower fell in 1757 and there is now a single bell in a cote on the w. gable. The whole of the interior is close carpeted, and the chairs are a simple design with arms, carried out in oak, and used to display individual memorial plaques. The C15 font has shields in the bowl panels – three chalices, St George's cross, the *Trinity* emblem, and a floriated cross. Round the stem, four angels carrying books, three mitred bishops carrying scrolls, and one mystery person wearing what one might be forgiven for calling a medieval bowler. Over the s. door is a good 5ft. x 6ft. set of *Stuart Royal Arms*, undated but the design points to the 1620s. In the chancel there is an attractive *pillar piscina* with a flower design in the drain. The marble *reredos* of 1879 has mosaic inlay Alpha, Omega and Chi-rho symbols. On the chancel s. wall, a portrait medallion of Thomas Mann (1886) by C. Stoatt – a prosperous Victorian with dundreary whiskers, spiky eyebrows and a benevolent expression:

Born at The House, Albion Brewery, Mile End Road...owner of the Thelveton estate which parish he entirely remodelled. He zealously promoted religious and secular education, also the moral and social welfare of his tenants and labourers.

Themelthorpe, St Andrew (G3): There are all the signs of a C13 building here – slim unbuttressed tower, *lancet* windows in the *chancel* and tower, and the re-set *jambs* in the outer *porch* door-way, but the foundation is older. There are no dressed *quoins* at the *nave* corners and the *herring-bone* pattern of masonry also suggests an earlier date. The nave and chancel are one, and although there were the remains of a *rood screen* as late as the mid-C19, they have gone. There is a simple *trefoil*-headed *piscina* and stepped-sill *sedilia*. *Poppy-heads* have been rescued from the C15 benches and re-used in recent work. By the font there is a good *brass* to William Pescod (d.1505), a 13in. figure in a long gown with deep sleeves and an inscription below. Three other brass inscriptions are screwed to the n. wall.

Thetford, St Cuthbert (E7): A town church comfortably settled among shops and pedestrian streets. Well maintained overall, inside it is warmly welcoming. It is so much restored that few details of real interest remain. Its w. tower was rebuilt in 1854 in *Perpendicular* style, including its stylishly traceried *sound-holes*. The s. door is C13 and attractive, with slim rounded shafts to each side, flat *capitals* and a trim arch. Its *porch* is of slightly later, *Decorated* period origin, and though much restored, retains a good outer arch with neat figure niche above. The s. *aisle* is the oldest part of the church (there is a contemporary piscina in its e. end) though the 'Y' tracery in its windows is all replacement. The best thing in the church is the C13 double piscina in the *chancel*, though how much is original, how much is restoration/replacement, it is difficult to say. It has fine little *corbel* heads to its arches and some original colour though, as noted, one has to be cautious in deciding how much.

Thetford, St Peter (E7): Not far away from St Cuthbert's, at a busy traffic intersection, is St Peter's, now serving largely as a meeting centre/chapel in association with St Cuthbert's. The tower deserves a close look – it is a 1789 rebuild, and very well done too, its buttresses lavishly decorated in flint and stone chequerwork. Notice the w. door, tall and slim and mildly fanciful in its classically-inclined side shafts and in its flowing arch, more Gothick than gothic. The tower's window traceries are perhaps not so successful, having used the 'Y' tracery design of around 1300. The body of the church is strongly *Decorated* in character, though much restored. Inside, *nave* and n. *aisle* are cleared for use as meeting rooms, while the *chancel* is furnished as a chapel. The nave has its original C15 *Perpendicular* windows on the s. side and trim *arcade* with the n. aisle – the aisle has its original roof, with carved *spandrels* including the keys of the church's dedicatory saint, *Peter*. The e. end of the aisle, arched through to the chancel, appears to have been a later addition, though the intervening arcade is a faithful copy of that between aisle and nave. Heraldic glass in nave and aisle windows is C18; there are remains of (remodelled) *rood stairs;* and *Royal Arms* of George III. The church has a good ring of 8 bells, tenor 18-0-1 cwt.

Thompson, Collegiate Church of St Martin (F6): A college of canons was founded here in the year of the *Black Death* (1349) and the chaplains met to say matins, vespers and a daily mass for the souls of the Shardelowe family, who founded it, until the Dissolution. This is a beautiful little church, set deep in quiet countryside and a pleasure to visit. Mostly of the early C14, with a particularly pretty w. window and a lovely range of tracery in the *chancel* windows that has, alas, been blocked up for years. The s. *porch* has a fine triple niche over the door which looks suspiciously like a blocked window. As the roof was lowered and replaced in 1608 there could well have been an upper room here. The *aisle*less *nave* is broad and high and here we have a *scissors-braced roof* of the type beloved of C19 restorers but not often seen in Norfolk as an original. A calm and lovely interior with oak pews the colour of old cider with a touch of silver, and a pale red brick and *pamment* floor. Two of the pews are dated 1625 and 1632 but this must surely refer to the curious chip carving panels of thistles on some of the ends. There is a full scale *Jacobean* family pew on the n. side and two-decker pulpit opposite which has a strange hotch potch of a pew in front for the *parish clerk*, made up of two C15 bench ends and fragments of C17 panelling. The pulpit proper is fitted with a steeply canted book rest all round and the *tester* has decorated wheelspokes on the underside, the whole standing on a turned stem. The early-C14 chancel *screen* has turned shafts painted barber's pole fashion, with varied tracery circles above the *ogee* arches. The base is plain, with diaper painting, but look behind the pulpit to find an *elevation squint* which is a carefully cut *cusped* circle – much superior to the normal crude cross or bored peephole. In the chancel, the stalls of the college fellows have been replaced and four retain their *misericords* – two with the Shardelowe arms, one with a bishop's head and one with the head of a woman. The *Decorated piscina* and *sedilia* are grouped very handsomely under a square label and the *spandrels* between the *ogee arches* have three little *Green Men* peeping out. There is an *aumbry* in the n. wall and two *consecration crosses*. The *communion rails* are tall early-C17 turnery with a mighty odd top rail – concave, tilted and with a bottom lip. Perhaps it was designed to take the place of a *houseling cloth* and catch stray crumbs of the communion bread should they fall (another section which matches this rail survives at Griston below the gallery). Going back to the nave, note that a *ledger slab* before the pulpit has been robbed of its *brass* and re-used for crudely lettered memorials to Robert and Marie Futter – one at each end. The little C15 s.

transept chapel has the lower half of its *screen* and the huge *Perpendicular* window was originally in the e. wall, as you can see outside. The chapel was dedicated to St James and Sir Thomas Shardelowe lies before the altar – and did so long before the present chapel was built. Across the nave, the Commandment board behind the organ is dated 1826 and is the only example in Norfolk that bears the king's initials. At the w. end note that the *Royal Arms* are dated 1705 for Queen Anne but were originally early *Stuart*. The C14 font has varieties of shallow tracery in the bowl panels and the cover is probably contemporary – simple *cruciform* pinnacle with rudimentary *crockets*. No less than three chests are in the corner – a square C13 dugout with a decayed top, a later model with a half tree trunk top, and a plain C17 successor. The large painting on the s. wall of Jacob recoiling in horror at the sight of Joseph's coat is by Jacques Berger, the French painter whose patron was the Bishop of Derry – the Hervey who built Ickworth House in Suffolk.

Thornage, All Saints (G2): Perched above the village street, the church was rather brutally restored twice in the late C19 and early C20, and the interior is bleak. Outside there are indications of *Saxon long and short work* at the n.w. angle of the tower, and *Norman* windows remain in the *nave* and *chancel*. The s. *aisle* has disappeared, but the arcade can still be seen. There is a *Renaissance*-style tomb chest of Sir William Butt (d.1583) on the s. side of the chancel, opposite the very pretty little 1812 chamber organ by Thomas Elliot: with its mahogany case and gilded pipes, it was made for Squire Atkinson at Swanton Novers Hall. See also the *ledger-stone* to Rector Francis Fesquet (d.1734) 'who left his Native country for the sake of the true Protestant Religion'.

Thornham, All Saints (D1): A well-proportioned, good looking church. Largely *Perpendicular*, with a rather plain tower and a big two-storey *porch*. Inside the porch are the remains of a canopied *holy water stoup*. The inner s. doorway here is lovely *Early English* work of about 1280, with pairs of slim little pillars to each side. The C15 door itself is notable, being richly panelled and inset with a neat little *postern door*. On the inside, its lock casing has I – R 1759 – the church-wardens, no doubt. A spacious interior, the lofty *nave* being 27ft. wide. Adding to the effect is a fine *hammer-beam* and *arch-braced roof* on deep *wall posts*, which in turn rest on chunky stone *corbels*; five big three-*light*,

Perpendicular clerestory windows each side; and a fine *arcade* of five bays which is a mixture of Perpendicular and re-used C13 work. There is a fragment of ancient wall painting on the w. wall; a *Tudor* arch, with figure niches set into the *jambs* each side, leads through to the tower; font with elaborate carving, with shields on its panels, and some painted with the *Instruments of the Passion*, St Andrew's Cross and other subjects. In the nave are some good *poppy-head* bench ends with a lively variety of carvings on the elbows – a post-mill, a unicorn, and a fox in priest's clothing, preaching energetically while a couple of geese stick out from under his habit – a popular way of poking fun at the clergy. *Jacobean* pulpit, dated 1631. The base of the *rood screen*, with donor's inscription dated 1488, has 16 panels of figures, each with a scroll and 'name plate' – David the Psalmist and eleven of the Old Testament prophets, *Lazarus, Paul, Barbara* and *Mary Magdalene*. The *chancel* is Victorian, being a rebuild of 1877 without much character. The e. ends of the two aisles were also rebuilt at this time.

Thorpe Abbotts, All Saints (H8): Close by a bend in the main Scole to Bungay road, and lately bereft of the line of elms that used to fringe the churchyard. The tower is a plain *Saxon* drum up to the level of the *nave* roof, then a plain octagon stage topped by another with two-*light* bell openings and *flushwork* dummies between. A walk round the outside reveals that there are no *quoins* used in the n.e. corner of the nave, and so that wall probably survives from when the tower was first built. The n. doorway is C13, and there is a blocked *Early English lancet* in the n. wall of the *chancel*. The s. *porch* is *Tudor* brick, and the side windows have three oddly shaped lights over the two main ones below. The early-C14 doorway has been given new *headstops* and the door itself is early and of very coarse workmanship, with lattice bracing on the back. Inside, the nave roof has been renewed but, except for the angels at the bottom of the *wall posts*, the chancel roof seems largely original. Until 1840, the font was plain and unadorned, and then rector William Wallace experimented a little with his pocket knife and found that it had been carefully plastered over in defiance of the image breakers. So we now can see a wonderfully crisp and clean set of carvings in the bowl panels – *Evangelistic Symbols*, and angels bearing shields: a floriated cross, St *Edmund's* crown (the parish belonged to the Abbey at Bury – hence its name), St *George's* cross. Look particularly at the symbol

for St *Matthew* – an angel with a scroll lying across his knees – it is in pristine condition. The C15 *rood screen* has two complete bays of good tracery, between two others that have been cut in half to fit the arch. The bottom panels and most of the centre rail have been ruthlessly cut away for some reason. The sanctuary has attractive panelling but unfortunately it is faced with oak veneer, and this is cracking and lifting in places. The set of *Royal Arms* above the tower arch are *Stuart* – altered for George III, and are nice enough to warrant cleaning if this were possible.

Thorpe Episcopi, St Andrew (I5): Close to the Yarmouth road out of Norwich, the church looks well from the green by the river. The little brick and flint tower which stands by the roadside is all that remains of the medieval church, save for a fragment of the *nave* wall nearby. It was a tiny building and was demolished in the 1880s. Before that, in the 1860s, a new building was designed by the eccentric architect *Thomas Jekyll*, to which a tower with a 150 ft. spire was added in 1881. The latter was damaged by bombs in 1944 and was dismantled in the 1950s, being replaced by a stumpy pyramid. The building of *knapped flint*, brick and stone is in C14 style and entry is through the base of the tower. The plain C13 font came from the old church and, above it in the w. wall is a large and decorative rose window filled in 1969 with symbols of the Apostles in stained glass by Dennis King. Jekyll's sense of design was wayward to say the least, and the *arcade* is a prime example – stumpy round *piers* with enormous *capitals* decorated with *pelicans* and busts of angels. The *rood screen* is in open C15 style with roundels above an *ogee* centre arch. The base panels have an extraordinary range of apostle figures to which have been added faces based on C19 people. Painted by A.Kingston Rudd, they include Bishop King of Lincoln, General Sir Dighton Probyn VC and an anonymous American actress, none of whom had any connection with the church as far as is known. The screen was inserted as a war memorial in 1920, but the rood figures above are C18 and were installed in 1943. 'The Lamentation' a C16 painting on a wood panel by an anonymous artist belonging to Lambert Lombard's circle of Flemish artists hangs on the n. wall. The tower contains a ring of 8 bells which are at present unringable.

Thorpe Market, St Margaret (I2): In 1796 local magnate Lord Suffield engaged a Mr Wood to build him this little exercise in 'churchwarden's gothick', and although it has attracted abuse in the past ('The ugliest place of worship I ever entered' was local historian Walter Rye's comment.) it is delightful for those who have some feeling for the period. A plain rectangle with twin *porches* on the s. side and corner turrets, dressed overall in faced white flint, its interior is beautifully kept. The pale blue coved ceiling is picked out in yellow and red, and the windows have a pleasing pattern of blue and orange diamonds. The most surprising thing is the arrangement of two tall *screens* – slender wood columns with glazed panels at the top. That at the *chancel* end has painted glass panels of Moses and Aaron plus a recent addition of George III's arms in the centre, while the other has another set of *Royal Arms* dated 1796. The font was saved from the old church and so were the excellent memorials in the chancel. One on the n. wall is to Sir Thomas Rant:

> ...his sovereign Charles ye first was driven from London by the tumult when retireing into his native countrey he lived hospitably and honourably in composing differences between his neighbours and was chosen a Member of the Healing parliament.

The tablet opposite to Robert & Elizabeth Britiffe (1712) is an outstanding piece by *John Ivory*; good architectural composition with three cherub heads below and a curly *pediment* with arms above – very like his Mackerell monument in St Stephen's Norwich.

Thorpe-next-Haddiscoe, St Matthias (K6): A peaceful spot, where the little churchyard is perched among trees above the level marshes that stretch away to the Herringfleet Hills. Another round tower – this time an interesting hybrid. The lower stage is *Saxon*, so look for the window arches carved from a single piece of stone and the small round window high up under the roof inside. Saxon too the *arcading* round the middle stage, but above that the double windows with central chunky shafts are *Norman*. They are now half bricked up unfortunately. Having ducked your head through the low Norman doorway, look to the left and you will see a large double *aumbry*; an unusual position – they are normally to be found in the *chancel* – but this possibly housed the the salt and napkins used for baptisms. The shallow font is a big square *Purbeck marble* piece that is probably Norman. Beyond it stands one of those satisfying *Jacobean* chests with simple

blank arcading in shallow carving, with a matching frieze along the top. There are rudimentary steps cut in a n. wall window embrasure that gave access to the *rood loft*, while a blocked arch on the opposite side shows that there was once an additional chapel there. The chancel is an all-brick rebuilding of 1836 – seemly but not exciting.

Threxton, All Saints (E5): Quite a steep drop down a narrow lane to the church lying just within the entrance to Church Farm. It was probably built on the site of a Roman villa, and when it was restored in the 1860s, foundations of a *Saxon* church with an *apsidal chancel* were found – there is still Saxon masonry in the s. wall. The round tower is *Norman* up to the belfry stage where it breaks back slightly. The bell openings have late-C13/early-C14 'Y' tracery and there are three rather than the usual four – w., n.e., and s.e. A single long slope of roof covers half the *nave* and the narrow n. *aisle*, and when the chancel was shortened during restoration, the old e. window of three stepped *lancets* was found embedded in the wall and was re-used. At the same time, the early-C13 s. doorway was taken out and became the entrance for a new *porch*. Before the C19 alterations, the n. aisle had been blocked off and used as a mausoleum, but when the late-C13 *arcade* was opened up again, the original decoration came to light and it is the church's most striking feature. The arches of the four bays have deep red leaf trails in the chambers and there is a band of decoration below the *capitals*. The *piers* vary slightly in their detail, and the *respond* at the w. end terminates with a single thick and curly leaf. The C14 octagonal font has a pleasing variety of shallow carving in the bowl panels, including 'window' designs of *reticulated* and interlaced tracery. The simple *Jacobean* pulpit, standing on a new base, matches the reading desk, and on the latter is carved 'Edward Gofe his gifte 1613'. The good C19 oak pews were made from a single tree, and look under the front bench on the n. side to find a metal top-hat rack – something seldom seen anywhere. The hat was inverted, and the brim slid between the metal frame and the underside of the seat. Beyond the C19 *screen* to the right, the large embrasure of the blocked *low side window* you may have noticed outside. There is a jumble of C15 glass fragments in a n. aisle window, and on the s. nave wall, a memorial to the four sons and one daughter that the Stewart family lost in a mere two months of the Spring of 1797. They, who 'sparkled, blossom'd and were exhal'd to Heaven' were all very young, and the verse ends:

> And till we share your Joys, forgive our Grief:
> These little rites, a stone, a Verse receive,
> 'Tis all a Father, all a Friend can give.

Thrigby, St Mary (K4): The C14 tower has an odd mixture of bell openings. Two of them are the same period but of differing shapes, while the other pair are late *Perpendicular*. The *sound-holes* are tiny *quatrefoils*. There was a wholesale restoration in 1896 when the *nave* walls were raised, *chancel* arch constructed, and the *Decorated* windows put in the chancel. Look for the three little *Norman* or even *Saxon* fragments set in the wall above the chancel arch. The four windows in the nave have wooden *mullions* and look to be late-C18. Best feature of the church is the C14 doorway. The deeply moulded arch has a trail of flower ornament at the outer edge, and big *headstops* (one has been heavily re-cut and given quite a sultry expression). *Royal Arms* of George III are opposite the entrance above the n. door and are nice enough to merit a better position on the s. wall – they could then be seen with the light instead of against it. The chancel has two big *consecration crosses*, the one on the e. wall retaining its colours. In the base of the tower there's a reminder that communion wafers were sometimes baked in the church – the square recess in the n. wall was an oven, and still has its flue.

Thurgarton, All Saints (H2): This largely C14 church, now in the care of the *Churches Conservation Trust*, has had its *nave, chancel, porch* and vestry all splendidly re-thatched. The round tower fell in 1822 and on either side of it in the w. wall there are *lancets* that probably date from the early C13. The vestry in place of the tower was added in 1923. When the nave was re-structured in the mid-C14, three windows with flowing tracery were inserted in the s. wall and new doorways were provided. The chancel has a Y traceried window and *priest's door* of the early C14, and it had a chapel on the n. side. In the C18 the e. wall was rebuilt and a new window was inserted and there is a strange little flying buttress on the s.e. corner that may have been needed as a support prior to the alterations. The colour-washed porch is tall, and its upper story houses a single bell removed from the old tower. Above the clean and light interior, the reed of the new thatch can be seen, laid on the *scissors-braced* timbers of the medieval roof, and a fine iron-bound C15 chest stands in the n.w. corner. The plain C14 octagonal font has a C17 cover with carved brackets rising to an acorn *finial*. Just to the e. of the entrance door there is an example of Elizabethen 'fruitful and profitable sentences' that were painted on church walls for the congregation's edification, although most of the text and decorative surround have gone. Another like it in similar condition has survived on the n. wall alongside two small image niches. Thurgarton's best feature is the range of excellent bench ends in the nave. They are broad with well carved *poppy-heads,* and on some of the elbows there are some interesting carvings. Although somewhat damaged most have recognisable subjects – n. side from the w. end: a man playing a lute, a lion, a man playing bagpipes (see the bag under his right arm and the two pierced pipes in his hands), a man in armour with shield and huge arrow shaft, an elephant with its howdah, and a tun (a *rebus* on the village name); s. side from the w. end: seated figure with wings and a cloth folded over his knees, a figure creeping up to the dog on the other side of the poppy-head which has a fox or a lamb across his back (see the way the dog's ear is flopped over the captive's back), a *griffin* with a curly tail, a winged beast with a human head between its paws, and another tun. Close by the large *ledger stone* commemorates William (1761) and Elizabeth (1732) Spurrell:

> He was a Father to the Fatherless
> He helped the Widows in their Distress
> He never was given to Worldly Pride
> He lived an honest man and so he dy'd
> They was tender parents our Loss was great
> We hope that both eternal joys will meet.

In the n.e. corner of the nave is the doorway to the *rood loft stair* which is complete up to loft level in the wall. The medieval *rood screen* was sold in 1897 to raise funds for restoration and Edwin Windsor Sandys-Reed the rector made the light-weight replacement. The small square stone bracket that juts from the face of the chancel arch on the s. side is interesting because it is pierced, and almost certainly secured the cord that was used to raise and lower the *Lenten Veil* which in this case would have covered the *rood* rather than the altar in the chancel. The *hammer-beam* chancel roof probably dates from the C17 and the *communion rails* are C18 turned and painted work, but in the sanctuary there is the plain C14 *piscina*, with *sedilia* alongside. The large blocked archway in the n. wall will have led to the vanished chapel on that side. The church's only *brass* is a small C16 inscription for John Bakon on his ledger stone in the chancel floor.

Thurlton, All Saints (K6): A handsome C15 tower with an elaborate *flushwork base course*, and it looks very well with the long range of thatch over *nave* and *chancel*. A walk round the outside is important here, otherwise you will miss the *Norman* doorway on the s. side. It is squat and rich, with zigzag moulding enclosing a pretty curl motif with incised dots. Also on the s. side there is a dumpy *rood stair* turret, and the n. wall of the chancel has a blocked C13 *lancet* and, to the w. of it, the faint outline of a low door of the same period. *Thomas Jekyll* carried out a restoration here in the 1850s when he re-clad the roofs, reglazed throughout, and inserted a new window in the tower and re-floored the lavish n. *porch*. The C15 inner doorway has angels swinging *censers* in the *spandrels* and the arch is inset with crowns, flanked by demi-figures of angels. Within, there is a mighty figure of S. *Christopher* on the n. wall; the Christ child carries a staff with a pennant and the saint's staff sprouts leaves against a pale red background. Jekyll was very active inside – repairing the font and the pulpit (to which he added a new stone base and stair); an *hourglass* stand survives on the wall behind. Oak benches were installed in the *nave* and seats for children in the tower. Jekyll also restored the *rood screen* which has delicate flower trails on a white ground decorating the leading edges of the uprights, and the heads of the remaining panels have pretty sprays of flowers. He and provided choir stalls for the *chancel* where, in the n.e. corner of the sanctuary you will find Ann Denny's enigmatic epitaph of 1665:

Reader stay and you shall heare
With your eye, who 'tis lyes heare.
For when stones do silence brake
Th' voice is seene not heard to speake.

The church has a ring of 5 bells, tenor 10 cwt.

Thurne, St Edmund (K4): The C14 tower has a most curious feature in the ground floor chamber. A circular peep-hole some 8in. in diameter runs through the w. wall at eye level. It aligns with St Benet's Abbey, one and a half miles away across the river, and the suggestion is that it was used to summon the monks in time of need, by lighting a candle within the tower. The interior of the church is plain, with an unpretentious *arch-braced roof*. There is a

simple late-C13 double *piscina*, and the original *rood beam* divides *nave* and *chancel*. The late-C17 *communion rails* are solid, with good *balusters*, and would be even better for having the old black paint removed. The e. window has good panels of mid-C20 glass – the risen Christ and Mary at the tomb, with flanking roundels.

Thurning, St Andrew (G3): In a pretty situation, with one cottage for company. C14 unbuttressed tower and three attractive *Decorated* windows in the s. *nave* wall. There was a *chancel*, but by 1719 only the n. wall was left and the rector was excused by faculty from rebuilding it. Its late-C13 e. window, with lovely *reticulated* tracery, and the blocked *priest's door* are re-set in the present e. wall. So we have an C18 reduced church and what a delightful example it is. The n. *aisle* is furnished with a range of *box pews* which were allocated to the various village farms, the squire, and the rector. The Hall and Rectory servants had their own pews at the w. end, and these still have the brass uprights for draught-excluding curtains. The corners of the servants' pews are rounded, and the joinery throughout is excellent – fielded panels, crisp mouldings. The body of the nave has plain open benches, and as late as the 1920s the congregation still clung to the old convention of 'men on the right, women on the left'. The *three-decker* was moved across to its present position in the 1830s, and the pulpit itself was made up out of panelling from Corpus Christi, Cambridge. William Wilkins pulled down the old chapel there in 1823 to make way for his new design, and Thurning (being a Corpus Presentation) had, through the good offices of Sir Jacob Astley of Melton Constable, the benefit of its discarded fittings designed by 'that ingenious

Thurning, St Andrew: Three-sided altar rails

architect' *Sir James Burrough*. And very good they are. Not only the pulpit, but a lovely set of three-sided *communion rails*, with slim turned *balusters*, a broad inlaid top rail, and a deep plinth – plus the sanctuary panelling wherein are set the *decalogue* and Lord's Prayer. On the e. wall a tablet to William Wake (d.1750) is a potted biography of an Indian nabob who died on the way home before he could fully enjoy his rich rewards, and also on the same wall, an excellent tablet in variegated marble to Caleb Elwin (d. 1776). The lettering is particularly good, as it is on Elizabeth Wake's memorial in the nave (1759) by *William Tyler*. This has a big scrolly *pediment* supporting a shell and, again, coloured marble panels. The hat pegs for the men and boys, which cost £2 18s 0d in 1840, still line the s. wall. No wonder C18 churchmen preferred worship in such surroundings to the draughts, muddle and dirt of the average church of their fathers. Here are dignity, intimacy, and comeliness, with a proper regard for the niceties of social distinction – the age caught like a fly in amber.

Thursford, St Andrew (F2): Nothing unusual about this church as you approach it down the park drive to 'the big house'. Assorted gothic, it seems, with an elegant early-C14 tower. But inside it is rather extraordinary, rather gloomy and features a Victorian *chancel* that either exasperates or enchants. High Victorian pantomime *piers*, two-deep, look through to a resoundingly ugly *transept* raised about 6ft. higher than the rest of the church, like the public gallery in a courtroom. This was, in fact, the family pew of the Chadds of Thursford Hall, its elevation explained by the fact that their burial vault is underneath. Back in the chancel, typical Victorian *encaustic tiles* cover the floor and a dominant mosaic *reredos* backs the altar. If you like Victorian glass, then here you will find some of the finest, in the e. window of about 1862 in particular. It was made by *Powell & Sons* from cartoons designed by the painter Albert C. Moore. It was Moore's only complete window and one of the outstanding works of its time. *Powell's* n. and s. chancel windows, designed by *Harry Ellis Wooldridge*, are equally good. In the *nave*, a central column holding up the n. arcade is 'a Victorian disgrace' (*Pevsner*). On the other side, the *arcade* looks original, but is so individual (a long tradition, evidently, at Thursford) that one hesitates to place it, but the s. aisle itself is mainly C15 work. Under the tower, a good marble monument to Sir Thomas Guybon, 1666, signed by the London sculptor, *William Stanton*

Thursford, St Andrew: E. Window detail

(1639-1705). Don't miss, in the vestry, the small, stained glass Arms of England, inscribed for Elizabeth I, 1579. A pity it's tucked away there – a most interesting item. As you leave, note the fine doorway – it's the oldest part of the building, said to date from the early C13. Walk round outside and see the wildly fanciful *gargoyles* which complete the Chadd chancel.

Thurton, St Ethelbert (J5): An unspoiled little place in its high village setting with sentinel fir trees around it. It is a 'single hall' construction, having no separate *nave* and *chancel* and is thatched overall, including the *porch*. Even the slim little tower has been 'built in' to make it look as if it sits on the w. gable end of the nave, like a *bell turret*. The upper part of the tower, in brick and *knapped flint* chequerwork, and with brick corner finishings, is *Perpendicular. Norman* in origin, the body of the church as we see it now is all (or nearly all) C14 – 'Y' tracery, *lancets*, intersecting tracery, and an e. window with *reticulation* and a *priest's door* on the s. side. Fine *corbels* to the s. windows of the nave – animals, birds, and one carved with two human heads, one male, one female, very fine-boned and wearing curious headgear. Inside the little porch with its wooden wicket gate under the rounded outer arch, is a splendid Norman s. doorway, with a richly carved and decorated arch and *capitals*, set on receding pillars. Norman too is the blocked n. door-way. A cosy place inside, with a white plastered barrel ceiling, heavy timber *wall plates* and *wall posts* and a n. wall which leans outward at a crazy angle. Furnishings are modern, though the font is probably C17. Curiously, the 'wrap around' construction of nave to tower produced two tiny little windowless rooms, each having a *Tudor* style doorway. Many fragments of old glass, C16 to C18, in the windows, most of it foreign, a collection both diverse and colourful; the glass in the e. window came from Rouen Cathedral, having been brought to this country by Lady Beauchamp. In the centre, St *Ethelbert*, with St *Andrew* above and Christ below. Other windows have lovely roundels showing scenes and emblems, and in the w. window, more saints. St Ethelbert is an unusual dedication, the only one in Norfolk and shared with Hereford Cathedral, where the saint was buried. Before you leave the churchyard, note that on the church's s.e. corner, carved into one of the *quoin* stones, is a *mass dial*.

Thuxton, St Paul (G5): Despite heavy restoration over the years, this little church presents a very distinctive outline if walk to the top of the churchyard, and view it from the north. The C14 *Decorated* square tower has a projecting stair turret, capped by slates, an octagonal belfry with a slate cap, and a nice 'Y' traceried w. window. The *nave* has a little *clerestory*, with windows which look as if they should belong to an ancient house rather than to a church, but they have no *aisle* to look over – that has long since disappeared, leaving only the stone outline of its arches in the walls; and a smaller arch outlining one of the *lancet chancel* windows. On the s. side, *Tudor* windows, topped with alternating pink brick and flint; the *porch* is heavily restored but retains C13 small pillars in two corners and a rebuilt *holy water stoup*. There is an agreeable little three-lancet e. window to the chancel, in which the *spandrels* either side of the centre *light* have been filled in with flints – a rather pleasing effect. Inside, a charming and simple interior, much restored, with modern roofs and chancel arch, the latter with overblown *corbels*, like those supporting the chancel *wall posts*.

The tower arch is C14 – elegant little *capitals*, with tiny *quatrefoils* and flower motifs topped by a 'battlemented' course. The *Early English* arches and pillars outlined on the s. wall show the position of the vanished aisle. The tower too has a large filled-in arch. A much smaller arch in the chancel s. wall has remnants of a large table tomb. Above, a window with a modern *Paul*. Either side of the window are two *brasses* for: l., Mary Seffowle, 'second wife to Gregory Pagrave was', who died 'the XIth of Jvne. M.D. Eight & Seventy' (i.e. 11th June, 1578); and r., the lady who:

> was third wife of Gregory Pagrave,
> Katherine Pigeon was her first name. Rich
> in faythe and honest fame Whos vertves &
> works breifly to declare Many poor folks did
> fele what they were.

She died in July 1596: 'The yere of grace. M.D. six and nyenty... Hir sovle rest in Ioy by Gods fre mercy'. Two seemly echoes of life, and death, 400 years ago. The chancel has an e. window of deep set, heavily mullioned triple lancets and a *reredos* the width of the sanctuary with a modern frieze across a series of small arches with beautiful pencil-slim round pillars and carved leafy *capitals*; in the s. wall, a *piscina* with a *trefoil* arch and low two-seat dropped *sill sedilia*; then an odd square hole. It had a door, as the marks of the hinges still show, but if it was an *aumbry* it was an odd position for it. *Norman* font, with odd projections on its massive round bowl; a *Jacobean* pulpit; a fine modern eagle lectern; and the *Royal Arms* of Charles I, dated 1637, which are said to have been made by a local craftsman.

Thwaite St Mary, St Mary (J6): A pretty little building in a humpy churchyard, with no windows to the n. so that from that side its plain rendered wall and thatched *nave* roof look for all the world like the side of a cottage. The simple C14 tower has no buttresses and little decoration of any kind save three blank shields above a brick niche. To compensate, halfway down the s. wall of the nave is a splendid late *Norman* doorway with no porch to hide it. The arch has a roll moulding like a heavy twisted rope, and scallop carvings on edge round the outside. Pairs of columns flank the entrance and all the *capitals* vary. The design on the inner rim of the doorway laps over onto the inside edge, and the same scooped-out orange segment motif that can be seen at Heckingham near Loddon occurs again here. Sections of the hood and one capital have been very recently renewed in a cream coloured stone and it will be interesting to see how this weathers. There is what may be an original *consecration cross* cut in the e. *jamb* (equal length bars with tails) and a very well defined *mass dial* low down on the w. face with two fainter ones above it. The brick chancel dates from 1737 and its neatly boarded ceiling has been painted blue. The *screen* is a heavy C18 country gothick with *trefoil* arches, and behind it nestles a tiny chamber organ with a *Regency* case and pretty blue and gold pipes. The C15 font is in the local family style of octagonal stem with attached columns, but like all families, one member is plain, and the bowl of this one has no decoration at all.

Thwaite, All Saints (H2): The round *Norman* tower is smooth and tapers slightly up to the C14 bell openings. There is a blocked doorway low down on the s. side and inside, the outline of a tall and narrow original arch can be seen. The C15 *rood screen* has been cut down to the middle rail, but the remains of *gesso* decoration show that it must have been beautiful. Little canopied figures on the buttresses are very like those on the screen at nearby Aylsham. The plain dark tall pulpit, backboard and *tester* are dated 1624. Somebody later unfeelingly put the steps in and cut half across the screen in so doing. The builder of the *aisle* chapel was John Puttok (d.1442), and a *brass* to him and his wife Alice lies before the altar there. The same family's arms can be seen on the end of the *box pew* at the front of the nave, which, like the rest, has very crude *poppy-heads*. For such a small church the size of the chest is extraordinary and it's completely swathed in iron bands. Equally lavish is the C19 Sunday school room. Complete with fireplace and hat pegs at all levels, it opens off the *chancel* on the n. side. For some reason a window in the s. aisle attracted the local graffiti specialists. Among other mementos scratched on the glass one reads, 'J. Spurgeon Aldborough January 26 1832 Glazier.' – his version of a trade card!

Tibenham, All Saints (H7): In this area of long flatland vistas, Tibenham's tower stands as a noble landmark for miles. It is splendidly tall and cleanlined early-C15 *Perpendicular*, with the *Emblems of the Evangelists* carved on its four corners; battlements adorned with *flushwork* and shields; flint and stone chequerwork down the faces of the big buttresses; finely traceried belfry and w. windows; and tall *sound-hole* slits on two sides with *cusped* arches cut from single pieces of

stone. The lowest points of the buttresses, and the *base course* all round, are ornamented in a striking diamond pattern of flint and stone. Early and developed *Decorated* period windows, and later Perpendicular examples, alternate around the body of the church, but on the n. side of the *nave* is a filled-in *Norman* slit window, deeply splayed. The *porch* is Decorated, with slim rounded pillars, and carved floral motifs studding the inner and outer rim of the arch. The interior of the church has a wealth of good woodwork: the nave roof, massively *arch-braced* and *tie-beamed*, in bleached timbers, with deep *wall posts* punctuating enormous moulded *wall plates*. Below them, three-*light clerestory* windows. The pulpit is octagonal, with arched panels – a first-class *Jacobean* piece, complete with *tester* and backboard. Beside it, severe in contrast, the lectern, of similar date. There is an abundance of *box pews* and *poppy-heads*. Another interesting Jacobean piece at the back of the church is a low four-sided reading desk; beside it, a panelled chest of similar vintage. The *arch-braced roof* in the s. *aisle* is good, with excellent open carving and shields in the *spandrels*. Then there is the Buxton Pew, a massive family pew, shoe-horned into the e. end of the s. *aisle*, right under the roof, with its own cumbersome bannistered staircase leading up from the eastern-most corner. A special faculty for this was granted in April 1635 by *Laud* to the Buxtons, an important Norfolk landed family. The pew is big enough to seat a score and provides a fascinating insight into social history. Faded *Royal Arms* of George I. In the corner of the aisle, the *piscina*, and the Buxton *brass*, dated 1572, on the wall. One of the Buxtons' *hatchments* hangs on their pew's w. side. The nave *arcade* is early-C14, with *quatrefoil* pillars and moulded capitals; the C14 octagonal font has Decorated tracery designs carved on bowl and stem and standing on eight little round-pillared legs. In s.e. corner of nave, the *rood stair* exit; and in the *chancel*, a deeply recessed piscina, with slots each side for a *credence shelf*; adjoining *sedilia* under a plain recessed arch, and a looking stone armrest. The C19 *decalogue* is painted on the chancel walls. The church has an excellent ring of 6 bells, tenor 18-1-3 cwt.

Tilney All Saints, All Saints (B4): It looks good from across the fields, the squatly powerful tower, bracing its shoulders under a sturdy stone spire and big corner pinnacles. Close to, the impression of strength is further reinforced by the bravura detail and truly massive angle buttresses, one of them containing a stair to the ringing chamber, the other a small room. The lower half of the tower is C13, with a beautiful w. door flanked by miniature buttresses topped by *crocketted* pinnacles, and on three sides there are big triple *lancets* within bold *arcading*. The upper half, including the spire is C14 with good window tracery. On the e. face the ridge line of an earlier roof is outlined, together with a filled-in *sanctus bell opening*. The rest of the church presents, on first appearance, a largely *Perpendicular* character, but this is but a C15 stamp upon an essentially *Norman* building. Look at the upper walls of the *chancel* and notice the outlines of Norman windows. These were part of a *clerestory* which once continued along the whole length of the church before the C15 reconstruction. The chancel n. *aisle* has rather good C14 flowing tracery to its windows and note on the same side the *rood stair turret*. The s. *porch* is C15 but the door within is C13, with delicate foliage *capitals* to the trim little pillars. The interior has a rugged splendour to take your breath away – one long, uninterrupted *nave* and chancel under a superb double *hammer-beam roof*, and a memorable *arcade* of eight striding bays from tower arch to sanctuary. First the roof. It has angels on all the hammers, spread-winged on the *purlins*, and carrying shields at *wall plate* level, with more in relief on the wall plates themselves. The lushly carved *wall posts* have figures under crocketted canopies, and more boldly carved figures as decorative *corbels*. At every point the timbers are adorned with carving and moulding. The chancel roof is an 1880s replacement effected with tact and skill. Now the arcade – a real beauty; seven fairly low, solidly plain round arches on big square capitals, carved with stiff foliage or fluting, some of the pillars round, others irregular or in clustered shafts. Notice that the westernmost bay is distinctively *Early English* and complements the lovely tower arch – bay and tower were added to the church about 1250, some 70 years after the last Norman arcade was built. It has been suggested that there was a Norman tower where this additional bay now stands, that it probably collapsed, and that its replacement was built slightly further w. In the vestry behind the panelled-in bay on the s. side, a blocked stairway, large window and unexplained niches high in the e. wall combine to suggest that here could have been a two-storey 'clergy house' for the priest. The handsome font of 1618 is something of a curiosity; apart from its extrovert carvings, and arcading round the stem, its bowl has inscriptions in Latin and English, the latter eccentrically reading, 'SEE,

Tilney All Saints, All Saints: Royal Arms

HERE IS / WATER: WHAT / DOETH LET ME / TO BE BAPTIZED / ACTS.8.36.' The remnants of an ancient font bowl are nearby in the n. aisle, together with two C13 grave slabs. One of these is carved with the *Knights Templar*'s *cross patée* and may belong to Baron Frederick de Tylney, knighted by Richard I while on Crusade. A man famous for his strength, he fell at the siege of Acre (1291) and his body was brought back here for burial. Set into the *pier* immediately to the e. is a little *piscina* under a lovely *trefoil* head and, at the far end of the aisle, another, equally attractive under a multi-*cusped* arch. Now into the chancel, and look for the outlines of the Norman windows. The e. window came four centuries later and fills almost the whole wall. Yet with its clear glass allowing the light to stream in, and with its uncluttered lines, it enhances the Norman detail. Of the same period are the piscina and *sedilia*, all under cusped *ogee arches* below an embattled square hood with tracery in the spandrels. Appealing *Jacobean communion rails* with open carving, elegant C15 *screens* to the aisles, and some modest *misericords* of the same date. The chancel *screen* is unusual, having been erected as late as 1618 (the same year as the font). It is not a subtle piece and its general heaviness suggests a craftsman more used to pompous country house commissions. Don't overlook the very good Queen Anne *Royal Arms* at the w. end of the s. aisle – dated 1711 and topped by a little traceried half wheel inscribed 'Love God, Honour the King'.

Tilney St Lawrence, St Lawrence (B4): The layout and profile of this heavily restored church is so irregular that it gives it a special character. Its long low *nave* is dwarfed by a much higher *chancel*, and by big n. and s. *transepts*, with the stubby w. tower balancing the grouping at the other end. Cement rendering covers the body of the church overall, which can never be any help to the look of a building; but the old *Decorated* tower is of natural stone and *carstone*, providing a pattern of subtle colours which is most attractive. Low on the w. buttress, s. side of the tower, notice on the s. face an incised coat of arms in a panel; and on the e. face, a boldly carved mason's mark. Very pretty w. doorway, with several slim shafts supporting a deeply moulded arch: a contrast with the wholly plain s. door of the same early-C14 date, whose only adornment is two heavy and much-defaced *headstops*. Inside all has a positive Victorian stamp, with heavily timbered, barn-like C19 roofs throughout, and the plainest of deal pews of the same date. There is a C14 *piscina*, much restored, in the sanctuary, complete with its wooden *credence shelf*. Opposite, the *screen* into the vestry appears to have some old remnants built into it. On the chancel s. wall is a monument whose naive style and lettering accentuates its poignancy:

> Heere ly Mary the wife of Mr John Beckham who left this life the 7th of Ivne 1673 and 4 sonns who dyed as Followedth Iohn the Eldest in 1661 Iohn the 2nd sonne 1668 Iohn the 3rd 1669 and Iosiah dyed 1673.

Did the poor woman die in childbirth – or just of a broken heart? Above is a large tablet setting forth how this church was saved from decay:

> This parochial chapel which had fallen greatly into decay and become much defaced and mutilated through age and neglect, was entirely restored by the pious munificence and at the sole expense of Mrs Mary Mann of South Lynn, Norfolk, The walls in some places having been rebuilt, the transepts restored and the tower repaired and surmounted by a spire, AD 1846.

That spire, incidentally, has long since gone. Back in the nave, a special feature on the s. wall is the *Royal Arms* of James I, dated 1620, in the big original wooden frame. The set survived, most fortunately, against all the odds. In the early C20

it was found in the base of the tower – being used to hold up the coke heap. Rescue and restoration followed.

Titchwell, St Mary (D1): A tiny, picturesque church, hugging the edge of the salt marshes. It is given special character by its *Norman* round tower with tiny round headed windows, including two blocked ones which made way for the later, higher *nave* roof. The body of the church is *Perpendicular*, though the fabric is much older, the *chancel* in particular showing evidence of its Norman origins. Outside, notice at the n. e. corner of the chancel the foundations of the circular *rood stair*. Entering through the C13 *Early English* s. doorway, with its trim pillars supporting a crisply moulded arch, to a simple interior – a tiny church of considerable atmosphere. Restorers with an evident feel for history have left in indented outline, first, the original e. window; next, the partial outline of a Norman window. Some years ago there were discovered the remnants of a lovely piscina under an *ogee arch*, which had been broken into to make way for a Perpendicular window. Traces of original colour can be seen on the old window *jambs*. On the chancel n. side is part of the arch of a tomb recess – broken into by a *Tudor priest's door*. Very faint colour is to be discerned on the simple, square headed wooden *screen*. The big, plain, Norman tub-font stands on modern, 'spiralled' shafts.

Tittleshall, St Mary (E3): Two massive horse chestnuts guard the gate and, with mature limes around the churchyard, make a handsome setting. The C14 tower has a two-*light* w. window with *Decorated* tracery and there are canopied niches in the w. buttresses; round *sound-holes* n. and s., with four-petal tracery, and a wide niche above the w. window. The C14 *chancel* has fine flowing tracery in the windows on the s. side, and the five-light e. window has a lovely web of *reticulated* tracery in the head. On the n. side of the chancel, a big and rather forbidding early-C18 mausoleum used by the Coke family for 150 years before the vault at Holkham took over. The *nave* interior is plain and spacious, with a broad centre *aisle* and a deeply moulded C14 tower arch. Octagonal *Perpendicular* font, with *quatrefoils* on the bowl and panelled tracery on the shaft. Above the n. door, a fine and well restored set of Hanoverian *Royal Arms* signed by the painter – L. Cobbe of Kings Lynn. Tittleshall is famous for its Coke monuments and there is a useful potted history of the family available in the church. Winefrid Coke was the first to be buried here in 1569, and her tablet to the left of the chancel arch has a pretty pink alabaster surround, gilded and with shields above and below. The full richness is in the chancel, and on the n. side, Sir Edward Coke's first wife Bridget has what is probably the finest C16 monument in Norfolk; framed in alabaster enlivened by coloured ribbons and shields, she kneels within an arch with her children at prayer below. The whole piece avoids all the heaviness of its contemporaries and is graced by sensitive carving. Perhaps remembering that, as a *Paston*, she brought a dowry of £31,000 and bore ten children, it says 'Many daughters have done virtuesly (sic) but thou surmountest them all'. Her husband, the Lord Chief Justice, 'a famous pleader, a sound counsellor', prosecutor of Essex, Raleigh and Guy Fawkes and founder of the family fortunes, asked that his body be brought home to lie beside his first wife and it lies in the great tomb of black and white marble by *Nicholas Stone* on the n. side of the sanctuary. Four Virtues loll on the broken *pediment* and the recumbent figure is crisply carved in pure white marble – attributed to John Hargrave, Stone's assistant. Opposite, an even bigger monument for Thomas Coke, earl of Leicester 1759 (not to be confused with the later 'Coke of Norfolk'). The excellent busts of the Earl and his wife are by *Louis Francois Roubiliac*. Next to it, one of only two pieces by *Joseph Nollekens* in the county, the 1805 monument to Jane Coke, first wife of 'Coke of Norfolk'; this is a lovely bas-relief composition, with the lady leaning on a column being encouraged upward by an angel above and a cherub below. It so happens that the other Nollekens piece is a bust of Charles James Fox at Holkham – he was named leader of the Whigs and was a close friend of Coke. Before leaving the chancel, see the *ledger slab* of the Rev. Dixon Hoste whose son, Sir William Hoste was the dashing young sailor who flew the signal 'Remember *Nelson*' at the battle of Lissa.

Tivetshall, St Margaret (H7): The *chancel* used to be thatched, and even now the steep pitch of the pantiles cocks up a little over the apex of the *nave* roof. The e. end of the building dates from the early C14 (see the deeply moulded *priest's door* and 'Y' tracery window by it). The plain unbuttressed tower has small *Decorated* bell openings and *flushwork* battlements, with a stubby stair turret to the s. The outer arch of the homely little *porch* has an endearing list to

Tittleshall, St Mary: Bridget Coke's monument

starboard, and within there is quite a handsome doorway under a square label. The *spandrels* have shields of the *Trinity* emblem and the *Instruments of the Passion*, and there are floral motifs in the moulding. Inside, the walls are dazzling white (except for a patch on the s. side where there are fragments of C16 black letter text), and even the plainest of fonts has been given a coat of whitewash. The pale timbers of the roof have interlaced *bosses* in the centre of the panels. There are nine medieval bench ends, one with a niche, and their tall *poppy-heads* are surprisingly varied. The arms once supported carved figures but not much of them is left. The *screen* has the remains of excellent tracery in the panels and this, with the rail, has been carefully regilded. There is a line of big tracery rosettes along the bottom similarly treated and the whole thing must have been quite splendid originally. By it, a *trefoil piscina* for a nave altar, and there is another like it in the chancel with heavy *finials* in the wall over it. On the n. side, an *Easter Sepulchre* recess under a trefoil arch, with an early-C13 tomb slab (pre-dating most of the chancel) set in the bottom. Now we come to

Tivetshall's special attraction. The whole of the chancel arch above the screen is filled with a *tympanum* on which is painted a sumptuous set of *Royal Arms* and the commandments. It is dark with varnish, and one needs to sit and accustom the eyes to the light. Even then, binoculars are a real help to distinguish the details. This combination of Elizabeth I's Arms and the *decalogue* is one of the most remarkable in the country. It was set up in 1587 – twin inscriptions either side record that Richard Russel, Geoffrey Neve and Humphrey May 'in there tyme they caused this for to be done'. The le Neve family produced two Kings of Arms later, and this may explain why the heraldry here is so elaborate. Not only have we Elizabeth's own achievement in the centre, but there are badges for all the *Tudor* sovereigns – the centre shield with a falcon crowned is Anne Boleyn's badge adopted by her daughter Elizabeth, and the four banners carry: top right the rose of Henry VIII, bottom right the portcullis of Henry VII, top left the phoenix of Edward VI, bottom left the pomegranate of Mary. Under the words 'O God Save oure Quene Elizabeth' there is a text from the Bishops' Bible and the date 1587. The whole is painted as an architectural composition, with the lion and dragon supporters using the *pediment* for a foothold, and with pinnacles at the corners; the large panel at the foot is filled with the commandments in black letter, and each initial is picked out in red. There was a crude repainting in 1862, but this was on top of the old varnish, and perhaps one day it may be possible for this remarkable survival to have the careful restoration it richly deserves.

Toft Monks, St Margaret (K6): The church stands well away from the village and its distinctive octagonal tower has bell openings which form part of a complete *arcading* of tall *lancets*. The *Norman* arch inside and the round headed doorway above it means that the C13 exterior probably encases an earlier original. When going in look up at the bold wooden head *corbels* of the *porch* roof – one has split from top to bottom but still has a lot of character, and the one in the corner has his tongue out; all retain traces of original colour. The C15 font with its angels and *Evangelistic Symbols* round the bowl has obviously been moved nearer the tower, for under the *arch-braced roof* to the e. you will see the beam from which the font cover was originally suspended. For another sign of the way in which things change, observe how

the arch-braces of the *nave* roof drop down over two windows to finish in mid air – the *Perpendicular* style windows were inserted later to give more light but nobody bothered to match them up with the roof timbers. The C13 *chancel* has bold modern glass in the e. window designed by Thomas Derrick and made by Gilbert Sheedy in 1952. On the floor just w. of the sanctuary, a little *brass* to Edward Howlet (d.1607) has a thoughtful variation on a common theme:

As I was so be yee, as I am yee shall be.
That I gave yt I have, that I spent yt I had.
Thus I end. All my cost, yt I left yt I lost.

Toftrees, All Saints (E3): The square C15 tower has *sound-holes* near the top and either the belfry stage was never completed or it was reduced at some time to its present height. There are early *carstone quoins* at the w. end of the *nave* and the shape of a *Norman* window is outlined in tile on the s. wall. The s. doorway is C13 and its n. counterpart is now blocked. Inside, the font immediately draws the eye. One of the finest Norman examples in the county, its square oatmeal-coloured bowl has barbaric animal heads at each corner which hold the ends of a knotted rope trail in their mouths. The patterns in the panels are highly individual, and it stands on five stumpy columns with cushion *capitals*. In the *chancel* there is a set of C17 *communion rails*, fairly coarse country work but pleasing, and a nice black and alabaster memorial on the n. wall to Sir Henry Clifton and his wife (1620, 1603). The relief decoration is very cautious with a delightful little allegorical roundel in the *pediment*. *Royal Arms* of George III on the *nave* s. wall, and a single *hatchment* at the w. end. Note as you go that the *priest's door* in the chancel is only 21in. wide, and also the stump of a *churchyard cross* by the gate. After the war this church was in very poor state and threatened with closure. It shows full well how a community can revitalise, repair and restore – given the will – and Toftrees has had that all right.

Topcroft, St Margaret (I6): A pleasant walk between tall sycamores leads to the s. *porch*, and on the brick *chancel* a plaque announces that it was rebuilt in 1712. The whole building has lived through many changes, and even the tower is of three periods. The round base is *Norman*, and then in the C13 an octagonal stage replaced the old top – where the cement rendering has fallen away note the thin brick and tile *quoins* at the angles. Then in the C15 the top was rebuilt, and, like nearby Bedingham, there are pretty *flushwork* patterns on four sides in *Perpendicular* tracery, although the bell openings themselves have lost their tracery. There are lovely grimacing *gargoyles* and a moulded *drip course* decorated with floral motifs below the battlements. The tall porch has a *holy water stoup* outside and faint traces of a *mass dial* high on the s.e. buttress. Both inner and outer arches have *corbel heads*. Inside, the C14 *arcade* has a pronounced tilt outwards and the small *trefoil piscina* at the e. end of the *aisle* shows that there was once an altar there. The C15 font is the familiar blend of angels and lions. Those round the square shaft have all lost their front paws. Above the tower arch is a very dark set of Georgian *Royal Arms* and it would be nice if they could be lowered and cleaned, together with two *hatchments* on the n. wall. Passing the *rood stair* in then. wall, one comes to the chancel and despite its being an uninspired structure, there are some very good memorials. Susanna Smyth died in 1765 at 29, and it is good to know that, 'Her amiable Character Placed her out of the Reach of Censure During Life, And needs not the Support of Panegyric after Death'. Beyond, and flanking the *priest's door*, are the memorials to James and John Smyth (1787 and 1808), At first glance they match, but notice that the carving of the earlier one is crisper and more confident. A handsome pair nonetheless, surmounted by oval urns, coats of arms in roundels above, cherub heads below – all in white marble on black ovals. By the chancel arch, an earlier tablet for Richard Wilson (1637) catches the eye – a circle of black marble in a simple frame, enlivend by his arms in colour at the top.

Tottenhill, St Botolph (C4): A lonely little church approached by narrow lanes in deep countryside, the graveyard to the e. a sea of whispering bracken. It originally belonged to the vanished hamlet of West Briggs, but when Tottenhill's own church fell into ruin this one was taken over, despite its isolation from the village. The *carstone* tower is C15 and once had a spire but the body of the church is *Norman* and within the *porch* there is a lovely small scale doorway; the single columns have interlace patterns on the *capitals* and in the *tympanum* there is a cross ringed with a coil of rope, the ends of which are drawn out across the lintel of the door. Norman too, the blocked n. door and small *lancet* in a deep splay in the n. wall. The late-C12 *chancel* arch has bold zigzag ornament but the

outer band of decoration was added in 1877 and may or may not repeat an original design. The recesses either side will have been for *nave* altars (see glossary, *guilds*) but the C19 restorations robbed them of their shape although the chancel e. window, with its intersected 'Y' tracery of around 1300 was apparently undisturbed, like the plain *piscina* nearby. Under the tower is a *Royal Arms* board of George III dated 1763 but it is now so faded that one can hardly read the name below of churchwarden Thomas Jake. Churches never cease to surprise and delight, for who would expect to find in this secluded spot a tablet dedicated to perhaps that most English of C18 composers Thomas Arne, whose 'Rule Britannia' still evokes the spirit of the age? As far as one knows he set not a foot in Tottenhill, but the daughter of his wife's niece attended his deathbed and was determined that he should not be forgotten. Read about him behind the organ, next to the strange encapsulated life story of a Dickensian ward in chancery, Cecilia-Maria Henslowe who died in 1859. That begins: 'O my Mother, my mother! – words can never tell...', and opposite there is a strange cry from the heart of a parson who lost his son, Lt Col. Patrick-John Henslowe of the Bombay Grenadiers, in a minor insurrection at Mhow in 1882: "Tis hard indeed to think that God / Could so afflict – so ill reward / Both thee and us'.

Trimingham, St John the Baptist's Head (I2): The dedication of the church is most unusual. Before the *Reformation* swept away such things as saintly relics, a local will mentioned the head of St *John the Baptist* at Trimingham Church. But had that been so, this would have been a place of pilgrimage to rank with Compostella in northern Spain. In fact what was almost certainly kept here was one of the alabaster representations of the Baptist's head, which were manufactured at Nottingham and Burton-on-Trent in alabaster mined nearby in Derbyshire. As it was, records the 'History, Gazetteer and Directory of Norfolk', 1854, in ancient times Trimingham was visited by pilgrims who 'came to see the head of St *John the Baptist* which the wily priests pretended they had got'. Which is probably very near the mark. A pleasant church this is today, mainly in the *Perpendicular* style, with some earlier work built in, and a solid squat tower dating from about 1300. By 1854 the building was in a state of total neglect and *Thomas Jekyll*, the Norwich architect, entirely rebuilt the *nave* and part of the *chancel*, keeping close to the original. He restored the *piscina, sedilia, holy water stoop* and C15 *rood screen* which had been discovered hidden in a barn. His too are the pulpit, lectern, benches, choir stalls and *reredos*. Notice that the screen's meticulous carving is in a double-layer. Then it has lovely paintings, date about 1500, of eight saints: left to right – *Edmund, Clare, Clement, John the Baptist* (holding aloft his own head on a dish, underlining the church's very rare dedication, there being only one other such, in Kent), *Petronella, Cecilia, Barbara* and, again, *Edmund, King and Martyr*. The chancel arch above is beautiful in its simplicity, as is the lovely little pink stone double-headed piscina by the altar. Those wooden braces across the angles of the walls, to either side of the altar, are puzzling, with their original-looking *billet* moulding – until you realise they are artistic cosmetics to hide metal braces doing a practical wall-holding job. Note the fairly rustic chancel windows, square headed within Perpendicular recesses. The font is C14, early Perpendicular. All around the church are highly distinctive carvings, all the work of the Rev. Reginald Page, rector here from 1909 to 1923 and including his own memorial in the chancel, dated 1953, which – unless someone is a very clever style copyist – he prudently carved for himself in advance.

Trowse Newton, St Andrew (I5): If not the most attractive of churches outside (A cement rendered *chancel*, ugly modern s. chapel adjoining the chancel, an uninspired n. *aisle* added in 1901 and much restoration overall.), it is nonetheless a place with many attractions. Of considerable and especial interest is the e. window, in which the tracery, though renewed, is known to be exactly in the form of the original – and closely dateable. Below and to the right of it are the sadly decaying remains of a stone-panelled, Latin inscription, telling us that 'Wilemus de Kirkebi Prior Norvic me...'. Only half the inscription remains, but fortunately it was fully noted by Charles Cox in 1910, setting down that William, Prior of Norwich Cathedral (from 1272 to 1288) made this window to the Glory of God, which gives us a clear dating of a C13, *Early English* design, seen in the boldest *quatrefoil* tracery. Above the inscription is a large figure niche, attractively arched and hooded in pink brick (probably from the late C15 to early C16). The *nave* has good *Perpendicular* s. windows; the tall, over-slim tower (recently excellently restored and repointed) has splendidly fierce *gargoyles* at each corner, belfry windows

with most delightful tracery (Perpendicular, but still with a touch of *Decorated* style exuberance), and a neat *Tudor* w. window. The two storey C15 *porch*, with queer-looking *corbel* heads on the ends of its outer arch, has a nice little *groined* roof and a deeply inset *holy water stoup*. Inside the church, there is a strong flavour of Victoriana: nonetheless an arresting interior, with two things in particular taking the attention. First, a modern pulpit which would be fairly ordinary, if it did not have three astonishing, life-size wooden figures seated around it on little fixed wooden seats – with even a footstool for King David, centre, playing his harp, and at either hand an androgynous angel energetically blowing a trumpet. Possibly C18, these figures were acquired originally by the Colman family (the mustard people) and may have come from a Flemish organ case. Second, the three-dimensional carved wooden *reredos*, which presents The Last Supper with most Eastern detail, and to each side of the altar, two rather overwhelming, larger-than-life figures, in Gothick painted frames, of gesticulating saints (four different ways of hailing a taxi, as someone irreverently but descriptively quipped). These, together with the enormous C18 Ascension of Christ painting hanging in its original frame on the s. wall (Roman soldiers fleeing in disarray before a levitating Jesus) came from St Michael Coslany Church in Norwich – and were yet more acquisitions, displaying a curious collecting taste, of the Colmans. There is a handsome *pelican* lectern, C18 again, on a Victorian base much barnacled with *crocketting*. The rather fine C15 font has splendidly snooty lions carved around its octagonal bowl, alternating with angels bearing shields variously representing the *Trinity*; around the base, *griffins*, winged lions and various figures all, alas, beheaded. Nearby is a *brass* to Elizabeth Dalyson, 1585, 'loving wyef of Roger Dalyson', but unfortunately this is sealed off from view by a fixed carpet. A rubbing on the adjacent wall reveals it as very good, she in beautifully detailed ruff and gown. In the churchyard, look for a little gravestone, to be touched by the tragedy and the out of wedlock shame, of a nine months old babe, who lived and died in 1829: 'Bold. Infidelity. / Turn pale and die. / Beneath this stone, / Infant, asleep, lie.'

Trunch, St Botolph (I2): A trim, neat church with a fairly plain tower (the little cross-shaped slits in the s. face are air/light holes to the tower stair). A *Perpendicular* church throughout, though the tracery in some of the *aisle* windows is so *Decorated* in its flowing character that it must be very early Perpendicular – compare with the 'pure' version of the style in the *chancel*, particularly in the fine e. window. The *clerestory*, still later, has flattened arches of *Tudor* character. On the s. side of the chancel, note the charming and unusual feature of a Perpendicular *porch* over the *priest's door*, with a buttress 'seated' on its roof (see also Warham St Mary); the doorway itself is earlier, of the Decorated period. Once inside the church (via the C15 Perpendicular porch) there is no question about what dominates the attention – the astonishing and beautiful oak font canopy, one of only four of its kind in England (the others are at St Peter Mancroft in Norwich, Luton and Durham), a carved, crested, canopied and gilded creation standing on six legs set around the plain C15 font, and richly carved in foliage, flowers, birds and animals (including a pig wearing a bishop's mitre) – a memorable sight. Above is a fine *hammer-beam roof*, adorned with angels, with lush carving in the *spandrels*, and long *wall posts* between the *clerestory* windows (note some remnants of ancient glass in the centre window, n. side). The four-bay *arcade* is of the Decorated period; at the e. end, in both aisles, are slots in the arcade pillars which indicate where *parclose screens* were once fitted to enclose side chapels. On the top stone of the pillar facing into the s. aisle chapel is a faded 'star' outline which could possibly be a *consecration cross*. Below the tower is an open ringing floor, supported on a splendid painted wooden arch. The chancel *screen*, dated 1502, is very good, with painted saints in 12 panels, with really beautiful carving above them. The saints and symbols on the left side are *Thomas*; *Philip*; *James the Less*; *Matthew*; *James the Great*; *Peter*. On the right are *Paul*; *Andrew*; *John*; *Jude*; *Simon*; *Bartholomew*. The chancel is full of interest: on n. side, note *squint* through wall (more probably to a *sacristy* than to an *anchorite's* cell); set into the base of a window, what looks like an *Easter Sepulchre*; on the s. side, over the *priest's door*, an intriguing monument to Robert & Ann Thexton, whose initials stand outside a circle containing the *Instruments of the Passion*; two *piscinas*, one angled with an *aumbry* above, built into the base of a window, the rest of which is let down as *sedilia*. The carvings and scratchings all over the friendly old choir stalls probably date back to 1700 when the chancel was used as a schoolroom (note the ink-well holes!). More interestingly the stalls are raised up on sounding-boxes, to give more resonance. There

Trunch, St Botolph: Priest's door

are half a dozen good old C14 *misericords*, carved with grotesques, angels, winged animals and a devil.

Tunstall, St Peter and St Paul (K5): Once a large and beautiful church to serve this hamlet on the edge of the marshes, but now the tower is riven, its top like a rotten tooth, and grass grows between the walls of the ruined *nave*. Open *putlog holes* can be seen in many places, and there are remains of the *Decorated* tracery in the windows, with the shape of a *holy water stoup* by the doorway. Even in 1704 the parish petitioned the Diocesan Chancellor, 'to sell the bell in the decaying steeple to repair and adorn the *chancel*' for 'by reason of dilapidations and fall of roof no service has been held for 40 years'. Ruined churches are not a new thing in Norfolk. They did repair the chancel, and in fact extended it eastwards in red brick, so that the C13 double *piscina* with its simple *cinque-foiled* arches and centre column is now outside the sanctuary and partly masked by pews. The chancel arch was bricked up and a stone tablet over the little door reads, 'This rebilt by Mrs Elizabeth Jenkinson the relict of Mils Jenkinson of Tunstul esq and Mrs Anne Kelsall daughter of ye said Miles and Elizabeth 1705'. It was repaired again in 1853, and it looks as though the bowl of the C15 font with its good tracery was re-cut then. *decalogue boards* flank the altar, and looking w.

you can see the shafts and *capitals* of the old chancel arch and the line across it at high level suggests that there was once a *tympanum*. Early on there was a chapel s. of the chancel, and the arches of the *arcade* show on the outside with just a sliver outlined within. At least one service is still held in the church each year and the building is now vested in the Diocesan Board of Finance who have stabilised one of the nave window embrasures with new brickwork.

Tunstead, St Mary (J3): This is another of the great churches raised on the rich back of the medieval *wool trade* in this part of Norfolk. Building went on from 1327 until the *Black Death* called a halt in 1349. Work started again in 1371. The s. facade is striking; where one would expect a *clerestory*, there is a band of *blank arcading* in *flushwork*, and the *chancel* is almost as tall as the *nave*. The windows of the *aisles* and chancel match in size, and a prominent *drip course* runs below them for the whole length, giving a strong unity to the design. It is interesting to see how the *reticulated* tracery of the *Decorated* style in the aisle windows was used in conjunction with the tall and slender *Perpendicular*, *quatrefoil* piers in the nave – an example of how architectural fashions merged and overlapped sometimes. The C15 *arch-braced* nave roof had *tie-beams* added in 1683 but they were not enough to prevent the *arcades* being pushed outwards. This forced a major restoration 1952-56 when the n. arcade was taken down and rebuilt. The n. aisle wall still has a decided list. The feature of the church (unique in England) is the stone platform at the e. end of the chancel. It has a door on the s. side by which one descends into a barrel-vaulted chamber running the whole width and lit by an iron grating in the top. The platform is reached by steps on the n. side, and no one has produced a definitive answer as to its function. It may have been used for the exhibition of relics, with the chamber serving as a strong room; the presentation of mystery plays has been suggested and scorned in equal proportion. There was once a painted stone *reredos* for the high altar and fragments are preserved in situ behind glass. In 1771 the e. window was bricked up in desperation because the village children persisted in throwing stones at it (nothing changes!) and now a huge cross worked in dried flowers, grasses and foliage hangs before it. The *rood screen* of 1470, tall and very like the later one at Worstead, has much of its original colour, and the paintings of the named saints on the panels are virtually untouched. The floor of the

Tunstead, St Mary: C14 ironwork on S. door

rood loft is still there and above it the *rood beam* itself, standing on large brackets and with most of its colour intact. Lastly, be sure not to miss the quite exceptional C14 ironwork on the s. door. The ring is at the centre of a 4ft. cross fantastically decorated with curly tendrils from which spring little *trefoil* leaves. The church has a ring of 8 bells, tenor 10-3-10 cwt.

Tuttington, St Peter & St Paul (I3): Apart from the round *Norman* tower with a spike on top, the church was rebuilt in 1450, although some of the window tracery takes earlier forms. The shallow s. *porch* is two storied but has had its upper floor removed. The *chancel* has no step and the few stalls are set well back to promote a welcome feeling of space. The *rood loft* stairs are in the n. wall and one of the stone *corbels* for the beam itself remains. The C15 font has shields round the bowl and rests on a very short panelled stem. The 1638 cover is a pleasing design of scrolls radiating from a centre post. The pulpit is dated too – 1635; it has barleysugar *balusters* to the stairs and is fitted with an *hour-glass stand*. In the chancel lies Ann Elwin (1697) who seemingly died somewhat preoccupied with lineage: 'only daughter & heires of Thomas Seamier of Heveingham Esq., & great Grand daughter of Edmund Seamier, formerly Lord Bishop of Norwich'. But what one remembers

Tuttington, St Peter & St Paul: Bench end

about Tuttington are the bench ends. They have a splendid variety of unusual carvings on the arms which are full of character – the Elephant and Castle has a face peeping out of the window, men play lute and tabor, a milkmaid regards her churn, a fox steals a goose, animals thieve from a woman's basket – a little gallery of fable.

Twyford, St Nicholas (G3): That this was a *Norman* church can be seen by the w. wall mixture of flint and *carstone*, and there is a *lancet* window with a deep splay. The w. wall is uneven up its centre line and there were traces of a door in the C19, so the original building probably had a western tower, although this suggests that the window has been repositioned. Now, there is a homely brick C18 tower serving as a s. *porch*, with a most engaging cupola to house the bell. Backed by great trees it is a beautiful combination. *Nave* and *chancel* are one, but the e. end is largely undisturbed C13 work, with a fine triple lancet window and a simple *piscina*. The chancel roof was given a ceiling in the C18 and one mourns the upholstered *box pews* and *three-decker pulpit* that were here then. The C13 font is a massive cube relieved only at the corners, standing on four pillars with a centre column. Small is beautiful and so is the hymn board – don't overlook it. It has an inset limewood panel carving of a branch of the vine, with grapes and a tiny butterfly perched on the stem, A sinuously carved *pelican* in her piety is set upon the top.

Exquisite. Admiral Sir Edward Ellis (d.1943) is commemorated thoughtfully: 'Life is eternal and love is immortal, and Death is only an horizon and an horizon is nothing save the limit of our sight'. A table tomb near the porch illustrates a very likeable trait – Robert Framingham was a shoemaker. His grandson, Henry, became Mayor of King's Lynn and High Sheriff of Norfolk, but he built a fine tomb for his 89 year old grandfather who died in 1683.

Upper Sheringham, All Saints (H1): With the original Sheringham village clustered comfortably about it, some little way from the sea, All Saints is basically C14 and improved and enlarged a century later. At that stage the handsome s. *porch* was added, with its excellent *flushwork, crocketted pinnacles* and fine outer doorway. Inside, the really exciting feature is the *rood loft*. The C15 *screen* is good but not unusual – it is the survival of the loft front parapet and floor that is remarkable, together with the original bottom door to the stairs, complete with ring handle. There are carved dragons in the *spandrels* of the loft, one with the head of a crane. Many bench-ends with good large grotesques on the arms – cat with mouse, mermaid, *griffin, chrysom child*, monkey, etc. There was originally a large cover for the C14 font, and the painted beam from which it was suspended remains above. Wall monument in the *chancel* to Abbot Upcher (d.1819) – a cold but impressive piece by *Bacon* & Manning (who often exhibited at the Royal Academy) commemorating the owner of Sheringham Hall, who never lived to see Humphrey Repton's landscape work completed – his widow weeps disconsolate upon a fallen column.

Upton, St Margaret (J4): The tower had been ruined for centuries before its rebuilding in 1929,

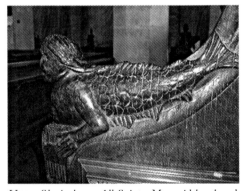

Upper Sheringham, All Saints: Mermaid bench end

and the rest of this C15 church has been extensively restored. It is memorable for its magnificent font which is unusually interesting. Dating from about 1380, it stands on three steps, and the shaft is surrounded by richly canopied figures. They represent the two Sacraments of mass and Baptism, and godparents flank the mother with her swaddled baby, while priest and bishop occupy the other side. Little angels in the corona above hold rebec, crowth (an early square form of two-string violin), and an open music book with the ancient four line score. All the figures are of high quality. The base of the *rood screen* has painted panels of the *Four Latin Doctors*, and *Saints Etheldreda, Helen, Agatha* and *Joan of Valois* (the latter a very rare bird – how she came to Upton is an interesting query). The way the two outer panels have been cut away suggests that the screen originally stood further west. There is a nice pair of *piscinas*, one in each *aisle* chapel, with prettily pierced tracery heads. On the way back to the gate, see the memorial on the e. wall of the s. aisle to John Cater (d.1781) which has two attractive cherubs, and this verse: 'Afflictions sore long time I bore, / Physicians were in vain. / Till God was pleased to give me ease, / And free me from my pain'.

Upwell, St Peter (B5): A very large, spread-out church. It is largely a *Perpendicular* building, though its offset tower, n.w. from the *nave*, is C13 – an octagonal, embattled top sitting on a square base, and picked out with interesting window shapes and traceries. A big and impressive Perpendicular *porch* was added on to the tower's n. side: it is fine with its battlemented gable, and a bold squareheaded window to its second storey bounded by figure niches with elegantly *cusped* and *crocketted* canopies. Inside, it has a good vaulted stone ceiling; the *Tudor* n. door has devilish *headstops* to its *hood mould*. The body of the church is powerfully Perpendicular in character, *clerestory*, *chancel* and *aisles* bearing the same bold imprint. The big e. window, though wholly faithful in detail to the rest, is in fact modern: the original was blasted out by a gale in 1912. The 1842 battlements all the way round the building somewhat overbalance the whole. Perched on the n. e. corner of the chancel is a curious, much-weathered little turret – was it a chimney? At the s.w. corner is a most unusual *sanctus bell turret*, of irregular shape, in old pink brick and stone, topped by a crocketted pinnacle. It is built directly over the interior *rood stair* – a canny double use of resources. At the w. end,

Upton, St Margaret: C14 font

the nave's big four-*light* window complements the tower, having early-C14 cusped and intersecting tracery (though renewed). It points to the origins of the present nave at that time. However, as we see inside, the striking six-bay *arcades* are Perpendicular, with above them a fine C15 roof. It has massive, generously carved *tie-beams* and braces, and tracery in the *spandrels*; along the ridge are a profusion of angels, and more thrusting spread-winged from the *wall plates* (notice that some of them hold the *Instruments of the Passion*). There is another extremely good roof in the n. aisle, with still more angels, and richly carved *wall posts* which sit on carved stone *corbel* heads. It can be viewed at close hand from the C19 *gallery* which runs all along this aisle, complementing another at the w. end – the only virtue of these redundant survivals, which apparently were erected to accommodate, and to keep separate from good Upwell people, the folk of neighbouring dependent parishes then without their own churches. A curiosity fixed on the n. face of the aisle gallery are two enormously long poles, with massive cast iron hooks on the ends, designed to drag burning thatch from houses in pre-Fire Brigade days. At the w. end of this aisle is an incised stone cross, let into the wall, with a remnant of another on the e. wall – they are said to be *consecration crosses*, but one puts a question-mark over this. The nave boasts two sets of Victorian *Royal Arms*: that under the w. gallery is very notable, being the largest in the county. It is splendidly carved in wood and on a grand scale. Octagonal Perpendicular font, with half-figures of angels. Hugely heavy pulpit, with equally massive, pineapple-shaped *tester* above it, of uncertain date. The lectern is C15 and of that lovely buttery texture and patina which brass assumes with great age – notice that the 'eagle' is decidedly cockerel-like, with a cock's-comb to prove it. To each side of the chancel arch (note the very distinctive shape at the angles of the arch) are the stubs of the old *rood beam* supports. An ancient *brass* is mounted on each of the chancel walls: that on the s. is extremely good, the figure of Henry Martyn, 1435, being shown under a resplendent canopy. Both he and the figure opposite, William Mowbray, 1428, were priests, and are depicted in their vestments. Big plain *piscina* in the sanctuary; and *sedilia* under a square hood inset directly into the wall under a window, and embellished with restrained moulding and tracery. On the chancel n. wall is a plaque recalling days when medicine had little answer to raging epidemics – a commemoration of 67 people of the parish who died in 1832 from the Asiatic cholera which swept the country at that time. Nearby is a memorable brass inscription to one Jane Bell, 'late wife of Sinolphus Bell', who died in 1621 at the age of 62, in the sure confidence of who was who in Upwell:

> Here lyeth buried of whome may be sayd
> For parentage equall with most in this land
> Noe wyves maydes or widdowes more hartely prayd
> Then she in her Closset whose liberal hand
> Was ever releeving the poore in their neede
> Her name was Jane Coltropp as being a mayde
> Her mother a Rookwood of awcient discent
> She maried a Bell and never delayde
> By deeds and good vsage to geve him content
> Children she had eleven whereof davghters fovr
> Of whome remayn seven alive at this Hower.

Very faintly, above the inscription, may be seen the engraved figures of mama and papa, five sons and four daughters, assiduous polishing over the years having almost erased them – though not the memory of them and their illustrious Upwell kin.

Wacton, All Saints (H6): The outline of this little church, and its range of beautiful windows,

at once arrests the eye. The round tower is almost certainly *Saxon*, and it is curious in that it narrows quite sharply towards the top, like a massively squat chimney. *Nave* and *chancel* are a continuous range, giving the initial impression that a spacious nave has lost its chancel. This is a complete creation of the second quarter of the C14 with five great windows to n. and s., all with elegantly flowing *ogee* heads and handsome tracery in two distinct patterns – a fine example of the *Decorated* period. The huge e. window is a sympathetic replacement. The s. door has splendid decorative ironwork contemporary with the building and richly ornamented with leaves (only the impression of a matching centre boss survives on the n. door, plus hinges). Charming interior, with a timber panelled modern roof, and white walls. Largely modern furnishings with some exceptions – the late-C17/early-C18 *communion rails*, with their curly, twisted *balusters*; a restrained pulpit, complete with door and little interior seat; and the tall C14 *screen* has rounded, ringed, slim shafts supporting its heavy tracery. The C14 piscina and triple *sedilia* lie under continuous ogee-headed arches. On n. side of nave, a complete and quite unusual *rood stair* is set into the side of a window with its exit emerging at the *rood loft* level. To the w., hung on a frame on the wall, is a tiny roundel of ancient glass which was discovered when the e. window was restored in 1977: it's thought to be C17-C18, from the Low Countries or Northern France, and represents Christ instructing the *Apostles* to go out and preach. On the opposite wall, a beautifully lettered little *brass*, in Latin, to John Knyvett, 1623. On w. wall, the *Royal Arms* of the Hanoverian Georges. Good *Perpendicular* font, with the *Symbols of the Evangelists*, and angels bearing shields, carved boldly around the bowl, and four butter-in-mouth little lions below.

Walcott, All Saints (J2): An elegant church, all of a piece in its late *Decorated* and *Perpendicular* lines, standing up against the blustering coastal winds. The big C15 tower has stepped battlements, finely decorated with *flushwork*; and below, a good flush-panelling *base course* all round; the big bell openings have Perpendicular tracery. An unusual feature, on the tower's s. side, is the V-shaped stairs turret. The *nave* windows are Perpendicular but the n. door is Decorated, as are the flowing traceries of the n. and s. windows of the *chancel* – the e. window is a Victorian replacement. Inside the church is spacious and light. The C15 *screen* has been restored, but the delicately carved upper part has that lovely soft look of very old wood. The screen under the tower arch has uprights and *balusters* that are *Jacobean*. Nearby is an enormous C17 chest. In the lofty chancel, there is an excellent modern *reredos*; and a spendid *piscina* and triple *sedilia*, each with its traceried arch and little clustered columns. In the chancel floor, an eccentric *ledger stone* – across the top, a text in Hebrew; then, in Latin, a long eulogy to John Collingnes, Doctor of Divinity (1690): 'protagonist of truth, the hammer of error, but not unworthy example of human courtesy'. Finally, lines are added in Greek for good measure.

Walpole St Andrew, St Andrew (B4): One of the big Marshland churches, St Andrew's was taken into the care of the *Churches Conservation Trust* in 1986. It replaced an earlier church and was rebuilt from e. to w. between about 1420 and 1470, although the roofs were not leaded until 1504. Dressed stone was used for facings and windows, but the prime material is brick, a fact self evident in the tower and visable in the walls where the plaster has fallen away. The tower stair rises to an octagonal turret topped by a weather vane and the clock on the w. face has recently been handsomely restored. The big turrets at the e. end of the *nave* house extensions of the twin *rood stairs* within, and provide easy access to the roofs; between them, a platform at the apex was designed for a *sanctus bell cote* like the one at Walpole St Peter. Have a look at the s.w. buttress of the tower – uniquely adapted to make a small room which extends in lean-to form within the space between buttress and w. door. Apparently an afterthought (it interrupts the tower's *base course*), it has been described as an *anchorite's cell* but they were normally placed to give a clear view of the high altar via an internal window. Here, we have a door, windows each side, and a niche on the e. wall within that matches the one to the left of the main w. door of the church. A more likely explanation is that this was a convenient shrine for travellers setting out across the treacherous fens into Lincolnshire – especially if you remember that King John lost his jewels in this very parish while making for Long Sutton in 1216. Inside, the church is spacious, with light flooding down from the ample *clerestory*. Immediately, the eye is caught by the tall *arcades* – not only for their grace, but also for the extraordinary erosion of the pillars. The only reasonable explanation is that for a long period

Walpole, St Andrew: Anchor hole or pilgrim's shrine?

the nave lay unroofed and open to the weather. The tower arch is less elaborate and probably later than the arcades; over it, early-C19 *Royal Arms* of George III and below, the ringing *gallery* has a *Jacobean* balustrade that may have been made from old *communion rails*, but could as easily have been designed for the job. Leaving the w. end with its simple C15 font, note that both aisles have double *aumbries* halfway along and that the s. aisle has a rich *piscina*; its embattled top matches the *transoms* of the aisle windows and the mould running up to the multi-*cusped* arch is set with floral motifs. The early-C17 pulpit, with typical shallow carving, stands on a very solid C16 stone base decorated with rosettes and incorporating steps. There is a fine wrought iron *hour-glass* bracket and the hour-glass itself is no modern reproduction. Above the pulpit, the painting of the two Marys with the dead Christ, by Sebastiano Ricci, was originally an altarpiece and is the only work by him in an English church. The *rood* was served by two stairs and the s. doorway shape is echoed by a blank arch alongside; from the shaft between springs a large stone bracket, nicely moulded and completing a very clever ensemble. This supported a pulpit, but remembering the C15 pulpit base opposite, it may have been used only for reading the gospel. There is a nice touch in the n. aisle – two shepherd's crooks 'laid-up' in 1964; they are relics of the local Shepherd's Club founded in 1841, 'to relieve the sick, bury the dead, and assist each other in all cases of unavoidable distress.'

Walpole St Peter, St Peter (B4): To some, the w. Norfolk landscape may be dull and flat, but it boasts some of our finest churches, and St Peter's deserves its title 'Queen of the Marshland'. First impressions are of great richness and size, especially from the s. – lavish detail and mighty windows, although the tower is markedly plain by contrast. That is because it was built about 1300 and was the only part of the church to survive a great flood in 1337. Then came the *Black Death* in 1348, and only after another decade did work begin on the new *nave*. Nave and *chancel* were one until the 1420s when the present chancel was added, and the design was completed by the s. *porch* 30 years later. To walk round the outside on a fine day is pure pleasure; a mighty copper beech spreads over the tombs close by the s. *aisle*, and to the e. is one of the church's most interesting features – the chancel extends to the very edge of the churchyard and a passageway passes under the sanctuary, as it does at St Peter Mancroft in Norwich. Known locally as 'The Bolt Hole', it enabled processions to circle the church and yet remain within consecrated ground. It is stone flagged and has a *vaulted* roof enhanced by *bosses* – seek out the sheep's head that shows where the money came from to build the new church. Parishioners left their horses here during service time until the C19 and fragments of the tethering rings remain in the walls. The church has a complete set of matching battlements, all intricately panelled and set with tiny shields; one on the s. side of the chancel is dated 1634 – perhaps the date for the whole range but more likely marking a repair or extension. The nave gable is very impressive – octagonal stair turrets rising to *crocketted* pinnacles flank a beautifully delicate *sanctus bell cote* to which the ancient bell has been restored. On the n. side, see how the stair turret rests on a worn carved figure at ground level – the mythical Atlas maybe, or perhaps the local and equally fabulous Hickathrift, the Fenland giant. Passing the n. porch (now a heating chamber), return to the s. porch. Its lush facade has a big three-*light Tudor* window above the arch with deep canopied niches either side, the pedestals supported by

Walpole St Peter: C17 Cradle & Poor box

lions and eagles holding shields carved with St Peter's keys. The two-stage buttresses are capped and niched, while above the doorway are the arms of the donors, complete with helm and mantling. The upper room served as the village school for a century until 1812 and another door was inserted on the w. side in 1728 so that the children did not have to go into the church. A notice close by tells you what to do if you are wearing pattens, and a pair hang overhead in case you had forgotten what they were. The *groined* roof has a superb set of *bosses*; the large centre one nearest the door shows the Last Judgement, with the souls of the righteous cared for on the right of the Father and the jaws of bestial Hell devouring the damned on the left; the second large boss is the *Assumption*, with the Virgin crowned and angels holding the surrounding canopy; elsewhere, a muzzled pig, a tail-biting dragon, and beyond the Last Judgement, a homely hound with floppy ears has just caught a rabbit. The vaulting comes down to rest on wide corner niches containing battered figures and the one in the n.w. is a *Pietà* representation – very rarely found. The entrance doors are original and have excellent embattled tracery like patterns for a *Perpendicular* window, with a thick band of niches at the edge. Within, the great church opens up, with light streaming through the *clerestory* and the huge aisle windows. The medieval stained glass was never destroyed here – it merely fell into decay, and the remnants were later gathered to form a panel in the n. aisle Lady chapel. The gargantuan deal table on six sturdy legs by the door may be plain but it is an unusual survivor of the 1640s when the congregation sat round it to take communion – doubtless for other meetings as well. By the tower arch is another rarity – a grey sentry box called a hudd, which was used until the late C19 to shelter the minister at the graveside. Within the tower arch, see the sturdy *Jacobean* ringing *gallery*, and then turn to one of the building's most memorable features, the 1630 w. *screen* – arcaded panels and turned *balusters* from wall to wall, with tentative classical details framing the three sets of doors. Beyond it, the font has panels with *ogee* arches and is inscribed 'Thynk and thank 1532' at the base, plus another battered inscription commemorating its donor, parson Whetsom Jannes. The cover is a tour de force of about 1600 which totally encloses the bowl; two segments of the octagon hinge outwards for access and all the panels have perspective arches set between rich double *pilasters*; above them are carvings of pagan centaurs wearing curly caps, and the whole is surmounted by a conical spire with openwork panels that reaches to the arch of the *arcade*. If the infants are overawed by all this, there is a sweet hooded rocking cradle close by – and a 1639 poor box for the alms of the sponsors. The nave has a good set of oak *box pews* at the back, and beyond, a matching set of open pews with square ends and a trail of carving along the backs – all of around 1630. The nave roof has been restored but is largely original, and a splendid chandelier, purchased in 1701 and of a size to match the church, hangs from one of the beams. Over the third *pier* from the e. look for the sockets of the *rood beam* that divided nave from chancel before the present chancel was built in about 1425. The s. aisle has pews facing inwards in tiers which are an interesting amalgam of C15 and C17 work. The s. aisle chapel now contains the organ but its *parclose screen* is still in place – *ogee* arches and good tracery. The early-C16 lectern has a close affinity with Snettisham's – the same defiant eagle minus its claws, and across the nave stands a high Jacobean pulpit complete with *tester* and a book-rest which is supported by quaint two-dimensional gilt cherubs blowing trumpets. The base of the C15 *rood screen* has indifferently painted saints in the panels but some are easily recognized – on the n., *Catherine, John, James* and *Thomas*; on the s., *Paul* and *Andrew*. The ancient *sanctus bell* on the roof still does duty – see the rope with its bright sally to the n. of the screen. The processional way provided the base for an impressive sanctuary raised high above the rest of the chancel and the view westward from the top of the steps is grand. The chancel walls have shallow *arcades* with little vaulted canopies as a backing for the stalls – do not miss the lovely variety of tiny faces carved on the *bosses*. The C15 stalls themselves have been extensively restored but there is a good head of St *Edmund* with the wolf on the s. side, and camels on either side of the entrance; two of the original *misericords* remain behind the screen on the n. side, with carvings of a *pelican* in her piety and an eagle. The *piscina* and *sedilia* are contained within part of the wall arcades, but their canopies were chopped back in 1730 to make way for commandment boards – which in their turn have gone.

Walsoken, All Saints (A4): In the springtime, orchards to the e. are a mass of blossom and very beautiful but Walsoken is now effectively a suburb of Wisbech. From the outside there is a complete contrast between the stone tower and the rest of the building which has been rendered and painted a pale cream. The C13 tower is a marvellous example of the *Early English* style, with a deeply recessed w. door flanked by triple columns with stiff-leaf *capitals*. The mouldings are excellent and note that the door arch itself still clings to the *Norman* shape rather than the pointed outline of the blank *arcades* on the buttresses. Above the door, twin *trefoil lancets*, their shape echoed by the *blank arcading* at that level, and then a third range of arcading – this time very tall and plain. The short bell stage and the stone spire were added in the C14. Walking round, note the unusual C13 *corbel table* under the eaves of the n. *aisle*, the massive *sanctus bell cote*, and the barred windows of the two-storey *sacristry* which forms part of a C15 rebuilding of the s. aisle chapel. Note also that the C13 *porch* retains its original gable cross and that the line of an earlier, steeper *nave* roof shows on the e. wall of the tower. Inside, one can see immediately why Walsoken has been called the finest Norman parish church in Norfolk. Dating from the mid-C12, the round arches of the mighty nave arcade are richly moulded with deep horizontal zigzags, and the alternating circular and octagonal *piers* have intricately scalloped capitals. It is most interesting to see how the style develops in the *chancel*, where the westernmost *responds* sprout *crockets* that herald the Early English style. The chancel arch, too, shows the shift towards Gothic; dating from around 1200, its arch still retains the zigzag motif but is pointed not round, although the multi-ringed flanking shafts are a Norman rather than an Early English feature. Blocked upper windows in the chancel survive from the original building and you will see the shafts of a C13 e. window (probably a group of lancets) either side of the C15 replacement. There is a very small blocked Norman doorway on the n. side of the chancel and a narrow, simply carved frieze follows the line of its arch before continuing round the sanctuary. The building of the sacristry entailed blocking off a C13 arch – see the outline in the s. wall. The font stands on a very spacious plinth of two steps and is a fine and intricately carved *Seven Sacrament* example. Although the heads of the figures have been defaced, the scenes are more easily recognisable than usual and they are, clockwise from the e.: mass, ordination, marriage, extreme unction, crucifixion, baptism, confirmation and penance – all under shallow vaulting within crocketted *ogee* arches. In addition, the shaft niches have a good and interesting range of saints; clockwise from the e.: Saints *John the Baptist, Dorothea, Peter, Catherine, Paul, Margaret, Stephen, Mary Magdalen.* At the bottom is the donors' inscription interspersed by shields carved with the *Instruments of the Passion,* 'Remember the souls of S.Honyter and Margaret his wife, and John Beforth, chaplain 1544'. Thus it was one of the last additions to the church before the *Reformation.* Above the tower arch is a large and rather strange C17 wooden figure of King Solomon in the centre of a painted scene of his judgement. At the opposite end of the nave, a matching King David with his harp over the chancel arch. The nave *hammer-beams* are small and tucked up against the roof; the angels on them are coloured as are the little figures that stand under canopies against the *wall posts.* Below, there are four original bench ends at the e. end of the nave, with heavy *poppy-heads* flanked by seated figures with standing effigies below – all in the style of the famous series at Wiggenhall St Mary. At the e. end of the s. aisle, a *parclose screen* with exceptionally pretty tracery in two complete ranges one above the other, the upper being unusually intricate and close-set. It has traces of colour and there is a *piscina* close by. The early-C15 screen in the n. aisle is much simpler and has been extensively repaired. Close by it is interesting evidence of a heart burial. Medieval wills sometimes stipulated that the person's heart be buried separately, and here we have, set in the wall, a worn carving of hands holding a heart under a pinnacled trefoil canopy. Beyond the organ, the n. chapel is now

arranged as a meeting room, but note the C13 piscina and a large mutilated tomb recess in the n. wall. Both here and in the s. chapel there is bold carving on the principal roof timbers. The stalls in the chancel have some fine original heads carved on the arms, including a bishop with a windswept mitre in the n.w. corner. A rector who served the parish for 36 years and died in 1717 had a son who rose to become Primate of all England. 'In grateful memory of his excellent parents', Archbishop Herring raised a tablet in 1750 and you will find it on the s. side of the sanctuary. Before going, have a look at the compact late-C16 communion table at the w. end of the n. aisle and note that there is a piscina just w. of the s. door, showing that a *guild* or *chantry* altar stood there before the Reformation did away with them all.

Warham, All Saints (B1): The tower has gone (stubs can still be seen) as have the *aisles*, excepting their last bays, which remain as *transepts* with their C14 *arcades.* Walls are partly *Decorated* period, but with several *Perpendicular* and later windows added. *Chancel,* early-C14. All heavily restored by the Rev. C.F. Digby, rector 1874-1923, who was thorough in his prime – C19 pitch-pine pews, floor tiles and all. There is a stiff and spiky alabaster *reredos,* 1897, 'in memory of those who have entered into rest'. Overall, something of a contrast with the taste and refinement of the 1800-1 restoration of the village's second church, St Mary's. Note that here at All Saints there are two fonts: a square Norman one, which came from St Mary's, and in the n. transept, another old Norman font, rescued from a nearby rockery. In chancel, a *low side window,* a simple *angle piscina* and *dropped sill sedilia.* A brass to William Rokewode, 1474, a nice little 18in. figure in armour (near s.w. door). In s.e. corner of sanctuary, a big stone effigy – unusual for Norfolk and pleasing, though defaced – of a civilian, about 1300, carrying what could be a horn or a roll.

Warham, St Mary (B1): *Decorated* tower with later battlements, attractive in flint and stone, and some *Norman* work at base (plus a blocked n. door-way). The rest is mainly Decorated with some *Perpendicular* windows inserted. There is a delightful *priest's door,* good early Perpendicular, on s. side of *chancel,* with a buttress rising immediately from its top. Inside the church a pleasing surprise – a 'lovely interior, calm and moving, [and] one of the most memorable in the whole of East Anglia'. It has its C18 high

Warham, St Mary: Three-decker pulpit

box pews, three-decker pulpit, plus a 'bird bath' font – that delighted Sir John Betjeman – and the *Royal Arms* on canvas of George III. There's some fine glass, splendidly glowing Flemish work, mostly of the early *Renaissance* and English medieval glass, all collected by the rector, the Rev. W.H. Langton, who in 1800-1 'beautified' the interior – and who lies in the chancel. There's a melancholy mausoleum to the Turner family on the n. side of the chancel, probably contemporary with the pews and pulpit. In the sanctuary, a *brass* to James Wigfall, priest, 1638. A nice homely touch – the C18 hat pegs on the n. wall of *nave*.

Waterden, All Saints (E2): There is no village now, and a wide grass track leads down from the lane to this tiny church in the midst of open fields. It is disused, and not so long ago was sinking to decay among the undergrowth. But thoughtful and energetic friends have brought it back to life with the help and encouragement of the *Norfolk Churches Trust*. Undistinguished architecturally, but so old that its magic seems to rub off as you touch the stones. Everywhere

is a patchwork of alterations down the centuries; two blocked *Saxon* windows under the eves on the n. side, the doorways are either Saxon or early *Norman* and are bare of decoration; the little *porch* has *Early English quatrefoil* windows and a *nave* n. window of the same period had a *Tudor* replacement inserted. The e. window was blocked up to take four Tudor *lancets* in a brick frame, and the s. side tells the same story. There was a s. *aisle* once and the *arcade* lies like a fossil in the wall. The tower fell at some stage and a heap of rubble lies below a blocked w, end topped by a small wooden turret. Inside, nothing very much except peace and quiet. A simple font on a plastered brick column is tucked up between n. wall and the back pew – one of a good set of C19 deal *box pews* grained and varnished in yellow ochre. Over the harmonium, a text, 'Lo, I am with you always', and the church is ready for the village to come back. Well – who knows?

Watlington, St Peter & St Paul (C4): Walk round the outside first to pick up one or two points of interest. The late-C13 tower was given an additional storey when the *nave* roof was raised and it was then that the curiously truncated red brick stair turret was added on the s. side. The s. *aisle* was given a new parapet too, but the old *gargoyles* still stick out at their original level. The C14 *chancel* has very nice *butterfly tracery* in the side windows and the large e. window is a good example of quite lavish flowing *Decorated* tracery. There was once a n. chapel and you will find the *piscina* and two *aumbries* embedded in the outside of the chancel wall, with a roof line above. The C13 s. *porch* has steps which lead down to an *Early English* doorway and a door which is partly original – see the narrow trail of carving round the edge. Inside, the tower arch is very tall and narrow and the old roof line shows above it, together with the outline of a *sanctus bell window*. There is a single *hatchment* in the n. aisle and, close by, a fine early-C16 font with unusual pendant arches below the bowl, with vaulting behind them over tall figures round the shaft. These, like the pairs of saints in the bowl panels, have all lost their heads. The *Jacobean* font cover has spindly columns supporting a spire and on top, a large and rather gawky *pelican*. Above the C14 *arcades*, a *clerestory* with square-headed windows and a good *arch-braced roof*. The nave benches have lovely pierced backs and carved figures on the arms – look for the pensive woman with a rosary second from the back on the s. side. There are some excellent reproductions interspersed and these may be by the same late-C19 vicar who restored the chancel *screen* so well; only the upper panels on the s. side are original C14 but the rest blends beautifully. The s. aisle chapel has a double piscina and there is a long *squint* through the wall to give a view of the high altar. Above it, a tablet to Thomas Gawsell and his wife (1600), but the two painted kneeling figures have lost their heads. The pulpit is a standard late-C16 or early-C17 design with blank arches in the panels, and just beyond the screen on the s. side is a good monument to John Freak (1628); he kneels in his black M.A. gown and ruff within an alabaster niche. The piscina and *sedilia* are very pretty, contained within a line of *cusped ogee* arches carried on free-standing columns, and opposite you will see the blocked doorway to the former n. chapel. Simple Jacobean chest in the n.e. corner of the sanctuary and a rather unusual C15 model by the choir stalls – very small, with *trefoils* carved in the front panels. Going back down the church, note that the chancel arch was cut with mortices to hold the old *tympanum*, and at the w. end of the nave pause to have a look at the fine early *ledger slab* incised with a floriated cross. It

originally carried a *brass* and the inscription in *Lombardic script* round the edge identifies it as the grave of Sir Robert de Montalt who died around 1330.

Watton, St Mary (F5): No doubt the town needed the extra 220 additional seats in its church in 1840, but there is no denying that the building was much more handsome in its old state with two little *aisles* and a n. *porch*. Now, the wide, blunt gables of the Victorian rebuilding overwhelm the *Norman* round tower with its pretty octagonal top. Inside, the arches of the *arcades* match, but while the pillars on the s. side are C14, those on the n. are later. Both sets are gloss painted in grey, which seems an odd finish for honest stone. The C13 *chancel* has a plastered ceiling – nice, in deep blue with gilt stars, and there is the simplest form of *piscina* cut into a window sill. In the n. wall, a large *aumbry* (or perhaps an *Easter Sepulchre* – it has a *corbel* set in the back). The *priest's door* has been blocked by pews but you will find that the *low side window* still has its grill and has been fitted with a robust replacement shutter. Just in front, a section of exuberant secular *Jacobean* woodwork, complete with caryatids, has been made up into a stall. Watton has a quite splendid Victorian brass lectern; the eagle puts one foot forward and turns its head, and the steps have flashy brass rails, with an art nouveau angel bearing a torch aloft at the corner. Close by, a piscina under a *trefoil* arch. The *Royal Arms* of George II are painted on wood and hang at the w. end. Below them, a unique poor box; it is the wooden figure of a man holding a bag in his left hand into which one may still slip money. Tradition has it that it is a portrait of the vicar William Forster, and across his breast is carved 'Remember the poore 1639'. The church has an excellent ring of 6 bells, tenor 7-1-4 cwt.

Waxham, St John (K3): The church is only a field away from the dunes that protect this little village from the sea. The C15 tower has an outside stair shaft up to the belfry on the s. side, at which level there are blocked square *sound-holes*. The w. window is blocked and the bell openings are boarded, but it is now in sound condition. The *nave* has one *Norman lancet* in the n. wall, and in the recently repaired s. wall there are three later C13 windows with Y tracery. A previous roof was steeper than the present one – its line shows on the e. wall of the tower. The ruins of the *chancel* are now separated from the rest of the building and the jagged walls reach up almost to their full height. The *priest's door* has traces of three arches and one of them is unusually tall rather like the one at Castle Acre. The tall *Perpendicular* s. *porch* has a line of blank shields in quatrefoils over the outer arch, and the inner C14 door has worn *headstops*. Within, there is a *holy water stoup* recess to the right, and the C14 font has quatrefoils in the bowl panels, a panelled shaft, and stands on two circular steps. Another clue to the building's Norman beginnings is the blocked lancet embrasure in the s. wall and across the nave a *banner-stave locker* is rather oddly placed. The old chancel arch has been blocked in and *decalogue boards* are mounted on the new wall. The small *piscina* to the right will have served a nave altar originally, and the sanctuary is enclosed in nicely serpentine rails. The best single item in the church is the early Elizabethan monument on the n. side. It is the tomb of Thomas Wodehouse who died in 1571 – no effigy but tasteful classical detailing with *Corinthian* columns flanking the recess above the tomb chest.

Weasenham, All Saints (E3): A small church with rather an odd history. The tower collapsed in 1653 and a second storey of brick was built on top of the *Perpendicular* s. *porch* to serve as a belfry. Then the s. *aisle* was demolished in 1796 and the porch was tenuously connected to the church by a short brick wall. In 1905, a new s. aisle and *chancel* were built, and the porch came into its own again, discarding the brick excrescence and gaining a new parapet. It is very attractive, with floral motifs round the arch, canopied niches either side, and a line of crowned M's below them; there is a recessed *flushwork base course*, with pointed *quatrefoils* above it. Just inside the *Early English* doorway, have a look at the endearing 1890s watercolour (in Grandma Moses style) that shows the church as it was then. The early-C14 *arcade* has not been disturbed but you can see that there was once a *clerestory* above it. The *Jacobean* pulpit has tall arcaded panels, with new base and stairs, and there is a handsome and substantial reading desk opposite made to match it. The top of the *screen* is modern but the C15 base has painted panels; they have been cruelly defaced, but the labels show that the four on the left depicted the *Four Latin Doctors* of the Church: St *Ambrose,* St *Augustine,* St *Jerome* and St *Gregory.*

Weasenham, St Peter (E3): An 1870s restoration made quite a difference to the look of this church standing close to the main road.

Pinnacles and battlements were added to the C13 tower and to the *nave*, the *chancel* was rebuilt, and a vestry complete with chimney was added on the s. side. The n. side of the nave is very impressive and has large *Perpendicular* windows with two sets of embattled *transoms*; there is a panelled *base course* with a line of pointed *quatrefoils* above it, and there are more set in the buttresses. The whole of the n. *porch* frontage is *flushwork*, and its gabled buttresses have recessed panels matching the base course. Walking round, note the *Early English lancet* and quatrefoil *sound-holes* in the tower, and the pretty *Decorated* flower tracery in the *aisle* w. window. Inside the porch, a *holy water stoup* to the left, and the Perpendicular doorway has an embattled hood that matches the nave windows. With windows of such a size, the interior is very light, and the effect is emphasised by sleek modern pews in parana pine and a C15 *arcade* with extraordinarily slim pillars. The font in the s. aisle has a deep and heavy bowl decorated with quatrefoils on a short panelled shaft, and although it has 1607 carved on the s. side, it is more likely to be C15. The s. aisle chapel *reredos* is modern but in traditional style, as are the pulpit and lectern, and the carving on the latter is particularly good. The old *rood stair* is on the s. side with a solid doorway decorated with floral motifs and shields over the lintel. A harsh yellow predominates in the 1857 glass of the e. window by *William Warrington*, but in the nave there are two lovely C15 panels reset low in the n. windows where they can be examined easily; St *Margaret* with her dragon is in the centre, an angel to the right, plus a small shield to the left

Weeting, St Mary (D7): Modern Weeting, in a spick-and-span profusion of bungalows, has crept back around its ancient church, which is a nice turn of events in a county of depleted villages. The church is an attractive building in which all the detail looks crisp and fresh. Not surprisingly so in the case of the slim round tower – it was rebuilt in 1868, replacing a *Norman* original. The steeply-pitched *nave* has big *Perpendicular* windows – very handsome with their 'embattled' *transoms*. The chancel, a *Decorated* period construction, has a mixture of contemporary and Perpendicular (restored) windows, but notably a very fine e. window of five *lights* with eloquently flowing *reticulated* tracery, balanced at the top by a multi-*cusped* circle. A most attractive Decorated window of two lights, generously cusped, has been filled in on the n. side, leaving its outlines flush with the

Weasenham, St Peter: C15 glass St Margaret

wall. Most agreeable, spacious interior, beautifully maintained and cared for under a prodigiously timbered roof (again C19), which impressively sports *tie-beams* with vigorously springing *king posts*. Pretty little early-C14 *arcade* of four bays, on lovely *quatrefoil* pillars which are separated by pencil shafts barely an inch across. Decorated also the big chancel arch, though slightly later than the arcade. On either side of the e. window are elegantly tall figure niches with cusped heads, which were discovered during the Victorian restoration which accompanied the tower rebuilding. The filled in n. window, already mentioned, is outlined in relief within its deep splay, and makes an eye-catching feature. Interesting are the late-C13 pair of quatrefoil *piscina* bowls which are cut directly out of the window sill on the sanctuary s. side. This is the simplest known arrangement; there are other examples at Frenze, and Watton. In the n. *aisle* (remodelled by the Victorians) are *poppy-head* benchends on solid rustic benches.

Welborne, All Saints (G4): Amid parklike fields, and in an immaculate churchyard, stands this equally well maintained church. A round tower of positively military plainness, with only a tiny arrow-slit on the s. and a *lancet* low down

on the w.; on top, a conical cap with tiny dormers, rather like that at Little Snoring. Restoration lies evidently but elegantly on this church – all is beautifully done, from the replaced square-topped *nave* windows to the wholly Victorian, rebuilt *chancel* of 1874-76, with its geometrically patterned windows in the *Decorated* style. The *porch* is basically original *Perpendicular*, if much restored – nice little rounded pillars to the outer arch, with battlemented *capitals*; and over, a square hood with blank shields in the *spandrels*. Notice that one of the porch windows has a sombre jig-saw of bits of medieval glass, said to come from the same source as that at North Tuddenham. Inside, the church is ornate in detail but in faultless good taste – a serene interior dominated by a richly gilded and coloured *screen*. This colouring, upon an old plain screen, was done between the world wars; how much underneath the paint is old, how much modern, it is not possible to determine. There is a handsome Perpendicular *piscina*, with a *cusped* and *trefoiled* arch, to right of the screen, and a much plainer one on the opposite side. The Victorian chancel is very good indeed, with its piscina and marble-pillared *sedilia*, gleamingly ornate *reredos*, copious stained glass and generously carved choir stalls, the latter installed in 1902. Back at the w. end, the plain font, with its coarse battlemented rim, is possibly Perpendicular, C15 to C16 and looks rather out of place in this refined and gilded setting. A curiosity and a puzzle is the large, deeply-splayed, filled-in *lancet* window shape in the w. wall. If the tower is *Norman*, i.e., C12, how come we have an *Early English* lancet, i.e. C13, in this position?

Wellingham, St Andrew (E3): The un-buttressed tower has bell openings which have been reduced to half height and there are C19 battlements. C13 *lancets* remain in the *chancel*, with one in the *nave*, but in an 1896 restoration the whole of the s. side was rebuilt on new foundations. The interior is a hall of nave and chancel with no intervening arch and the *arched-braces* of the old roof were retained in the chancel. The interesting thing here is the *screen*. Only the base remains but the fragmentary inscription on the top rail dates it 1532 and names the donors as Robert Dorant and his wives. There are four painted panels; from left to right: a pair of figures, St *Sebastian* (or perhaps St *Edmund*) and a saint in a green cloak and ermine cape over armour, holding sword and spear; St *George* with the dragon transfixed by a broken spear under his horse's feet, while the court looks on from the battlements of a miniature castle and the princess kneels in prayer with her lamb beside her; next, St *Michael* with wings and feathered cape, sword in one hand and scales in the other – little black and red devils are balanced by a pair of kneeling souls in white and the Virgin lays her rosary on the balance in favour of the blessed; lastly, a half panel of the Resurrection with the wounded Christ surrounded by all the *Instruments of the Passion*, plus Pilate's disembodied hands being washed.

Wells-next-the-Sea, St Nicholas (F1): On Sunday morning, 3rd August, 1879, the church was struck by lightning and in two hours completely gutted by fire, leaving only the walls and tower. It was wholly restored – nicely done, but a bit dull – on its original C15, *Perpendicular* lines. Two side windows in the *chancel* retain old tracery, and a chancel door-way re-uses old mouldings. Over this doorway is a *brass* – text only, no figure – to Thomas Bradley, rector, 1499. The *rood loft* stair remains on the n. side within the wall. There's a large coffer-type, iron-bound chest dated 1635; and a fine medieval brass lectern, an eagle with three lions at its feet, all smoothed by the centuries and with that lovely buttery look of old brass. The church has a ring of 8 bells, tenor 16-3-16

Wendling, St Peter & St Paul (F4): Divided from its village by the Dereham by-pass, this once quietly set church now resounds to the roar of traffic. It is a clean-lined, beautifully balanced building, largely a blend of *Decorated* and *Perpendicular* styles, though the fabric is said to be of C13 origin. Neat battlemented early Decorated tower, with crisply *cusped* contemporary windows to the belfry and a good late Perpendicular w. window. Notice too the deeply incised *mass dial* low on the s.w. buttress, s. side. Perpendicular *nave* and short s. *transept*, the latter with an impressively large, four-*light* C15 window; Decorated chancel. Very simple interior, given a sense of spaciousness by the large windows, not least that in the transept, and by the big Decorated chancel arch. The *Tudor* doorway to the *rood stair* is outlined behind the pulpit; there are battered and faded *Royal Arms* of George III, dated 1824; a nice little pipe organ; and a *seven sacrament font* notable for the crudity and engaging ham-fistedness of its carving. Several of the panels are badly defaced, but they can be identified as (starting from the e. face and moving round clockwise): matrimony, extreme

unction, the baptism of Christ, baptism, confirmation, penance, mass and ordination. In the sanctuary, the dropped – sill *sedilia* and *piscina* set into the sill look like modern reconstructions.

Wereham, St Margaret (C5): The main road thankfully skirts the village now, and the church is nicely clustered round with cottages. Most of the building dates from around 1270, and the evidence is in the details of the tower w. doorway, the tall *lancets* that light its ground floor, and in the *chancel* where there are lancets again, with three in the e. wall set in deep splays. The top of the tower is a C16 variation, with brick battlements, pinnacles, and *Tudor* bell openings; one of them on the s. side is half covered by a large and handsome sundial dated 1725. Entering by the w. door, note that the C13 tower arch is framed by the outline of a *Norman* predecessor, and so there must have been an earlier church altogether. In 1866, a thatched roof made way for a successor with rather ugly timbering, although the *arch-braced* s. aisle roof was left alone. The C14 *arcades* have curiously smooth caps and bases, with arches typical of no period – one assumes that they were partially rebuilt at the time of the restoration. The large *Royal Arms* on a shaped board (w. wall) are very dim but appear to be Hanoverian, although they carry the vicar and wardens' names of 1866. The *nave* and aisles, with pitchpine pews and indigestible stone pulpit, are rather glum, but the wide and open chancel has been painted white and given a pale blue ceiling sprinkled with small golden stars and is refreshing. On the s. wall is a simple tablet to John and Martha Heaton (1779), but on the deep shelf above it stands a remarkably good bust of the husband; it is a fine period piece showing him in close wig, stock, and stylish coat – unsigned but in the *Thomas Rawlins* or *John Ivory* class.

West Acre, All Saints (D4): Sir Edward Barkham, whose magnificent tomb is at nearby Southacre, virtually rebuilt this church in 1635-38, though largely retaining its *Perpendicular* character. He added an enormous vestry to the n. of the *chancel*, placed his coat of arms on tower, vestry and *nave* and his initials over the n. door. In the centre of the rounded outer arch of Sir Edward's *porch* is a carved 'deaths-head' serving as a keystone; did this, like the carved panel to the right of the inner door, come from the nearby priory ruins? (The gatehouse of the old priory is immediately adjacent to the e. end of the church). The panel in question is both interesting and rare. It is C13, shows a seated figure, and was perhaps itself originally a keystone in an arch. A pleasing, well cared for interior of surprising spaciousness. Modern roofs and most furnishings; a *hatchment* over the n. door; and rather fine *Royal Arms* of George III on the s. wall. Good C14 chancel arch; interesting C17 *communion rails*, pierced in simple fretwork. The *reredos* and altar frontals have carved wooden panels showing various religious scenes or individual figures – possibly C15 Dutch. A profusion of C18 and C19 monuments adorn the chancel walls: notably a roof-high memorial in white marble to Anthony Hammond, 1822, and his wife, with a life-size winged angel taking flight from its upper half. To left of the altar, again in white marble, a female figure in classical dress leans weeping against a sarcophogus – this is for Frances Ann Hammond, who died in 1820 aged 16.

West Barsham, The Assumption of the Blessed Virgin (F2): A small church in a charming setting by the Hall entrance, with a surround of neat close-cropped lawns. There was once a *Saxon* central tower but the only trace of this now is a line of masonry in the s. *chancel* wall and a window above the chancel arch inside. Entry by way of a curious s. doorway which began as a plain *Norman* piece and was modernised in the early-C13 when a decorative surround and shafts were added. An early window above the s. *porch*, and high up on the n. side, two Saxon porthole windows over another plain late Norman doorway. The chancel dates from about 1300. The church was run down and unused for a long time, but now the interior is a delight and shows how well the benefactors have done their work – a plaque at the w. end behind the C18 font commemorates them. Everything is fresh and uncluttered, with a new arch shaped like the prow of an upturned boat between *nave* and chancel. Excellent benches designed by Margaret Tarrant in a pastiche of C15 style – varying pairs of animals and birds on the arms, imaginative *poppy-heads*, and traceried backs. Equally good is the modern lectern – look for the mouse at the foot of the carved barley fronds – reminiscent of *Robert Thompson's* work. In the chancel, a plain *Early English piscina*, and on a window ledge a little C15 marble bas relief of the Adoration of the Shepherds; all the heads are defaced but it is a nice swirling composition. There is an early-C15 chest decorated with simple *blank arcading*, and in a niche in a n. window

West Barsham, The Assumption of the Blessed Virgin Mary: detail of Margaret Tarrant lectern

embrasure a good 12in. wooden figure of St *Francis* attended by animals and birds.

West Bilney, St Cecilia (D4): This is a very rare dedication – only three medieval churches in all England have it. A gale in 1976 wrecked the tower and the building had to be closed. Talk of demolition was parried by steadfast local opposition and a will to move forward. Comprehensively restored, blessed with a good congregation, and leased to the *Norfolk Churches Trust*. it is a pleasure to visit. The *Perpendicular* tower has decorative flint panels in the battlements, and the only evidence of the *nave's* Norman identity is the blocked circular window high in the n. wall. Just beyond, note a worn but lively 1706 *cartouche* of Freake family arms – powerful and wealthy Lords of the Manor until 1750. It may have been moved when material from the derelict *chancel* was used to make a new e. end in the early C18 and all the church's windows were renewed. Enter by the s. door into a bright interior. *Quatrefoils* alternate with rosettes in the panels of the C14 font, and beyond is the blocked *Early English* n. door. Above hangs a nicely restored set of *Hanoverian Royal Arms*, and a C17/early- C18 *bier* stands in the tower. It is an unusual design with additional drop-handles allowing the weight to be shared among more bearers – another like it can be seen at Stradsett. The arched recesses in the n. and s. walls probably backed a pair of nave altars. The e. end was re-ordered in 1881 and pins of a large medieval *brass* survive on the long slab in front of the sanctuary steps. *Decalogue boards* hang on the e. wall and below lies the *ledger-stone* of Francis Dalton (d.1807), 'Lord of the Manor of Bilney'; on the s. wall a namesake who died eleven years earlier had an oval cartouche cut for him by Eldredge of Lynn.

West Bradenham, St Andrew (F5): A pretty situation, with the churchyard ringed with Scots pine and chestnut above the shallow valley of the Wissey. The w. end of the *nave* has a very tall three-*light* window, and a gable line above it shows that the roof was originally lower. The early-C14 s.w. tower has a bulky stair turret that doubles as a buttress, and above the 'Y' tracery bell openings there is a dainty band of chequered *flushwork* under the parapet. The base of the tower forms the *porch* and leads to a late-C13 doorway flanked by pairs of columns, with a deep niche overhead under an attractive moulded arch. The whole interior is painted flat white, including the *quatrefoil piers* of the late-C13 *arcades*. The nave has a simple *arch-braced roof* which still bears traces of colour on the *wall plates*, ribs and *bosses,* and the very narrow *aisles* have good tracery in the *spandrels* of their roofs. The C14 font sits on rather unusual carved stops at the corners of the base moulding, and by the door there is an interesting *Jacobean* chest. Given by the rector in 1818, it came from Ely Cathedral; the carved front panels are separated by thick fluted columns and it has a coved lid instead of the usual flat top. There is a *piscina* in a square recess in the s. aisle and the *rood stairs* go up from that side. The late-C13 *chancel* retains its original side windows but the e. window is renewed. The piscina and stepped *sedilia* are grouped under plain moulded arches with good *headstops,* and behind the free-standing columns the wall has been scooped out to give more room. In the n. wall, a *Decorated aumbry; crocketted* pinnacles rise beside an *ogee* arch that encloses a niche above the new door. It is so elaborate that one wonders whether it was originally an *Easter Sepulchre,* with the niche containing a light. To the left of a blocked *low side window* on the s. side, see the memorial to James Bentham, the rector who gave the chest and who was son of the historian of Ely Cathedral – they sprang from an unbroken line of clerics stretching back nearly 300 years. In the chancel floor below is a thing not often seen – a *ledger stone* with *rococo* decoration for the Rev. Henry Topping and his wife, 1779.

West Dereham, St Andrew (C5): This village was well blessed in the Middle Ages – not only two parish churches, but an Abbey of White Canons for good measure. Fragments of St Peter's lie hidden in the undergrowth w. of the present church. The round *carstone* tower of St Andrew's is massive, with walls nearly 4ft. thick and it is over 17ft. in diameter – largest of its type in Norfolk. It is stepped slightly halfway up, with a deep *lancet* above the 1860s w. window. The belfry stage is a C16 octagon with five bell openings in mellow red brick, a decorative frieze of arches above them, and a plain parapet. The C15 *porch* has a barrel vaulted roof, and a Dutch gable was added in the C17 without disturbing the image niche which has a small head at the top of the *trefoil* arch. There is a *holy water stoup* set very deep in the wall, and the early-C14 doorway has a heavily moulded arch and single flanking columns. The matching *Early English* n. doorway has been blocked, and the heavy *Norman* tower arch is filled with a modern glazed *screen.* Beyond it, within the cool and roomy tower is a fine late-C17 oak *bier,* dated and carved with the wardens' names; it is lower than most and has finely turned legs, plus the usual drop handles. The main fabric of the church is probably as old (or older) than the tower, but all the windows are *Perpendicular* insertions. The *chancel* was restored in 1895, and a few years later the *nave* roof gave way and had to be replaced, although one of the old *tie-beams* remains at the w. end, resting on the original *corbels.* Simple C14 font, and a *Jacobean* pulpit with stubby blank arches, fluted *pilasters,* chip carving lozenges in the lower panels, and a book rest on carved scrolls. The reading desk opposite incorporates a matching panel that may have been the pulpit's back board. By it, the *rood stairs* lie in the angle of the wall. On the chancel n. wall, a monument in *touchstone* and alabaster to Robert Dereham and his father (1612); miniature shields surround the epitaphs, with coat-of-arms above and skull below. Next to it, an especially decorative panel of Florentine work for Sir Thomas Dereham (1722); coat-of-arms, two crests, exuberant mantling that fills the rest of the frame, and small bronze stags' heads at each corner. But the pièce de résistance stands opposite – a life-size marble figure, framed by an arch and heavy *pediment.* Finely sculpted by Robert Singleton, Colonel the Hon. Edmund

West Dereham, St Andrew: Col. Soame's monument

Soame (1706) wears armour and a full-bottomed wig, and strikes a suitably martial pose – one of the best standing monuments in Norfolk. The long inscription tells us in passing that he was 'immaturely cutt of when he was in pursuit of and ready to be raised to the Highest Military Honours'. His sister not only commissioned his memorial but provided the lovely set of three-sided *communion rails*, with twisted *balusters* and heavy mouldings. There is a jumble of C15 glass in the top of one of the nave s. windows, but look for the two angels (minus their heads) and three pairs of eagles perching on the remains of canopies. The e. window contains more C15 fragments which are said to have come from the Abbey – at the bottom there is a disembodied hand swinging a *censer*, and at the top, the head of the Blessed Virgin crowned; the C17 arms are those of the Jenyns/Soame family. By the door, as you leave, note the turned pillar poor-box, with a quote from the Book of Tobit over it.

West Harling, All Saints (F7): It is a long way down the stony track, so perhaps it is wise to enquire for the key first. But what a lovely setting – a calm and peaceful meadow, with sheep grazing, and only their cries mingle with the sough of the wind in the thick pine forest. The *Churches Conservation Trust* took over here in 1976 and have cared for the building well – repointed

the tower, gilded the weathercock, and given the inside a fresh coat of lime and tallow. The *chancel* is late-C13 and there was a chapel to the s. which had become ruined by the time it was pulled down in 1733. There is a line of *quoins* in the wall to show where it was, and the double *lancet* with *plate tracery* above may have been resited then. The C14 tower had a stone spire until 1756 when it was taken down, and the tower partially rebuilt (The small *trefoil* niche is rather unusually placed low down on the s. side, was it moved?) The chequer *base course* stops short at the n.w. corner. The plain n. door has animal *headstops* and at the eaves of the chancel gable, an odd pair of human/animal heads to the s. and a single head to the n. The C15 font has a panelled stem and routine shields and roses in the bowl panels. There are *rood stairs* in the n. wall, and a tall plain niche behind the Victorian pulpit. Opposite is the lancet/plate tracery window, and notice how the mould meets the column of a corner *piscina* – this makes it difficult to agree that the window was re-sited, but if not, how did the s. chapel fit on? The chancel has the drains of a double piscina set in a squared off recess that gives no clue as to its original form, and the same goes for the *sedilia* – except that a fragment of diaper painting with fleur de lys survives on the back wall and may well have been part of the chancel's original decoration. Over the *priest's door* is an excellent portrait bust of Richard Gipps (c.1780) set in a dished recess, and at your feet, a *ledger-stone* that tells of three generations of Cresseners who were rectors here for 130 years: 'none of them ever contending in Law suits under Unjust Extortions of their Just demands'. There are fine *brasses* too; w. end of the *aisle*, the 2ft. effigy of a priest who died in 1479, blessed with a singular, and we hope appropriate, name – Ralph Fuloflove. Further along, William and Margaret Berdwell (1508), he in armour, she with long tailed *kennel head-dress* and purse hung from her girdle; next, another William Berdwell (1490) with his wife Elizabeth – he wears heavy spurs, has his sword hung behind him, and keeps his hair very long. Just w. of the chancel arch is the Victorian manorial pew, and it must have been most gratifying for Evelyn Lady Nugent to come to church on Christmas morn 1893, to find that her son George and his wife had presented her with a personal reading desk, suitably inscribed. There are two marble tablets on the n. wall – one by Gaffin of London for Nicholas William Lord Colborne, the other by Ruddock of Lopham for the Rev. Charles Ridley. Both are

1854 and it is instructive to compare the London fashionable with the country cousin.

West Lexham, St Nicholas (E4): Perched on a high mound, in picturesque surroundings above its little village – but something of a disappointment when you get to it. Its rough old round tower, of early *Norman* date, is so encased in cement and generally battered by the years as to look like an industrial relic. The body of the church was virtually entirely rebuilt in 1881 by the Earl of Leicester, but there are remnants of the place's ancient past – the neat s. doorway is of the *Decorated* period; the ancient low tower arch remains; good early-C14 Decorated *chancel* arch; very odd *piscina* (like a coarse two-*light Saxon* window, with a solid, square pillar down the middle) in the basically *Early English* chancel; and opposite, an *aumbry* given a chunky, *cusped* wooden surround. The offertory box, given in 1967, is charming – it is carved in relief on its front face with an ass who breathes docility and humility, and on the top, flowers in scrollery – lovely!

West Lynn, St Peter (C3): In a trim churchyard, which reflects the lovingly cared for interior of the church, stands this pleasant building, across the river from Lynn and the dominating outline of St Margaret's. The cement-rendered tower is *Decorated*, with attractively *cusped* and traceried belfry windows, and distinctive *sound-holes* which feature traceries of four cusped *quatrefoils* in a square frame. The little leaded spire is said to be of C18 date. The high, steeply pitched ridge line of an earlier roof and a filled-in *sanctus bell opening*, can be seen on the tower's e. face. *Nave* and *transepts* are all of the *Perpendicular* period, though at different phases of the style. The nave w. end is probably the latest, in *Tudor* red brick. Is the sturdy little red brick *porch* of the same era too? On the s. side was added in 1922, as a Great War memorial, a little vestry in exactly corresponding red brick and old-style tiles – it harmonises most beautifully. The *chancel* collapsed and decayed at least two centuries ago and the chancel arch was walled over. In 1934 a new chancel was built – and thoughtfully the builders set into its outside walls numerous fragments of *Norman* carving and moulding which were discovered during digging of the foundations. They also re-used the e. window and its glass (a representation of the Three Marys at the Sepulchre) which had been inserted into the filled-in chancel arch in the mid-C19. The glass is by William Jay Bolton of Cambridge

whose finest work is in Holy Trinity church, Brooklyn, N.Y. This is his only large piece in this country and is important for this reason. On the e. gable of the nave is a neat *sanctus bell turret* whose bell is thought to be the original medieval one – it did service in the early C20 as the local school bell, but was returned to its turret in 1934. An impressively spacious interior, flooded with light, the nave being very wide, and running into the short modern chancel whose division is marked by a vast arch which barely interrupts the eye, save to invite admiration for the elegance of its proportions and lines. The arch is of C14 date, but it has been suggested that its masons re-used Norman materials. The nave roof is a good C15 *tie-beamed* and *arch-braced* example, alternating with *hammer-beams* and arch-braces carved with angels carrying symbols such as the *Instruments of the Passion*. The tie-beams have good open traceries in the *spandrels*, and deep *wall posts* carved with figures of the *apostles* (each carrying his distinctive emblem) and sitting on stone *corbels*. The roof in the chancel is a modern interpretation of hammer-beam, and enormously attractive in natural scrubbed-look pine. The chancel rebuilding made possible the re-opening of the large *squint* from the n. transept. The roof just noted perfectly complements the choir stalls and old nave pews, which are all stripped and scrubbed to their clean natural texture. There are some intriguing *poppy-heads* in the nave – a knight's head bounded by twin eagles; angels' wings and feathered lion-like beasts. On the ends of the two front pews are figures set within sunk niches, one a bishop, the other a priest with a chalice, both set against backgrounds of sun-rays – and fairly poor workmanship though full of character. Elegant octagonal *Jacobean* pulpit, with typical 'Romanesque' arches in squared panels; and a couple of ancient *misericordes*, with seat rests carved with big initials in circles. Don't miss the little *brass* in front of the *communion rails*, a most attractive figure of a priest in his vestments, both figure and inscription being preserved in mint freshness. But it is his name which completes the appeal: Adam Outlawe, chaplain ('Ade Outlawe Capellani') who died 2nd August 1503. *Seven sacrament font* of the C14 in simple carving. The panels show (starting at the e. face and moving round clockwise): baptism, extreme unction, matrimony, ordination, God the Father, mass, penance and confirmation. The God the Father panel, though mutilated, is rather fine: an awesome Old Testament figure, regally crowned, sits on a bench with the Child held between his knees, all against a background of traceried windows.

West Newton, St Peter & St Paul (C3): One of the group of w. Norfolk churches built of the local *carstone*. The simple early-C14 tower has a large niche with an *ogee arch* s. of the w. window which itself has restored 'Y' tracery. An 1881 restoration for the Prince of Wales effectively Victorianised the rest of the outside, when the n. *aisle* was rebuilt and the s. aisle given wide, almost domestic, *mullioned* windows. Inside, the easternmost arches of the low C14 arcade are wider than the rest, so there were probably stub *transepts* originally. The tall tower arch is C14 too, and below is a simple C15 font which has a dark, pinnacled and *crocketted* cover that is C15 in style – but does not look quite right. Is it C19? A vivid window by Karl Parsons in the n. aisle commemorates the men of Sandringham who fell at Suvla Bay, Gallipoli in 1915, and to the left, a tablet to young Robert Graves who in 1854, 'fell nobly fighting for his country at the glorious battle of Inkermann, when 8000 British and 6000 French troops gallantly repulsed the Russian army of 60000 men!'

> Soldier rest – thy warfare's o'er,
> Sleep the sleep that knows no breaking!
> Dream of battle fields no more,
> Days of danger – nights of waking.

West Rudham, St Peter (E3): Following major restoration in 1994 funded by English Heritage and the *Norfolk Churches Trust*, the church is well cared for by the latter. The stolid C14 tower has *Decorated* bell openings below a plain parapet. A *porch* once stood where there are now two steps down to a C13 doorway flanked by pairs of columns. Within, the *aisle* and the low *arcade* are of the same period, and note the stiff-leaf decoration on the w. *respond* which proves that the narrower w. bay was not an afterthought; the three *corbel* heads on the s. side probably date from a C16 alteration. At the w. end there is a plain C15 font and a set of George IV *Royal Arms*, and the three small *poppy-heads* in the aisle are C15 although the remainder are C17 versions – the same age as the tiny poor box on the back pew. In the tracery of the *nave's* n. windows look for the following from the w.: a feathery angel, the Christ of Pity wearing the Crown of Thorns and displaying his wounds above a blue robe; centre window: four figures comprising the *Annunciation* and Coronation of the Blessed

Virgin; e. window: a pot of lilies (one of the Virgin's emblems) and S. Mark holding a scroll. Christopher Woodeforde recognised the similarity of this C15 glass with schemes at Stratton Strawless and Norwich St Peter Hungate – he thought the quality of the colour and line here pointed to a Kings Lynn workshop following the designs of the more skilful Norwich glaziers. The small *trefoil*-headed recess in the e. respond of the arcade may have been prepared for a *heart burial*. The *chancel* was rebuilt in 1456 and in the sanctuary there is a *piscina* under a battered *ogee* arch decorated with *Instruments of the Passion*. As you leave have a look at Barned Steel's fetching epitaph outside the s. door – you will find some of the lines repeated on other stones in the churchyard.

West Runton, Holy Trinity (H1): The heavy western tower is *Early English* with a w. *Decorated* window. Apart from the s. range of C15 windows (two in the *chancel* unusually large), most of the others are Decorated. The e. window and the roofs are C19, and it was then that the former *clerestory* disappeared. This was all part of a drastic remodelling by *Thomas Jekyll* in 1854-6 using plans by the Aylsham builder Robert Bartrum. The benches are a simplification by Jekyll of *Pugin's* 1844 set at Wymeswold, Leicestershire. The *sedilia* and *piscina* in the chancel are rather ponderous C14, but the font is a fine member of the late-C14 'family' which crops up in this district (eg., Roughton and Sheringham) with eight attached shafts below a traceried bowl. There is a pleasing portrayal of worshippers down the ages in a n. aisle window by H.J. Stammers of York, dated 1959.

West Somerton, St Mary (K4): Round tower with C14 octagonal top, thatched *nave* and *porch*. Of the many traces of medieval wall paintings, only the Last Judgement on the s. wall remains to any extent. In it, a king and a bishop wake, along with the hoi-polloi, to the sound of the Last Trump. There is a good early-C15 *screen*, with a *crocketted* centre arch. By it stands a contemporary pulpit with unusual concave panels; note the hinge at the bottom of one of the front uprights, showing that the door has been repositioned. Outside, look in the n.e. corner of the churchyard for the C19 grave of Robert Hales, the Norfolk Giant. He was 7ft. 8in. tall and turned the scales at 33 stone. Also a headstone on the way to the porch with its chatty epitaph to a good lady who 'toiled and muddled through her life.'

West Walton, St Mary (A4): The great bulk of the detached tower rears up spectacularly in the level marshland and quite overwhelms the little village street that snakes round it. The church itself was built between 1225 and 1240 but the tower is slightly later and is sited on the firmest land in the parish. The four open archways of the base have *dog-tooth* decoration and each of the massive corner shafts carries capacious niches like sentry boxes under gabled roofs. In the second stage, the buttresses are faced with tall *blank arcading* which continues and matches the form of the triple openings in the walls, behind which a passage runs. The bell openings take up the whole width of the walls and the deep mouldings have dog-tooth decoration, with a circle of *plate tracery* set above the twin *lancets*. *Blind arcading* completes the scheme to the top, but a parapet with corner pinnacles was added later. Through then to the church itself, and the s. *porch* lavishly complements the tower behind us. A deeply moulded arch, again with dog-tooth, is flanked by buttresses which are arcaded below with columns to match the doorway and continue up with blind arcading to finish in conical caps. The incongruous crowstepped gable is a *Tudor* afterthought. When the *aisles* were widened in the C14, the porch was cut back to one and a half bays and the original C13 doorway re-used. This is a beauty, with a deep range of arch mouldings supported by four shafts a side and lovely stiff-leaf *capitals*. The pattern of the mouldings is repeated in the hunched up little arches either side. Walking round to the w. end you will see that the main entrance was even more impressive – before two huge and ungainly buttresses were applied to save the facade from collapse. As with the s. porch, there were once C13 buttresses here too, and fragments of the *arcades* peep out from behind the rescue operation. Nevertheless, the w. doorway is still a fine sight, with its pair of pointed arches separated by a shaft and set within a deeply recessed round arch. It rests on four attached columns each side, with stiff-leaf foliage capitals (renewed) and the typical dog-tooth ornament crops up again. There are vestiges of it round the *Perpendicular* replacement w. window above. The n. doorway is a slightly less exuberant version of its partner and is equally good. Continuing round, note a *piscina* in the n. wall of the *chancel*, showing that there was a chapel there, and on the s. side see how the *priest's door* and one of the church's original C13 windows were re-used when the aisle was widened. The small *clerestory* lancets occupy every

West Walton, St Mary: Bell tower

third space in a continuous run of arcading and are obscured on the n. side by the slope of a later aisle roof. Once inside the real quality of this exceptional building is plain to see. The columns of the *nave* arcades are graced by four *Purbeck* shafts which rise to a ring of deeply undercut stiff-leaf foliage round the capitals that is not surpassed anywhere. The spacious nave and aisles set them off admirably and the chancel arch matches the design. In contrast to the outside design of one in three, the clerestory windows internally are contained within a range of larger blank arcading, so that every other space has a window. The dull red wall paintings between the windows date from the time the church was built. Within the chancel, parts of the arcades to the vanished side aisles can still be seen, with eight Purbeck shafts to each column. Unfortunately, the chancel was shortened by about 9ft. in 1807 and a beautiful C13 double piscina was destroyed in the process. The e. window dates from then but the wall arcading on either side is original. The simple C15 font on its three steps has a very spacious setting at the w. end and the alarming outward lean of the last arcade bays shows why those huge outside buttresses were added. There are a number of freshwater springs under the church and one can only congratulate the builders of the tower on their choice of site. The C15

Wheatacre, All Saints

hammer-beam roof is not exceptional but the angels bear shields carved with the *Instruments of the Passion*. The roundels just above the nave arcades were overpainted in the C18 with emblems of the tribes of Israel and perhaps the most easily recognisable is the lion of Judah on the s. side. At the n.e. corner of the n. aisle, a large table tomb with a brass inscription of 1552 on top but lacking its border and shields. Close to it, the effigy of a C13 priest in *Purbeck marble* which once lay in the chancel. It was taken out, probably at the *Reformation*, and the pieces were scattered all over the parish. Reassembled by determination and good fortune in 1847, it probably represents Prior Albert who built the church or Hugh of Northwold, Bishop of Ely. The front of the body has been sliced off where it was turned over and used as a doorstep but the worn, tonsured and bearded head has still much dignity and authority. Despite the extensive programme of restoration in the 1960s, the parish is still struggling with repairs and upkeep, trying to pay its way and avoid closure, but at least the bell tower is no longer a problem. Having been declared redundant by the diocese, the bell tower was extensively repaired by the Department of the Environment before being placed in the care of the *Churches Conservation Trust*.

West Winch, St Mary (C4): The big, early-C15 *carstone* tower has a flint *flushwork base course*, with tall matching panels on the w. side. There are large niches flanking the w. door with elaborate canopies, and the *sound-holes* have centre shields carrying the arms of the Cholmondeley family. Walking round, you will see that there is no n. *aisle* and the high wall on that side is broken only by a blocked *Early English* door and two large, (renewed) *Perpendicular* windows. Apart from later additions, the early-C14 *chancel* has an e. window of three *lancets* contained within one arch, and a single lancet on the n. side. The C14 s. *porch* looks decidedly odd because it rises above the s. aisle roof, but it is quite enterprising on a small scale. The flint chequerwork front has a sundial of 1706 over the arch, the side windows boast pretty *Decorated* tracery and the heavy ribs of the vaulted roof rest on big *corbels* – one still recognisable as a head with the hair held by a fillet bearing a cross. Inside the Early English doorway with its worn *headstops*, is a plain C14 octagonal font, and a s. *arcade* which is a chronological mixture. The first two bays are early-C14, with tiny *ball flower* decoration on the *capital* of the w. *respond* – the *quatrefoil* pillar has shafts that are keel-shaped rather than round, and the next octagonal respond has *dog-tooth* decoration; then comes a break in the design and the last bay is plain Perpendicular. There seems to have been a series of alterations to the s. side of the church – look, for example, at the placing of the Decorated aisle w. window and the very large walk-through *squint* by the chancel arch. Above it is an opening that presumably connected with the *rood loft*. The *screen* itself is no longer there but its base, with a carved trail on the centre rail and a renewed top, is under the tower arch. Nearby, some old bench ends with *poppy-heads* of an unusual design. The chancel has been given a tiled floor recently with changed levels and the C17 *communion rails* have been brought forward to a new step just within the arch – an enterprising variation that complements the placing of the altar and preserves the proper distinction between *nave* and sanctuary. The rails have substantial half-figures on the posts and the two in the centre hold cup and loaf, symbols of the eucharistic elements. In the chancel floor, two *ledger slabs* with fine epitaphs; Henry Cremer's ends, 'Go Thou and doe like wise and be happy. Farewell. He Began his pilgrimage Decemb. 18 1597 and returned to his owne cuntry Feb 8 1657.' Of the Morehouse family (1736/63), the elegy begins, 'Within this Grave three Faithful friends are laid'. If it is unlocked, have a look at the *sacristry* on the n. side of the chancel. It has a *tunnel vaulted* roof with transverse ribs like the *porch* at nearby Runcton Holme, a five-leaf *piscina* and two *aumbries*, one large and oblong, the other a small one with a *trefoil* arch.

Westfield, St Andrew (F5): The *chancel* has long since gone, leaving just tower, *porch*, *nave* and the appearance, in an open position, of a charming country chapel. It is a largely *Decorated* style building – see the tower's belfry windows and the fine windows of the nave, all very good, flowing tracery of the first half of the C14. The e. window is in sympathetic style – it is not known exactly when the chancel disappeared and this window was probably inserted around 1700. Inside, the charm of the exterior is warmly mirrored – utter simplicity, with its plain *arch-braced roof* and cream-painted walls. Visible in a corner of the sanctuary is the indentation of the *rood stair* entrance. There is a plain C14 font; restrained *decalogue boards* either side of the altar; a homely *Jacobean* pulpit and, of similar period though probably slightly later, the neat and domestic *communion rails*. They are a set which was three-sided. Unspoiled and welcoming, with an atmosphere that both soothes and satisfies.

Weston Longville, All Saints (H4):

April 16, 1775. We went to church this morning at Weston, and Cooke read Prayers and preached for Mr Howes (the curate). I administered the H. Sacrament this morning at Weston Church being Easter Day – I had near 40 Communicants. N.B. No money collected at the Sacrament, it not being usual at Weston. My clerk is a shocking hand. The worst singing I ever heard in a church, only the Clerk and one man, and both intolerably bad.

Thus *Parson James Woodforde* first appears on the scene at Weston Longville, and through the diary that he kept continuously for 43 years until his death in 1803, we are privileged to eavesdrop on Norfolk village life in the last quarter of the C18 – a long voyage of discovery and delight that charms by its harmony and its tranquillity. For many people, this is Woodforde's church – his squire lies buried outside the e. window, his own memorial is in the *chancel*, and the signposts all around point to villages he knew so well. Apart from this special association, the building has a great deal of intrinsic interest. The tower is C13,

and the C14 chancel has exceptionally pretty tracery in the s. windows, As you go in, glance up at the shield above the niche – not that of a noble family, but of the Company of French Merchant Adventurers – now isn't that strange! Local man Thomas Curyng gave money for the *porch* in 1481 so perhaps he provides the connecting link. The C14 s. door has hinges that stretch almost the full width and retains its original closing ring. Inside, tall C14 *arcades* give a nice sense of space, and (on weekdays anyway) serried rows of bright embroidered hassocks line the pew ledges and give the place a glow. The tower arch has a modern *screen*, glazed at the top to light the ringing chamber, and to the right, a portrait in oils of Parson Woodforde himself, painted by his nephew Samuel in 1806 from a sketch taken in 1785. The plain font with its thick shaft and four *Purbeck* columns is unremarkable, but take a look at the step on the w. side; on it, the outlines of a small *Saxon* Calvary show up plainly. It may have been part of an altar *reredos*, discarded at the *Reformation*, and used again here simply because it was the right size and shape. At all events, it must be the oldest artefact in the church. On the wall of the n. *aisle*, a large *Jesse Tree* painted some time after 1350; this is in much better condition than most, and some of the heads are particularly good. For a detailed critique, see the framed description on the wall below. The chancel arch is flanked by two other C14 paintings; to the left an elongated figure of St *John the Baptist*, and behind the pulpit, the top half of a figure of St *John the Divine*. The Square headed C15 *screen* is good and solid, but the entrance arch is relieved by a light fringe of lacy *cusping*, and the main uprights have a decorative flower trail. The bottom panels have heavily restored paintings of saints that all cast sidelong glances towards the entrance, and carry scrolls of the creed. The work may be crude but the effect is vigorous. From left to right: St *Peter*, St *Andrew*, St *Simon*, St *Matthias*, St *Jude*, St *Matthew*, St *John*, St *James the Great*, St *Thomas*, St *James the Less*, St *Philip*, St *Bartholomew*. Under the mat in front of the lectern is a fine 2ft. 3in. brass to Elizabeth Rokewoode (1533), with her two sons kneeling on either side. She wears a *kennel head-dress* and an ample furred gown from which her toes peep demurely. The family was evidently well established in Weston, for there is a small white marble tablet to Henry Rookwood at the e. end of the s. aisle dated nearly 200 years later. It has a delightfully individual style of lettering, plus a skull and alabaster flourishes above and below.

The old *rood stairs* rise through the wall nearby, and the spacious enclosures of the Custance family pew take up that end of the aisle. In the early-C14 chancel, a *piscina* and *sedilia* of exceptional quality, compactly grouped under a square label. The five-leafed *ogee arches* are *crocketted*, and there are *Green Men* within the angles. Across the sanctuary, a plain *aumbry* keeps company with a pretty little niche which now has a statue to fit. During the 1880s restoration, the old *mensa* was moved from the *nave* back to the sanctuary and, by peeping under the hangings, you will see that it now rests under the altar. (To do so will provide an excuse not to look at the Victorian reredos.) On the way out, detour via the s. aisle to see the mid-C15 glass in the heads of two windows. There are angels from the Norwich workshops in the second and fifth *lights* of the easternmost window, and further w., restored figures of St *John*, St *James the Great* (He has whelks on his coat this time – not *scallops*.) and St *Philip*. The church has an excellent ring of 6 bells, tenor 10-2-17 cwt.

Westwick, St Botolph (I3): The church lies just within the park of Westwick House, and tall trees hug it close on three sides. The late-C15 tower is well proportioned and has a *base course* of shields carrying *Passion Emblems*. The *sound-holes* are particularly attractive, each with a shield encircled by little *quatrefoils*. The outside of the rest of the building has the slightly petrified look common to restorations done in the 1840s. There is a good early-C16 font with the usual four lions squatting round the shaft and the bowl decorated with foliage. The *rood* and *parclose screens* have been extensively restored and then grained, but there are painted panels of the *Apostles*. The *chancel* had its n. windows blocked to accommodate Burney and Petre monuments which are worth looking at, and for this it is well that the *priest's door* has been replaced with leaded *lights* to brighten the gloom of the e. end.

Weybourne, All Saints (H1): The present church grew out of a C13 Priory of Augustinian Canons, which itself took over the site and building of an earlier church. The impressive ruins of the *Saxon* tower remain to the n. of the present *chancel* and much of the outlines of the Priory can still be seen. The canons added a s. *aisle* for parish use and the old *nave* forms the present n. aisle. Handsome tower with nice *sound-holes* and *flushwork* added in the C15, as was the *porch*. This is prettily chequered and had an upper chamber used as a chapel – note the blocked *squint* which gave a view of the high altar. An impression of the old Priory seal is displayed on the s. wall of the nave.

Wheatacre, All Saints (K6): In a county dominated by C15 flint, an early-C16 tower in brick makes an agreeable change, and here we have an imaginative designer as well. The entire surface is a chequerboard of red brick and dressed flint, and the w. front has a masterly combination of multi-recessed doorway and *mullioned* window above. The whole thing glows in the sun if you are lucky with the weather. The rest of the building outside is hard Victorian restoration. The C14 s. doorway has a strong *ogee hood mould*, with fine heads of a king and queen as stops. Restoration has laid a heavy hand inside too, but it would seem that the e. end dates from the C14 and that the *nave* was rebuilt when the tower was done. The C15 font is oddly placed in the s.w. corner and is picked out in colour – some possibly original. The cover, on a counterweight, is distinctly odd – traditional *cusps* and *crockets* all mixed up with flatly carved art nouveau flowers and fruit. The *chancel screen* has modern mouldings and heavily carved cornice reminiscent of Devon work, but the tracery in the *lights* is original. The 1904 screen between chancel and n. chapel looks to be by the same hand as the font cover, but in a more solid and restrained mood.

Whinburgh, St Mary (G5): A lovely setting, with a mid-C14 square *Perpendicular* tower offset from the rest of the church to the s.w. The windows in the tower are *Perpendicular* – but their free-flowing tracery harks back to *Decorated* freedom of form, even though it is a bit coarse. The big two-*light* Decorated window on the s. side of the nave, against the tower, has that touch of coarse workmanship too, with a big six-leaf shape in the head of its tracery. Next to it, a three-light *Tudor* window. On the opposite side of the nave, there is a good example of *plate tracery*. Notice that all the windows, as well as the entrance arch into the tower and the nave's n. door, have substantial *drip stones* and hefty *corbels*. The e. and w. windows are C19. Inside, a spartan church, with a single-framed roof, basic pews with *poppy-heads*; a rough brick, *herring-bone* floor; plain C14 octagonal font; *rood stair* on n.; and in front of the *chancel* steps two tiny shields are all that remain of a large memorial *brass*. The chancel is a total C19 rebuild. There are two windows here by *Lavers, Barraud & Westlake*, bright and colourful in their portrayal of scenes surrounding the birth and boyhood of Christ. As you leave, look for the rough outline in the angle of the tower and its s.e. buttress of a *holy water stoup*.

Whissonsett, St Mary (F3): Set in the heart of its village, it has a spruce *Decorated* tower with neat *Perpendicular* battlements, panelled and *flushworked* and with *crocketted* corner pinnacles. The body of the church is of *Early English* foundation (the little *priest's door* on the *chancel* s. side appears to date from then) but *Decorated* (chancel) and Perpendicular (*nave*) now predominate. The tower w. window, and possibly the *porch*, are late Perpendicular. The e. window is an unfortunate modern hybrid, the chancel s. windows even less fortunate modern restorations. The hand of past restoration lies heavily on the interior. The vastly wide nave (some 30ft.) is plain to the point of austerity, an effect not helped by the common-or-garden clear glass of the windows. Big unadorned octagonal font on a Maltese cross base; restored *holy water stoup* by s. door, with matching replacement stone *screen*. Big figure niches to right and left of e. window and right of chancel arch in the nave, the latter containing the finely preserved head of an *Anglo-Saxon* cross (dug up from the churchyard in about 1900), the cross pierced and the shaft decorated with interlacing carving. In the two e. corners of the nave are *piscinas*, one with a stone *credence shelf*. Evidently there was much *guild* involvement here in pre-*Reformation* times. Another piscina, in the sanctuary, appears to be of early date; the nearby triple *sedilia* are so totally restored that it is difficult to judge their authenticity. In the n. wall opposite, an ancient *squint* gives a view of the high altar from the modern vestry – pointing to the presence here of a room in medieval times. The church has a good ring of 6 bells, tenor 6-3-22 cwt.

Wickhampton, St Andrew (K5): This was once a prosperous community when, like other villages round about, it lay on the banks of the great tidal estuary. When C16 reclamation formed the grazing marshes Wickhampton declined, and now the church with its cluster of cottages and farm buildings stands on the very edge of the level meadows that stretch away to Breydon and Great Yarmouth in a windy solitude. The *chancel* was originally *Norman*, but you can see from the outside that there were *Early English lancets* before the C15 e. window was inserted. The present *nave* was built about 1300, and both the s. door and the windows on

that side have charming *headstops* – one man and one woman to each. The tower details are a mixture of *Decorated* and *Perpendicular* and it dates from the late C14. The *base course* is very like that at Halvergate, a mile away across the fields, and the tiny window in the tower stairs matches the Halvergate *sound-holes*. Here there are regulation-size sound-holes, and two of them (n. and s.) have excellent and varied tracery with traces of carving on the moulded surround. The corner pinnacles each have a weather vane – unusual in this part of the country. Wickhampton's treasure, however, is inside. Open the door and you are faced with one of the finest ranges of C14 wall paintings in the country. They cover most of the n. wall and are in three parts. At the w. end there is the legend of *The Three Living and the Three Dead*; under the skeletons a hare runs from the leashed greyhounds held by a youth in the centre, and the king on the right has a hawk on his wrist. Next, there is a huge St *Christopher* (10ft. x 5ft.), and then a fine series of The *Seven Works of Mercy*, each set in a 3ft. x 3ft. architectural panel, with rudimentary perspective. The eighth panel is a Resurrection scene. There are useful water colour drawings of 1849 with annotations, framed below the paintings. The series was uncovered in the 1840s but deteriorated badly until they were described a century later as 'almost indistinguishable'. Happily, the Pilgrim Trust financed their restoration in 1963 when much more detail was brought to light. Another treasure in the chancel – two splendid C13 effigies lying under restored *crocketted* canopies. They are Sir William Gerbrygge and his wife. His 6ft. figure has a lion at the feet, and he is dressed in short tunic and carrying a shield which has his coat of arms in relief. He wears sword and spurs and his head rests on two pillows. His wife, in plain gown and *wimple*, has a pug dog minus nose for company. Sir William was Bailiff of Yarmouth in 1271 and patron of this church. Between his hands he holds a stone heart (inscribed by some C19 oaf 'RMD 1832'), and this wove itself into a local legend which surfaced in Clyde's 'Norfolk Garland' – too long to quote here, but the extract is neatly typed and framed by the tomb. Don't overlook the little C19 chamber organ in the chancel – it has a very fine mahogany case with an extraordinary number of panelled doors.

Wicklewood, St Andrew & All Saints (G5): From the road, which loops around it, the outline of this church catches the eye. It has a big tower offset to the s.w., the base of it serving

Wickhampton, St Andrew: C14 wall painting of the Seven Works of Mercy

as entrance *porch*. Church and tower are mainly *Perpendicular* throughout, though it is interesting that the pillars of the porch arch into the tower are rounded and substantial – possibly use of materials from an earlier church. The e. window is a 1979 replacement. On the s. side of the *chancel* is one small Decorated window. Inside the porch under the tower is a sturdy timber-raftered ceiling, with chunky wooden shields and deep corner wooden *wall posts*; and below, the remains of a *holy water stoup*. Within, the church has *arch-braced roofs*. There's a C16 octagonal font, with shields in the panels and little *cusped arcades* round the stem. A square niche by the s. door once held a holy water stoup. In the s.e. corner of the *nave* are the remains of a fine *piscina*, with a carved trefoil head; beside it, set into the wall, a curiosity: a weird carved head, more animal than human, more pagan than Christian. Opposite, behind the pulpit, is the filled-in outline of the *rood stair*, its *rood loft* exit in the angle of the walls above. At the back of the nave are a few old *poppy-heads*; the rest are modern, but very well done, in full medieval spirit, with faces, birds, biblical texts and floribunda carved in lively fashion. In the sanctuary, a Perpendicular piscina, with a cusped arch in a square mould and with the base projecting from the wall: it has one large bold flower carved underneath, which still has traces of its original colour. It adjoins very low, arched *sedilia*, recessed into the

wall. If you can arrange access to the tower, it is worth making the ascent to see, at the first level, an enormous fireplace, big enough to roast a pig; and at the next level, immediately underneath the bell chamber, a much smaller fireplace. They have been called *wafer ovens*, though their size points to domestic use, as at Great Snoring. On leaving, note that either side of the s. door are massive holes deep into the walls to take the door's draw-bar.

Wickmere, St Andrew (H2): Lonely and in a big churchyard where the grass often lies flat in the wind. The round tower and the *nave* w. wall have much *carstone* and may be pre-Conquest. The *aisle* and *chancel* windows have pretty *Decorated* tracery and although renewed, the alternating circular and two-*light clerestory* windows are strikingly attractive. The facing between them and also on the s. *porch* is of dressed white flint which flashes in the sunshine. Inside, some of the benches are medieval, and one in the s. aisle has a carved and painted inscription for the donors, with the lily emblem of the Virgin in a shield on the *poppy-head*. Another at the w. end of the nave has a mutilated satyr figure on the arm, and on the left hand stall in the *chancel* a little man plays the lute with his legs crossed negligently. The C15 *screen* has been largely restored, but four of the panels retain their paintings of saints, although only

St *Andrew* with his cross can be recognised. The pulpit dates from 1938, and the two panels with C15 paintings of donors came from Wolterton Hall and were probably taken from the screen of St Margaret's, Wolterton which has been ruinous for some 300 years. As a result, the Walpole family adopted Wickmere and their *hatchments* hang in the chancel. There too, is the *ledger-stone* of Horatio Baron Walpole, 'a useful Co-adjutor to his brother (the famous Sir Robert) in directing the Councils of England and the Peace of Europe'. In the n. aisle, the fifth Earl of Orford (d.1931) has a massive tomb chest with robed figure attended by angels on top. The crown of his head already has a faint sheen and one feels that the whole effigy may gently weather in time. (Sir Robert Walpole was created first Earl of Orford. The title became extinct with the death of the fifth Earl. The Barons Walpole of Wolterton continue at Wolterton Hall). The most memorable memorial in the church is a white marble *cartouche* with cherub heads at the corners, on the wall at the w. end. It is to Henry Spelman (d.1765) who, 'having distinguished himself by his Intrepidity and Conduct as a Soldier at Dettingen and Fontenoy, died at Calcutta in ye Kingdom of Bengal'. Two of his friends brought back the standard 'under which he has often bravely fought', and its bamboo shaft with pointed filigree head is still there on the wall above. As you go out, admire the excellent C14 ironwork on the door.

Wiggenhall St Germans, St Germaine (B4): Snuggling down below the bank of the wide River Ouse is this little church in intriguing outline – a very slim tower, tall and slim *nave* with *clerestory,* a s. *aisle* of extremely generous proportions, wholly overlapping the *chancel* and with its own separate, pitched roof; n. aisle in the usual 'lean to' construction, and a charming, though neglected and unused n. *porch* in pink brick, of C16 date. The lower and sturdily buttressed part of the tower, with its rough and colourful mixture of brick, flint and *carstone*, is C13, with tall, pencil-slim *lancets*. The upper part, in neatly dressed stone and with stone, flint and brick chequerwork in the battlements, is C15. As you approach the church, the view of the n. aisle is rather striking – three splendidly confident windows, one with 'Y' tracery, two with flattened *Tudor* heads, and the wall in a conglomeration of materials which present great character in colour and texture. At its w. end pink brick vigorously dominates; at the e. end a fine three-*light* window with interlacing tracery

is the focal point. Big, good looking Tudor windows to the n. aisle, though much restored; very elegant ones of the same period in the clerestory. On the e. gable of the nave, a delicate and weathered little *sanctus bell turret,* with a neat nave e. window below it. The nave is especially effective inside: big, barn-like roof timbers; bold clerestory; lovely four-bay C15 *arcade* on *quatrefoil* pillars; and beautiful *Early English* tower arch topped by a hood crisply carved in *dog-tooth* mouldings and with mask-like *headstops.* Panelled pulpit, dated 1631, complete with *hour-glass* and iron stand. Above is the filled-in loft level exit of the *rood stairs,* the stairs themselves contained within the massive pillar at this corner. Nearby, a small iron bound chest, and a good C17 reading desk. The best thing here, however, is the collection of remarkable medieval pew ends, of terrific character, detail and variety. They include massive *poppy-heads,* single and grouped figures and animals on the arm rests, with more figures carved within niches on the faces of the bench-ends – among saints with their emblems will be found *Stephen, Simon, Andrew, Jude, John* and *Peter.*

Wiggenhall St Mary, St Mary (B4): Apart from one or two houses, the church is well away from the village, and Wiggenhall St Germans has become the focus of parish activity for both communities. Having become redundant in 1980, it is now in the care of the *Churches Conservation Trust.* As with Wiggenhall St Mary Magdalen, the base of the tower is C13 but, with the exception of the doorways, the rest of the building is C15 and carried out in red brick which shows up attractively on the tower with its double angle turrets widely splayed. Note outside that the *aisle* windows have oddly paired *headstops* – one animals, one human. A sundial of 1742 over the entrance to the early-C15 *porch,* with its tunnel-vaulted roof like Clenchwarton, and then a C13 s. doorway with pairs of detached shafts, bell-shaped *capitals* and finely moulded arch. The n. doorway is similar but slightly later in date judging by the style. The *arcades* within are C15 but the style of the *piers,* with their heavy shafts bearing individual capitals, harks back to the previous century, and it is strange that the *clerestory* windows have three *lights* on the n. but only two on the s. side. The bowl of the plain octagonal font curves gently in to join the moulded shaft and the *Jacobean* cover is exceptionally lively. It stands on four turned shafts which carry pairs of arches separated by pendants; it bears initials of the donors or

Wiggenhall St Mary, St Mary: Tomb of Sir Henry Kervil

churchwardens, dated 1625, is picked out in pale colour, and the solid pinnacle cap is embellished with a large *pelican* in her piety. Also Jacobean is the unusually large alms box – of a size to double as a parish chest, with C18 dates and initials cut into the top. St Mary's great glory is the magnificent suite of benches – they are surely the finest in the county, both in terms of quality and completeness. There is a marked difference between the n. and s. ranges; those on the n. side are more elaborate and the details of costume (the hats and broad toed shoes particularly) point to the late C15 or early C16, while on the s. side, the costume and hair styles are more typical of the late C14 or early C15. The *poppy-heads* are large and luxuriant and figures crown the square buttresses either side. Large statues stand within deep niches facing the aisles and the backs of the benches are heavily moulded, with a variety of pierced tracery on the n. side and *quatrefoils* with the letters V.R.A. (Virgo Regina Ave) on the s. This differencing applies to the standing figures too – those on the s. side are mainly of the Virgin within an aureole, with the letters V.B. (Virgo Beata) and one has the attribute of her *Assumption*, the pot of lilies. In particular, seek out the following (counting from the w. end in each range): n. side of *nave*: no. 5 St *Agatha* with the knife over her breast; no. 6 St *Mary Magdalen* wearing a headdress of 1490-1550; no. 8 the seated figure on the e. side probably St *Ambrose* with his beehives; no. 9 e. side, St *James the less*; no. 10 St *Leonard* with a book in one hand and shackles in the other, s. side of n. aisle: no. 4 St *Matthew* to the e. and it may be St *Vincent* with his saw to the w.; no. 6 w. side St *Jude*, e. side St *Simon*; no. 7 w. side a headless St *Lawrence,* e. side St *Stephen* with the stones of his martyrdom, s. side of nave: no. 2 e. side a headless St *Agnes* with her lamb; no. 5 w. side a headless St *Margaret* with the rear half of her dragon; no. 7 w. side St *Andrew* n. side of s. aisle: no. 2 e. side St *Hugh* if the bird is a swan or St *Martin* if it is meant to be a goose. The base of the *rood screen* was replaced in the C19 and the panels bear the name of Humphrey Kervil who died in 1526 – the costumes of the figures coincide with that date; from left to right they are: Saints *Mary Magdalen, Dorothy, Margaret, Scolastica* (?), *Catherine* (?), *Barbara, the Blessed Virgin, John the Baptist*. In front stands a fine brass lectern given by Robert Barnard in 1518. The lion feet and the inscription on the flange halfway up the shaft are like the one at Oxborough and others from the same workshop may be found in St Martin's Salisbury

Wiggenhall St Mary, St Mary: Bench end figure of St James the Less

and St Nicholas' Bristol. The Jacobean pulpit, with its inlaid *tester*, has a large *hour-glass* stand. The s. aisle chapel has a *parclose screen* and within is the imposing alabaster tomb chest of Sir Henry Kervil (d.1624), the last of his line. He wears full plate armour, with his feet resting on a pair of gloves, while his wife is in stomacher and farthingale, with a deep hood over her head; on the wall above, twin columns and strap-work frame the inscription, with the Kervil leopard's head arms contained within a curve of the cornice topped by the goat of the family crest.; more heraldry on the tomb chest and the figures of a daughter and a *chrysom child* in the centre panel; traces of original colour survive overall. There is a plain *piscina* nearby and a *consecration cross* on the wall. In front of the chapel altar is an interesting example of a *heart brass*; two of its four labels remain and it commemorates Sir Robert Kervil who died abroad about 1450. His wife despatched a monk to retrieve his heart and it was buried here in an iron casket.

Wiggenhall St Mary Magdalen, St Mary Magdalen (B4): A grand church for this small village by the Great Ouse, and remarkably similar in design to Wiggenhall St Mary. The *nave* roof was raised in the C15, making room for a generous range of *clerestory* windows and this makes the tower look shorter than it is. Twin stair turrets capped with pinnacles rise from the e. corners of the nave on either side of a *sanctus bell turret* and contribute to the very handsome profile. The lower part of the tower is C13 but it has *Decorated* bell openings contemporary with the *chancel*. Apart from the C18/C19 e. window and one in the n. wall of the chancel, all the windows are *Perpendicular* and those in the *aisles* have heavy battlemented *transoms*. The tower is a mixture of *carstone,* flint and various other materials, but the body of the church is all red brick which shows through the plaster rendering here and there. The *porch* is warm red brick too, with a *Tudor* outer arch and an inner doorway which has shields and roses in the *spandrels*. There was once an upper room (see the stairway) and part of a *holy water stoup* remains by the entrance. Tall C14 *arcades* divide the wide nave and aisles, with a good roof above – *tie-beams* with *queen posts* alternating with small *hammer-beams* bearing angels. The w. end is curiously blank, with only a low doorway into the tower and either side of it are panels crudely painted with the *Evangelistic Symbols* which once formed part of the *rood screen*. Sections of the C15 *parclose screens* that originally enclosed chapels at the e. end of the aisles have been re-used to form a vestry in the n.w. corner. Simple C14 octagonal font and rustic oak benches in the nave with rudimentary *poppy-heads*. In the n. aisle windows there is a remarkable sequence of C14 and C15 stained glass. The tracery *lights* are filled with 40 little figures of saints, bishops and popes, many with identifying labels, and there is the head and shoulders of a bishop in one of the main lights. The *rood screen* must have been quite a feature of the church and, remembering the turrets outside reaching to the roof, see how there are stairways on both sides of the chancel arch to give access to the rood and how the height of the upper doorways proves that the screen was exceptionally lofty. There is an image bracket over

the door on the s. side and the chancel arch is notched on the e. side to take the *rood beam*. The chancel *weeps* markedly to the n. Mid-C17 panelling covers the e. wall; it has been painted white but the carving is quite lush, with a vine motif recurring. To the s., a plain C13 *piscina* with an *aumbry* on one side and simple *sedilia* on the other. When leaving, note the iron-banded chest and C13 grave slab by the door.

Wighton, All Saints (F2): There are many similarities with Great Walsingham here. The body of the church is all C14 and has an impressive range of large, three-*light clerestory* windows giving a spacious and airy feeling to the interior. Everything is on a large scale, with a *chancel* arch some 20ft. across. The early-C14 tower collapsed in 1965 in a gale, and for eleven years the church presented an unfamiliar silhouette on the skyline. Then, from over the Atlantic, came Canadian businessman Mr. Leeds Richardson, whose ancestors had worshipped here at All Saints, who paid for the tower's rebuilding in 1976. His generosity did not end there. In 1980 he paid for a peal of six bells to be hung in the tower, including the one original Wighton bell, first cast in 1657 and now, in its recasting, inscribed with the fitting words: 'With determination, success is inevitable'. The other five bells came from a redundant church in Maidstone. Inside the church there is a good *rood loft staircase* and the font has a range of shields around the octagonal bowl, with the *Instruments of the Passion* included in the subjects. Sheep graze in the churchyard around the timbers of the medieval bell-frame from the old tower.

Wilby, All Saints (G7): Its tall, handsome *Decorated* tower of the C14 stands clear in the surrounding flat countryside. It impresses at once with its neat, *quatrefoil*-traceried *sound-holes* in circular 'frames'; and not least with its magnificent w. window of opulent flowing tracery. The church as a whole is of fine proportions, though judging by the pitch of the old roof visible on the tower, it was even grander before its C17 remodelling. The *chancel* looks superb, with an enormous e. window with richly *cusped,* flowing tracery, tall and graceful side windows, and an elegant *priest's door* on the s., all proclaiming the Decorated period. Notice also, on the chancel n. side, the *put-log holes* outlined in stone of the original scaffolding. The *nave* windows are good *Perpendicular* with little battle-mented *transoms*; with the exception of an

Wiggenhall St Mary Magdalen, St Mary Magdalen

ambitious Decorated window on the s. side. Decorated too is the lovely n. door, with its flowing *ogee* head and *drip mould,* topped with a large *crocket.* The *porch,* whose battered outer arch is inset with little floral motifs (as at nearby Eccles) and tiny shields, is C15 Perpendicular; inside is a hacked-away outline of a *holy water stoup.* The church interior has a lovely surprise: for what we see is virtually unchanged since 1633. At that time a fire gutted roofs and furnishings and all was replaced in *Prayer Book Church* fashion. We have therefore a splendid *Three-Decker Pulpit,* complete with backboard and *tester* and placed well up the nave; *box pews,* open pews with chunky 'cut-out' bench ends in a fleur de-lys pattern; and a solid, sensible low *screen* and attractive gates across the chancel arch. Contemporary with all this are the fine roofs; the excellent timber 'ceiling' over the ringing chamber in the tower; the *gallery* rails to the chamber with their double set of *balusters,* dated 1637; and the *communion rails* in the chancel. In a church packed with interest, of special note are: the faded St *Christopher* painting on the n. wall; the acute outward lean of the n. wall (thus the outside brick buttresses to support it); the fine

Royal Arms of Charles I over the s. door; the C13 stone coffin slabs against the w. wall; the C14 font, with battlemented rim and architectural carvings round the bowl; the poorman's box (dated 1639, as at neighbouring Quidenham), standing on a turned shaft and attached to the rear pew. On the s. wall are the imposing coats-of-arms of important local families of the C17, which will be found repeated in several *ledger-stones* throughout the church. Nearby is a coarsely restored *piscina* niche, indicating a *guild altar* here in pre-*Reformation* times; opposite, an un-lovely shore-up job in brick (from the 1630s remodelling?) where the old *rood stair* was removed. Through the beautiful, tall Decorated chancel arch now into the nobly tall chancel: the gorgeous *communion rails* have been noted already; there is also a grandly styled piscina, adjoining *dropped sill sedilia.* There is another niche, without drain, behind the altar – was this an *aumbry*? In the n. wall of the sanctuary are no less than three further recesses: at least two of them were aumbries. But what of the third, nearest the rails? If you put your head inside it (writers of church guide books are inspired to do silly things like that) you will see that it has a chimney flue going high up inside the wall – so was it a *wafer oven*? Or a welcome warmer for cold curates? In the sanctuary floor is a ledger slab to Robert Wilton, 'faithful patriot and true lover of his country', carved not only with his own coat-of-arms but with those of his three wives, who died in 1635, 1643 and 1652 respectively. Evidently a true lover of ladies too – though not, depending on which way you look at it, a very lucky one. The church has a ring of 5 bells, tenor 8-1-0 cwt.

Wilton, St James (D7): The early-C14 tower carries a graceful stone spire – one of the very few in Norfolk and most of the building is of the same period. The s. *porch* and the majority of the *nave* windows are *Perpendicular,* but note that two of them have 'Y' tracery of around 1300, and all the *chancel* window tracery is *reticulated.* The blocked *low side window* is not only unusually small, but its *trefoil* head is out of the ordinary – they were normally designed so that a shutter could be fitted easily. Walking round, notice the *holy water stoup* in the angle of a buttress by the blocked n. door and the mark of another in the s. porch, and also the fine examples of C17 headstones on the s. side; look particularly for the epitaph of Thomas Wethered and his three young children – they all died together in 1620: 'Here Root and Branches in ye Grave are laid...'. Both nave and chancel lie under single framed *scissor roofs* and, as at neighbouring Feltwell St Mary, there is a beautiful suite of C15 benches, with carved top rails, pierced backs, and figures on the arms; two sentry box groups symbolising Mercy ministering to prisoners are to the left of the door, and there is a fine shepherd with his flock on the first bench end on the right going up the nave (if you sit in the pew you will see his dog as well, with a slain wolf hung by a nail). A number of bench ends are modern replacements and it is good practice to pick them out. All the Perpendicular nave windows have deep *dropped sills* with tall image niches in two of them, and it is likely that there were *guild altars* in front of them. Behind the Victorian pulpit is the outline of the door to the *rood loft stair,* and the way that the late-C15 *screen* tracery is truncated at the sides indicates that it once stood further to the w. It has been extensively renewed, but don't overlook the original carvings of *Green Man* heads at the top of the e. side. Within a big *ogee* arched tomb recess on the n. side is a superb honey coloured chest, with a pattern of flat rosettes lying within roundels, themselves forming part of an overall window tracery pattern. Estimates of its age vary, but I favour C14 and think that it has been

altered and possibly reduced in length. The little *piscina* also looks as though it too was more elaborate once, and below is a very rare thing – a floor piscina 1ft. 9in. square. This was probably installed as an easy method of converting a single to a double piscina in the late C13 when they were in vogue. (See also Barton Bendish).

Wimbotsham, St Mary (C5): A church that has seen many alterations but which is basically *Norman.* You will notice this first in the doorways; that to the n. is fairly simple, but the s. doorway has double shafts, one pair with a spiral pattern, the other with *chevron* decoration. The arch has *billet,* rope and bobbin motifs and there is a creature's head at the top – this was probably the main entrance originally. The stumpy C14 tower has small two-*light* bell openings, a C15 w. window and a decorative set of C19 battlements. Within, a fascinating mixture of styles and periods. The *chancel* arch is pure and massive Norman, with double columns to the w, and simple roll mouldings. Beyond it, an 1853 chancel with an incredibly elaborate neo-Norman *apse.* When the chancel was rebuilt, there were traces of a Norman arch within the e. wall and the foundations of the original apse were uncovered outside. And so, the original form was recreated with typically Victorian bravura. The *nave* walls were heightened to carry a new roof but the panelled form was retained and the original leaf *bosses* re-used – some of them have grotesque faces and there are two angels at the e. end. The *rood loft* stairs go up from a window embrasure on the n. side of the nave and there is an *angle piscina* opposite with all the stonework re-cut. The bench ends are carved with a fine array of animals and grotesques, with a cowled figure at the front on the s. side and, in place of the usual *poppy-head* on the next pew, a large standing figure holding a shield. The muzzled bear and the pig are particularly satisfying and have that true medieval feel, both literally and visually. And then we find that everything here was carved by that C19 master craftsman James Rattee, born at Fundenhall in 1820 and creator of the *reredos* at Ely. There is a strange and telling contrast between the monstrous drum of a font or the fungoid *corbels* in the chancel and this honest, vivid artistry in wood. They both sought to recreate the past, but the carver succeeded where the mason failed.

Winfarthing, St Mary (H7): A neatly proportioned little church of the *Decorated* and *Perpendicular* periods, characterised by a most agreeable range of window traceries which are alike in looking as crisp and correct as if they were completed yesterday. What we see today is in three progressions: the *chancel* came first, with its graceful 'Y' traceried windows to n. and s. and the e. window in typical intersecting form. Next, the *nave* and s. *aisle* – on the n. side, and in the w. end of the s. aisle, lacey *reticulated* tracery, but contained in very tall, slender arches, compressing but in no way detracting from the tracery, and giving a most individual effect; on the s. side, Perpendicular windows of late insertion. *Clerestory* of *quatrefoils* in round frames – though those on the s. side are Victorian replacements, albeit in exact replica of the C14 originals. Then in the C15 came the tower and *porch* – though the tower, interestingly, has belfry openings which faithfully mirror the C14 spirit of the rest of the church, 'Y' traceried on the e. side and crisply geometrical on the other three. Inside, the church is rather sparse and plain, but appealing, under timbered roofs so spruce you might think they were as zealously dusted as is the rest of this lovingly cared for little place, and with walls overall immaculately colour washed. Though nave and chancel roofs are modern, that in the s. aisle has its original C15, *arch-braced* timbers, with battlemented *wall plates* and moulded *wall posts*. The *arcade* is C15 with octagonal pillars – with a slot in the easternmost pillar where a *parclose screen* would have been fitted round an aisle chapel in pre-*Reformation* days. Where the altar of that chapel would have stood is now a massive C16 oak chest, but the *piscina* is still there in the s. wall – very large, with a big, cusped *ogee* arch. Starting well up the wall in the n.e. corner are the steps of the old *rood stair*. In the serene, uncluttered chancel is another piscina, again very large, with a boldly *cusped* arch and an eight-leaf drain; adjoining it are plain *dropped sill sedilia*. In modern stained glass (1957) by George King & Son in the n.w. window of the chancel, an ancient curiosity of Winfarthing is recalled – a figure kneels, emotionally, head dropped in exhaustion, holding a great sword. In the s. aisle chapel there was once preserved a sword, known as 'The Good Swerde of Winfarthing', left there by a thief who had taken sanctuary here and subsequently escaped. It came to be regarded as a relic and was visited by pilgrims, what happened to it, no-one knows. Lastly, to an existing curiosity, the *Norman* font – it is large and bulbous with a plain octagonal top on an equally large round base which stands on a square stepped pedestal, with little stumpy legs at the corners, two of them carved with

inscrutable, 'classical' faces which might look down from an early Greek temple, one leg plain, the rest spiralled like barley sugar. The church has a ring of 6 bells, tenor 9-0-4 cwt.

Winterton, Holy Trinity & All Saints (K4): A very lofty (132ft.) tower, begun in the C14 and completed or remodelled in the C15. The design has a satisfying unity, due partly to the clever variation on the corner buttresses, from square at the bottom to diagonal at the top. The *base course* and the parapet with its *gargoyles* and pinnacles are of high quality. In late spring, yellow wall-flowers bloom in patches all up the s. face – not good for the fabric perhaps, but endearing. The C15 *porch* is a large ambitious piece which now lacks its upper room. The carving in the arch *spandrels* has come to look like a sponge, but the dedication inscription above the door can still be read, and the coats of arms point to a connection with Sir John Fastolf of Caister Castle (Shakespeare is said to have based the name of his memorable character Falstaff upon him – though not the character himself, for this Caister Sir John was a fine and noble soldier). There was a full-scale restoration of the church in the 1870s and little of the original work in the C14 *chancel* and C15 *nave* can be seen: but the interior is impressive, and the modern roof spans no less than 34ft. Just beyond the *screen*, on the *chancel* n. wall, is a memorial with an unusual Christian name – 'Persis', the wife of John Lens. The modern *communion rails* have flame tracery of very high quality. At the w. end of the church is the unique Fisherman's Corner, where everything is made from ships or has been to sea.

Witton (near Norwich), St Margaret (J5): A tiny, well-cared for church, only a step from the busy A47 yet seemingly in deepest, peaceful countryside. Heavily restored and re-roofed in 1902, with a *chancel* rebuilt in 1857, little of its early fabric is in evidence – the *nave's* original structure is probably C14, but the window traceries are replacements. Presumably there was originally a western tower, as can be seen from the layout inside (tower arch and stair turret) but there is now a rather attractive octagonal *bell turret* perched on the w. gable of the nave – possibly C17. Inside, the Victorian chancel in *Early English* style, including the somewhat overstated chancel arch, is rather agreeable, with plenty of colour. In the *nave*, the pulpit is modelled on one at Croydon designed by *Sir Gilbert Scott*. The neat font is crisply carved with miniature 'windows', largely showing detailed *Decorated* tracery at its high phase. Nearby, by the entrance door, a nice little figure *brass* to Juliana Anyell, about 1500, with an inscription revealing her as a widow and *vowess*. There's a rubbing of it on the n. wall adjacent.

Witton-by-Walsham, St Margaret (J2): Distant from its village, this attractive church has a fine round tower, the lower part possibly *Saxon* (opinion varies), the upper section – where flint is delightfully mixed with sun-glowing pink brick – is a C15 addition. Very probably Saxon too, tucked in behind the tower, are the s.w. *quoins* of the *nave*, large rough blocks of *carstone*. The nave n. side presents an intriguing prospect: there is a *clerestory* range with rather coarse early-C14 Y-tracery – but no *aisle* below; above the modern vestry (built around the ancient n, door) are two tiny round windows, deeply splayed, which are thought to be part of a range in an earlier Saxon church of C10, or even late-C9 date; then come two square *Perpendicular* windows. The *chancel* windows are all renewed. The church's interior is serene and full of interest. A good *arch-braced roof* to the nave, with simply carved *wall plates* and heavy, deep *wall posts* descending between the clerestory windows. The tower stair juts into the nave. Simple C15 font. Attractive *arcade* on s. side, C14 like its aisle. The easternmost column of the arcade looks earlier, possibly C13 *Transitional*, contemporary perhaps with the remains of a filled-in window immediately behind the C15 chancel arch. The aisle has early Decorated window tracery in three windows, a fourth with Y-tracery. The easternmost window is cut away to form a low-sill seat, with a *piscina* adjoining, its plainly carved head cut from one piece of stone. In this corner are some rudimentary old *box pews*. The chancel is graced by beautiful two-seat C13 *sedilia*, with graceful arches and *dog-tooth* moulding. Below the simple piscina niche are two *brasses*, one of especial interest. It reads:

> Heare lyeth berried the boddyis of
> Thomas Parmenter and Francis his wife
> who weare maried 47 year together, and
> Thomas Paramenter died 12 days before
> Hollimvs 1631. His wife died one St
> Stevens day 1627.

That is a rare and interesting use of 'Hollymus' for Christmas. Nearby is an inscription without date to Henry Hemsley, once vicar here. To l. of the altar, a third inscription, invoking prayers for Thomas Calke, 1519. On the n. wall are two

splendid C18 monuments to members of the Norris family, that to Elizabeth Norris, 1769, being as opulent and unusual in its rococo design; its wording is a moving offering of a husband's radiant love and devotion to his young wife, for Elizabeth – 'She looked like Nature in the world's first spring' – died aged 28.

Wiveton, St Mary (G1): A handsome *Perpendicular*. The tracery in the big, fine windows has flowing forms contained within Perpendicular *mullions* reaching to the top of the arch, suggesting the *Decorated* forms used before the *Black Death*. C15 *clerestory* windows. They include an e. end *nave* window, which lit the *rood loft*. The tower is basically earlier than the body of the church. The large e. window in the *chancel*, with its graceful, simple interlacing tracery, is of the early part of the C14. Standing outside the e. window, look at the interesting *flushwork* panelling set into the chancel walls; it might well be some of the very earliest on record, possibly as early as 1316. The church has two fine *porches*, n. and s. Inside, St Mary's is severe but grand. Roofs are simple *arch-braced* and the nave has a C15 five-bay *arcade* and matching tower arch. The chancel arch is probably contemporary. Over the chancel arch, *Royal Arms* of the Hanoverians. Below the arch, remnants of the *rood screen* which is said to have been in its original place until 1863, when *Thomas Jekyll* directed repairs and restoration; he clad the roofs internally, repaired some of the windows while preserving sills and mouldings. He directed that 'as little distinction as possible shall exist between appearance of new and old work' and it is difficult to tell the one from the other. The octagonal font, on its carved and canopied base, is C15. In the *aisles*, all the windows are set within *arcades*, and are let down to provide seats – as at Cley, Blakeney and Tunstead. In s. aisle, a huge iron-bound 'charity chest'; and above it on the wall, a *brass* to Raulf Grenewey, 1558, citizen and alderman of London, with merchants' marks, arms of the Grocers' Company, and his bequests to Wiveton which still operate. In chancel, a *piscina* and *dropped sill sedilia*; the e. window has slim *jambs*, with tiny, moulded capitals – typical *Early English*. The church has some good brasses: before the pulpit steps, a fine set, complete with coat-of-arms, for George Brigge of Letheringsett, 1597, and Ann his wife; beside the pulpit, a 'cadaver' brass for George Brigge's great-great-grandfather, Thomas Brigg, 1470; nearby, in centre of chancel, a little brass to a priest, William Bishop, 1512. Outside, several headstones in the churchyard are worth examination. The church has a ring of 6 bells, tenor 12 cwt.

Wolferton, St Peter (C3): The byroad to the church is lined with rhododendrons and tall pines, and the setting itself is beautiful. Mainly *carstone* here, and the early-C14 tower has large round *sound-holes* and *Decorated* tracery in the bell openings. The rest of the building is the same period – *reticulated* tracery in the e. window, doorways of about 1300, pretty Decorated tracery in the *porch* windows and a fine pointed gable over the *priest's door*. Three restorations in 20 years – the last by the Prince of Wales in 1886, wrought a great change and much of what one sees now is new work. The C15 *nave* roof was first lowered and then altered, although the *tie-beams* and the tall *wall post* figures are original; the *chancel* was given a lush angel roof and new pews and pulpit came in. The *aisles* and w. end are clear of pews now, and this has given a wonderfully spacious feeling to what is a large church anyway. The pink flush on parts of the C14 *arcades* bears witness to a fire that gutted the building in 1486, but note that the windows have the *ogee* shape or the *cusped* 'Y' tracery of the C14. Another survival is very puzzling – a pair of blocked ogee arches low in the w. wall of the n. aisle. Wolferton is very close to the Wash marshes so was this perhaps a travellers' shrine like the one at Walpole St Andrew? The deep C15 font bowl has panelled sides, and above the tower arch are the *Royal Arms* embroidered by the vicar's daughter in 1844. Also at the w. end, some C12/C13 stone coffins and by the n. door, a fine C17 Florentine wooden lectern in black and gilt, with masks on each side. Many churches had *wafer ovens* to bake communion bread and the one in the base of the tower has a flue that emerges outside not far from the ground. The s. aisle chapel is enclosed by a late-C14 *parclose screen* with graceful ogee arches and a delightful range of delicate tracery; most of it is original, and the rest very good C19 work, including some of the tiny heads. The late-C15 n. aisle *screen* is much plainer, with a narrow band of tracery at the top and the chapel there has a heavily carved Elizabethan melon-legged table. The top of the *rood screen* is modern, but the C15 uprights are nicely moulded although very little remains of the painted figures in the panels. That is compensated for by a huge wall painting over the chancel arch. The Christ in Majesty at the top is C19 and much of the rest was touched up, but there are tall angels either side holding the shafts of square banners which bear the *Instruments of the Passion* – look for the pincers, sponge, dice and knife on the n., and the cock crowing atop a pillar on the s.; above, two more angels float, blowing long trumpets. The bright, clean gleam of the fine silver lectern catches the eye even from the w. end – given by Queen Alexandra in 1871 when she was Princess of Wales. In the chancel, the C14 stepped *sedilia* have five-leaf arches and free-standing smooth columns. Most of the church has been refloored, but see how light dapples the old *pamments* round the font – a beautiful effect.

Wood Dalling, St Andrew (G3): The C15 tower is very handsome – four *drip courses*, good *sound-holes* and, like the *clerestory*, dressed white flints. The *chancel* is C13, with three *lancets* in the n. wall and a tall *priest's doorway* akin to that at Castle Acre. The e. window has good flowing tracery and the *ogee arch* of the *piscina* has an exceptionally nice headstop – the finely moulded features are perfect. The C15 s. *porch* has an upper chamber reached by a stair which ends at a door 6ft. above the floor, a possible indication that it was used as a treasury. The e. window of the s. *aisle* has a space below it designed for a *reredos* but no trace remains. There is a fine recumbent effigy of a priest at the e. end of the n. aisle but the head, neck, and hair have been re-cut. There are *brasses* to Robert Dockyng (d.1465) priest, (s. aisle), John Crane (d.1507) – a 17in. figure by the pulpit, and to John and Thomas Bulwer (1517), (e. end of *nave*). The last has only the inscription and two attendant children, and the stone was used again in 1726.

Wood Norton, All Saints (G3): The tower has a warm red brick C18 upper stage with battlements, and the arched bell openings are filled with honey-comb screens of brick. The C14 s. *porch* is of much better quality than the rest and probably came from a wealthy donor. The arch is tall and thin, and there are *crocketted* pinnacles, angle buttresses decorated with little hoods on the *set-offs*, and the porch has its own *gargoyles*. The bowl of the C14 octagonal font has an unusual curved profile and stand on a short plain stem; its C17 painted cover is topped by a gilt dove. Just why a wicker bath chair is in attendance is not clear. The *chancel* is C14 but the *angle piscina* with its slender column is about 1300, and so is the *priest's door*. There is a big head of a pig with extended tongue as a *stop* to the blocked arch in the s. wall. The pulpit is a curious Victorian essay – three panels on a plinth that was going to be the real thing but then lost confidence. For epitaph hunters the churchyard yields a rich harvest – mainly C19 but some C18, ranging from the quietist 'This Mortal must Put on Immortality' (Susan Dewig 1713 s. of *nave*) to 'Dear George is safe, all his sorrows are o'er' (George Wright 1868 s. of nave).

Wood Rising, St Nicholas (F5): This tiny village with fewer than forty people has a right to be proud of its little church. The tower collapsed some time before 1740, and the rubble lies where it fell, in a grass-covered mound. The medieval bell frame was put together again and now squats under a deep thatch in the corner of the churchyard, with one C19 bell that can be chimed. The s. *porch* has been restored and there are *Perpendicular* windows in the *nave* and *aisle*, but the fabric is largely C14. This is the period of the little *trefoil* window within a circle at the w. end of the s. aisle and of the *chancel* e. window. There was a time when *barrel organs* were quite common, but now Norfolk has only five in working order, and one is here on the C19 w. *gallery*. Built by Flight and Robson in 1826 and restored in 1957, the little pipes in their Cuban mahogony case look very sprightly. One of the three barrels was replaced in 1960 (the only order from a church for 80 years!) and the repertoire of 30 hymns is now reserved for special occasions. The C14 font is fairly coarse work, with a simple pattern of shields, and the *Jacobean* pulpit is similarly modest. There is only one aisle, with its floor raised 15in. above the rest at the e. end, and this gives the interior a most agreeable lack of symmetry. To add to that effect, a table tomb is set within an arch between aisle and chancel and there are substantial *squints* cut through the walls at either end of it. By the alignment one can assume that there were once two altars in the aisle – one at the e. end and one further w. The early-C15 tomb itself has no inscription and the *brasses* have gone from the shields that lie within *cusped* lozenges on the sides, but it is likely that one of the de Witchinghams (lords of the manor before the Southwells) is buried here. In the chancel there is a *double piscina* (late-C13 or early-C14) and the stepped *sedilia* have a later arch superimposed. Carefully lift the carpet in front of the altar and you will find Sir Francis Crane's grave, with a splendid coat of arms engraved on a brass oval. He had gone to Paris to be operated on for the stone in 1636 but was not as lucky as Samuel Pepys and died, having 'behaved himself like a

Wood Rising, St Nicolas: chancel arch corbel

stout and humble Christian and member of the Church of England' throughout his painful ordeal. He was Clerk to the Commons, and Charles I's secretary when Prince of Wales, but he is chiefly remembered as the man who established the famous tapestry workshops at Mortlake in 1619. In the n.e. corner of the sanctuary is the impressive tomb of Sir Richard Southwell (1564); his alabaster figure in full armour is enclosed by a table tomb supported on four fluted Doric columns, with coats of arms set in a semi-circular recess above. All is very cool and restrained, but Sir Richard the man was hardly that. His father dying young, he was brought up with Henry Howard, Earl of Surrey, and his career was typical of the unscrupulous place-seeking courtier of the C16. He was pardoned for a murder committed in 1531 on payment of an enormous fine, and then made a killing of another kind when the monasteries were suppressed. It suited him to betray his childhood friend, and Surrey was executed for treason in January 1547 – his father escaped the same fate only because Henry VIII died in the same month. Southwell flourished briefly under Mary but life in Elizabeth's reign was less kind and he fades into obscurity. It was his grandson Robert – Jesuit, poet, martyr, whom history rightly honours. Holbein's painting of Sir

Richard – clean shaven with a cold and calculating eye, is in the Uffizi Gallery, Florence, and the drawing for it is at Windsor. As you leave, do look at the chancel arch *corbel* on the s. side – absolute amazement, medieval style!

Woodbastwick, St Fabian & St Sebastian (J4): There is no other church dedicated jointly to these saints in England, and it is picturesquely sited by one of the most photographed village greens in Norfolk. It underwent a thorough-going restoration by *Sir Gilbert Scott* in the 1880s, and apart from the tower *sound-holes* and the C14 *chancel* windows, not much of the old fabric can be identified. The high thatched roof is terminated by pretty crowstepped gables in red brick, and within, it has braced *king posts* which are not often seen in Norfolk. Scott inserted an unusual *tie-beam* across the chancel to delineate the sanctuary. The C15 *screen* has a beautifully solid look at the head because the two layers of tracery of the arches have an infill cut to shape between them. The tracery above the arches is beautifully delicate and reminscent of Scarning, near East Dereham. There is a series of very well designed modern mural tablets to the Cator family who were Lords of the manor.

Woodton, All Saints (I6): Well away from the nucleus of the village, backed by a range of big trees and approached up a pleasant grassy track. The round *Norman* tower has a C15 octagonal top with *flushwork* in the battlements. Before going inside, have a look at the e. window of the s. *aisle*. The *reticulated* tracery has beautifully intricate mouldings and the *hood mould*, crowned with a *crocket*, has a pair of attractive female *headstops*. *Nave* and *chancel* date from about 1300 and the s. aisle was added a little later. Its *arch-braced roof* is unchanged and has delicate tracery in the *spandrels*. The aisle chapel must have been quite lavish, either as a Lady chapel or for a village *guild*. The inside of the window matches the quality of the outside, with a bearded head at the apex of the arch and a band of Michelmas daisy floral motifs in the outer moulding. There are dainty little figures in medieval glass of St *Catherine* and St *Margaret* in the tracery *lights*. Two image ledges in the s. wall and a large *squint* through to the high altar complete the picture. Woodton Hall used to stand nearby, and the old road ran to the n. of the church. For that reason, the main entrance was the n. porch (now the vestry) and it has a good, small scale, arch-braced roof. By the time of the 1880 restoration the road had been re-routed and so the s. porch

was added. Standing on a new stone base, the *Jacobean* pulpit is satisfyingly solid – perspective panels with lots of split-bobbin mouldings. Behind it is the stair to the old *rood loft*, with an odd and tiny window halfway up. The chancel C13 *piscina* is quite unusual – there are stumps of pillars each side of the *trefoil* arch and the drain is set in a half-round *corbel*. The e. window has *reticulated* tracery and twin attached columns each side with *dog-tooth* decoration running between them and continuing over the arch. Below the window is an excellent example of a double *aumbry* (the doors are not original). The glass in the e. window by *Lavers & Barraud* dates from the 1830s and was made for Tenderton in Kent. When it was restored in 1932, the parish there took a dislike to the devil that should figure in the centre scene. The rector of Woodton seized the opportunity to buy the lot and brought it back here. Then it was found that it wouldn't quite fit, and so the devil had to go anyway – or most of him. In the scene of the Temptation in the Wilderness (centre panel) you can see the remains of one olive green wing just below Christ's right hand. The Suckling family were lords of the manor here from time immemorial until 1810. In 1749, Catherine Suckling married the Rev. Edmund Nelson at Beccles and gave birth to one *Horatio Nelson* at Burnham Thorpe rectory in 1758. So it is that we have a lovely portrait memorial to the great-great-grandmother of England's hero in the sanctuary at Woodton. She was Ann Suckling who died in 1653 and her alabaster figure, with one hand on her breast, is beautifully and sensitively sculpted, kneeling within an arch under a curly *pediment* and cluster of shields. The church has an excellent ring of 6 bells, tenor 7-2-4 cwt.

Wormegay, St Michael & All Angels & Holy Cross (C4): The village clusters round its castle mound, but the small church is over half a mile away to the e. along a stony track, and its C15 *carstone* tower rises gaunt above the fields. Until the Dissolution of the Monasteries, Wormegay had an Augustinian priory down by the river Nar, dedicated to the Virgin, St John and Holy Cross and the rectors of this church and of Tottenhill were appointed by the Prior. It is said that the worn Crucifixion panel halfway up the w. face of the tower came from the priory and its theme certainly fits the dedication neatly. The tower, with its small *quatrefoil sound-holes* and *Perpendicular* bell openings was the only part of the church that escaped a virtual rebuilding in the 1890s. The Perpendicular e. window looks right but was apparently preceded by an original that had *Decorated* tracery. Inside, a C14 font with slightly sloping sides and small shields set in pointed quatrefoil panels. *Nave* and *chancel* are under one roof with no intervening arch, but on the n. side there are blocked doorways that led to an outside *rood stair,* and the two blocked *lancets* between the modern windows show that it was a C13 chancel. There are still two large niches in the e. wall with rather battered *ogee arches cusped* and *crocketted,* and their interiors are still painted with mock vaulting complete with *bosses* and simulated curtains hang from rods below. In the sanctuary, a rough chair has been made by using the backboard of a C17 pulpit. It has side carvings of eagles and the top panel is carved: 'Cathedra 1624 Wormegay'. Not to be outdone, a C19 rector had the lower panel inscribed 'Henslowe 1848 ministro'. It stands on a C13 grave slab, and on the window ledge opposite there is a fragment of a larger and much more splendid slab which has beautifully undercut stiff-leaf foliage in the edge moulding, a floriated cross, and recessed *trefoils* in the corners. This too, no doubt, came from the priory and perhaps also the fragment of a *pillar piscina* lying close by.

Worstead, St Mary (J3): William Paston, 1378-1444, wrote to his cousin Robert, 'I shall make my doublet all Worstead, for the glory of Norfolk.' Though the riches of the *wool trade* that made the name of this village known throughout the world have long since gone, its church is very much a part of 'the glory of Norfolk', Apart from the mid-C15 vestry, the whole church was built in one continuous operation from the *chancel* in 1379 to the tower twenty years later. It replaced a smaller predecessor and the size is impressive – 130ft. long. The 109ft. tower with its big *sound-holes* is splendid; a double *base course* is topped by *flushwork* arcading and the w. door and window are linked within a single composition. The n. door has no *porch* but is embellished with flower carvings and a line of shields above. Entry is by way of a sumptuous s. porch, two storied with its own stair turret. There are triple niches over an arch enriched with decoration and the *groined* ceiling has a Coronation of the Virgin on the centre boss, with the *Symbols of the Evangelists* around it. Once inside the church, the impact is one of great space and light. Improvements in the C15 gave the whole building more height when the *chancel* arch was lifted and the great *hammer-beam roof* inserted. The strain that this

subsequently caused probably accounts for the afterthought *flying buttresses* over the aisle roofs. The chancel *screen* is one of the tallest in the county, and has a nice folded label inscription along the middle rail which referred to John Arblaster and his wife Alice who gave it in 1512. There is a little *brass* to him just in front of the screen, and it is a nice touch that it is protected now by a thick fleecy rug made locally. The paintings on the screen panels have been so confused by Victorian essays in restoration that a competent listing is difficult. Apart from the *Apostles,* the two at the extreme right are probably St *William* and St *Uncumber.* Both n. and s. chapels also have screens with painted panels; those on the n. are Saints *Bartholomew, Philip, Lawrence* and *Thomas of Canterbury*; those on the s. are Saints *Peter, Paul, John the Baptist,* and *Stephen.* Notice how the screens were originally linked by matching painted patterns across the walls and arches n. and s. of the chancel arch. The n. chapel has an interesting and unusual survival – the original altar *reredos* has gone, but the painted frame remains with a panel of beautifully varied decoration below it. The ringers' *gallery* under the tower has an elaborately carved front with an inscription:

> This work was made in ye yer of God MCCCCCI [1501] at ye propur cost of ye catell [probably meaning candle] of ye chyrche of Worsted callyd ye batchellers lyte yt God preserve wt all the benefactors of ye same now and ever, amen, then wer Husbondes [ie. wardens] Christofyer Rant and Jeffery Deyn.

The screen below is beautifully delicate and could well be taken for original work, but an early-C19 engraving does not show it and another of the same period describes it as 'lately erected'. This squares with the painted panels on it which are copies of Sir Joshua Reynolds' work at New College Oxford, The font stands imposingly on three steps with the top level in the shape of a cross, and the bowl has an overall pattern of *quatrefoils.* The cover is really only the skeletal remains of quite an elaborate construction, but it was well restored in 1954 and is very graceful in its present form. The *nave* has a most satisfying suite of oak C18 *box pews.* The interiors have been modified but the chest-high doors with beautifully made fielded panels are intact. The tall draught screens at the w. end have little fluted pillars at the ends. An arduous programme of restoration has been in progress since 1964 and there has been a gradual transformation. Work

Worstead, St Mary: Font & cover

on the roof has been completed – it looks superb, and memories of leprous green stains and general decay have given way to clean creamwashed walls and general good health. It is a heartening example of what can be achieved by local initiative, faith and hard work, backed by national support. Links with Worstead's famous past are maintained by St Mary's Guild of Weavers Spinners and Dyers, and there is a fascinating array of 14 looms in the n. aisle with much work in progress.

Worthing, St Margaret (F4): A tiny church isolated from its equally tiny village. The round

tower had lost its top in the C18 and now has a flue running up the angle – with a faintly domestic chimney pot on top. The *chancel* has completely disappeared. There is a simple C12 n. doorway (blocked), but the s. doorway is confident *Norman* work – single columns with spiralled *capitals*, and a bold zig-zag arch. There is a well defined *mass dial* on the left hand side that will have been used before the *porch* was built. Notice that some care was taken with the outer arch – there are floral motifs on the inside as well as the outside moulding. The diminutive cream-washed interior has one or two surprises – the font for example. The base of an old Norman font rests on a cube of brickwork, and on top of that there are two sections of a *churchyard cross*. The upper one has been hollowed out to form a bowl, and this is now the font. Not beautiful, but a fascinating example of local ingenuity. Close by, a good *Jacobean* chest, with rustic *blind arcaded* panels and chip carving above them. The blank e. wall shows the line of the old chancel arch, and to the left there is a lovely little C14 niche. It has everything in miniature – vaulting, canopy, *crockets* and pinnacles; two tiny birds jut out as brackets, and even the canopy has two miniscule niches of its own. There is a stone that rests outside against the porch which tells its own sad story. Marsham Pigg died in 1748, when he was only three months old: 'O cruel death that would not spare / One favourite child that was our dear'.

Wramplingham, St Peter & St Paul (H5): Charming hilltop position over the little village, with views across to Barford. The round *Norman* tower has a tall brick *lancet* to the w. and another, later one to the s. which *Cautley* called a *low side window*. If so, it is unusual, particularly as the *chancel* has its own. The C14 octagonal top of the tower has *Decorated* bell openings. A walk round the outside first, to see the plain *Norman* doorway (re-sited further e. when a new n. *aisle* was added in the 1870s – they used the Decorated windows again too), and then on to the chancel. This is the really memorable feature of Wramplingham. It was built about 1280, and has a range of lancets n. and s.. Seen from the outside, the *hood moulds* are linked, and at each end a *headstop* looks inwards towards its opposite number some distance away. Though worn with time and weather, these little heads are finely cut and very individual. The e. window is an 1863 version of *Early English* that does not measure up to the real thing. Inside, the chancel is the attraction again. The deep splays of the lancets are separated by slim shafts, with six marvellous *headstops* and stiff leaf decoration on the rest. A measure of the quality is the fact that each shaft has a concave chamfer each side with a *trefoil* hood, and from them peep tiny heads not much more than an inch across. With such a design it is strange that a two-*light* window was placed over the *sedilia*; only the stumps of the double *piscina* canopy remain. *Communion rails* of 1939 – a very good piece of work, and some medieval bench ends in the n. aisle, with remnants of animals on the arms and one complete face.

Wreningham, All Saints (H6): When the C13 tower collapsed here in 1852, the lower part seems to have escaped much damage and there is a small brick niche above the w. window – with a decayed stone figure of a lion in it that may not always have been there. When the tower was rebuilt and the rest of the church restored, a n. *transept* was added and the old windows from the n. wall of the *nave* were re-used in its e. and w. walls. The C15 font has *quatrefoil* panels in the bowl and there is a squareheaded *piscina* with a multi-*foiled* arch. The interior, with its new oak roofs and clean white walls is welcoming and neatly kept, but there is little to quicken interest. The churchyard, however, has a very pleasing array of C18 headstones; the top profiles vary a lot, and cherubs blow trumpets with abandon in the carved heads.

Wretton, All Saints (C6): The unbuttressed tower has a *lancet* w. window and two more very narrow lancets with *trefoil* heads in the second stage – probably C13, although the bell openings have later 'Y' tracery. The brick parapet, like the one on the s. *aisle* is C17 or C18 and the pinnacles were added in the late C19. Like many another the tower once had a spire on top. The s. *porch* of brick and flint nestles close to the ground and steps go down within to the entrance – a doorway which, like its blocked partner on the n. side, was probably *Norman* in origin. The *Perpendicular* e. window is tall and thin and there is one *Decorated* window in the *chancel*. Inside, the s. *arcade* of around 1300 has a crudely cut *corbel* head on one of the pillars which will have supported an image at one time. Above the tower arch, a very faded set of George III *Royal Arms* dated 1816 has most luxuriant mantling and the words 'Springfield & Sons Painters' can just be read below the motto (the only example I know produced by a named firm). Some new benches were provided in the C19, but the range

on the s. side of the *nave* is dated 1627 on one of the ends and also on the front row, where the initials of the churchwardens are carved – 'CW : IC : RW' for John Cowell and Robert Watson. The back rails of the benches have a pretty leaf design in shallow carving and this crops up again on the panelling of the reading desk – probably by the same craftsman. The C18 pulpit is in plain oak panelling, with a heavy half-round carved moulding on the rim. Behind it, note the blocked top and bottom doors to the vanished *rood loft*. The *screen* itself has been renewed and given a new cornice but some of the tracery is original. Little of note in the chancel, but there is an *aumbry* in the n. wall and the *piscina* survives within a square plain niche. One can assume that All Saints once had its quota of medieval stained glass and two fragments remain in the window by the pulpit – one of them a golden *chalice* and *host* right at the top.

Wroxham, St Mary (I4): In one of the centres of the popular Broads holiday area, the church is quietly sited above a steep bluff, and looking west, the view is all treetops and greenery. The C15 tower has good angle buttresses, well defined *string courses*, and pretty four-leaf *soundholes*. Entry is by way of an excellent *Norman* doorway with a deep blue colouring. Triple miniature columns with plaited rings carry *capitals* which sprout little grotesque heads and figures; the concentric rings of the arch have a whole variety of decorative carvings. The C15 *porch* had an upper room at one time, but only part of the stairs now remains. The entrance door is at least as old as the porch and the handle may well be two hundred years older. The s. *aisle* was re-built in 1825, and the crude and graceless *arcades* may date from then but could be earlier. At the n. end of the n. aisle is a monument to Robert Blake-Humfrey, who lost a leg serving with the Buffs in the Peninsular, but still survived to the ripe old age of 91. The glass in the e. window by *William Wailes* is dull in spirit, garish in execution, and dear at £101 15 0d in 1851. Much nicer is the 1882 s. window by Thomas Curtis: lots of flowers and foliage around Christ and Mary in the Garden – she with a great mane of crinkly hair. It's probably significant that the first essay in ecclesiastical gothic by *Anthony Salvin*, was the Trafford mausoleum of 1829 in the churchyard, n. of the tower. He went on to remodel Norwich Cathedral s. transept and Norwich Castle, with more enthusiasm than sensibility. The church has an excellent ring of 6 bells, tenor 9-2-0 cwt.

Wymondham, St Mary & St Thomas of Canterbury (H5): The abbey church has a setting to match its own magnificence, and the long approach paths from the town are bordered by tall and craggy Scots pine which provide a perfect foil for the uncompromising bulk of the mighty towers. This is patently no ordinary parish church – the size alone betrays it, and one has to go back to the C12 to trace its story. *Norman* knight William D'Albini held office under Henry I and had been rewarded after the Conquest by grants of land which included Wymondham. His brother was Abbot of the great Benedictine foundation at St Albans, and so when William decided to establish a monastery that would also serve as a parish church for his manor, Wymondham became one of the many offshoots of St Albans – a Priory with an initial complement of twelve monks. Building began in 1107 and was completed in 1130 – a huge church over 200ft. long with twin towers at the w. end, a big centre tower with *transepts* n. and s. of it, and a presbytery with chapels to the e.. Cloisters, chapter house and domestic buildings were grouped on the s. side. The 'dual use' concept of the founder proved disastrous and for the next 300 years monks and parishioners bickered and fought over their rights, with a climax in 1249 when the dispute was carried to the Pope in Rome. As a result the parish were allotted the *nave*, n. *aisle* and the n.w. tower, while the monks controlled the rest. In the C14 the *crossing tower* became unsafe so the monks pulled it down and built another further w., and this is the tower now at the e. end of the church. Walk round the outside and you will see the humps in the ground that mark the old crossing, and then look up to admire the soaring arch and octagonal double stage above it – a ruin that is dramatically beautiful. Having borrowed the n.w. tower for their bells, the monks then moved them back and blocked the entrance of it so that the parish could not use it, and this triggered off another sulphurous dispute that was bad enough for Henry IV to send the Archbishop of Canterbury down to sort it out. As a result, the parishioners won the right to have their own bells, and 3800 of them signed a petition to the king to let them build a new tower. After a further twenty years of wrangling and the advent of a lord of the manor with a talent for diplomacy, the great 142ft. w. tower was put in hand in 1448 and rose to the w. of the old twin towers. The size of the churchyard makes it possible to stand away from it and take in its fine proportions and massive

strength – and also to regret that the steady upward march of the richly panelled buttresses was never completed by pinnacles and battlements. One of the stages of the tower is strongly marked by a band of chequer work and the massive double bell openings lie under lovely *ogee hood moulds*. The w. doorway is deeply recessed, with tall niches either side, and above it in the centre of a line of blank shields is a helm and coat of arms. The effect of the w. window is largely destroyed by the ugly reinforcing shaft up the centre. Not content with a new tower, the parish rebuilt the n. aisle on a much grander scale, doubling its width, and by this time the old Norman nave had been given a new *clerestory*. Its range of three-*light* windows have deep splays adorned with decorative carving and shields, under hood moulds crowned by *finials*. The n. side has *flushwork*, and note how it is enriched by relief panelling in the two easternmost bays to correspond with the sanctuary within. A traceried parapet was begun at the w. end but never completed. The n. *porch* is part and parcel of this mid-C15 surge of rebuilding and matches its richness and solidity. The stepped battlements are pierced with *quatrefoils*, and the pair of windows of the upper room are flanked by canopied niches. Under them, a row of quatrefoils with shields and crowned 'M's alternating, and the *spandrels* of the doorway have the *censing* angels of the *Annunciation*. After the turbulence of its early history, the Priory became an Abbey in its own right in 1448 and lived out its last hundred years at peace with its neighbours; in 1539 the last Abbot, Elisha Ferrers, quietly transformed himself into the Vicar of Wymondham and, having briefly tasted higher preferment, was buried in the sanctuary in 1548. The parish by that time was busily rebuilding the s, aisle, using the now disused parts of the Abbey as a quarry for materials. And now for the inside. The first impression is one of an enduring solidity – mass vying with space. The Norman nave pillars have largely been squared off, but those at the w. end are complete, and have between them the half round shafts rising towards the roof that remind one of Norwich Cathedral. Over the nave *arcades*, a beautifuly compact triforium (arcaded wall passage) has coupled columns on the inner faces, and if you look at the easternmost bays on the s. side you will see the window and slits that the monks made in the early C15 to keep an eye on what the parish was getting up to, from the dormitory they had built over the old s. aisle. The C15 nave *hammer-beam roof* is a beauty –

Wymondham, St Mary & St Thomas

steeply pitched, with a host of angels. They stretch out from the braces and there are more perched on the *wall plates* (note that these are larger and more elaborate over the sanctuary). Ridge and main intersections are embellished with flamboyant flower *bosses* and the whole roof has a richness in execution and unity of design that mark it as one of the best – if not the best in the county. Standing under it, the visitor may experience a curious feeling of being cut off and enclosed, for unlike most churches, here there is neither e. nor w. window. When the Benedictines built their new e. tower in 1400, out of prudence or pure spite they threw a wall 6ft. thick across the arch and cut the old vista brutally in half. And so it remained until the C20 when the great *reredos*, designed by *Sir Ninian Comper*, was erected in 1919 as a war memorial. A separate benefaction added the *tester* and *rood* (which rests on the same *corbels* that supported its predecessor), Christ in Glory is surrounded by the figures of the Madonna and 14 saints – bottom row left to right: the Annunciation, St *Peter*, St *Thomas of Canterbury*, The Blessed Virgin, St *Alban*, St *Paul*, the *Visitation*; middle row: St *George*, St *Margaret*, John the Baptist, St *John the Divine*, St *Andrew*, St *Michael*; top row: the East Anglian saints: St *Felix*, St *Etheldreda*, St *Edmund*, St *Hugh*, Mother *Julian*, St *Fursey*. Rich canopies and tabernacles, the figures and the great *rood* itself, all of it has a dull golden sheen which glints here and there as the light catches it, and imparts an incredible richness that is not easily forgotten. Turning to the w. – again no light from the blocked window, and the dark recess of the tower arch houses the elegant case of an organ expressly designed for the church by James Davis in 1793 (its original console is on show in the glass case under the *gallery*). The w. door has also been blocked off and a small gift/souvenir shop has been neatly fitted in. Above it, a fine and large *Royal Arms* of George II on canvas. The n. aisle is large enough to be a church in itself and its sumptuous roof vies with that of the nave. The *spandrels* of the hammer-beams are full of tracery, and the whole length is filled with panels enriched with *cusping*. The four easternmost bays are painted with crowned 'M's for the dedication, and form a *canopy-of-honour* over the sanctuary. Look for the angel over the second window from the e. end – it still has its original colour. The Lady chapel altar there now has a canopy-of-honour and a backdrop of rich dark blue velvet to match the *Laudian* altar cover. With no adornment save the cross and candlesticks, it is stunningly impressive. Just to the w. of the

communion rails (made from the old organ gallery) is one of the best candelabras in the county – rotate beneath to find out who made it, who gave it, and when. By the door, the font stands on three steps and dates from 1410. In the bowl panels, the *Symbols of the Four Evangelists* alternate with angels carrying shields – the *Trinity* symbol, the three crowns of Ely, three chalices, and one blank; round the stem the remains of lions and smaller figures of *woodwoses*. In 1962 it was given a tall and elegant cover in green and gold as a memorial to a former vicar. In the sanctuary to the right of the Comper *reredos* is a terracotta facade, said to commemorate the last Abbot, Elisha Ferrers. It dates from about 1525 and is probably by the same craftsman who made similar ones at Oxborough and Bracon Ash. Certainly it seems to have been cut down rather awkwardly to fit into the surrounding Norman arch. There are three deep niches panelled overall, and above a double cornice, three half round sections have short columns in front – all overlaid with attractive *Renaissance* decoration. On the second *pier* from the w. of the n. arcade is an oddity – a crowned 'M' and 'T' in *flushwork*, set in back to front. Perhaps it found a home there when the n. aisle was rebuilt, who knows! The Abbey has many good wall tablets and it is a pity that the vestry screen in the s. aisle prevents all but the tallest of us having a good look at one of the best – that to John Drake 'of this Town Esq. Captain of the Militia' (1759). It is by *Thomas Rawlins* and is a lovely piece – grey obelisk with urn and swags in front; a scrolly *pediment* over a tablet framed in pale brown marble, with two cherub heads below. As you retrace your steps towards the town, remember that Queen Elizabeth I held her court at Wymondham in 1573, and look for that date and 'R.E' on a n. clerestory buttress. Remember also rebellious Robert Kett (see glossary under *isolated churches* for detail of his place in Norfolk history) who was hanged at Norwich castle in 1549, but his brother William swung from the great west tower behind you. The church has an excellent ring of 10 bells, tenor 26-2-2 cwt.

Yaxham, St Peter (G4): A compact little church in its snug circle of trees, with a round *Saxon* tower that adds to its charm; the upper range, with two-*light* windows, is C14. In the lower section, notice the layers of *carstone* among the flints; and more pieces in the s. *aisle's* w. end wall and in the *nave* n. wall. The church is largely *Perpendicular*, but the fussy *chancel* windows are C19. Inside, all is serene. The Saxon tower arch is rough and powerful. The arch above is was probably the only entrance to begin with, when the tower was needed as a refuge. The Perpendicular *arcade* between nave and s. aisle has pillars which are alternately octagonal and *quatrefoil* and sit on rough rubble bases, around which seats may originally have been placed. The *clerestory*, the s. aisle and the nave roof are all early-C15, the latter with *arch-braces*, plus handsomely carved *wall plates*, and deep *wall posts* resting on carved *corbel* heads. There is a lovely braced arch with pierced carving in the *spandrel*, plus traces of original colour, at the e. end of the aisle. The rest of the roof is covered with flat sheets, which a villager cleverly painted to look like timber boards. There is a Perpendicular *piscina*. Opposite, the *rood stair* door, which probably linked up with the odd indentations in the wall behind the pulpit. The *screen* between aisle chapel and nave is modern; but at the w. end there is a small screen which probably once served the same duty, as a *parclose* around a chapel. The C15 chancel screen is elegant and clean lined. Furnishings generally are modern, but in the s. aisle see how the carver created a splendid array of birds and beasts on the bench ends, including on the front pew a copy of the *pelican* in the glass by *Powell & Sons* in the nave window opposite. The C14 font is superbly carved and in wonderful condition. In the window splay behind the pulpit, notice a remnant of medieval wall painting: you can just see the Christ child with a hand raised in blessing. In the chancel, some C17 wood carving in the back of the choir stalls; a good *arch-braced roof*, its *wall posts* supported by winged angels carrying shields; a ponderously restored piscina, and *dropped sill sedilia* alongside. The literary connection here is with 'England's sweetest and most pious bard', as George Borrow called William Cowper. The poet was a close friend of John Johnson, rector of Yaxham for 36 years and Johnson it was who subsequently edited Cowper's letters. See also East Dereham. The church has an excellent ring of 6 bells, tenor 12-1-14 cwt.

Yelverton, St Mary (15): It is the tower which attracts the eye. Though built of flint, it is trimly dressed at corners, parapet and around the windows in red brick and was rebuilt in 1673-

74. There are tablets on the s. side of the tower which give the names of the masons who did the work. The body of the church is largely *Decorated* and *Perpendicular*, though traces of its *Norman* fabric can be found. On the *chancel* s. side and at the w. end of the s. *aisle* are flowing C14 Decorated windows; and on the n. side a Saxo-Norman slit window next to a 'Y' traceried example of about 1300. Notice, from this spot, that the *nave* n. wall is extended upwards to make a *clerestory* to match that over the s. aisle. The s. clerestory has been renewed in recent times, but the n. side the windows are edged with *Tudor* brick. Soft brick also makes notable the small Tudor doorway – flattened arch under a square hood – in the s. aisle: not a *priest's door*, but giving access to a chapel originally. The enormous wall monument to its left, framed in similar brick, is dated 1705 and 1711. Inside, the church is light and spacious, with a handsome modern roof to the nave, a pale blue panelled one for the chancel – and the medieval *arch-braced roof* for the s. aisle, with carved *bosses*, and wheel traceries in the *spandrels*. The *arcade* is C15; the square font is obviously medieval, but has been recut. There is a fine wall monument in the s. aisle, exuberantly carved and gilded, and elegantly lettered, to Humphrey Rant, 1661; below is a *ledger-stone* to his daughter, Anne, who died aged 66 in 1698, on which is set out in forceful detail her Will & Testament of land in the parish whose income was 'forever' to be divided between the Minister and the poor of the parish – her directions to be rigidly adhered to, 'upon pain of forfeiture of the said land'. The *rood loft* entrance between aisle and nave (matching the steps in the window embrasure on the opposite side) have been ingeniously re-used to form a *sanctus bell turret*. The base of the C15 *screen* remains (with a Victorian top fitted), painted with angels and a scroll commemorating the donors, 'Thomas Hotte and Betreis ys wyf'. Thomas is remembered in one of the several *brass* inscriptions in the floor just in front of the screen; another of these brasses has a little figure, about 6in. long, with a mass of hair down to her waist, a girl named Margaret Aldriche, who died in May 1525 'in her floryching youth' – as we see her here, snub nosed and pert mouthed. In the chancel, some *poppy-heads*; a restored *piscina* and *dropped sill sedilia*.

Glossary of Terms

Abacus: A flat stone slab set on top of a pillar or pier to take the thrust of an arch springing from it. Most often seen in *Norman* and *Early English* architecture. (Compare with *impost* and *capital*).

Adam style: The four Scottish Adam brothers were distinguished architects and interior decorators. Robert and James developed an architectural style, distinctly their own, of elegance and charm and classical line. They were especially renowned for their interior work – fire-places, ceilings, furniture and other woodwork – which all showed a very Grecian influence. (See Gunton, St Andrew.)

Agnus Dei (The Lamb of God): When *St John the Baptist* saw Jesus coming he said, 'Behold the Lamb of God who takes away the sin of the world'. The words were used in the mass as early as the C5 and by the C9 wax medallions were being made on Holy Saturday from remnants of the previous year's paschal candle. In the Middle Ages, the lamb bearing a cross or flag was widely used in painting and sculpture as a symbol of Our Lord.

Aisles: The parts of the church to the n. and s. of the *nave*, and sometimes of the *chancel*, under sloping roofs which give the impression of 'extensions' to the main building. Which indeed they often were, being added to accommodate side altars (see *chantry* and *guild* altars), as well as larger congregations, and to provide processional paths – an important proviso before the *Reformation* (see under *banner stave*

lockers and *Galilee porches*). The word 'aisle' in this sense is not to be confused with the 'aisle' down which the bride demurely steps – more properly referred to as the 'pavement'.

Anchorite/anchoress (female)/**anchorite's cell:** An anchorite – the word being derived from the Greek anakhoreo, to retire – was a religious recluse who chose to be confined in a cell attached to the church, in order to devote his or her mortal existence to prayer, meditation and piety. A small outer window gave light and a way for food to be passed in – and for people to receive advice, consolation or encouragement from the recluse. Another small window, or *squint*, gave a direct view of the altar so that he or she could watch the celebration of mass. See *Julian of Norwich* and entries for Norwich St Julian's Church and Norwich St John the Baptist and the Holy Sepulchre; Fincham, King's Lynn All Saints, and Walpole St. Andrew.

Angle piscina: See *piscina*.

Anglo-Saxon: The Anglo-Saxons were the Teutonic invaders who overran Britain in the 'Dark Ages'. Between the fifth and seventh centuries Norfolk and Suffolk were settled by the Angles, who gave their name to East Anglia. *Saxon* architecture, distinctive in its simplicity, existed until it was superseded by Norman building following the Conquest of 1066 (see Appendix 2).

Annunciation: Annunciation representations are a regular subject for stained glass scenes, as well as wood and stone carvings – the Archangel Gabriel bringing the Virgin Mary the news of the Incarnation, that she would conceive a child of the Holy Ghost (Luke 1, 26-38). A splendid Annunciation may be seen in C15 glass at Bale, and a lovely C15 carving in the porch at Great Witchingham. The Feast of the Annunciation is March 25th – otherwise known as Lady Day, an important date too in the rural calendar, when tenant farmers' rents were due, and new tenancies were granted.

Antiphonal lectern: The antiphon (literally – 'before voice') is a sung verse immediately preceding the psalm, or the Canticle for the particular office or service (i.e. before the Benedictus at matins, or the Magnificat at vespers or Evensong). It was sung by the Cantor who during this office stood at the Antiphonal Lectern, on which his music was placed. (See Ranworth, St Helen, and Norwich, St John Baptist Maddermarket).

Apse/apsidal: Rounded end of a building, usually the *chancel* at the e. end in churches. Derived from Romanesque architecture, semi-circular in shape, or consisting of five sides of an octagon, and often dome-roofed or vaulted; and generally associated in Britain with *Norman* churches. (See Fritton, Hales, Heckingham, Kirstead).

Arcades: A series of arches – i.e. those down each side of the *nave* of an *aisled* church – supported by pillars. Sometimes arcades are 'closed', 'blind' or 'blank' – a decorative outline on a wall or tomb or furnishing; or when, as may often be found, an aisle has been demolished and the arcade bricked up, but leaving its pillars and arches outlined.

Arch-braced roofs: A roof carried on a simple, braced arch. (See *Roofs*, fig. 4.)

Assumption of the Virgin: The translation of the Blessed Virgin Mary, body and soul, into heaven – a theme often represented by medieval artists in painting and sculpture. The Feast of the Assumption is August 15th, a festival first initiated in the year 582 by the Roman Emperor Maurice. The Eastern Orthodox Church, with a poetic touch, celebrates the Assumption as 'The Feast of the Falling Asleep of Our Lady'. See Hemsby, Great Witchingham, Denton, Seething, Bridgham, East Harling, Walpole St Peter and Wiggenhall St Mary.

Aumbry: A small cupboard or recess in which were stored the Holy Oils used in Baptism, Confirmation and Extreme Unction (anointing of the dying person by the priest); also to house the sacred vessels used for mass. Sometimes the aumbry held the Reserved Sacrament – the consecrated bread, 'reserved' from a mass (see also *Easter Sepulchre*). The aumbry is generally found on the north side of the *chancel*, but sometimes near the *piscina* – on the south side – and in a few cases may be near the font. Originally very few parish churches had *sacristies* for storing the plate and valuables: the priest robed at the altar, his vestments being kept in a parish chest, the vessels for altar and font being placed in the aumbry. Thus chest plus aumbry equals the later vestries. Occasionally the aumbry was used in the C15 as a safe for documents, not only belonging to the church, but to parishioners, as it would be secured by door and lock. Very few of these wooden doors remain today, though the hinge and latch marks in the stone can often be made out. One complete survivor, however, can be seen at Great Walsingham.

Bacon, John the Younger (1777-1859): One of the most representative memorial sculptors of his time. One of his grand marble monuments is at Sprowston, to Lady Maria Micklethwaite, 1805, symbolising her death in childbirth. Something of a child prodigy – he was already sculpting monumental works at the age of 11 – examples of his artistry may be seen in many churches throughout England.

Ball Flower: An early C14 decorative ornament in sculpture. See 'Decorated period', Appendix 2.

Baluster: A short, decorative column, often bulging at the middle and tapering at top and bottom.

Banner-stave locker: In the late medieval period, *parish guilds* proliferated – St Peter Mancroft Church in Norwich had nine – and all had their banners to be carried in the processions which in medieval times were an important part of services on Sundays and Feast Days (see also: *Galilee porches*). Between times, the banners would be placed in the *guild chapels*, and the staves in their lockers – which explains the long, narrow upright niches in the walls of some churches. A most unusual example is at Castle Rising in West Norfolk, where the locker is highly decorated, and its position and character suggest that it was used to house a processional cross rather than just the simple banner staves. See also Hassingham, Sea Palling, Strumpshaw, Waxham, Barmer, Dunston, Pulham Market, Shotesham All Saints and Stoke Holy Cross.

Barrel organ: A mechanised organ played by turning a handle, which in turn revolves a cylinder, 'set' with several tunes; often a regular part of the fittings at one time of many rural churches. Now these delightful curiosities, complete with several cylinders of good old hymn tunes, are few and far between, but Mattishall Burgh, Belton and Wood Rising have examples.

Bar tracery: Tracery in the heads of windows, constructed in separate pieces, as distinct from *plate tracery*, where the pattern is cut directly through the masonry. See 'Early English', Appendix 2.

Base course: A horizontal layer of masonry, decorative in character, usually at the base of towers. See *Courses*.

Bell cote/turret: Not to be confused with *sanctus bell cote*. When a church had no tower, a miniature single or double turret was placed on the w. gable end of the nave to take one or two small bells. Brundall, Witton and Sisland have attractive examples.

Biers: Some churches – and particularly, for obvious reasons, those with a long path between *lych-gate* and church – have a platform to carry the coffin to and from the funeral service. These curious conveyances can often be seen, discreetly tucked away at the back of the *nave* or in a side *aisle*. Occasionally ancient, but usually Victorian. Of particular interest are those at Gissing, Old Buckenham, Bressingham, Illington, South Wootton, West Bilney and West Dereham.

Billet: Billet moulding or decoration was particularly used in *Norman* work – it was formed by cutting notches in two parallel and continuous rounded mouldings in a regular, alternating pattern.

Black Death: A modern expression for a horrific epidemic of bubonic plague during the 1340s. It began possibly in China, and by 1348 it had reached the south of France where it devastated the Papal city of Avignon. By the end of the year it had crossed the Channel and begun the ravages which, in 12 months, would leave between a third and a half of the nation's population dead. It also cut off in its prime the greatest flowering of English architectural beauty (see 'Decorated', Appendix 2). It may have destroyed whole village communities, leaving their churches isolated – see under *Isolated Churches*. On January 1st, 1349, Edward III issued a proclamation postponing Parliament because 'a sudden visitation of deadly pestilence' had broken out in and around Westminster, and by June the full fury of the plague had reached Norfolk. Hunstanton may serve as an example of what must have been repeated in scores of parishes. In the two months of September-October 1349, 63 men, among them the priest, and 15 women died of the pestilence; during the next six months, the total reached 172. In that dreadful year ending 1350, it has been estimated that at least half, and probably more, of the population of Norfolk and Suffolk was swept away. Plague broke out again at intervals over the next three centuries (the city of Norwich was ravaged by it after Queen Elizabeth's visit early in her reign) until the last major outbreak, culminating in the Great Plague of London in 1665, when a quarter of the inhabitants died. What is remarkable, in considering the Black Death in relation to our churches, is that it was followed by one of the greatest ages of church building.

Blank/blind arcading: See *arcades*.

Blomfield, Sir Arthur William (1829-1899): Son of a bishop of London and one of the most successful architects of the Victorian era. He established his own practice in 1856 and was president of the Architectural Association in 1861. He carried out important cathedral restorations at Canterbury, Salisbury, Lincoln, and Chichester, and he designed many churches in England and abroad.

Blomefield, Francis (1705-1752): An historian and map-maker, best remembered for his 'An Essay towards a Topographical History of the County of Norfolk'. This was incomplete when he died and was carried to its conclusion by Charles Parkin, Rector of Oxburgh. Blomefield, who was born at Fersfield, near Diss, began collecting material for his history while he was still at school at Thetford, but it was not until he became Rector of his home village in 1729 that the work began to take shape. He sent out a comprehensive questionnaire to more than 200 people, and travelled extensively in the county, collecting and verifying information. It was he who first discovered the Paston Letters (see *Paston family*) at Oxnead. After many difficulties, he set up his own press and volume one of 'The History' appeared in 1739. He got as far as page 678 of the third volume – before being struck down by smallpox and died in 1752. The completed edition of his great work, which is still a source of valuable information today (many things which he meticulously recorded, or sources to which he had access, having since disappeared) was published in 1805-10. (See Fersfield entry).

Bosses: The carved ornamentation seen at the intersections of roof beams or of the ribs in vaulted (see *groining*) ceilings. Usually they represent foliage or grotesque animals or figures, but may often be intricately worked with biblical scenes, with portraits, heraldic arms and symbols, or lively scenes like that in the porch at Cley St Margaret, where a fox, chicken in jaws, is being pursued by an old woman.

Box Pew: Large pews panelled to waist height or higher, often with seats on three sides, and entered by a door from the aisle. Nicknamed 'box pews' from their similarity to horse-boxes or stalls. They came into favour in the late C17 and early C18 and were often embellished with curtains, cushions and carpets. Most disappeared in the wave of C19 restorations, but there is a fine set at Bylaugh St Mary. See also *Prayer Book Churches*.

Brasses: Incised memorial portraits, usually found set into the floor, though some brass inscriptions may be seen fixed to walls and furnishings. Brasses are made in an alloy called latten, a mixture of copper and zinc. This was chiefly manufactured at Cologne, where it was beaten into rectangular plates for export to Britain, the Low Countries and elsewhere. Such memorials were for long favoured by a wide range of classes: from the nobility, through the priesthood, scholars and monks, to merchants and families of local standing. The earliest brass to be seen in England is said to be that of Sir John d'Abernon at Stoke D'Abernon in Surrey, dated 1277 in the reign of Edward I. It was not until the first half of the C17 that the fashion finally petered out. Norfolk is particularly rich in brasses, with two of the finest at Kings Lynn St

Margaret and a very late one at Acle, 1627, one of only six known from the reign of Charles I. North Walsham has a good inscription brass with coat-of-arms, from only a couple of years earlier. At a time when Norwich was, in wealth and consequence, the second city of the kingdom, it had its own prolific group of brass craftsmen, as well as drawing on the work of London workshops and of other provincial centres. But brasses are more than memorials: they are remarkable, pictorial commentaries on four centuries of our history, martial armour, manners, customs, dress and fashions. Particularly fine examples in Norfolk are those at Felbrigg, and at Elsing. A rare variant is at Morston – the only brass in the country to an Elizabethan clergyman. See also, *chalice brass, palimpsest brass, shroud brass,* and *heart brass.*

Browne, Sir Thomas (1605-82): Physician, scientist, writer, scholar, antiquarian, philosopher, sage, and a distinguished son of the city of Norwich – where he spent most of his life, and where he was knighted in 1671 during a Royal visit to the city by Charles II, in recognition of his steadfast Royalist loyalty and for his antiquarian scholarship. His writings are renowned for their sonorous prose and rich use of language, not least in his personal confession of Christian faith, 'Religio Medici', with its fascinating diversions upon all matter of things touching upon man's religious quest; and in the 'Hydriotaphia or Urn Burial', in which Sir Thomas, set off by the discovery of some ancient burial urns in Norfolk, contemplates the many and various ways of burial and the great unknown that follows: 'But the iniquity of oblivion blindly scattereth her poppy'. Sir Thomas's statue sits, deep in thought on a plinth on Norwich's Hay Hill. His memorial is nearby in the sanctuary of St Peter Mancroft Church.

Burne-Jones, Sir Edward (1833 1898): Meeting *William Morris* at Oxford University was a formative influence on Burne-Jones. His work is notable for its medievalism, for its mystical and dreamlike air, and its exotic and symbolic themes – qualities, which in his day earned him great popular fame and a baronetcy. He created numerous glass and tapestry designs for William Morris. And among good examples of their collaboration in stained glass to be found in Norfolk is a typically brilliant one at Horstead; and a splendidly bold one at Langham.

Burrough, Sir James (1681-1764): Amateur architect, and successively graduate, don, master and vice-chancellor at Cambridge. His skills as an architect earned him a considerable reputation at the university, where he was responsible for many projects – new buildings, re-mouldings and 'beautifications'. But Norfolk has something fairly unusual of his: a set of rather fine church fittings, originally in Corpus Christi College Chapel, and now in Thurning Church.

Butterfly head-dress: 'Butterfly' was a name given in the C16, and used ever since, for a style fashionable in the previous century, from about 1450 to 1485. Its high fashion status is indicated by its appearance on effigies of the period in brass and stone. The head-dress consisted of a wire frame, fixed to a close-fitting ornamented cap, supporting a gauze veil spreading out above the head on each side like a pair of diaphanous butterfly wings. Stibbard, East Dereham and Ditchingham have examples. An interesting preliminary to the style, in the decade up to 1450, is meticulously carved on a *corbel* at Howe – a close skull cap with large 'bunny ears' rising on each side. See also Bylaugh and Mattishall.

Butterfly tracery: A pattern development of the flowing form at the height of the *Decorated* period, towards 1350. See Fig. 18, Appendix 2.

Camden Society: The Cambridge Camden Society was founded by J. M. Neale and B. Webb in 1839 to study church art. It encouraged interest in ecclesiastical architecture and traditional Catholic worship and had a powerful influence on the later C19 liturgical and ceremonial revival in the Church of England.

Canopy-of-honour: See *celure*.

Capital: The usually decorated and ornamented top of a column/pillar, from which springs the arch which the pillar supports (compare with *impost* and *abacus*).

Carstone: 'Gingerbread' stone it used to be called in Norfolk. It is a soft sandstone which you can see in the cliffs at Hunstanton, not far from the old Snettisham quarries. Carstone is mostly seen in buildings in the n.w. of the county, though an ancient example of its use is in the Anglo-Saxon tower on the other side of Norfolk at Bessingham.

Cartouche: Sculptural representation of a curling sheet of paper, seldom contained within a formal frame. Latin: carta, paper.

Cautley, Henry Munro (1875 1959): Suffolk architect, antiquarian, expert on heraldry, and authority on church architecture and fittings. His two books, 'Suffolk Churches and their Treasures' (1938) and 'Norfolk Churches' (1949) remain essential for student, specialist and enthusiast.

Cavell, Nurse Edith (1865-1915: At Swardeston Church one of England's heroines is remembered, not only in stained glass and by mementoes, but by an annual service. Her father was vicar there for nearly half a century. While serving as head of a nursing school and clinic in occupied Belgium during the First World War, she hid allied soldiers and helped them escape. At length she was arrested, quickly tried and sentenced to be shot by in the early hours of October 12th, 1915. The result was a propaganda catastrophe for the Germans; the international outrage was such that it helped swing neutral opinion against the Kaiser. But all this is incidental to the gentle, steadfast, God-fearing woman, who loved children, the countryside and flowers. How apt that in the church where she was so happy she should be recalled each year by a flower festival and service on the Sunday nearest the date of her execution. She is buried at Life's Green, outside Norwich Cathedral; and in nearby Tombland, there is an imposing monument to her.

Celure: Or 'canopy-of-honour'. A panelled and painted section of the roof of a church, either over the altar, or at the eastern end of the nave over the position occupied by the *rood*. Wymondham has a good example.

Censer: Also known as a thurible, it is a pierced metal container used for the ceremonial burning of incense. The incense is burned on charcoal and the censer is usually suspended on chains, so that it can be swung in the hand of the thurifer as he censes the alter, the priest and the congregation – thus fanning the charcoal and directing the smoke. An acolyte bearing a boat-shaped vessel containing incense for replenishing the censer sometimes attends the thurifer.

Chalice: The goblet or cup used to contain the wine consecrated and offered to the congregation at the Eucharist or Holy Communion.

Chalice brass: Small memorial brasses, surmounted by a representation of the *chalice* and *host*. There are about 40 such brasses in Norfolk, all dating from the early C16. These may all have been the work of a single craftsman working in or near Norwich. Good examples can be seen at Salthouse, Bintree, North Walsham, Scottow, Attlebridge, Colney, Surlingham Norwich St Giles, and Diss. See also *brasses* and *palimpsest brasses*.

Chancel: The e. end section of a church, containing the altar. Before the *Reformation*, the chancel was restricted to the clergy and the celebration of mass, the people occupying the *nave*. Separating the two was a carved and traceried *screen* – thus the derivation of the word from the Latin cancelli (lattice). See *rood loft*; and *weeping chancels*.

Chantry chapels: Before the *Reformation*, it was the wish of every God-fearing man to have masses said for his soul after his death, especially during the month immediately following his demise. But for the rich there was the possibility of prayers and masses for ever, by establishing and endowing a chantry chapel, with attendant priests, where the donor's bones could rest, sometimes with those of his family. For those who could not afford all this, there was another way – through membership of a local *guild* of merchants or craftsmen. Even small parish churches might have several guild and chantry altars, with their 'lights' burning; in cathedrals there could be dozens: it is said that Lichfield had 87.

Chapling, J.C.: A Norwich sculptor in the C18. One of his monuments is to Sir Horatio Pettus, 1746, a member of an important Norwich family, which may be seen in Rackheath's remote and delightful little church.

Chapman, John: see *Pedlar of Swaffham*.

Charnel: A repository for bones removed from a grave to allow re-use of the plot.

Chevron: The chevron or zig-zag is a characteristic decorative moulding of *Norman* architecture, its bold 'V' shapes being used from the early C12 around open arches and arches of windows and doors. See Appendix 2.

Cheere, Sir Henry, 1703-1781: Only one example of this celebrated sculptor's work is

recorded in Norfolk, that being at St Giles's Church in Norwich, a wall monument to Thomas Churchman and his wife. His output included, in 1758, a chapel in Boston, U.S.A.; and on a less exalted plane, great carved chimney pieces for grand houses. He was knighted in 1760 by George III, and created a baronet six years later.

Christopher images: St Christopher representations are almost always to be found opposite the main entrance of the church, because of the belief that no harm could come to anyone who had seen the image of the saint on the day of a journey: sensible, therefore, to place him where, on opening the door, the traveller could see him in a trice, cross himself and be on his way, in safety, all in a moment. There was sometimes an inscription: 'The day that you see Christopher's face, that day shall you not die an evil death'. Norfolk has many fine St Christopher representations, notable being the wall paintings at Wickhampton and Hemblington. Probably every medieval church had some representation, in painting, glass or statue – though the latter is rare, a notable exception being at Terrington St Clement. See also St Christopher's background in Appendix 1.

Christmas, Gerard: Carver to the Royal Navy and pageant master to the City of London in the reign of James I, Christmas was an outstanding sculptor whose fine monument to Sir William Drury can be seen at Besthorpe.

Chrysom child: When a child was baptised, it was swaddled for the Christening service in the 'Chrysom' cloth or sheet, which often belonged to the parish. If the child died before its mother had been Churched (i.e., had been to church after the birth to receive the priest's blessing and purification) it was then buried in the Chrysom cloth, thus becoming a 'Chrysom child'. In this form it was represented on tombs and brasses – as, for example, on the John Clippesby brass, 1594, at Clippesby St Peter; see also Upper Sheringham; Ketteringham, Norwich St George Tombland, Pulham Market, St Mary Magdalene, Rougham and Wiggenhall St Mary.

Churches Conservation Trust: The Trust cares for the most beautiful and historic churches no longer required for regular worship by the Church of England. Over a million people a year visit the 338 churches in its care, of which

Norfolk has 29. Just over half of the Trust's income comes from government sources, but the support of hundreds of local volunteers is vital to its work.

Churchyard cross: See *preaching cross.*

Cibber, Caius Gabriel (1630-1700): Sculptor. Born in the German state of Schleswig-Holstein. As a young man he went to Italy, after several years moved on to the Netherlands, and towards the end of the Civil War arrived in England and took employment with John Stone, the youngest son of *Nicholas Stone,* master mason to Charles I. Three decades later he was appointed 'Sculptor in Ordinary to His Majesty' by William III. He was not responsible for many monumental works, but all those which he created are notable for their artistry and craftsmanship – as in his one Norfolk example, the alabaster statue of Clement Spelman (1672) at Narborough.

Cinquefoils: See *Foils.*

Clayton & Bell: A firm of stained glass manufacturers founded by John Richard Clayton and Alfred Bell in 1855 and still continuing under Michael Bell. Their studio was one of the largest of the Victorian period and they were notable for the brilliance of their High Victorian designs and consistency in their use of colour. Their work of the early 1860s was of a particularly high standard. Examples of their work can be found at Hedenham, St Peter and Ormsby, St Margaret.

Clerestory: An upper storey, standing clear of its adjacent roofs, and pierced with windows which usually correspond in number with the number of arches, or bays, in the arcade below. Its pronunciation – 'Clear storey' – explains the clerestory's function, clear glass windows letting in light on the nave below.

Collar beam: See *Roofs.*

Collar of Esses: A decorative collar of gold or silver composed of S's linked together. There are many theories concerning the origin of this mark of honour and what the 'S' stood for (Sovereign, Seneschal, etc.). The earliest effigy shown wearing it in this country dates from 1371 and so it cannot, as some have maintained, have been introduced by Henry IV. He did, however, issue a regulation in 1401 limiting its use to sons of the king, dukes, earls and barons and

to other knights and esquires when in his presence. During the reigns of Henry IV, his son and grandson, it was a royal badge of the Lancastrian house, with a white swan as pendant rather than the more usual portcullis. It was later restricted to the Lord Chief Justice, the Lord Mayor of London, the Heralds and Kings of Arms and the Serjeants at Arms. See Ashwellthorpe, and Burnham Thorpe, for examples dated 1417 and 1420.

Colonette: A small column.

Communion rails: The rails against which the congregation kneel to receive Communion which were originally installed for quite other reasons. They were to protect the altar from irreverent people and even less reverent dogs – and the balusters were to be set close enough to ensure this. Before the *Reformation,* the *chancel* was always closed off by a screen (*rood loft/screen*) usually fitted with doors, and the people normally never entered it. Except at great festivals, they watched through the screen as the priests celebrated mass and themselves received the sacrament. When general participation in services and the administration of the sacrament to the people became the norm, different arrangements were needed. Archbishop *Laud* ordered that the altar should be railed and not moved from its n.s. position, and the rails often enclosed the altar on three sides. Examples of three-sided rails are found at Merton, Thurning and West Dereham, although a number on in-line sets were clearly three-sided originally and have been adapted, as at Bawbugh. Whether there should be rails or no, Richard Montague, Bishop of Norwich, made his position quite clear in a Visitation question in 1638: 'Is your communion table enclosed, and ranged about with a rail of joiners and turners work, close enough to keep dogs from going in and profaning that holy place, from pissing against it or worse?' The Bishop further ordered that 'the communicants being entered into the chancel shall be disposed of orderly in their several ranks, leaving sufficient room for the priest or minister to go between them, by whom they were to be communicated one rank after another, until they had all of them received.' This was to come into conflict with the Puritan habit of demanding that communion should be received by the congregation seated in their pews. In 1643 communion rails went the way of other 'monuments of superstition and idolatry', but at the *Restoration* in 1660 old habits were resumed and the taking of communion at the sanctuary rail became accepted practice. (See also *Prayer Book Churches*.)

Comper, Sir Ninian (1864-1960): Distinguished and highly individual architect of the Gothic Revival, who in the course of 70 years built 15 churches, restored and decorated scores, and designed vestments, windows and banners for use all round the globe, from America to the Far East, for both the Roman and Anglican communions. The seated Christ in Glory, with accompanying saints, on the great *reredos* of St Peter Mancroft Church in Norwich, is Sir Ninian's work (1930), as also is the great reredos at Wymondham, erected in 1919. See also East Winch, Great Ryburgh and Mundford.

Consecration crosses: painted or carved – indicate the points at which the walls of the church, and the altar slab (the *mensa*) were touched with Holy Oil by the Bishop at the consecration of the building. On the altar were incised five crosses – one at each corner and one in the middle – signifying the *Five Wounds of Christ*. Twelve crosses were marked on the walls, three on each of the four walls, both inside and out, at a height above the ground so that they would not be brushed by passers by. To reach them, the Bishop used a small ladder that was moved round during the service of consecration. Comparatively few survive – painted ones in various states of preservation can be seen at Bale (good), Calthorpe, Great Walsingham, Lammas and Thrigby. Alby has four carved ones – and Holt a single one placed unusually into the back of a *piscina*.

Corbels: A support, set firmly into the wall, to carry a weight from above (see *Roofs*) and usually carved, either decoratively, or with heads which may be reverent or formalised, delightfully (and irreverently) portrait-like (see, among others, Barney, Cley, Burlingham St Andrew, Matlask). Corbels are also freely used decoratively on the ends of *dripstones* and *hood-mouldings*.

Corbel table: A continuous row of *corbels* set into a wall to support the eaves of a roof. The exposed *Norman* example on the exterior s. wall of the chancel at King's Lynn All Saints is especially interesting.

Corinthian: A column of one of the classical (Grecian) orders, comprising a cushioned base, the shaft or pillar itself (usually fluted), and a *capital* enriched with acanthus leaves.

Courses: A horizontal layer of masonry. A *base course* will usually be at the base of the tower – a purely decorative course, a little above the ground, designed to set off the tower visually. In Norfolk, the local flint is often used to great effect here, *knapped* and set flush into stone panelling (thus, *flushwork*) to create a most attractive contrast, as well as a visual impression of upward, vertical thrust. A *string course* is a moulding whose purpose is to indicate the divisions of a tower into its several stages, though in some cases – Brisley is a fine example – it is carried over the tower window(s) to create an impression of lightness and uplift. Finally, a *drip course* is a raised course doing the practical job of carrying off rain from the wall surface. (See also *dripstone*.)

Credence/Credence shelf: A shelf on which the bread and wine for the mass or communion are placed before consecration by the priest; usually found within the niche of the *piscina* beside the altar, or the site of a former altar. Can sometimes occupy a niche of its own.

Cresset: In St Giles's Church in Norwich is preserved a cresset or fire-basket which served as a warning beacon on top of the church tower – set there in 1549, a troubled time of rebellion and strife. From the French croisette, because beacons usually had crosses on their tops.

Cresset Stone: A stone drilled with holes that were filled with oil on which a wick floated, a primative form of candle lighting. (Blakeney)

Crockets/crocketting: An exuberant ornamentation of the *Decorated* period, in the first half of the C14, though it was to be carried through with enthusiasm into the later *Perpendicular* style. It is a little projecting sculpture in the form of leaves, flowers etc., used in profusion on pinnacles, spires, canopies and so on, both inside and outside the building.

Crossing/crossing tower: The crossing is the part of the church at the intersection of the cross shape of a *cruciform* church, where *chancel* and *nave* and n. and s. *transepts* meet. The *crossing tower* is the central tower built over this point.

Cross patée: The cross adopted by the *Knights Templar* in the early C12, though its significance for the Order is not clear. In shape the cross spreads towards the ends of its arms, or expands 'in three claw-like divisions'. The claw shape presumably explains the derivation of 'patée' from the French, une patte, a paw. The tombs of Knights Templar are generally adorned with the cross patée, as examples in Norfolk testify.

Cruciform: The cross-shaped ground plan of a church made by *chancel* and *nave* to e. and w., and *transepts* to n. and s., and sometimes also with a *crossing tower* built centrally at the intersection of the cross.

Cusp/cusping: The little projecting points on the curves of window and screen tracery, arches etc., which give a foliated, leaf-like appearance. From the Latin cuspis, a point (of a spear).

Dance of death: An allegorical subject in European art, in which the figure of death, often represented as a skeleton, is shown meeting various characters in different states of life and leading them all in a dance to the grave; German – the Totetanz of Holbein, French – Dance macabre. (Sparham)

Decalogue/Decalogue board: The decalogue is the ten commandments collectively. The decalogue board is a large board upon which the commandments are written. These became a regular part of church furnishings in the reign of Elizabeth I, when it was state policy to clear churches of the decorations and adornments which were regarded as 'Popish'. In 1560, Elizabeth ordered *Archbishop Parker* to see 'that the tables of the Commandments be comely set or hung up in the east-end of the chancel.' The following year more explicit instructions were given: the boards were to be fixed to the e. wall over the communion table. Decalogues were also set up on the *tympanum* panelling which filled the curve of the chancel arch to replace the discarded *rood loft* (See also, *Royal Arms*). In most cases today, the decalogue boards have long since been moved from their position behind the altar (as at Thurning) but are usually displayed on a convenient wall of nave or aisles.

Decorated: This was the high point of ornamented Gothic architecture in the first half of the C14. (See Appendix 2.)

Despencer, Henry le, Bishop of Norwich (1341-1406): A soldier/bishop who early in life fought in Italy for the Pope and was assigned the Bishopric of Norwich in 1370. Despencer is most remembered, however, as the man who in 1381 put down the Peasants' Revolt in Norfolk (this was a popular movement which broke out all over the country against serfdom). Despencer was at court when he heard of the Norfolk insurrection, and having raised a contingent at his manor at Burghley near Stamford, he set out for Norwich. Battle was finally joined near North Walsham, where the bishop himself led the assault on the rebels and joined in the fierce hand to hand fighting. Many of the peasants were killed and Despencer, acting as a judge in the King's Court, tried John Lidster the local leader of the rebels at North Walsham. He was sentenced to be hung, drawn and quartered, and then Despencer in his role as bishop took the condemned man to St Nicholas' church to hear his confession and absolve him. As Lidster was dragged at the cart-tail to the place of execution, Despencer went with him, holding up his head to spare him some of the rigours of that last journey. A contemporary cross beside the Norwich road going in to North Walsham marks the site of the battle. The bishop's later life was punctuated by feats of arms at home and abroad, and he finally came to rest in a grave before the high Altar of Norwich Cathedral. There, in St Luke's chapel, may be seen a *retable* which may well have been given as a thank offering for the suppression of the rebellion in 1381. (See also Norwich, St Mary in the Marsh).

Dog-tooth decoration: An ornamental carving of the *Early English* period (see Appendix 2) in the C12/C13, which looks like a four leafed flower. One suggestion is that it is based on the dog's tooth violet.

Dowsing, William (1596- 1679?): In August 1643 Parliament ordered a general destruction of altars, pictures, and images in all churches, and the Earl of Manchester, as general of the, eastern counties, appointed Dowsing as his visitor in Suffolk. Born at Laxfield, and later living at Coddenham and Eye, he toured East Anglia between January and October 1644, and is the best known of the despoilers simply because he kept a diary. The original manuscript has disappeared but a transcript was made in the early C18 and it was first published in 1786 (C.H.E. White edited the best edition in 1885) Dowsing employed deputies, but took a personal delight in wreaking vengeance on all that he considered 'popish', often exceeding his brief by digging up floors and disturbing tombs. An eyewitness to his work in Cambridgeshire said: 'he goes about the Country like a bedlam breaking glasse windowes, having battered and beaten downe all our painted glasse…and compelled us by armed soldiers to pay… for not mending what he has spoyled and defaced, or forthwith go to prison.' It should not be assumed that all villagers and ministers in this strongly Puritan area were averse to the purge, but some churches saved their particular treasures by guile or obstinacy. Nevertheless the man exacted a terrible reckoning, particularly in Suffolk. His was a very personal interpretation of the psalmist's 'Let the righteous put their hands into wickedness'. Of Norfolk churches, only Gorleston St Andrew figures in his diary.

Drip course: See *courses*.

Dripstone: A projecting ledge or moulding over the heads of doorways, windows etc., serving the practical purpose of carrying off the rain. When the same architectural addition is used inside a building, as a decorative feature, it is called *hood mould*.

Dropped sill sedilia/window: See *sedilia*.

Early English: This is the style developed during mid C12, which heralded the arrival of Gothic or pointed architecture in Britain – as well as the birth of a truly native style. (See Appendix 2.)

Easter Sepulchre: On the n. side of the *chancel*, a recess in the wall – ranging from the plain to the richly carved and canopied – housed the Easter Sepulchre (itself normally a temporary structure of wood). On Maundy Thursday, a host was consecrated and placed in the Easter Sepulchre, to be consumed at the following day's Good Friday mass. This practice still continues in the Roman Catholic and some Anglican churches today, the *host* being 'borne in solemn Procession... to the altar of repose', to be processed back to the High Altar the following day. Until the *Reformation*, the sepulchre would be watched over from Good Friday to Easter Day and sometimes, on Easter Morning, would be the setting for a dramatisation of the Resurrection. Most Sepulchres were disposed of during Elizabeth's reign, though in 1538, during the time of her father, Henry VIII, a list of 'superstitious lights' to be removed specifically excluded the light (i.e. a constantly burning candle) before the sepulchre. Good examples in Norfolk are at Northwold, Kelling and Baconsthorpe. We noted a possible 33 overall.

Elevation squint: Central to the Eucharist (mass) is the consecration of the bread and wine. During the Middle Ages, the standard practice was for the priest to raise the wafer of bread and the cup to symbolise the offering and for adoration by the people. Those kneeling in the *nave* close to the *chancel screen* could not gain a clear view, and the more determined sometimes bored a hole in the panel in front of their accustomed place so that they did not have to rise from their knees. These apertures have become known as elevation squints and can be found in a number of churches.

Emblems of the Trinity: Among the enormous variety of images found on medieval fonts and in stained glass, the Emblems of the Trinity are a regular feature. Among them: the equilateral triangle, the trefoil design, three interlocking circles, all representing the idea of the three persons of the Godhead – Father, Son and Holy Spirit, three in one and one in three; also the two interlocking triangles ('Solomon's Seal', borrowed from Judaism); a figure of God as king with Christ on the Cross and a dove of peace hovering over them; and lastly a shield design, linking indissolubly Father, Son and Holy Spirit, with, at the centre of the shield, Deus, God.

Encaustic tiles: The Victorians invented the process of burning-in different coloured clays onto tile and brick, to produce a stencil like effect. In churches built during the C19, and in others 'restored' and 'improved', these tiles were freely used on floor and wall, on *reredoses* and elsewhere.

Evangelistic symbols: See *Symbols of the Evangelists*.

Fan vault: A C15 architectural development, in which a roof was constructed in a fan pattern angled in a trumpet shape to a central point, all the ribs being of the same length, and the centre point often being ornamented with a *boss* or pendant. Examples are to be seen at Shelton and at Norwich St Giles. See also *groining*.

Finial: A carved or moulded ornament, often in foliage or floral form, or as a particularly decorative *crocket*, completing the points of arches, pinnacles or gables. Any finishing in this sense, no matter how plain or simple, is still technically a finial.

Five Wounds of Christ, The: On fonts (at Blakeney, for example) and elsewhere, The Five Wounds of Christ are often represented. They are the wounds of the Crucifixion – to hands, feet and side. See also the *Instruments of the Passion*, which often accompany representations of the Wounds.

Flaxman, John (1755-1826): Sculptor. He was a sickly child, but with a great gift for drawing which brought him, when he was only eleven a premium (repeated in 1769) from the Society of Arts. In 1775 he began work for the celebrated potter, Josiah Wedgwood, for whom he designed cameos and made wax models of classical friezes. Later he spent seven years working in Rome, which established his fame throughout Europe and settled the great success he was to enjoy after his return to England in 1794. See entries for East Dereham and Ketteringham, for examples of his work.

Flint-knapping: Flint split (knapped) across the middle, to achieve a shell like fracture – and a lustrous, flat surface (see *flushwork*).

Flushwork: This is the use of *knapped flints*, set flush into panelled patterns in brick or stone, a combination which adds visual beauty and striking impact to so many Norfolk (and Suffolk) churches.

Foils: From the C12, foils were a much used adornment in Gothic architecture. The *Early English* style produced the graceful *trefoil*, or three leafed shape: it is said that this was intended to represent the Trinity – three in one and one in three – and that St Patrick, in C5 Ireland, put together three leaves of shamrock to illustrate to his converts that profound mystery. The trefoil was followed architecturally by the *quatrefoil* (four leaf), *cinquefoil* (five leaf) and multi foil.

Four Latin Doctors: 'Doctor' here indicates one who is learned, a theologian. The Four Latin Doctors were the leading theologians of the early Christian Church in the west – Ambrose, Augustine of Hippo, Jerome and Gregory (more about them in Appendix 1).

Galilee porches: The western porch of a church – of which examples can be seen at Little Walsingham, Cromer and Cley, among others – was often called the 'Galilee porch' because it was the final 'station' in the Sunday procession. The priest at the head of the procession symbolised Christ going before his disciples into Galilee after the Resurrection. In medieval times these processions were an important part of the Sunday and Feast Day services and must have made an impressive sight with the colours of robes and banners. Garboldisham, and North Elmham have examples. (See also *banner-stave lockers*.)

Galleries: In churches, they have a fascinating pedigree. Before the *Reformation*, when every church had its *rood loft* in the chancel arch, singers might use the loft as a gallery, the singing being accompanied by a simple organ. In the couple of centuries that followed the Reformation and the destruction of the old rood lofts, galleries – usually at the w. end of the nave – became a common feature. There was housed the village orchestra (the enthusiastic, if not always entirely harmonious sounds, of clarinet, flute, bass fiddle, bassoon and hautboy). Village choirs were common, although the robed and surpliced variety were a mid-Victorian innovation. When organs again became popular they were sometimes placed in a western gallery, and there they can still occasionally be found – there is a delightful example at Hempstead. Many more galleries were inserted in the C19 to accommodate the larger congregations of the period, but only about 30 now remain in Norfolk.

Gargoyles: A spout jutting outwards from a wall so as to throw rainwater well away from the building. But there is much more to them than that. Almost always in ancient churches they are grotesquely carved in all manner of fanciful forms of weird beasts, dragons, devils and representations of human vices like the seven deadly sins. To appreciate good and beauty, it is necessary to recognise the face of evil and ugliness – and this medieval man knew and practised. As his mixture of reverence and superstition also inclined to the view that dragons and demons were always prowling evilly round his church, what better way of keeping them at bay than putting their own kind on guard... on the basis, presumably, of 'it takes a devil to catch a devil'.

Gesso: A system of coating a base, usually wood, with a thick layer of plaster of Paris, or with gypsum (one of the powdered minerals used to make up plaster of Paris). When it is hard, the artist/sculptor carves into it his chosen design, to produce an incised effect, which is then painted and, in church art, almost always gilded.

Gibbons, Grinling (1648-1721): An interior decorator, wood carver and sculptor of genius, who worked for Charles II, was master carver to George I, and collaborated with Sir Christopher Wren at St Paul's. He was especially known for the beauty and delicacy of his carvings of birds, flowers and foliage. One of his monuments is in Felbrigg Church, sporting, typically, large swags of flowers and fruit.

Green Man: The Green Man is a foliate mask, often of demonical appearance, probably representing the spirit of fertility, often having living vines issuing from its mouth, and as such, an occasional device in wood and stone carving – a touch of persistent Paganism in Christian art. A green man's head peers from below the rim of the old pulpit at Guist, and at Scottow that disconcerting face looks down from a *boss* at the centre of the porch roof. See also Moulton, Weston Longville, Thompson, Wilton and King's Lynn St Margaret's.

Griffin: Traditionally the guardian of treasure – but also used in church sculpture, carvings and paintings. The griffin – or gryphon – is a mythical monster with an eagle's head, wings and forelegs; and the body, tail and hind legs of a lion. Heraldry uses this fabulous creature too – there is a griffin on the Arms of the City of London, for example. In Oriental folklore, a couple of griffins pulled Alexander the Great in a magic chariot up to heaven – while he was still alive that is – just to have a look around. See Felmingham, Upper Sheringham, North Elmham, Old Buckenham, Rockland St Peter, Trowse, East Harling and Mundford.

Groining: The creation of a vaulted ceiling, divided into segments by raised, intersecting lines – these lines, between the angled surfaces, being the actual 'groins'. Found in carved canopies, as well as in roofs. Norfolk roof examples are usually in porches, though there is a fine *Early English* example in the elegant little chancel at Blakeney. Where groined vaulting is used on the large scale, it is very grand and impressive.

Groves, William (b.1809): A sculptor who first exhibited at the Royal Academy in 1834 and subsequently for many years at Burlington House. Apart from statuary and portrait busts, he was also responsible for numerous monuments for churches. Among them is an arresting tablet memorial at Catfield to Lt. Thomas Cubitt, 1848, featuring a 'peepul tree', a neatly philosophical allusion to the eastern scene of the young lieutenant's death. Groves also has a monument at Shouldham, to Thomas Allen, 1841, which was exhibited at the Royal Academy before being transported to its present setting.

Guilds/Guild altars: In corners of churches, at the e. ends of aisles and elsewhere, may often be seen *piscinas*, and occasionally *squints* which indicate the presence of a guild or *chantry* altar. Guilds were associations of those living in the same neighbourhood who remembered that they had, as neighbours, common obligations – an obligation to put into practice the commandment to 'love thy neighbour'. Their religious commitment would often be shown by having their own altar in their parish church, served by a priest whom they maintained. There were two main divisions: craft or trade guilds, whose purpose was the protection of particular work, trade or handicraft; and religious societies or, as they are sometimes called, 'Social Guilds'. The split was one of convenience rather than a real distinction founded on fact – all had the same general characteristic, the principle of brotherly love and social charity, and none was divorced from the ordinary religious observances daily practised in before the *Reformation*. Broadly speaking, they were the benefit societies and provident associations of the Middle Ages – a helping hand as ready to help the sick or look after poor children as to lodge pilgrims cheaply. Nearly everyone was a member of one fraternity or another. One distinct help to the parish was the provision of additional priests for the services of the church. Beccles Guild of the Holy Ghost, for example, had a priest 'to celebrate in the church', Beccles being 'a great and populous town of 800 houseling people...the said priest is aiding unto the curate there, who without help is not able to discharge the said cure'. (Note: 'housel' in Old English means 'sacrifice', and was used in the English Church from St Augustine to the Reformation to mean The Eucharist; 'houseling people' – those who had received communion). (See also *chantry chapels*, *houseling cloth*)

Hammer-beam roofs: A brilliant conception, architecturally and artistically, of the late gothic period, late C15 C16, in which the thrust of the roofs weight is taken on 'hammer' brackets. (See *Roofs*, figs. 6, 7, and 8)

Hatchments: Many churches display on their walls large, diamond shaped boards, bearing a coat-of-arms and either the motto of the family whose 'coat' it is, or the word 'Resurgam' (I shall rise again). Dating from the second half of the C17 through to the end of the C18, these boards were carried in procession at the burial of the holder of the Arms; afterwards for some months they adorned the dead man's house, and finally were transferred to the church. The composition of the boards followed a formalised pattern – the background is black on the left hand side if the dead person was a husband, black on the right if a wife; for a bachelor, widow or widower, the whole background would be black.

Headstops: The decorative 'stops' at the ends of *dripstones* and *hood moulds* over arches, doors and windows.

Heart brass: A memorial *brass* in the shape of a heart – the Sacred Heart of Jesus. It may simply be alone, with an inscription or, as at Helhoughton, held up by hands. See also Kirby Bedon, Brancaster, Wiggenhall St. Mary, Walsoken and compare with variations at Wickhampton and East Tuddenham.

Heaton, Butter & Bayne: A firm of stained glass manufacturers founded by Clement Heaton and James Butler in 1855, joined by Robert Turnill Bayne in 1862. They took over the role of the most original Gothicists from *Clayton & Bell* and produced an impressively varied series of high quality windows in 1860s, which were fine examples of the High Victorian style at its most accomplished. There was significant collaboration with *Henry Holiday* and other artists of the aesthetic movement in the 1870s and the firm continued to produce glass until 1953. Examples of their work can be seen at Dunton, East Dereham and Wereham.

Hardman, John (1811-1867) & Co.: The family were originally button-makers in Birmingham, but John Hardman met *Pugin* in 1837 and they became friends. The following year they were partners in a new metal-working business which set out to provide church fittings and accessories of all kinds, for which Pugin provided all the designs in medieval style. Starting with small projects, mainly in precious metals, the venture blossomed. As Hardman and Iliffe, the firm took part in the Great Exhibition in 1851 and the medieval court displayed an extraordinary range of Pugin's designs and Hardman's craftsmanship. The revival of memorial *brasses* was largely due to them and Hardman's became by far the largest suppliers, producing some notable designs. In the early days, Pugin's influence was pervasive and stained glass was added to the repertoire in 1845. He was the chief designer in this medium until his death in 1852, when the role passed to Hardman's nephew, John Hardman Powell who continued until 1895. The firm's early work set standards for the Gothic revival in stained glass and it is of high quality and beauty, for example at Bunwell.

Herring-bone work: A technique of positioning stones, bricks or tiles in 'arrow formation', like the bones of a fish, with alternate courses in different directions, giving a zig-zag effect. Not a decorative device, but a strengthening and supporting measure. The technique goes back to Roman times, but continued through the *Saxon* period and well into the *Norman* era. Many examples may be found in Norfolk churches.

Holiday, Henry G.A. (1839-1927): Artist, writer and one of the key stained glass designers of the C19. When his friend, *Burne-Jones*, left the *Powells* in 1861 he became their chief designer, working in his highly individual version of the *pre-Raphaelite* style. He also accepted commissions from Shrigley & Hunt and Saunders. Examples of his work in Norfolk can be found at Banham, North Pickenham, Pulham Market and Methwold.

Holy loaf: Before the Reformation a loaf was blessed and censed after Sunday mass, cut into pieces and distributed to the congregation who went up and received it from the priest, whose hand they kissed. Knife marks on the ends of some altars show where it was cut for distribution. It was a sign of fellowship rather than a sacrament, although some took it home for the sick. The faithful were encouraged to make an offering of a loaf each Sunday and the priest was allowed to keep what remained after the service. See Norwich, St George Tombland. See also *host*.

Holy water stoup: In the porches of many churches, and/or just inside the main entrance door, are basins, usually recessed into the wall. More often than not they are very plain in execution – though there are exceptions, like the very grand one at Stalham. The basins held holy water, which was mixed once a week before mass. On entering the church, worshippers dipped their fingertips into the water, and crossed themselves to remind themselves of their baptismal vows. For the preparation of the water, salt was first of all exorcised (the expelling of the evil spirit) and then blessed; in turn, water was exorcised and blessed. The salt was then scattered over the water 'in the sign of the cross' and another blessing was said over the mixture.

Hood mould: See *dripstone*.

Horns of Light: In North Tuddenheim church and also in Norwich Cathedral, may be seen representations in ancient stained glass of Moses with 'horns of light' springing from his ears. The reason for this inclusion by medieval artists is intriguing. In Exodus 34, v. 30, it is recorded that when Moses came down from Mount Sinai, the Israelites saw that 'the skin of his face shone; and they were afraid to come nigh him'. The Hebrew verb for 'shone' is also the root of the noun meaning 'horn'. In Latin it became 'facies cornuta' – and from as far back as the C11, artists chose to interpret this literally as 'horns'.

Host: The bread consecrated in the Eucharist and regarded as the body of Christ sacrificially offered. Prior to the *Reformation*, it was a wafer of unleven bread, but household bread was substituted by the Puritans and both have been used subsequently. See also *wafer ovens.*

Hour-glass/hour-glass stands: There was a time when long sermons were the rule rather than the exception, particularly so after the *Reformation*, in the Puritan period in the mid-C17, and in the C18. For their own guidance preachers often had an hour glass on or near the pulpit, to indicate the passing time – though when the hour was up it was not unknown for the glass to be turned over, sometimes in response to a cry from the congregation demanding more. Numerous hour-glass stands remain today in our churches – among Norfolk examples are those at Catfield, Salhouse, Burlingham St Edmund, Braydeston, Ingworth, Tuttington, Billingford St Leonard, Brooke,

Marlingford, Mundham, Thurlton, Bexwell, Breckles, Merton, Roydon, South Acre, Walpole St Andrew, Wiggenhall St German, and Wiggenhall St Mary.

Houseling cloth: A cloth sometimes held or stretched below the priest's hands when offering the *host* to communicants so that no particle should fall to the floor.

IHS: The Sacred Monogram of the name of Jesus. There are two schools of thought regarding its interpretation. One says that it is the first two and last letters of the Greek alphabetic spelling of Jesus: the other that it represents the Latin 'Iesus Hominum Salvator' – Jesus the Saviour of Mankind. Either way, IHS is regularly seen carved on fonts and represented elsewhere in our churches.

Impost: A simple bracket or moulding set as a 'lip' in a wall to carry a springing arch. A typical attribute of plain and massive *Saxon* architecture, in which field it is almost exclusively used in this book. (Compare with *capital* and *abacus*).

Instruments of the Passion: These are frequent among the symbols carved on medieval fonts and on the stonework of the church (for example – on an outer buttress at Blakeney). They are – Christ's Cross; the Crown of Thorns; the Spear that was thrust into His side; the cup of vinegar; the reed and sponge by which that vinegar was offered as Christ hung on the Cross (John 19, vv 28-29); the dice which were used to cast lots for His clothing (an example can be found in the top of the e. window at Poringland), and a ladder are additional symbols.

Isolated churches: Churches far removed from their villages, or from any habitation, inevitably invite the question: 'why?' A popular answer is that the *Black Death* was the culprit, either killing everyone in the village or removing so many that the remainder deserted the plague hole and built elsewhere. There is no actual documentary evidence for this having happened, however, although that does not mean that it did not happen. But it is a theory to be treated with caution, especially as there are some places with isolated churches that apparently suffered little or no loss at the time of the Black Death. Lords of the Manor sometimes built a parish church near to their house for their own convenience and not necessarily for that of the villagers.

Another reason was often to establish sheep walks. In the late C15 and early C16 century, the *wool trade* was big business in Britain and the Low Countries. From its profits arose some of our most magnificent churches. But apart from architectural glory, the wool trade also produced impoverishment, as landowners demolished villages, cleared huge areas and enclosed common pasturage in order to graze yet more sheep. This period is much more likely to have created isolated churches. There is another consideration still. In the late C17 and early C18, when landed gentlemen were making huge parks around their mansions, whole villages were demolished to make way. But this time there was reparation – which usually meant rebuilding the village at the park gates. Houghton, Gunton and Felbrigg are Norfolk examples. Broome is a classic example of a church that was sited alongside the lord of the manor's house for his convenience and well away from the village – the house has gone, but the church remains in the midst of fields. From all this it will be seen that the questions surrounding isolated churches are very open ones.

Ivory, John (?-1805): John Ivory was an apprentice of *Robert Page*, and in company with *Thomas Rawlins* was one of a group of talented sculptors unequalled in any other provincial city. He was responsible for numerous carved monuments in Norwich and Norfolk churches, and for three in the cathedral. Little is known of his life. See Thorpe Market, Norwich St Stephen's and Hockwold.

Jacobean: Style of architecture dating from early in the C17, specifically the reign of James I (1603-25). (See Appendix 2)

Jamb/jamb shaft: The upright of a doorway, or the side of a window opening: the 'shaft' is a decorative shaft or slim column at the angle of the window splay with the wall, and can often be used to remarkably beautiful and delicate effect.

Jekyll, Thomas (1827 – 1881): One of the C19's quirky, but highly creative designer architects who had something in common with *Pugin* and the *Pre-Raphaelites*. Many of his designs in metal were brilliant, winning international awards, and most of his church woodwork is of very high quality. The building styles he adopted ranged from 'Old English', through 'Queen Anne' to Anglo-Japanese, in which he was one of the first in the field. Jekyll was active in London and elsewhere, and in Norfolk he designed the Norwich Gates at Sandringham (made by Barnards of Norwich 1859-62) and restored a number of country houses. His only complete Anglican church was Thorpe Episcopi, St Andrew, although his virtuosity can be seen running riot in the Methodist church at Holt. Highly regarded in his day, his boundless activity and enormous output proved too much for him and he died insane. Apart from Thorpe, he was active at Banham, Carleton Rode, Forncett St Peter, Gt. Hautbois, Gt. Melton, Haddiscoe, Hempnall, Lt. Massingham, Scarning, Thurlton, Trimingham, W. Bradenham, and Wiveton.

Jesse Tree: Isaiah prophesied: 'And there shall come forth a rod out of the stem of Jesus, and a Branch shall grow out of his roots'. Medieval artists illustrated the human genealogy of Christ as a tree (often a vine) springing up from the body of Jesse with each generation as the fruits. The *Blessed Virgin* and Christ child were depicted at the top, and occasionally pagan figures, such as Virgil, slipped in. There is a C19 version in stained glass at Hunstanton St Mary, and an important carved medieval version at East Harling.

Julian of Norwich: See *Mother Julian of Norwich*.

Kempe & Co (Kempe & Tower): A firm of stained glass manufacturers founded by Charles Eamer Kempe in 1869, a designer who had worked for Clayton & Bell. His nephew, Walter Earnest Tower, took over in 1907 and continued until 1934. Their work is generally in C15 mode, intricate and often sentimental, with a distinctive steely colour range. Kempe was one of the most successful of the late-Victorian designers and there was little change in the style he adopted, even in the C20. His windows are sometimes signed with a wheatsheaf emblem, while those of Tower often have a castle superimposed on the sheaf of corn. Typical examples can be found at Langham, Glandford, Brundall, Belton, Gillingham, Newton Flotman, Norwich St Stephen, Old Buckenham, Sedgeford and Stanhoe.

Kempe, Margery (c.1373-c.1440): A remarkable 'religious woman' with a simple faith, the resilience of an early saint; and an unabashed fluency of tongue. Until the 1930s it was thought that the only writings of this

(King's) Lynn woman were some brief pages of 'The Boke of Margerie Kempe of Lynn'. Then, excitingly, a manuscript came to light – an autobiography which, late in life, she had dictated (for it seems she was illiterate herself) giving an account of the many religious experiences she had undergone and pilgrimages she had made. For astonishingly, this ordinary, unlettered woman had travelled to Rome, Jerusalem and Compostela in Spain. Nearer at hand, she met *Julian of Norwich*. Nothing daunted Margery Kempe; no one, no matter what his rank, intimidated her (she once swapped words sharply with the Archbishop of York); and all that she saw and heard she remembered and considered. At St Margaret's in Lynn, where she regularly worshipped, they would have forgiven her much after she had a vision in which St Margaret's was assured of being in the right in its dispute with St Nicholas' Chapel, for the right to baptize children and collect the fees.

Kennel Head-dress: A style of head-dress fashionable from about 1500 to 1540 – but not in fact given its name as we know it until the C19. It appears distinctively on figures on *brasses* and tombs of the period, and on carved heads of *corbels* etc., in several Norfolk churches. The head-dress consisted of a hood wired up to form a pointed arch over the forehead, with borders framing the face to each side. The early kind hung in their folds to the shoulders behind; but after 1525 the back drapery was replaced by two long pendant flaps which hung down in front, each side of the neck. Both kinds will be seen represented. Examples are at Bedingham, Frenze, Forncett St Peter, Norwich St Andrew, Norwich St Clement, Shotesham St Mary, Weston Longville, West Harling, Feltwell, Great Cressingham, Narborough and West Harling.

King posts: An upright roof beam set between horizontal cross beams; or between cross beam and roof ridge, to prevent sag and give greater stability. (See *Roofs*, fig. 3, for full description.)

Knapped/knapping: See *flint-knapping*.

Knights Templar: Originally a military Order founded in 1119 at the time of the Crusades, its founders took upon themselves the vows of chastity, poverty and obedience, and the duty of defending pilgrims to the Holy Land. Baldwin II, King of Jerusalem, gave them quarters in his palace, which was built upon the site of the great Temple of Jerusalem – thus the name of the Order. For nearly 200 years their valour and military honour were by-words. But their power, the wealth of the Order and the arrogance of its members grew in proportion. King Philip of France, and Pope Clement V, plotted their downfall – and the end began in 1307 with the seizing of the Grand Master of the Order and 140 of his followers. England, among all the European nations, was the least willing to bring charges against Templars, and did so only under the strongest pressure from the Pope. However the Order was suppressed here under Edward II and their lands, as elsewhere in Europe, given to the Knights of St John of Jerusalem. Reminders of the Templars in Norfolk may be seen at Carbroke, Southacre and Tilney All Saints. See also *cross patée*.

Lancet: The slim, pointed window that characterises the beginnings of *Early English* architecture from about 1200. (See Appendix 2.)

Laudian: This refers to Archbishop William Laud (1573-1644). His seven years as Archbishop of Canterbury, during which he tried to impose certain disciplines of worship on the English and Scottish churches, had far reaching effects – but resulted in his execution. Laud wanted to reform the English Church in a way compatible with Protestantism, yet without giving way to the sweeping changes and austerities called for by the increasingly powerful Puritans. Brought down to its simplicities, he wanted a disciplined order and form of worship which centred on the altar, placed against the e. wall of the *chancel*, with an enclosing *communion rail* around it; and with the communicants kneeling within the chancel to receive the sacrament. But these were matters of bitter and violent debate. From Elizabeth I's reign, the altar often had been placed 'table wise' – i.e. e. to w. – at the *nave* end of the chancel; or a temporary table was set up in the nave – the intention being in each case for the communicants to be within sight and hearing of the priest at the altar. But there were those who refused to kneel, or even to enter the chancel, and who certainly would not tolerate, in the e. end altar, what smacked to them of a Roman 'high altar', divorced from the people. The impression which comes down to us of the Archbishop is of a man of honest intent, but whose every action seemed to turn people against him. He was accused of 'popery' and blamed for disastrous moves against Scotland, both judicial and military, aimed at enforcing conformity. Then he issued instructions which appeared to many to enshrine the absolute rule and 'divine right' of King Charles I. In December 1640, Parliament impeached Laud for treason, and he was imprisoned in the Tower, but it was not until March 1644 that he was put on trial. The House of Lords had decided in advance that he was guilty of trying to alter the foundations of Church and State, but they hesitated to sentence him before relenting under pressure from the House of Commons. On January 10th 1644, staunchly declaring his innocence and good intent, William Laud died under the axe, parliament having graciously agreed that he should be excused the usual traitor's punishment of being hung, drawn and quartered. The irony is that, by the end of the century, the forms of service that developed in the Anglican church were much in sympathy with the things for which Laud fought and died. (See also *Prayer Book Churches, Communion Rails* and *Mensa slabs.)*

Lavers & Barraud (Lavers & Westlake): Stained glass manufacturers. Founded by Nathaniel Wood Lavers in 1855; he was joined by Francis Phillip Barraud in 1858, both men having been with *Powell & Sons* in the 1840s. Lavers was the craftsman and head of business, relying on competent artists to design his windows. Barraud was a prolific designer for the first decade of the partnership, specialising in small figure medallions. In the 1860s the firm was much favoured by the leaders of the Ecclesiological Society. From then on, major commissions were designed by Nathaniel H.J. Westlake and he became a partner in 1868, doing the majority of the figure work. At that time, their colouring was light and sweet, with a wide range of tints, and the leading was meticulous. Towards the end of the century there was a steady deterioration in aesthetic standards, with mass production methods being used to meet the heavy demand. Westlake was head of the firm in 1880 and continued to his death in 1921. Examples of their work can be found in Colton, Whinburgh and Woodton.

Ledger stone: When the art and use of monumental *brasses* declined in the first half of the C17, sculpture in stone began to come into its own in our churches. But while those splendid, opulent examples which adorn wall or table-tomb may be the first to catch the eye, it often pays to drop one's gaze to the floor to those dark, massive slabs in pavements of *chancel, nave* and *aisles,* incised with arms, crests and epitaphs. These are our ledger-stones, and a study in themselves, as many carry quite marvellous inscriptions – here a lusty hunting man, earthed at last 'by that subtile Fox Death' (Cantley); there a touching remembrance of a parish priest 'as good perhaps as ever lived' (Little Snoring); and again, a subtly bitter-edged lament on a little seven year-old's passing, 'what crowds will wish their time on earth had been as short as thine' (Knapton). To go into a holy place with eyes cast down can be rewarding in more than one sense!

Lenten Veil: It was the custom in medieval times to 'curtain off the altar during Lent with a Lenten Veil'. This was suspended from *corbels,* or hooks – of which a few examples remain in Norfolk churches – set into the chancel walls at a suitable height. See Antingham, Horsham, Haddiscoe, Old Buckenham and North Creake.

Lights: A 'light' is the space between the vertical *mullions* dividing a window. So if a window has just one central mullion, it is a 'two-light window'. The biggest examples are of six lights, where five tall mullions divide up the sections. Not to be confused with an occasional usage of 'light' in the sense of constantly burning candles, which in medieval times were maintained on *chantry* and *guild* altars and in front of images.

Linen-fold panelling: An innovation in wood carving of the C16 in the *Tudor* period – an elegant and beautifully restrained representation in wood of linen laid in crisp vertical folds. Seen on a range of church furnishings.

Linton, W. of Norwich (1666-1684): A Norwich sculptor, well known in his day, whose memorial to Edmund Hobart can be seen at Holt.

Lombardic script/Lombardic capitals: A calligraphic form of writing which developed in Italy after the Roman and Byzantine periods. A variant of it was used for Papal documents and for legal work in Rome until the early C13. From time to time it is used on tombs and memorials in English churches. Among Norfolk examples is the border inscription on an ancient coffin lid at Hickling. See also Stradsett and Watlington.

Long and short work: Distinctive of *Saxon* craftsmanship, upright stones alternating with flat slabs in the quoins at the corners of buildings. (See Appendix 2.)

Low side windows: Almost as much nonsense has been written about low side windows as about *weeping chancels*. These small, square or oblong windows were usually low down in the s. wall of the *chancel*, just e. of the chancel arch, and fitted with shutters so that the window could be opened. It has been suggested that these were 'leper windows' for these afflicted people to look in and thus share in the mass – a ridiculous assertion, lepers were not allowed to roam at leisure. Their actual use at the moment of the elevation of the *host* during the mass, a handbell would be rung through the opened low window, so that for a moment those in the vicinity, in village and field, might pause in their daily round, cross themselves, and thus share in the celebration. Most low side windows are now filled in, but a complete one can be seen at Saxthorpe; at Attlebridge, one is contained in the lower part of a large window; and, at Burlingham St Andrew, there is an interesting pointed one. But perhaps the most telling example is at Melton Constable, which has beside it a stone book rest and a hollowed-out seat. We have noted throughout the county a total of 49 low side windows. (See also *sanctus bell.*)

Lych-gate: The word 'lych' is derived from the Anglo Saxon 'lie' or 'lich', and from the German 'leiche', all meaning corpse. The purpose of the lych-gate is to provide a shelter and resting place for coffin bearers on the way to the church. In former times, the lych-gate would have had seats and a table, on which the coffin would be set. Poor people who could not afford a coffin might be placed – temporarily – in the parish coffin; but otherwise they would be wrapped in a sheet and placed straight onto the coffin table, where they would be received by the priest, who here speaks the first sentences of the burial service. Ancient lych-gates are rare, most being C19/C20.

Mandorla: (from the Italian for almond) Another term for vesica piscis: a pointed oval figure used as an architectural feature and as an aureole enclosing figures such as Christ and the Blessed Virgin in Medieval art.

Marshall, Joshua (1629-1678): He was Master Mason to the Crown, and carried out much work at the Royal Palaces for Charles I. He built, or helped rebuild, several of London's churches after the Great Fire of 1666, and is remembered as one of the greatest statuaries of the C17. The one example of his work in Norfolk is the monument for Lady Williamson in Loddon church.

Mass or scratch dials: On or near the s. porch or the priest's door of many old churches may be seen small patterns, usually about six to ten inches across, of radiating lines centred on a hole. In the hole was placed a metal or wooden peg known as a gnomon (Greek – indicator), whose shadow moved round with the sun and each time the shadow touched one of the radiating lines, it was time for mass. Later, largely in the C18, sun-dials became popular, providing a timepiece, sunshine permitting, for the whole day.

Mensas: Before the *Reformation*, the high altar and altars in chantry chapels were of stone, topped with a mensa (Latin, table). Each had five crosses carved upon it, one at each corner and one on the centre, representing the *Five Wounds of Christ*. After the Suppression of the Monasteries, begun in 1536 by Henry VIII, the chantries too were soon dissolved, and with them went their altars. But stone high altars remained, and in the reign of Henry's son, the boy king Edward VI – a convinced Protestant – a movement was led by two of his bishops to have them removed and replaced by wooden tables. This was realised in 1550 when the King in Council commanded every bishop to order this change in all the churches in his diocese. Hanworth has its mensa restored to its old position – it was found nearly a century ago, buried in the churchyard; Scottow has one framed as a memorial; and Salthouse has a foot-square one set into its present altar. This last one is interesting: it is a portable mensa, which would have been used for saying mass on unconsecrated altars. This was quite a common thing in churches in medieval times: indeed, it is recorded that, in 1367, there were 200 of them in the Archdeaconry of Norwich alone. We have noted some 22 mensa throughout the county. (See also *Consecration Crosses.*)

Misericords: In the *chancels* of many churches remain ancient stalls with hinged seats. Underneath, the tip-up seats are carved generally with very free expression and often with exuberant irreverence and humour: anything from the wildest caricatures to cartoonish domestic scenes and upsets. All are worth examining closely, wherever they are found. On the leading edge of these seats is usually a smooth, hollowed surface on which, during long services, the elderly – or just the plain sleepy – could lean and rest. Thus the name, from the Latin 'misericordia', pity, compassion.

Morris, William (1834 1896)/Morris & Co.: Architect, painter, designer, poet, and prolific writer on artistic, literary and political matters. But best known as the man who in 1861 founded Morris & Co. and thus revolutionised British taste in furnishings, interior decoration (his wallpaper designs are still famous and in demand), ceramics, textiles and stained glass, and exercised a considerable influence on industrial design. Himself a first-rate craftsman, he was devoted to the idea of reviving craftsmanship and old handicrafts in an age already embarked on mass production. While at Oxford he began a life long friendship with the painter *Edward Burne-Jones*, who made many tapestry and stained glass designs for Morris & Co. which were executed in the company's workshops. (See under *Burne-Jones* for examples in Norfolk of their stained glass collaborations.)

Mother Julian of Norwich: Julian was the C14 *anchoress* at St Julian's Church in Norwich, who wrote the book now regarded as one of the masterpieces of spiritual literature – 'Revelations of Divine Love'. She was born in 1343 – about the same time as Chaucer – and was almost certainly educated by the nuns at nearby Carrow, a Benedictine Priory. On May 8th, 1373, during severe illness, she received a series of 'showings' from God. She became an enclosed nun, living alone beside St Julian's Church. Her name is thought to be taken from the church itself. There, during the next 20 years, she wrote her book, the first known to be written in English by a woman. Julian's cell was in use until the *Reformation*. The church survived, only to be badly damaged by bombing in the last war. Today the church and cell have been rebuilt. The cell is now a chapel to which pilgrims come from all over the world. Mother Julian looks down on worshippers at Horstead, from a stained glass window, and a statue of her was added to the w. front of the Cathedral at the Millenium. See also Norwich St Julian's and Wymondham.

Mouchette: A tracery shape or motif, used principally during the *Decorated* period early in the C14. It is a curved dagger or spearhead shape, *cusped* and arched inside.

Myngs, Sir Christopher (1625 1666): Admiral Myngs was born at Salthouse, on the n.e. Norfolk coast, in 1625 at the manor house: later he was to acquire Salthouse Hall. He went to sea at an early age in a coastal vessel sailing out of nearby Blakeney. During the Four Days Battle, off North Foreland in 1666, Myngs was fatally wounded in the throat. His death moved a number of his men to offer themselves as a 'suicide mission' crew of a fireship, to exact revenge upon the enemy; and also inspired a popular song:

> So here's the grave of Sir Christopher
>   Myngs
> A great name greater than my lord the
>   King's
> He fought and bled for England
> He's lying dead for England
> And foul fall shame
> On England's name
> When Englishmen forget the name
> Of stout Sir Christopher Myngs.

He is remembered, at least, at Salthouse, in the proud church above the shoreline where a copy of that song hangs on a wall.

Narbrough, Sir John (1640 1688): One of Norfolk's several admirals, he was baptised at Cockthorpe Church on October 11th, 1640. He went early to sea, in a local vessel, possibly with *Admiral Myngs*, from nearby Salthouse. He was involved in the Battle of Solebay in 1672; and the following year was promoted rear-admiral and knighted. Following distinguished Mediterranean service (mostly against pirates) he was posted to the West Indies, where he caught fever and died.

Nave: The main 'body' of a church – from the Latin navis, a ship. Traditionally the nave was for the congregation, the *chancel* being for the clergy. Indeed, so much was it a preserve of the people that in ancient times, it was used for parish meetings, as a courtroom and perhaps for the performance of mystery plays.

Nelson, Admiral, Viscount (1758-1805): The naval career of Norfolk's 'essential hero', Horatio Nelson, is too well known to need relating here. Enough to note that he was born at Burnham Thorpe (where his father was rector) and that in his days of celebrity he was back in 'dear Burnham' whenever he could arrange it. In time, too, he would bring his mistress Emma, Lady Hamilton, to the county. After the deaths of both of them, their illegitimate daughter Horatia was to come to Burnham too. She married the curate, Philip Ward, at Burnham Westgate Church, opposite the elegant Bolton House (still there) where she lived for two years. You have to go to Trunch to find a memorial to her though: and then it is merely her name, tacked onto the end of a ledger slab in the chancel floor, inscribed to Philip's parents (see also Woodton).

Nine Men's Morris: In Act II, Scene II of Shakespeare's 'A Midsummer Night's Dream', Queen Titania of the Faeries says:

> The nine men's morris is filled up with mud;
> And the quaint mazes in the wanton green,
> For lack of tread, are indistinguishable.

What she was talking about was a game, generally played with counters on a board set out in a frame pattern of three squares, one within the other, with diagonal intersecting lines. Titania's shepherds, as did countrymen in Elizabethan England, carved it out in the turf – thus the 'quaint maze' in the 'wanton green'. But the game is much older than Shakespeare: in the n.e. corner of Norwich Cathedral cloister you can see traces of it scratched out on a stone bench. There's a frame on a table-tomb at Hickling, and on benches in the porches at Rollesby and Braydeston. Also known as The Mill the game is for two players, each having nine counters. And the 'morris'? That probably alludes to the similarity of its moves to those in an old 'morris' dance.

Nine Orders of Angels: The theme of the Nine Orders of Angels was only rarely employed by medieval church artists. But Norfolk has one magnificent series painted on the rood screen at Barton Turf, and part of a series in stained glass in the e. window of Salle church. There are several Biblical references to the 'orders' of these heavenly beings: in Ephesians 1,21, and Colossians, 1,16 in the New Testament; and in Isaiah 6,2 and Ezekiel – in that wonderful first chapter – in the Old Testament. It was around the year 500 however that a mystic and theologian, Dionysius the Areopagite, set out in one of his several treatises, 'The Celestial Hierarchies', an explanation of The Nine Orders of Angels and their mission as mediators between God and man. He arranged them in three hierarchies, each containing three choirs, in the following order: Seraphim (who inspire humankind towards divine love); Cherubim (who give forth endless wisdom); Thrones (flaming wheels with eyes, set about the Throne of God); Dominions (the instruments of God's almighty will), Virtues and Powers; and the lowest orders, Principalities, Archangels and Angels. Of these only the last two choirs have an immediate mission to men, for they are God's messengers, moving between Earth and Heaven. The word angel, in its Hebraic origin, means 'message'. But some early Christian writers saw angelic beings as ranged on two sides, some good, some bad (the Devil, after all, is a fallen angel), so that the message could be of God or Satan. (See also Banningham).

Nollekens, Joseph (1737-1823): The choice of fashionable London, Joseph Nollekens occupied in the sculpture of his time the equivalent role to that of the celebrated portraitist Sir Joshua Reynolds in painting. His sculpture extended to opulent chimney pieces and ceilings for great houses, as well as portrait busts for the nobility and urns and tablets and the like as memorials. But well paid and well patronised as he was – he left a fortune of £200,000 –, Nollekens was renowned for his miserly ways. There are examples of his work at Tittleshall for Jane Coke, and a grand one at Felbrigg, to William Windham, 1813.

Norfolk Churches Trust: The Norfolk Churches Trust was formed in 1976 in order to safeguard the future of a number of churches in the county which were no longer required for regular worship by the Church of England. By 2007, the Trust was leasing eleven churches, and in 2006 grants totalling nearly £300,000 were made to 79 parishes to help them maintain their buildings.

Norman: The 'Romanesque' form of architecture, with its distinctive rounded arches and massive round pillars, introduced to England following the Norman Conquest of 1066. (See Appendix 2.)

Norwich Glass: In Norwich there was a remarkable burgeoning of glass painting, beginning in the late C13 and reaching its summit in the C15, of what has come to be known as The Norwich School of Glass Painting. In the late Middle Ages Norwich was one of the leading centres of English art – not only glass painters, but artists working on screens, roofs and walls, producing rich work of which only a small part has been handed down to us. In churches like Bale, Salle, Norwich St Peter Mancroft, North Tuddenham, East

Harling and others, the work of the stained glass artists in the century before the *Reformation* can be appreciated – 'glass of high quality, of marked individuality, and of abiding interest'. The earliest glass – C13 – identified in any Norfolk church is at Saxlingham Nethergate.

O'Connor, Arthur and William: Stained glass artists whose father, Michael, began in Dublin as an heraldic painter before moving to London in 1823. He had studied with Thomas Willement and worked with *Pugin* and Butterfield. He took his sons into partnership in the 1850s and when Arthur died in 1873, William George Taylor joined the firm and managed it from 1877 onwards. Fine colour and an effective deployment of lead lines distinguish much of the O'Connors' work. Windows by them can be found at North Pickenham and Snetterton.

Ogee arches/curves: A lovely, flowing 'S' shaped arch or moulding – a convex curve flowing into a concave one. Usually they are not very large because, by their very nature, they cannot carry heavy loads. But their grace lends them to the heads of canopies, to *piscina, sedilia* and the like; sometimes also to doorways, giving them a curiously oriental look, as well as in the tracery of windows and screens. Adorned with *crocketting*, ogee arches are still more attractive. They came into general use in the C14, playing an important role in the development of the sumptuous windows of the late *Decorated* period, with their flowing tracery of which the ogee curve forms an integral part (See also Appendix 2.)

Page, Robert (1707-1778): A prolific and important sculptor in his native Norfolk, Robert Page occupies the position of perhaps the best in his field which this county has ever produced. In his Norwich workshops he developed his skilled use of coloured marbles, and showed a facility for *rococo* detail, seen in groups of cherubs' heads and in richly carved shields. Among a considerable list of his works in Norfolk churches, there is a fine one at Sprowston, with portrait bust; and others at Gateley, Dersingham, Melton Constable, Coulton, Colton and Catton; with a further list in Norwich itself, including his own memorial, carefully completed 'in advance' and placed where he now lies, in St John's Timberhill.

Palimpsest brass: A memorial *brass* which has been turned over – and used again by re-engraving it on its plain side. The word is also used in relation to writing material which has been 're-used', comes from the Greek palimpsestos, rub smooth.

Palladian: One of the foremost Renaissance architects in Italy was the Venetian, Andrea Palladio (d.1580) who took his inspiration from Imperial Rome. In the C18, there was a great movement in England, both in churches and in great country houses, to revive the Palladian ideal. Here in Norfolk is one of the finest examples in the kingdom, Holkham Hall, built between 1734 and 1761. Occasional Palladian features and details, however, are encountered in several churches in the county.

Pamments: 6 in.-12 in. unglazed floor tiles used all over East Anglia.

Parclose screen: Screens which separated *chantry* or side chapels, and/or aisles, from the main body of the church. (See also *Rood loft/screen*.)

Parish Clerk: Not the 'clerk to the parish council' of late Victorian, local government invention, but a paid office which was for centuries of central importance in church services. It was the job of the clerk to lead the singing and the responses to the prayers. Sometimes he filled the role of choirmaster; certainly he would 'give the notes' on a pitch pipe. After the *Reformation* in the C16, the clerk continued to exercise his role; indeed, he had a special seat in the *Three-Decker Pulpits* which appeared later. In the C17, under James I and later Charles II, the parish clerks, who had the dignity of being a London Company, were given new Charters which stipulated that 'every person that is chosen Clerk of the Parish should first give sufficient proof of his abilities to sing at least the tunes which are used in the parish churches'. He sang on until soon after Victoria ascended the Throne, when most of his duties were given to others. Then came the local government acts of the late C19, which finally consigned him to history: and left only his seat at the foot of the three-deckers to remind us of a 700 year tradition.

Parish Guilds: See *Guilds/Guild altars*.

Parker, Matthew, Archbishop of Canterbury (1504-1575): One of the most famous sons of Norwich, Parker is remembered by an annual sermon in the cathedral and another at St

Clement's Church on the same evening. He asked that a prayer be said for the souls of his parents by their tomb at St Clement's on that day – and so it is. At Cambridge University, Parker became closely associated with Protestant reformers inspired by the writings of Martin Luther – but he himself remained cautious. After serving in several parishes (including Burlingham here in Norfolk) he returned to Cambridge as Master of his old college; and soon after was elected vice-chancellor of the university. During the reign of King Edward VI, he grew in favour and was appointed to the rich deanery of Lincoln. However, his support for Lady Jane Grey (briefly hailed as Queen) meant that on the accession of Catholic Mary he had to go into hiding until the accession of Elizabeth brought him back into favour. He was her choice for Canterbury and from this time he was central in the movement that created the 'Anglican' philosophy, treading a careful path between Puritanism and Catholicism. He left behind him the record of a great benefactor of education, of great scholarship and of staunch defence of his church. This then is the man who, more than four centuries on, his native city still remembers each year. (See also Mattishall).

Passion Emblems: See *Instruments of the Passion*.

Pediment: The low triangular gable used in classical building but often employed on classically styled monuments in churches.

Pedlar of Swaffham, The: Riches, according to legend, came remarkably to John Chapman, the Pedlar of Swaffham – but his parish church at Swaffham benefitted greatly from his wealth. During its major rebuilding in C15 he paid for the new n. *aisle*. John the Pedlar had a dream – that if he went to London Bridge he would meet there a man who would make his fortune. He went, and there a shopkeeper asked why he, and his inseparable dog, were hanging about. He roared with laughter when told of John's dream and said: 'Why, if I heeded dreams, I might be as big a fool as you. I dreamt recently that at Norfolk at a place called Swaffham Market lived a pedlar called Chapman. In his garden was a tree, and buried under it a pot of gold'. John hurried home, keeping his knowledge to himself – and dug up a brass pot containing gold coins. Being thrifty, he put out the pot for sale with his other goods. A would-be purchaser translated for him an inscription on the pot

which revealed: 'Underneath this pot is one which is twice as good', John hurried home and dug again to reveal a second pot of gold.

Pelican: The pelican has long had a special place in religious symbolism and is often seen as a device used in medieval carving and embellishment known as the pelican in her piety – a pelican crowns the summit of the great font cover at St Peter Mancroft (Norwich), for example. There is a legend that the bird tore its own breast to feed its young upon its own blood – the source of the idea, it is suggested, being that the tip of the pelican's bill, which usually rests on this ungainly bird's chest, is touched with red. In medieval art the legend is transmuted into a symbolism of man's fall and redemption through the Passion of Christ. Here we find that the parent bird was said to kill its young in a moment of irritation – then, 'on the third day', to restore them to life by tearing its breast and letting its own blood pour over them. Brass lecterns sometimes have a pelican instead of an eagle – one fine example is the lectern under the crossing in Norwich Cathedral.

Pentecost: The Christian festival commemorating the descent of the Holy Spirit on the Apostles (Acts 2) on the 50th day after Easter. Better known as Whit Sunday – a name derived from the white robes of those presented for baptism, for which this festival became the traditional occasion. Medieval artists used the theme in stone and paint and glass – See for example Bawburgh, Saxlingham Nethergate and East Harling.

Perpendicular: The great age of church building, in the second half of the C14 and through the C15, in the style characterised by soaring upward lines in great windows and majestic towers. (See Appendix 2.)

Pevsner, Sir Nikolaus: Author of the monumental and remarkable undertaking 'The Buildings of England' series – 46 volumes, written between 1951 and 1974 by Pevsner himself. His two volumes on Norfolk appeared in 1962, following a 'grand tour' round the county lasting about four months in which Dr Pevsner – as he then was – visited every location personally:

> I found Norfolk to be the kind of county it is especially nice to do. People are proud of it, they like it, and it is a county in which one feels at home.

Revised editions edited by Bill Wilson were published in 1997 and 1999.

Pier: The 'architectural' word for a column or pillar.

Pietà: A carving or painting of the Blessed Virgin as Our Lady of Sorrows, seated with the dead Christ across her knees. There is an example at East Harling, St Peter & St Paul and more across the county.

Pilaster: A miniature pillar, rectangular in section, usually based in style on one of the Classical orders of architecture, and normally applied to a wall.

Piscina/angle piscina/double piscina/pillar piscina: A stone basin near an altar (its presence today indicates that there was formerly an altar there), usually set into a niche in the wall below an arch or canopy, sometimes projecting outwards on a bowl, which in turn may be supported by a small pillar. The piscina was used for cleansing the communion vessels after mass – thus it has a drain hole in its basin, which allows the water used in the cleansing to run down into consecrated ground. It was obligatory that where water had been blessed, or has come into contact with anything consecrated, it had to be returned to earth. Sometimes there is a small shelf in the piscina niche called a *credence*. The angle piscina is one built into the angle of a window or *sedilia*, and opened out on two sides. Double piscinas – two side by side – may occasionally be found. These had but a short span of fashion in the late C13-early C14: one was used by the priest for the cleaning of the vessels, the other for the washing of his own hands. A pillar piscina is one which protrudes from the wall, its bowl and drain standing on a miniature pillar, either attached to or standing clear of the wall. A corbel piscina has, instead of a pillar, its bowl supported by a *corbel*. See Barton Bendish and Wilton for very rare examples of floor piscinas.

Plate tracery: This is tracery in the heads of windows where the pattern is cut directly through the masonry; as distinct from *bar tracery*, which is constructed in separate pieces. (See 'Early English' in Appendix 2.)

Poppy-heads: The boldly carved floral ornament which graces the ends of bench pews – said to be derived from the French 'poupée',

puppet, doll or figurehead. It was during the great age of C15 church building and wood carving that poppy-heads came into being and achieved their highest artistic expression. The carvers often seem to have been given a free hand, with diverse and interesting results – animals, grotesques, faces and so on; or for a noble patron, a carved crest or coat-of-arms, like that of the Paston Family at Paston Church.

Porches: It was not until the C14 that porches came to be regarded as an essential part of the church plan, so few are found from before that date. It explains why *mass dials* will often be found beside the inner door, inside the porch, where the sun could not possibly reach them. The porch in those cases was a later addition. Having become established, the porch assumed a practical importance which we tend to forget today. Services of Baptism began here; sentences were spoken from the burial service, after the first pause in the *lych-gate*; women were 'churched' (i.e. purified and blessed) after the birth of a child; part of the wedding service was conducted here; in the porch the kneeling penitent received absolution; and the porch was one of the 'stations' in the regular Sunday and Feast Day processions (refer also to *banner stave locker* and *galilee porch*). Not least, the porch was a convenient meeting ground for the carrying out of much civil and legal business. Some porches also have a second storey originally intended as a priest's room – but later much used as the first and only school in the parish.

Postern door: A small door sometimes found inserted in a larger entrance door to a church, as at Thornham and elsewhere.

Powell, James & Sons: Stained glass manufacturers. Founded in 1844, the business had one of the longest histories in the trade and did not close until 1973. It was among the most important and progressive firms, making a significant contribution both in technology and in the art form. Many of their designs came from artists of the calibre of *Burne-Jones, Henry Holiday* and Christopher Whall. Examples can be found at Middleton and Garboldisham.

Prayer Book Churches: A phrase used to describe those churches where the furnishings and layout still embody the great shift of emphasis in church worship that came, first with the *Reformation* and then with the Puritans. The old, and strict, division of priest in *chancel* from people in *nave* was put away, and the English prayer book of 1549 required the laity to take part in all of the service – Matins and Evensong were to be conducted from the Chancel and everybody had to hear the Lessons. The altar became 'the table' for the first time in the 1552 revision. After the Civil War, Sunday services (except on infrequent Sacrament Sundays) were conducted entirely from the Reading Desk, and soon the convenient Reading Desk cum Pulpit became the rule (see *Three-Decker Pulpits*). In the C18 virtually every church in the land had its pews (often enclosed for each family – see *Box Pews*) arranged to focus on the Reading Desk and Pulpit. Then, in the 1830s, a 'new wave' of churchmen were inspired by *Pugin*, followed by John Newman's Oxford Movement', to sweep away these things. Their vision was to have truly Gothic churches again, and C18 domestic church interiors were anathema. Today, very few of the sensible and seemly furnishings of the 'Age of Reason' are to be found, but Norfolk has some examples – Warham St Mary, Bylaugh (excellent!), Thurning, Gunton, and Wilby.

Preaching/churchyard cross: In ancient times, when the churchyard was a gathering place, market and fair-ground, most churches had a preaching or churchyard cross, from which the resident priest, or wandering friars, might preach to the assembled people. The stumps of some of these crosses remain.

Pre-Raphaelites: The Pre-Raphaelite Brotherhood was a group of Victorian artists who sought to go back to principles before the Italian master, Raphael (d.1520) imposed his mark. The Brotherhood had only three members – Rossetti, Millais and Holman Hunt – and lasted only five years from its establishment in 1848. But, with its pre-occupation with biblical and literary subjects and the artists' urge for 'social realism', it had a great influence on several other artists of note, among them *Burne-Jones*. It was he who later, with *William Morris*, briefly tried to revive the brotherhood. Inevitably the Pre-Raphaelite movement left its impression on the church art of the period, as evidenced in Burne-Jones's work to be found in a number of Norfolk churches.

Priest's door: Most *chancels* have a small door, usually on the s. side, which was the priest's 'private entrance'. It fits into context when it is remembered that, until recently, the chancel was

the priest's particular responsibility, while the parishioners looked after the *nave*.

Pugin, Augustus Welby (1812-1852): English architect, born in London. He early became a Roman Catholic and he had a large share in the designs and plans for the Houses of Parliament in 1836. Through pressure of work he went insane, and died at the age of only 40. However, his influence on the interior furnishing of churches as we know them today was considerable. South Pickenham has a gorgeous 'High Gothic' organ case designed by him.

Purbeck marble: Frequently used for fonts and columns. The first in this material came during the *Norman* period, and it was used for long afterwards. The grey stone is not in fact marble at all, but a hard limestone full of shells: it comes from a strata stretching from the Isle of Purbeck, in s.e. Dorset (famous for its quarries for a thousand years) northwards to Aylesbury.

Purlin: The main horizontal supporting beam of a roof. (See *Roofs*, fig. 4.)

Put-log holes: The holes where the horizontal members of the (timber) scaffolding slotted into the walls during construction.

Putti (singular, putto): Little naked cherub boys first seen in that form in the work of *Renaissance* artists in Italy and regularly in the work of C18/C19 sculptors in England in the adornment of monuments and tombs. It is possible that these cherubs have their origin in the naked Eros and Mercury representations of ancient classical, pagan belief one of the many examples of 'Christianising' ancient deities, places and practices.

Pyx: The receptacle, suspended over the altar, in which the *host* is 'reserved'. Note the story of Saint *Clare* in Appendix 1.

Quatrefoils: See *Foils*.

Queen posts: Upright roof beams set in pairs on horizontal cross or *tie-beams* and thrusting up on each side to the main horizontal supporting beams, or *purlins*, of the roof. Designed, like the *king post* to prevent sag and give greater stability. See *Roofs*.

Quoins: The outside corner stones at the angles of buildings.

Rawlins, Thomas (1747-1781): Son of Thomas Rawlins the Elder, a mason and statuary in Norwich, Rawlins Jr. was trained in London whence he returned to his native city and in due course was mason for the building of the porch of St Andrew's Hall, a gothic creation in full sympathy with the great *Perpendicular* hall. Among the best in his field, locally and nationally, in his time, with great skills in the use of coloured marbles and in fine details, Rawlins has a particularly fine example of his work in St Giles' Church, Norwich, a monument to Sir Thomas Churchman, 1781; also a very elegant memorial, dated 1762, at Smallburgh. In Norfolk and Norwich there are many Rawlins' monuments, but it is not always clear whether they are the work of 'the Elder' or 'the Younger'. Among them are examples at Mendham, Wymondham, Costessey and Woodton, in several Norwich churches and in the cathedral. See also East Bradenham.

Rebus: A punning representation of a name or word by the use of symbols, normally in churches referring to the name of the place or the name of a donor. Thus, at Shelton there are carvings of shells on barrels (or tuns), and at Norwich cathedral, Bishop Lyhart is remembered by carvings of a deer (or hart) lying down.

Reformation: The great religious movement in western Europe during the C16, founded on a return to Biblical sources and their fresh interpretation, which led to the rejection of Rome and Papal authority and the establishment of 'Protestant' churches. In England the original motivations were more basic, being political and economic, rather than theological. Firstly, Henry VIII, intent on putting away one wife and taking another by whom he could beget an heir. Secondly, his calculating eye on the wealth of the monasteries – backed by his aristocracy and gentry. Even when he had broken with Rome, however, Henry did his best to minimise the impression of any break with the tradition begun in England by St Augustine a thousand years earlier. The true religious, reforming Reformation came with his son, Edward VI, who though young, was a fanatical Protestant.

Regency: Usually understood as the Regency of George, Prince of Wales, from 1812 to 1820, during the insanity of his father, George III. He succeeded as George IV in 1820 and died in 1830, having earlier wasted his considerable talents as wilfully as he wasted public money. The Regency style was a decorative style spanning the three decades to 1830 – a vogue for 'Chinoiserie' and for heavy furniture inspired by ancient Greek, Roman and Egyptian models.

Regnart, Charles (1759-1844): Regarded in his time as a very competent monumental mason, he was employed all over the country. Norfolk has just one example of his work, at Gissing church.

Renaissance: The age of 'the complete man', embodied in England in men like Elizabeth's 'perfect Renaissance gentleman', Sir Philip Sidney. Greek and Latin literature, and the inspiration of the Greek and Roman classical ages in architecture and architectural embellishment, were the visible and lasting signs. The Renaissance movement, this 'rebirth' of western culture, began in Italy in the C14 and in the C16 spread to the rest of Europe. (Refer also, in Appendix 2, to the *Jacobean/Carolean* periods.)

Reredos: The screening at the back of an altar, usually richly embellished in painting or carving. Few old examples remain, many having disappeared at the *Reformation* and in the century following. (See also *Decalogue* boards.)

Restoration: The period from 1660, following the Restoration of the Monarchy after the Civil War and Commonwealth, and the accession of Charles II.

Retable: A shelf or frame enclosing decorative panels above and behind the altar.

Reticulated: A form of 'flowing' tracery in windows which was developed at the height of '*Decorated*' achievement during the first half of the C14 (see Appendix 2). It is made up of circles flowing downwards to make *ogee* shapes. (Latin: rete, a net; reticulum, a bag of network – the link being that the tracery forms a netlike pattern.)

Reveals: Internal side surface of an opening or recess, especially doorways or windows.

Rib-Vault: This is a vaulted/arched ceiling which has diagonal, projecting ribs, which form a support for the in-filling of the ceiling. (See also *Groining*.)

Rib Vaulting: Furniture or architecture, mainly of the C18, characterised by an elaborately ornamental late-baroque style of decoration with asymmetrical patterns.

Rogation: On the Thursday following the fifth Sunday after Easter comes Ascension Day, marking Christ's Ascension to Heaven forty days after His Resurrection. The Monday, Tuesday and Wednesday of that week are the Rogation Days, in former times a period of fasting and preparation for the Ascension. The Sunday immediately preceding is Rogation Day, traditionally a festival to ask God for His blessing upon the crops and fruits of the earth – and definitely a pagan inheritance (in ancient Rome at this time of year came the Fontanalia, to honour the spirits of springs, streams and fountains). In England Rogationtide has for many centuries been the time of 'beating the parish bounds' – processions went all round the parish boundary, certain 'marker posts' being struck with rods. A notable representation of this ceremony is carved upon the remarkable C12 'Seasonal Font' at Burhham Deepdale.

Rood beam: See *Rood loft*.

Rood loft: In the individual accounts of churches in this book there repeatedly occur references to – rood; screen; rood screen; rood stairs; rood loft; and occasionally, to rood beam. Before the *Reformation*, all churches were separated into two – the chancel for the clergy, the nave for the people – by a wooden, carved *screen*, with secure door, from pillar to pillar under the chancel arch. Immediately above, sometimes included in the screen's construction, was the *rood beam*, which supported a *loft* or platform on which were placed a great Crucifix or rood, with images of the Virgin and St John on either side. This loft was approached by a *staircase* let into the wall. At the Reformation, the rood and its images were almost universally torn down and their images destroyed in violent reaction against Rome and 'popery'. The fact that we have so many screens surviving – Norfolk is especially rich in them – is due to Queen Elizabeth, who in a Royal Order of 1561 directed that while the great rood and its figures should go, the screens themselves should remain, and be topped with a suitable crest or with the *Royal Arms*. Where screen as well as rood had already been destroyed, a new screen (or 'partition', as the wording had it) was to be constructed: for the Elizabethan view was quite clearly that the church should be

partitioned into two distinct sections. In its heyday, the rood loft might be used by choristers, or even do service as a small organ loft; and mass might be said there on the Feast of the Holy Cross. The issue of screens and their role was to rumble on for another century. In 1638 Richard Montague, Bishop of Norwich, was pointedly asking his clergy: 'Is your chancel divided from the nave or body of your church, with a partition of stone, boards, wainscot, grates or otherwise? Wherein is there a decent strong door to open and shut (as occasion serveth) with lock and key, to keep out boys, girls, or irreverent men and women? And are dogs kept from coming to besoil or profane the Lord's table?' While rood stairs and screens are common in Norfolk, rood lofts are very rare – examples can be seen at Little Sheringham and Attleborough. (Refer also to *Communion rails* and *Laudian period*.) Rood beams survive at Banningham, Blakeney, Potter Heigham and Tunstead, Costessey and Bawburgh.

Rood screen: See *Rood loft*.

Rood stairs: See *Rood loft*.

Roofs: The development, structural variety and embellishment of church roofs is a fascinating field in itself. Here is a potted guide to a richly complex subject:

Coupled rafter roofs are a simple variety, which also serve to indicate the roof components (Fig 1). The principal rafters, the feet of which are secured to a wall plate, have a collar beam to support them and prevent sagging. More support is given by the collar braces, with struts lower down giving more strength.

Another framing system is the scissors beam (Fig 2), which can exist with the cross-beams only, or with a supporting collar. As a precaution against spreading of the roof, a tie beam was often added between the wall plates (Fig 3); but as tie-beams have a tendency to sag in the middle a central king post served to prevent this.

The arch-braced construction is where the roof is carried on a braced arch which incorporates 'in one' the strut, collar brace and collar beam (Fig 4).

The function of the tie beam has already been seen in Fig 3. With a low-pitched roof, it is often used simply with struts upward to the principal rafters, and downward on brace and wall post to a corbel set into the wall (Fig 5) well below the wall plates.

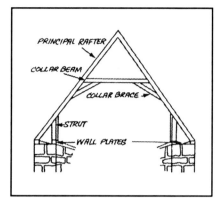

Fig 1.

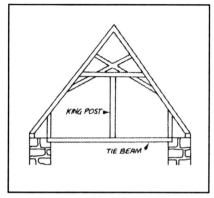

Fig 3.

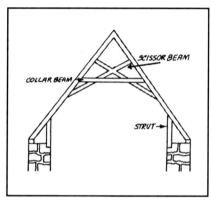

Fig 2.

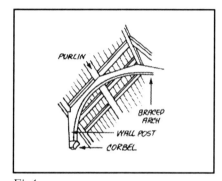

Fig 4.

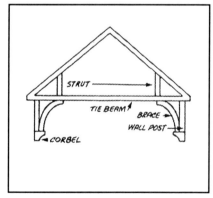

Fig 5.

With the advent of the hammer-beam development (Fig 6), a new splendour was added to the roof builder's art. Trunch is a superb example which comes to mind. Instead of a tie beam spanning wall to wall, there are hammer-beam brackets, from which spring vertical struts, upward to the principal rafter at its intersection with the purlin (refer again to Fig 4), the main horizontal supporting beam. Continuing upward, curved arch-like braces meet either at the ridge beam; or at a collar beam, set very high (Fig 7). From there it was a natural development to the double hammer-beam. Fig 8 is self explanatory – of which a glorious example may be found at Knapton. The ends of the hammer-beams are often embellished with angels or decorative carvings, as Knapton wonderfully illustrates.

Roubiliac, Louis Francois (1705-1762): Sculptor. A native of Lyons, Roubiliac came to England in the early 1730s. By happy chance, he attracted the interest of Sir Edward Walpole, who introduced him to *Sir Henry Cheere* whose assistant he became. Commissions for busts and monuments were to follow from all over the land, and he was the finest of the C18 sculptors. Two excellent busts – of the Earl and Countess of Leicester – can be seen at Tittleshall.

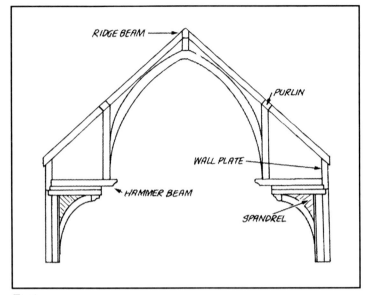

Fig 6.

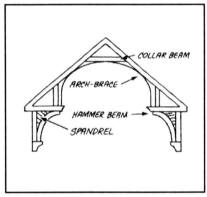

Fig 7.

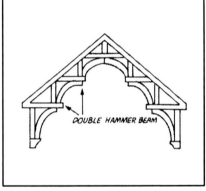

Fig 8.

Royal Arms: Many churches display Royal coats of arms, usually square and framed, painted on wood or canvas; though they may also be found in carved wood or stone, cast in plaster, or set in stained glass. Occasionally the arms are set up and painted in a lozenge shape, like a *hatchment,* but this is unusual (Briningham, Field Dalling and Caister-on-Sea, have examples). It was only during the reign of Henry VIII, when he assumed complete control of the English Church, that Royal Arms began to come into regular use. Catholic Queen Mary was later to order their removal, but with Elizabeth's accession, they began to reappear; indeed Elizabeth directed their use and indicated that

the *tympanum* was the place to display them. Inevitably many disappeared during thr Commonwealth, and Parliament ordered 'the removal of the obnoxious Royal Arms from the churches'. In that same year, at St Margaret's, King's Lynn, the Arms were 'taken Downe & Burnt by Mr Bartholomew Wormell then Alderman'. The 1660 shield is still there, though altered for subsequent reigns (something which often happened). The *Restoration* Parliament in 1660 made Royal Arms compulsory in all our churches – a practice continued generally until Victoria's accession – ordering that 'the Armes of the Commonwealth wherever they are standing be forthwith taken down, and the

Kings Majesties armes be set up instead thereof'. Bearing this in mind there is an interesting rarity at North Walsham – on one side, the Commonwealth, on the other, Charles II. Hosts of Royal Arms will be found throughout the county, but several, in addition to those noted above, may be specially mentioned. Thursford, and Banham, have Elizabeth I's Arms in stained glass; excellent Elizabethan examples at Ludham, Tivetshall St Margaret and Kenninghall. James I Arms are far from common, but good examples are at Marsham, Blo Norton, Burston, Kimberley, Moulton and Tacolneston, Helhoughton, Hilborough, Marham and Tilney St Lawrence. Two of the best sets of Arms for any reign to be seen in the whole county are those of Charles II at Stow Bedon and William III at Shelton. The rarest of all are those for James II's short reign, before he fled the country in 1688 – Little Snoring has a fine set. (Next door, in Great Snoring, they followed suit by updating with an added 'I' their James I Arms). Upwell takes the prize for the biggest set of Arms in Norfolk – those of Victoria magnificently carved in wood and set up at ground level so that one can appreciate them to the full. When the full complement of crest, mantling, shield and motto are present, the whole is called an 'achievement'.

Sacred Monogram: See *IHS*.

Sacring Bell: A small bell rung at that point in the mass when the priest holds up the *host* above the altar (the action known as the Elevation). See Earsham and East Dereham.

Sacristy: A room, often with specially strengthened doors and windows, where the vestments, church plate and other valuables were stored.

Salvin, Anthony (1799-1881): Architect, Gothic revivalist. In Norfolk, he remodelled Norwich Cathedral s. transept and Norwich Castle – with more enthusiasm than sensibility; and his first essay in Victorian gothic was the Trafford mausoleum in the churchyard at Wroxham. During his working lifetime, Salvin restored and/or added to an enormous list of buildings, provided designs for the construction of several new churches and restored many others, including Castle Rising in the 1840s.

Sanctus bell cote/turret: At the point in the Eucharist at which the priest elevates the *host*

the 'sanctus' (Latin – sacred, holy) is rung. Some churches have a little bell turret over the w. end of the chancel to house the bell, specifically for this purpose, which was rung from within or from a *low side window*. Banham's is on the spire.

Sanctus bell opening/window: Frequently seen high up in the w. wall between tower and nave, inside the church. From there the sanctus could be rung, with the ringer having a clear view of the high altar, enabling him to sound the bell 'on cue'. See also *low side windows*.

Saxon: The period, with its distinctive architecture, preceding the Norman Conquest of 1066 – a vital era in the general establishment of Christianity in these islands. See *Anglo-Saxon* and 'Saxon' in Appendix 2.

Scallop-shell: Traditionally the symbol of pilgrimage, but most closely associated with St James the Great (see under *Saints*). Pilgrims to James's shrine at Compostela wore a scallop shell in their hats; but it became a general symbol of pilgrimage, including the 'martial pilgrimage' of the Crusades, on return from which noblemen included a scallop in their coats of arms.

Schorne, Sir John: See 'Sir John Schorne' under *Saints*.

Scissors-braced roofs: A roof in which the beams are crossed and interlocked diagonally in the shape of an opened pair of scissors. (See *Roofs*, figs. 2 & 3).

Scott, Sir George Gilbert (1811-1878): Master of Victorian gothic, foremost 'restorer' of his age and builder of that most ornate of railway terminals, St Pancras Station. He is credited with having been the architect, or restorer, or the compiler of a report, on more than 700 buildings or projects – cathedrals, hospitals, churches, mansions, colleges and public buildings. In Norfolk he was responsible for a thorough-going restoration of Woodbastwick Church, among others. The pulpit of Witton Church is exactly modelled on one designed by him. See also King's Lynn St Nicholas.

Scratch dials: See *mass dials*.

Screen: See *Rood loft*.

Sedilia: These are seats (usually made into decorative and architectural features, with miniature columns, arches and canopies, and detailed carvings) on the s. side of the chancel. Generally there are three seats. These can be all on the same level, 'stepped' (i.e. on descending levels), and/or 'graduated' under separate arches but contained within a composite pattern, frieze or frame). In many cases, a simple seat is created by building a low sill – called *dropped sill sedilia,* for the window above. The three seats were specifically for the priest, the deacon (who read the gospel), and the sub-deacon (who read the epistle). The three retired to their seats while the choir sang the Kyries ('Kyrie eleison' – Lord have Mercy), the Gloria and the Creed. Though three seats are the norm, there can be just one seat (sedile, singular), two, four, five (as at Yarmouth St Nicholas) and even eight. They may be found beside subsidiary altars, as well as at the chancel high altar – as at Harpley and again at Yarmouth. In places where the seats seem impracticably low, it may well be, that the floor has been raised in more recent times.

Set-offs: The sloped, angled surfaces on buttresses at the points where the buttress 'sets-off' another stage further out from the wall it is supporting.

Seven Deadly Sins, The: A colourful theme for medieval artists – as at Crostwight, for example where it is represented in a fine C14 wall painting in the form of a tree. The Seven Sins are Pride, Anger, Covetousness, Lust, Gluttony, Envy, Sloth.

Seven Acts/Works of Mercy: Based on Matthew 25, vv 34-39, these acts or works of mercy are: to give food to the hungry; to give drink to the thirsty; to make strangers welcome; to clothe the naked; to visit the sick; and to visit prisoners. The additional seventh is normally the burial of the dead. This was a favoured allegorical theme of medieval artists and can be seen, among others in Norfolk, at Potter Heigham and at Wickhampton. The latter is an especially fine example presenting, in small square architectural panels.

Seven sacrament font: Among the great treasures of Norfolk's churches are its seven sacrament fonts; almost all date from the C15 (a few may be slightly later); all octagonal and exquisitely carved – if often mutilated – in each of the eight panels. Seven panels contain representations of the seven holy ordinances or sacraments: Baptism, Holy Communion (Eucharist or Mass), Confirmation, Confession and Penance, Ordination to Holy Orders, Marriage and Extreme Unction (anointing of the dying). On the eighth panel the choice of subject varies – the baptism of Christ, perhaps, as at Sloley, which has the best preserved of the seven sacrament fonts in the county. Great Witchingham is remarkable for the excellence of the original colouring and, with Bridgham, has *Assumption* panel – very rare; still others have a Crucifixion. Gresham All Saints is another fine example. It will be noted that those being confirmed are always shown as very young – as was the custom in medieval times.

Shovel, Sir Clowdisley (1650 1707): One of Norfolk's several Admirals, Clowdisley Shovel was baptised on November 25th 1650 at Cockthorpe. He went early to sea, at the age of 14, under the care of *Sir Chrystopher Myngs,* of nearby Salthouse – the start of what was to be a most distinguished career. After Myngs' death, Shovel's career was closely associated with that of *Sir John Narbrough,* probably a relation – and also baptised at Cockthorpe. An interesting connection can be seen on a big table tomb below the s. transept window at Cley Church, to James Greeve 'who was assistant to Sir Clowdisley Shovel in burning ye Ships in ye Port of Tripoly in Barbary Jan 14th 1676, and for his good service perform'd was made Capt. of the Ship called the Orange Tree of Algier, in 1677 presented with a medal of Gold by King Charles ye 2nd'. On the way home from the Mediterranean in Oct. 1707 his fleet was hit by bad weather and driven among the rocks of the Scilly Isles. His own ship, the 'Association', foundered and broke up. Shovel was thrown ashore, still alive, but a fisherwoman found him – and for the sake of a ring on his finger murdered him.

Shroud brass: A monumental brass in which, the figure of the person commemorated is seen as a cadaver or as a skeleton, wrapped in a shroud. This curious practice began shortly before the middle of the C15 and continued to the end of the C16; and for some reason, was most common here in the eastern counties. The shroud is usually knotted about the head and feet, and sufficiently open to expose the chest and knees of the dead figure. It is said that these memorials were frequently laid down during the life-time of the persons they were intended to commemorate, in order that they might constantly be reminded that they were but mortal. Wiveton, Frenze, Bawburgh and Kirby Bedon, are among Norfolk examples.

Solemn League and Covenant: This was an agreement between the Scots and English parliaments in 1643. The English aim was military, to get Scots support against the forces of Charles I in the Civil War. The Scots aim was religious, a 'conjunction and uniformity of religion' between the churches of the British Isles. It brought a 20,000 strong Scottish army into England – but not the wholehearted commitment to Presbyterian disciplines that the Scots were looking for on the English side. Parishioners throughout England were ordered during the Commonwealth to consent to the Covenant by signature in their local parish registers. At the *Restoration* the offending or embarrassing pages were nearly everywhere torn out. Copies of rare survivals are preserved at South Walsham church.

Sound-holes: At the 'first floor' level of innumerable towers will be seen small openings – rounded, oblong, square, geometrical – often treated most beautifully with delicate traceries. Their purpose is not, as might be supposed, to let out the sound of the bells – the belfry openings serve that purpose. But rather to serve the ringing chamber, both to let in light – and to allow the ringers to hear the bells they are ringing.

Spandrels: The triangular space between the curve of an arch or the supporting braces of a roof, the wall or upright brace, and the horizontal line above. Often filled in with rich and delicate tracery (see *Roofs*).

Squinch: A straight or arched structure across an internal angle of a square tower or other feature to carry a superstructure of a differing form. There is an example at East Ruston.

Squint (also called hagioscope): An opening cut obliquely in a wall or pillar to give a view of the high altar from side chapels and *aisles*. For priests officiating at side altars, it enabled them to elevate the *host* simultaneously with the elevation at the high altar. When squints are found on the outside walls of chancels, the suggestion that they connected with an *anchorite's cell* is only rarely true.

Stafford, Francis: Little is known of the life of this sculptor, whose well carved architectural monuments, all created in a brief span from 1740 to 1744, adorn several Norfolk churches. That to Mrs Hodgson, at Dersingham is his best. See also Cranworth and Saxlingham Nethergate.

Stanton, Edward (1681-1734): Son of William Stanton, through whom he was early admitted to the Masons' Company. In 1719 he became Master of the Masons' Company, a status which he consolidated the following year when he was appointed Mason to Westminster Abbey, a post he held until his death. He is notable as one of the most prolific of English statuaries, providing monuments for a considerable list of cathedrals and churches – among them Gissing.

Stanton, William (1639-1705): A London sculptor of note, who became Master of the Masons' Company and whose skills were employed by churches all over the country. Memorials by him in Norfolk are at Hethersett (1699), Thursford (1666), and in Norwich Cathedral (to Dean Fairfax, 1702).

Stations of the Cross: These are a series of (usually) 14 representations in pictures or carvings, of the scenes of the Passion of Christ from Pilate's presence to the Cross outside the walls of Jerusalem: Pilate 'washes his hands' of Him; Christ takes up the Cross; His first fall under its weight; the meeting with His mother; Simon of Cyrene is taken from the crowd to carry the cross; Veronica wipes His face with her veil; He falls a second time; the exhortation to the women of Jerusalem; the third fall; His clothes are stripped from Him; Christ is crucified; he dies; the body of Christ is taken down from the Cross; He is buried in the tomb provided by Joseph of Arimathea. Processions took place from station to station, with devotions at each. Note also processional details under *Galilee porches*. There is an interesting modern set at Hempton, Holy Trinity.

Stone, Nicholas (1586-1647): Greatest sculptor of his century, he was born the son of a quarryman in Devon, but soon moved to London, then to Holland, to gain greater experience. By 1614, Stone was back in London as mason and statuary; and quickly gained such a reputation that he was employed by the king. He was made master mason to James I, and in 1626 Charles I confirmed him in that appointment. In Norfolk there are a couple of the splendid Jacobean style monuments for which he is best known. Dame Katherine Paston's at Paston, 1629 (though next to hers, that to Sir Edward Paston is coldly classical, and hardly seems to be from the same hand). At Tittleshall there is the noble tomb, in contrasting marbles of black, white and grey, to Lord Chief Justice Sir Edward Coke, 1634, the man who founded the fortunes of the Cokes of Holkham. At Oxnead, an impassive white marble bust to Lady Katherine, wife of the fourth Sir William Paston, shows Stone not at his expressive best. Another of his productions is the Hewer tomb of 1631 at Emneth.

Stops: See *head-stops*.

Storey, George (1733 1759): A Norwich sculptor of variable skills and, apparently, of variable temper, if one can believe a contemporary letter written by the mason Andrews Jelfe to architect Matthew Brettingham, with whom he had been working at Holkham Hall for the Earl of Leicester: 'After I had parted with you at Norwich, I talked to George Storey, who I do not like and will have no further dealings with'. Storey has a large and ugly monument at Scottow, but there are better things at Holt and St Peter Mancroft, Norwich.

Stoup: See *Holy water stoup*.

Street, George Edmund (1824-1881): Architect, born at Woodford in Essex. He began his career as a student under *Sir Gilbert Scott* and designed and restored many churches as well as the Law Courts in the Strand. His work in Norfolk can be seen at Castle Rising and Roydon (near King's Lynn).

String course: See *Courses*.

Stuart: The Royal House of Stuart, who inherited the Scottish throne in 1371 and the English throne, on the accession of James I, in 1603. The 'Stuart period' is taken to cover the reigns of James I, Charles I, Charles II, James II, William & Mary, and finally Anne, who reigned 1702-14.

Symbols of the Evangelists: On fonts and screens, in stained glass etc., the Symbols of the Evangelists are represented as man (St Matthew), eagle (St John), lion (St Mark) and ox (St Luke), all winged. The biblical source is in the vision of St John the Divine: 'The first living creature was like a lion, the second was like an ox, the third had a face like a man, the fourth was like a flying eagle' (Revelations 4, v.7).

Talbots: In heraldry, and in sculptural/architectural adornment, talbots are dogs – they perch on the pinnacles of the C15 chancel at Rollesby, for instance. See also Hockering, Castle Acre and Swaffham.

Transepts: Projecting 'arms' of a church, built out to n. and s. from the point where *nave* and *chancel* meet, to form a cross shaped or *cruciform* ground plan.

Tester: Flat canopy above a pulpit, acting as a sounding board.

Teulon. Samuel Saunders (1812-73): An architect of the High Victorian period, whose churches and large houses are remarkable for their eccentricity and panache. His compositions are often irregular and characterised by harsh, spiky detailing, often combined with polychromy. Although his work has acquired a reputation for extreme ugliness it does not always deserve it, and his work at Brettenham in the 1850s bears this out.

Thompson, Robert: The craftsman of Kilburn in Yorkshire (known popularly as 'the mouse man') who produced much fine furniture in the 1920s and 1930s. His use of the adze as a finishing tool was distinctive and he always signed his work with a diminutive mouse carved unobtrusively somewhere. Although most of his pieces are found in the north of England, including York Minster, I have identified two East Anglian examples – at Middleton in Norfolk and Marlesford in Suffolk.

Three-Decker Pulpits: After the Civil War, the normal Sunday morning service was conducted entirely from the Reading Desk, and only on the infrequent Sacrament Sundays would Minister and people move to the altar. Convenience demanded that pews be grouped round a focal point, and the C17/C18 solution was a three decker pulpit. The service was read from the second tier, and the Minister climbed to the pulpit above to deliver his sermon (if the curate took the service, the rector would sit in the pulpit until sermon time). The *Parish clerk* led the responses, and conducted the singing from the bottom compartment. Fitted out with cushions on the book ledges, candlesticks, *hour-*

glass, and even a wig stand and a peg for the Minister's gown – it was the centre of congregational worship, though not the apex – that was always the altar. Examples are at Ingworth, Salle, Thurning, Warham St Mary, Belton, Bylaugh (best in the county), Fritton St Edmund, Reymerston, Brisley, East Walton and Wilby. See also *Prayer Book Churches*.

Three Living and Three Dead: At Wickhampton, Heydon and Paston there are examples, in wall paintings, of this intriguing allegorical theme. A popular subject for medieval artists, though of some 30 examples remaining nationally only about a dozen are complete enough to give an idea of its importance. Based on a C13 French poem, the 'story in pictures' tells of three spirited young courtiers (always represented in English examples, in royal and hunting guise) who encounter three Deaths in the form of skeletons. The first young blade flees, as the first skeleton dolorously tells him that 'As I am so shall you be'. The second young courtier, though he greets the skeletons as heaven sent, is rewarded with the leveling observation that 'Rich and poor come to the same end'. Courtier number three expounds philosophically on mortality confirmed by his skeleton's 'No one escapes'. See also Belton, Haddiscoe and Seething.

Thurible: See *Censer*.

Tie-beam: The wall-to-wall cross-beam or truss supporting a roof. (See *Roofs*.)

Tithe barn: Tithes (literally tenths) were until relatively recent times a form of 'in kind' tax levied on landowners of all degrees in a parish to support the church and its priest – payable in corn, or fodder, for example. These were stored in tithe barns, often buildings of fine dimensions and superb internal timber work – Paston has a fine example. In the C19 a rent charge was substituted.

Touchstone: Smooth fine-grained black quartz, jasper or basalt once used to test gold and silver coinage.

Transitional: Though 'transitional' can refer loosely to any change from one phase of architecture to another, it is particularly applied to the transition from the 'rounded' Norman to the 'pointed' Gothic, in the second half of the C12. (See Appendix 2.)

Transoms: The horizontal cross-pieces in window tracery, most noticeable in *Perpendicular* windows.

Trefoil: See *Foils*.

Trinity: See *Emblems of the Trinity*.

Tudor: The dynasty founded by Henry Tudor, who was crowned Henry VII in 1485; Henry VIII followed, then Edward VI, Mary I, and finally Elizabeth I, who died on March 24th 1603. For the church, it was a cataclysmic time – various aspects of this are dealt with under the headings *Communion Rails*; *Laudian*; *Mensas*; and *Royal Arms*. If the interiors of churches were changed beyond recognition during this era, the Tudor influence upon church architecture as such was negligible. (See Appendix 2.)

Tudor roses: A typical flower decoration of the period.

Tunnel Vault: A ceiling (usually of a porch or passage) which is semi-circular in cross-section. Examples at Bridgham and Anmer.

Tyler, William (d.1801): A director of the Society of Artists, and a founder-member of the Royal Academy in 1768, he was a sculptor whose work ranged from decorative interior features like marble chimney pieces, through portrait busts, to church monuments of considerable charm. Examples of his work are in Thurning (1759) and Earsham (1762) churches.

Tympanum: Space over head of door, or in head of filled-in arch, plain or carved. See also *Royal Arms* for special connection, and refer to Tivetshall St Margaret, and Marsham, for especially interesting examples.

Visitation, The: Having been told by the Archangel Gabriel that she would bear a son, whose name would be Jesus and whose kingdom would have no end (Luke, chap.1) the Virgin Mary hurried to tell the news to her cousin Elizabeth, already near her time with the child who would be John the Baptist. This meeting is commemorated on July 2nd as The Visitation. There is a gorgeous representation in stained glass in a panel of the e. window of St Peter Mancroft in Norwich, the Virgin robed in blue and gold, Elizabeth in yellow and dark red. See also Wymondham.

Vowess: At Witton is a small brass, dated about 1500, revealing in its Latin inscription that it is a memorial to a 'widow & vowess'. A vowess was a woman, especially a widow, who had taken a vow of chastity for the remainder of her life, and would henceforward wear a habit of blue dress and white hood. She was not a nun, though 'vowess' could be used to mean one who makes a vow of devotion to a religious life, as that of a nun. See also Frenze, and Necton.

Wafer Ovens: A very few churches still have small ovens which were used to bake the wafers for the mass. Thrigby, Overstrand and Braydeston, have examples; also Mundham, Seething, Wicklewood, Burnham Norton, Wilby(?) and Wolferton.

Wailes, William: His Newcastle firm was one of the busiest stained glass suppliers in the C19. He made glass for *Pugin* in the 1840s and received commissions from *Scott*, Butterfield and other key architects in the 1850s and 1860s. The firm maintained a high standard, but was resolutely conservative and resisted artistic innovation. Their handling of colour and pattern is normally good, and the style is quickly recognised. Wailes died in 1881, and the firm continued for a while under his son-in-law as Wailes & Strang.

Wall plate: See *Roofs*.

Wall post: See *Roofs*.

Ward & Hughes: Firm of stained glass manufacturers founded by Thomas Ward and James Henry Nixon in 1836. They traded as Ward & Nixon until 1850 when Henry Hughes became chief designer. After Hughes' death in 1883, the firm continued under Thomas Curtis until the 1920s and some later windows are signed by him. They were the largest suppliers to Norfolk and Suffolk in the C19, and their 1850s-1860s High Victorian work was well drawn and often pleasing in design and colour. In 1870, their massive production was rationalised and was often dull, repetitive and poorly designed thereafter, although they have a good window at Ellingham.

Warrington, William (1833-1866): He described himself as an 'artist in stained glass, heraldic and decorative painter, plumber, glazier and paperhanger'. He designed in medieval styles and some of his detailing was distinctly fanciful. The firm continued under his son James until 1875. Examples of his work can be found at Brampton and Sutton.

Weeping chancels: Much nonsense has been written (and is still being perpetuated in some church guide books today) about chancels which incline away from the rectangle formed with the nave. The popular fallacy is that this is intended to indicate the drooping of Christ's head on the cross onto His right shoulder, as He is always shown in medieval representations of the Crucifixion. There are as many chancels which 'weep' left as right, however. The explanation, is that mathematical accuracy was not the forte of medieval masons – and the chancel being 'out of true' with the nave was a result of ground plan inaccuracy or expediency. Cley, Clenchwarton, Lammas and Wroxham are among numerous Norfolk examples.

Westmacott, Sir Richard: Sculptor, born 1775. In 1793 he went to study in Rome and returned home in 1797 and set up his own studio, which within six years was handling in one year commissions worth the then staggering sum of £16,000. The famous Waterloo Vase which now stands in Buckingham Palace gardens is his work, as is the group of sculptures in the *pediment* of the British Museum. He died in 1856. Stradsett, Walsingham and Ketteringham have examples of his work.

Wherry boats: Not so long ago the Norfolk Broads were the preserve of a distinctive craft, the wherry, which plied these waters in the way of lively local trade. A century ago there were hundreds of them; now only two or three remain. Not surprisingly, the wherry has found its way into the ornamentation of several Broadland churches like Horning.

William & Mary: The 'joint' reign of William III (1688 1702) and Mary II (1688-1694). A period of gracious houses and fine furniture.

Willis, 'Father' Henry (1821 1901): 'Father' Henry Willis was the founder of the great London organ building firm – a name synonymous, for all organists, choristers and churchmen, of fine workmanship, excellence of tone, ingenuity of design and perfection of execution. Apart from installing the mighty organ in the Albert Hall, Willis supplied or rebuilt organs in half the cathedrals of the realm and in innumerable colleges and churches. In Norfolk we have a lovely example of his small scale work, a charming little instrument at Hanworth, built in 1865 at a cost of just £75. Recently it has been restored so that its true Willis tone can be fully appreciated.

Wimple: A piece of fine white linen or silk, tucked into the top of the gown and then drawn up and pinned to the top of the head, under a veil, to frame the face. Worn by women in the late C12 to early C14 period, and still a part of the habit of some nuns. Memorial *brasses* and other effigies in our churches occasionally illustrate it: Lady Alethia de Narborough (1293) at Narborough, for example, and the fascinating graffiti at Beachamwell.

Woodwose: A wild man of the woods, bearded and hairy and usually carrying a club – as he can be seen in some churches in carvings on fonts (e.g. Acle), on pulpits (e.g. Felmingham), on furnishings (e.g. old *misericords* at North Walsham). The woodwose appears to have some ancient fertility deity significance, closely allied to that of the *Green Man.*

Woodforde, James (1740-1803): During his time as Rector of Weston Longville, from 1774 to his death, Parson Woodforde kept a diary: a detailed, observant, loving and humorous account which affords a wonderful description of English village life in the second half of the C18. The diary was first published in 1924-31. See Weston Longville.

Wooldridge, Harry Ellis (1845-1917): Stained glass designer. As a painter, musician and critic, he had a wide influence on the educated taste of his time. He was a friend of *Burne-Jones* and designed many windows for the *Powells*. He worked in the *Renaissance* manner, with correct drawing and pre-determined colours. There is one of his windows at Colney.

Wool Trade: The great C15/C16 wool boom, which brought great wealth to East Anglia and, from its profits, Anglia, and from its profits some of our finest churches, like Worstead. (See also *Isolated Churches*).

Wounds of Christ: The wounds of the Crucifixion in hands, feet and side, symbolising the triumph of sacrificial love. In devotional literature they were sometimes called 'wells' of mercy, eternal life, grace and good comfort, and were objects of devotion in the Middle Ages. (Ashmanhaugh).

Appendix 1 – Saints

'For all the saints, who from their labours rest' is the opening line of a well-known hymn, and on rood screens, on fonts, in woodwork and stained glass, a panoply of saints is represented in Norfolk churches. Almost all of them have some identifying emblem – which adds yet another element of interest for the church visitor. The following is a list of those to be found in the county, with emblems, brief story background and some representative locations.

Agatha: Represented either with pincers in her hand or with her severed breasts upon a dish, indicating the horrid nature of her martyrdom in C6 Sicily. She vowed her virginity to Christ, refused to yield to the lust of the local governor, who took ghastly revenge. She is invoked against fire (another of her tortures) and against diseases of the breasts. Agatha is also patron saint of bell founders. (Upton, Dersingham, Mileham and Wiggenhall St Mary).

Agnes: Her symbols are a sword, often thrust into her neck or bosom, and a lamb (Latin, agna, a pun on her name). Ancient Rome, about 300 AD, and 13-year-old Agnes refuses to marry the prefect's son. She was publicly stripped – but her hair miraculously grew long to cover her. They tried to burn her – but the flames declined to help. So at last she was stabbed. (Cawston, Plumstead; Denton, North Elmham, North Tuddenham, Beeston, Dersingham, Garboldisham, Litcham, Sandringham and Wiggenhall St Mary).

Alban: Often represented with a tall cross or a sword, he was Britain's earliest martyr. He was a Roman knight who had been converted to Christianity here in Britain in the C3. He was ordered by his superiors to sacrifice to pagan gods, refused to do so, and was condemned to be executed at Verulamium – the city that became St Albans. He converted the first executioner who tried to despatch him. The second was more successful and beheaded the saint – whereupon the man's eyes dropped out! Alban is the only saint to have enjoyed a continuous cult in England from Roman times. (Norwich St Peter Mancroft, Wymondham).

Ambrose: One of the *Four Latin Doctors:* usually represented with a beehive – allusion to the story of a swarm of bees which settled on the baby Ambrose's cradle. Also seen wearing his bishop's robes and holding whip or scourge, recalling penance he imposed on the Roman Emperor Maximus Theodosius to atone for a frightful massacre. Ambrose became Bishop of Milan in 374. Central figure in early church, with powerful influence on the Roman Emperors (Cawston, Foxley, Great Witchingham, Houghton St Giles, Ludham, Denton and Wiggenhall St Mary). Refer also to *Four Latin Doctors.*

Andrew: The saltire – X-shaped cross, Scotland's part of Union Jack – and fishing net are his symbols. One of the Twelve Apostles, he was a fisherman before he became a disciple. Legends of his later life are legion – including one that he visited Scotland, thus becoming its patron saint. Martyred by crucifixion, it is said, upon an X-shaped cross. The locations where he is represented are too numerous to mention.

Anne: Usually represented teaching the Virgin – a homely allusion, since Anne was the Virgin Mary's mother. Save for minimal biblical references, little is known about her. In medieval England, many parish *guilds* adopted her as their patron (King's Lynn, East Barsham, Houghton St Giles, Elsing, Saxlingham Nethergate, Hingham).

Anthony of Egypt: Pigs and bells are this austere saint's particular symbols, and occasionally an Egyptian cross like the letter 'T'. Born about 251 in Egypt, he lived in the desert as a hermit, where he was tempted by the devil. Founded a monastery, returned to civilisation to refute heresies, worked miracles and wrote letters which are still quoted. The reliquary for his bones in Alexandria was looked after by Hospitallers who attracted alms by ringing little bells. The pigs? – the Hospitallers' pigs were allowed to roam freely in the streets! (Smallburgh, Swanton Abbot, Tacolneston, East Rudham, Gressenhall and Middleton(?)).

Apostles: The title given in the Gospels to Christ's twelve chief disciples. They were Simon Peter, James the Great, James the Less, Thomas, Philip, Bartholomew, John, Simon, Jude, Matthew, Andrew and Judas. Judas was replaced by Matthias, and in the Acts of the Apostles, SS Paul and Barnabas are both called Apostles. The 12 may be seen grouped together at Ranworth, Westwick, Worstead, Mattishall and Carleton Rode.

Appollonia: This saint is most often seen having her teeth forcibly removed with huge pincers – or herself holding aloft a tooth representing the torture which preceded the martyrdom by fire of this aged deaconess in Egypt in 249. Not surprisingly, she is invoked against jaw and toothache. (Barton Turf, Ludham, Norwich St Augustine's, Sandringham).

Armel: A Breton saint of the C6, he is seen in only one representation in Norfolk, on Litcham screen, where he is shown with the dragon which he miraculously subdued when it was causing havoc around the city of Rennes. He took the beast to the top of a hill (having tied it up with his stole), and ordered it to hurl itself into the river far below – which, being a properly reformed

dragon, it obligingly did, to the gratification of the citizens of Rennes. When England's King Henry VII (d.1509) was in danger of being shipwrecked off the coast of Brittany, he called upon Armel for aid. His ship was saved, and in thanksgiving he placed a statue of the saint in Westminster Abbey, where it can still be seen today.

Audry: An alternative name for *Etheldreda*. In her Audry incarnation she can be seen on the *screen* at Gateley.

Augustine of Canterbury: Always seen in medieval representations as a bishop. In the C6, Pope *Gregory* sent Augustine, at the head of a band of monks, to convert England. King Ethelbert of Kent received him civilly – and was soon himself converted. Augustine made Canterbury his base and built the first cathedral there. But he also travelled much to spread the word. The wisdom of Gregory guided Augustine and laid down those precepts that enabled the new Christian religion to assimilate, gradually and quietly, the pagans and their sacred places – don't destroy the pagan temples, but just their idols, advised the Pope, then convert the place to Christian use. (Belton, North Elmham, North Tuddenham, Norwich St Peter Mancroft and Gateley).

Augustine of Hippo: One of the *Four Latin Doctors* of the early church; a profound and sustaining influence through the centuries on the church's thought and teaching. Often represented holding a flaming heart in his hand; or in his bishop's robes (he was Bishop of Hippo in N. Africa for 35 years to his death in 430) and carrying a pastoral staff. His saintly adulthood followed a dissolute youth, from which he was rescued by St *Ambrose*. Augustine, a man of flesh as well as spirit, is credited with the memorable prayer: 'O Lord, make me chaste but not yet' (Hemblington, Cawston, Foxley, Great Witchingham, Houghton St Giles, Ludham).

Barbara: A tower, and a chalice with the *host* above it are her emblems. She was an early Christian convert in godless Italy, to the fury of her pagan father, who shut her up in a high tower. When she tried to escape, he beat her up then handed her over to a judge who condemned her to death. She was tortured and decapitated – whereupon, very properly, both father and judge were consumed by bolts of lightning.

Barbara is thus patroness of firearms, and also protectress from thunderbolts and lightning or any form of explosion. (Edingthorpe, Trunch, Barton Turf, Filby, Hemblington, Trimingham, Bawburgh, Denton, North Elmham, Ringland, Mileham, Thornham and Wiggenhall St Mary).

Bartholomew: One of the Twelve Apostles, his emblem is the butcher's flaying knife – for thus, it is said, he was martyred somewhere along the Caspian Sea, being first flayed alive and then beheaded. He is sometimes seen in medieval art carrying the skin of a man, with the face still attached to it. It follows that he is the patron saint of tanners (Edingthorpe, Trunch).

Benedict/Benet: Usually seen as an abbot holding a bishop's crozier with which he belays howling little devils around his feet. Or he may be seen with his fingers to his lips, commanding monastic silence, as in the statue by the Cathedral's great w. door, marking the Millenium. Roman nobleman who became a hermit and lived in a cave. His example of piety and worldy renunciation drew others to him, enabling him to found his monastery at Monte Cassino where he devised The Benedictine Rule, the great guiding injunction of Christian monasticism in Europe. (Burlingham St Andrew, Horning, North Walsham, North Elmham).

Blaise: During the persecution of Christians around the year 300 by the Roman Emperor Diocletian, innumerable martyrs died various and nasty deaths. Blaise, Bishop of Sebaste, in Armenia, was first torn with iron combs, and then beheaded. A large comb is thus his symbol in medieval art – and it also made him patron saint of wool combers. Interesting to note that *Parson Woodforde*, in his diary, describes a solemn procession in the saint's honour in Norwich in March, 1783. The only medieval representation of Blaise in Norfolk, is at Harpley.

Blessed Virgin Mary: See *Mary the Blessed Virgin*.

Blide or Blida: A Norfolk saint of Royal blood, usually shown crowned and/or holding a bible. Chiefly celebrated as the mother of St Walstan of Bawburgh, patron saint of farm workers. Her shrine was at Martham.

Botolph: No definite symbol, though he is properly represented as an abbot, occasionally holding a church in his hand. Many churches are dedicated to him, including Boston in Lincolnshire where in the C7 he was abbot of a monastery founded by himself. No representations of him noted: but churches are dedicated to him at Hevingham, Banningham, Limpenhoe, Trunch, Westwick, Morley St Botolph, Grimston, Stow Bedon and Tottenhill.

Bridget (or Bride): One of Ireland's favourite saints. In Norfolk only one representation of her, at Sandringham. After living the life of a consecrated virgin in her own home in mid-C6 Ireland, Bridget brought together a small community of like-minded followers. Later she was to establish several convents, notably at Kildare. Charming stories are told of her. She was so immersed in the spiritual life and heedless of material things, that she absentmindedly hung her cloak on a sunbeam but was practical enough to turn her bathwater into beer upon the arrival of some unexpected and thirsty visitors.

Catherine of Alexandria: The emblem of this saint is a wheel, set with spikes and knives, on which she is said to have been martyred in C4 Egypt and which in turn inspired the spinning firework. The wheel, however, flew to pieces as she was spun on it, the knives, etc., skewering her persecutors. Her head was then cut off and from the wound flowed milk, not blood, which could explain why she is patroness of nurses. The number of is too numerous to list here, though Hardley and Sporle, have especially interesting examples.

Cecilia: Patroness of music – and thus always seen with an organ or other musical instrument. Much hymned in words and music of the centuries. A Roman virgin of the C3, her colourful tale credits her with such numerous conversions that the local prefect ordered her to be suffocated in the baths. That failed to work. So a soldier was despatched to lop off her head. Three times he struck, but could not sever it. It was three days before she died meanwhile preaching to her hordes of converts, who came to collect her blood (Burlingham St Andrew, Trimingham, Filby, North Elmham and Litcham(?)).

Christina: Represented with an arrow, and occasionally with a millstone, or a wheel and pincers. Her story is insubstantial and accounts vary. They agree however that she lived in the C3 or C4, was converted to Christianity – and then was variously ill-used for refusing to sacrifice to pagan gods. Attempts were made to burn her – which failed; then to drown her thus the millstone emblem – but that did not work either; and finally she was shot with arrows a legend, it would seem, which is an amalgam of several saints. Compare with Saints *Agatha*, *Appollonia*, *Catherine* and *Lucy*. (North Elmham, has the only representation in the county).

Christopher: The saint everyone recognises – a gigantic figure spanning a river, his huge staff in one hand, the Christ-Child on his shoulder, or sometimes in an outstretched hand. Tradition has it that he was a pagan giant who wished to give his service to the most powerful man in the world. He found a great king – but saw that he crossed himself as protection against the devil. Judging therefore that the devil must be the stronger, Christopher forsook the king and went to Satan. But then his new master carefully avoided a wayside cross – the symbol of Christ, the giant learned: here, at last, must be the mightiest of all. But how to find him? A holy hermit advised him to use his strength for Christ, by carrying travellers across a dangerous river. Then came the day when he carried a child, who grew heavier and heavier, taxing even his strength until he learned that he had 'carried the weight of the world upon his shoulders'. See also *Christopher images*. Representations are legion.

Citha: See 'Zita'.

Clare: Clare's emblem is a *pyx* or monstrance. This is the Clare of Assisi, spiritually beloved and influenced by St Francis, who founded the Order of Poor Clares, vowed to a life of absolute poverty. She spent her life as abbess of her convent at Assisi and never left the town. When she was old and sick, Assisi was threatened by the Saracens of the invading emperor Barbarossa's army. Clare was carried before them, deep in prayer and carrying a pyx containing the Blessed Sacrament whereupon the invaders fled. (Trimingham, Norwich St Julian's, North Tuddenham (?)).

Clement: His emblem is an anchor – the object which was hung about his neck by the envoy of the Emperor Trajan, around 100 AD, before he was hurled to a watery death in the Black Sea. His offence – too much efficiency in converting the local heathen, following his Black Sea exile

from his bishopric of Rome. He is usually represented as a pope. (Trimingham, Houghton St Giles, Barnham Broom, Norwich St Julian's, Terrington St Clement).

Columba: No special symbols. He was a prince of C6 Ireland with a talent for founding monasteries. He left Ireland in 563 when he was 41 and with a small group of companions headed for Scotland and the island of Iona, where he established his own monastery and lived there until his death in 597 – still during that time establishing more monasteries and churches in Scotland and Northumbria and converting en route the Pictish king, Brude. He was also scholar and poet, and transcriber of the gospels; work survives which is believed to be his. Norwich St Peter Mancroft, has the only representation of him in the county.

Denys/Dionysius: His symbol is a severed head. Patron saint of France and first bishop of Paris – where his missionary zeal so roused the fury of the pagans that they put him to terrible tortures from which he emerged miraculously unharmed. So they took him to Montmartre and beheaded him. But 'Anon the body of St Denys raised himself up, and bare his head between his arms' and walked to his chosen resting place at St Denis: which is why the kings of France were buried there. He is usually represented as a bishop, holding his mitred head in his hands. Though at Hempstead he is a monk, complete with head, plus a tonsured head in his hands.

Dorothy: Usually shown holding a spray of flowers and/or a basket of fruit – as most beautifully at North Tuddenham. Strangely beautiful too is her legend. During the persecution of the Emperor Diocletian in the early C4, she was threatened with terrible tortures unless she rejected her Christianity and married the Prefect. Her reply, it is said, was: 'Do to me what torment thou wilt, for I am ready to suffer it for the love of my spouse, Jesu Christ, in whose garden full of delights I have gathered roses, spices and apples'. On her way to execution, she was mocked by a young lawyer who scornfully asked her to send him some of them. After she had been beheaded, an angel appeared to the lawyer, bringing from Dorothy in Paradise the requested gift – where-upon he was converted and followed the saint to martyrdom. (Barnham Broom, Denton, North

Elmham, North Tuddenham, Litcham, Walsoken and Wiggenhall St Mary).

Edmund, King & Martyr: His symbol is an arrow – or sometimes a wolf, guarding his severed head. King of East Anglia, defeated by the Danes in 870, he was shot with arrows, then beheaded, the head being contemptuously hurled into the undergrowth. But there it was guarded by a great grey wolf until it was found by the Faithful (its singular ability to call out 'Here, here' must have helped); whereupon the wolf followed the funeral cortège into Bury St Edmund's. Representations of him are numerous, but see especially Fritton and Pulham St Mary.

Edmund Rich, of Abingdon c.1180 – 1240: Archbishop of Canterbury. Born at Abingdon of pious parents. He had an early reputation for austerity and sanctity; Treasurer of Salisbury cathedral c.1222 and Archbishop of Canterbury in 1233. He tried ineffectually to prevent royal mismanagement and Papal exactions. When the Papal Legate Otto came at Henry III's request to help him exploit ecclesiastical wealth and patronage, Edmund retired to Pontigny in self-imposed exile. Canonised by Pope Innocent IV in 1247. He is remembered for his association with the University of Oxford and commemorated in St Edmund Hall, the sole surviving medieval Hall in Oxford, built it is supposed, on the site of his house. The screen at Fritton St Catherine has a partial figure than may be a portrait of him.

Edward the Confessor: Usually seen wearing a crown, and holding aloft a ring. This deeply pious king of England, immediately before the Norman Conquest of 1066, built Westminster Abbey – the price for not having kept his vow to make a pilgrimage to the Holy Land. Confronted once by a beggar asking for alms, the king, having no money, slipped a ring from his finger and gave it to him. The beggar, it seems, was really St John the Evangelist, who returned the ring to English Pilgrims in Palestine and foretold the king's imminent death. (Burlingham St Andrew, Hemblington, Barton Turf, Ludham, Stalham, Barnham Broom, Denton, Saxlingham Nethergate, Harpley).

Eligius, or Eloy: Patron saint of farriers, his symbol is a blacksmith's hammer and tongs, and occasionally a severed horse's leg, as on the C15 screen at Hempstead. Eligius was a bishop in C6 France and Flanders, much given to good works. His most famous exploit was to lop the leg off a difficult horse which was refusing to be shod, fix the shoe to the offending limb then put the leg back again and make the sign of the cross whereupon the again-complete beast trotted happily away. (Potter Heigham).

Elizabeth: No distinguishing symbol – but usually represented at the moment of The *Visitation*, when the Virgin Mary came to tell her of the visit of the Angel to announce Christ's birth, Elizabeth already being near her time with the child who would be John the Baptist. (Houghton, St Peter Mancroft, Norwich and Earsham).

Elizabeth of Hungary: Rarely represented, though one of the painted figures on the screen at Barnham Broom could be her. Daughter of a C13 King of Hungary, she married a prince and lived in great happiness with him – until he died on his way to the Crusades. A woman of immense charity and kindness, she now took to a life of poverty and severe personal austerity, and to nursing and tending the sick. She died at the age of 24, in 1231, worn out by her labours, and was canonised four years later by Gregory XI.

Emeria/Emerita: No special emblem and an obscure saint, who nonetheless has found her way onto the screen at Houghton St Giles. One of two virgin sisters (St Digna was the other) brought before a judge in C3 Italy for their Christian belief, probably in the persecution of Emperor Valerian. They were stretched between four stakes, cruelly beaten and burned alive.

Erasmus: His symbol is a windlass. He fled from Roman persecution, about 300 AD to a cave, where he was cared for by a raven. But later, when he resumed his inspirational preaching, his death was ordered by the emperor Maximian and he is said to have been martyred by having his bowels uncoiled and wound upon a windlass. Which explains why he was invoked against colic and stomach troubles. (Sandringham).

Ethelbert: Rarely represented. There are eleven East Anglian dedications to him. He was King of East Anglia in the late C8, and was executed by King Offa of Mercia – for 'political offences', say some sources; through the machinations of King Offa's wife, goes a more likely story.

Handsome Ethelbert arrived to seek the hand of Offa's daughter, who was much smitten by him but so was her mother who, in jealousy, persuaded her husband to lop off the visitor's head. Thurton has a representation of him in glass (the only one in the county), and like Alby, East Wretham and Larling, is dedicated to him.

Etheldreda: No special emblem, but generally represented as a royally crowned abbess. Daughter of a C7 king of East Anglia, she was twice married before becoming a nun. She founded a nunnery at Ely, became its first abbess and was known for her deep devotion and piety. After death her body remained incorrupt; its miracle working powers made Ely a great centre of pilgrimage. (Burlingham St Andrew, Upton; Barnham Broom, East Dereham, North Tuddenham, Wymondham, Belton, Sandringham). See also Saint *Audrey*.

Fabian: A dove fluttering down and settling on his head assured Fabian of election as Pope in C3 Rome and he became a memorable and revered pontiff. He converted the emperor Philip to Christianity but when Decius succeeded Philip, he had Fabian beheaded. Woodbastwick Church has a unique dedication jointly to St Fabian and St Sebastian.

Faith: Her symbols are a palm branch and a grid-iron upon which latter object she was unpleasantly roasted to death in France about the year 287 – just a few years after St Lawrence suffered the same martyrdom in Rome. Legend has it that a thick fall of snow came down to veil her body during her suffering. (Horsham, Marsham, Little Witchingham).

Felix: Usually seen as a bishop. One of our East Anglian saints, who came here in the C7 from France to preach the Gospel, and in 630 became the first Bishop of Dunwich, in Suffolk. For the 17 years of life that remained to him, he worked steadfastly to establish the Church on the eastern seaboard, founded schools, and preached extensively, with the friendly support of the King of the East Angles. (Norwich St Peter Mancroft, Wymondham, Kenninghall.)

Four Latin Doctors: The Four are Saints *Ambrose, Augustine of Hippo, Gregory* and *Jerome*. See entry in main glossary for explanation of their joint title. They can be seen grouped together at Morston, Salle, Stratton Strawless, Suffield, Upton, Fritton St Catherine, Saxlingham Nethergate, Burnham Norton, Castle Acre, Gooderstone, Griston, King's Lynn St Margaret, Weasenham All Saints.

Frances: Uniquely in England, she can be seen on the *screen* at Sandringham. In early C15 Rome she founded a monastery of nuns who became known as the Collatines. After her husband's death, she entered the community and became its Superior. Only four years later she followed her husband to the grave in 1440, much honoured for her piety. It was her particular blessing, so it is recorded, to be attended constantly by a visible angel which could explain why, five centuries on, Pope Pius XI was to name her Patron Saint of motorists!

Francis of Assisi: Usually seen as a friar holding a cross, often accompanied by the animals and birds with which he is always associated; sometimes also with the 'stigmata' – the wounds of Christ. Oddly this much loved saint is only occasionally represented in medieval art, though his story is so well known – his birth in wealthy circumstances in C12 Italy; his decision as a young man to devote himself to poverty, prayer and charity; his establishment of his Franciscan Order; his healing powers; and not least, his rapport with wild things. He died, aged only 45, in 1226, and was canonised two years later. (Cringleford, Little Melton, West-Barsham).

Fursey: A C7 Irish abbot who became an East Anglian saint. He came to these shores about the year 630 and established himself at Burgh Castle, near Yarmouth; though later he went to France where he set up another monastery, and died there about 650. (Burgh Castle, Wymondham).

George: The martial knight, armoured and mounted, and England's patron saint, famed for his exploits in rescuing the beautiful maiden from the terrible dragon, and then killing the fire-breathing beast. Represented in C15 stained glass at North Tuddenham, and dramatically in an ancient wall painting at Fritton St Catherine. All this took place in Palestine – where subsequently George was horribly put to death for refusing to sacrifice to idols. It was during the Crusades that he was adopted as England's patron – King Richard Coeur-de-Lion is said to have had a vision of him, assuring him of safety and victory in a forthcoming battle against the Saracens. Representations of the saint in Norfolk churches are numerous.

Geron/Gereon: Rarely represented, but seen in a splendid representation at North Tuddenham, in armour and with a falcon on his arm. He was of noble birth in late C3 Germany but became a priest and, according to one account, went as a missionary to Holland, where he was martyred by the Danes. Another version is that he was a knight of Cologne who with several companion soldiers was put to death for refusing to renounce the Christian faith. See also Suffield, and Litcham.

Germanus: Rarely represented, but seen as bishop at Garboldisham, with cross and crozier. A nobleman and subsequently bishop, in C5 France, he came to Britain and brilliantly combated heresy at a gathering at Verulamium (St Albans) in about 430. He also gave useful advice to the British army in their struggle against attacking Picts and Saxons. On his instruction, the soldiers set up a united triple cry of 'Alleluia' as the savages attacked at which the invaders turned tail and fled in terror. He died in Ravenna while on a mission to the Emperor, and his shrine became a celebrated centre of pilgrimage. In the form of 'Germaine', he is the dedicatory saint of Wiggenhall St Germans church.

Gervasius & Protasius: This is the unique dedication of Little Plumstead Church. The two, twin sons of a Roman consul in the C2, were honoured as the first martyrs of Milan, during Nero's reign. They refused to offer pagan sacrifice before one of the emperor's military campaigns into Germany, and were put to death.

Giles: His emblems are a doe or hind at his side, sometimes an arrow piercing his hand or leg, he being dressed as a monk, or abbot with crozier. He lived as a hermit in C8 France, with his doe for company. One day a king and his companions hunted the doe, which fled to the saint for protection. However, an arrow loosed off by the king by chance struck Giles. In penance the king built a monastery on that very site, Giles becoming its first abbot. About 150 churches in England are dedicated to him (Colby, Smallburgh, North Elmham, Norwich St Giles, Sandringham).

Gregory (the Great): Represented as a pope, with a dove, and a roll of music in one hand.

One of the *Four Latin Doctors*, he was born of noble Roman stock in 540. He became a monk and founded several monasteries, into one of which he retired. It was he who, seeing fair-haired British slaves in the Rome slave market, commented: 'Not Angles, but angels'. It is said he came briefly to Britain as a missionary but was recalled to be elected, much against his will, as Pope. It was he who sent St *Augustine* to these islands; and gave his name to Gregorian Chants (thus the symbolic roll of music). (Burgh next Aylsham, Cawston, Foxley, Great Witchingham, Houghton St Giles, Ludham, Barnham Broom, Bawburgh, North Tuddenham, Norwich St Giles, Litcham).

Heiron/Hieron: A saint of notable obscurity who for equally obscure reasons is discovered in the C16 screen at Suffield. He was one of 33 Armenian martyrs who suffered under the Emperor Diocletian, about the year 300.

Helen(a): Represented wearing a crown and holding a cross – sometimes an Egyptian cross, like a letter 'T'. Mother of Emperor Constantine the Great, but her own parentage is mysterious. One story says she was an inn-keeper's daughter. Another says she was the daughter of King Coel of Colchester – Old King Cole of the nursery rhyme. What is certain is that she married an emperor and bore another: and that as an old lady she set off on pilgrimage for the Holy Land, where she found fragments of The True Cross and brought them to Europe. (Cawston, Upton and Litcham).

Henry VI: Though modern scholarship may suggest that King Henry VI of England, 1422-61, was a bad and unjust ruler and a worse judge of character and counsel, medieval tradition saw him in a very different light: a man of piety, charity, fortitude and saintliness, and a great patron of learning. Never formally canonised, but much venerated in this part of England and the north. He appears, youthful and kingly, with orb and sceptre, on the screens at Gateley, Barton Turf and Ludham. See also Foulden.

Hubert: Born into a noble family of C7 France, he was a great hunter – until one day, during a chase, a stag appeared before him with a shining crucifix between its horns. Hubert prostrated himself upon the ground – and from that moment his way of life was changed. He went on a pilgrimage to Rome, was ordained, and thereupon consecrated by the Pope as Bishop of Liège. Legend says that St Peter appeared to Hubert and gave him a key which had the power to cure lunatics. Another version says that at his ordination the Blessed Virgin appeared to him and gave him a white silk stole with which he was able to cure hydrophobia. He is patron saint of huntsmen and hunting. See him with his stag as Dersingham and Litcham.

Hugh: A C13 Carthusian monk and bishop, born in France, but invited to this country by Henry II to become Prior of a monastery in Somerset. The establishment flourished under his charge, so Henry chose him to be Bishop of Lincoln. He is said to have been the most learned monk in the land. He rebuilt his cathedral, established schools; and was much called on for his wisdom as a judge. His reputation was for simplicity and kindness, yet of being wholly immovable on matters of truth, doctrine and principal. (Wymondham and Wiggenhall St Mary).

Ignatius: Uniquely represented in England on the *screen* at Sandringham. He was Bishop of Antioch, having been personally appointed by St *Peter*. He was arrested during persecution of the Christians by order of the Emperor Trajan and taken to Rome – where his fate was to be thrown to the wild beasts in the Colosseum.

James the Great: Usually seen with a sword, or with the pilgrimage necessities of staff, wallet and *scallop-shell*. One of the apostles closest to Christ and subsequently, one of the leaders of the church, he was executed by Herod Agrippa in AD 44 (Acts 12,2). Many traditions surround him; enough churches claim relics to make up half a dozen bodies. Strongest however is the belief that his body was put into a boat, without sails or rudder, which travelled unaided out of the Mediterranean, round Spain and fetched up near Compostella, on the western coast, where James's shrine became throughout the medieval age one of the greatest places of pilgrimage. Representations of him are legion, but an especially notable one is at Hales.

James the Less: His emblem is a fuller's club – a curved implement like a hockey stick, used by a fuller (a 'cloth cleanser') to beat cloth – with which he was killed by a blow on the head after he had survived either being stoned (one version) or being hurled from the pinnacle of the temple in Jerusalem. This occurred after James, one of the Twelve Apostles, presided

over the great Synod in Jerusalem which reached agreement on how far Gentile converts to Christianity should be made to observe Jewish rites and customs. Representations of him are very numerous.

Jerome: Usually seen with a cardinal's hat; sometimes with an inkhorn; and with a lion at his feet. One of the *Four Latin Doctors*, he became secretary of the Roman See, about 381, after much travel and study. (This office was held by a cardinal: thus Jerome's representation.) Later he travelled again, coming at last to Bethlehem, where he founded a monastery, and fulfilled his ambition of translating the New Testament from Hebrew into Latin: The Vulgate of the Roman Church (thus the inkhorn). There is a charming story that a lion came to his monastery with an injured paw: the saint healed it, and the animal stayed on as his faithful companion (Cawston, Foxley, Great Witchingham, Houghton St Giles, Ludham).

Joan of Valois: No special emblem and rarely represented – though she can be seen on the screen at Upton. She was the deformed daughter of Louis XI of France; married off at 12 to the Duke of Orleans; later, to her joy, released when he obtained a grant from the Pope to divorce her. Thereafter she devoted her life to good and pious works; founded the Order of the Annunciation for women in 1500; and five years later died aged 41. See also Barnham Broom.

John of Bridlington: A rarely represented figure – but he is seen on the screen at Hempstead, as a monk and holding a crozier. A figure of renowned piety and a worker of miracles, he became prior of his own monastery at Bridlington, about 1360. Ten years after his death his shrine became a place of pilgrimage, though he was never formally canonised.

John the Baptist: The man who baptised Christ and 'led the way', and who died at a whim of Herod's daughter Salome. Representations of him are legion, though the wall painting at Seething is an interesting variant. See also Trimingham and the stained-glass interpretation at North Tuddenham.

John the Divine/the Evangelist: As one of the four Evangelists (see also *Symbols of the Evangelists*) he is represented with an eagle, and also with a chalice or a cup from which a snake or devil is leaping – a reference to a story that he was given poisoned drink, but made it harmless by making the sign of the cross over it. John – 'the disciple whom Jesus loved' – was hurled into boiling oil in Rome: but he emerged unharmed. His is the last book of the New Testament, 'The Revelation'. Representations are very numerous.

Jude, also known as Thaddaeus: Most often seen holding a boat, though sometimes with a club or carpenter's square. One of the Twelve Apostles, he is said to have preached in Mesopotamia, Russia and finally in Persia where he was attacked and killed by pagan priests, says one tradition; another, that he was hung on a cross at Arat and pierced with javelins. Representations are numerous.

Julian of Norwich: See *Mother Julian of Norwich* in the Glossary of Terms.

Julian the Hospitaller: His symbol is an oar – an allusion to his work in maintaining a hospice and ferry on the bank of a river, in a setting as mythical as his story. This work was penance for having killed, by horrid error, his father and mother. At length a diseased and stinking traveller came by; Julian, in pity, cared for him. Whereupon the figure was transfused with heavenly light, and revealed as a messenger sent to announce divine acceptance of Julian's penance, and of the Saint's imminent death. St Julian's Church, Norwich, is dedicated to him.

Juliana: Not often represented, but when she is, as on the screen at Hempstead, she has the devil haltered on a rope held in her hand. It is recorded in the 'Golden Legend' that she refused to marry the governor of her district unless he became a Christian. She was thrown into prison, where she was tempted by the devil in the form of an angel but won the day through steady prayer. See also North Elmham, and Litcham.

Lambert: Seen as a bishop holding a sword. He was bishop of his native city of Maastricht, in Germany, from 670. There, according to the 'Golden Legend', he 'shone by word and by example in all virtue'. But around 709 he was the victim of a revenge killing. Unknown to him, his servants killed two brothers who looted his church and the relations of the two took their revenge on the bishop.

Lawrence: He shares with St Faith the emblem of a grid-iron – both were martyred by being roasted on one. He is usually shown in the vestments of a deacon, an office he held under the martyred Pope Sixtus II. During the persecutions of the Emperor Valerian in the C3, Lawrence was ordered to reveal the treasures of the church. Whereupon he disappeared into the alleys of Rome to return with a retinue of cripples and beggars; 'These are the church's treasures', he declared. It was an answer which earned him an agonising death. (Hemblington, Brundall, Hempstead, Hunworth, Ludham, Smallburgh, Worstead, North Tuddenham, Norwich St Giles, Norwich St Julian's, Harpley, Wiggenhall St Mary).

Lazarus: Brother of Martha and Mary Magdalene, he was raised from the dead by Jesus (John 11.43). Later, he was present with his sisters when the Apostles received the gift of tongues (Acts II, 3). Later still, a miraculous journey was to take him to Marseilles, where he became bishop – and suffered martyrdom. He can be seen in company with 15 saints on the C15 *screen* at Thornham, the only representation of him in the county.

Leger: Bishop of Autun in C7 France. His political partialities and involvements earned him the hatred of a royal chamberlain, one Ebroin. When Ebroin rebelled and sent an army against Autun, Leger offered himself so that the inhabitants might be spared. Ebroin promptly had the his eyes put out, later subjected him to horrible tortures, and finally beheaded him. His emblem is the auger (tool used for boring holes in wood) with which he was blinded. Representations of him are rare: the only one in Norfolk is at Harpley. Footnote: The celebrated horse race at Doncaster has no connection with our martyr – it takes its name from Colonel Anthony St Leger, who instituted this oldest of English classic races in 1776.

Leonard: His symbols are chains or fetters in his hands, his robes those of an abbot. This courtier-turned-monk was given land near Limoges in C5 France by King Clovis, at whose court he was brought up, and there founded the monastery of Noblac, of which he became first abbot. The king gave him the right also to release any prisoner whom he visited – and he is thus the patron saint of prisoners. (Hemblington, North Tuddenham, Gressenhall, Sandringham and Wiggenhall St Mary).

Louis: Louis IX was King of France in the mid C13, a model Christian monarch noted for his piety and spartan way of life, his patronage of friars and building of churches. He twice went on Crusade to the Holy Land and died in Tunis in August 1270. He was canonised only seven years later. Representations usually show him as a king holding a crown of thorns and a cross of three nails – recalling the sacred relics he brought back to France and housed in the Sainte-Chapelle in Paris. (Gateley and Litcham).

Lucy: She is represented holding a sword, or with a sword driven through her neck; or with light issuing from her gashed throat; or holding aloft a plate or a book on which are two eyes Martyred in Syracuse about the year 303, she was sentenced to death and nothing could move her; even oxen yoked to her could not budge her from the spot. So faggots were piled around her and lit – but the flames declined to burn her. At last she was killed by a sword thrust to the throat. The rays of light, and the eyes, are thought to stem from her name suggesting the Latin lux, light. (Guestwick).

Luke: One of the Four Evangelists, his special symbol is an ox (see *Evangelistic symbols*), probably a reference to the sacrifice in the temple at the beginning of his gospel – while tying in neatly with Revelations 4, v. 7. 'The Beloved Physician', and thus the patron of doctors and surgeons. Of artists too, some portrayals showing him painting Christ or the Blessed Virgin. (Belton, Burgh St Margaret, Great Witchingham, Stratton Strawless, Suffield).

Margaret of Antioch: Her emblem is a writhing dragon, which she transfixes with a cross. Thrown into prison in Antioch for her Christian belief, she was tempted by the devil in the guise of a terrible dragon. Some have it that the dragon was miraculously decapitated; others that he swallowed her but burst when her cross stuck in his throat; others still that she simply made the sign of the cross and he faded away. That she is guardian of women in childbirth presumably has something to do with her 'caesarian' irruption from the dragon. There are frequent representations of her, an especially notable example being at Kimberley.

Mark: One of the four Evangelists, his symbol being the winged lion (see *Evangelistic symbols*). The significance of the lion is intriguing – in ancient lore it typified the Resurrection, based on the curious idea that the lion's young were dead for three days after birth – and were then brought to life by the roaring of their parents. Mark's story as evangelist, and his missionary travels, thread through the New Testament. There is a tradition that later he went to Rome, then to Alexandria, where he became the city's first bishop, and was subsequently martyred during Nero's reign. What is certain is that in the C9 his relics were taken to Venice, whose patron saint he became. (Belton, Great Witchingham, Little Witchingham, North Tuddenham, Stockton).

Martin: Rarely represented despite the popularity of this figure who typified the saintly virtues of simplicity, piety, charity and concern for others. When he is portrayed, it is generally as a bishop offering alms to the needy. He was born in C4 Hungary and trained as a soldier; but after giving half his cloak to a beggar on whom he took pity, he dreamed that night that he saw Christ wearing the half of the garment he had given away – and was straightaway baptised. He founded a monastery, became known for his piety and, much against his own wishes, was made Bishop of Tours. His reputation for miracles and healing, and his St Francis-like rapport with animals, grew from this time. Churches in Norfolk are dedicated to him at Glandford, Hindringham, Overstrand, and New Buckenham. At North Tuddenham there is a scroll in ancient stained glass in the porch inscribed 'St Martin', with the figure of a bishop above it, but it is unlikely that the two belong together. He is represented on the C15 screen at Dersingham; in medieval stained glass at Harpley; and in carved wood at Wiggenhall St Mary.

Mary Cleophas or Clopas: As on the screens at Ranworth and Houghton, she is generally seen with her four sons – *James the Less, Joseph, Simon* and *Jude*. She was half-sister to the Virgin Mary.

Mary Magdalene: Mary Magdalene appears in St *Luke's* gospel as one of the women whom Jesus 'healed of evil spirits and infirmities'. Later she witnessed from afar the Crucifixion and, more centrally and importantly, the Resurrection. She is the prototype Christian penitent, realised as the woman kneeling in tears before Jesus and annointing His feet with ointment – the ointment pot thus being her usual symbol in medieval art (Ludham, Garboldisham, Thornham, Walsoken, Wiggenhall St Mary).

Mary Salome: No special emblem – but recognised by the presence of her two sons, the apostles *James the Great* and *John*, as on the screens at Ranworth and Houghton. She is said to have been one of the women present at the crucifixion and at the taking down of Christ's body from the Cross.

Mary the Blessed Virgin: The mother of Christ, pre-eminent among the medieval patron saints. Daughter of Joachim and Anne. Early in C5 she was acclaimed as 'the Mother of God'. See also *Annunciation* and *Assumption*. Her usual emblem is the lily and/or a crowned 'M'.

Matthew: Several are the emblems of this former tax collector who became Apostle and Evangelist. His evangelistic symbol is an angel with the face of a man; but he may be represented as an old man, with the bible or his own gospel in his hand; or with a purse and a money box. But also he may have a sword or even an axe (avoid confusing him therefore with *Matthias*). Representations of him are frequently encountered.

Matthias: Though not in the least martial, Matthias is usually depicted with an axe, spear or sword. The connection is that he was beheaded in Jerusalem by the Jews. He was the disciple chosen by lot to take the place of Judas Iscariot, after the betrayer's death. (Cawston, Norwich St Julian's, Hingham (?), Pulham St Mary the Virgin, Weston Longville, North Tuddenham, Castle Acre, Gooderstone, Great Cressingham).

Maurice: Represented as a knight in armour, with sword, axe or banner. A Christian commander in the army of Emperor Maximian, late in the C3. On an expedition into Gaul, the emperor ordered a sacrifice to the pagan gods of Rome. When Maurice and his fellow Christians refused to participate, Maximian ordered their execution. Briningham has the only representation of him in the county.

Michael: The feathered, winged and armed angel of light who strikes down the dragon of evil; or the glorious Archangel, judging souls in his scales of justice. These are the usual representations of this popular dedicatory saint. (Filby, Irstead, Ranworth, Aslacton, Moulton,

Norwich St Julian's, Wymondham, Gressenhall (?), Ryston (especially notable) and Wellingham).

Nicholas: Three golden balls? The pawnbroker's sign, of course. Also that of St Nicholas, for the balls represent the three bags of gold which, on three consecutive nights, this good priest tossed through a poor man's window so that his daughters might have dowries. And thus he became, via a corruption of the Russian 'Sant Niklaus', Santa Claus. He is patron saint of pawn-brokers too! While he is a favourite dedicatory saint of countless churches, he is rarely represented in art (the one at Horstead is modern). But when he is, it is usually as a bishop – with three little boys in a pickling tub. In the C4, he was bishop of Myra in Asia Minor; his most celebrated miracle was restoring to life three boys who had been cut up by an inn-keeper and pickled in a tub! See also North Walsham, and Litcham (?).

Olaf (or Holofius) of Norway: A battle axe and loaves are this saint's curiously mixed symbols where rare representations of him are shown. There is just one in Norfolk – on the C15 screen at Barton Turf. King of Norway, 1016-29, he became a Christian and helped England fight the Danes; after which he returned to Norway and seized the throne. He ruled well and brought Christianity to his kingdom. But rebellion came and he was exiled. When he tried to regain his throne he was killed in battle, and duly buried. Whereupon a spring gushed from his grave, its water proving to have healing properties and miraculous virtues. The loaves were prompted by his Latin name sounding like 'whole loaves.'

Paul: A sword is this apostle's symbol, usually pointing down – though on the Ranworth screen it points up. With this weapon his head was struck off at the order of the Emperor Nero, about the year 66 in Rome, when his success in converting eminent people to Christianity became too much for the Emperor to tolerate. Upon his beheading, it is said, milk flowed from the wound. Representations of him are very numerous.

Peter: 'Thou art Peter, and upon this rock I will build my church... I will give unto thee the keys of the kingdom of heaven' (Matthew 16.18): Christ's words to his apostle. And so, Peter's symbol is keys. The gospels tell his story during Christ's ministry on earth. But not his ending.

He was crucified in Rome by the Emperor Nero – upside down, at his request, as he did not consider himself worthy to die in the same way as his Master – at about the same time that Paul was beheaded there. Examples of Peter and his crossed keys are many.

Petronella: Legend has it that she was a daughter of St Peter, so she is always shown holding a key, or a key and book. Her shadowy story says she suffered from paralysis, from which Peter miraculously cured her. But in health she was so beautiful that a Roman count desired her. To escape this fate, she gave herself up to fasting and prayer, praying that she might die – a fulfilment which came three days later. (Trimingham, North Elmham, Litcham).

Philip: One of The Twelve, Philip is seen either with a cross – for like his Lord, he was to suffer Crucifixion, at the hands of pagans in Asia Minor; or with a basket of loaves and fishes, recording his connection with the biblical story of Christ's feeding of the 5,000. Representations of him are numerous.

Puella Ridebourne (of Ridibowne): Uniquely in England, and for no clearly explainable reason, this obscure holy lady is represented on the screen at Gately, in company with several other fairly rare figures. She may have been the subject of a strictly local celebrity or cult; or she could possibly be Christina of Redburn (near St Albans in Hertfordshire), who lived as an *anchoress*. The 'Puella' may be merely a prefix, being Latin for girl or maiden – thus 'The Maiden of Redburn'.

Remigius: Not often depicted, but when he is, it is usually with the dove which helped him out of a rather embarrassing situation. During his 73 year reign as Bishop of Rheims up to his death in 530 AD (he was elected 'by popular acclaim' at the startling age of 22) he had the satisfaction of baptising Clovis, King of the Franks, who had for long proved particularly stubborn to conversion. But when the moment came, the good bishop realised that the holy oils had not been prepared at which, serenely on cue, a dove descended from Heaven bearing a brimming vessel of the sacred liquid. Remigius is seen in a rare medieval stained glass representation at Dunston: this church, like Hethersett and Seething is dedicated to him, as is Roydon.

Roche: This saint's identification is plague marks, usually displayed on his upper left leg – as on the restored screen panels at Stalham, one of the very rare representations of this saint in England. Son of a nobleman in C14 France, who devoted his life to the relief of poverty and sickness, in particular of plague. Whenever he went where the plague was rampant, the epidemic ceased. Eventually he did catch it himself, but recovered – only to be hurled into prison as a spy during his wandering pilgrimages. There he died five years later, in about 1355. See also North Tuddenham.

Scholastica: Twin sister of St Benedict. She became a nun and possibly an abbess. She and her brother were deeply attached to each other; but though they lived in nearby communities, they are said to have met only once a year. Representations of her are rare – there is a question mark even over the one possible painting of her in Norfolk on the *screen* at Wiggenhall St Mary where she is shown, as in European medieval art, as a Benedictine abbess.

Sebastian: Recognisable at once, the saint riddled with arrows – or at least holding an arrow in his hand. This fate befell him in early Rome, where the saint preached and converted, and comforted Christian prisoners – until the vengeance of the emperor Diocletian fell on him. There is a unique dedicaton to St Fabian & St Sebastian at Woodbastwick. See also Colney, North Tuddenham, and Wellingham.

Silvester: No particular emblem where his very rare representations are found; but when he is, as at Houghton St Giles, he appears robed as a pope and carrying a double cross. Legend has it that Silvester, pope in the early C4, baptised the Emperor Constantine and cured him of leprosy. Also, he is credited with having slain a terrible dragon near Rome which daily was killing 300.

Simon Zelotes: Simon, one of The Twelve, is usually seen with a fish; or with a saw, relating perhaps to one tradition that he suffered martyrdom in Persia by being sawn in two. He is said to have preached in Egypt, as well as Persia; and even, one story says, in Britain. There are numerous representations of him in the county.

Sir John Schorne: Rector of a Buckinghamshire parish around 1300, he is said to have wiled the devil into a boot and there kept him prisoner – as he is represented here in

Norfolk in Gateley, Suffield and Cawston churches, wearing his academic or clerical robes, and holding a boot from which Satan peers. Never formally canonised, Sir John was honoured for his piety and for his working of miracles.

Stephen: Shown always with a heap of stones in his hands, or on a platter or book for he was stoned to death, the first Christian martyr, by the Jews of Jerusalem, when he fearlessly answered their charges of blasphemy (Acts, 6 and 7). Representations are numerous.

Swithin: No special emblem, but generally seen as a bishop – as at Bintree, for example. Everyone knows at least this much about St Swithin, that if it rains on his dedicatory day, July 15, then it will rain for 40 days afterwards. Bishop of Winchester in the early C9, counsellor to King Ethelwulf, and a man of piety, great charity and modesty, he was buried at length outside his cathedral. A century later it was decided to move his remains to a great shrine inside a project hampered and delayed by a month and a half of continuous rain. Bintree, together with Ashmanhaugh and Frettenham, are among the infrequent dedications to him.

Thaddeus: See *Jude*.

Theobald: Very few representations of him are found, but he is seen as a bishop on the screen at Hempstead. Born to wealth in Paris early in the C11, he chose poverty and solitude rather than wealth and became a hermit. Later, he went on pilgrimage to Compostella (see St *James the Great*) and then to Rome. After which he again took to the solitary life and a spartan existence. So why represent him as a bishop? It could be that the C15 artist confused him with the Theobald who was Archbishop of Canterbury from 1139-61.

Thomas: One of the Twelve Apostles, he is represented carrying a spear – for it was with spears, it is said, that he was martyred in India. What we know of 'Doubting Thomas' – he who would not believe in the Risen Christ until he had seen Him, and touched Him with his own hands – is wholly contained in the gospel of St John (chapters 11, 14 & 20). Representations of him are numerous.

Thomas of Canterbury, (Thomas Becket): Represented always as an archbishop.

Occasionally he may have a sword or an axe – reference to his famous martyrdom at the hands of four of Henry II's knights in Canterbury Cathedral at Christmas, 1170. Thomas's shrine became a place of veneration and miracles. Four centuries later, Henry VIII branded him traitor, rather than saint – which is why representations of him are often defaced with particular savagery and thoroughness. (Burlingham St Andrew, Burlingham St Edmund, Sparham, Stalham, Worstead, East Dereham, Wymondham, Attleborough, Dersingham, Harpley).

Uncumber: A lady with a long beard, and thus not likely to be mistaken (see Worstead. Uncumber, also known as Wilgefortis, was the daughter of an early king of Portugal who pledged herself to a life of pious virginity. When her father insisted she marry, and produced a suitable husband, she prayed to be made ugly so the suitor would not want her. Whereupon, miraculously, she grew a long beard. Her father, foiled and enraged, responded by having her crucified.

Ursula: Very few representations of her are found. But she is portrayed on the C15 screen at Barnham Broom, crowned, a sheaf of arrows in one hand, and young women in some profusion at her feet and under her cloak. She was a king's daugher in early Britain who, to escape the attentions of an unwelcome suitor, set off for Rome accompanied by 11,000 handmaidens. It has been suggested that this startling entourage stems from an early translation error. Ursula's maid was called Undecimilla, which could have led to the confusion. Be that as it may, Ursula and entourage arrived in Rome where the Holy Father received her – and perceived in a dream that she was to suffer martyrdom. At which intelligence, he put off his triple crown and, together with several bishops, set off with the crowd for Cologne. There they were beseiged by the Huns, who took the city and slew every last one of them – with the exception of the beautiful Ursula, whom the Hun prince wanted to marry. When she refused, he transfixed her with an arrow – thus the sheaf at Barnham Broom. See also Litcham.

Vincent: Recognisable in medieval art by the hook which accompanies him – just one of the implements with which he was tortured and torn during the persecution of the Emperor Diocletian about the year 300, for his Christian faith, teaching and ministry in Spain. Legend says that his broken body was thrown into the fields, where a raven guarded it. Then it was hurled into the sea but the waves returned it to shore. At last it was rescued by Christians and buried in the church at Valencia, where it is still venerated. (Norwich St Julian's, Harpley, Sandringham, Wiggenhall St Mary).

Walstan of Bawburgh: Norfolk's own farmer saint, patron saint of farm workers, usually shown crowned (denoting his royal blood) and holding a scythe (as at Ludham, Norwich St Julian's, and at Martham, site of the shrine of his mother, St *Blida*). The son of a prince, he chose a life of poverty, taking a job as a farm-worker at Taverham. After his many years of faithful labour, Walstan's master wanted to make him his heir. But Walstan declined – and asked instead for a cart and a cow in calf. She produced two fine young bulls, which he trained to pull his cart. In his old age, Walstan received a divine visitation foretelling his death, which came as he worked out in the fields. His body was placed on his cart and, unguided, his bulls set out. They paused at Costessey – where a spring sprang up and continued to give water until the C18. At last they came to the saint's birthplace at Bawburgh – passing clean through the solid wall of the church, and leaving behind them yet another spring, which as St Walstan's Well was famous for centuries, and survives in the farmyard close by. His shrine attracted many pilgrims until it was destroyed at the *Reformation*. (Martham, Ludham, Burlingham St Andrew, Sparham; Barnham Broom, Bawburgh, Denton, Norwich St Julian's Litcham and Kenninghall)

Wandregisil: He is rarely depicted, and has no special emblems, but he is on the pulpit at Horsham. Though a wealthy and well married courtier to the King of the Franks, he opted for the religious life, became a wandering pilgrim, and at length a monk, establishing an abbey at Fontenelle which was a by-word for spartan discipline.

Wilfrid: Born of noble parents in Northumbria in 634. A pious man, a great ecclesiastical authority, a notable builder of churches and abbeys, a patron of art. Yet still, it would seem, a most quarrelsome gentleman too, for he fell out with

kings, archbishops and fellow bishops throughout his long life. He died in 709, having but recently (through the intervention of the Pope) patched up his final quarrel with his archbishop. There is but one representation of him in Norfolk, at Harpley.

Wilgefortis: See *Uncumber.*

William of Norwich: Represented nailed to a cross, or holding a cross, hammer and nails. This pious eleven year-old boy is said to have been strangled and crucified by Jews in Holy Week 1144 and his body buried on Mousehold Heath, just outside the city walls. Five years later a nun discovered the grave, guarded by a raven, and the body was incorrupt. (Loddon, Norwich St Julian's, Litcham.)

William of York: Represented very infrequently, and then as an archbishop, as at Worstead and Garboldisham. He was for a time Archbishop of York in the early C12, before being dethroned on papal authority. After a few years, however, he was reinstated. Such was the popular enthusiasm that vast crowds collected on his return to York – and a wooden bridge over the river, on which many people were gathered, gave way under the weight, hurling all its occupants into the water. But through William's speedy prayers, none was drowned! Only a month later, William died, poisoned, it was thought, which made him a martyr. Miracles occurred at his tomb – and in 1226 he was canonised.

Withburga: A Norfolk saint, shown as an abbess, crowned to denote her royal blood, and with two does at her feet – as at Burlingham St Andrew. Brought up at Holkham, she later established an abbey at East Dereham and was its abbess for many years. Her community lived in poverty: during one especially hard period, it is said that two does appeared and their milk sustained the nuns until better times came. (Burlingham St Andrew; Barnham Broom, East Dereham, Holkham).

Zita (also known as *Citha*): A devout servant girl in C13 Italy who became known for her piety and for the help given her by angels. She can be seen on the screen at Barton Turf and on the font at Hemblington, Denton and North Elmham.

Appendix 2 – Styles of Architecture

From the days of the Saxons, before the Norman Conquest of 1066, through to the Georgians in the C18, architecture both sacred and secular has passed through many developments and details, fads and fancies, inspirations and inventions. The names we use to describe those phases – Early English, Decorated, etc. were coined only in the C19, and given convenient, even precise dates. But such dating can be more than misleading. Just as fashions in costume took time to filter through from city or court to provincial outposts, so changes in architectural ideas were only gradually assimilated. In Norfolk there are plenty of examples of styles being stuck to stubbornly long after they had been overtaken by new fashions. Not least, there are those instances of

the *Decorated* style still appearing after the *Black Death*, well into the 1360s and '70s – where, presumably, masons with the old skills had survived the pestilence. For our purposes here, we shall place the emphasis on the clearest line of styles – as shown, that is, in window shapes and tracery, which are undoubtedly the most useful guide for the layman:

Saxon: From the C7 to the Conquest. Characterised by roughness of construction, crudely rounded arches and triangular-headed window openings (as in the Saxon round tower at Bessingham); see figs. 9 & 10. Equally distinctive of the period is their 'long and short' work at corner angles of buildings. This is where upright stones are alternated with flat slabs,

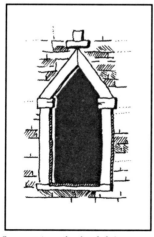

Fig 9. Saxon triangular-headed form.

Fig 10. Typical saxon round-headed window with crude arch.

often re-using Roman tiles and other materials, salvaged from local remains. Always exciting when one finds these old quoins included in later buildings – as at Barney, for example and Rockland All Saints.

Norman: From the Conquest to about 1200, including the *Transitional* phase, spanning the reigns of William I & II, Henry I, Stephen, Henry II and Richard I. Massive walls and pillars are typical features, mighty rounded arches and, still, small round-headed windows, though they might be used in groups, with heavy pillar-like mullions between them. But after the Saxon crudity, here is growing craftsmanship and artistry, with rich, bold ornamentation (the fine

Fig 11. Norman slit window – interior view of typical deep 'arrow slit' embrasure.

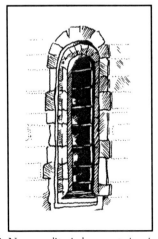

Fig 12. Norman slit window – exterior view.

arcade at Walsoken, and in part at Binham, are good examples). The small windows of the period are usually deeply splayed – see figs. 11 & 12. These would originally have been filled with parchment or oiled linen – glass came later.

Transitional: This is the phase of the changeover from the rounded, Romanesque architecture of the Normans to the Gothic movement in England – the triumph of the pointed arch. It took three or four decades, to about 1200, for the changeover to take full effect. Massive pillars during this time became slimmer and lighter, and might sometimes bear a pointed arch, carved in Norman character, as at Walsoken. These attractive, slimmed down columns were also used in clusters – and would continue to be so used during the full flowering of Early English.

Early English: Gothic has now fully arrived and, with it, the first really native English architectural style. The style spans roughly the 100-year period from the end of the reign of Richard, through John and Henry II, and into the time of Edward II, to about 1300. The simple, elegant lancet made its appearance, first used singly (fig. 13) then in groups. As ideas developed, the space between the heads of two lancets placed together was pierced with an open pattern, cut directly through the masonry: this is known as *plate tracery* (fig. 16). From there it was but a step to fining down the tracery by constructing it in separate pieces – that is, *bar tracery*, of which it has been claimed that we have in Norfolk (in competition with Westminster Abbey) the earliest example in England, in the great bricked-in west window of Binham Priory, which can be accurately dated between 1226 and 1244. Intermediate, however, about the year 1300 (and a most useful dating device) came a most distinctive phase, the 'Y' traceried window (fig. 14 is self explanatory; a development of this was the extension of the Y's through three or four lights, producing the simplest interlocking tracery with slim and graceful pointed heads). Everything at this time became finer in conception; bold buttresses, effortlessly thrusting arches, beautiful foliage carving and – most distinctive of this period – the trefoil, or three-leaf decoration (see also, *Emblems of the Trinity* and *Foils*), much used in window tracery and in decorative carving. Also popular was the *dog-tooth moulding,* which looks like a square, four-leafed flower, said to be based on the dog's tooth violet.

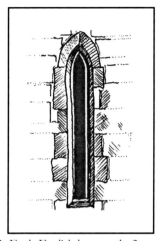

Fig 13. Early English lancet – the first arrical in England of pointed Gothic.

Fig 15. Early English lancets composed in a group.

Fig 14. The typical 'Y' traceried window of around 1300.

Fig 16. Simple geometric 'plate' tracery.

Decorated: This supreme time of architectural achievement and marvellous confidence in the use of shape and decoration had but a half century of full life – during the reigns of the first three Edwards – before the catastrophe of the *Black Death* struck Europe in 1349-50. This was then, the high point of ornamented Gothic. Windows grew larger, tracery became progressively more flowing and adventurous: from the 'geometrical', with circles, trefoils, quatrefoils, lozenges, etc. (see *Foils*), dominating the tracery, it burgeoned ultimately to the dazzling virtuosity of *reticulated* or net-like tracery (fig. 17) and the creative beauty of form as seen in fig. 18. Rich ornamentation and carving abounded, including the distinctive *'ball flower'*, a perfect little globular flower whose carved petals enclose a tiny ball; and also a sculptural explosion of pinnacles and *crocketting*, both inside and outside the church, from gable ends to tombs. Of many examples in Norfolk of fine Decorated work, the tracery of the e. window of the ruined s. transept at Cley may be especially mentioned.

Perpendicular: This style takes us from the aftermath of the *Black Death*, through Richard II's reign, and successively those of Henry IV, V & VI, Edward IV and Richard III to the time of Henry VII, until around 1500, when the *Tudor*

Fig 17. The flowing beauty of the Decorated style's 'reticulated' form.

Fig 19. The classix Perpendicular window, its mullions thrusting to the head of the arch.

Fig 18. Decorated artistry in imaginative flow – the butterfly motif.

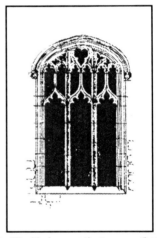

Fig 20. The Tudor contribution – a flattening of the arch over a Perpendicular window.

adaptation took place. The Perpendicular style was virtually created in one project by the monks of Gloucester. The style, as its name implies, is one of soaring upward lines, drawn in great windows by vertical *mullions* (fig. 19); by majestic, clean-lined towers; and by meticulously panelled buttresses and parapets and the ornamented bases of walls (see also *Flushwork*). Rich decoration is typical, though it usually has more of the grandly formal than of purely aesthetic. The important point is that, after the catastrophic plague, this magnificent, yet basically simple design was a godsend in places where all the old masons had been wiped out and only inexperienced men remained. Yet out of this

grim necessity arose some glorious constructions, of which Norfolk has many splendid examples. It was also a blessing that at this time wood carving and glass painting reached a peak of achievement, with Norwich craftsmen producing stained glass of a quality to rank with any in the land. Roof building equally reached a zenith of craftsmanship – Tilney All Saints, Knapton, St Peter Mancroft in Norwich, Swaffham and Trunch are but a handful of the inspiring examples to be seen in this county.

Tudor: Here we are talking of roughly the century to 1600 spanned by Henry VIII, Edward

VI, Mary and Elizabeth. Not so much a style as an adaptation, in that the 'Tudor' mode, as far as churches are concerned, is basically the flattening of the Perpendicular arch, while otherwise retaining the same features (fig. 20). Often seen and attractive embellishments are the lovely Tudor rose; and the heading of arches of windows and doors and open arches with elegantly used pink Tudor bricks.

Jacobean/Carolean: From the early C17 with the reign of James I (Latin, Jacobus), 1603-25), and continuing with the reigns of Charles I and II (Latin, Carolus). It was during James's reign that a stirring towards a *Renaissance* expression of architecture truly began in England. It was a style, and a movement, which employed the principles of the ancient Greek Classical building concepts – much 'classical' detail and ornamentation, and as in the Elizabethan period, a copious use of bricks. This stylised approach found much expression in furniture too, as will be found by many examples in Norfolk churches. During James's reign, the Renaissance movement found its resident genius in Inigo Jones (d.1652) whom James appointed Surveyor General of the Works. After Jones came another genius, Sir Christopher Wren. And if his masterpiece, St Paul's Cathedral, remains one of our greatest Renaissance buildings, it was nonetheless in country houses and grand mansions that the Renaissance spirit was most evidenced. Here in Norfolk, Blickling Hall is a magnificent Jacobean example; the Marquess of Townshend's seat, Raynham Hall, an elegant product of the Inigo Jones period. In our churches, the Jacobean title applies as often as not to wood carving – pulpits, typically high bench backs, etc. – and to aristocratic monuments.

Printed in the United States
117134LV00001B/33/A